After the Projects

After the Projects

Public Housing Redevelopment and
the Governance of the Poorest Americans

Lawrence J. Vale

OXFORD

UNIVERSITY PRESS

Library of Congress Cataloging-in-Publication Data
Names: Vale, Lawrence J., 1959- author.
Title: After the projects : public housing redevelopment and the governance of
the poorest Americans / Lawrence J. Vale.
Description: New York : Oxford University Press, [2018] |
Includes bibliographical references and index.
Identifiers: LCCN 2018012937 | ISBN 9780190624330 (hard cover) |
ISBN 9780190624347 (updf) | ISBN 9780190624354 (epub)
Subjects: LCSH: Public housing—United States—Case studies. |
Urban renewal—United States—Case studies. | Low-income housing—
United States—Case studies. | Legal assistance to the poor—United States—Case studies.
Classification: LCC HD7288.78.U5 V35 2018 | DDC 363.5/850973—dc23
LC record available at https://lccn.loc.gov/2018012937

9 8 7 6 5 4 3 2 1

Printed by Sheridan Books, Inc., United States of America

Contents

PART VI: CITIES OF STARS

Preface

Few topics in the fields of either American urban history or American planning history have lingered as long as the subject of public housing. And few topics have been subjected to as much constant disparaging and despair. Now, however, "the projects" are disappearing from municipal landscapes—one painful process at a time. What comes after these projects is neither foreordained nor consistent from city to city—as revealed in this book by examples of redevelopment efforts drawn from New Orleans, Boston, Tucson, and San Francisco. As exercises in policymaking and as experiments in place-making, crafting the postproject world has much to teach us about the challenges of governing the poorest Americans.

I view *After the Projects* as the final piece of an informal quartet of books I have written over the last two decades about public housing history, design, politics, and society. This includes a three-hundred-year prehistory, narrated in *From the Puritans to the Projects: Public Housing and Public Neighbors* (2000); a mostly hopeful saga of resident-centered urban reinvention in *Reclaiming Public Housing: A Half Century of Struggle in Three Public Neighborhoods* (2002); and a cautionary tale about the persistent inequities of redevelopment, *Purging the Poorest: Public Housing and the Design Politics of Twice-Cleared Communities* (2013). *After the Projects* takes the Boston focus of both *From the Puritans to the Projects* and *Reclaiming Public Housing* to a national scale, while also providing some additional positive directions for future planning practice. In so doing, *After the Projects* is both a sequel and companion to *Purging the Poorest*, since it demonstrates that such "purging" is often far from necessary.

METHODS AND SOURCES USED IN THE BOOK

Methodologically, the book relies on more than fifteen years of research that has included approximately two hundred semistructured interviews with key participants in the four redevelopment efforts. It is also grounded in multiple site visits conducted over many years and relies on archival and

secondary accounts of the larger history of each housing project, its neighborhood and its city's politics, and the redevelopment plans themselves. The
text has been greatly enriched by considerable access to internal documents
pertaining to each public housing redevelopment process, obtained from
developers, housing authorities, architects, neighborhood organizations,
and residents. Drawing upon both interviews and the language of surviving
documents made it possible to assess how various players viewed the actions
of others: Who was central, who was peripheral, and who was neutralized?
How did tensions wax and wane during implementation? Having access to
copious real-time minutes and accounts of meetings made it possible to rely
on more than just retrospective recollections that are inevitably colored by
self-justifications.

In the two cases where larger numbers of former public housing residents
have returned to redeveloped public housing (i.e., those in Boston and in
San Francisco), I have undertaken formal processes to interview representative samples of tenants. In all cases, the book has benefited from candid
conversations with a wide variety of individuals engaged in public housing
reform—including developers, designers, leaders of community-based organizations, and housing officials—enabling the book to attempt multifaceted portraits of these complex redevelopment processes. My goal has been
to try to see the evolution of each place through the eyes of diverse players.

I began this inquiry with the observation that public housing redevelopment has proceeded quite differently in various American cities, even
though each place relied centrally on the same federal funding mechanism
and thereby needed to embrace its aims. Still, in each specific key place,
different major players came to the fore. Sometimes redevelopment was
led by the public sector, but sometimes private for-profit developers gained
more unfettered sway. In other cases, not-for-profit organizations—whether
nonprofit housing developers or neighborhood-based advocacy groups—
achieved greater ascendency. And, in some cases much more so than others,
low-income resident leaders from the community acquired considerable
influence. While every redevelopment initiative included the same full
range of participants—bridging across the public, private, not-for-profit, and
community sectors—the balance of power among these skewed quite differently from place to place. As a result, I realized that I needed some more
systematic framework for describing the governance-in-practice that I was
observing.

Through process tracing, I attempted to construct plausible causal
narratives that could explain how and why governance in a particular case
gets weighted toward one of the four sectors more than the others. I began
by making relatively crude diagrams that simply called out the names of the
various institutional players in various fonts. Fonts, by definition, have both

typeface and size. Sometimes the most assertive font could signal a well-functioning housing authority, depicted in a modestly proportioned modernist **Helvetica**, but elsewhere another project diagram could highlight a dominant private developer, rendered in 60-point **braggadocio**.

I arrived at the visual metaphor I call "governance constellations" only after fifteen years of interviewing and close observation of the behavior of actual individuals and groups during the course of project implementation, based on analysis of extensive paper trails. Utilizing evolving word clouds of fonts enabled me to track and document my growing clarity about the relative power of the individuals and groups I was studying, but had two obvious limitations. First, the collections of words conveyed hierarchy but not linkages, and therefore did not easily help sort the players into sectors. Second, the resultant images seemed entirely dehumanized.

Shifting to a more spatial diagram, I situated the various players in four quadrants: the public, private, not-for-profit, and community sectors. Next, I switched from font sizes to differently sized circles, still intended to signal a hierarchy of influence of each institutional player on a particular process of public housing transformation. To this point, the diagrams accorded relative visual primacy to categories such as private developer, city council, neighborhood nonprofits, but did not disaggregate the players within each category.

As a final step, I translated typefaces into actual human faces inscribed within each circle. Although every star in my constellations is representative of larger categories—such as mayor, private developer, legal aid attorney, or public housing resident—I wanted to acknowledge the roles of specific people in the stories I was telling, even though each diagram of governance is also still intended to convey a more structural message. In short, the diagrams depict the relative visibility of particular human stars but also step back to reveal how those stars may become aligned into particular, nameable constellations.

Acknowledgments

I am grateful for the patience and graphic talents of Suzy Harris-Brandts, who endured all too many iterations of the constellation diagrams with good humor. A project of this duration has benefited from earlier significant research assistance, most of it generously provided to me since 1990 by my career-long academic home: the Department of Urban Studies and Planning at MIT. In particular, I acknowledge the support from Kim Alleyne, Kassie Bertumen, Esther Chung Byun, Kristin Simonson Carlson, Carla Morelli Francazio, Yonah Freemark, Erin Graves, Annemarie Gray, Stephanie Groll, Nick Kelly, Zach Lamb, Steve Moga, Tony Petropulos, Shauna Rigaud, Jeff Schwartz, Diana Searl, Callie Seltzer, Annis Whitlow Sengupta, Jonathan Tarleton, Andrew Trueblood, and Carrie Vanderford.

In addition to all those interviewed for this book, and support from the staff and collections of MIT's Rotch Library and the Loeb Library at Harvard (where I spent much of 2009 as a visiting scholar), I am grateful to many others in each of the four cities discussed in this volume.

In New Orleans, my account of the transformation of the St. Thomas project into River Garden has been greatly enhanced by having full access to the unparalleled files assembled by Hope House director Brother Don Everard, himself a key participant in the process. I also received help from the New Orleans Public Library staff, as well as from Annemarie Gray, Zach Lamb, Aditi Mehta, and Jeff Schwartz. I wish also to acknowledge consistent support from other former students now doing great work in their home city, including Jeff Hébert and Seth Knudsen.

My debts to the assistance of others go back furthest in the Boston part of the book—all the way to 1993, when my interviewing at the Orchard Park development began. At the time, I imagined that fifty-three interviews with residents of the not-yet-redeveloped project would largely serve as part of a "control group" intended to help calibrate the findings of *Reclaiming Public Housing*, a book focused on the experiences of residents of three other public housing projects that had already undergone extensive redevelopment. Now, though, these old interviews serve as the first of three successive waves of interviews, supplemented in 2005-2006 and 2013-2014 by interviews

at the new Orchard Gardens, and I am especially grateful for the work of
Carla Morelli Francazio, Kim Alleyne, and Shauna Rigaud in facilitating
that triple set of conversations. For a quarter-century, the staff at the Boston
Housing Authority has been highly responsive to my period requests for
materials and interviews, and I particularly thank Sandi Henriquez, Bill
McGonagle, Kate Bennett, Joe Bamberg, and Lydia Agro. I am also thankful
for materials on Orchard Gardens from architect Fernando Domenech, the
Bostonian Society, Trinity Management, and the Madison Park Development
Corporation. Jonathan Tarleton provided both first-rate research assistance
and a close read of my draft chapters on Boston. Finally, it has been my
great privilege to work with Shomon Shamsuddin—once my postdoc and
now a treasured colleague—on two previously published pieces about other
aspects of the Orchard Gardens redevelopment achievement.

In Tucson, my work gained a significant jumpstart from Lydia Otero's fine
book *La Calle*, coupled with her kindness in sharing materials and contacts.
I first heard about the remarkable redevelopment of the Connie Chambers
project into Posadas Sentinel by attending a conference presentation given
by that project's architect-planner, Corky Poster in 2002. Corky later loaned
me his extensive cache of materials about the redevelopment process and
facilitated my access to the city's Community Services Department (now
the Department of Housing and Community Development), where, over the
years, I gained access to additional materials from Olga Osterhage, Emily
Nottingham, Bobbi Stone, and Erin Arana. Library staff at the University
of Arizona also proved universally helpful, and I truly appreciate the close
read of my draft Tucson chapters by sociologist Debbie Becher.

In San Francisco, my first thanks go to Tan Chow, whom I first met when
he attended a talk I gave in Chinatown in 2007. Since he was, coincidentally,
a resident of North Beach Place, I was thrilled to be able to hire him as a
multilingual research assistant to conduct interviews. Tan, along with Cindy
Wu, also facilitated access to a trove of internal documents and project files
held by the Chinatown Community Development Center, which proved crucial to understanding the evolution of the North Beach Place redevelopment process. I also appreciate access to San Francisco Housing Authority
files provided by Barbara Smith, materials from HOPE VI consultant Libby
Seifel, as well as additional assistance from the public library staff of the
San Francisco room at the San Francisco Public Library, as well as from
staff at the University of California Berkeley Library and Archives. I also
benefited greatly from the willingness of employees from BRIDGE housing
and the John Stewart Company—two of the codevelopers of North Beach
Place—to provide materials and site access and to speak openly about their
experiences. Ahsha Safai took me on a memorable tour of various parts of
the San Francisco public housing landscape, highlighted by attending Mayor

Gavin Newsom's speech at the Alice Griffith development. In addition, Amy Howard, author of an excellent book about San Francisco public housing, consistently proved to be a generous and delightful colleague, and Hilda Steckel provided welcome hospitality in Berkeley.

Although almost no material from this book has appeared elsewhere in publication, I have gained immensely from presenting pieces of it at a variety of conferences, media venues, and invited symposia over the last decade, as well as through other more informal conversations. In the course of all that, I have benefited substantially from Rit Aggarwala, Danielle Allen, Nick Allen, Martine August, Bernadette Baird-Zars, Jack Bauman, Bob Beauregard, Debbie Becher, Eran Ben-Joseph, Larry Bennett, Ronit Bezalel, Ariel Bierbaum, Nick Bloom, Rachel Bratt, Neil Brenner, Xav Briggs, Bob Bruegmann, Bob Buckley, Jim Buckley, Ken Burns, Sarah Burns, Tom Campanella, Naomi Carmon, Manuel Castells, Karen Chapple, Rob Chaskin, Liz Cohen, Susanne Cowan, Margaret Crawford, Alex Curley, Prentiss Dantzler, Matt Desmond, Ingrid Ellen, Shawn Escoffery, Susan Fainstein, Bob Fairbanks, Roberta Feldman, Raphaël Fischler, Stephanie Forbes, Jim Fraser, Archon Fung, George Galster, Matthew Gebhardt, Miles Glendenning, Ed Goetz, Kian Goh, Erin Graves, Andrew Greenlee, Taryn Gress, Penny Gurstein, Jim Hanlon, Tali Hatuka, Joseph Heathcott, Amy Howard, Brad Hunt, Derek Hyra, Aseem Inam, Alison Isenberg, Sandy Isenstadt, April Jackson, Mark Joseph, Dawn Jourdan, Michael Katz, Jerold Kayden, Nick Kelly, Lang Keyes, Amy Khare, Thomas Kirszbaum, Rachel Kleit, Lili Knorr, Seth Knudsen, Nancy Kwak, Shinwon Kyung, Matt Lasner, Mickey Lauria, Lisa Lee, Nancy Levinson, Diane Levy, Li Li, Donlyn Lyndon, Lynne Manzo, Peter Marcuse, Michael McGandy, Dave McMahon, Tim Mennel, Justine Minnis, John Mollenkopf, Harvey Molotch, Michelle Norris, Deirdre Oakley, Max Page, Sandra Parvu, Mary Pattillo, Rolf Pendall, Sue Popkin, Bill Rohe, Jane Rongerude, Brent Ryan, Lynne Sagalyn, Rob Sampson, Adèle Santos, Hashim Sarkis, Katie Schank, Susanne Schindler, Alex Schwartz, Richard Sennett, Cassim Shepard, Wayne Sherwood, Jeff Shumaker, Elaine Simon, Mario Small, Peer Smets, David Smiley, Janet Smith, Shomon Shamsuddin, Michael Snidal, Valerie Stahl, Justin Steil, Walter Stern, Jim Stockard, Laura Tach, Phil Thompson, Fritz Umbach, Florian Urban, David Varady, Alex von Hoffman, Laura Wainer, Sam Bass Warner, Paul Watt, Gretchen Weismann, Rhonda Williams, and Yan Zhang.

The process of developing a manuscript into a book has been ably guided by James Cook at Oxford University Press, who immediately championed this project and who secured two extremely constructive reviews. At the Press and its partner Newgen, I received consistent support during book production from Emily Mackenzie and Cheryl Merritt. Closer to home, the manuscript also benefited considerably from the attentive editorial suggestions of Julie Dobrow.

Finally, for a book project that began when I had four small children and is now published while they are in college, graduate school, or beyond—the passage of time has not dimmed my deepest gratitude to Mira, Aaron, Jeremy, and Jonathan, and to Julie, for the unfinished project of building and sustaining our family.

Abbreviations

ACC	annual contributions contract (for public housing)
AFDC	Aid to Families with Dependent Children (welfare)
AMI	area median income
BHA	Boston Housing Authority
BRA	Boston Redevelopment Authority
CCCD	Coalition for Community Control of Development (Boston)
CCDC	Chinatown Community Development Center (San Francisco)
CCH	Creative Choice Homes
CCHO	Council of Community Housing Organizations (San Francisco)
CCU	Council of Civic Unity (San Francisco)
CDB	central business district
CDBG	Community Development Block Grant
CDC	Community Development Corporation
CRC	Chinatown Resource Center (San Francisco)
CRP	Community Resource Partnership (New Orleans)
CSD	Community Services Department (Tucson)
CSS (CSSP)	community and supportive services (program)
CURE	Citizens Urban Renewal Enterprise (Tucson)
DSNI	Dudley Street Neighborhood Initiative (Boston)
EDN	Eviction Defense Network (San Francisco)
ELI	extremely low income
FHA	Federal Housing Administration
FIC	Family Investment Center
FSS	Family Self Sufficiency program
GBC	Greater Boston Committee (on the Transportation Crisis)
GNOFHAC	Greater New Orleans Fair Housing Action Center
GRIP	Greater Roxbury Incorporation Project (Boston)
HANO	Housing Authority of New Orleans

HOPE VI	Housing Opportunities for People Everywhere (initially Homeownership and Opportunity for People Everywhere)
HOPE SF	Hope San Francisco (local variant/successor to HOPE VI)
HRI	Historic Restorations, Inc.
HUD US	Department of Housing and Urban Development
IBA	Inquilinos Boricuas en Acción (Boston)
IG	inspector general
JSCo	John Stewart Company (San Francisco)
LIHTC	Low-Income Housing Tax Credit
MINCS	Mixed-Income New Communities Strategy
MOU	Memorandum of Understanding
NAACP	National Association for the Advancement of Colored People
NBRMC	North Beach Resident Management Council
NBTA	North Beach Tenants Association
OPTA	Orchard Park Tenants Association
PCIC	Pima County Interfaith Council (Tucson)
PHA	public housing authority
PHMAP	Public Housing Management Assessment Program
PRC	Preservation Resource Center (New Orleans)
PRWORA	Personal Responsibility and Work Opportunity Reconciliation Act
RAD	Rental Assistance Demonstration
RFP	request for proposals
RFQ	request for qualifications
RMC	Resident Management Council (North Beach Place)
RMC	Resident Management Corporation (New Orleans)
SFHA	San Francisco Housing Authority
SFRA	San Francisco Redevelopment Authority
SHPO	State Historic Preservation Office
SPUR	San Francisco Planning and Urban Research Association (originally founded as San Francisco Planning and Urban Renewal Association)
STICC	St. Thomas Irish Channel Consortium (New Orleans)
STRC	St. Thomas Resident Council (New Orleans)
TANF	Temporary Assistance for Needy Families
TCB	The Community Builders
TCC	Tucson Community Center (later Tucson Convention Center)
TEL HI	(formerly rendered as Tel-Hi) Telegraph Hill Neighborhood Center
THA	Tucson Housing Authority

TPC	Tenants Policy Council (Boston)
TUPHP	Tenants United for Public Housing Progress (Boston)
ULI	Urban Land Institute
WACO	Western Addition Community Organization (San Francisco)
WPA	Works Progress Administration
WRT	Wallace, Roberts & Todd

After the Projects

Part I

DEVELOPING, REDEVELOPING, AND GOVERNING PUBLIC HOUSING

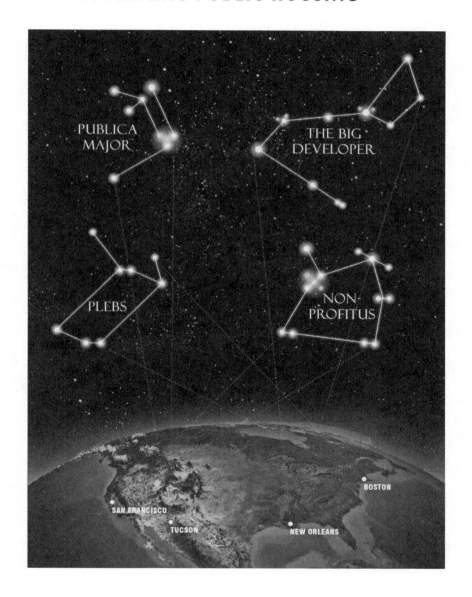

1

Public Housing, Redevelopment, and the Governance of Poverty

At its most straightforward level, this book is about American public housing and the contested efforts to redevelop it. Yet, precisely because such efforts are hardly straightforward, I am necessarily drawn to larger questions. How, and where, does an overwhelmingly wealthy polity like the United States provide help to house its poorest citizens? And, in turn, what do public housing practices reveal about American attitudes about poverty and how the poorest should be governed? Why are some governance practices more equitable than others, and how can more equitable practices be encouraged?

Climate change and nuclear weapons may constitute the planet's preeminent existential threats, but for millions of families the quotidian struggle for affordable housing is a more immediately pressing challenge. At a time when full-time employment at low wages fails to provide adequate income for a household to affordably rent market-rate apartments in most American cities, just one in four low-income households receives a housing subsidy. The persistent underfunding of public housing has been one of the greatest public policy failures of the last century—and one of the most revealing.

The eighty-year history of public housing in the United States offers an illuminating window—albeit a broken one—into evolving attitudes toward the poorest Americans. This is more than a decline-and-fall narrative about the stigma of those places known individually and collectively as "the projects." This book adds a new chapter, with a new plot twist centered on ideas of revitalization and rebirth: the nationwide set of efforts since the 1990s to replace the extreme poverty of public housing with new mixed-income communities. Not surprisingly, such mixing has not happened easily. Political and economic choices about which people to throw into the mix depend not just on the nature of the housing market in each specific location but also on the larger political history of each city. This book investigates the social, political, and economic pressures that undergird this trend toward mixed-income redevelopment. Yet the central puzzle here is that the trend is not uniform. This book focuses on approaches undertaken in four very different American cities: New Orleans, Boston, Tucson, and San Francisco.

When faced with the common challenge of redeveloping public housing in a gentrifying neighborhood, each place responded quite differently—with significant consequences for the poorest residents. Why is it that the leadership in some cities chooses to remove the poorest from highly desirable locations, whereas others willingly—even eagerly—rehouse them in such places?

To answer this question involves undertaking detailed examinations of the actual processes of public housing development and redevelopment in each particular place, but also entails asking broader questions about how political will gets forged and how decision-making power gets distributed. To make sense of the complex and conflicting trajectories of public housing, I have needed to find a new framework to make sense of urban governance. I call this framework a *governance constellation* and will explore it in detail in chapter 2. For now, though, I can pose another question: What governance conditions make it possible for leaders in some American cities to resist gentrification and to continue housing the poorest, even after the projects are gone?

To grapple with the governance of the poorest in the American city entails addressing several interrelated questions that link real-estate development to ethics: Who benefits from the redevelopment of public housing and how can the range of beneficiaries be expanded? How can stigmatized public housing be redeveloped in a way that removes the stigma without also removing the residents who most need the housing? Under what circumstances is it possible for the poorest residents to retain a central place in a newly crafted successor community? In short: after the projects, where—and how—should the poorest be housed?

CHOOSING THE PUBLIC FOR PUBLIC HOUSING

Most analysts situate the origins of American public housing in Franklin Roosevelt's New Deal and its robust expansion of the public sector, but it is deeply rooted in many older forms of policies that offered housing assistance to the poor—everything from seventeenth-century almshouses to the Homestead Act of 1862.[1] Still, the public housing launched under the Public Works Administration and the Housing Act of 1937 assumed an unprecedentedly large role for a public sector that underwrote construction. In exchange, these initial iterations of public housing expected rent payments by residents to be sufficient to cover the operating costs of the housing. This implied selecting residents with adequate income to be reliable rent payers and meant that little of the initial housing would be targeted to the poorest of the poor. Razing the slums did not necessarily entail raising the slum-dwellers—at least not the same ones who lost their homes. Instead, three other compelling public interests could be served. Politically, constructing public housing could ease unemployment in the building trades; aesthetically, public housing could remove "slums and blight" from cities; and economically, public housing could assist municipal finances by eliminating districts that paid little in property taxes but required large public outlays for city services. Selective admission to public housing also proved a way to reward good people who had been economically waylaid by the Depression and, subsequently, to reward others who had served their country during wartime. Well-staffed housing authorities carefully vetted applicants for stable employment history, "proper" family composition, and suitable housekeeping skills. Many households appreciated the "honor of selection" and viewed public housing as providing "status and social currency."[2] This need to govern selection has always remained central.

These first deals on public housing occupancy also had more nefarious aims. They frequently shifted mixed-race areas into new segregated zones, based on ill-conceived principles about the previously dominant "neighborhood composition." In some cities, this meant more than black-white segregation; it could also entail steering some project occupancy toward particular ethnicities—often Irish, Italian, or Mexican. At the same time, public housing worked to reward particular kinds of family structures: two-parent households with a young child or two rather than multigenerational families, gay or lesbian couples, single individuals, or any arrangement that included lodgers or unrelated kin. In all these ways, public housing could be considered a mechanism for enhancing public virtue—a way to replace chaotic, dangerous, and financially dysfunctional slums with a more regularized and regulated alternative that identified and rewarded only the most worthy among the needy. And, by the 1950s, once public housing was formally paired with urban renewal, it could also be the mechanism needed to free up desirable land for its "highest and best" use by implicitly removing its lowest and worst people and housing them elsewhere. In all these ways, the project of "the projects" entailed both spatial and social engineering.

Launched in the 1930s and 1940s to provide short-term homes for the upwardly mobile working poor, public housing by the 1960s was increasingly spurned by the white working class, which embraced other housing opportunities that were systematically excluded from nonwhites. Title I of the Housing Act of 1949 expanded the availability of mortgage insurance programs that could make suburban homeownership more attractive than urban living, but discriminatory lending practices kept large parts of suburbia off limits to most nonwhites.[3] This increasingly left public housing to become the long-term domicile for large numbers of the nation's most economically disadvantaged, and most housing projects built for families soon housed a nonwhite majority. Ever since, in most large cities, policymakers and politicians have explored ways to pare back this housing, while none-theless acknowledging the ever-present need to house the poorest. In some cases—first and most notoriously with the implosion of Pruitt-Igoe in St. Louis that commenced in 1972—city leaders have simply sought to eliminate public housing. This did little to solve the underlying problem, however, since the growing need for housing subsidy remained. Even as some new kinds of voucher-based subsidies burgeoned, the lingering problem of the older public housing projects remained both politically fraught and distress-ingly visible.

Since the early 1990s, many city officials have embraced opportunities to raze and redevelop public housing. In some cities, this seemed no more than the latest desperate attempt to infuse capital into disinvested areas, but sometimes public housing in city districts with robust real-estate markets could attract interest from private sector developers. In such neighborhoods, public housing redevelopment emerged as a powerful, if unlikely, new source of urban gentrification. When developers help city officials reimagine public housing sites located adjacent to reviving downtowns, the poorest have frequently struggled to keep their place. Instead, efforts to reinvent public housing often entail both displacement of the poorest residents and replacement by higher-income denizens more in keeping with rising com-munity fortunes. The national and local policy environment now favors mixed-income housing as an alternative to public housing that housed only the poorest, but local leaders define this mix very differently. The leader-ship of nearly every city touts the advantages of efforts to deconcentrate poverty, yet communities experience this process in markedly divergent ways. Sometimes, public housing gets redeveloped in ways that maximizes the possibility for the poorest to remain, whereas in other instances the goal seems to be to find ways to rehouse the least possible number of the poorest while targeting most of the revitalized housing to those who are able to pay market rates or who need no more than a shallow subsidy.

THE PROBLEMS OF POVERTY

In a masterful essay written near the end of his life, historian Michael Katz asks and answers a vital question: "What kind of problem is poverty?" Looking across more than two hundred years of American interpretive traditions, Katz sees six valid levels of responses that have emerged successively:

- Persons: poverty is the outcome of the failings of individuals or families.
- Places: poverty results from toxic conditions within geographic spaces.

- Resources: poverty is the absence of money and other key resources.
- Political economy: poverty is the byproduct of capitalist economies.
- Power: poverty is the consequence of political powerlessness.
- Markets: poverty reflects the absence of functioning markets or the failure to use the potential of markets to improve individual lives.[4]

Each of these six frames implies different kinds of policies, though all carry resonance for understanding public housing and its redevelopment. Most American discourse, Katz notes, "gets stuck" at the first or second level and devolves into arguments about people-centered or place-based solutions. Yet a focus on persons misses how much of poverty remains outside of an individual's control, while a focus on places risks "overemphasizing the causal power of concentrated poverty or residential segregation and missing the political-economic forces that produce uneven geographies." Likewise, Katz argues, viewing poverty as a problem of "market failure or absence" falls short of grasping "how market-based societies produce poverty," while other frames that root poverty in power or political economy too often remain at the level of critique, without proffering "realistic and potentially effective strategies." All six of these frames get aligned, however, in a common preoccupation over "the question of work."[5]

At base, both public provision of housing and welfare policy entail judgments of worthiness as well as neediness—closely tied to the capacity and willingness to engage in paid employment. Public housing began as an employment effort for the construction industry that, in turn, chiefly provided homes for those with stable jobs. Then, when public housing devolved into welfare housing for the predominantly jobless, it came wrapped in new stigma. It should then come as no surprise that public housing reform emerged in tandem with welfare reform, specifically in the Quality Housing and Work Responsibility Act of 1998. More generally, as Katz discerns, "Identifying and administering the grounds for exclusion has remained the quintessential act of policy."[6]

Two decades later, this is what President Donald Trump's budget director, Mick Mulvaney, means when he questions the size and contours of the safety net and seeks to "try and figure out if there's folks who don't need it that need to be back in the workforce." Increasingly, programs such as Medicaid and food stamps seem headed for work requirements, at least in some states, with public housing soon to follow. It is also the cold moral calculus behind the insistence of Trump's US Housing and Urban Development (HUD) secretary Ben Carson that poverty is largely "a state of mind." For those with the "right mindset," Carson insists, "You can take everything from them and put them on the street and I guarantee in a little while they'll be right back up there," whereas for those with the "wrong mindset, you can give them everything in the world, and they'll work their way back down there." In 2015, prior to taking over at HUD, Carson made his policy views clear: "I have a strong desire to get rid of programs that create dependency in able-bodied people." And, in 2017, the HUD secretary went further: "For me," he told a *Time* reporter, "success is not how many people we get into public housing, but how many we get out," by which he meant that the poor should gain "life skills that will allow them to be independent."[7] For Mulvaney, Carson, and Trump, as for many other conservative policymakers, poverty stems from poor personal choices rather than from poor wages.

These are not aberrant beliefs: a poll conducted by the Kaiser Family Foundation and the *Washington Post* in 2017 found that nearly two-thirds of Republican respondents believed "a lack of effort" rather than "difficult circumstances beyond their control" is generally to blame for a person's poverty. Overall, men were twice as likely as women to blame poverty on a lack of effort, and Christians were more than twice as likely as non-Christians to hold this view.[8] Given this larger political and cultural context, the persistent stigma of public housing is hardly surprising. Yet, as of 2016, fully 90 percent of the nation's public housing households were headed by someone who is elderly, has disabilities, worked (or had recently worked) or was subject to work requirements through another program.[9] Many are dependent on public housing, but this is not the same as a culture of dependency. The persistence of thinly veiled contempt for the poor as lazy or un-American has limited the political capacity to expand housing subsidies.

A SHIFTING AND SUBSIDING LANDSCAPE OF SUBSIDY FOR LOW-INCOME RENTERS

In the course of eighty years of experimentation in public housing and its public-private offspring, the federal government has launched many different kinds of policies yet still managed to subsidize only a small fraction of the nation's poorest households. In late 2013, then-HUD secretary Shaun Donovan observed that Americans were in the midst of "the worst rental affordability crisis that this country has known."[10] That crisis has persisted, especially for those with the lowest incomes. In March 2018, the National Low Income Housing Coalition (NLIHC) released its annual analysis of the affordable housing gap. It showed that the United States had "a shortage of 7.2 million affordable rental units" available to those with extremely low incomes (ELI)—defined by HUD as those earning less than 30 percent of the area median income (AMI).[11]

It is not that the United States lacks a commitment to housing subsidies for those with the lowest incomes; it is that this commitment is much too small.

Nationally, the United States still has more than a million units of conventional public housing (i.e., housing financed, owned, and operated by the public sector) and provides an additional 3.5 million households with deep housing subsidies through other mechanisms such as vouchers and privately owned projects. For a subsidy to be considered deep, this typically means that a household pays no more than 30 percent of its income in rent. This is the current threshold at which housing is deemed to be "affordable," Such deep housing subsidies overwhelmingly serve ELI households and yet come nowhere near closing the gap. The 2018 NLIHC study found that, nationally, there are just thirty-five affordable and available units per one hundred ELI households, a gap that inheres partly because those with higher incomes occupy many of the units that would be affordable to ELI households. Moreover, for those with incomes at 15 percent of AMI or less (what the NLIHC terms deeply low income, or DLI)—a 2016 NLIHC study showed a more extreme gap: There are just seventeen available and affordable housing units for every one hundred of those particularly impoverished families. The shortage of affordable housing creates significant dilemmas for the most economically vulnerable households. Nearly three-quarters of ELI renters have been stressed and stretched into paying more than half of their income for housing and utilities, forcing them to squeeze all other expenses, like food. And, for DLI renters, the situation is especially dire—fully 93 percent face such a severe burden. [12]

Since housing subsidies in the United States have never been considered entitlements like Social Security or food stamps, more than three-quarters of those earning less than 50 percent of AMI receive no housing subsidy despite being income-eligible for other forms of support.[13] As of 2015, this meant that 8.3 million US very low-income households paid more than half of their income for rent, lived in severely inadequate conditions, or both—and received no government housing assistance.[14] Many of those left out face frequent disruptions not just to their housing but to their very lives, as painfully illustrated by the ethnographic and statistical findings in Matthew Desmond's *Evicted: Poverty and Profit in the American City*.[15]

Even as the need for deeply subsidized housing has grown, public housing projects have inexorably dwindled in number and size since the early 1990s. As of 2018, urban officials had demolished at least 20 percent of the national stock, which peaked in the early 1990s at about 1.4 million apartments.[16] Skeptics often regard this as good riddance, given pervasively poor conditions in many large cities, and point to alternative options for providing subsidies. It is certainly true that alternatives have proliferated. Starting in the 1960s and accelerating in the 1980s and 1990s, the idea of conventional public housing has been supplemented, even supplanted, by a variety of other public-private ventures. These include more than two million of what are now called housing choice vouchers (tenant-based subsidies that subsidize rent from private landlords). In 1994 the voucher program surpassed the unit volume of the conventional public housing program itself and is now more than twice its size. The supply of deeply subsidized housing also includes more than a million vouchers allocated to subsidized apartment projects built and managed by the private sector (known formally as project-based Section 8 vouchers). These constitute a second form of "projects" that are a much less often discussed.

Cumulatively, despite the terrible reputation that public housing has held for decades, the nation's overall commitment to deeply subsidized housing rose steadily for five decades—even though it continued to fall well short of the actual need. Since the early 2000s, however, the stock of deeply subsidized housing has stopped growing and has actually lost considerable ground, given that the national population has risen by about 15 percent during this same period. Figure 1.1 reveals the place of the public housing program in this larger realm of federally sponsored efforts to generate deep subsidies for low-income families through public-private housing. The clear message here is that conventional public housing, while certainly the pioneer program, has long since been numerically eclipsed by other efforts. Public housing stands out far more starkly in people's minds than it does in the world of actual housing supply.

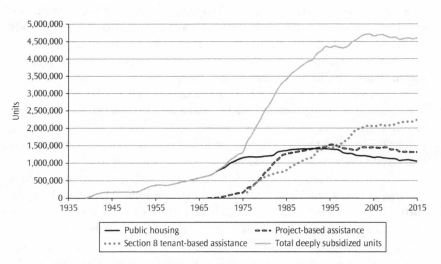

Figure 1.1. Trends in Deep Subsidies for Federally Assisted Rental Housing
Public housing, once the only approach to deeply subsidized housing in the United States, is now the third largest program. Overall, these subsidies expanded significantly over several decades, but have slowed dramatically during most of the last twenty-five years, in tandem with a decreasing reliance on the conventional public housing program.
Source: Vale and Freemark, "The Privatization of American Public Housing."

Moreover, there is a fourth major type of subsidized affordable housing, produced with the assistance of Low-Income Housing Tax Credits (LIHTCs), which were first made available to investors in 1986. These tax credits—managed by the US Treasury Department as part of the tax code, not by HUD—provide wealthy corporate investors with lucrative tax deductions in exchange for investing funds that reduce the cost of producing housing. This development subsidy, in turn, makes it possible to lower the rents this housing needs to charge to tenants. As figure 1.2 shows, affordable housing supported by tax credits is now the single largest program, with well over two million subsidized units. The LIHTC housing, however, does not—on its own—provide the same kind of deep subsidy as the other public housing programs. It is, instead, a form of public-private shallow subsidy, since it does not attempt to cover the difference between what HUD considers to be a "fair market rent" and thirty percent of a tenant's income, as deep subsidies currently do. LIHTC beneficiaries pay reduced rents, but these rents do not vary with their income. Instead, LIHTC subsidies target those with incomes in the range of 40-60 percent of AMI. This reaches those are technically still poor but tend to have stable employment and earn well beyond the minimum wage. This so-called workforce housing therefore does not substitute for public housing that reaches the poorest. Unless the tax

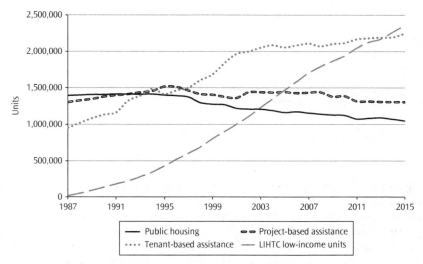

Figure 1.2. The Low-Income Housing Landscape in the United States: Thirty Years of Dramatic Change
The Low-Income Housing Tax Credit (LIHTC) has become the nation's most popular funding mechanism for new subsidized housing, with more than two million units created since 1986.
Source: Vale and Freemark, "The Privatization of American Public Housing."

credits are paired with additional subsidies from the conventional public housing annual contributions contract (ACC), LIHTC subsidies assist a different group of people. Then-HUD secretary Andrew Cuomo put this quite explicitly in 1999: LIHTC "can't house the poorest of the poor."[17]

Who then *will* house the poorest of the poor? Despite the rise of public-private alternatives to conventional public housing projects, the overall provision of deeply subsidized housing has failed to keep pace with the growth of the American population.[18] As figure 1.3a reveals, since the early 1990s there has been a steady erosion in the percentage of American households receiving deeply subsidized rental housing. This is true even if one counts that portion of the LIHTC subsidies that get paired with additional public housing ACC support. Moreover, as figure 1.3b shows, even if one also adds the portion of the LIHTC-supported housing that provides only a shallow subsidy and targets those with somewhat higher incomes, the trend is still downward since the early 2000s. The reality is stark: public housing

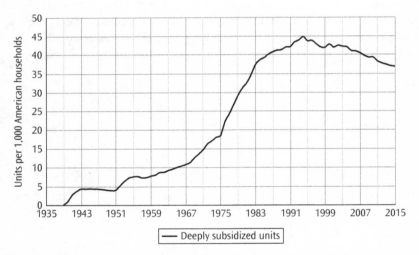

Figure 1.3a. Deeply Subsidized Rental Housing in the United States: A Declining Commitment?
The provision of deeply subsidized housing units in the United States exceeded the growth of overall housing units for much of the period since the Great Depression, especially in the spurts following the Housing Acts of 1937, 1949, and 1968. Since the early 1990s, however, the number of deeply subsidized units has declined from 45 to 37 per 1,000 households (figure 1.3a). Even when accounting for the rapid growth in the number of units produced through the LIHTC program that are targeted to low-income households but which do not receive deeper subsidies (see figure 1.3b), the number of federally subsidized low-income units per household has still declined slightly since the early 2000s.
Source: Vale and Freemark, "The Privatization of American Public Housing."

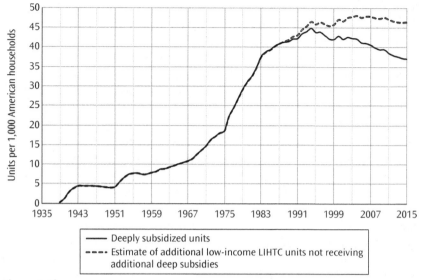

Figure 1.3b.

provision is declining, and alternative subsidy programs do not keep pace. Meanwhile, underscoring the crisis, the needs of extremely low-income households forced to pay more than half of their income for housing continue to mount.

In this context, efforts to redevelop the remaining stock of conventional public housing—the country's most visible reminder of subsidized housing—have remained fraught. Many public housing projects have simply been demolished, but hundreds of others have undergone more nuanced attempts at replacement, usually involving some form of a mixed-income approach. Details matter a lot here: all public housing redevelopment efforts are not alike, and the distribution of benefits varies greatly. This book attempts to distinguish between redevelopment efforts that contribute to the loss of well-located public housing, and those that attempt to preserve and enhance the opportunities that remain available to extremely low-income households.

PUBLIC HOUSING REDEVELOPMENT: THE HOPE VI PROGRAM

In 1992, HUD launched the chief national effort to reinvent public housing, known as both the Urban Revitalization Demonstration and, more lastingly, as HOPE VI. The HOPE VI acronym initially stood for Homeownership and Opportunity for People Everywhere, terminology diplomatically accepted by the incoming Bill Clinton administration to symbolize continuity with the earlier set of HOPE homeownership initiatives promoted by the outgoing administration of George H. W. Bush. Within a few years, as homeownership within public housing proved to be a less prominent aspect of HOPE VI, the moniker quietly shifted to a more generic wish to provide housing, expressed as Housing Opportunities for People Everywhere. HOPE VI initially provided grants of up to $50 million to public housing authorities to remake projects. Over the next two decades, this program invested more than $6 billion, leveraging tens of billions more, in comprehensive redevelopment attempts. Carried out in more than 130 different cities, HOPE VI targeted 260 of the nation's public housing projects judged to be most "severely distressed." In turn, the HOPE VI program has been both lionized and lambasted. Supporters, epitomized by the volume *From Despair to Hope*, coedited by Clinton's first HUD secretary, Henry Cisneros, viewed HOPE VI as the "new promise" of public housing in American cities. In sharp contrast, others found little of redeeming value in a program that has caused one city's poor to be "driven from New Orleans" and that, viewed nationally, disproportionately displaced African Americans in ways that left little more than "New Deal Ruins."[19]

HOPE VI, which derived much of its inspiration from the work of the National Commission on Severely Distressed Public Housing and its report in 1992, focused central attention on the issue of concentrated poverty and sought ways to end it. Drawing heavily on William Julius Wilson's book *The Truly Disadvantaged*, HOPE VI proponents downplayed the parts of Wilson's work that emphasized the larger forces of deindustrialization and suburbanization that had contributed to the decline of many central-city, black, ghetto areas, and instead drew attention to the neighborhood effects of concentrated poverty itself. In this view, the overriding goal for public policy involved facilitating escape from inner-city neighborhoods. Although some early HOPE VI developments permitted redevelopment in communities that remained 100 percent public housing, the program's emphasis quickly shifted to strategies for mixing incomes.[20]

In *Clearing the Way: Deconcentrating the Poor in Urban America*, Edward Goetz trenchantly critiques the "deconcentration of poverty" trope. Following Goetz, this idea has continued to be vociferously debated among scholars yet has remained dominant among policymakers.[21] The most comprehensive quantitative analysis to date of the HOPE VI program as a whole, by sociologists Laura Tach and Allison Dwyer Emory, found that the program did indeed bring statistically significant changes to "poor, minority *places*" but concluded that the drop in neighborhood poverty "came from the net displacement of poor, minority *people*," rather than from increases in the number of wealthier households.[22] Some of this surely resulted from the deliberate reduction in public housing units at most of these sites, though it is also true that HOPE VI developers frequently failed to construct as many market-rate and homeownership units as had been wishfully proposed in the initial HOPE VI applications.[23]

Even if HOPE VI mostly promoted the deconcentration of poverty by requiring the poor to leave, much of the rhetoric about the program has focused on its ties to broader trends in neoliberal urban development. As a term, *neoliberalism* has frequently been both overused and underdefined. Seeking to pin it down, geographer Jason Hackworth's *The Neoliberal City* usefully contrasts the neoliberal present to an earlier brand of "egalitarian liberalism" steered by a Keynesian welfare state that viewed governmental intervention as necessary to cope with the failure of markets. The neoliberalism ushered in during the 1980s and 1990s represents a return to an earlier classic liberalism, with its view that the chief purpose of government is to protect the free exchange of goods and services. Seen this way, neoliberal restructuring entails "the removal of Keynesian artifacts (public housing, public space), policies (redistributive welfare, food stamps), institutions (labor unions, U.S. Department of Housing and Urban Development), and agreements (Fordist labor arrangements, federal government redistribution to states and cities)," while simultaneously supporting new forms of "government-business consortia" and policies that require work to receive government benefits. In the American city, this has entailed a "reduction of public subsidies and regulations, the aggressive promotion of real estate development (particularly spaces of consumption), and the privatization of previously public services."[24]

HOPE VI fits with this neoliberal project largely because of its reliance on public-private development partnerships, preference for private management, and frequent support for requiring work as a precondition for housing. As Matthew Gebhardt puts it, neoliberal public housing redevelopment is "consistent with a broad strategy to reorganize cities to support capital accumulation" because it "opens opportunities for real estate development, provides housing and consumption activities for middle and upper class residents, and improves the image of cities as safe places to live and invest."[25] In this way—at least in those neighborhoods that manage to entice private developers—the neoliberalism of HOPE VI must also be considered as part and parcel of gentrification.

HOPE VI AND GENTRIFICATION

At first glance it may seem odd to think of public housing as a site for gentrification, especially if gentrification is seen as a process of upgrading existing structures rather than a process of wholesale demolition and new construction. That said, the definition of gentrification has continued to widen, and use of the term now regularly includes "new build" processes that are led by a neoliberal state (or at least state facilitated), rather than by small-scale, private, upgrading initiatives. As Loretta Lees, Tom Slater, and Elvin Wyly argue, residential gentrification remains a prime way to close the "rent gap"— the widening difference between the economic return from the rights to use land, given its present use (known as the "capitalized ground rent") and its "potential ground rent"—the more lucrative return that this land could earn if "put to its optimal, highest, and best use." Robert Chaskin and Mark Joseph describe Chicago's efforts at mixed-income public housing transformation as nothing less than "planned gentrification."[26] Such redevelopment has often become caught up in these larger processes of class-based neighborhood regeneration, whether as the final piece or as the leading edge.

To many urban leaders, such practices hold understandable appeal. Seen most positively, gentrification contributes to the stabilization of declining areas, transforms deeply stigmatized images, increases social mix, reduces the pressures on suburban sprawl, lifts property values, reduces vacancy rates, augments local fiscal revenues, encourages additional development and makes this development more viable, and supports both state-sponsored and private development. As Robert Beauregard observes, many sorts of city boosters have every reason to support gentrification, including "redevelopment bodies, local newspapers, 'city' magazines, mayors' offices, real-estate organizations, financial institutions, historic preservationists and neighborhood organizations comprised of middle-class homeowners." Each of these, he notes, "has an interest in increased economic activity within the city and an affinity for the middle class who function as gentrifiers."[27] Local government law scholar Gerald Frug pointedly observes that for some cities such as Boston, exclusive dependence on property tax receipts means that "the only way to raise revenue is to gentrify: to raise the value of the property."[28] In recent years, state-led gentrification has become increasingly intertwined with efforts at place marketing, cultivation of the so-called creative class, and expansion of growth coalitions, all concerned with putting forth the best possible competitive advantage for a particular city.

At the same time, gentrification brings many other negative consequences: residential, commercial, and industrial displacement due to rent or price increases; psychological distress to those being forced out; community resentment and conflict; loss of affordable housing; homelessness; new housing demand pressures on adjacent areas; more expensive local services; and new local expenses for lobbying and marketing. It may lead to a loss of social diversity if a community shifts from socially disparate to uniformly wealthy and may have disproportionately dire effects on racial minorities.[29] All of this is, of course, quite market specific, linked to vacancy rates and prices. Moreover, such markets do not always remain stable.

When the larger economic context shifts in the middle of a project's implementation, as happened in many HOPE VI projects that took many years to implement, this becomes a chance to observe governance in action. Whose preferences win out when the initial economic calculations get upended? To a great extent, especially in cities with relatively strong housing markets, the contested efforts to implement HOPE VI are a proxy for larger conflicts over gentrification. Given the powerful political and economic forces behind such growth-driven initiatives, it is actually rather surprising that some cities, under some circumstances, have been able to use HOPE VI as a brake on gentrification, rather than its accelerator.

HOPE VI raises important questions for the future of what geographers Elvin Wyly and Daniel Hammel dub "islands of decay in seas of renewal." In many cases, HOPE VI brought new investment to neglected corners of cities, while in other places—such as those discussed in this book—HOPE VI brought new investment and new occupants into well-located areas already attracting considerable interest from private capital. These are instances where, as Edward Goetz puts it, "HOPE VI redevelopment plans attempt to take advantage of local housing markets poised to take off, awaiting only the removal of worn-down public housing to set tremendous neighborhood changes in motion." Goetz observes that it is "difficult" to calibrate new investment so that "it is sufficient to produce neighborhood improvement but modest enough to avoid triggering wholesale gentrification"—and many city leaders may not even wish to try to avoid it. Planner Peter Marcuse puts the central dilemma into the language of gentrification, asking whether "the expansion of the spaces of the gentry displaces the poor" and whether "the expansion looked to by the gentry can be made consistent with the deconcentration of [public] housing and opportunities for the poor." Marcuse worries that "investment by the gentry and income mixing in public housing, if not carefully handled, may in fact come together with the same undesirable result: a disproportionate worsening of housing opportunities for poor and African-American families." If the term *gentry* here is read to connote something more like "bargain-hunting middle class," this nicely sums up the challenge put before those seeking to implement HOPE VI.[30] The leadership in some cities does wish to "carefully handle" the balance between seeking investment and minimizing displacement, but the responses vary quite a lot.

Sociologists Deirdre Oakley and James Fraser argue that HOPE VI exemplifies "a pervasive neoliberal discourse that assumes, polemically, that the only way to address concentrated poverty in traditional public housing is to destroy it and reinvent it as new mixed-income redevelopments."[31] Yet the story of neoliberal privatization of public housing paints its critique with too broad a brush. Although there are indeed many neoliberal purges at work, there are sometimes also more heartening outcomes from HOPE VI. Rather than a uniform set of practices operating in lockstep exploitation leading to displacement and gentrification, this complex program warrants closer scrutiny of what Neil Brenner and Nik Theodore term "actually existing neoliberalism." Instead of assuming uniformity, they call for analysis that is "intended to illuminate the complex, contested ways in which neoliberal restructuring strategies interact with pre-existing uses of space, institutional configurations, and constellations of sociopolitical power."[32] To do so with HOPE VI means paying close attention to the overarching political history of urban development in each city while remaining alert to signs of productive pushback and unexpected victories. The dominant picture may indeed reveal an unraveling welfare state, but one cannot understand the fraying without paying close attention to the fray.

Especially in places where neighborhood activism has been honed by previous battles over displacement induced by urban renewal and highway projects, the boundaries of what could be considered politically possible shift. As Robert Fairbanks points out, the urban renewal era commenced with lingering ideals about shared civic obligation to support programs that would be "for the betterment of the entire city." If the ill-housed faced the wrenching consequences of displacement, this could be justified as necessary for improving the overall health of the metropolis. By the 1960s, however, public discourse shifted "from protecting the public good to promoting the rights (and self-defined needs) of citizens," thereby threatening "the agenda of business-led city governments preoccupied with growth."[33]

The mid-century period of close government-business cooperation epitomized by the shared governance of the urban renewal program rapidly disintegrated once other community-based voices demanded to be heard. Christopher Klemek has charted the "transatlantic collapse" of this "urban renewal order" during the 1960s and 1970s and notes that planning and design professionals only later came to "confront the complexity of economic viability (as opposed to idealized modernist form alone) or the volatile force of democratic political resistance."[34] Urban renewal had come to the fore because cities needed a way to restore fiscal stability through enhanced property values and taxation, and that imperative never went away. In the 1990s and 2000s, HOPE VI provided a renewed mechanism to confront these fiscal and planning challenges, now rendered more complex because of community-based contestation. HOPE VI—not unlike the initial Housing Act of 1937 or the urban renewal efforts of the 1950s and 1960s—was a national program implemented differently in each local situation because of wide variation in political and economic conditions.

In short, rather than either some consistently conspiratorial evil or, alternatively, some welcome panacea, the national transformation of public housing has been implemented in wildly different ways, with markedly different intents, yielding dramatically different results. In this book, I present four detailed case studies, offering a detailed comparative analysis to explain this variation in the HOPE VI program. I identify ways that housing for the poorest Americans can sometimes be retained or reclaimed, rather than slated for demolition or lost to gentrification. At base, public housing redevelopment under HOPE VI occupies a continuum between two poles: one that favors creation of communities that minimize the post-redevelopment presence of the poorest, and one that attempts to retain public housing residents as the majority in the new community, while nonetheless seeking to mix incomes in more subtle ways.

Most commentators about HOPE VI seem to assume that the various deployments of the program are all pretty similar, but HOPE VI data supplied by HUD reveal an extreme range of income-mixing practice nationwide. This diversity matters. Figure 1.4 conveys the multiplicity of mixed-income practice in terms of levels of subsidy. Looking only at the percentage of units allotted for occupancy to public housing residents in HOPE

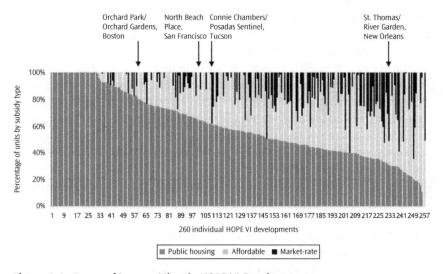

Figure 1.4. Range of Income Mixes in HOPE VI Developments
The HOPE VI program has varied dramatically in terms of the allocation among public housing, affordable, and market-rate units. The four examples featured in this book fall at very different points along this spectrum.
Credit: Author, based on data supplied by HUD for the entire HOPE VI program, January 2015.

VI developments (shown in medium gray) clarifies that projects range all the way from those with no public housing units to those with all public housing units. The variation encompasses 5 percent of developments that have fewer than one-fourth of units allocated to public housing residents, and fully 40 percent that have kept public housing residents in the minority. But at the opposite end of the spectrum, another 13 percent of HOPE VI developments are entirely devoted to public housing occupancy.

Figure 1.4 also shows a large amount of variation in the distribution of units not allocated to public housing residents. The middle-range "afford-able" components of these mixes (shown in light gray)—typically achieved by deployment of LIHTC-supported apartments—range from zero to more than 80 percent of units. Finally, the market-rate components (shown in black) range from zero to more than 60 percent of units. This book, by fo-cusing on approaches undertaken in New Orleans, Boston, Tucson, and San Francisco that fall across this spectrum, seeks to explain the reasons for such disparate implementation, while keeping the focus on how the poorest residents are treated under each place-based scenario.

Taken overall, about half of HOPE VI developments still exhibit a low-income skew, meaning that they overwhelmingly house residents whose in-come is below 60 percent of AMI. At the opposite extreme, 12 percent of HOPE VI efforts feature a high-income skew—places where public housing residents constitute a minority, and where more residents pay market rates than occupy units designated as affordable. Another 7 percent of HOPE VI efforts exemplify a polarized low-high mix—a sharp disparity between a majority of extremely low-income households and another group paying market rates, with the middle tier of affordable housing de-emphasized. Finally, the remaining 30 percent of HOPE VI sites house a broad continuum of incomes, defined as having a minority of units allocated to public housing households, but where more of the remaining households receive a shallow subsidy (usually resulting from LIHTC) than pay market rates. These four basic types are illustrated in figure 1.5.[35]

Despite four distinct types of actual practice, many academic studies, professional reports, and journalistic accounts seem to assume that HOPE VI mixed-income redevelopments typically fall into the broad-continuum type—with roughly equal allocations of public housing, market-rate, and "affordable" units. In reality, only about one-third of all HOPE VI projects have even as much as 10 percent of their units allocated to each of these three categories. This misperception may have arisen because so much of the mixed-income scholarship has focused on Chicago and Atlanta, where such one-third/one-third/one-third mixes have often been intended, if not always realized. By contrast, the majority of HOPE VI projects have allocated more than half of redeveloped housing units to poor households eligible for

Remaining units

		More affordable than market rate units	More market rate than affordable units
Public housing	>50% of total units	Low-income skew 52% (n = 135)	Polarized low-high 7% (n = 17)
	<50% of total units	Broad continuum 30% (n = 77)	High-income skew 12% (n = 31)

Figure 1.5. Four Types of HOPE VI Allocation Mixes
All of the 260 HOPE VI examples can be categorized as one of four types, based on their allocation of public housing, affordable housing, and market-rate housing units. Source: Vale and Shamsuddin, "All Mixed Up."

public housing.[36] Much previous scholarship has thus focused on atypical cases that have attempted broad income mixes while overlooking the majority of projects that kept most redeveloped units for low-income families. By exploring a wider variety of examples, this book will help redress this imbalance (figure 1.6).

In addition to variety in the allocation of income mix, the mixed-income communities developed under HOPE VI also vary significantly in other dimensions.

Importantly, income mixing differs substantially in the intended proximity of the mix. In some HOPE VI communities, apartments housing families with different types or levels of subsidy live as next-door neighbors. Elsewhere, developers prefer more attenuated income mixing, with market-rate or LIHTC-supported households located in separate buildings, or even on disconnected sites. Such decisions about how and where to build a mix seem likely to affect social interaction in the development. Similarly, the mix in HOPE VI developments also varies in terms of opportunities for rental versus ownership. One-quarter of all HOPE VI grant recipients proposed developments that would be entirely occupied by renters, but the rest attempted to construct a mix of housing tenures; 57 percent are at least two-thirds rental but include some ownership. A third kind of tenure mix— accounting for 17 percent of HOPE VI cases—is more balanced between ownership and rental opportunities, containing at least one-third of each. Finally, a few HOPE VI developments skew much more heavily toward home-ownership, and there is even one case—Washington, DC's Townhomes on Capitol Hill—that is wholly composed of cooperative homeownership units.[37]

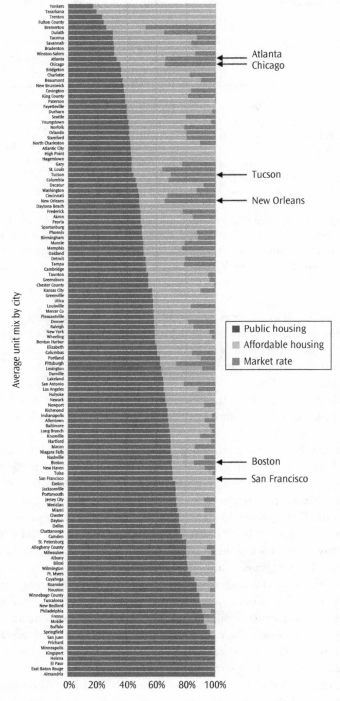

Figure 1.6. HOPE VI Public Housing Share in Six Cities
The share of mixed-income housing devoted to public housing residents varies widely
by city, not just by individual HOPE VI project. At one extreme, the four HOPE VI

Scholars of communities frequently view the presence of homeowners as a marker of stability, since they are usually tied to long-term mortgages and are also likely to invest themselves heavily in both their home and their neighborhood. With HOPE VI, however, simplistic assumptions may not hold since, following redevelopment, it is often low-income public housing renters that remain the longest. Here, too, the nature of the mix carries important social consequences and underscores the need to pay close attention to individual communities.

THE SIX HOPES OF HOPE VI

At base, HOPE VI embodies six hopes, many of them quite contradictory. First there is the hope of *reimaging*, that the reputation of cities will benefit from the removal of dangerous and unattractive projects. Dramatic before-and-after images convey this hope, ironically reminiscent of an earlier generation of slums juxtaposed with new public housing projects. Second, there is the hope of *reinvesting* with new capital spending that can revive distressed and disinvested neighborhoods. Third, proponents share the hope of *reforming residents*, who will benefit from the chance to live in a new, mixed-income community where they can find role models and gain greater self-sufficiency. Fourth, there is a countervailing hope of *releasing residents* from the shackles of life-constraining projects; they will then "move to opportunity" with the assistance of a fortuitously deployed portable voucher. Fifth is the hope of *reinventing housing authorities* as asset managers[38] who can learn from best practices of the private sector. Sixth, and most controversially, the hope of many housing authorities has entailed *reprioritizing beneficiaries*.

Many housing authorities now favor attracting higher-income tenants able to pay correspondingly higher rents as one way to offset declining federal funding. At the same time, revising the tenant economic profile

---

Figure 1.6. continued
cases in San Francisco, on average, provided 71 percent of units for public housing occupancy, and Boston, with five HOPE VI developments, reserved 70 percent of its units as public housing. Tucson and New Orleans are closer to the national average, with 44 percent of units devoted to public housing in Tucson (three developments) and 48 percent used for public housing in New Orleans (four developments). At the other extreme, the two cities receiving the most scholarly attention and national publicity— Chicago and Atlanta—are outliers. The nine HOPE VI developments in Chicago proposed, on average, to devote 35 percent of units to public housing, while Atlanta, with seven HOPE VI developments, targeted just 32 percent of units for public housing. Credit: Author with Nicholas Kelly, compiled from data supplied by HUD in January 2015.

upward also accords with the desire to reward only the "deserving poor." Public housing redevelopment typically requires existing residents to move off-site during construction, and this provides an opportunity to rethink who should be able to come back. Although most tenant groups negotiate some kind of "right to return" agreement, HOPE VI redevelopment efforts usually entail a shift to private management. Such companies frequently impose increased levels of screening, coupled with new rules and policies that some former residents may judge to be onerous or intrusive. Saddled with the difficult task of governing some of the poorest Americans, these new managers pursue ways to improve a development's image and marketability. For all of these reasons, housing authorities and their partners have frequently used HOPE VI to move away from housing the least-advantaged families and instead attract working families at the higher end of income eligibility for public housing. Clearly, however, not everyone shares the same hopes. These first six hopes—centered on reimaging, reinvesting, reforming, releasing, reinventing, and reprioritizing—are viewed chiefly from the top-down perspectives of housing authorities, mayors, federal officials, and developers. From a resident's point of view, the hope is often much simpler: I hope *I won't lose my home.*

These multiple, contending hopes make clear that judging success in HOPE VI redevelopment can never be simple and should never be uni-dimensional. Instead, a wholly transformative version of HOPE VI—the aim of future housing policies—needs to embrace the goals of as many parties as possible. At the same time, though, a truly equitable successor to HOPE VI ought to place the well-being of the least-advantaged public housing residents as the sine qua non in any definition of a successful outcome.

THE EVOLUTION OF HOPE VI

There are at least three reasons why it is a mistake to consider HOPE VI as a single entity. First, HOPE VI goals—and implementation of those goals—varied dramatically across the country, depending on particular constellations of forces: the housing authority, the housing market, the local political climate, the power of neighborhood groups, the strength of tenant advocacy organizations, and neighborhood experience with prior urban renewal efforts. Second, HOPE VI practice has varied significantly even *within* cities, depending on the real estate development climate around a particular site, as well as the power of particular neighborhood interests. And third, HOPE VI evolved as a program in significant ways over nearly twenty years, frequently subjected to differing institutional priorities and regulatory constraints.

When HOPE VI awarded its initial grants in 1993, the program seemed little more than a way to provide greater funding for bricks-and-mortar reconstruction, although this was augmented by language emphasizing residents' empowerment and allowed up to 20 percent of the grant to be used for social service provision. Still, the focus remained on upgrading a severely distressed housing project and assisting its residents. At first, talk of concentrated poverty and public-private partnerships for mixed-income redevelopment seemed secondary. And so did outright demolition. This quickly changed once Republicans gained a congressional majority following the midterm elections of 1994 and demanded major changes at HUD. As Clinton's HUD secretary, Cisneros scrambled to reinvent HUD to forestall Republican threats to demolish the entire agency. At a time when bipartisan support seemed necessary, HOPE VI offered timely opportunities for "policy entrepreneurs" to put forth novel ideas. HUD policymakers soon offered unprecedented flexibility to local housing authorities and their partners, part and parcel of the era's larger efforts at government devolution and welfare reform. As Yan Zhang and Gretchen Weismann observe,

> In a very short time, the primary focus of the HOPE VI program moved from a concern about the isolation of families to a concern about the isolation of housing authorities [from the marketplace]; from a government housing program targeting poor people to a market-driven, mixed-income housing program for the deserving poor and even the well-to-do; and from a modest attempt to cure the ills within the projects to an ambitious plan to revitalize urban communities.[39]

St. Louis–based developer Richard Baron proactively got the attention of Cisneros, and HOPE VI soon entered into a brave new world of ambitious mixed-finance efforts to remake neighborhoods. Two important factors converged: Cisneros and Congress wished to reduce the concentration of poverty in public housing, which opened the door for emphasis on attracting a broader mix of incomes; and HUD general counsel Nelson Diaz delivered a favorable opinion concluding that it would be legal for private entities to own public housing. This meant that HOPE VI could be used to leverage additional private capital such as that available through Low-Income Housing Tax Credits. Starting in 1995, HUD required HOPE VI applicants to identify potential leveraging partners and in 1996 strongly encouraged applicants to propose mixed-income developments. HOPE VI quickly became dubbed "HOPE VI Plus."[40]

Cisneros also attracted much greater interest in HOPE VI from private developers by working with Congress to overturn the long-standing requirement that any sold or demolished "hard units" of public housing must be replaced on a one-for-one basis. In place since 1969, except for a brief period in the mid-1980s, this mandate for replacement revealed the extent of concern about the loss of low-rent housing due to urban renewal clearances. By 1969, Edward Goetz argues in *New Deal Ruins*, "Urban renewal was so widely used and demolition of low-cost housing so common, that Congress felt the need to ensure that public housing development would keep up with the removals." HUD's reversal of this approach, initiated provisionally in 1995 and soon made permanent, accelerated the shift of deeply subsidized public housing in the direction of vouchers, while making it possible to envision many different kinds of mix under the thoroughly ambiguous banner of "mixed income" redevelopment. Between 1993 and 2010—when the Obama administration superseded HOPE VI with the Choice Neighborhoods Initiative—the main HOPE VI program redeveloped 260 sites, and a separate demolition-only program provided grants to raze additional public housing in 287 communities. Ultimately, for a public housing program that experienced a net loss of 250,000 units in this period due to a combination of HOPE VI and other programs, Goetz concludes, "The most important part of the evolution of the HOPE VI program was how it moved from an orientation toward rehabilitation to a program that relies on demolition."[41]

In its early years, aided by the opportunity to deploy mixed-finance approaches, HOPE VI practices evolved largely without promulgating new regulations. Instead, HUD tweaked the program with each successive notice of funding availability (NOFA) that suggested new priorities. In 1994, it was HOPE VI Plus (the initial suggestion of mixed income and leveraged finance); in 1995, with the use of computers and the internet rapidly expanding, the NOFA proposed a "Campus of Learners" concept; by 1996, HUD encouraged applicants to adopt "new urbanism"—a return to traditional architectural styles and street patterns. HUD and the Congress for the New Urbanism even issued a joint publication, *Principles for Inner City Neighborhood Design*. In 1997, the HOPE VI NOFA's annual theme stressed provision of services for a postwelfare clientele. Other NOFAs encouraged respondents to think about everything from public-private partnerships to resident homeownership to defensible space strategies to program managers.[42]

Most significantly, however, HOPE VI implementation changed *after* an award of funds, during the negotiation of grant agreements at each site. Often, the local public housing authority (PHA) significantly reworked the original proposal, yielding unanticipated tensions. HUD required HOPE VI applicants to consult with the existing public housing community and surrounding neighborhood before submitting an initial application, but this did not mean things could not change thereafter. It is common for any complex real-estate deal to go through multiple iterations, yet this proved particularly contentious in neighborhoods where city leaders and private developers regarded the lingering presence of distressed public housing as a barrier to the flourishing of an otherwise robust local real-estate market.

To outsiders, public housing redevelopment under HOPE VI may seem a straightforward result of winning a federal grant and implementing the proposal that had received funding. Yet, in place after place, the actual process as experienced on the ground could not be more different. The plans that yielded successful receipt of HOPE VI grants were, most commonly, treated as little more than suggestions—subject to changes as circumstances and preferences evolved, both locally and nationally. Senior HUD officials charged with monitoring the HOPE VI program point out that many cities submitted their original applications before they "had a chance to think their plans through very carefully." Thereafter, many plans evolved over time due to changes in the housing market, the failure of developers, as well as changes the PHAs made after collaborating further with HUD. Especially in the mid-1990s, as HUD pressed PHAs to introduce then-novel mixed-finance approaches, some HOPE VI teams worried, "Oh my god, how are we going to do this?" and changed their estimates about what might be possible.[43]

PHAs and their consultants invariably needed to pull together applications for HOPE VI revitalization very quickly, even if they had earlier received an initial grant to assist them with their planning. HUD mandated that no application could be submitted without involving affected residents and the broader community and explicitly required a resident training session and several public meetings. Yet such requirements remained vague, so actual practices varied quite a bit. Residents needed to be consulted, but participation could often be rather rushed and limited, especially if a local tenant organization had leaders who were not broadly supported or well engaged with the full range of constituencies in the development. Because of this, in some cases a nervous sign-off often came only after reassurances about particular kinds of unit mix and carefully articulated expectations about the terms of return to the new community. Perhaps most importantly, these proposals marked an initial agreement with a community but could not possibly address all of the contingencies that would later arise. Although public housing residents and their neighbors might understandably regard HOPE VI application as a kind of promise, in reality this grant was merely a first step in a long process. A successful HOPE VI application brought funding from HUD but did not yet delineate a full set of development partners needed to actually carry out the implementation.[44] And, as the number of financial players expanded and diversified, the project parameters often shifted.

The wrenching consequences for community morale and cohesion of such shifts in strategy and intent can hardly be overstated—even if they are eminently explainable by financial exigency. Instead of some single "HOPE VI Plan" that gets funded and then executed, there can sometimes be a succession of evolving proposals—each with different assumptions and different beneficiaries. At times, the evolution bends to the demands of residents or their advocates; more often, the shifts—from pre–HOPE VI to various iterations of HOPE VI to the final disposition of investment in the site—are driven by the calculations of developers, the pressures of neighbors, and the whims of politicians.

It is deeply revealing that HUD's own data management system for HOPE VI provides no way to account for most of the broken promises felt most deeply by residents. This is because HUD does not count the baseline for project delivery as commencing with the submission and award of a HOPE VI grant. Instead, the "project estimates" get recorded only after a subsequent grant agreement has been reached and revised to reflect what a PHA and its development partner eventually conclude will be a financially and logistically feasible way to proceed. In real-estate terms, this makes perfect sense; in human relationship terms, this is often highly problematic.

Adding to the flux, HUD frequently chose not to fund HOPE VI grants in the full amount requested. That shortfall, in itself, forced difficult decisions over what to include or exclude in a revised plan. If everything promised in the grant application cannot be delivered, then what remains and what does not? And who remains and who does not? Moreover, HUD wanted HOPE VI to leverage additional nonfederal funding. This meant that the actual viability and ultimate form of a HOPE VI project depended largely on the availability of funding from other sources that may not have even been considered at the time of the initial application. Again, in putting together complex real-estate deals, this kind of stressful mutability is standard. To developers, this accounts for much of the financial risk—and financial reward—of entering into such ventures. To low-income public housing residents, however, the stakes are different. To them, this is not some real-estate tabula rasa. Their sign-off on participation—or even partnership—in a particular HOPE VI grant represents a clear set of stipulated promises about their present and future homes.

In the early years of HOPE VI, grant recipients regularly reported that they expected a majority of original residents would return to live in the redeveloped sites. In 1999, for instance, the fiscal year 1993–1998 grantees collectively estimated that 61 percent would get to come back. Over time, however, both estimates and realities continued to plummet, especially as HOPE VI pivoted to serve increasing numbers of residents who did not have extremely-low incomes. By 2003, those same early grantees now indicated only 44 percent would return, and even that number proved highly inflated. In part, a General Accounting Office study determined, this was because "grantees lost track of some original residents for a number of reasons." HUD "did not emphasize the need to track original residents until 1998 and did not require grantees to report the location of residents until 2000." Moreover, HOPE VI sites almost invariably faced disputes about *when* to start counting original residents with a right to return—especially in cases where the housing authority deliberately accelerated vacancies in the long run-up to redevelopment. As a whole, HUD-reported data as of 2014 for the HOPE VI program as a whole estimated that, on average, just one in four relocated households returned to redeveloped HOPE VI sites.[45] This figure almost certainly overstates the rate, both because so many of the original households were lost and because some original households could be counted twice if they were split at the time of return to provide a separate unit for an adult child with a family.

While HOPE VI's critics on the left stressed displacement and the loss of units, the Right assailed the slow pace of development. In many cases, HOPE VI redevelopment efforts took much longer to realize than had been promised, adding to the frustration of everyone involved. As of late 2014, about one-quarter of all HOPE VI projects still had uncompleted units, and one-third of those had been launched back in the 1990s. In other words, many quite early HOPE VI initiatives, especially some of those on very large sites, have remained unfinished more than two decades after the award of funds. While such delays are quite common in intricate real-estate endeavors, each extra year in limbo made it less likely that households would return to the completed project. Susceptibility to property market swings worsened with the Great Recession that began in late 2007, markedly curtailing some HOPE VI development—especially in cases that emphasized units that would be sold or rented at market rates.

Housing consultant Jeffrey Lines, who was the principal author of the national commission report that helped inspire HOPE VI, has subsequently assisted or managed HOPE VI grants with seventeen different housing authorities across the country through his firm TAG Associates. Asked about what types of things changed between HOPE VI applications and subsequent implementation, Lines stresses the difficulties of implementing homeownership, especially if it required subsidies. "Mayors didn't want a bunch of rental housing. They wanted some folks that would also pay property taxes." In some application rounds, HOPE VI NOFAs suggested that including a homeownership component would make proposals more competitive, "So there were certainly some things that folks did to *be* more competitive." After winning the grant, though, "They had to figure it out in reality." Then, once reality meant recession, "The economic implosion beat up a lot of homeownership plans." In the worst-hit markets, "You could not get someone to underwrite anything that wasn't an assisted unit. So unless there was some form of public assistance, it was not something for which an equity investor was going to put equity in. Period."[46] Meanwhile, HOPE VI kept to the premise that grant recipients would be required to leverage large amounts of other funds.

At base, HUD and Congress deliberately chose not to scale HOPE VI grants to cover the costs of replacing the public housing that this new program sought to demolish; the initial grant maximum of $50 million got reduced to $40 million in 1996, $35 million in 1997, and $20 million in 2002.[47] In the unusual cases where one-for-one replacement of "hard units" ensued, it either happened early in the program before the height of the mixed-income push, or else resulted from strong local pushback. Most often, implementing HOPE VI has meant downsizing public housing—at the risk of increasing homelessness. Even the required social service component sometimes seemed a short-term measure to cope with the initial political backlash against the program. These provided a way to invest in the well-being of vulnerable residents who were being involuntarily displaced, and to help them deal with the fact that the redeveloped housing communities would no longer be scaled or oriented in a way that would include most of their former, extremely low-income residents. The service component also provided an appealing—if often illusory—promise that additional exposure to job training and other supports would be enough to cause an upward shift in income sufficient to make more of them into desirable tenants (or even homeowners) in the new communities. As with the first round of public housing construction—when few former slum-dwellers were invited back to occupy the new homes built upon the site of their razed dwellings—so, too, HOPE VI represented no more than a highly selective reprieve.

By framing the problem of public housing as one of concentrated poverty (instead of emphasizing more structural problems of racism, low wages, and poor education) HOPE VI proponents assumed all could benefit. Viewed through this lens, those who did not return to the revitalized development would still gain simply by no longer living in "severely distressed" public housing. The voucher carrot paired with the HOPE VI stick promised release from the violence of the projects. Anything other than those places would, almost by definition, constitute an improvement. For some people—those able to find private landlords who would honor their vouchers and able to cope socially and financially with their new circumstances in "opportunity neighborhoods"—this did prove to be a desirable solution. For others, though, an involuntary move out of public housing either meant a move into other nonrenovated public housing in an unfamiliar and sometimes unwelcoming neighborhood or a gamble with a private sector landlord, often located in an area almost as impoverished as the former housing project. Moreover, as sociologist Robert Chaskin points out, "For many voucher holders, even where initial moves were made to safer, less poor neighborhoods they were often followed by subsequent moves to high-poverty, racially segregated, socially isolated neighborhoods." Frequently, moves onward and outward from concentrated poverty yielded homes in safer places, but this could be undercut by the cost of diminished social networks and enhanced expenses for transportation, utilities, and childcare.[48]

Just as careful and copious research has found no more than limited support for the economic value of "moving to opportunity," so too researchers have also consistently found that HOPE VI developments themselves have fallen short of fulfilling many of the most cherished assumptions of ardent proponents. "Public housing transformation that began under the Clinton administration," Janet Smith observes, "was not an evidenced-based policy decision."[49] Rather, this serial experiment in social mixing got launched with wishful thinking.

HOPES AND REALITIES

Most research on mixed-income housing commenced only after the federal government chose to make a heavy investment in it. Social scientists Mark Joseph and Robert Chaskin, together with their colleagues in Chicago and more recently at the Cleveland-based National Initiative on Mixed-Income Communities, have spent more than a decade evaluating mixed-income communities, while also developing ways to categorize and assess the claims made for their success.[50] Drawing on their own work in Chicago, but also taking into account the findings of a wide range of other researchers, Joseph and Chaskin show that supporters justify mixed-income housing as facilitating four distinct kinds of gain—at least in theory. The presence of higher-income residents is said to provide (1) increased social capital for low-income residents; (2) direct or indirect role modeling of social norms for work and behavior; (3) informal social control leading to safer and more orderly communities for everyone; and (4) gains for the broader community through enhanced engagement of political and market forces.

Regarding the first proposition about social capital, researchers have found little empirical evidence that mixed-income development will lead to changes in residents' social networks. "Most studies," Joseph determined, "have found little interaction across income levels, and those that have found such interaction have not been able to demonstrate that it has led to information about jobs or other resources." Similarly, Joseph notes that "the presence of middle-class role models has become a fundamental and commonly accepted rationale for mixed-income development," but that researchers have consistently found little substantiation that it occurs, especially in terms of "proximal one-on-one interactions across income levels." Chaskin and Joseph's subsequent empirical work confirmed that "social interaction among residents in these communities—and particularly between residents of different races, incomes, and housing tenures—is restricted, overwhelmingly casual and of limited instrumental benefit."

Joseph's literature review found more empirical support for the third proposition—the notion that mixed-income housing could promote greater informal social control—but concluded that this resulted mostly from "strong property management" rather than simply the actions of residents. The power of mixed-income communities to deliver greater social control depended on the willingness of "higher-income residents, particularly homeowners," to be "more stringent about upholding rules and regulations." Finally, Joseph found the most empirical support for the idea that mixed-income communities could exercise positive influence on the overall "political economy of place." In other words, having additional higher-income individuals—who could be presumed to bring greater stability and spending power—would leverage greater external resources by encouraging new neighborhood investment, thereby raising the stakes and expectations for everyone involved.[51] Measuring progress on these particular four presumed benefits of mixed-income communities is not the only way to assess the success of such places, but it does engage many of the most debated issues.

That said, as geographers James DeFilippis and Jim Fraser trenchantly observe, all four of the most frequently voiced rationales for mixed-income policies are "largely based on the (hegemonic) mantra that low-income people themselves are the problem, and that a benevolent gentry needs to colonize their home space in order to create the conditions necessary to help the poor 'bootstrap' themselves into a better socioeconomic position." Framed this way, "Poor people . . . come to be simply 'a problem' that we need to spread out—and the language of 'fair share' or 'regional equity' that is often heard sounds remarkably similar to how people involved in environmental justice movements talk about things like waste transfer stations or incinerators."[52]

Ultimately, decisions to include or exclude the poorest in a new HOPE VI community are not merely individual judgments made about particular people. Instead, attitudes toward the poorest are developed and cultivated in a more collective manner over a long period of time. Conversely, the attitudes of the poor toward municipal authorities are also rooted in deeper histories, tied to community power relations linked to class, race, and gender inequities that long predate anything known as HOPE VI but still help to condition its reception. HOPE VI may appear to many of its protagonists as fundamentally about a real-estate deal. To impoverished tenants, however, it is linked to many other kinds of deals that have previously governed their lives.

How can we best unpack the concept of HOPE VI? It is, simultaneously, a real-estate deal, a management experiment, a community replacement strategy, and a social engineering venture. Pursuing each of these goals entails different measures of success. If it is primarily a real-estate deal, success could be assessed in terms of a return on investment, and its capacity to yield a high-quality product for its residents. This is already hard to do, but at least we know some ways to measure this, and the best firms win frequent awards. If it is primarily a management experiment, other factors enter in. First is the question of public and private responsibility; HOPE VI asks us to consider whether the private sector is always a better choice. More pointedly, the choice of management is linked closely to issues of rules and rule enforcement. Does the threshold for good management entail setting so many barriers to entry that only the most easily managed tenants can get in and remain? Every manager or landlord only wants good tenants, but the HOPE VI experiment asks whether we have mechanisms that are fine-tuned enough to screen out criminals, gangbangers, and drug dealers without also rebuffing good low-income citizens whose only crime is their poverty as expressed through poor credit histories, low education, few skills, persistent disabilities, and frequent joblessness.

If the principal aim of HOPE VI is to be a mechanism for replacing a community, must it always demonize the community that previously existed and lionize the new one? How do we come to terms with the work of ethnographers who have studied distressed public housing communities and found deeply valued social networks providing childcare, as well as other forms of personal and financial support? Finally, if HOPE VI is primarily a social engineering venture, success comes in still different forms. Should it be judged by how well very different subcommunities can coalesce in a single place? Building diverse communities is never easy, and, as Oakley and Fraser summarize, "Purported benefits of social mix for low-income residents have been elusive," and, sometimes, "interaction may mean conflict."[53] Although the social science research on HOPE VI and other mixed-income communities has so far shown very little positive mixing, such copious evidence has not been allowed to get in the way of the aspirational myth, the hope. Ultimately, the quality of interclass mixing should not be the only measure of success. More than this, low-income urban residents—just like all others—are in search of respect.

STRUCTURE OF THIS BOOK

After this introductory chapter that provides an overview of HOPE VI aspirations and practices, Part I concludes with a second chapter examining how cities develop distinctive governance constellations that shape attitudes toward low-income housing. The impetus behind HOPE VI can differ from city to city, and neighborhood to neighborhood, because different key players stand out as more influential than others. Specifically, the relative empowerment of low-income residents and their allies helps set the terms of each HOPE VI experiment, coloring what is politically possible in each place. Some of this relates to the real-time machinations of dealmaking and opportunities during HOPE VI implementation itself, but much of this is more deeply rooted in a larger political culture. Much of each city's political culture has been shaped and buffeted by past efforts to redevelop low-income areas. In those cities where past backlashes against perceived excesses in land taking and displacement led to lasting citywide movements to resist this disruption from happening again, there seemed to be much greater protection for the poorest citizens once HOPE VI arrived on the scene. These governance constellations are diagrams of power and influence. As such, they are about more than regimes focused on the relationship between government and business and can include more players. By examining particular instances of HOPE VI processes in the context of previous rounds of urban renewal in that particular city, we reveal the pattern of power sharing.

In Parts II, III, IV, and V—which each contain multiple chapters—the narrative shifts into detailed empirical analysis of four specific HOPE VI sites, located in New Orleans, Boston, Tucson, and San Francisco. Although the focus remains on one place-saga in each city, this is treated in the broader context of city and neighborhood history.

These four in-depth cases begin on one side of the HOPE VI spectrum (see figure 1.4) by examining an example from New Orleans. The St. Thomas to River Garden transformation has been judged successful by many local observers but has also been vociferously denounced by low-income residents and their advocates because the push to achieve mixed-income redevelopment shifted most of the poorest residents out of a desirable central neighborhood. Building fifteen hundred apartments in St. Thomas cleared a mixed-race community to create what was initially an all-white project. The Housing Authority of New Orleans (HANO) constructed a great deal of public housing across the city, but city leaders largely refrained from implementing urban renewal efforts during the 1950s and 1960s. While this allowed many neighborhoods to escape the wrecking ball, it also meant that New Orleans did not develop the kind of community-empowering backlash against perceived redevelopment excess that came to the fore in many other cities. New Orleans developed a strong white-dominated clientele for historic preservation, but—despite a long succession of black mayors—did not have a comparable network of citywide tenant advocacy organizations, not-for-profit housing developers, or elected officials committed to the well-being of low-income residents of color. By the 1960s, St. Thomas rapidly moved toward all-black occupancy, and HANO entered in a period of protracted dysfunction. When the possibility of HOPE VI funding arrived in the mid-1990s, redevelopment at St. Thomas meant heavy reliance on private developers, plus a deal-saving commitment to add an enormous Walmart to the site. Despite significant contention from residents and their allies, redevelopment minimized the presence of extremely low-income households in the new community of River Garden; just 12 percent of the original St. Thomas households were able to return.

By contrast, Part III focuses on Boston's transformation of Orchard Park to Orchard Gardens, which successfully retained centrally located public housing as a resource for the poorest. In contrast to many places where redevelopment into mixed-income communities has offered the poorest either marginal status in a community or has forced them to scatter to other impoverished communities, Boston's leaders chose to mix incomes without mixing out most of the poorest residents. Instead, many of the city's poorest were able regain their dominant presence in a desirably located HOPE VI community. When Orchard Park first opened in the early 1940s, it housed 774 households, most of them white. After an initial stable period, conditions at Boston Housing Authority (BHA) properties plummeted and vacancies skyrocketed, lurching the mismanaged agency into an unprecedented court-ordered receivership during the early 1980s. By the time HOPE VI came around, Orchard Park remained deeply scarred by drug-related violence yet still featured a vibrant tenant organization and a committed community. Most importantly, the political climate for redevelopment in Boston had dramatically shifted. Famous for its dramatic embrace of a massive urban renewal program under the direction of Ed Logue, there was also a corresponding backlash. Still riven by the (pre-Logue) total clearance of the city's West End and further fractured by the central-city clearance associated with ill-advised highway projects, Boston developed a rich array of countervailing social movements and not-for-profit housing developers. Armed with mayoral support and a revitalized BHA, maximizing—rather than minimizing—the return of public housing residents became a political necessity. At Orchard Gardens, fully 85 percent of apartments remained as public housing. The BHA set goals for income mixing but agreed that these could be met slowly. The BHA, like other public housing agencies, wished to "deconcentrate poverty" yet chose not to blame residents for creating the problem. They resisted rehousing families that had been causing trouble with drugs and violence but otherwise welcomed back Orchard Park households wishing to remain in the redeveloped neighborhood. The redevelopment did entail a loss in the overall number of units, but the BHA greatly reduced this loss by deploying an innovative multiphase effort to scatter and spread new housing onto vacant lots in surrounding areas. In stark contrast to the displacement that occurred in the transition from St. Thomas to River Garden in New Orleans, nearly 70 percent of the households from Orchard Park returned to live in the new Orchard Gardens.

That said, the rate of resident return should not be the sole measure of HOPE VI success. The return rate often reveals a municipality's underlying attitude toward the poorest of the poor, but there are other ways to engage in respectful treatment, even if the return rate is not so high.

Part IV considers the case of Connie Chambers in Tucson, a far more politically conservative city than Boston, where willingness to build public housing in the first place proved quite limited. While Tucson erected a total of just fifteen hundred public housing units, the city had no shortage of experience with urban renewal. In 1966, Tucson's housing authority constructed the two-hundred-unit Connie Chambers project in the Santa Rosa barrio, just south of downtown Tucson. Importantly, this was but one small part of a clearance effort nearly twice the size of the one that razed Boston's West End. And, just as in Boston, the devastation of homes in Tucson had lasting repercussions. The lingering resentment in the city's Mexican American community meant that any future public housing redevelopment needed to proceed with great caution. Thirty years later, after a period of decline and a perception of extreme isolation, the city's Community Services Department (CSD) received a HOPE VI grant to redevelop Connie Chambers as Posadas Sentinel, part of a broader effort to revitalize the larger barrio. The overall development plan also included a child development center, learning center, health center, expanded recreation center, and grocery store, with a housing complex for seniors constructed nearby by a nonprofit organization.

The transformation of Connie Chambers into Posadas Sentinel stands near the middle of the HOPE VI spectrum of income mixing (see figure 1.4) but is certainly no middle-of-the-road solution. Tucson's CSD preserved all of Posadas for subsidized occupancy and sought to diversify the income range and type of housing tenure without including any strictly market-rate residences. It did so in several innovative ways. By staging the demolition and development of the project in phases, just as Boston did, the CSD offered residents greater opportunities to remain on-site. For those who preferred to leave, however, the housing authority acquired 130 scattered-site public housing units, many of them in newer subdivisions being built across the city. On the site itself, the CSD replaced 60 public housing units and added 60 units funded with LIHTC, plus 60 additional subsidized homeownership units. In contrast to other housing authorities, such as those in Atlanta or Chicago, that emphasized the provision of vouchers that required public housing-eligible residents to seek housing with landlords in the private sector, Tucson's leadership found a way to reduce concentrations of poverty through city-owned, scattered-site public housing while also working to maximize the ability of the lowest-income residents to remain on site. Unlike many HOPE VI efforts that endured protracted arguments about a "right to return," in Tucson the process of getting resident agreement proved much less contentious (though hardly without detractors). This alternative mechanism for mixing out the poorest, in combination with sincere efforts to also mix them in as part of the redeveloped site, suggests that all HOPE VI does not have to be the same. Just 22 percent of Connie Chambers households returned to live in Posadas Sentinel, but the Tucson CSD provided most of the rest with other excellent public housing options.

As the book's final HOPE VI saga, Part V considers San Francisco's North Beach Place. Completed in 1952, this 229-unit project replaced a low-income industrial and residential area in a predominantly Italian neighborhood near Fisherman's Wharf. Initially a development overwhelmingly occupied by whites (which led to a landmark racial discrimination suit when blacks sought entry), North Beach Place gradually became highly diverse, with substantial African American and Chinese populations. Thousands of San Francisco's blacks lost their homes when the city razed the Fillmore District during urban renewal, and the city became a hotly contested battleground against development-induced displacement in Chinatown, all coupled with antihighway protests elsewhere. As in Boston, San Francisco developed a broad constellation of forces determined to help low-income households stay put once HOPE VI money became available.

With North Beach Place located on either side of the terminus of a major cable car line, by the 1980s huge numbers of tourists attempting to reach Fisherman's Wharf found themselves disembarking in a dangerous and crime-ridden housing project, uneasily located just across the street from several upscale hotels. Rather than join the whirl of high-end, market-rate development, the San Francisco Housing Authority's HOPE VI proposal—lifted by the city's strong nonprofit housing community, empowered tenant groups, and a supportive mayor—sought to preserve public housing occupancy for low-income residents, while eschewing entirely the option of a market-rate component. At North Beach Place, unlike the other cases discussed in this book, the SFHA achieved one-for-one replacement of all public housing units *on the original site*. Still, the overall mix of incomes places it toward the middle of the HOPE VI spectrum (see figure 1.4) since the SFHA's plan both densified this site and broadened the range of resident incomes by augmenting the public housing with 112 units of LIHTC-supported housing. In addition, the redeveloped complex included a new supermarket, additional below-grade parking, and new street-level retail.

Faced with an even greater degree of high market-rate demand than what had caused leaders in many other cities to hand prime land over to private developers and retain only the minimum number of low-income residents that would be politically and financially palatable, San Francisco's leaders did the opposite. They sought to maximize the number of affordable housing units on the site while still taking care to produce a community that could be secure and appealing to both residents and neighbors. Thirty-six percent of the original households returned to the redeveloped site—far higher than the average HOPE VI rate—though many others preferred to relocate with vouchers.

In short, the particular constellations of players in Boston, Tucson, and San Francisco chose to go much further in accommodating the needs and presence of the lowest-income households than did the leadership in New Orleans. In these three cities—prodded by some combination of lingering resentment over past displacement, pressures from tenants and their advocates, the influential presence of not-for-profit housing developers, the engagement of local elected officials, or the opportunities afforded by unusual housing market conditions—the impulse to minimize the presence of the poorest in central parts of the city has been actively resisted. Importantly, the Boston, Tucson, and San Francisco variants followed three quite different paths from the developer-centered approach pursued in New Orleans. In narrating these four stories, each of the book's case study parts will emphasize a different structure of governance.

LEARNING FROM HOPE VI AND HOPING FOR MORE

As these brief descriptions of Parts II to V suggest, I am seeking to understand the lived practice of HOPE VI in four quite different, relatively large American cities. I have selected New Orleans, Boston, Tucson, and San Francisco to convey a broad range of regions and urban trajectories, revealing the reasons behind wildly differing approaches to income mixing and to, by extension, the management of poverty. By focusing on one public housing community in each of these cities, tracing it across its full planning history, I seek to understand the structure of its sociopolitical context in ways that can clarify the complex collective decisions about how—once the opportunity of HOPE VI funding became available—the redevelopment of particular places has occurred. Keeping the comparison meaningful in the context of the evolution of HOPE VI as a program, all four examples benefited from grants received in 1995 or 1996. This situates them in the early middle part of the program—late enough so that each needed to address HUD's preference for mixed-finance approaches right from the start, but early enough so that they have been completed and it is possible to assess them as occupied places. To narrow the four-city comparison a little further, I look at those neighborhoods in each city where private development interest ran particularly high. To do otherwise would risk confusing places that are centrally situated and hotly contested with other places of isolated abandonment that may well be located elsewhere in the same cities. Although I concentrate on one particular public housing development in each city, I set this investigation in the context of other redevelopment practice in that city, thereby revealing both commonalities and anomalies (see figure 1.6). In contrast to past accounts that have either praised or vilified the HOPE VI program as a whole, I demonstrate that there really is no such thing as a typical HOPE VI project and explain how and why this is the case. There is, instead, a single named program that yields multiple variants in practice, each revealing different ideological positions about the place of the poorest.

Ultimately, in the book's concluding part, I attempt to explain why some housing authorities have chosen to redevelop communities in ways that retain substantial numbers of extremely low-income households, while others have chosen to disperse or eliminate the presence of the least advantaged. What factors encourage some cities and some neighborhoods to redevelop the best-located public housing in a way that preserves its availability to larger numbers of the poorest households? And, conversely, what explains why some jurisdictions have used the HOPE VI program to restrict reoccupancy by extremely low-income households that had previously lived on the site? Framed a little differently, this raises key political questions: Who benefits from redeveloped public housing? And what institutional or neighborhood factors contribute to the variation?

My emphasis on the explanatory power of urban history and planning history is also a response to other scholars who have struggled to explicate HOPE VI variation in terms of quantitative economic geography. Jason Hackworth attempted to explain the broad variance in HOPE VI practice between projects skewed toward public housing provision versus market-rate units and could find little statistical evidence that it was driven some pattern of award size, race, income, amount of private funding, or local economic geography. Instead, he surmises that "deeply ingrained geo-institutional differences that manifest themselves through housing authorities are far more to blame for such uneven responses to HOPE VI."[54] Similarly, planning scholar Shomon Shamsuddin's analysis of all HOPE VI projects found no strong statistical relationship between housing market indicators, race, or poverty and the relative proportion of HOPE VI units devoted to redeveloped public or affordable housing (as opposed to market-rate housing), and he suggests that "unobserved variables like local politics may have an underestimated effect on housing redevelopment strategies."[55] In keeping with this more institutional lens, I believe that a lot can be explained by examining each city's previous experience with urban redevelopment efforts. Those places that faced the largest backlash against the perceived excesses of slum clearance and urban renewal—that is, Tucson, Boston, and San Francisco—seemed later to be more willing to adopt HOPE VI policies that advance the needs and rights of the poorest. This finding, in turn, illuminates the double aim of the book: to demonstrate the range of innovative approaches to public housing redevelopment in American cities, and to reveal what close observation of the HOPE VI program can teach us about the nature of urban governance.

2

After Urban Renewal

Building Governance Constellations

Urban redevelopment processes vary among cities even when they are implementing the same federal program. Examining how and why different types of actors have gained greater or lesser amounts of power in remaking public housing in a given city makes it possible to explain the variety of approaches undertaken with HOPE VI. To do so is more consequential than simply charting variations in implementation of a particular policy. It is also possible to characterize these approaches as types of urban governance, a process that, I contend, can be productively conceptualized through the spatial metaphor of constellations. Before turning in detail to the structure of governance constellations, however, it is worth underscoring the extent to which these patterns are produced over time. To understand how the stars become aligned differently in ways that help us explain divergent outcomes for HOPE VI, we must look first to each city's particular history of urban planning.

Much of the variation in HOPE VI approaches, as I will demonstrate, is rooted in a city's experience with earlier efforts at slum clearance, urban renewal, and central-city highways, especially in cases where these mid-twentieth-century redevelopment efforts sparked lingering resentment in residential areas. Those cities that experienced both significant urban renewal and subsequent outrage often developed strong institutional mechanisms to thwart future rounds of displacement. Sometimes, this backlash yielded broadly inclusive constellations of governance that favored preserving more public housing for low-income occupancy. The four case studies are not simply stories about implementing a housing policy; they are windows into what it means to govern the poorest Americans. The tales from New Orleans, Boston, Tucson, and San Francisco remind us that HOPE VI is heir to a half-century of efforts to manage poverty and promote economic development through displacement.

THE CHANGING GOVERNANCE OF PUBLIC HOUSING

The development and subsequent redevelopment of American public housing have taken place in tandem with changing conceptions of urban governance. Public housing projects are more than objects in the landscape; they are exercises in governance. As such, public housing is constructed both literally and ideologically. The initial mid-twentieth-century production of public housing involved several key decision-makers, but—a half-century later—public housing redevelopment has needed to contend with a vastly more populous array of potentially influential players. I characterize the different blends of decision-makers and the forces acting upon them in each city by using the metaphor of constellations.

Over time, tightly configured governance constellations once oriented by the polestar of the state have both expanded and diversified. Demands for participation by citizens and civil society institutions have burgeoned. Geographers and political scientists now regularly point to the influence of governance beyond the state. This includes what Michel Foucault characterized as governmentality—the tactics and technologies for implementing rules and policing spaces. Enhanced and broadened participation can sometimes lead to genuine power sharing, but sometimes may yield little more than an illusion of inclusion, masking the increased domination of private economic actors. Geographer Erik Swyngedouw warns of the "Janus Face of Governance-beyond-the-State," a useful reminder of the need to turn a critical eye to each type of governance constellation. Swyngedouw himself briefly refers to "a new constellation of governance" but does not pursue the metaphor further. Instead, he sees only "a proliferating maze of opaque networks, fuzzy institutional arrangements, ill-defined responsibilities and ambiguous political objectives and priorities."[1] In this book, however, I train a more sharply focused telescope on the governance constellations of New Orleans, Boston, Tucson, and San Francisco. By looking closely at the configuration of those constellations when applied to HOPE VI implementation, we can see urban governance with greater clarity.

To understand the historical origins of HOPE VI variation does not entail returning to the origins of the known universe, but I will nonetheless deploy an astronomical (or perhaps astrological) metaphor. In the beginning, by which I mean the 1940s and 1950s, the governance constellation had a public housing authority as its orienting polestar. When public housing was built, federal dollars entered localities through a relatively simple—if frequently corrupt and discriminatory—form of governance. Figure 2.1 illustrates the tight constellation of well-connected players. Not all of them were always white males, as in this image of the Boston Housing Authority board from the 1940s, but most authorities of this era had no more than

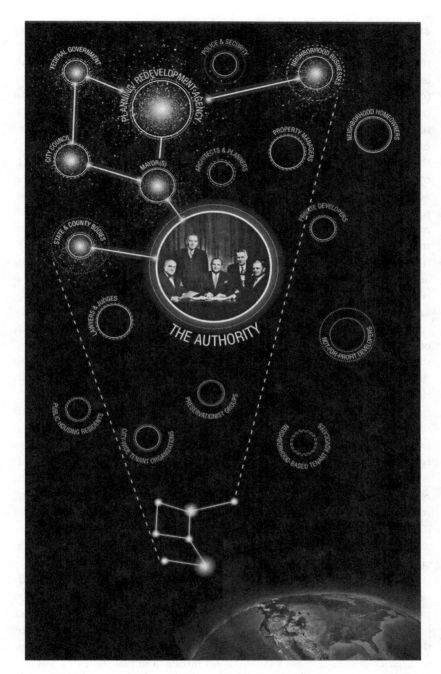

Figure 2.1. Distant and Telescopic View of Public Housing Governance Constellation in the 1940s and 1950s

In its earliest decades, public housing governance appeared as a tight constellation of public sector "stars." Zoomed in, as if through a telescope, the governance constellation of early public housing appears as a tight cluster of particular public sector players. Given the connection to urban renewal in the 1950s, however, the constellation also reveals an important link to private businesses. Still, its orienting pole star remains a public "housing authority."

Credit: Author with Suzanne Harris-Brandts.

token representation from women or nonwhites. This would become an issue in many cities once the clientele for public housing shifted toward female-led households and nonwhite occupancy far faster than did the constellation that governed them. Initially, public housing governance remained very much an insider's game. Mayors appointed all or most of the members of a housing authority board; city councilors sometimes involved themselves in site selection but otherwise left this to planning and redevelopment agencies. Occasionally, individual counties set up their own housing authorities, but few other individuals or agencies had the power to dictate policy. The federal government allocated funds and approved plans. Since residents for the new housing would not be chosen until its completion, they played no role in decision-making. Similarly, public housing construction had no role for neighborhood service organizations or legal aid groups, and the notion of not-for-profit housing developers did not yet exist. As a result, a small set of decision-makers asserted the capacity to choose how, and where, public resources could be allocated to house a city's poor. By setting the terms of selection for public housing, they got to choose which of the poor would be served and which would not. This combination of high selectivity and paternalist management meant that those who lived in the "slums" cleared to build public housing did not need to be chosen to live in the new developments built on the sites of their former homes.

Public housing facilitated a larger urban redevelopment agenda centered on the imperative of reviving downtown economic growth. As political scientist Clarence Stone puts it, "In many places political and business leaders came together and created arrangements to pursue economic growth and, as much as possible, keep it uncluttered by other concerns."[2] As a result, Stone and colleagues continue, "The poor, near poor, and other nonaffluent residents of the central city were thoroughly marginalized—displaced and disregarded, never part of the power-wielding body of insiders who set agendas, targeted investments, and guided the public discourse about the city's future."[3]

By contrast, the half-century of urban housing policy between the advent of postwar urban renewal and HOPE VI has continually been forced to grapple with the challenge of community participation. The Housing Act of 1954, which put forth "urban renewal" as the term of choice in lieu of the "urban redevelopment" language in the Housing Act of 1949, opened up greater possibilities for rehabilitation rather than just total clearance of urban sites. This provided some modest requirements for community participation. As part of demonstrating that it had a "Workable Program," each city needed to set up citizen advisory boards. However, this often entailed no more than token involvement of members from affected communities. Such groups, as legal scholar Audrey McFarlane concludes in her historical

survey of community participation, led to "very little meaningful participation in important redevelopment decisions." This is not the end of the
story, however. As McFarlane observes, the "unintended consequence" of
suppressed voices during the urban renewal era "may have been partially responsible for galvanizing the importance of including meaningful measures
for citizen participation in future urban development programs."[4]

In places with more deeply seared collective memories about past
excesses, new battles could be framed as efforts to rectify past mistakes—
or at least not to repeat them. Political scientist James Q. Wilson makes
clear that this backlash began even while urban renewal was very much
still underway. Whereas "many of the earliest redevelopment projects
were completed with little organized opposition," he commented in 1966,
"somehow . . . people have learned from the experience of others," and
now "planners often find prospective renewal areas ready and waiting for
them, organized to the teeth."[5] Alternatively, in cities that were not able
to consolidate a broadly shared understanding of some past neighborhood
injustice, each successive contested development setting has to organize its
protests around a specific place in the present. This distinction—between
cities with galvanizing events, long memories, and broad coalitions formed
to support the needs of the poor and cities that lack such things—seems
quite salient. Implementing HOPE VI programs has almost always been
controversial, but the structure of each controversy differs based on the
previous level of activism in that particular city. Much of this has to do
with shifting expectations about the surprisingly complex concept of
participation.

During the War on Poverty in the 1960s, programs such as the Economic
Opportunity Act's Community Action Program (CAP) famously called for
"maximum feasible participation of the poor," a requirement as vague as
it was bold.[6] Recognizing this ambiguity, McFarlane argues, the contemporaneous Model Cities program operated more cautiously. "In contrast
to Community Action's mandate . . . , Model Cities contained a general requirement of 'widespread citizen participation' but attempted to minimize
participation by channeling funding of development through state and local
governmental agencies instead of directly to community groups." Next, in
1974, the Community Development Block Grant (CDBG) program replaced
Model Cities and other programs. This program, McFarlane contends, "had
the dubious distinction of replacing the strong participatory mandates of
the Great Society with minimal citizen participation mechanisms," since it
required no more than public hearings. Still, this system did include funding
for local community development activities, which led to greater expectation for consulting with citizens. This did not yet affect public housing,
however. Legal scholar Georgette Poindexter notes that "the law continued

to exclude tenants from the public housing decision-making process long after initiatives such as CAP acknowledged the importance of community involvement."[7] Public housing residents acquired "a statutory right to participate in the redevelopment of their projects" only in 1984, when Congress amended the Housing Act of 1937 to require that any plan to demolish or sell public housing could not proceed unless the PHA's application "has been developed in consultation with tenants and tenant councils . . . who will be affected by the demolition or disposition."[8] Once HOPE VI emerged in the 1990s, there would be ample opportunities to test just what "consultation" might mean.

To Poindexter, the ambiguous language about consultation granted too much leeway to residents and their lawyers to stop the implementation of HOPE VI projects if they did not like a revision to the plan. "The scope of 'meaningful consultation' remains undefined. . . . Therefore, a tenants' association unsatisfied with a proposed revitalization plan of the local Housing Authority can use litigation to halt development. Practically speaking, this bestows great latitude and power upon tenant organizations while holding housing authorities to an undefined and changeable standard."[9] Poindexter points to a redevelopment effort in Atlanta where the tenants, the Atlanta Housing Authority, and the developer (a foundation) signed an agreement that carried both legal and psychological significance:

> For the tenants, the document represented an ending point. It symbolized closure of a long negotiation and served as an inalterable development blueprint. For the Housing Authority and the Foundation it functioned as a starting point, an initial outline that would be revisited and modified as the development process unfolded.[10]

Poindexter views this contradictory interpretation as prompting an unfortunate legal challenge from tenants once the developer decided that some aspects of the plan "were not reasonable market strategies" and made alterations. The residents' association "fought this bitterly," driving "a final wedge into the already tense and distrustful relationship," and then sued. The residents lost their suit, but it caused delays in completion of the community, prompting Poindexter to ask, "Why did it have to be so difficult?" She blames excessive resident empowerment. "The ambiguity of 'resident participation' can backfire when it creates an unrestrained power center in the hands of the tenants' association. Unchecked empowerment produces a strong incentive to resist everything and concede nothing." Instead, Poindexter calls for an approach to governance that would "ensure tenant voice while stopping short of a tenant veto."[11] Others, however, worry more about the risks of silence.

Legal scholar Lisa Alexander is also concerned about the ambiguity of "meaningful" consultation but seeks ways to ensure greater empowerment for marginalized residents. Alexander laments that the legal structure of HOPE VI does not "resolve the historic tension between rigid mandates for participation and broad privatized networks in which the meaningful participation of marginalized stakeholders can be easily undermined." Given that her work focused on Chicago, where gains for impoverished tenants largely depended on the rare resolution of lawsuits into consent decrees, her skepticism about the ability of "new governance" theories of jurisprudence to resolve the asymmetrical power relationships among HOPE VI players seems understandable.[12] Still, many HOPE VI fights have been more than just feisty. Some have yielded significant gains for residents even without the need for protracted litigation.

PARTICIPATION AND ITS LIMITS

Sherry Arnstein's classic "Ladder of Citizen Participation" identified eight rungs rising from nonparticipation (manipulation, therapy, informing) through token participation (consultation, placation) to citizen power (partnership, delegated power, and—at the apex—citizen control).[13] Arnstein, who served as the chief citizen participation adviser to the Model Cities Administration at the time her article was published in 1969, viewed participation as meaningful only when it actually empowered low-income citizens to affect the *outcome* of a development process in a way that let them "share in the benefits." Still, the ladder did not really clarify the relationship between strategy and outcome, and it assumed just one form of participation in any given process, rather than tactics for managing additional ascension. Arnstein's model did not account for multiple voices or acknowledge how racial or ethnic discrimination might delimit such participation (or how participation by racists, sexists, or others with antisocial attitudes might *enhance* such discrimination). As an artifact of the 1960s, when community development programs depended chiefly on top-down federal largesse, Arnstein's ladder arose before community development corporations or mixed-finance public-private partnerships became prevalent. This limits its utility for explaining the implementation of today's more complex deals. Specifically, as Rachel Bratt and Kenneth Reardon argue, the old ladder misses many newer, direct, bottom-up strategies and institutional mechanisms that can provide low-income residents with the capacity to negotiate partnerships, develop alternative plans, organize new coalitions, or engage in disruptive protests. Moreover, all ladders are not similarly situated; support varies considerably, depending on a longer community history, the outcomes of past political skirmishes, and shifting economic conditions. To grasp what Manuel Castells theorized as the relationship between "the city and the grassroots," urban social movements must be seen as the full interplay of dominant interests and citizen resistance.[14]

Today, seen outside the context of the civil rights and Black Power movements of the late 1960s, Arnstein's invocation of citizen control over urban policy decisions may seem like dated overreach, yet the HOPE VI battles of the 1990s and 2000s very much deployed language that recalls the rickety upper treads of her metaphor. Public housing leaders and their allies (including lawyers) did not wish merely to have their voices heard in a process run by others. Nor did they wish to remain stuck on any particular rung. Rather, they regularly insisted upon a HOPE VI outcome that would grant them a legally mandated role as a partner. Instead of a public-private partnership between a housing authority and a developer, public housing tenant organizations frequently demanded to become the third named participant in the deal. Sometimes, residents explicitly sought a particular role in the resultant community delegated to them, whether through some form of tenant management corporation or through oversight of the community's social service provision. To a great extent, these aspirations for true resident control proved unrealizable. Such paper partnerships often proved either elusive or illusive. This caused protracted angst and disillusionment, especially if resident leaders felt that the promises made to them in an initial HOPE VI application had been broken. Still, at least in some HOPE VI processes, resident groups made significant inroads, shaping development in ways that proved to be profoundly empowering. Elsewhere, though, residents found themselves manipulated and marginalized.

AN EXPANDING UNIVERSE: THE GOVERNANCE CONSTELLATIONS OF HOPE VI

The vexed issue of resident expectations for participation and influence often proved central to implementation challenges for HOPE VI, but it is linked to a much larger constellation of interests. In sharp contrast to the circumstances when public housing was first built in the 1940s and 1950s, municipal public officials no longer carried the same centrality. In some cities, mayors and city councils certainly held sway. Yet, because HOPE VI is financially structured as system that uses public sector grants to leverage (often much larger) private sector funding, the result is a form of public-private housing.[15] This means that the universe of players claiming a stake in the outcome is now far larger, and expanding. As Robert Stoker, Clarence Stone, and Martin Horak argue more generally, "Governing capacity no

longer rests with a cohesive body of elites in command of an array of resources responding single-mindedly to the decline of a city's economic
core. Governing power is now less concentrated, and today's urban movers
and shakers are less single-minded about the city's business core and find
themselves thinking more about how to reconcile bundles of social and economic challenges."[16] Reconciling such challenges now involves many more
players.

HOPE VI proposals for transforming public housing are therefore much
more than the results of ideas offered up by a local housing authority,
and governance extends well beyond the role of the state. Moreover, in
sharp contrast to the practices of the 1940s and 1950s, these expanded
constellations increasingly feature development professionals and community leaders who are mixed in terms of gender and much more likely
to include members of racial and ethnic minority groups. In many HOPE
VI governance constellations, the housing authority—once at the center of
the public housing universe—now appears as little more than a dwarf star.
Instead, other powerful players—especially mayors or private developers—
judge the housing authority to be weak or dysfunctional, a barrier to
obtaining federal largesse rather than a conduit. Given this, city leaders
frequently delegated production of their HOPE VI application to an outside
consultant.

As figure 2.2 shows, at least fifteen other urban governance components
may play important roles in carrying out a deal:

1. One or more successive mayors
2. A planning/redevelopment agency
3. A city council
4. States or regional bodies that bridge the city-suburb boundary
5. Federal agencies (especially in cases where there is direct oversight of
   a local housing agency)
6. For-profit private housing developers
7. Not-for-profit affordable housing developers
8. Architects and planners (who may be aligned with the housing
   authority, the developer, or with residents)
9. Lawyers and judges (especially in the case of litigation)
10. Nearby neighborhood groups (such as homeowners' associations)
11. Neighborhood business interests
12. Citywide tenant advocacy organizations
13. Neighborhood-based tenant advocates (including service providers)
14. Preservationist groups
15. Sometimes most important of all, the public housing residents
    themselves

Figure 2.2. Governance of Public Housing under HOPE VI
In contrast to the small cluster of public sector players and private business interests
that formed the constellation of public housing decision-making at the time when
most projects were initially constructed, in the HOPE VI era of the 1990s and 2000s
there is a much broader universe of relevant participants. Each HOPE VI case aligns
a different set of stars, although distinct patterns emerge, permitting distinct
constellations to become visible.
Credit: Author with Suzanne Harris-Brandts.

And, once a housing development is built, two additional players typically assist in its governance:

16. On-site property managers (who may vary quite a bit in terms of capacity and independence)
17. Security personnel (whether police or private forces), who may play new roles

The relative strength and visibility afforded to each of these seventeen components in turn causes each HOPE VI effort to appear as a distinct constellation. The universe of potential players may be the same, but, in each specific case, some shine forth much more brightly than others. And, sometimes, HOPE VI processes face sudden interventions from outside agitators, not unlike the passage of a comet or meteor.

In recent decades, political theorists such as Archon Fung have developed increasingly sophisticated ideas about deliberative democracy and "empowered participatory governance," seeking ways to make collective decisions more robustly shared and action-oriented, what Xavier de Souza Briggs calls "democracy as problem solving."[17] This certainly has relevance for understanding HOPE VI, yet these housing redevelopment processes have only rarely been set up as structured exercises in dispute resolution, consensus building, or power sharing, so it seems forced to impose such framing upon them. HOPE VI projects in some cities, such as Chicago, yielded "working groups," but even such formal or informal governance structures did not systematically include all stakeholders, let alone attempt to mediate a process. Instead, because these complex development processes are driven by the divergent agendas and priorities of multiple, distinct actors, it seems more faithful to the structure of the process to view these as contested narratives, and to try to understand them from the perspective of each protagonist. The list of players may be similar from place to place, but their relative power is not. This is why I call it a constellation of governance: out of the universe of stars, some stand out as most prominent. If we connect the brightest points, it becomes possible to visualize the operative diagram of power relations at each site.

The first challenge is to situate each constellation in its broader universe. As figure 2.3 shows, the various individual stars fall into one of four celestial quadrants. Viewed across the horizon, two are predominantly private-sector actors, whether for-profit or not-for-profit, while the other two are primarily public-centered, whether in the sense of the state or the community. And, if seen in terms of relative altitude, two can be seen as prone to more top-down action—the public sector and the for-profit private sector—while the

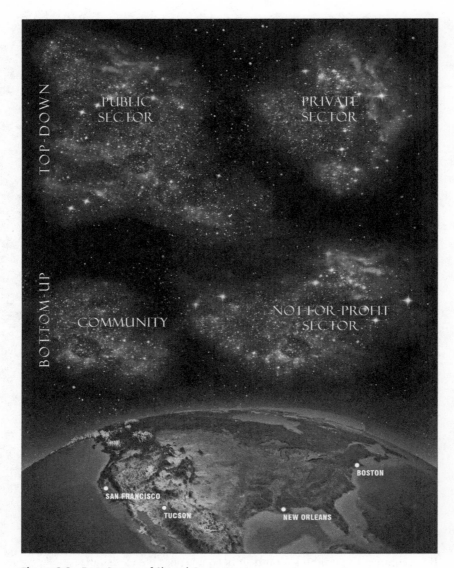

Figure 2.3. Four Sectors of Shared Governance
The complex nature of poverty governance under HOPE VI includes people and institutions from the public sector, the private for-profit sector, the private not-for-profit sector, and community members. Within this broad universe, each city develops its own constellation of stars, skewed toward one or another of these sectors.
Credit: Author with Suzanne Harris-Brandts.

other two—the community and the not-for-profit sector—operate in a more bottom-up manner. Importantly, because poverty governance constellations are broad partnerships, they connect across such sectors. They do not, however, link up evenly. Rather, they are skewed toward one or another corner of the visible universe in a distinctly imageable way. Each constellation has stars of varying brightness in all four quadrants but does not occupy the sectors equally.

Constellations contain many stars, but it is still possible to give a single name to the whole: think of Orion, the Big Dipper, Ursa Minor, or Pegasus. In astronomy and astrology such names are often allusions to myth. In the astropolitics of poverty governance, few central players attain such mythic status. As the four examples in this book will show, HOPE VI governance constellations can take at least four forms, what I call the Big Developer, Publica Major, Nonprofitus, and Plebs (figure 2.4).

The first type, the Big Developer, is named for its private sector dominance. Big Developer constellations subsume many other players but never let the primacy of private profits fade from view. In this realm, progress would be unimaginable without a private developer as its organizing image. River Garden in New Orleans epitomizes the Big Developer type.

By contrast, a Publica Major constellation retains a strong role for the state. Many private actors have roles, but central direction comes from public-spirited elected and appointed officials in the public sector. Tucson's Posadas Sentinel typifies such an approach.

Third is the constellation type I term Nonprofitus. In this configuration, not-for-profit organizations—whether developers or community-based organizations—carry special import. They are linked to others in the public and private sectors, but also have strong commitments to low-income residents. San Francisco's North Beach Place emerged from such a Nonprofitus constellation.

Finally, there is Plebs. Here, low-income residents themselves remain the sine qua non of the governance constellation. All of the other models must account for citizen participation, but in a Plebs constellation residents are key decision-makers, not just tolerated obstructionists. While some might today view the term *plebs* as derogatory, I use it here in a more neutral way, signifying the role of the general populace. The constellation governing the construction of Boston's Orchard Gardens truly respected its plebs.

In one reading, a governance constellation can be viewed as a meaningful arrangement of the brightest stars. Others of a more conspiratorial bent, however, may see a governance constellation as no more than a cosmic take on the same neoliberal regime: not only are business and political interests aligned, they are also coupled with co-opted resident association leaders who have been misled by complicit self-styled supporters from neighborhood

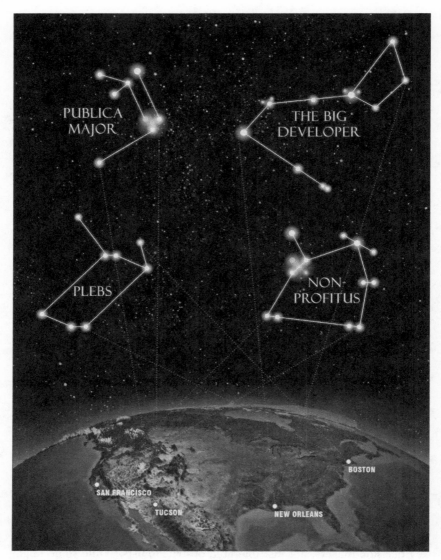

Figure 2.4. Four Types of Governance Constellations
As viewed from across the United States, HOPE VI governance constellations vary
greatly, but fall into four basic types, each skewed toward a different sector of the
sky. The first type, the Big Developer, is named for its private sector dominance.
By contrast, a Publica Major constellation retains a strong role for the state. In a
Nonprofitus constellation, not-for-profit organizations—whether developers or
community-based organizations—carry special import. Finally, there is Plebs,
where low-income residents themselves remain the sine qua non of the governance
constellation. The four cities in this book—New Orleans, Tucson, San Francisco, and
Boston—each illustrate one of these basic constellation types.
Credit: Author with Suzanne Harris-Brandts.

non-for-profit institutions that are excessively dependent on tainted money from foundations. These pseudo-progressive advocacy forces, in turn, foster a captive quiescence in the face of ongoing oppression. Pretending to share a struggle for spatial justice, they instead encourage a capitulatory compromise that works against the interests of the minority poor.

At the opposite extreme, champions of HOPE VI (and related sorts of public-private partnerships for other forms of public housing redevelopment) see a program wholly worthy of its Innovations in American Government award from Harvard's Kennedy School.[18] In this view, HOPE VI is a public-spirited, private sector rescue of failed public bureaucracies and once-decrepit physical environments. Supporters see investment in the creation of mixed-income new places, with private managers capable of enforcing rules, as a triumphant alternative to "concentrated poverty." Where there had once been dangerously dysfunctional social systems that failed to warrant being dignified with the term *community*, HOPE VI advocates have seen neighborhoods steadied and readied for new investment. Moreover, they claim, nearly all former residents will benefit. Even if they do not return to the newly developed community, voucher-armed low-income households will now be released from lives previously relegated to dead-end, racially segregated ghettos and given the choice to find opportunity elsewhere.

Is a governance constellation just a descriptive shorthand to describe structural economic failure—no more than a diagram of a rigged system—or is there room for historical contingency and individual agency that reveals significant local variation? I argue that governance constellations are not all the same or easily reducible to some single integrated co-opted complex. In some cities—and in some neighborhoods within them—quite different types of stars burn brightest. As a result, the overall patterns hold different meanings. HOPE VI governance constellations are not always dominated by a profit-driven private sector and its public hostages. The Big Developer constellation does not describe the only possible type of stellar alignment. Instead, the worlds of Publica Major, Nonprofitus, and Plebs suggest different ways of understanding governance. Much urban theory assumes that low-income residents will always be uniformly victimized by the forces of capital, yet how can that fact be squared with the great variation in HOPE VI practice in terms of the range and proportions of incomes present in a given project?

To understand a phenomenon such as HOPE VI, urban theory needs to catch up with the complexity of urban practice. Clarence Stone acknowledges that "the 'narrative of failure' is deeply entrenched" but contends that this "should not prevent us from seeing that social-equity gains can be real." But neither should it keep us from recognizing the forces that limit such gains in so many places. In any case, it seems increasingly clear that these gains and losses are now measured through a much more diffuse model of governance. Stone observes: "What had once been an urgent task of saving the city by refashioning the central business district morphed into a more complex undertaking as policy elites began to see that economic aspirations and community problems could not be neatly separated. . . . Accordingly, the policy domain of distressed neighborhoods is now populated with players and practices not prominent when downtown-centered redevelopment reigned as the distinct action priority for cities."[19] Urban regime analysis, including Stone's own famous work about "the informal partnership between city hall and the downtown business elite" in Atlanta, exposed the "privileged status of economic development," but this cannot fully account for what happened as cities moved into a postindustrial political economy.[20]

Starting in the 1970s, urban scholars developed explanatory frameworks more rooted in the political economy of cities and neighborhoods. They have argued that, far from following the "natural" processes of the Chicago human ecology school, the dynamics of urban growth and development are carefully plotted and created through economic and political mechanisms that produce the capacity to act. As articulated by John Logan and Harvey Molotch in *Urban Fortunes*, much of urban development is a product of a particular city's "growth machine"—a heady confluence of real-estate speculators, political leaders, business owners, insurance brokers, and universities. Others emphasize extralocal factors contributing to the priority on growth—national trends such as deindustrialization and economic cycles or broad policy initiatives such as tax incentives, rather than approaches centered at the scale of the individual city. Many others adopt a more global perspective when seeking to identify the drivers of urban change: enhanced residential investment (leading to gentrification) in centrally located neighborhoods is closely tied to a broader effort by cities to attract international firms with high-wage service sector employees. Whatever the scale, these observations support Logan and Molotch's "growth machine" model, revealing the dynamics that undergird the close relationship between municipal officials and the business community.[21]

At base, Logan and Molotch criticize growth-centric regimes for prioritizing the "exchange value" of property in the marketplace over the "use value" of neighborhoods that provide daily life benefits for residents. This basic tension continues to be a useful frame for understanding present-day development controversies. Still, this model, too, remains excessively time bound. Stone's famous account of Atlanta's regime covers more than four decades but is a demonstration of how a single type of regime—a development-oriented one centered on growth—persisted across multiple mayoral administrations and major racial change. This analysis does not explain how such a regime might shift to one of Stone's other types, such as a "middle-class progressive" regime, even though this kind of change did happen in cities such as Boston and San Francisco. As Stone and colleagues have more recently concluded, neither regimes nor growth machines can properly explain cities in "deep transition" because they "neglected to put policy and politics into an ongoing flow of time."[22]

Two of Stone's intellectual descendants, Peter Burns and Matthew Thomas, have recently proposed the concept of "political arrangements" to convey "a body of relationships that gives a city its policy-making character." Usefully, they apply this framework to a city undergoing change— New Orleans following the 2005 Katrina disaster—so they directly confront the issue of regime change over time. They also ask whether a given political arrangement is strong enough to remain cohesive over a long period of time, or whether its duration remains weak and limited. Burns and Thomas inquire whether a city has a "unified political arrangement" or instead one that may differ according to the type of policy arena, such as housing or education. Diagrammatically, they depict political arrangements much like an archery target, with the agenda-setting actors in the bullseye, supporters and beneficiaries near the center, those seeking to influence or redirect further out, and those "least served" at the margins.[23] All this makes sense and shares some commonalities with the governance constellation approach just described. What the governance constellation concept adds, however, is a more nuanced capacity to diagram relationships, convey hierarchies, and visualize the relative prominence of public, private, civil society, and community actors. Additionally, the governance constellation notion is concerned about more than policy formation; it is centrally deployed to visualize the power dynamics of policy *implementation* under particular local conditions. As a form of political arrangement, governance constellations evolve over time, and this dimension deserves special scrutiny. Applied to the poverty governance of HOPE VI, constellations as a mode of interpretation can shift as particular stars fade in and out of importance in the course of a contested creation. Still, if one steps forward to view the constellation from the time the new community is actually occupied, the overall pattern stands out. This pattern reveals not just the implementation of a particular program of the 1990s and 2000s but also lays bare a deeper multigenerational set of urban political conditions.

Regime analysis and its political-arrangements variant provide a potentially more inclusive frame than does an elite-led growth machine paradigm, yet both need to allot a greater role for historical memory. Sociologist Mary Pattillo's observation about Chicago seems more widely true: "The ghost of urban renewal is always present."[24] To assess the trajectory of HOPE VI or any other complex redevelopment project in any particular place, the starting assumptions matter. Those starting assumptions—the sense of "This is what is politically possible *here*"—are rooted in the historically contingent conditions facing each city's governance constellation, shaped by the successes and the frustrations of past neighborhood battles. A governance constellation—like a regime, a growth machine, or a political arrangement—can also only represent a single moment in time. My point is that such moments share a basic and traceable structure that has been in place for a long period, and that those structures are highly differentiated.

Sometimes, HOPE VI marks no more than the latest round of federally funded marginalization of the poorest. On other occasions, though, the pattern of shared benefits is quite different. In McFarlane's terms, low-income residents engage in "meaningful participation" that signals "an act of resistance." In such cases, resident empowerment is more than a way "to tinker with the process;" it can "redirect the emphasis away from uses and developments that gentrify centrally located neighborhoods, displacing poorer residents or channeling the resources of the city exclusively to the downtown business district."[25] Stone and colleagues observe that neighborhood actors frequently now play a more central and sophisticated role. "In earlier times, faced with what they regarded as a hostile agenda, neighborhood leaders mobilized to protest and resist freeways and other development projects." Now, in a postindustrial world where developers and city officials may need to pay more attention to broader constituencies, "Neighborhoods still find reasons to protest, but the strategic goal has changed. Rather than seeking to protect neighborhood integrity by a go-for-broke effort to derail an intrusive economic development agenda, neighborhoods can seek to participate in a policy process and make claims for the sake of community improvement."[26] In the complex politics of HOPE VI implementation, residents and their allies seem far more oriented to leverage than to derailment. Observing the ideas and actions of players within a given city's governance constellation can therefore help us understand more about the particular power dynamics of that city.

James Fraser and Edward Kick's study, "The Role of Public, Private, Nonprofit and Community Sectors in Shaping Mixed-Income Housing Outcomes in the US," sets out some of the groundwork for what a fuller analysis of HOPE VI governance might entail. They usefully point out the importance of examining a broad set of key actors across all sectors and observe that such players often pursue substantially different goals and operate with significantly different capacities—even within the same sector. These questions of capacity and orientation matter a lot, especially given the sort of protracted public-private partnerships that complex HOPE VI arrangements necessarily entail. Some players (particularly private developers seeking to attract new investment) may be more fully focused on place-based changes, while others (such as residents, their advocates, and community-based organizations) may be more fully centered on people-centered gains for existing dwellers. Yet, especially because they must work together, nearly everyone espouses both place-oriented and people-oriented aims. Still, as Michael Katz astutely noted, the real complexity of efforts to govern the poor must also cope with issues of resources, political economy, power, and markets.[27]

Fraser and Kick's analysis proposes the "admittedly ideal type hypothesis" that "if mixed-income initiatives are fueled by stakeholders that have common goal sets and high capacity, then favorable space- and people-based outcomes are highly probable," while, conversely, "if stakeholder goal sets are disconsonant and capacities are uniformly weak, the probabilities of success are low." They correctly predict that complex and contentious mixed-income housing ventures will not align so neatly. Accordingly, though their own paper provides illustrative accounts of two mixed-income efforts in North Carolina and Tennessee, they call for further "intensive case studies of housing initiatives" that emphasize "implementation" and "embed . . . their analyses within the context of the city in which they are deployed, focusing on the capacities of different stakeholders and the governance of projects in which they are involved."[28] This book attends to that call by endeavoring to situate each HOPE VI saga in its larger municipal setting—a situation that is anything but static. In this way, by emphasizing the urban history and planning history that preceded HOPE VI, I attempt to explain not just the capacity of various players, but the roots of their passions and the sources of their powers.

Complex governance structures, each with a city-specific or even neighborhood-specific constellation, shape every attempt to implement a HOPE VI project because important decisions about post-redevelopment community makeup are steered by the relative power of the players. When it comes to the provision of affordable housing, however, such governance structures are deeply rooted in long-standing local practices; such structures long precede the investment opportunity afforded by HOPE VI. Specifically, the neighborhood change made possible by HOPE VI takes place in the aftermath of each city's previous experiences with slum clearance and urban renewal. In some places this has empowered private development forces to press forward again in ways that are supported by local politicians and cannot be curtailed by neighborhood groups or residents. In other places, however, low-income residents and their allies have capitalized on these deep histories of mistrust to try to steer HOPE VI investment away from practices that contribute to urban gentrification.

When analyzed with respect to the microrelations of observed practice, the hybrid governances of HOPE VI can help us understand the puzzle of why a single program has been implemented locally with such high variation. Some "HOPE Sixed" sites re-emerge as 100 percent low-income communities, while others become dominated by a clear majority of high-income new residents and contribute to gentrification. Sometimes, even new communities that are primarily low income can support gentrification simply because they have resulted from the demolition of some vilified project and its replacement with a more benign community presence. This is often signaled by a correspondingly pastoral name change, invoking reassuring terms such as "Commons," "Village," or "Gardens." Governance, in these contexts, represents the confluence of contending authorities vying for influence over neighborhood investment. By identifying the diverse sorts of governance coalitions that can structure an approach to HOPE VI and by observing the outcomes that result, this book's case-based analysis of HOPE VI practice can help us rethink and refine established notions of "urban regimes" and "growth machines" that have shaped recent discussion about the development of cities.

POVERTY GOVERNANCE AND NEOLIBERAL PATERNALISM

In their landmark volume *Disciplining the Poor*, Joe Soss, Richard C. Fording, and Sanford F. Schram point out that poverty is "a problem of governance" because "the needs and disorders that arise in poor communities, and the difficulties they pose for societal institutions, must somehow be managed."[29] Their book dissects and documents the most recent trends in poverty governance, but remains centrally a critical analysis of welfare reform, with barely a mention of housing. Even so, the book's cover features a boarded-up mid-rise at Chicago's Cabrini-Green. The book may be about the policy tools and administrative arrangements of welfare reform, but when such policies need visualization, postwelfare HOPE VI projects seem a good place to look. Soss, Fording, and Schram's book offers more than an analogy; it provides an untapped way to ground the experience of HOPE VI in urban theory and practice.

Housing is more than an epiphenomenal offshoot of neoliberal welfare reform. It is, instead, a reminder that poverty governance takes place in *communities*, not just households; it affects *places*, not just individuals. HOPE VI dramatically brings together the policy discussion about work versus welfare with the dynamics of neoliberal property development and management practices. Disciplinary efforts to modify the behavior of the poor take place not just through paperwork or in meetings at the offices of social service providers but also in the selection processes for entry into mixed-income housing and in the shared physical places of neighborhoods, under the watchful gaze of private managers and their security personnel.

HOPE VI, brought forth in tandem with welfare reform, imposed new levels of selection, surveillance, and sanction on a system of public housing management seen to have grown far too lax. To Soss, Fording, and Schram, the current practices of poverty governance result from the confluence of paternalism and neoliberalism. Applied to welfare reform, paternalism arises from "a more directive and supervisory approach to managing the poor," in which the availability of assistance is "recast to emphasize behavioral expectations and monitoring, incentives for right behavior, and penalties for noncompliance." Receipt of benefits has, in short, been "made conditional on good behavior." This approach to behavioral monitoring intersected with neoliberal efforts in the 1990s to value "the state as an instrument for creating market opportunities, absorbing market costs, and imposing market discipline." In welfare reform, this meant deploying "work first" strategies and "personal responsibility" contracts, aimed at turning the poor into better citizens. This has a direct parallel in HOPE VI, where readmission to the new mixed-income community is often premised on a willingness to enter into "self-sufficiency" programs or, at least in some cities, to meet an outright "work requirement" as a condition of re-entry. Such demands, Soss, Fording, and Schram point out, fail to give "serious attention to the disabilities, life problems, family needs, and resource deficits found among the poor. In the process, they actively diminish opportunities to acquire education and other forms of human capital that people need to get better jobs." Given the mismatch between education and skills needed for jobs, an "aggressive work-enforcement system . . . willfully ignores the conditions of labor markets and poor people's lives." The result, they argue, is that these social service initiatives become little more than "tutoring programs that service low-end labor markets, thereby eroding the boundary between state and market."[30]

Provision of housing assistance has long been part of state efforts to sort, evaluate, regulate, and reform low-income populations.[31] At least since the arrival of the Puritans to Massachusetts in the 1630s, city leaders have sought to determine the causes of poverty by casting a cold eye on any incapacity of household heads to engage in paid work. For centuries, the American state has sought ways to identify and assist chiefly the "deserving poor"—those whose poverty was attributable to no fault of their own and who were otherwise engaged in upwardly mobile behaviors—while resisting the "undeserving poor"—those whose poverty could be rooted in their own behavioral failures.[32] In facilitating this moral selection, paternalism is not just an attitude; it is a spatial practice that is facilitated by some forms of designed environments much more than others. In contrast to the anonymity of either the unpoliceable back alleys of the early twentieth-century slum or the vast open spaces of the mid-century modernist superblock housing project, the neotraditional New Urbanist streetscapes of HOPE VI provide a return to surveillable space. As Soss, Fording, and Schram observe, "The 'new paternalism' bears a striking resemblance to earlier forms of paternalism, including the ideologies that attended nineteenth-century poorhouses, agencies for outdoor relief, and scientific charity movements. Indeed, even the major areas of behavior emphasized in poverty policy today—work, sex, substance abuse, marriage, child rearing, and so on—echo the main targets of earlier crusades to uplift and normalize the poor." Applied to mixed-income housing developments, as articulated by Chaskin and Joseph, the push is to make the poor adhere to "what development professionals often describe as 'market norms.'" Such "mechanisms of poverty governance reproduce marginalization and create new dynamics of social exclusion within the context of spatial incorporation."[33]

Just as HOPE VI ramped up, Congress passed, and Bill Clinton signed, the Personal Responsibility and Work Opportunity Reconciliation Act (PRWORA). This terminated welfare (AFDC) as an entitlement program and replaced it with the Temporary Assistance for Needy Families (TANF) program. Supporters cheered when welfare caseloads plummeted by about two-thirds in the first decade, but critics pointed out that those exiting from "temporary" support rarely did so because they no longer needed it. AFDC could be blamed for "making people dependent on welfare handouts," and TANF could be cast as "rewarding people who work hard and play by the rules by helping them achieve independence," but this wishful reframing masked the lack of economic progress by those most in need of income supplements in an era of economic restructuring that undercut wages and reduced opportunities for the low-skilled poor.[34] Similar arguments quickly arose as HOPE VI displaced tens of thousands of extremely low-income households from the neighborhoods that it purported to revitalize.

Public housing reform did not simply follow parallel efforts to impose conditional and behavior-centered welfare reform. Instead, the Quality Housing and Work Responsibility Act of 1998 marked a forceful return to the kind of conditional and behavior-centered provision of housing that existed when the public housing program began in the 1930s. In the earliest decades, some new public housing projects elicited so much demand that the gatekeepers of the housing authority could afford to interview ten households for each available apartment, choosing only the most desirable from among those who seemed to be income eligible (meaning that their incomes were neither too high nor too low). Within twenty years, however, most large, urban, public housing authorities had evolved into institutions that accepted all applicants—regardless of their financial or social circumstances—once they had reached the top of a waiting list. HOPE VI and the rest of the public housing reforms of the 1990s and 2000s sought firm ways to restore this earlier sense of reward and selectivity. Poverty governance, in the guise of neoliberal paternalism, has again attempted to "reconfigure the ways that poor people freely choose to conduct themselves."[35] This proffers the carrot of self-governance coupled with the stick of punitive recrimination if such responsibilities are not properly exercised. In public housing, this invocation of self-governance has taken the form of periodic flirtations with the idea of resident management corporations—an idea that carried ideological appeal but which rarely proved feasible. More typically, HOPE VI has delivered new forms of private management demanding stricter rule compliance. This has arguably improved safety, though not without significant contestation over cultural norms and social practices.

GOVERNANCE CONSTELLATIONS AND THE LEGACY OF URBAN RENEWAL: FOUR EXAMPLES

The first part of this book has outlined the evolving political, social, and cultural roles of public housing in the United States that led to promulgation of the HOPE VI program, while asking why this program has varied so much from city to city. To frame an answer, I have proposed the notion of governance constellations and suggested some ways that these may deal with the management of poverty, citizen participation, and gentrification. The governance constellations for public housing under HOPE VI are strikingly different from the ones that facilitated the initial creation of this housing, and it seems vital to document and diagram this fundamental change. I have postulated that the particularities of new constellations may have emerged in response to each city's past experiences with urban renewal and other forms of development-induced displacement of low-income residents. It is this, in combination with other aspects of the city's evolving political culture, that has shaped the attitudes toward rehousing the city's poorest residents in HOPE VI developments.

To test this entails rigorous and detailed engagement with the implementation of HOPE VI in particular places, paying close attention to the reasons behind the variation. In some cities, such as Tucson, a Publica Major HOPE VI process can be driven by a well-regarded housing authority. In Boston, a Plebs constellation shows support from a strong mayor and a reformed housing authority that granted particularly powerful roles to resident leaders. In other cities, though, weak or failing housing authorities—such as the one in New Orleans—permit HOPE VI to be led by the strength and deference accorded to a for-profit Big Developer and site-based property managers. But other cities with a weak housing authority, such as San

Francisco, behave differently: the presence of influential not-for-profit affordable housing developers and the power of tenant advocacy movements
can shape a Nonprofitus approach to HOPE VI. Undergirding this jockeying
for influence, urban leaders in cities such as Boston, San Francisco, and
Tucson have been forced to grapple with the contested racial legacy of urban
renewal, while those in New Orleans faced few such pressures. These four
windows into the spatial politics of HOPE VI collectively reveal how complicated it is to shape a future for public housing after the projects are gone.

Part II

THE BIG DEVELOPER IN NEW ORLEANS

Figure II.1. The Big Developer Constellation: New Orleans
Viewed from New Orleans, the Big Developer constellation shines prominently in the private sector of the sky.
Credit: Author with Suzanne Harris-Brandts.

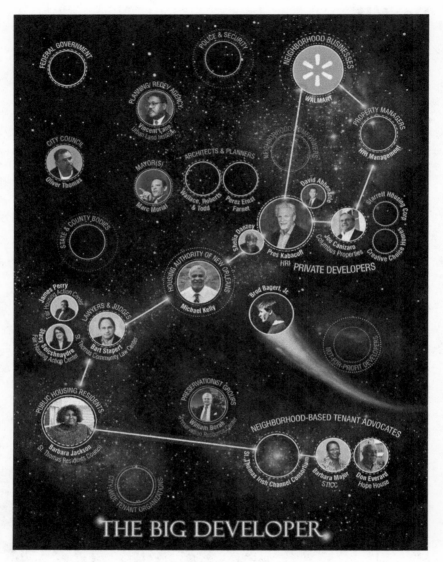

THE BIG DEVELOPER

Figure II.2. The Big Developer Constellation in New Orleans: Telescopic View
This telescopic view of the Big Developer constellation depicted in figure II.1 has
developer Pres Kabacoff as its orienting pole star. St. Thomas community members
and their not-for-profit allies also matter, but the constellation is skewed toward the
private sector, with the housing authority and the rest of the public sector playing a
secondary role.
Credit: Author with Suzanne Harris-Brandts.

HOPE Sixes are nothing more than finding a way to attract market rate. The subsidized are coming, but if you lose your market rate, you return to what was.

—Pres Kabacoff, developer of River Garden

OVERVIEW: PURGING THE POOREST AND SATISFYING THE DEVELOPERS

Part II of this book depicts one dominant strand of HOPE VI practice—the confluence of a weak housing authority and a strong developer in a city that failed to breed a robust tradition of coordinated resident advocacy and tenant empowerment. This discussion of New Orleans is spread across three chapters. Chapter 3 traces the rise and fall of the St. Thomas development, while chapter 4 follows the tortuous course that led St. Thomas to its redevelopment as River Garden, revealing the machinations of a governance constellation centered on the prerogatives of the Big Developer (figures II.1–II.2). Redevelopment remained hotly contested, and chapter 5 reveals the challenges of inhabiting and managing River Garden.

The St. Thomas development in New Orleans, completed in 1941 and extended in 1952, replaced a mixed-race "slum" area with public housing for white tenants. The fifteen-hundred-unit development shifted to primarily black occupancy following desegregation in the 1960s and subsequently underwent disinvestment that led to a protracted decline. Located in a part of the Irish Channel neighborhood that became rebranded during the early 1970s as the Lower Garden District,[1] the struggling housing project had multiple suitors eager to launch a transformation. Many powerful players regarded St. Thomas as "a crucial missing link needed to complete an unbroken chain of economically valuable city neighborhoods" from the French Quarter to Uptown. Within this part of New Orleans, St. Thomas stood out as "an isolated island of African-Americans in concentrated poverty." Still, despite (or because of) its "pivotal location," the redevelopment effort faced a long series of false starts and endured multiple lawsuits and setbacks.[2] Eventually, championed by maverick developer Pres Kabacoff, this yielded the mixed-income community of River Garden, completed in phases between 2001 and 2009.

Although the initial HOPE VI application had proposed a majority of low-income housing on the site, subsequent proposals shifted to plans emphasizing market-rate and tax-credit housing, with additional scattered-site public housing for large families long promised but never constructed. Eventually, however, market conditions soured and the actual development that got built has far less market-rate housing than this mid-course correction had sought to deliver. At each stage, old promises gave way to new financial realities, to no one's satisfaction. In New Orleans, given the poor reputation of the housing authority, there was ample reason and leeway for strong private sector developers to take the lead. Ultimately, a key $20 million needed to close the financing gap in the deal came from Walmart, whose Supercenter and supersized parking lot adjoin the development, to the great consternation of the city's preservationist community.

The St. Thomas saga typifies many other instances where the catalytic power of HOPE VI provided little more than an excuse for displacement. Rather than an investment that would create a "win-win" combination of a revitalized neighborhood and genuine opportunity for the former neighborhood's least-advantaged residents, the redevelopment process, slowly but surely, shunted public housing tenants to the margins—both literally and figuratively—and also failed to construct the market-dominated community that the developer wanted. Framed by policymakers as a "deconcentration of poverty," this strand of HOPE VI instead purged the poorest and failed to yield either an equitable outcome or a just process.

3

The Rise and Fall of St. Thomas

TWO SCALES OF HISTORY

In New Orleans, as elsewhere, understanding the dynamics of a complex project like public housing development—or public housing redevelopment—entails analysis of urban history at two different scales. Most obviously, there is the history of the project itself in two eras. That history traces the decision to clear "slums" and construct public housing and charts the corresponding process of clearing public housing and constructing a new mixed-income community. To participants, those processes happen in real time; they mark the tortuous path from promises to implementation of a particular project. But there is also a second time-frame at work, a deeper history that grounds the specific implementation saga of any particular project in a larger set of entrenched expectations about what is politically possible—and what is not. This larger history clarifies who can be trusted and included and who cannot and thereby establishes the structure of each city's governance constellation.

The public housing during of the 1940s and 1950s emerged during a simpler era of racialized governance. Fewer voices could be articulated, and those in positions of political and economic power faced few consequences from neglecting to listen. New Orleans had operated with machine-style politics since the nineteenth century, and "the dominant concerns for most local officials were patronage, power, and personal wealth." One study of fifteen large American cities found that, between 1931 and 1980, "New Orleans was second only to Chicago as the most corrupt city in the United States."[1]

In the 1990s and 2000s, however, public housing redevelopment straggled forward amid a much broader constellation of interested parties, many of them buttressed by those who held law degrees. At one level, this protracted contestation simply traces the evolving negotiation over what would built in a particular place and is thereby temporally bounded by the period between an initial project proposal and its eventual realization. Seen in a different register, however, the contestation is rooted in the prehistory of the proposal. This larger political dynamic, much of it rooted in racial animosities, determines what can be proposed in the first place. In New Orleans, as in every city with its own unique political and economic history, these baseline expectations will differ.

HOPE VI is not just a grant; it is both a process that extends from pre–HOPE VI to post–HOPE VI, and it is also a catalyst for larger neighborhood change being sought by prominent constituents of the governance constellation. HOPE VI is also not some single plan, though this is how it is usually framed. Rather, it is an iterative process of plan-making and promise-proffering. To developers, this is all part of finding what is needed to make a deal financially and politically feasible. To residents, however, it can feel like a constantly shifting set of agreements and expectations, a saga ultimately skewed to favor the needs and priorities of others.

Residents may enter this process with some genuine degree of buy-in, especially since the HOPE VI application required that housing authorities be able to demonstrate that residents were on board. In New Orleans, as in many American cities where housing authorities remained perpetually dysfunctional, launching a redevelopment process meant contending with deep-seated mistrust. As bad as conditions had become in the development, residents depended on it as their central social world and predominant support system, especially if they lacked stable employment elsewhere. To live in what others readily condemned as "severely distressed public housing" surely remained difficult, but to be displaced from these same troubled homes without a viable alternative could be even worse. Residents sought to exercise their voice, but successive waves of transformation proposals typically treated tenants as the object of development, rather than as its subject. At St. Thomas, like other public housing imposed onto existing communities, mistreatment of the poorest has deep roots.

THE UNEASY RISE OF ST. THOMAS

Origins and Development: The First Purge

Shortly after its establishment on March 15, 1937, the Housing Authority of New Orleans (HANO) commenced work on two projects: St. Thomas for whites and Magnolia for blacks, both of which opened in 1941 (figure 3.1). By early 1942, HANO had also opened four other developments: Iberville for whites and Lafitte, Calliope, and St. Bernard for blacks. In warmly embracing the concept of public housing, HANO quickly produced 4,881 apartments, all operated in accordance with prevailing Jim Crow "separate but equal" racial segregation principles that comported with the US Housing Authority's own "neighborhood composition" rule.[2] Previously, many older

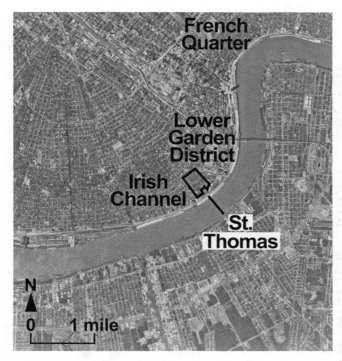

Figure 3.1. St. Thomas, the Lower Garden District, and New Orleans
The St. Thomas development, located along the slightly higher ground of the
Mississippi River's natural levee, emerged from the cleared slums of the Irish Channel,
a neighborhood later rebranded as the Lower Garden District.
Credit: Author with Jonathan Tarleton; aerial photograph 1VCUI00010057 courtesy of
the US Geological Survey.

portions of New Orleans featured racially mixed neighborhoods, so these
monoracial projects represented an increase in concentration, and actually
served as "the first implementation of legally enforced residential segregation in the city." Still, since the quality of housing provision between black
and white projects seemed similar, and since these projects represented a
marked improvement over poor-quality private housing, the racial segregation of public housing drew less immediate attention in New Orleans than it
did elsewhere in the country.[3]

Whatever the acceptance of segregation, however, residents certainly
objected to displacement. While the Magnolia Street neighborhood project
replaced an almost entirely black area with a project built for other blacks,
the situation at St. Thomas proved more complex. The piece of the Irish
Channel neighborhood cleared to build St. Thomas for whites housed many

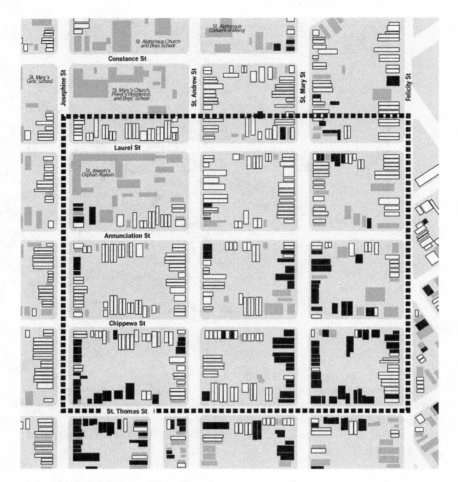

Figure 3.2. Racial Composition of St. Thomas Area as of 1930
To make way for the all-white St. Thomas housing project, the Housing Authority of
New Orleans (HANO) cleared a mixed-race neighborhood. Dwellings shown in black
were black-occupied as of 1930.
Credit: Author with Jeffrey Schwartz, Andrew Trueblood, and Yonah Freemark, derived
from the 1930 manuscript census.

black households (figure 3.2). At the beginning of the 1930s, analysis of the
manuscript census reveals that blacks constituted nearly one-third of the
neighborhood's residents.

On average, families contained four persons, but large families—almost
universally with two parents—frequently included six or more children. At
the opposite extreme, many single individuals lived as boarders in larger,
multifamily dwellings. Bigger families were more likely to own their homes,

but 85 percent of households in the neighborhood rented their units, at a cost of less than ten dollars a month for individuals and up to thirty dollars a month for larger families. With the Great Depression underway at the time of the census, most household heads were out of work; those that held jobs chiefly worked nearby on the wharves, though many black women did laundry work or served as maids in wealthier parts of the city. Conversely, twenty-five neighborhood residents owned their own businesses.[4]

At the end of the decade, clearance forcibly shifted occupancy to all white, forestalling what had otherwise been a shift away from white occupancy. When displacing residents to build St. Thomas, HANO acknowledged that "the number of Negro tenants was almost one-half of the total." HANO rules said that those 597 households displaced from the 237 parcels acquired by the housing authority should end up in "habitations no worse than those vacated." It worried, at least a little, about where such households could go, given that the citywide vacancy rate for appropriate alternative accommodation was considerably less than 1 percent.[5]

Undaunted, staff members "called together outstanding groups of Negro leaders including the clergy, educators, newspapermen, labor leaders, business leaders and others of that type to whom these people were accustomed to look for guidance." HANO officials "explained frankly" the goals of public housing, insisting that "no attempt was made to disguise the fact that certain hardships and inconveniences must be endured by many of the families." The housing authority then asked the leaders of the black community to accept their "civic responsibility" to help bring about the "success of the movement." They noted that "an appreciable percentage of those families who were removed from the sites would be eligible under the regulations for tenancy in the new units." HANO promised "ultimate redemption from the evils of sanitation and blight," but this did little to explain how "these people" who were being "removed" would find their way into the all-white project that replaced their neighborhood. Invocation of "the movement" of public housing could do little to disguise the more painful movement out of private housing.[6] Poverty management in New Orleans entailed managing the media as well.

HANO worried that this massive relocation of thousands of people from the first two public housing sites might receive bad press, largely because whites—worried about what might happen to their "domestic and other employees"—had "divulged information on the situation" to newspapers eager to print "human interest" stories. HANO quickly recognized that "any publicity that might appear prior to the complete organization of the Authority's resources might cause serious impediments." They rejected "bear stories" being "circulated by alarmists and others not well informed" that claimed the blacks displaced from the St. Thomas neighborhood would be "thrown in the street," would find it "impossible to locate new homes," and "ultimately might become public charges." Instead, HANO officials congratulated themselves for having successfully kept "the evacuation of 2000 families" entirely out of the press. "Had any stories of this kind [of hardship] found their way into print they would have created a situation that the Authority might have found extremely difficult to handle." HANO worried that "the enthusiasm of their leaders probably would have been dampened, interference from well-meaning but meddlesome outsiders would have followed naturally and the whole operation might have suffered." Fortunately, "The newspapers rendered the Authority the desired cooperation," and HANO could claim that "the mass migration [was] effected without a single instance that claimed unfavorable public notice."[7] Apparently, "out of press, out of mind" was enough (figure 3.3).

To build the St. Thomas project in lieu of a network of modest wooden homes, HANO undertook a substantial number of condemnations to gain full possession. With the neighborhood thoroughly transformed, the new housing project emerged as a large set of superblocks with solidly constructed brick apartment buildings ornamented by attractive cast-iron metalwork. Architects Allison Owen and H. T. Underwood arranged 970 units in long rows and around large courtyards planted with live oaks that would become strikingly capacious as the decades progressed (figure 3.4).[8]

Tenanting St. Thomas

With tens of thousands of applicants to choose from during the 1940s, HANO's one-hundred-person tenant selection team approached its task with great care. The authority wanted to find low-income residents coming from substandard housing but also intended its apartments to be rewards for good citizenship, offering an explicit preference for servicemen and veterans. In those cases—obviously quite common in the 1940s—HANO dropped the requirement that families needed to have come from substandard accommodation. It sought two-parent households with children and expected the household head to be gainfully employed. HANO geared rents to apartment size and to family income, with five different rent grades.[9] St. Thomas, like other prewar New Orleans public housing, served mostly working-class, employed households, with no more than 20 percent permitted to be on relief.[10] As HANO phrased it in 1942, "The Housing Authority of New Orleans . . . must collect rentals in order to function. It is not possible for tenants to remain in projects whose financial difficulties cannot be solved in a manner which will enable them to meet their accrued and future obligations to the Authority, or whose behavior cannot be modified in line with the best interests of the community."[11] Similarly, in 1946,

NEW ORLEANS HOUSING—BEFORE AND AFTER

The 970 homes in this St. Thomas Street development replace the colony of shabby slums (bottom) formerly occupying the site. The 3-story houses are characteristic of housing design in Louisiana.

Figure 3.3. St. Thomas Neighborhood, before and after Public Housing
HANO cleared a "colony of shabby slums" (note presence of black children) to build the St. Thomas development, "characteristic of housing design in Louisiana" (note presence of white children).
Source: Housing Authority of New Orleans, Annual Report, 1941, 33.

Figure 3.4. St. Thomas Housing Development and Its Extension
HANO completed 950 units of the St. Thomas development in 1941, much of it
oriented around courtyards. The barracks-style extension, taking up the blocks nearer
to the river, was completed in 1952.
Credit: Author with Kristin Simonson.

HANO observed that "having no income or practically no income is a
problem in low-rent public housing operations." To retain a "stable" community, the "norm will be a family unit with a head, usually a married man as
chief wage-earner, and minor dependents." This will "preclude" the "serious
problem [of] a 'pauper or relief' community."[12] In its early years, the project
offered a broad range of amenities, services, and opportunities, including
a playground and spray pools, Boy Scout and Cub Scout troops, a teenage

club, an athletic club, outdoor movies, classes in homemaking, health education, adult recreation, a bookmobile, and home-nursing courses.[13]

During and after World War II, the nonwhite population of New Orleans grew faster than the white population, and whites in public housing moved out faster, largely due to higher incomes and their ability to access more of the private housing market without facing racial discrimination (figure 3.5).[14] With the revival of public housing construction in the late 1940s and early 1950s, pressures from the private real-estate industry caused HANO to build many of its new projects as extensions of the old sites, rather than attempt to enter entirely new neighborhoods. The extensions to these projects, such as the one at St. Thomas that added 540 more apartments in 1952, lacked the attractiveness of the original, used lower-quality materials, and abandoned much of the earlier ambition to construct model communities. The St. Thomas extension accommodated more large families; the majority of the new apartments had either three or four bedrooms. With its full complement of 1,510 apartments, St. Thomas typified the New Orleans preference for sizable projects (see figure 3.4), but other kinds of large projects faced additional barriers.

Figure 3.5. Twenty-Five Years of HANO's White Male Leadership, 1937–1962
To mark HANO's twenty-fifth anniversary in 1962, the authority provided a gallery of those who had served on its board to date.
Source: Alvin M. Fromherz, "Development and Operation . . . the Early Days," in Housing Authority of New Orleans, *Twenty-Five Years of Community Service in the Field of Low Rent Housing* (HANO, 1962), 28–29.

THE LIMITS OF URBAN RENEWAL IN NEW ORLEANS

In the years before urban redevelopment and urban renewal legislation offered major federal subsidies to facilitate land assembly and clearance, HANO had embarked on several "slum clearance" schemes that yielded the city's plethora of early public housing projects. Yet in Cold War America, as historian Arnold Hirsch observes, "the coincidence of the civil rights revolution with the era of urban redevelopment and renewal" forced New Orleanians into a new and uneasy relationship with a federal government that was "itself perceived to be in crisis and susceptible to the most insidious influences." Hirsch sees "what passed for urban planning" in 1950s New Orleans as both "race-based and politically driven"—a kind of reprise of Jim Crow segregation, now using "new tools." Caught between concerns about black protest and resentment of federal overreach, New Orleans leaders "tried to resuscitate the principle of 'separate but equal' through redevelopment, even as the Supreme Court rendered that principle a nullity." Ultimately, "A highly mobilized hard-line opposition, fueled by a reflexive distaste for federal authority and a deeply rooted local populism, exploited the perennial factionalism of Louisiana politics to kill all subsequent efforts at urban renewal for a decade and a half." In 1954, shortly after the *Brown v. Board of Education* court decision, state legislators repealed the enabling legislation that in 1948 had authorized Louisiana's participation in the future federal program. This action prohibited municipal exercise of eminent domain powers for anything other than direct public uses. It permitted public housing but meant that the city could not acquire "slum" properties for clearance and resale to private parties. That effectively barred New Orleans from taking advantage of the urban renewal provisions enacted through the Housing Act of 1954.[15]

The relative lack of urban renewal implementation and backlash in New Orleans did not result from any lack of dramatic proposals. In 1952, the St. Louis–based, nationally prominent planning firm of Harland Bartholomew & Associates prepared a "25 Year Urban Redevelopment Program" for New Orleans that envisioned ambitious ideas for "clearing and rebuilding the slum areas." The firm proposed fourteen different projects intended to clear more than fourteen hundred acres of the city, an area larger than City Park. Implementing the Bartholomew plan would have required the displacement of 17,519 families—71 percent of them black, in a city that was then still two-thirds white.[16] But such big plans went nowhere.

The Housing Authority and Planning Commission prepared a report to the mayor and city council in late 1952, noting that "cities can no longer afford to keep their hopeless slums." They supported an initial slum clearance effort based on the Bartholomew program, but worried about the "high cost of [acquiring] slum property" and observed that relocation might prove a major obstacle, since "experience has shown that families displaced by housing project land clearance are not eligible for low-rent housing project occupancy and yet do not have sufficient income to rent or purchase a minimum-standard dwelling elsewhere."[17] Segregationist mayor Chep Morrison (in office from 1946 to 1961) faced objections from real-estate interests and worried that the city lacked available residential units to accommodate those who would be displaced. He decided that the city should instead pursue more modest efforts at rehabilitation. Councilman Victor Schiro, another segregationist who would later succeed Morrison as mayor, voiced a different objection to urban renewal: the intrusion of big government. "Why don't we turn over to the federal government the entire city?" Schiro rhetorically questioned. "You might as well resign yourself that you are not living in a democracy anymore when you depend so much on Uncle Sam."[18] Similarly, long-serving New Orleans–based US congressman Edward Hébert complained that urban renewal ignored "the right of an individual to keep his home," and other groups fulminated about its anti-American communism.[19]

When Louisiana eventually reintroduced legislation enabling urban renewal in July 1968, it was the very last state to do so. New Orleans did not receive its first funds until 1970.[20] By that time, of course, most other cities had already turned against a system seen as unfairly providing "land grabs" for private developers, and "the program had largely run its course."[21]

The city's principal belated urban renewal venture then stalled out amid acrimony, taking decades to build. Seeking to establish a jazz-oriented cultural complex in the mode of New York's Lincoln Center, the city contradictorily "leveled eight blocks of historic Creole cottages and music halls, as well as other community structures, and tore out the streets where the music flowed." In exchange for these deeply resented losses in the Treme neighborhood, New Orleans eventually gained a single-building performing arts theater, a lot of surface parking, and Louis Armstrong Park—part of which was later leased out to become the New Orleans Jazz National Historical Park.[22] Another pre-urban renewal redevelopment project, launched in the 1940s, cleared a near-downtown area to build a modernist civic center, including a new City Hall and public library during the 1950s.[23]

New Orleans also took advantage of the Model Cities program to invest in neglected neighborhoods and improve infrastructure but still mostly missed out on the largest clearance schemes, other than the ones that had already made way for public housing. As Hirsch comments, it was too late for urban renewal to "transform the face of New Orleans."

The somnolent Crescent City had earlier dozed through the age of industrialization; it missed urban renewal in much the same way. More dynamic

cities with more vibrant economies ripped their cores, bulldozed their
neighborhoods, and sent thousands on an urban trail of tears looking for new
accommodations. For better or worse (and either case could be made), New
Orleans opted out.[24]

Certainly, belated and limited arrival of urban renewal spared the city some
of the controversies of total-clearance neighborhood plans, which proved
to be so problematic in many other American cities during the 1950s and
1960s, including Boston, San Francisco, and Tucson.

At the same time, however, this meant that New Orleans could not use
those same decades to build up neighborhood-based resistance to such intrusive plans. Nor could there be the same sort of lingering resentment
about destroyed communities that would fester for decades in so many
other cities and inspire lingering commitments to prevent major redevelopment from ever happening again—at least not without a big fight. Instead, in
New Orleans, the absence of enabling legislation meant that backlash could
be confined to the realm of verbal sparring and stalled projects, rather than
played out in fractious community meetings and contesting coalitions.

That said, the fraught politics of neighborhood disruption reached New
Orleans anyway. In addition to the civic center and cultural center projects,
New Orleans neighborhoods faced the consequences of bringing the nascent
interstate highway system into the heart of the city. Here, too, the racial politics of planning greatly favored the claims of white residents over those of
blacks. White-led preservationist groups successfully averted a six-lane elevated freeway along the Mississippi River that would have clipped the edges
of the historic French Quarter. This proposal for an inner-city beltway had
its origins in a 1946 plan proposed by none other than New York's Robert
Moses, but the advent of interstate highway planning revived the Riverfront
Expressway idea in the 1950s and 1960s (figure 3.6). Mayor Schiro and a
Central Area Committee—whose "powerful members controlled every commercial interest in the city"—welcomed a highway that would "bring shoppers
to the foot of Canal Street" and the central business district. Armed with initial city council support, the new piece of interstate seemed a done deal.
Once it became clear that highway planners wished to extend the Vieux
Carré expressway westward along the riverfront through the Lower Garden
District and Audubon Park, however, squawking preservationists gained a
broader set of allies. Eventually, the antihighway coalition—supported by
good lawyers, wide social networks, carefully orchestrated national publicity, and an increasingly wary secretary of transportation—saved the Vieux
Carré. Federal officials stopped the project. In *Divided Highways*, Tom Lewis
argues that "the revolt in New Orleans helped to define the future relationship between the highway and the city for urban areas across the nation."[25]

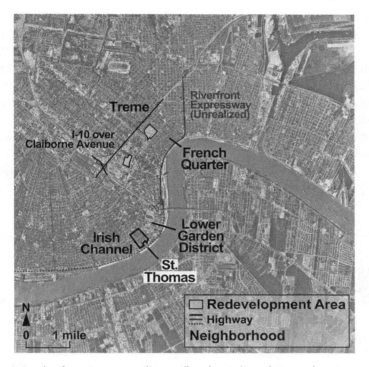

Figure 3.6. Riverfront Expressway (Stopped) and I-10 through Treme (Not Stopped)
Preservationists and allies stopped construction of the Riverfront Expressway that
would have separated the Vieux Carré from the Mississippi River, but did nothing
to stop Interstate 10 from destroying Claiborne Avenue with an elevated highway.
A proposed extension to the Riverfront Expressway would have carried it up river
through the Lower Garden District past St. Thomas.
Credit: Author with Jonathan Tarleton; aerial photograph 1VCUI00010057 courtesy of
the US Geological Survey.

In the meantime, however, just across the city of New Orleans, the relationship soured.

The effort to construct an antihighway coalition on preservationist
grounds failed to include the predominantly black midcity communities
along North Claiborne Avenue. Instead of a long-treasured "neutral ground"
with its grand allée of live oaks, its black Mardi Gras parade route, and its multiplicity of community gathering places, transportation officials delivered
a hulking stretch of I-10 through Treme, passing just a few hundred feet
away from the area cleared for the proposed cultural center (see figure 3.6).
Moreover, as historians Mark Rose and Raymond Mohl found, "The highway
builders rammed an elevated expressway through the neighborhood before
anyone could organize or protest." They continue, "In southern cities, where

blacks had little political leverage at the time, building a freeway through the black community was not only the most common choice, but the choice that generally had the support of the dominant white community."[26] Today, memories of the earlier North Claiborne Avenue urbanism linger chiefly in the succession of murals painted onto the concrete highway supports, although post-Katrina replanning has included serious consideration of removing the elevated expressway.

New Orleans certainly faced its full share of neighborhood-ripping highway projects, but there is simply not the same rich history of cumulative neighborhood struggles over urban renewal that continue to resonate in so many other American cities. In other places, the backlash against urban renewal prompted a fundamental realignment in the city's governance constellation, enabling far greater political representation from neighborhood leaders determined not to replicate high-handed property takings. New Orleans has faced no shortage of contestation over downtown development projects, let alone the protracted fights over post-Katrina planning priorities throughout the city, but there is still no single touchstone event that gets consistently invoked in the more recent round of struggles. New Orleans lacks an emblematic kind of "never again" moment. Consequently, New Orleanians never developed a strong and unified citywide countermovement emphasizing tenants' rights. Despite hard-fought battles over particular sites, aggrieved parties did not coalesce into a larger force that could make significant headway into electoral politics or trigger widespread citizen activism. When it came to fighting for the future of St. Thomas, this helps explain a curious omission. In sharp contrast to activists, city officials, and private developers in other cities, none of the key participants in the St. Thomas redevelopment saga ever seems to mention any other iconic community development struggles when situating this case. To be sure, St. Thomas itself has now become a touchstone in subsequent battles over the future of post-Katrina public housing in New Orleans, but for St. Thomas itself, the relevant past seems only to be the past struggles of *that place*.

RACIAL CHANGE OVERTAKES ST. THOMAS

St. Thomas has had no shortage of struggles to recount. As a "white" project in a city that would become majority black during the 1970s,[27] St. Thomas exemplified the tensions that arose because residential and economic opportunities for whites remained far more prevalent than did those for blacks. By the early 1960s, vacancies started to mount, necessitating mass mailings from HANO to neighborhood employers and churches to solicit interest from potential tenants.[28] White turnover remained high, despite the continued desirability of the housing. With passage of civil rights legislation, HANO commenced the racial integration of St. Thomas in 1964; within a year, 110 black families had moved in. At least initially, the racial transformation did not cause any immediate mass exodus of whites. The transition proceeded without much rancor or resentment. Still, as legal scholar Martha Mahoney comments, "Lower-income whites simply stopped viewing the projects as housing they were willing to accept. It was a decision that they could afford to make."[29] By the later 1960s, residents started experiencing more acts of burglary, vandalism, and "fights or rowdy groups," and the St. Thomas Neighborhood Council urged them to be more vigilant about calling the police.[30] Whites steadily moved out. By 1969, whites no longer constituted a majority in the project, and they constituted only about one-quarter of households by 1972. Nearly all of the remaining whites left by the end of the 1970s. A survey of St. Thomas residents in 1977 found that 57 percent were well satisfied and planned to stay, but half complained about crime, poor drainage, and the ineffectiveness of the St. Thomas Resident Council.[31]

Unfortunately for those who found their way to St. Thomas in the 1960s and thereafter, nearby jobs open to blacks began to decline. Mahoney observes, "The existing industrial base had diminished rapidly. The port soon modernized to handle containerized cargo, requiring far fewer employees than before. Jobs were available for whites, but not blacks, in the suburbs."[32] Black male unemployment more than doubled between 1970 and 1990, approaching 50 percent in some parts of the development. And, by 1990, nearly 80 percent of the households were headed by a female.[33]

THE TENANTS STRIKE BACK

Barbara Jackson and her children moved into St. Thomas from a nearby neighborhood in 1979, when she was in her early thirties. She has remained a powerful force in this place for nearly four decades, so her presence resonates across the early tenant activism of the 1980s, the HOPE VI battles of the 1990s, and the new River Garden community that eventually ensued. As Jackson reflected in 2013, "I think I was sent here for a reason, and I've been here ever since." Prior to moving to St. Thomas, Jackson had never even "walked past a housing development," despite "living right down the block." Reflecting back on her early years in the development, she expected "safe and decent and sanitary conditions," but discovered a place of rampant neglect. She blames this on HANO's reaction to the racial shift in resident makeup. "When the faces of the people changed" from white to black, she opines, "the quality of taking care of the site went down."[34]

Jackson found a community full of conviviality on porches and stoops, but also observed HANO's disinterest in enforcing its own regulations and worried that residents were too isolated. Because she was a newcomer who evinced concerns about fellow residents, she recalls, HANO sought her out for a leadership position. With resident council elections due in 1981, Jackson says she was "conjured in by the housing authority." Obligingly, residents chose Jackson as St. Thomas Resident Council (STRC) president. Jackson knew that HANO expected her to "direct the residents and keep them from doing this kind of stuff that was going on." In supporting the candidacy of Jackson, however, HANO leaders got far more than they expected. Jackson came to consider HANO "a dictator" that expected to "just tell you what they want and you do it." Instead, she felt she had been elected "to do some things that was going to change the quality of life" for fellow residents.[35]

Jackson soon began to take control of meetings. HANO leaders were "shocked" when she told them that the housing authority was not welcome to attend STRC meetings unless they explicitly asked to be put on the agenda for particular items. As Jackson puts it, "Nobody can make a change but us, and we are going to do it because we know what we are going through." As an elected leader, she toured the development and found "total neglect" of the physical conditions: "I went into some apartments and they didn't even have a door to the bathroom. . . . Another woman I went in to talk to said, 'I haven't had water in my bathroom for two months. I have to put water in my toilet.'"[36]

In July 1982, Jackson and fellow St. Thomas resident Fannie McKnight helped lead a two-day sit-in at HANO seeking "to roll back recently imposed rent and utility rate increases, to improve maintenance, and to foster real, meaningful democratic input from residents on how their communities were run." A month later, the two launched a nearly yearlong rent strike at St. Thomas to protest against the utility charges and poor maintenance of the development. The housing authority accused residents of illegally withholding funds even after maintenance concerns had been addressed and sought to evict sixty-two tenants. As Jackson puts it, "I was trying to prove that these people were not *not* paying their rent. They *were* paying their rent. But they were being evicted for non-payment of utilities" that residents could not afford and that HANO had not actually metered. During the course of the strike period, HANO sought punitive actions against the strikers and allowed vacancies to increase from 6 percent to 13 percent in the development. This encouraged vandalism to escalate. Attorneys from the New Orleans Legal Aid Corporation demonstrated that residents had been keeping careful records of rent deposits into an escrow account totaling $250,000; a judge agreed and issued an injunction against evictions without individual hearings to assess tenant complaints. Soon afterward, the parties reached a settlement that contained additional subsidies for utility payments (and eventually caused these separate utility payments to be once again eliminated). The residents ended their strike, and HANO started filling vacancies again, while also dedicating a $21 million modernization grant to improve conditions in the development.[37]

The battles at St. Thomas during 1982-1983 clearly demonstrated the power of resident organizing but also marked this project as "the most combative in the city."[38] It can be debated whether or not this feistiness had anything to do with St. Thomas being put forth for redevelopment under HOPE VI more than a decade later, but the rancor did little in the interim to forestall the continued downsizing of public housing budgets and, soon, the downsizing of the public housing developments themselves.

By the late 1980s, public housing in New Orleans housed an estimated forty to fifty-five thousand residents, spread across ten developments and 1,697 scattered sites. This meant that HANO, then the sixth largest housing authority in the country, housed about 10 percent of the city's population.[39] Increasingly, HANO lost control over of the management and maintenance of these projects, as crime and violence escalated and public housing residents struggled to find other sources of support.

HOPE HOUSE: SUPPORTING ST. THOMAS RESIDENTS

Even before the STRC commenced operations in 1972, residents had another ally in the neighborhood. Well in advance of HOPE VI, there was Hope House. Hope House began in 1969, when two Mercy sisters moved into a house at the corner of St. Andrew Street and Laurel Street and began offering assistance to their neighbors in the immediately adjacent St. Thomas development. As Hope House evolved, it became a "a place for men and women to learn to read or get counseling; a helping hand in times of emergency; somewhere for children to play."[40] Hope House's most famous leader, Sister Helen Prejean, moved to St. Thomas in 1981 and soon founded her prison ministry, which commenced after she started corresponding with a death row inmate, made famous through her book *Dead Man Walking*.[41] The subsequent film was shot on-site at Hope House and St. Thomas.[42] To Prejean, St. Thomas in the early 1980s was "not death row exactly, but close," because "death is rampant here"—"an explosive mixture of dead-end futures, drugs, and guns."[43] Even the youngest were not safe: between April and November 1989, four St. Thomas children between the ages of three and five were shot in separate incidents; two of them died.[44]

Brother Don Everard joined Hope House in 1983 and remains its leader thirty-five years later. He lived in the St. Thomas development from 1983 to 1996, prior to moving into a nearby house, so he experienced the ravages of its decline directly.

> I had water dripping from the ceiling; I had broken pipes; I had windows that were broken and you couldn't get them to replace them; the screens were out, and people were just living with that all the time. It was quite miserable.

As vacancies mounted in the 1990s, conditions worsened, since "the empty apartments were just an easy access to all sorts of drunk folk, molesters—anybody that wanted to could find a place to stay and nobody could do anything about that."[45]

Press reports frequently cited the perils of St. Thomas, seen as "one of the most dangerous neighborhoods in the city," a place of "brazen violence" and "crime rampage," and "no place for the faint of heart." One reporter referred to the Lower Garden District as "a microcosm of New Orleans' best and worst"—a "place of meticulously kept private homes and beleaguered public housing." Another described "the graffiti filled walls [that] show no signs of a future Michelangelo, only expressions of frustration and despair."[46] In December 1993, *Times-Picayune* columnist Iris Kelso opined: "Let's face it. The St. Thomas housing development is not an asset to the city or to its residents. With its crowding, its dilapidated apartments and its high crime rate, it is considered one of the most desolate public housing developments in the country."[47] Journalists focused on the drug ring known as the Cutthroat Posse, fighting for "control of heroin distribution near the river."[48] The New Orleans police named its major antidrug campaign "Operation St. Thomas" since the investigation began there, even though the actual police work occurred throughout the city and beyond.[49] Once St. Thomas had become designated as a useful shorthand for mayhem, reporters often identified crime scenes as "near the St. Thomas development" or involving "residents of the St. Thomas area," even when incidents did not actually occur on development property or involve its tenants.[50]

At other times, though, the press picked up "feel good" stories—a community garden turned into a profitable business by St. Thomas residents tilling land at the nearby Kingsley House social service organization; another garden at the Sixth Baptist Church with produce made available as gifts to needy neighborhood shut-ins; a US Department of Agriculture grant to St. Thomas women to start a homemade pasta business; a plan by teenagers to make and market St. Thomas Hotsauce from seven kinds of homegrown peppers; the success of students and athletes from St. Thomas in spite of their home surroundings; the power of a men's group dedicated to resolving neighborhood conflicts, through St. Thomas Peace Keepers and Black Males United for Change.[51] When it came to the unkept peace in St. Thomas, however, there was no shortage of well-placed *white* males "united for change." Many of these were real-estate developers with very different changes in mind.

4

The Tortuous Road from St. Thomas to River Garden

REDEVELOPMENT PRESSURES BEGIN

In 1988, Mayor Sidney Barthelemy's administration issued its Housing Plan for New Orleans. This is more commonly referred to as the Rochon Report, since it was produced by the firm of Reynard Rochon, a well-placed political consultant who had been HANO's first African American board chair during the mayoralty of Maurice (Moon) Landrieu in the 1970s. The Rochon Report stepped up developer interest in housing redevelopment. It proposed cutting HANO's public housing holdings in half (including St. Thomas, envisioned as 750 units instead of 1,500) while privatizing all public housing site management and eliminating HANO completely.[1]

To developers convinced that public housing projects remained a serious drag on larger neighborhood development efforts, the Report seemed to invite new opportunities. Joseph Canizaro, who had worked for Landrieu both before and after his mayoralty, quickly entered the fray. A long-standing major player in the interrelated realms of real estate and politics, Canizaro wished to turn underdeveloped, low-income neighborhoods into sources of profit. At the same time, however, by engaging directly with communities to try to find ways to help more people benefit, he engendered long-standing mutual respect.[2] Meanwhile, Pres Kabacoff, who had recently launched Historic Restorations, Inc. (HRI) with the celebrated luxury apartment conversion of the Federal Fibre Mills warehouse—entered the fray more contentiously, despite believing he came with the best of intentions.

As Kabacoff tells the story, "I called Moon Landrieu and Rochon to my apartment in the Fibre Mills and said that the riverfront, our gold— particularly on the uptown side from Canal to Carrollton—was interrupted by the St. Thomas project, which was tough, concentratedly poor, all the stuff we know about." Kabacoff challenged them to help him "figure out how to deconcentrate poverty and give these people homeownership and improve our riverfront—a win-win for everybody." Not all of these prospective "win-winners" had been at this meeting, however. As word of Kabacoff's ambitions reached St. Thomas, neighborhood advocate Barbara Major asked to meet with him at Kingsley House, the settlement house that had served the area since the late nineteenth century. Kabacoff recounts the story of his initial comeuppance:

> We sat in the center of a big room with a wall of people around it, and [Major] said: "Who are *you* to suggest how to deal with people when they're not at the table?" And I said, "Well, you make a good point. My presumptions on what works for you should not be recommended without hearing what you think works for you."

Kabacoff describes himself a "not your typical developer" because he is a well-read "policy wonk type of guy," "very civically engaged in early childhood programs," and "a poverty expert"—so he took this on as a personal challenge. "I thought of myself as pretty smart on the subject, but they were absolutely right. I was being presumptuous by suggesting what they ought to do with their land." Kabacoff retreated, at least for a little while. But, nearly a decade before HRI would be chosen to redevelop St. Thomas, he knew that his initial foray into the complex battleground had "caused a lot of rifts in the community."[3]

Faced with new interest in their community from outsiders, suspicious residents sought ways to shore up relations with their allies. Tenant association advisers Barbara Major and David Billings argued that the STRC needed to have a way to make area social service agencies more responsive to the needs of residents in their community. This led to the creation of the St. Thomas Irish Channel Consortium (STICC), established as a 501(c)(3) corporation in 1990. STICC's "Accountability Statement" articulated the need for greater "self-determination" and "the liberation of peoples of color from racism, oppression, and cultural subordination"—rooted in the ideological stance of its instigators from the People's Institute for Survival and Beyond. STICC's leaders wanted the organization to be accountable to "the independently-directed, low-income and indigenous poor of the area" and insisted that "no intermediaries, be they a local church, a non profit group or other type of organization or institution have the right to enter" the community "based on outside determinants or 'needs' factors."[4]

By melding the name of the St. Thomas development and the Irish Channel neighborhood into a single consortium, the organization made its mission clear. Moreover, despite the increasing use by others of the term *Lower Garden District* to describe the adjacent environs, this was never going to be the STLGD consortium—and not just because that acronym lacked the assertive sound of *STICC*. This STICC resisted any carrots proffered by Lower Garden District gentrifiers. STICC, with Major its first president, insisted that nonprofits wishing to do work in the area must consult first with residents and build programs from those expressed needs. The New Orleans governance constellation would need to contort to include a new star.

At St. Thomas, as in many other public housing developments nation-wide, advocates who were themselves residents often found themselves led by resident advocates from outside. As private development interest gradually closed in on St. Thomas, residents and their allies could either fight redevelopment pressures or seek to negotiate the best possible deal. Ultimately, they chose to do the latter. During the 1990s, developers put forth five separate deals to remake St. Thomas, each with very different implications for residents and for the larger community.

THE FIRST DEAL: JOE CANIZARO AND THE URBAN LAND INSTITUTE

As ideas percolated for development initiatives in the broader Lower Garden District neighborhood during the summer of 1992, Joe Canizaro convinced a variety of organizations to come together. STRC, STICC, the Preservation Resource Center, the St. Thomas Economic Development Corporation, and representatives of other neighborhood organizations agreed to form a new organization: the Community Resource Partnership (CRP). The initial funding came from Canizaro, who also served as its director. The CRP group debated the future of St. Thomas, with residents arguing for investment in rehabilitation, and other community members urging that the development be razed and replaced. Canizaro, casting himself as a mediator, convinced the group to bring in a team from the Urban Land Institute (ULI)—the nation's major not-for-profit organization focused on land use and real-estate de-velopment research, education, and consultancy—to offer an independent assessment. Canizaro sat on the ULI's board (and would become its chair in 1995). The New Orleans team served as part of ULI's Inner-City Community Building program—intended "to involve the private sector more extensively in inner-city issues and bring the resources of ULI's membership to bear on urban problems."[5]

Canizaro chose Chicago developer and Chicago Housing Authority chairman Vincent Lane to lead the nine-member New Orleans team. The ULI group visited in December 1993 and issued a report the following April. The parts of the report that centered on St. Thomas couched the discus-sion in the language of "rehabilitation" rather than "demolition" but evinced great wariness about the development. The ULI team viewed St. Thomas as a double problem—for its residents, and for its neighbors. Residents faced "high vacancy rates, social ills, economic despair, and government ineffec-tiveness" that had "turned this potentially historic housing development into a dangerous disaster area." But the report also stressed that "the development is reflecting negatively upon the larger community and hindering private investment." As one way to knit St. Thomas back into the rest of the Lower Garden District, the ULI team called for "opening the community to mixed-income residents" through adding market-rate "renovated and new infill units" that "should be woven into the boundaries of the existing St. Thomas." Framing the plan this way, the report seemed to suggest that constructing carefully phased mixed-income housing could minimize displacement of existing residents. ULI's goal of "de-densification" could be achieved by selective "building elimination and combining existing units to create larger ones."[6] Still, the report made clear that any viable "New St. Thomas" would need to be both smaller and more income diverse.

The ULI report provided "a roadmap for the CRP's actions and activities over the next several years" and recommended that St. Thomas be downsized from 1,510 to 950 units, with only half of those apartments to be occupied by very low-income households. Since St. Thomas still housed eight hundred families as of 1994, those residents who did not return would be offered Section 8 vouchers to move elsewhere. In fact, the ULI proposal—with a good deal of ambiguity—put forward an income mix that technically could include *entirely* low-income households: one set of 475 units for households earning less than 50 percent of AMI (which could either be public housing units or units subsidized with Low-Income Housing Tax Credits, or both), and the other 475 targeted to "market rate" (which they chose to define as including those earning 50 to 80 percent of AMI). Perhaps not surprisingly, Vince Lane had recently tried this brand of narrow income-mix in Chicago with Lake Parc Place—touted as the first example of his Mixed-Income New Communities Strategy (MINCS). At the same time, the ULI team seemed open to housing substantial numbers of large families: the proposal suggested that the New St. Thomas could have three-bedroom and four-bedroom apartments constitute fully 50 percent of its apartments.[7] Clearly, at least in this regard, the team envisioned working with substantial numbers of existing St. Thomas households—a far cry from the proposals that would emerge from others in the years that followed.

Still, at its core, the ULI plan for the New St. Thomas marked a fundamental departure from the existing St. Thomas: extremely low-income households would have fewer than one-third of the public housing units that currently covered the site. ULI team member Lewis Bolan put it bluntly: "St. Thomas is too large, too dense and too bleak."[8] Vincent Lane agreed that, with improved safety and "a de-densification of the number of units," there was hope, but otherwise St. Thomas would "become the negative anchor which prevents anything from happening. Crime will probably continue to increase until St. Thomas is standing there vacant. But you'll also have this blight there and nobody will make investments in the area." He argued that the negative spillover would "start affecting maybe the edges of the Garden District and you won't see [the nearby small-scale retail of] Magazine Street begin to come back."[9]

Since Lane had cochaired the National Commission on Severely Distressed Public Housing—whose report in 1992 paved the way for legislation that created the HOPE VI program—this newly launched federal program inevitably entered the discussion around St. Thomas. Accordingly, the report proposed that New Orleans apply for a HOPE VI grant to assist with the financing. It also called for the creation of a community center, a childcare / Head Start center, barbecue facilities, basketball courts, and a large playfield (for softball, soccer, and football), plus "resident-owned and operated stores" within the revitalized district. The report recommended that, in creating the "New St. Thomas," the resident council "should become a 51 percent participant" in the partnership that would develop and own the development—an appealing prospect to tenants, but one that received little detailed explication. This was no mere passing allusion, though. Rather, the ULI team explicitly opined that "resident ownership and management of St. Thomas will be a critical component for its successful redevelopment as a mixed-income community." Organizationally, ULI suggested that the CRP would be responsible for carrying out the redevelopment, a decision that underscored the marginal role of HANO, while also removing the process from usual channels of debate within city government.[10] Remarkably, and indicative of its "troubled" status, HANO was not mentioned even once in a ninety-six-page document centered on remaking one of its properties.

Brother Don Everard participated actively in the ULI discussions and would remain a central player in the long saga of redevelopment. Looking back twenty years later, he views this initial planning discussion as the most encouraging stage of the whole long process. The ULI team "had some really wonderful folks," and "you could see that they loved their work." They were interested in obtaining "all the input from people that they could get." As a result, "Public housing residents really appreciated them, because they actually drew models based on what people said. It was an exciting time."[11] Seen more darkly, the ULI strategy, in sociologist-activist John (Jay) Arena's view, led to promises that would not be kept. To him, the process of gaining greater resident buy-in depended on conciliatory roles of groups like STICC. "Supposedly grassroots nonprofits," Arena contends, "helped to forge a hybrid form [of neoliberal ideology] that combined promarket ideas with anti-racist notions."[12] In other words, acquiescence in the privatization of the development could be touted as the best means for self-determination through joint ownership and management. In New Orleans, as elsewhere, developers gained initial support by floating vague promises for governance structures that seemed to promote resident empowerment—even as those same notions would quietly disappear in subsequent iterations of plans.

Clearly, this first major plan for remaking St. Thomas had much to offer residents—and also much to withhold. Seen most optimistically, the plan offered an impressive array of promised amenities, carefully couched in the language of resident empowerment. Less auspiciously to some, however, the plan's starting premise assumed a drastic reduction in the number of extremely low-income tenants that currently called St. Thomas home. Resident leaders would need to negotiate versions of this basic contradiction between social goals and market goals for many years to come.

Most immediately, attracted by the possibility of new investment coming to their community, the St. Thomas Resident Council geared up to play a key role in the creation of a "public/private partnership" to facilitate realization of the ULI's vision. Led by STICC president Barbara Major and STRC president Demetria Farve, St. Thomas residents and their community partners started assembling consultants needed to help them successfully implement their 51 percent share of the partnership for the "New St. Thomas." Minutes from a September 1994 meeting suggest that residents knew this would not be easy. They wanted to take the lead but worried about "the training of residents in management, maintenance and accounting," since they understood these to be their responsibility "after renovation." They worked with Vince Lane to develop a proposed budget of between $100–$110 million, brainstormed ways to obtain federal grants and loans to cover this, and selected a team to be their construction manager and architect. An organizational diagram prepared by one of their consultants, Turner Associates (whose president had been a member of the ULI team) made clear the central role that STRC expected to play in directing the "joint venture" (figure 4.1).[13] Never again in the process would residents loom so prominent.

In addition to the ULI visit and report, HANO and CRP commissioned Perez Ernst Farnet Architects & Planners to produce a master plan for St. Thomas in 1994 and, in 1995, CRP asked the Philadelphia-based firm Wallace, Roberts & Todd to develop a revitalization plan for the larger Lower Garden District, with specific attention given to St. Thomas.[14] As the CRP moved forward with plans for St. Thomas, HANO commissioned yet another plan of its own.

In 1994, newly elected mayor Marc Morial reconfigured the HANO board, adding Joe Canizaro and placing him in charge of a strategic planning committee. In turn, that August the board hired Robert Tucker, a political associate of Morial's, to produce a strategic plan, which was released in late May 1995. The plan covered all of New Orleans public housing and contained a fifteen-page "Viability Report" on St. Thomas. Tucker's team found a

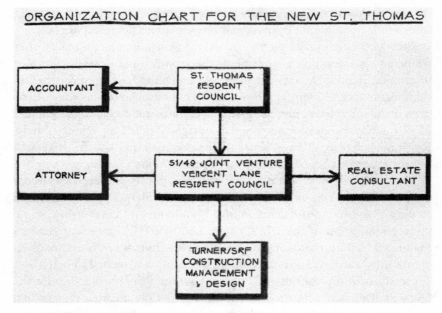

ORGANIZATION CHART FOR THE NEW ST. THOMAS

Figure 4.1. Wishful Thinking for a Resident-Dominated Governance Structure
For a brief period in 1994, consultants encouraged the St. Thomas Resident Council
(STRC) to believe they would have a 51 percent stake in a "joint venture" development
partnership. This diagram, supplied by Turner Associates, reveals a high point in
expectations for resident control. This would not last.
Source: Turner Associates, Atlanta, Georgia, Hope House files.

deteriorated development that was only 56 percent occupied, with a disproportionately large number of one- and two-bedroom apartments—too small
for the needs of the current population. Echoing others, the report called
St. Thomas "an island in stark contrast to its immediate neighborhoods."
As a strategic plan for St. Thomas, the report called for establishment of a
resident management corporation, which would partner with a private developer to "aggressively implement" recommendations from the ULI report
and also take on board the master plan prepared by Perez Ernst Farnet.[15]

In February 1995, while the Tucker report was in preparation, the HANO
board brought in Michael Kelly as executive director. Kelly, an architect-
planner, had previously led the San Francisco Housing Authority prior to
becoming a "troubled agency recovery specialist" at HUD, so he was certainly well suited to take on HANO. Morial and the board gave Kelly a mandate to downsize the agency by decentralizing the management of the city's
ten largest public housing complexes. Kelly soon embarked on an initial
promise, approved by HUD, to demolish 954 apartments.[16] Optimism grew

among key city players. In late 1995, HANO commissioner Canizaro told the *Times-Picayune* that on two occasions HUD secretary Henry Cisneros had already promised $50 million to redevelop St. Thomas. Kelly confirmed the promises, but cautioned, "We've not had firm commitment from HUD on that."[17] Presumably, even in the closely networked world of housing politics, New Orleans would at least need to submit an application.

THE SECOND DEAL: THE STARRETT INTERLUDE

The second major plan for St. Thomas entailed a competition among would-be developers, in advance of an application to HUD for federal funds to assist with this. In developer-friendly New Orleans—unlike other cities that typically first sought a federal HOPE VI grant and only subsequently sought competitive bids from developers to implement the grant—the city began by first seeking out a private developer to do the work.

In late 1995, five development teams submitted proposals to HANO for a master plan to redevelop St. Thomas. These included two teams from Boston, an Atlanta-based consortium, one bid from a New Orleans partnership, and one from New York City's Starrett Housing Corporation.[18] HANO official Peggy Landry insisted that the selected developer "will be an equal partner with residents" in decision-making.[19]

Meanwhile, continuing a "period of intense conflict and jockeying between HUD and the city government over control of New Orleans's public housing authority," HANO remained an unstable and mistrusted partner.[20] In February 1996, during the midst of the St. Thomas developer selection process, HUD took over control of HANO through a wishfully named "Cooperative Endeavor Agreement." This eliminated the HANO board and put the authority under an "executive monitor"—Tulane senior vice president and general counsel Ronald Mason, an African American—with additional oversight from HUD. This stopped short of a full judicial receivership, which had also been considered for an agency that had been on HUD's "troubled" list since 1979. HANO now had the lowest Public Housing Management Assessment Program score in the country, but the partnership offered hopes for what the *Times-Picayune* called "movement . . . in the right direction." Mike Kelly remained in his executive director post until 2000, and demolition plans continued to proliferate.[21] In this climate of high uncertainty, any new plans for St. Thomas drew high scrutiny.

In March 1996, a joint panel of HANO administrators and a law firm representing St. Thomas residents selected the Starrett team, which proposed to partner with Wallace, Roberts & Todd (WRT). Although this plan offered some general direction, it stopped short of supplying guidelines for the mixture of housing and incomes that would characterize the new St. Thomas community. This would need to be negotiated with their resident partners and sorted out in terms of financial feasibility. STRC president Demetria Farve and vice president Fannie McKnight wanted residents to be properly credited as "the driving force behind the plans for a new St. Thomas" but felt denigrated by press coverage that treated the tenant group as a "mere participant."[22] This struggle for voice and recognition would continue.

Starrett, however, did not last long on the scene. As fellow developer Kabacoff assesses it, after a year, stymied by "the complexity of working with the neighbors and the reality that they were probably $40 to $50 million short, they picked up their bags and left town." With Starrett gone, the next step in the transformation would necessitate reliance on the HOPE VI program.[23]

THE THIRD DEAL: HOPES FOR HOPE VI

HANO, under HUD oversight, used the ULI plan—augmented by the work of WRT—to apply for HOPE VI funds. Not surprisingly—and not unlike the practice around the country—HANO contracted out responsibility for crafting its HOPE VI proposal to a private firm. Wallace, Roberts & Todd worked closely with STICC and other tenant advisers to develop a plan during summer 1996, in keeping with the HUD requirement that all HOPE VI grants needed to demonstrate "full and meaningful involvement of residents." HUD's HOPE VI Guidebook high-mindedly articulated "four key principles of the HOPE VI program with regard to affected residents: Collaboration, inclusion, communication and participation." "The goal," HUD insisted, "is a 'spiritual' partnership with residents."[24] At St. Thomas, however, the interaction remained more spirited than spiritual.

According to director Kelly, it was never easy to work with STICC: "The Neighborhood and the tenants were working in concert," an approach Kelly attributes to pioneering community organizer Saul Alinsky. "They would say, 'Here are our demands. Do you meet them, yes or no?'" Resident leaders insisted on a cosignatory role. "It really was about [making it so the] housing authority could not make decisions without the resident council legally being in a position to counter and control whatever those decisions were." To Kelly, the "spirit of decision-making" mattered even more than the specifics:

> It was just the dynamic of being in a very hot, tight room with folks in a circle, heads down praying, prior to whatever decisions we would be making, and

having to be there until whatever we were talking about [got addressed], what the respect circle demanded. It wasn't like I could just take a phone call and leave.[25]

HANO held two public meetings with St. Thomas tenants, on August 7 and August 8, collected sign-in sheets from those meetings, obtained a resolution of support from the ten-member STRC board on August 30, and formally notified residents and community members about proposed HOPE VI activities on September 10.[26] That same day, HANO duly submitted the application to HUD.

Submitting a HOPE VI proposal with the necessary consent from residents—at least from their leadership—signaled that St. Thomas tenants believed that this was the best deal they could hope to get under current New Orleans political conditions—even though the redevelopment plan would entail a drastic reduction in the number of homes for public housing households.

The HOPE VI proposal for what was then still called the "New St. Thomas" envisioned a new development of only 775 units—a reduction not only from the 1,450 apartments on the site (as of 1995), but also a smaller total than the 950 offered up in the ULI "roadmap." Moreover, at a time when more than 90 percent of the 776 households still living in the development earned less than 30 percent of AMI (meaning that they earned less than $10,400 for a family of four), the HOPE VI grant allocated only 240 apartments for public housing occupancy at or below this income threshold. The proposal included 150 additional rental apartments for low-income households earning between 30 and 50 percent of AMI, and a further 195 units for those with incomes above 50 percent of AMI—intended for working-class households in units built with tax credit subsidies. The remaining 190 apartments would be intended for homeownership—the only true market-rate housing in the initial HOPE VI proposal. In short, despite a having already lost half of the apartments to vacancy and attrition, the HOPE VI application assumed that only about one-third of the remaining seven hundred or so extremely low-income households would be able to return to the redeveloped community.[27] HANO justified this shortfall, in part, by suggesting that the seventy households with incomes above 30 percent of AMI could access the next income tier of residences, and that another fifty households likely had such incomes but lacked incentive to report it.[28]

As always, the most contentious social and political questions about composition of a post-redevelopment community are embedded in the details of the plan. Sometimes this is expressed quite overtly through clear statements about changes in the number of overall units, but often the implications require a bit more digging. Once mixed-income strategies enter into the equation, development deals take on a complex set of requirements that are tied to the rules for each type of subsidy used. Since the affordability restrictions associated with the shallow subsidies of Low-Income Housing Tax Credits are targeted to those with incomes of between 40 and 60 percent of the area median, they fall into a socially and politically contested gray area. On the one hand, they target those who are income-eligible for public housing (although there is no guarantee that such households won't pay more than 30 percent of their income for rent), but, on the other hand, the LIHTC income targets are really intended to reach working-class, employed households that have much higher incomes than those extremely low-income households typically residing in the developments prior to the arrival of HOPE VI. In other words, though the language sounds similar, there can be a major disconnect between units described as "public housing" and those intended for households that are merely "public housing eligible." Although masked by technical or evasive language, this distinction can easily translate into a stark difference: in lieu of a plan designed to rehouse the same households that lived on the site pre–HOPE VI, it is instead a deliberate effort to socially re-engineer the community to bring in a higher-income variety of poor people.

As is so often the case in public housing redevelopment, HANO's original 1996 "New St. Thomas" HOPE VI proposal exploited this terminological ambiguity between "public housing units" and "public housing *eligible*" units. The proposal left unclear what percentage of units should be counted as "public housing," "subsidized housing," and "market-rate housing." Depending on the political point one wished to make, the income mix for the New St. Thomas could be portrayed as either overwhelmingly targeted to "public housing eligible" households or as drastically squeezing out actual public housing residents whose extremely low incomes made them unable to afford most of the units. And because the proposal very loosely— and very cleverly—defined "market rate" units as targeted to households earning more than 50 percent of area median income (which implied that some residents paying market rates might also have low incomes), this also allowed the proposal to be read as 50 percent market rate / 30 percent public housing / 20 percent subsidized. In practice, most St. Thomas residents, their advocates, and HANO seem to have read it this way.[29] By contrast, critics seeking to maximize the difference between this original proposal and subsequent revisions that increased provision of market-rate units preferred to minimize the market-rate component implied in the 1996 application.[30] Since only about 25 percent of the total units were intended to be wholly nonsubsidized—and therefore unambiguously "market rate"—this reading also seems legitimate. In the years that followed, various participants and academic analysts repeatedly clashed over exactly what had been proposed in both the "original" HOPE VI application and in its subsequent alternative iterations.

Other aspects of the initial HOPE VI application held particular appeal for tenants and their advisers. This proposal seemed to promise residents a controlling stake in the project, since they would be "a 51 percent partner in a joint venture with an experienced multifamily housing developer"— just as the ULI team had first suggested. Similarly, the proposal retained the idea of a resident management corporation, seeming to offer resident control over both management and tenant selection.[31] As HANO director Kelly recalls, "Marcus Dasher, [HANO's] director of development, negotiated a 51 percent / 49 percent policy document MOU. The agreement was that we'd be shoulder to shoulder with these guys."[32] In short, the proposal respected STICC principles, in the questionable belief that these could survive both a HUD application process and a HANO developer selection process.

On October 8, 1996, HANO received a $25 million HOPE VI grant to redevelop St. Thomas. In New Orleans, as with many other HOPE VI grants, the award fell short of what had been requested. And, as always, the consequences of a financial shortfall carried both social and political implications for the kind of community that would result. Instead of the full $40 million that the city had requested, HANO and its private partners would need to sort out a way to fill a sizable gap in the budget. A HUD inspector general audit later explained the shortfall, stating that the assessment panel "closely examined the facts and circumstances" before deciding to allocate reduced funds. The panel "felt strongly" that HANO had sufficient unspent comprehensive grant resources "to effectively carry out the revitalization plan," especially given "the strength of the surrounding neighborhood and the potential for private funding." Still, to those coping in real time with a budget shortfall, this called all initial assumptions into question. Promises about the number of public housing units could now get renegotiated, since the city now had to choose a developer willing to take on the project.[33]

The *Times-Picayune* editorial announcing the HOPE VI grant emphasized that this "great experiment" would turn "an isolated community into a district that relates to and blends in with the larger neighborhood." The newspaper emphasized that St. Thomas would be replaced by 575 new, single-family townhouses, "190 of which will be sold to low-and middle-income residents." Noting that the new plan would retain just 200 on-site refurbished apartments, the editorial said little about the fate of current residents except to note that "displaced families will go to private apartments whose rent will be subsidized by an additional $7.2 million

[HUD grant]." Readers were left to assume this was fine by residents, since the paper explained the transformation by noting that "the St. Thomas Resident Council was a key player in pushing to improve St. Thomas."[34] The *Times-Picayune* quickly moved on with a business writer's article entitled "Neighborhoods Rejoice: Lower Garden District, Irish Channel Renovators Thrilled about Plans for New St. Thomas."[35] With St. Thomas soon to be gone, the area would reward the early efforts of "pioneer" gentrifiers and allow this process to continue more fully and more safely.

Especially given the funding shortfall, moving forward on implementing the HOPE VI grant would not happen quickly or easily. This did not prevent HANO and HUD from pressing forward with clearance of the site. In March 1997, HUD approved total clearance of all 540 units of St. Thomas Extension, and 626 units of the original St. Thomas, leaving just 344 apartments remaining on the site—only 16 of which had more than two bedrooms. HANO indicated that those remaining 344 apartments would be further reduced to 200. To satisfy the State Historic Preservation Office (SHPO), HANO indicated that those remaining buildings contained "the most historic value, within a context of adaptability" and promised that their renovation and reconfiguration would "meet SHPO guidelines." Because the HUD appropriations act of 1997 had extended the repeal of the one-for-one replacement rule, HUD deputy assistant secretary Michael Janis informed HANO that "we are able to approve this demolition application without a plan for providing replacement housing." On the same day, Janis wrote a much more detailed letter to the Louisiana State Office of Public Housing, adding that "the Department is under no obligation to provide the replacement housing requested as a condition of this demolition approval."[36] HUD's message could not be clearer—demolish now and figure out the rest of it later.

More pointedly, the letter to the state office contained additional justifications for the demolition, blaming HANO for failing to have approached previous "modernization" efforts at St. Thomas "in a comprehensive manner." Janis noted the "high costs of rehabilitation due to historic designation"—and viewed the "problem" of St. Thomas as the reason "homeowners and investors are reluctant and unwilling to make major investments to the nearby neighborhood." Further, Janis stated, "There is a more critical contrast in the demographics between the surrounding neighborhood and the St. Thomas development." Not content to couch the matter in class terms as one of thwarted gentrification, he observed that "the demographics of the St. Thomas development are racially, socially and economically in sharp contrast with the surrounding neighborhood."[37] In other words, St. Thomas needed to be demolished not just because too many of its residents were poor; it also needed to be removed because too many of its residents were black.

THE FOURTH DEAL: A CREATIVE CHOICE GOES ASTRAY

In the summer of 1997, HANO issued a request for qualifications (RFQ) for a developer to implement the HOPE VI grant. Ten teams submitted bids, and a selection committee composed of representatives nominated by STICC, STRC, HANO and the mayor selected Creative Choice Homes (CCH). This Florida-based developer team notably featured Vince Lane (who had resigned as Chicago Housing Authority chairman in 1995)—someone already well known to New Orleans residents and officials due to his role with the initial ULI initiative. On September 26, 1997, HANO and HUD formally signed the grant agreement for the St. Thomas HOPE VI redevelopment.[38]

Since the STRC was to be a formal development partner and since HANO was still operating under HUD oversight, negotiating the terms of the plan—especially the amount and distribution of developer fees—proved a lengthy process, lasting into late March 1998.[39] Meanwhile, internal divisions within the tenant leadership increased. Barbara Jackson, who had returned to her role as STRC president, pressed for an agreement and convened a meeting that attracted four hundred people. Joined by Vince Lane from CCH and former STRC vice president Felton White—a member of the Black Men United for Change collective who had recently moved out of the development and become CCH's paid liaison to residents—Jackson wanted action. She said residents would take their case to the media, engage in a protest march, and refuse to cooperate with relocation if HANO failed to finalize its negotiations with CCH immediately. With a partnership on the line that offered residents a major role in future management of the development and would let STICC coordinate the social service component side of the grant, the stakes remained high.[40] To the consternation of many, however, the deal lasted only a few months.

In midsummer 1998, following up on a "private citizen's confidential complaint," a report from HUD's inspector general called the choice of developer into question, claiming that HANO had "lost control over the selection" process. The report alleged that it had been "both a perceived and an actual conflict of interest" to permit residents "with no fiduciary duty to the Authority" to be so heavily involved in choosing a developer, since they might just pick the one that "offers residents the most jobs."[41] Moreover, the report contended, in addition to "irregularities in the procurement process," the residents were not qualified to select a developer and "did not fully understand the process"—even though a well-regarded consultant, Abt Associates, had provided thirty-two hours of resident training. The HUD IG report also argued that CCH had made "unrealistic assurances to residents" because it requested a far higher than usual development fee while proposing the Resident Council be a partner that would gain a percentage of this enhanced fee. In the final vote, according to the HUD IG report, the HANO votes on the selection committee were "split" between CCH and another developer, Corcoran Jennison, which was well known for its work on the Harbor Point mixed-income development in Boston, whereas the three resident votes plus that of the STICC representative all favored CCH.

The HUD IG report recommended that HUD direct the housing authority to "convene a new panel consisting of Authority employees and re-procure the developer."[42]

Before HANO could move on to another process and another developer, however, CCH issued its own blistering twenty-six-page response to the accusations and findings. CCH blamed the complaint on "local politics, personal envy, and petty jealousies."[43] HANO disregarded CCH's rebuttal completely (though it did have to make a "substantial payment" in 2001 to settle litigation) and went ahead and rebid the St. Thomas redevelopment contract.

Most St. Thomas residents involved with the developer selection process supported the choice of CCH and roundly condemned HUD's insistence that the process be rebid. Some New Orleans critics, attuned to expect that corruption will have many layers, alleged that the destruction of the Creative Choice option had more to do with internal deal-making among well-connected Democrats, eager to help Mayor Marc Morial's friend Pres Kabacoff get the St. Thomas contract, even though the *Times-Picayune* found that Kabacoff's initial bid had "ranked toward the middle of 10 candidates"[44] in the first go-round.

THE FIFTH DEAL: HISTORIC RESTORATIONS, INCORPORATED

When the developer selection was rerun with a different jury evaluating the bids, STRC boycotted the process. While HUD's rebidding was still underway, the STRC's Barbara Jackson sent two letters to HUD secretary Andrew Cuomo and Mayor Morial to complain. "We have reason to suspect that HUD's decision to reprocure was made as part of a (backroom) deal that would favor your political allies," she wrote. "We understand from our sources," Jackson continued, "that you made your deal to select Historic Restorations, Inc. . . . or, as we have come to know it, Pres Kabacoff Company, as your developer of choice." Miffed by the decision to overrule the residents' preferred choice, she angrily concluded, "It is clear to us that what happens to the people of St. Thomas is of no consequence to you and yours."[45] The reapplication from Kabacoff's firm, Historic Resources Incorporated, switched his architectural team to feature Billes/Manning, described in the press as "a major campaign contributor to Morial."[46] More directly, the HRI application included a generic letter of support from the mayor and pointedly listed HANO director Michael Kelly as among those prepared to provide references—thereby underscoring its significant local ties. Especially since Morial and Kelly were also responsible for picking the selection panel, this could only have helped. Seven teams submitted bids, and four finalists made oral presentations on September 15. At the beginning of October 1998, Marc Morial named Kabacoff and his father, Lester Kabacoff, as recipients of his medal of honor for community work; at the end of the month, Kabacoff's HRI won the right to rework the community of St. Thomas.[47]

A core group of St. Thomas residents erupted in protest over this news. Forty of them, led by Barbara Jackson, marched over to HANO and boisterously entered the boardroom. "I submit there is a conflict of interest now," Jackson accused the HANO leadership. "We refuse to be a part of this scam. There's a strong smell of back-room deals here, when the tenants want something different from the politicians/dealmakers." For his part, now that the selection process was finally over, Pres Kabacoff promised "intense collaboration" between HRI and St. Thomas residents.[48] He knew that doing so would not be easy: "I understand that these folks are suspicious of developers, and my immediate assignment will be to go to the neighborhood and develop a sense of trust."[49] Recognizing that residents felt "very upset" after their preferred developer had been "terminated," based on his previous experience he also knew that he had work to do. Kabacoff's recollection of what came next is as jaunty as it is implausible: "Given my experience at Kingsley House, I put some undo-racism classes together, and I got our development team and the residents together in one of those programs, and we kumbayaed."[50] Such "undo-racism" workshops were hardly the invention of the white developer; these had been introduced to St. Thomas by the People's Institute for Survival and Beyond during the early 1980s and had been a core part of STICC's repertoire for years. To residents, such workshops remained a ticket of entry for those they mistrusted.[51]

Meanwhile, residents and their attorney, Bart Stapert from the nonprofit St. Thomas Community Law Center,[52] debated whether to sue to try to get the project back in the hands of CCH. Barbara Jackson advocated a return to the STRC's more confrontational style of the 1980s. Instead, due to the largesse of Joe Canizaro in response to a request from Jackson, the residents procured the services of ex-CCH employee Vince Lane as their adviser in their dealings with HRI and HANO for the next six months. Lane counseled residents that their best option was to stick with HOPE VI, since this was their best (and only) chance for substantial resources to improve conditions. Then—in a remarkably swift shift of allegiance—once his six-month stint advising residents was up, Lane took a job with HRI, helping them to implement their version of the plan.[53]

HRI skillfully managed to engage St. Thomas residents while simultaneously working to contain their influence. With Lane's assistance, HRI supported former STRC member Felton White "to form a rival tenant organization to challenge the legitimacy of longtime tenant leader Barbara Jackson." Meanwhile, the firm brought on two other well-placed African Americans—ex-mayor Sidney Barthelemy to help negotiations with public officials, and Shelia Danzey, Barthelemy's former director of housing, to help manage resident input.[54] As Kabacoff sees it, Danzey "was a housing pro, a tough love kind of person—certainly sympathetic to racial disparities but very hard on anybody that was not producing." To explain his reticence about power sharing, he notes, "She was always very discouraged about me making a deal with the residents, saying, 'This will blow up in your face; they won't do the work.' "[55] In the first instance, however, making a deal with the residents entailed clearing them off the site.

RELOCATION FROM ST. THOMAS

During late 1999 and early 2000, the remaining six hundred or so households in St. Thomas received notices that relocation and redevelopment would soon begin. Aided by an additional $3.5 million demolition grant from HUD that provided funds to tear down 701 units,[56] the destruction of St. Thomas moved forward. If residents wished to continue receiving federal housing subsidies, HANO offered them the option of relocation to another HANO public housing development or a voucher that could be used with a private landlord. Yet HANO had no capacity to manage this. As Don Everard recalls, "I remember one of the first meetings that we had for relocation. They had a two-page list of apartments for Section 8. We had probably six hundred families that were looking for Section 8 apartments, and they had a *two-page* list." Even though they knew "there was going to be an influx of poor people looking for places to live . . . they had done no preparation on building up the landlord listings."[57] Of the first 501 households relocated, HANO records show that about one-third took up the option to relocate to another HANO development. Poor conditions in other housing projects, not to mention the prospects of moves to distant parts of the city, made that option less appealing, especially since relocation of St. Thomas residents to the rival turf of the St. Bernard project led to considerable discord and deadly violence.[58] Another 17 percent of St. Thomas residents left the HANO system completely, while the remaining half chose to relocate with Section 8 vouchers, then known in New Orleans as HAP/HOP (Housing Assistance Payment / Housing Opportunity Program).[59]

The voucher option, too, had its downsides. Residents had to locate a unit from a willing private landlord within 120 days and needed to make a one-time deposit to establish electricity, gas, and water accounts (estimated to cost $75–$150 in total). If their new apartment lacked a refrigerator or stove, they were invited to purchase their HANO appliances. The biggest financial challenge for most, however, concerned utilities. Although the rent would remain pegged to 30 percent of household income, many residents worried they could not cover the additional cost of utilities. HANO had resumed including those costs in public housing rents, but private landlords charged extra.[60] In spring 2001, residents displaced from the St. Thomas and Desire developments filed a federal lawsuit to demand that HANO increase its utility allowance to allow them to be able to afford to live in rent-subsidized private apartments; residents with minimal incomes reported that utilities costs were actually several times more than their monthly rent, and that HANO's utility subsidy only covered about half of their actual costs for electricity and gas.[61]

At an even more basic level, residents knew that it was not always easy to find landlords willing to accept them and their vouchers. One survey found that fully 85 percent of New Orleans landlords resisted housing voucher holders, despite the appeal of a reliable check from the government covering 70 percent of the "fair market" rent. For some, this merely reflected ignorance about the operation of the program, while for others the prospect of having their unit inspected to demonstrate its suitability for the program proved a significant disincentive. Evelyn Stevens, HANO's director of the Section 8 program, observed that some displaced tenants found that their only real choice was to move into another nonrenovated public housing development across town, noting that this was "not the ideal situation" nor how the "[HOPE VI] program was supposed to work." "The idea," she continues, "was to decentralize public housing developments, not repopulate them."[62]

The Hope House leaders, Brother Don Everard and Dominican nun Sister Lilianne Flavin, worked hard to keep track of where St. Thomas households went following their displacement and obtained addresses for about six hundred of the last seven hundred households. They started a weekly newsletter, *Keeping the Ties*, intended to prevent "misinformation." The future of St. Thomas mattered in a pretty fundamental way to Hope House, given that fully two-thirds of those they served came from the now-scattered project.[63] Everard worried that HRI's new development would have little room for St. Thomas residents seeking to return and insisted that "families that had to put up with awful living conditions in St. Thomas during the bad times should be afforded every opportunity to return to the neighborhood and enjoy the good times."[64] He described HANO's relocation process as "unorganized and pathetic," noting that STICC had to step in "because HANO was struggling so bad." Even with STICC's help, "80 percent of the families headed from one 'poverty neighborhood' to another."[65]

To Kabacoff, moving residents out of St. Thomas was in their own best interests, because "concentrated poverty" is what "creates eighteen murders a year" in the project. Wherever else they went had to be an improvement on that. "They're now in neighborhoods that are better," Kabacoff says. Critics need to have realistic expectations: "It's not nirvana. New Orleans is very poor. We didn't send them to Shangri-La."[66]

HRI DEVELOPS AND ADJUSTS ITS PLANS

As residents moved out, HRI continued to refine its plans for what would come next and for who would be welcomed back. In January 2000, HRI and HANO submitted an initial revitalization plan to HUD. The plan underscored the sharp distinction between the existing development (which HRI noted once held 1,510 units) and the new development that would have only 143 public housing units—to be joined on the site by 808 additional non-public housing apartments. The HRI team masked the extent to which the new development mix underplayed public housing by noting that 253 units could be for "public housing eligible" residents, and that 52 of its 127 for-sale units would be "affordable." The remaining units included 221 market-rate rental units, a 250-unit Continuing Care Retirement Community, and 100 units of residential condominiums. Residents had hoped that additional units for extremely low-income households could be built on a scattered-site basis, but the new plan matter-of-factly reported that "the funding for developing off-site housing under the HOPE VI grant was not available." In other words, because the HOPE VI grant did not receive full funding from HUD, the new community would need to forgo much of the public housing that had been promised in the grant application. Other kinds of housing could be built, along with substantial retail and commercial facilities, but the new plan dramatically marginalized the sorts of extremely low-income families that HUD typically served. All HRI could offer was the "intent to work closely" with HANO and with for-profit and nonprofit community development corporations "to develop 240 units of public housing rental units to accommodate larger families['] needs."[67] Meanwhile, HRI would focus on building its own preferred version of a mixed-income and mixed-use community to replace St. Thomas and its environs. In the developer's interpretation of the new financial reality, it did not matter what sorts of promises its predecessors might have made.

To Brother Don, HRI's first draft of a revitalization plan came as "a bomb-shell for the residents." Instead of a partial rehab of the development, the new plan proposed total demolition.

> It included barely half of the public housing units proposed in the grant appli-cation. It also proposed to build mostly 1 and 2 bedroom apartments, despite the fact that hundreds of St. Thomas families needed 3 and 4 bedroom units. It was clear that large families, especially poor and African American large families, were not a part of HRI's vision for the new St. Thomas. The Resident Council revolted and threatened to derail the whole project.[68]

At base, there is a major disconnect between the way the process looked to HRI and the way it looked to residents. When the developer stated to HUD that "the Master Planning process for the revitalization of the St. Thomas Housing Development began in early 1999, following receipt of HOPE VI Grant Funding,"[69] this was true in only a narrow and one-sided sense. Residents and their allies may have inherited HRI as a new partner in 1999, but this hardly marked the beginning of a "master plan" for *them*. Rather, this was the fifth different forced marriage. With HRI, this process would continue for much longer, with divorce impossible.

In July 2000, faced with pushback from residents and their allies, HRI and HANO submitted yet another version of the HOPE VI revitalization plan. This next iteration proposed to replace the 1,393 public housing units that had existed at the time of the HOPE VI grant with 899 market-rate units and 343 "public housing eligible units." The careful terminology of the latter category meant that these units would house residents earning no more than the eligibility threshold for entry into public housing: 80 per-cent of AMI. With additional commercial projects, the developers prom-ised to leverage the initial HOPE VI grant into a total investment volume of $317 million.[70] To the Big Developer governance constellation, maximizing private investment counted most.

Even after another round of revision that slightly upped the number of subsidized rental units, the HRI version of the HOPE VI grant promised remarkably fewer on-site public housing units targeted to those with ex-tremely low incomes than did the pre-HRI plans. The developer could frame the revised plan as providing 358 units of "affordable housing." But many of these were one-bedroom apartments for seniors or subsidized home-ownership opportunities at costs well beyond the reach of those with the lowest incomes. Just 70 of the total were to be both on-site and targeted to families earning less than 30 percent of AMI. With average income for HANO tenants only 17 percent of AMI and the average income of former St. Thomas households even lower—only about 11 percent of AMI—the income categories proposed for HRI's carefully structured mix of units ensured that few of the previous households from St. Thomas could afford to return. Stated differently: if HRI kept to its targets, then the eight hundred or so former St. Thomas households whose incomes fell below 30 percent of AMI would be forced to compete for one of just 70 units if they wished to return.[71] HRI's seemingly magnanimous assurance that "every resident has the right to return"[72] to the New St. Thomas represented little more than empty, cynical rhetoric.

Moreover, 100 units of the 358 "affordable units" represented little more than wishful thinking—and those wishes are quite revealing. These last 100 units—to be built off-site by a separate nonprofit agency—were to house low-income households needing the largest apartments. Intended to contain the only four-bedroom apartments in the development, the decision to locate them off-site meant that River Garden itself would not need to house any of the large black families that once called St. Thomas home. When hundreds of households were relocated out of St. Thomas in 2000–2001, HANO records show, 301 households were large enough to be entitled to at least a three-bedroom apartment, and 82 households needed four, five, or six bedrooms.[73] This is hardly surprising, given that more than two-thirds of the St. Thomas Extension apartments contained at least three bedrooms, as did about one-quarter of those constructed in the initial portion of the development.

The developers may have genuinely believed that removing such households from a large, multifamily project would be in their own best interests, but it was not in the best interests of HRI to make this a priority. HRI clearly did not want large households on-site, even though the original HOPE VI application had specified 277 low-income three-bedroom units and 64 low-income units with four bedrooms, all arranged into two-family "camelback" townhouses (i.e., homes with a partial second story toward the rear).[74] By shifting the large units to an off-site phase and by specifying that no HOPE VI dollars would be used for them, HRI made them contingent on finding additional funding and on employing an additional developer.[75] Don Everard could foresee the result. "HRI remains vague about its involvement in this piece of the plan," he noted in June 2000. It wants as little to do with it as possible. The only reason it seems to show any interest in it . . . is to get the residents off its back."[76]

Barbara Jackson, as STRC leader, found this unacceptable and asked that further demolition and relocation be halted until "HRI shows documented progress on the off-site program that will allow for these 100 units to be built along the same phases as the units on-site." She reminded Kabacoff and new HANO executive director Benjamin Bell that "the development of the off-site program was the only reason why STRC agreed to the tremendous loss of units on-site." Jackson warned, "If the off-site units will not be built at the same time as the on-site housing, we will do everything we can to stop the on-site program as well." She further charged that "HRI is treating the off-site program as a stepchild, an afterthought to be accomplished at some point in time," adding, "We can already see the excuses down the line: no resources, no time, it just didn't work. We will not let it get that far." Jackson indicated that STRC had reached the point where "we seriously need to re-assess our participation in this 'revitalization' process."[77]

Undaunted by such concerns and threats, Kabacoff turned to the press to make broader points about the value of the project. He underscored the real estate rationale: "This area has been cut off in so many ways from the rest of the city, physically, socially and economically, by St. Thomas." As usual, though, the developer's outside-in framing—based on the need to open up St. Thomas to investment from the city—sharply contradicted the framework adopted by residents, who viewed the prospect of redevelopment from the inside out. As Jackson put it to a reporter in 2000, "We were here first, and they have to un-derstand that we're not going quietly." Jackson and the STRC had signed on to a HOPE VI application in the hope that 50 percent of the residences could remain public housing. Instead, as the *Times-Picayune* reported, "For St. Thomas, it's 15 percent for on-site public housing, or 28 percent if the units for the elderly and subsidized off-site homes are included." Jackson, though disillusioned, felt she had done her best: "It became a business arrangement, and I had to work as hard as I could for the residents. . . . I might not have had a three-piece suit on, but that didn't mean I don't know what I'm talking about." Attorney Frank Nicotera, who succeeded Ronald Mason as HANO's HUD-appointed executive monitor, explained HANO's challenge: because HUD offered to fund less than two-thirds of the $40 million requested in the HOPE VI grant, this significantly compromised HANO's bargaining position and encouraged the developer to leverage greater funds from elsewhere.[78] Handed this extra financial burden, it is hardly surprising that HRI would interpret the shortfall in the HUD allocation as reducing the number of units that would target those with the lowest incomes. Making suitably evasive use of the passive voice, HRI explained that "during the Master Planning process, it was determined that larger bedroom units would be built off-site."[79] When asked directly about this, however, Pres Kabacoff was, as usual, quite upfront about his preferences:

> I didn't want those on-site. I thought that would be too many people. This may sound callous, but the trick in this thing is to keep market-rate people. . . . This is *hard* to make work. I think I was absolutely right on the mix, in not allowing too many large family sizes in.[80]

To him, it mattered little that the former St. Thomas community had signed off on a different HOPE VI vision.

With the off-site units seemingly on indefinite hold, STICC and the STRC fought to have St. Thomas applicants gain priority for all on-site public housing units, countering HRI's wish to prioritize those earning 30–60 percent of median income over those earning less.[81] Everard calculated that, given an estimated federal subsidy of $225–$260 per month per apartment, HRI could meet its need to average $350 per month in rent for each public unit even if the occupants were earning as little as $500 per month in income. Given this, he wondered aloud to his allies, "Why do HRI and HANO insist on income-tiering?" He listed several "possible reasons":

- They feel that having too many very low income families in the new St. Thomas will scare away more affluent folk targeted for market-rate apartments and home ownership units.
- They fear that equity investments will be less enthusiastic about investing in the new St. Thomas, if too many very low income households are allowed.
- They feel that by keeping the standards high they will encourage former residents to work extra hard in order to be able to return to the new St. Thomas.
- They can make more money with income-tiering than without it.
- They just have no regard for poor people

"In the final analysis," Everard concluded, "these reasons have little to do with the aspirations and needs of former residents of St. Thomas."[82]

The STRC, their legal adviser Stapert, and their "numbers cruncher," housing consultant Jerry Salama, valiantly tried to get HRI and HANO to agree to put more public housing units on the site. The STRC insisted that they "could not commit to a set number of public housing/affordable units if we do not know the total number of units." The tenants wanted no less than the 50 percent "public/affordable" units promised in what they termed the "original" HOPE VI application, and urged that this be 50 percent of a larger total number. Oddly, however, their baseline demand now merely asked HRI to stick with a 50 percent market / 20 percent affordable / 30 percent public housing mix—while seemingly ignoring (or misrepresenting) the fact that the *actual* "original" HOPE VI proposal had, arguably, called for 50 percent public housing (albeit with some income tiering) and much less market-rate housing.[83] In the three and a half years since the original application had been submitted, the residents had seemingly stepped back from demanding fulfillment of the earliest promises—a reticence that would be unheard of in many other cities. Presumably, though, this can be explained by the fact that the most relevant number to public housing residents and their allies is the percentage of units devoted to those with extremely low incomes. They were determined not to have that number fall below 30 percent of the total, whatever that total number might become. But even that bottom line proved extremely difficult to retain.

Meanwhile, HANO itself continued to be an unreliable partner, both for the developer and for residents. In 2002, the agency was forced into federal receivership and management by HUD, thereby adding an important Washington, DC, address to the New Orleans governance constellation.[84] HANO would not again have its own executive director until late 2014. Instead of one-for-one replacement of public housing, this ratio would be applied to HANO itself.

With HANO and St. Thomas already flattened, the St. Thomas resident leadership felt pretty crushed, too. Exasperated by HRI's unwillingness to commit formally to the one hundred units of off-site housing until all elements of the rest of the deal were settled, on September 3, 2001, Barbara Jackson and STRC attorney Stapert simply walked out of a meeting with HANO and the developer. They told the press that they had broken off relations with HRI and wished to consider asking HANO to rebid the development contract yet again.[85] Shortly thereafter, Dutchman Stapert left New Orleans to return to his native country, leaving behind a much-heralded five-year record directing the St. Thomas Community Law Center.[86] Fortunately, STICC and STRC still had other allies.

On October 1, 2002, at a press conference organized by STICC and held at Hope House, a comet passed through the St. Thomas constellation. Brod Bagert Jr.—a young, recent graduate of the London School of Economics with a politically powerful New Orleans pedigree as the son of a namesake former councilman turned poet—publicly released a version of his master's thesis.[87] Entitled "HOPE VI and St. Thomas: Smoke, Mirrors, and Urban Mercantilism," the thesis spelled out the blatant discrepancy between the initial mix of units proposed for the "New St. Thomas" and HRI's then-current proposal for its replacement.[88] Pointing to the enormity of the "bait and switch" between the original HOPE VI application and the HRI proposal, Bagert alleged that the proposal had gone from 50 percent public housing, 30 percent "affordable" housing (for those earning up to 60 percent of AMI), and only 20 percent market rate to a community that would have 78 percent market-rate units, 13 percent low-income "affordable" units, and just 9 percent public housing. In clarifying the magnitude of change since the original application, Bagert also underscored that "non-profit resident ownership of 51 percent of the development" had been replaced by "full private ownership by HRI and its investors" and stressed that, instead of a "Resident Management Corporation and a resident-controlled tenant selection process," HRI's private management division would run a "unilaterally determined tenant-selection process, which will exclude most public housing tenants." In sum, Bagert charged, HRI now proposed "a completely different development" that "represents incomparably less provision, both for former St. Thomas residents and for the public sector's investment." Not just a change of plans, this constituted "a radical betrayal of what originally was agreed upon with the St. Thomas Resident Council"—all while taking advantage of what he calculated to be "more than $100 million of public money."[89] And, not content merely to issue a press release and a thesis, Bagert soon got himself on the agenda for city council hearings.

Two weeks after Bagert unleashed his report, Kabacoff responded by challenging all of his numbers. He insisted that federal and local officials plus STRC had already approved any changes to the 1996 HOPE VI plan before HRI came on board. In any case, he made clear, it would be a big mistake to undertake a remake of St. Thomas that was anything less than 60 percent market-rate housing.[90] "Bagert thinks what the cities ought to be doing is putting all their money into affordable housing," Kabacoff told a reporter. "I think he's wrong." Acknowledging that gentrification was "a national concern," he insisted that New Orleans had just the opposite problem. With "25,000 vacant, abandoned sites," Kabacoff jabbed back, "we could use a little gentrification." By getting "some market rate back in here," the city would gain "money to take care of the poor." He accused Bagert of "skewing reality" by suggesting that the new mixed-income community would house "rich people"—a deliberate rhetorical strategy designed to anger the poor. "You see what he's doing? 'It's the fat cats, it's Kabacoff trying to get his snoot in the public trough and trying to steal from the public,' and it's all kinds of hyperbole."

To HRI's leader, Bagert had quickly become "a pain in the ass." Kabacoff cast himself has someone civically "taking on the difficulties of public housing," noting that "it really wasn't that tough until Bagert threw his missile in here. And what he's promising, he can't deliver."[91]

Reflecting back on this, Kabacoff recalled a "tough negotiation." He expected "the affordable crowd" seeking entry to his new development to be "*all* former public housing, there was not a gradation of income levels—it was basically mothers with children on welfare." "If I had that crowd, I knew that going much beyond 40 percent [affordable housing] would keep the market rate people from coming." In Kabacoff's mind this reflected a basic business truth: "HOPE Sixes are nothing more than finding a way to attract market rate. The subsidized are coming, but if you lose your market rate, you return to what was—at least that's my belief. And so I held the line at 40 percent."[92]

At base, Kabacoff flatly rejected both the desirability and the feasibility of the original HOPE VI plan: "The original grant called for 563 affordable units and 200 market rate. You could not do it, and I would not do it." Even accepting Bagert's figure that the average HOPE VI unit costs $142,000 to produce (though Kabacoff would prefer "nicer houses that would attract market-rate people"), he posed a basic math problem created by the proponents of HOPE VI:

> If you multiply 563 by 142,000, that's about $80 million. We got a HOPE VI grant of $25 million. . . . I knew damn well it couldn't work. So I do what I do, which is find sources of money to make it work.[93]

This is indeed the fundamental disconnect behind the concept of HOPE VI. If left to for-profit private developers to "do what they do," this is hardly a surprising outcome. Unless there are countervailing pressures from other parts of the city's governance constellation—tenants, their advocates, or from government officials—HOPE VI projects will rarely be skewed to attract low-income majorities. HRI's capacity to outshine opponents once again demonstrated the extent that, in New Orleans, the governance constellation takes the overall form of a celestially prominent developer.

As residents and their advocates reiterated demands in the face of changing proposals from HRI, however, much of HRI's own focus remained centered on an entirely different priority: obtaining an additional large infusion of funding that could make the market-rate portion of the housing more marketable.

WALMART: SUPERSIZING RETAIL WHILE SHRINKING PUBLIC HOUSING

Inspired by a visit to New Orleans by Harvard Business School professor Michael Porter, founder of the Initiative for a Competitive Inner City, HRI CEO Kabacoff viewed landing a big-box retail giant as key to making the numbers pencil for the overall post-St. Thomas neighborhood. Kabacoff learned from Porter that "these big boxes had overbuilt in the suburbs" but—worried about poverty and land assembly—"had really never entered the city." He saw an opportunity to help such retail "penetrate" into "inner cities that [had] lost their shopping tax base" and "to attract what America had decided it wanted—quantity and low prices."[94] HRI had quietly worked for three years to assemble nearly all the land between the St. Thomas development and Tchoupitoulas Street, negotiating with twenty-five separate owners, and had finally found the partner to make this deal pay off. As Kabacoff spins the yarn, "I went out to all the typical players—Lowe's, Home Depot, Toys 'R' Us. We couldn't get any of the big boxes. I flew up to Bentonville and Walmart said, 'If you can get us a Superstore that we've been trying to get to penetrate the cities, we'll play.' I got down on my knees and said thanks."[95] Kabacoff knew that Walmart would "have to play ball" with a wide variety of preservationists, community activists, and civic groups,[96] and the ensuing battle did not fail to disappoint.

Kabacoff and HRI, battling public housing tenants on one front, now had an entirely new constituency of detractors. Kabacoff had previously told reporters that he was engaged in a "social experiment: market-rate folks living next to welfare mothers"; now he had to see if he could successfully marry a Walmart Supercenter and a supersized preservationist community.[97] The same upper-middle-class white community that had championed the removal of the St. Thomas housing and its residents reacted with much less enthusiasm to the prospect of a mega-Walmart in the newly rebranded Lower Garden District. Groups including the Irish Channel and Coliseum Square[98] neighborhood organizations joined with the Preservation Resource Center and the Historic Magazine Row Association and the Urban Conservancy.[99] In short, to implement the proposed deal, Kabacoff and HRI had to forge a delicate balance between the demands of preservationists, local city-planning officials, and the corporate bottom line expectations of Walmart—all while also making sure that substantial numbers of St. Thomas tenants would view the coming of Walmart as positive. Getting the stars aligned would not be easy—but once again the politics of developer-friendly New Orleans proved tractable.

Fighting the preservationists seemed the comparatively easy part, since he had previously learned a key design strategy from "New Urbanist guru" Doug Kelbaugh when Kabacoff sought ways to put a large supermarket into central New Orleans. Kabacoff asked Kelbaugh: "How do you plop one of these in the center of the city and get beyond the preservation crowd?" He learned that the key thing was to "put your auxiliary stuff on the outside and create entrances and make it a street scene." He hoped that this would work with Walmart, too: "I can make it like the old industrial cotton warehouses. I'll wrap it in brick, and we'll do all the right things. I'll design it within the parameters that I learned" from the New Urbanists.[100] More broadly, HRI invoked the ideas of Michael Porter about the importance of inner-city markets "to legitimate its Wal-Mart proposal as not only fiscally realistic but also consistent with leading business theory." Kabacoff could use "these claims of legitimacy to solidify political support from the local chamber of commerce, the mayor, and city council members."[101]

Residents, meanwhile, could construe Walmart as necessary to ensure the fullest possible complement of public housing replacement units would be built. Kabacoff told the *Times-Picayune* in September 2001 that Walmart "is an essential piece of a complex financing package needed to start work on the hundreds of market-rate and low-income houses and apartments." To Kabacoff and HRI the merits of the deal seemed obvious. Bringing

Walmart to St. Thomas offered a way to finance the rest—at relatively little cost to Walmart. With the Supercenter's grocery and other departments expected to generate annual sales of $76 million on a site that had previously contributed almost nothing to the tax coffers of New Orleans, HRI sought to capture some of the upcoming new tax windfall. On every dollar of merchandise sold, New Orleans charged a 5-cent local sales tax. HRI quickly figured out that it would be politically difficult to capture the 1.5 cents of this that was targeted to the Orleans Parish School Board, but proposed that the other 3.5 cents—which would typically be divided between the city and the Regional Transit Authority—be instead diverted into a "tax increment financing" mechanism, or TIF. Those funds would then be used to help pay off $15 million in bonds issued to build the new housing—an arrangement that would run for twenty years or until the bonds were paid off. On top of this, HRI called for Walmart to make an equivalent payment in lieu of taxes, or PILOT, that also would help pay off an additional $6.5 million in residential bonds.[102]

Pres Kabacoff's strategy and political connections carried the day, because he gained the trust of the mayor and city council. "I had to convince [Mayor] Marc Morial that if I put one of these big boxes in," HRI could get "a tax stream, and we'll go monetize it." The mayor agreed. "We made that deal. He said, 'If you can land it, I'll agree to not object to the TIF.'"[103] Without the Walmart and the TIF arrangement, Kabacoff told the press, he couldn't "guarantee to former residents that the low-income units will be built."[104] Moreover, since residents had been told that the one hundred units of promised off-site public housing would depend on HRI's capacity to raise additional funds beyond HOPE VI, this also encouraged them to get on board with the Walmart project.

In fact, however, Kabacoff did not expect to use the funds leveraged from Walmart to support the subsidized portion of the housing; he simply wished to be able to bring down the cost of the *market-rate* housing in order to make it more financially attractive. Kabacoff contended that HRI faced a special challenge since its units would be built to market standards but could not charge full market prices. As inducement to middle-class people, "You'll get 15 to 20 percent more house or apartment. I'm hoping people will say that the price seems so good that they'll give it a chance."[105] In other words, the extra funding from diverted city taxes would be used to subsidize the cost of market housing so that the developer could offer what looked like bargain rates—a discount meant to compensate for the potential liability of living near to some former St. Thomas residents.[106]

Meanwhile, Preservation Resource Center (PRC) members continued to object, raising everything from aesthetic concerns to diatribes against suburban sprawl and "the drive-through fast-food vendors and other camp followers who always, always travel behind a Wal-Mart." PRC board member Tony Gelderman stressed HRI's blatant financial self-interest in the deal in an op-ed published in the *Times-Picayune*:

> Kabacoff and a partner bought several parcels of land adjacent to St. Thomas shortly after HANO named him the exclusive HOPE VI developer. Kabacoff then saw to it that St. Thomas was torn down to the ground. Now that St. Thomas is gone, Kabacoff tells us the only way he can build a mixed-income neighborhood on the St. Thomas site, as is required by a $25 million federal grant, is to build a Wal-Mart on his property. What's more, he wants the taxes on Wal-Mart sales to finance the construction project for which he and his firm will be paid tens of millions of dollars in fees. Now, who really benefits from this Wal-Mart?[107]

In response, Kabacoff's own op-ed defended the deal and noted that HRI was "disappointed by the actions of the Preservation Resource Center and its colleagues who have denounced us as enemies of preservation." "Nothing could be farther from the truth!" he opined. Kabacoff reiterated that "a sensitively conceived, well-designed Wal-Mart 'fits' appropriately along the heavily commercial Tchoupitoulas corridor—among massive warehouses, a concrete mixing plant, a 750-unit apartment complex, electrical power stations, truck marshaling yard, wharves and convention center." Rather than allow preservationists to treat "the site" as a small-scale residential neighborhood backing up on the economically vulnerable small businesses of nearby Magazine Street, Kabacoff recast the context as a mixed-use, high-density, riverfront commercial corridor—a far cry from the vision conjured up by constant references to the "Lower Garden District." Pointing out that all Walmart positions pay more than minimum wage, Kabacoff added that many low-income New Orleanians were in "desperate need of discount shopping, affordable housing and jobs with benefits." For the city, however, the stakes could not be higher—HRI brazenly cast the Walmart-fed redevelopment of St. Thomas as "a national model for community revitalization and creative financing" and warned that "the opportunity to rebuild New Orleans as a prosperous 21st-century city hangs in the balance on the outcome of this struggle." He then turned up the heat by noting that "some of the opposition is motivated by reasons of race or class status and thereby is tragically distorting the noble cause of historic preservation."[108]

HRI helped foment the racially tinged Walmart-versus-PRC battle by allowing its public relations consultants to coordinate incendiary events. The developer employed former St. Thomas resident Felton White to rally a group of other former St. Thomas residents, joined by ministers, on the site of the proposed Walmart to urge its construction. At the rally, Reverend Marie Galatas charged that "the preservationists seek the resegregation of St. Thomas."[109] Kabacoff later acknowledged that both Galatas and White, like some others, were under contract to HRI, but insisted that they "performed legitimate services." "We had no payoffs," he insisted. "And we have no regrets." Kabacoff explained that he had hired Galatas "to do community organizing and to get the truth out on Wal-Mart and the housing." As part of what he called "a campaign for the hearts and minds of the community" against "very vocal opposition," this seemed an important investment. Galatas said she had favored the Walmart long before becoming a paid advocate, castigating its opponents as "devout racists." She likened her work to a political consultant hired to put up campaign signs and organize election-day workers."[110] Brother Don Everard, as cochair of STICC, viewed things quite differently. Everard charged that "in an effort to undermine STICC and the St. Thomas Residents Council HRI has spent considerable time and money creating misinformation and a small organization of former residents to voice that misinformation."[111] HRI managed to play all sides very well, working to undermine St. Thomas leadership whenever needed, while also seeming to support low-income black residents by selectively teeing up the opportunist argument that traditional preservationists were racist and elitist.[112] Not surprisingly, this complex posturing did not always sit well with some of Pres Kabacoff's former allies.

To Kabacoff, HRI's preservationist battles represented a shocking turn of events. Back in the early 1980s when "Historic Restorations, Inc." really did connote the innovative adaptive reuse of structures in the Warehouse District, he had been "the darling of the preservation community," winning an "Honor Award" from the National Trust for Historic Preservation in 1999. With the Walmart battle, however, Kabacoff felt vilified. "I've become a lightning rod," he lamented. "I am now a robber, I'm insensitive, I'm greedy, I've lost sight of the beauty of our city, I'm parodied on Mardi Gras floats."[113]

HRI's disputes with preservationists proceeded on two fronts—outright resistance to siting Walmart at all, and objection to demolition of adjacent historic warehouses to accommodate the retailer's insistence on a huge parking lot that would take up even more ground space that the store itself.[114] A parking lot of this scale would entail "unconscionable" removal of much of the city's late nineteenth-century Amelia Cotton Press and Kupperman warehouse complex, located at the downriver corner of the site.[115] Eventually, following another visit to Bentonville to discuss the possibility of a slightly smaller parking lot, Kabacoff gleefully reported that "Wal-Mart blinked." A mere 825 parking spaces could suffice, apparently sweetened by an agreement that overflow parking could take place within the residential portion of the development. Vastly relieved to have ended what he called a virtual "war with my staff," Kabacoff had successfully preserved his project. By shifting the focus from whether or not to accept

Walmart to the narrow question of whether the outskirts of the parking lot would need to displace a cotton warehouse, he had skillfully reframed the issue. "I can lose the Kupperman" preservation issue, Kabacoff commented. "But I can't lose Wal-Mart." PRC president Muffin Balart was "very pleased" to save the last cotton press structures, observing that "these buildings are ripe for adaptive re-use."[116] And, indeed such reuse would come—the unmarked structures now shelter the SWAT team vehicles used by the New Orleans Police Department. Apparently preservationists could cotton to that.

Meanwhile, the city council continued to debate the advisability of the TIF, following a refusal by its own budget committee to make a recommendation. With a newly elected council now in place, new member Renée Gill Pratt (whose district included St. Thomas) questioned whether the HRI plan would generate too few low-income units to justify the TIF. She got HRI to agree to an extra fifty units of off-site subsidized homeownership units. In late October Kabacoff sent the council a letter saying, "We have had enough." He threatened to pull out or just drop the market-rate housing completely and build only low-income housing at the St. Thomas site along with the Walmart, since the low-income housing did not need tax support from the store.[117]

Eventually, on the November 22, 2002, the full city council convened for its final vote. Much of the two-hour hearing featured the actions and voices of Walmart detractors. Some brandished signs saying, "The New St. Thomas Is a Lie," "Keep the Promise to St. Thomas," and "No Wal-Mart," while speakers told the council that the redevelopment plans are "an outrage," "a bad deal," "a social injustice," and "an incredible breach of public trust." Brod Bagert Jr., who received two standing ovations from most of the audience during the course of his own remarks, termed the proposed redevelopment "an incredible wasted opportunity" to help solve the city's public housing crisis, calling the Walmart TIF plan "a subsidy for gentrification," and repeating his estimate that only seventy former St. Thomas families would be able to afford to live in the replacement community. Despite the objections, the council voted unanimously to support the TIF and the attendant plan to support both Walmart and the new housing.[118]

Although it took more years and more money than HRI had expected to spend on pollsters and PR, ultimately Pres Kabacoff's strategy and political connections carried the day. Kabacoff hailed the council's decision and used the occasion to cast himself as the savior of public housing. Using entirely unsupportable figures to describe the HOPE VI grant, he boasted that HRI was "able to take a $25 million federal grant, which would have produced

33 affordable housing units, and now are able to deliver 414 affordable units, many of which will be available for former residents of St. Thomas."[119] Kabacoff's statement blatantly ignored the fact that the initial HOPE VI grant actually promised 563 affordable housing units. Similarly, he glossed over the fact that the now-proposed 414 affordable units included 150 to be located off-site with financing still uncertain. Still, Kabacoff seemed relieved to have dodged comet Bagert in the eyes of the council—and to have emerged physically unscathed. Bagert "whipped the poor—who are getting more than they bargained for—into a frenzy," Kabacoff observed, "because they're so desperate."

> It's a terrible thing; it's wrong and it's misleading and it's dangerous, actually. When I was in the City Council meeting, somebody came up to me and said, "If I had an incendiary device I'd throw it on you."[120]

Ultimately, though, Kabacoff regarded the poor of New Orleans—and their advocates— as little more than an irrelevant distraction. He acknowledged the "real power" of "the anti-Wal-Mart crowd," but concluded that, "the poor, at the end of the day, don't have the lobbying strength to make a difference." Given the Big Developer governance constellation in New Orleans, even Bagert had to agree with his adversary: "A lot of people became informed and have taken a very strong position on this," he noted. "And it didn't do a damn thing." At base, Bagert observed, "There's not a strong enough tradition of powerful community organizing in this city."[121]

Walmart opened on August 25, 2004, with "a traditional ribbon-cutting and a second-line led by the Storyville Stompers jazz band." The store, which did a robust business right from its first hour, offered some concessions to its preservationist critics. Although the interior was the size of six football fields, the vast parking acreage was somewhat softened by tree plantings and division into five smaller lots, paved in ways meant to conjure cobblestones. No single large blue Walmart sign dominated the facade. Although not clad in old brick, designers did their best to make it fit in with the lingering cotton warehouses. Walmart rejected the idea of separate exterior entrances to high-traffic departments, a New Urbanist nod, but did tweak the suburban prototype by agreeing to two entrances and two exits, plus a café entrance on one corner, and extra landscaping along Tchoupitoulas.[122] Inside the store, Walmart offered 587 jobs, more than three-quarters of them full time. Former St. Thomas residents gained 200 such positions, even though they would need to commute back to the neighborhood, since the first apartments on the site had not yet opened.[123]

Lost in the debate over the warehouses was the fact that half of the Walmart Supercenter itself—and not just its vast parking acreage—sat directly on the site of eight buildings of the former St. Thomas housing project, with four other former St. Thomas buildings now replaced by parking. Once the St. Thomas site had been leveled, *Times-Picayune* reporters started to refer to Walmart as "nearby" or "adjoining" the former St. Thomas or, more ambiguously, as "at the end of the St. Thomas site." One story about archaeological findings noted that "until recently, the site was occupied by the Pelican Cotton Press," making no mention of the public housing that had also been pressed out of existence.[124] In other words, once the residential buildings of St. Thomas extension had been obliterated, the distinction between building Walmart *adjacent* to public housing versus building it *on* public housing conveniently disappeared, as a comparison of figures 4.2, 4.3 and 4.4 readily attests.

Figure 4.2. Walmart and Its Parking Lots
The Walmart Supercenter and its vast parking lots dominate the vista from a River Garden mid-rise apartment building. The SWAT headquarters in the former Kupperman warehouse is visible on the left. The Mississippi River can be seen in the distance beyond the levee since there is no Riverfront Expressway extension to obstruct the view.
Credit: Author.

Figure 4.3. Housing Removed for Walmart and Its Parking Lots
The Walmart Supercenter and its parking lots are located not just "adjacent" to the
new River Garden but actually on top of ten buildings of the St. Thomas Extension
(outlined). This aerial photo from the 1950s has been highlighted to show part of
what was removed to make way for Walmart. The commercial structures between
the housing units were also removed to make way for the main part of the parking
lot, while the Kupperman warehouse and Amelia Cotton Press are shown in the
foreground.
Source: Adapted by author and Suzanne Harris-Brandts from Housing Authority of
New Orleans photograph.

COMMUNITY AND SUPPORTIVE SERVICES: ANOTHER BATTLEGROUND

Much of the appeal of Walmart to St. Thomas residents revolved around the
possibility of jobs—a key aspect of the HOPE VI program's ambition to foster
economic "self-sufficiency" among the poor. The HOPE VI grant for St.
Thomas provided $4 million for community and supportive services (CSS).
This marked a vital departure from past modernization funding focused
solely on "bricks and mortar" solutions, and the St. Thomas effort seemed
poised to make a major investment in local partners STICC and Kingsley
House. The underlying logic of the CSS component assumed that St.
Thomas residents would benefit from services whether or not they returned
to the development and that, for some, the advent of job training and other

1 River Garden Apartments
   1a Phase 1
   1b Phase 2
2 River Garden, For Sale Homes
3 River Garden "Historic Apartments"
4 River Garden, Elderly Apartments
5 Boettner Park
6 Walmart
7 Parking
8 Kupperman Warehouse / Amelia Cotton Press / SWAT Headquarters
9 Kingsley House
10 Hope House
– – – – original St. Thomas project boundary

Figure 4.4. River Garden and Walmart Replace St. Thomas
Rental and ownership phases of River Garden have completely replaced the former St. Thomas project, though five of the original buildings have been rehabilitated as "historic apartments." Walmart and its parking dominate the riverfront side of the site, covering up some of the former public housing, as also shown in figure 4.3. Credit: Author with Kristin Simonson, Yonah Freemark, and Jonathan Tarleton.

supports would be sufficient to give them the skills and employment income necessary to make them desirable tenants (or even homeowners) in the future community. Much of this proved little more than rhetorical fantasy, however. In practice, the quickly dissipating funds from the CSS program could, for most recipients, do little more than smooth over what became a difficult one-way transition out of their public housing community. Moreover, the failure of the CSS program to empower local agencies to deliver services would soon signal another betrayal of promises made in the original HOPE VI proposal. In this way, too, poverty management shifted markedly toward private sector control.

Control over the CSS program became inextricable from the question of which St. Thomas residents would benefit from the redevelopment. HRI's Shelia Danzey made clear that only those residents who had been actively participating in CSS would be eligible to return, and added that there would also be additional screening criteria. HRI initiated discussions with HANO about these criteria for the place it still referred to as the New St. Thomas, which included a requirement that the head of household must have "some form of income"—whether from earned wages, Social Security, Supplemental Security Income, pensions, TANF, or workers' compensation. HRI also proposed background checks to judge "past performance in meeting financial responsibilities, particularly rent; criminal activity; records of eviction (taking into account dates and circumstances) and income verifications." Finally, HRI said it wished to review the "record of each prospective family relative to disturbance of neighbors, destruction of property, or living and housekeeping habits at prior residences that may adversely affect the health, safety, or welfare of other tenants."[125]

Initially, in April 2000, HRI told STRC president Barbara Jackson that it wished to devise a CSS program "that will be acceptable to HUD and that will allow the residents to manage this process."[126] From the beginning, however, HRI seems to have doubted the capacity of STICC as the "implementing agency" to manage CSS for St. Thomas residents. HANO held HRI responsible for implementing this part of the HOPE VI contract, but HRI cautiously offered a "performance-based sub-contract" to STICC, which was then cochaired by Brother Don Everard from Hope House.[127] HRI's relationship with STICC remained sticky at best. As soon as the agreement was signed in the fall of 2000, HRI's Shelia Danzey embarked on repeated efforts to discipline its "independent" contractor. Danzey felt it necessary to repeatedly "clarify" what she termed "the chain of command."[128]

Eight different members of HRI staff spent at least part of their time on St. Thomas CSS activities—including not just Danzey and former mayor Barthelemy, but also Vince Lane—whose own "program monitor" contributions to the St. Thomas project cost HRI "approximately $6,800 per month." Jackson and Everard considered the $81,600 a year allocated to Lane to be "highly excessive for the monitoring of CSSP-activities." Pushing back on procedural grounds, they also questioned whether HRI had "followed its own procurement policy in the hiring of Mr. Lane," and explicitly raised the matter of his recent conviction for fraud (unrelated to either his CHA or New Orleans activities), for which he was about to be sentenced to prison. "Based on principles of equity and the adage 'what is good for the goose is good for the gander,'" Jackson and Everard opined, "we believe it to be highly inappropriate for Mr. Lane to be serving in any oversight capacity over CSSP or any funds related to the St. Thomas HOPE VI-grant." Jackson and Everard issued a threat: "We would like just like to warn our partners that our patience is running out; too many empty promises have worn it off."[129] The strained relationship continued through the fall of 2001.[130]

On January 31, 2002, with the fate of Walmart then still in flux and the financial future of the overall redevelopment uncertain, HRI formally severed ties with STICC and initiated plans for contracting out CSS programming directly with Kingsley House. Danzey told *Times-Picayune* columnist Lolis Elie that STICC never provided a viable plan for service delivery, adding that she had been worried for a year "that the residents did not have the capacity to perform." STICC staff countered that HRI had rejected three different implementation plans without offering any suggestions about how these could be improved.[131] In an effort to make press coverage more sensitive to resident needs, STICC board chair Everard wrote to Elie to lay blame on HRI for "falling very much behind schedule," calling efforts to blame STICC "a bit pharisaical."[132] Continuing a debate in the press over STICC's dismissal, Danzey reiterated, "The termination of the STICC contract had everything to do with STICC's inability to provide services to relocated residents of St. Thomas and its unwillingness to be held accountable to HRI and the relocated St. Thomas residents." In other words, HRI viewed STICC as insubordinate, whereas STICC viewed itself as having a long-promised role to support the interests of residents.[133] Long before the actual River Garden development opened, relationships among residents, their allies, and HRI had already faltered.

These seemingly minute details of CSS budgets, hirings, and firings are hardly trivial. Rather, these are indicators of power and control that set the pace of progress and, more fundamentally, eroded the trust among key players in the governance of the development process. Since a division of HRI would eventually have to manage the completed development, these earlier tensions established a baseline for subsequent relations. HRI had been trying to manage the development process long before there was an actual development to manage. In the larger dynamic of poverty governance, these are intimately interconnected.

CONSTRUCTION BEGINS

As construction commenced, many of the concepts that had initially drawn resident buy-in to the HOPE VI process had already disappeared from the table. Jay Arena succinctly summarizes the major changes that eliminated several aspects of what he calls the "people's capitalism" aspects of the plan: "1) resident ownership and managerial control over the new development; 2) the number of public housing apartments; 3) the right of return of St. Thomas residents and resident control of the admissions process; 4) resident-owned microenterprises; and 5) STICC control of the self-sufficiency component of the HOPE VI grant."[134] With their management roles eliminated, tenants and their allies focused on efforts to maximize the capacity of former St. Thomas residents to return.

In 2002–2003, residents gained some legal ground through a complaint championed by the Greater New Orleans Fair Housing Action Center (GNOFHAC). Barbara Jackson and nine other residents charged that they had been discriminated against due to "race and familial status." They argued that because the HRI plan approved by HANO contained no public housing units with more than two bedrooms, this "was designed with the intent to exclude former St. Thomas residents who are African American families with children from the 'new' St. Thomas." The plaintiffs documented that this caused three-quarters of relocated residents to end up in census tracts that were more than 80 percent African American, with most moving to areas that were at least 90 percent black. "Our participation in the HOPE VI process turned out to be a complete lie," these residents charged.[135] Attorney Stacy Seicshnaydre helped residents convince the HUD receiver team at HANO to reduce some of the intended income restrictions for the on-site units, thereby in theory increasing the number available to former residents all the way up to 304, with 62 three-bedroom public housing apartments promised in the first phase. The effort to make the project more equitable also entailed placing fewer limits on the capacity of former residents to return.[136]

Meanwhile, progress on building the new development faced additional objections from neighbors. In 2003, leaders from Historic Magazine Row, the Coliseum Square Association, and Smart Growth for Louisiana sued, claiming that silt runoff from the construction site exacerbated Lower Garden District drainage problems.[137] In 2004 and 2005, residents and local businesses launched additional complaints against HRI and its contractors. Heavy rains caused mud and water to overwhelm silt screens, inundating many homes, including the Josephine Street residence of erstwhile HRI ally Felton White. Always a good community organizer, White threatened to have a group of about forty homeowners "close down this project by any means necessary." Pres Kabacoff dismissed the claims about damage as opportunistic, disparaging White as a "disgruntled former consultant who's not on the payroll anymore."[138] In turn, local residents and businesses impacted by the neighboring construction activity sued, yielding a settlement—partly covered by HRI—that paid for some of the damage.[139]

With lawsuits beaten back or settled, HRI doggedly continued to build the first phase of what the developer now dubbed River Garden. HRI hired pollster Silas Lee to conduct focus groups to help determine the most marketable appellation. According to HRI chief administrative officer Eddie Boettner, "Participants strongly felt that a new name was necessary and selected River Garden from a number of choices." The new name, a *Times-Picayune* reporter observed, seeks "to avoid the stigma associated in many people's minds with the name St. Thomas, once one of the city's most blighted and crime-ridden housing developments."[140] HRI did its best to make the dissociation from the past as complete as possible.

5

Inhabiting and Inhibiting River Garden

RIVER GARDEN OPENS

The first residential units of River Garden opened in November 2004, and in March 2005, the new neighborhood received its first lengthy assessment in the *Times-Picayune*. Not surprisingly, reporter Elizabeth Mullener emphasized the stark contrast between a place that is "clean and cheerful and tidy as opposed to gloomy and chaotic and forbidding." Architecturally, instead of "blocky brick buildings, there are now brand-new frame doubles and four-plexes in classic New Orleans style, done up in pastel paint with jigsaw work and front porches and shutters. It was cheerless then; it's cute now" (figures 5.1–5.3).[1] HRI Properties marketed River Garden as "the restoration of an entire New Orleans neighborhood," terming this "old New Orleans living at its best."[2] Others recognized loss as well as restoration.

Hope House Journal devoted its lead article to the River Garden opening. The neighborhood's vital social service agency noted that "the families who have moved back to River Garden say that their apartments are indeed the best they've ever had" and praised "the conveniences of nearby public transportation, shopping, schools, churches, social services and medical facilities." That said, Hope House staff focused instead on conspicuous absences: "Our great regrets are that so few of our old neighbors will be able to return and that a side effect of the new development is a net loss of affordable housing."[3] At various points HRI has marketed the development as River Garden Apartments on Felicity and River Garden Apartments on St. Andrew. Needless to say, HRI did not call it River Garden Apartments on St. Thomas, even though that was true in a double sense.

HRI Management's president, David Abbenante, expected past St. Thomas residents to come streaming back into the development. "I'm going to have 122 affordable units," he told a reporter, and he "wanted them all to be filled by former St. Thomas residents." He hoped not to "have to go out on the market to fill them. I was thinking it would be like, wow, homecoming. How could anybody look at these units and not want them?" Yet, among the four hundred former St. Thomas households that had previously indicated

Figure 5.1. River Garden For-Sale Homes
River Garden for-sale homes and Boettner Park.
Credit: Author.

Figure 5.2. River Garden Rental Homes
River Garden rental homes, near the intersection of Felicity and Annunciation Streets.
Credit: Author.

Figure 5.3. River Garden Neotraditional Houses
Children play in front of River Garden homes.
Credit: Author.

their preference to return to live at River Garden, only seventy-five came forward when the first units were ready.[4] Abbenante explained "Some were hard to reach. Some did not respond at all. Some had already made a decision that 'we're not interested.' Others met, and when we revised the rules or came to meetings, said, 'Hmmm, thanks, but no thanks.'" Abbenante invited prospective tenants on "hardhat tours" of the site and made it clear that there would be some differences in management. "I felt that it was incumbent upon us as a management group to thoroughly explain . . . that this will be a privately managed property," he noted. "There will be rules that will be enforced; you will be required to pay utilities. This is a big difference from what you've had in the past when it's considered public housing." Sixty families indicated their eagerness to move in, and Abbenante had "no doubt, no concern, about any of those sixty. They were ready to come back in. . . . They couldn't wait for the day." He described "seeing residents cry" when viewing their new apartments. "One lady looked at her daughter and said, 'This isn't the projects anymore.'" Another asked, "'Where's the Laundromat?' And when I opened up the laundry doors . . . just the look on her face of 'That's mine?'—absolutely, and there's no coin slots, either. It's yours—that was what it was all about." Abbenante knew they were looking for "a better life."[5] They duly gained access to River Garden.

Many of those former St. Thomas residents entering River Garden appreciated the opportunity, even as HANO apologized for its past treatment of them. In June 2005, HANO's latest HUD overseer, Natalie Jarmon, candidly admitted to errors. "I have to publicly say that [relocations] weren't handled as well as they could have been." She promised not to "repeat the mistakes of the past." Jarmon also pointed out that the decision to move so many St. Thomas residents into the hotbed of St. Bernard had been undertaken under a previous HANO administration.[6]

Numerous factors discouraged other former St. Thomas residents from returning: the inertia of settling into other neighborhoods; concern that HRI's rules would be too numerous or strict; the appeal of keeping a treasured Section 8 voucher; lingering wariness about a place they had been forced to leave.[7] Meanwhile, as public housing options dwindled and existing housing was used for transfers during redevelopment efforts or deliberately kept vacant, HANO had 6,572 families—more than fourteen thousand people—waiting for public housing units, and more than twenty-five thousand people waiting for vouchers.[8]

Despite this, HRI struggled to find suitable public housing tenants for the remainder of the phase 1 subsidized units. Having "exhausted the list with repeated outreach to these people who were former St. Thomas residents who had expressed interest," in mid-August 2005 Abbenante's team received about five hundred inquiries from those living in other HANO properties, and prepared to consider those.[9]

Meanwhile, with River Garden formally opened for occupancy, HUD assistant secretary Michael Liu looked to the future. "As we go forward with the future phases of River Garden," he stated, "the continued involvement of all private—and I want to stress private—and public groups will be needed."[10] With HUD and HOPE VI coming under attack from congressional Republicans in the midst of a Republican presidency, HRI obligingly proposed ways to maximize private investment. In addition to 258 units of various forms of subsidized housing to be built on-site, HRI proposed 884 market-rate units. These consisted of 414 rental apartments, plus a $97.8 million, 312-unit continuing-care facility for the elderly (with charges of $3,000 a month or a one-time payment of $250,000–$300,000), one hundred luxury condominiums to be priced between $300,000 and $450,000, fifty-eight for-sale homes, plus the ongoing promise of 150 affordable off-site units. Taken together, these extra pieces were expected to cost $200 million. HRI hired Chan Krieger & Associates of Cambridge, Massachusetts, to join forces with the local firm Billes/Manning to complete the master plan for this phase.[11] Neither Hurricane Katrina (which struck in August 2005) nor the Great Recession (which followed a couple of years later) were included as part of that plan.

KATRINA'S IMPACT ON RIVER GARDEN

Due to its location on the relatively high ground along the Mississippi, River Garden remained substantially unscathed by either Katrina or the flooding from failed levees that followed. Despite the need for residents to evacuate during the storm, 90 percent of them managed to return. Normally, it is not an advantage to be "left high and dry," but for those sixty St. Thomas households that had made it back to the new River Garden pre-Katrina, this certainly proved preferable. For many others from the former St. Thomas, however, Katrina represented a particularly devastating blow. Don Everard comments that, during 2000 and 2001, "most of the residents moved from high ground to [Katrina-]flooded areas and never got back. The residents got screwed, pure and simple."[12] As attorney Bill Quigley, director of the Gillis Poverty Law Center at Loyola University, observed two weeks after the storm, many of those who left St. Thomas with vouchers had made fateful choices. "Thousands of people were systematically forced out to live in shabby Section 8 properties in the east that are now destroyed. Others literally died as the result of their displacement."[13]

Although River Garden escaped the post-Katrina flooding problem, the storm's aftermath nonetheless proved contentious. Post-storm, HANO requested that HRI lodge housing authority employees in the partially empty new development, leasing forty-four of sixty-three apartments reserved for public housing residents. This prompted administrative complaints from fair housing groups upset that former St. Thomas residents, and other low-income tenants, could now not access these not-yet-occupied apartments.[14] Pres Kabacoff blames the housing authority for creating the problem: "HANO asked us to put some people on-site, give them housing so they could keep their staff. We agreed to do that. Then the fair housing people sued us for putting HANO people on-site. It was in the 'No good deed goes unpunished' category, big time."[15]

Dasha Corner and her daughter had been approved for housing in River Garden just before Katrina struck, but when she returned to New Orleans that October following an evacuation to Houston, she was told her apartment had been rented to someone else. HANO said that Corner was now to be rejected because she was unemployed, though this was only due to a car accident that left her too injured to work. Even a doctor's letter explaining the situation did not convince HRI. It took a federal lawsuit to get Corner into River Garden.[16]

The legal settlement reached in the Corner case in July 2007 carried significant implications for HRI, HANO, and River Garden. In ruling against HANO for serving its own employees instead of low-income renters, US district judge Peter Beer blasted the authority for "the scorn and incompetence visited upon those citizens in such perilous need." He called the actions at River Garden "a new low for federally supported agencies," blaming the "self-serving, uncaring, 'pass the buck' bureaucratic swampland" and the "callous and indifferent 'leadership'" of HANO for "playing bureaucratic games with those whose lack of education or understanding left them essentially without an avenue of relief." Under the terms of the settlement, which Judge Beer termed "even-handed, impartial and essentially equitable," most phases at River Garden would remain as previously negotiated—122 of 296 units from phase 1 would remain allocated to public housing; fifteen of the seventy-three houses for purchase would be "affordable"; and the fifty-seven-unit building, which would open in early 2008, would remain targeted to low-income seniors. The settlement reiterated that five preserved structures from the old St. Thomas (which were nearly ready to open) would be used for thirty-seven "affordable" units, and reaffirmed that one hundred three- and four-bedroom apartments must be constructed for public housing residents on sites that HANO had acquired in 2004.[17]

The main change involved the next phase of on-site rental housing: the settlement now required all 125 of the "affordable" units in this 310-unit phase to be for HANO clients, not just sixty, and stated that former St. Thomas residents be given first preference for all of these. Despite the promises, however, GNOFHAC's fair housing attorneys had to go back to federal court to complain that HANO failed to provide adequate outreach to former St. Thomas residents. Of the 1,132 addresses HANO offered up, "38 percent stated that the families still lived at St. Thomas, which was demolished in 2001." Moreover, another 20 percent of the addresses were in other public housing developments that had been vacant since the storm. Under federal court pressure, two weeks later, HANO delivered a list of nearly three thousand names of former St. Thomas residents.[18] GNOFHAC executive director James Perry estimated that his organization eventually helped thirty or forty former residents of St. Thomas obtain placement in River Garden.[19]

David Abbenante praised the new long list of names from HANO, saying, "This is gold to me."[20] However, a decade later, with the development now as complete as it ever will be, the HUD records for River Garden—which are updated quarterly—list just ninety-two former St. Thomas households as having ever returned to River Garden. Certainly better than the seventy households that Brod Bagert Jr. had predicted would be accommodated—but not much.

OUT OF SITE, OUT OF MIND

Much of the shortfall in accommodating former St. Thomas residents resulted from the basic decision to allocate larger public housing units to some future off-site phase, to be built without recourse to HOPE VI funds. Predictably, both pre-Katrina and post-Katrina, this resulted in one snafu after another, interspersed with repeated promises that the units would still be forthcoming. Press Kabacoff blamed others for insisting that HRI use a different firm to build these additional units, commenting that "the city council wanted me to do a minority partner." In March 2003, following a selection process, HRI reached a development agreement with the accurately (if infelicitously) named Off-Site Minority Partners (OMP). Under the terms of this contract, OMP would be responsible for working with HRI and HANO to secure tax credits (together with project-based vouchers to further subsidize rents) to "acquire/rehab and/or newly construct" ninety off-site three-bedroom and four-bedroom apartments—to be scattered into groupings containing no more than ten units in any single quarter-mile radius without prior city council approval. One-fourth of OMP's 12 percent development fee would go to HRI for "coordination." OMP soon managed to obtain an allocation of state-issued Low-Income Housing Tax Credits, began purchasing some sites, and prepared designs in 2004.[21] So far, so good.

In 2005, however HRI encountered what it gently termed "legal issues" with OMP, causing HRI, HANO, and HUD to search for an alternative. While discussions continued, Katrina hit, flooding out some of the previously purchased sites. This caused HRI to reassess which places remained viable for renovation or new construction. HRI asserted that "those in safe areas will be developed when a new developer is selected"—but no such developer selection occurred. In March 2007, in an understatement, HRI noted that, "due to unforeseen circumstances, the program is temporarily on hold," but reassured HUD that "these issues should be resolved in the next couple of weeks."[22] In late 2009, with access to the tax credits already expired, HRI indicated that, "due to the challenging credit market," the work could not start. Through 2010 and well into 2011, HANO worked with a developer to find subdevelopers for both the one hundred off-site rentals and fifty homeownership units, but nothing progressed. In December 2011, HUD quietly agreed to "delete" the "off-site phase."[23] None of the long-promised, off-site apartments have ever been built—though the matter continues to be litigated.

There is plenty of blame to go around. An understandably frustrated Pres Kabacoff blamed HANO for the failure: "We had tax credits lined up; we had a million-dollar grant from the city, and then HANO went through a series of new administrations every year. It was really *impossible* to get anything done with them."[24] In any case, the nonappearance of the off-site housing happened just as Jackson, Everard, and Stapert had predicted back in 2000.

The other components of HRI's larger plan for a multipart, mixed-use replacement neighborhood for St. Thomas also faced a mixed fate in the years following Katrina. Before the storm, with the old St. Thomas gone and the new River Garden starting to emerge, neighborhood investment beyond the bounds of the former project began to increase, along with property values—just as HOPE VI proponents had hoped. In early 2005, University of New Orleans professor Wade Ragas found "enormous change" in neighborhood real-estate values. Both owner-occupied and rental property experienced price appreciation rates of "between 15 and 20 percent a year," as well as "a substantial increase in people buying property to renovate and redevelop."[25]

That June, HRI began work on the first of the spec-built single-family homes, with fifteen of the seventy-three houses intended to be subsidized for first-time buyers able to qualify for $100,000 mortgages. Given the need to transfer the land—as well as the house—to homeowners, HRI purchased six acres in the northern part of the St. Thomas site from HANO, with an understanding that the housing authority and HRI would split the proceeds once the homes were sold. The advent of Katrina at the end of August delayed this phase, but construction resumed in 2006.[26] After that point, though, several key market-rate components of the plan got shelved due to market conditions, and many of the lots reserved for high-end homes simply remained vacant. Another piece of the development puzzle—the retention and rehabilitation of a few pieces of the original St. Thomas project—proved to be slow but ultimately successful.

HRI'S SECOND PRESERVATION BATTLE

In addition to epic Walmart battles on the development's riverside flank, HRI fought preservationists on a second front. The developer initially wished to raze more than 99 percent of the site's public housing, including the more elaborately constructed courtyard housing dating back to 1941. Instead of preserving housing, "in order to preserve some of the history of St. Thomas," HRI proposed retaining a small triangle of land the far northeast corner of the site containing a maintenance and management building, along with a single four-unit residential structure. For the rest of the site, HRI initiated a "Section 106 Clearance process"—Historic Preservation Act terminology that in this instance sounded mostly like a cynical call for demolition.[27] That said, HANO director Kelly recalled that although HRI "really wanted to clear the site," the developer did value the live oaks: "Pres Kabacoff agreed that he would design around them."[28] This eventually yielded Boettner Park, named after HRI's cofounder.

The Louisiana State Preservation Office did not cave easily, however, and pressed HRI to retain one of the original courtyards. In a place where the surviving live oaks presented a more appealing opportunity for developers than did the preservation of dead housing, HRI initially framed the problem as one of lost parkland and as little more than an unwelcome distraction. However, once $2.3 million historic tax credits became available from the state Division of Historic Preservation, coupled with an allocation of Gulf Opportunity Zone Low-Income Housing Tax Credits, the transformation occurred quite quickly. Buildings that had been vacant and boarded up for six years received new plumbing and wiring, repointed bricks, new landscaping with preserved live oaks, and historically recreated ironwork. The $9.3 million renovation took less than a year to complete, and even included altered floor plans in four out of five structures. The results are quite striking (figure 5.4).

Even though HRI readily admitted salvaging the buildings only as a way to qualify for the tax credits, some preservationists and architects called for

Figure 5.4. Rehabilitated Housing in a St. Thomas Courtyard
Following pressure from preservationists, the development team agreed to rehabilitate five of the original St. Thomas buildings, including the ones in this courtyard, for use as tax-credit-subsidized rental apartments.
Credit: Author.

this—rather than total demolition—to be the new model for remaking public housing in New Orleans. Walter Gallas, the director of the New Orleans office of the National Trust for Historic Preservation, pointedly observed that "it puts the lie to the argument that 1930s public housing can't be rehabilitated. Look how quickly it can be done."[29] That said, since these beautiful apartments were financed with tax credits, they were not targeted to former public housing residents with the lowest incomes.

LIFE IN RIVER GARDEN

It is always complicated to judge the dynamic of life within a community, not least when that community results from a much-delayed and much-altered experiment in social engineering. River Garden, it would seem, has been both inhabited and inhibited. Despite HRI Management's efforts to find the most able and stable tenants for subsidized units, many extremely low-income households struggled socially and financially. One early site manager at River Garden, Ronald Baptiste, assiduously tried to enforce the rules of the lease and sent notes to residents about a variety of matters. In a single six-month period, one resident received separate violation notices regarding unregistered vehicles improperly parked in front of her home, a brother in residence without being on the lease, observations of an illegal pit bull, a bicycle left in a flowerbed, and a trash box kept on a porch. Meanwhile, this same resident faced extreme financial difficulties because her modest pay checks did not provide enough funds to keep up with bills for electricity or water—despite eligibility for subsidy from HANO. Distraught residents frequently sought assistance from New Orleans Legal Assistance. Often, they worried about the effect of job loss on continued tenancy. HANO policy and River Garden policy included stated preferences for housing households with jobs but technically could not require work as a condition of occupancy—although they could enforce HUD's requirement that able-bodied adult residents under age sixty perform eight hours per month of voluntary community service or engage in "self-sufficiency" activities (defined to include "education, training, counseling, classes, or some other activities that help an individual toward . . . economic independence").[30]

In practice, HRI and HANO struggled for many years to understand the difference in admissibility between a "work requirement" and a "work preference." David Abbenante believed that the settlement of legal disputes over occupancy gave HRI the right to insist that all nonelderly able-bodied tenants engage in work: "I've got a consent decree signed by housing advocates, fair housing, HUD, and a federal judge that says we have a work requirement," he stated in 2010. At the same time, since this issue remained contested, HRI said it would refrain from evicting anyone solely because the resident lacked income from a job.

> So we're not telling you, "Get a job tomorrow or you're out." We're saying, "You've got options—go get some training, go do this, go do that." As long as you're in jobs training and making that effort, that's what we need to see.

Abbenante felt that having a work requirement meant that River Garden would get "an individual that has options" as a tenant because "there is in essence a contract between me and that landlord. The deal is that he's going to provide me with a first-class apartment and I'm going to do my share to make that a healthy community and make the city a better place, by doing things for my family."[31] HRI Management's implied social contract with residents, however noble its aim, epitomizes just the sort of neoliberal paternalism that Soss, Fording and Schram disdained in *Disciplining the Poor*.

Site manager Don Gault, who succeeded Ronald Baptiste in 2008 and served in this role for several years, evinced much the same goal. River Garden offers "an opportunity to see what you can be with life," Gault said. "Get you out of that institutionalized public housing mindset. A move to work is a *good* thing. I don't know what the magic timeline is, but I envision it as developing people to make progress in their lives, and not subsidize their lives totally." He realized that there needed to be exceptions for "people who have supportive housing needs—people with issues"; his focus was on "people who are able, to compel them to the next point in life." Gault pointed out that, while "our selection criteria says that in order to initially qualify you must work a minimum of twenty verifiable hours, once you move in there's nothing—there's no teeth—to keep you working." He described instances where workers at the McDonald's in the Walmart "initially qualified" for entry to River Garden and then quit. Once you move in and are without a job, Gault commented, "Your rent goes down to [a flat] fifty dollars, and there's nothing to make you want to grow your life." Those on the minimum fifty-dollar rent also get refunds on their utility allowance—an overall operational cost of about $25,000 per month. Because HANO was not one of the initial three dozen housing authorities offered regulatory flexibility through the federal Moving to Work program, "HUD has told us that we can't make somebody work."[32]

Despite the pseudo work requirement, Gault estimated that three-quarters of public housing tenants from phase 1 were not working as of 2010. He acknowledged that "it's probably the economy in some instances," but for others unemployment "is a mindset." Gault saw some of the problem as rooted in the consent decree that "allowed former St. Thomas residents to have split families," meaning that those over eighteen could obtain a separate apartment. "So I have *grandchildren* who are living here, eighteen

years old, who've never had a home of their own, never really done anything significantly—I'm not debasing them when I say that—that now have a
brand-new apartment. They had to initially work, but then come in and quit
their job."

> I've got a group of girls that call themselves the Bout-It Thomas Girls—the
> BTGs—that are a nightmare. They're sixteen, seventeen, eighteen, nineteen
> years old and they just wail on each other. There are a number of them who
> have children from the same father, so it's like the Hatfields and the McCoys.[33]

From the perspective of management, many of River Garden's low-income
residents have created problems not just for themselves, but for the viability of a mixed-income community. At the same time, though, HRI
wished to support the aspirations of the most upwardly mobile among the
working poor.

When asked whether it would be possible to successfully manage a
redeveloped public housing development in New Orleans without a market-
rate tier, David Abbenante was aghast:

> That's not fair! That's not fair to the affordable residents. If the property is
> being torn down to come back with a new model, and you go to 100 percent
> affordable, that's letting down those sixty people that say, "I'm ready for a
> market-rate, mixed-income development."

To Abbenante, they are let down because being "trapped in areas that are
100 percent affordable . . . just limits the ability for growth"—growth that
depends on having better role models.

> You know, when you've got a neighbor next door who is an assistant professor
> over at Xavier, and they walk out and become friends with you, and you're
> a public housing resident struggling to work and they see your child who's
> fourteen or fifteen and kind of mentors them, works with them, and makes
> sure that they are going to get into Xavier, that's the beauty. That's what we're
> trying to offer. That's what I've bought into. It's going to provide opportunities
> for the affordable to step up to another level.[34]

At River Garden, as in other mixed-income developments, management
makes complex—and often controversial—moral judgments. Residents are
too easily characterized by their subsidy category and resented for having
their lives "totally subsidized." Meanwhile, the wishful assumptions about
role models coming to the rescue do not seem to be borne out empirically,
at least not frequently.

The most extensive effort to make sense of River Garden is found in a
dissertation by Kelly Owens, completed at the University of New Orleans in

2012.[35] Drawing on eight months of ethnographic fieldwork while living in the development during 2011, Owens reached out to forty-five River Garden residents, including eight homeowners, fifteen market-rate renters, and twenty-two residents receiving deep rental subsidies (either public housing or project-based vouchers), including some that had previously lived in the former St. Thomas. Overall, just as in most previous accounts of HOPE VI developments in Chicago, Boston, and Seattle, Owens found relatively little evidence of cross-tenure interaction.

Instead, Owens found "class divisiveness among African American neighbors" and demonstrated that "the struggle for contested space creates a neighborhood filled with tension." Although some respondents remained involved in the community and optimistic about the future of the neighborhood, she concluded that the majority lacked "any incentives or motivation to engage neighbors" across the divide of class and economic differences. "Rather than seeing their neighbors of different housing tenure as potential allies or resources, neighbors see each other as sources of discomfort." Because of HRI's need to "appease" market-rate tenants and homeowners, Owens learned, the public housing tenants felt "constantly monitored and regulated." Conversely, "Market-rate residents perceived River Garden to be 'rowdy' and 'dangerous' due to the presence of subsidized residents."[36]

The fact that HRI did not readily reveal the mixed-income nature of River Garden to prospective market-rate renters only added to the mistrust. Owens found that many market-rate residents expressed surprise that River Garden housed residents receiving rent subsidies. As one respondent put it, "The leasing agents don't talk about it at all, even with a positive spin. . . . They just talk about the fact that it didn't flood during Katrina. But they don't talk about the history of the area in any light, as even an experiment or a mixed-income place or anything like that." Similarly, without yet knowing that Kelly Owens intended to conduct research on the community, HRI's leasing agent mentioned nothing to her about the development's mixed-income nature.[37]

Many of the twenty-nine homeowners who bought into the property between 2004 and 2007 faced extreme financial challenges now that they were "stuck in the middle" of all the renters. River Garden was spared the floods of Katrina, but this did not prevent its homeowners from having their mortgages go underwater in 2008 with the larger market downturn. The double calamity in the New Orleans housing market meant that HRI did not build the larger community that realtors had promised to purchasers at the time of their initial buy-in. As one chastened homeowner commented,

> If he had said that . . . this is the second stage and then we're building some
> more rental homes over there on the other side of the park, I would never

have bought a house here. I don't want to be surrounded by rental homes on all sides. That's just idiotic. but the salesman said, "No, these are all going to be private condos."[38]

Just as ex–St. Thomas residents felt misled by a HOPE VI unit mix that minimized the presence of extremely low-income families and completely excluded the largest households, so too those early owners bought into HRI's bold promise of a new community of more than twelve hundred units that would be overwhelmingly composed of market-rate dwellings. They, too, faced dashed expectations when the "market" didn't "rate" as predicted.

Despite the temptations to remain guarded in their dealings with the community, Owens found some positively "engaged residents" living in all types of River Garden housing. These people sometimes interacted across boundaries of tenure and class, often because they used "the routine of dog walking for the purpose of meeting neighbors." Others with long-standing ties to the community, and broad social networks within the St. Thomas diaspora, also remained committed to the long-term future of the full new community. In short, engagement seemed most prominent among public housing residents and, at the opposite extreme, the homeowners. These two groups, despite their extreme differences, seemed most "wedded to River Garden due to constraints."[39] At base, neither could afford to leave.

In essence, the dramatic evolution of community visions and development realities yielded two kinds of broken promises. The disconnect between early prospects for a "New St. Thomas" and the Katrina-disrupted, market-battered partial version of River Garden that eventually resulted left few people happy. Former St. Thomas residents found fewer than expected places for themselves. And, at the other extreme, the much-coveted market-rate owners also felt betrayed once HRI understandably decided that it would be financially infeasible to follow through with much of the high-end investment initially planned for the site. Just like developers, residents also project the future of the community to make financial decisions.

River Garden is not a "gated community" in any larger urbanistic sense, but the doors to the mid-rise buildings require keycode entry, and the single-family homes at the rear are fenced and gated. Although the first wave of homeowners "lived fence-free for several years," residents then began erecting high, solid wooden barriers "to protect their properties from intruders who were creating routes through their backyards as shortcuts to get to the Phase II side of the development."[40] Meanwhile, in the poorer precincts of River Garden, residents faced the opposite problem—instead of excessive closure, they were blamed for undue openness. Owens identified what she terms "an informal 'stoop policy' that governs residents' abilities to socialize in front of their homes." Respondents reported that management employees, supplemented by police surveillance, "monitor the amount of activity in front of the units." HRI issued "written warnings" for having "too many individuals on one's stoop or porch." Many apprehensive public housing residents refused to be interviewed by Owens once they found out that HRI was aware of her research. Some former St. Thomas residents that had gained places in River Garden "did not want to be photographed," due to "fear that the research would share information with HRI and their participation would create additional tension between them and management."[41] Such observations resonate clearly with the work of Robert Chaskin and Mark Joseph in Chicago, where their studies of mixed-income communities revealed clear class-based "disagreement about what 'counts' as disorder, and what should be viewed as normative enjoyment of community space."[42] In contrast to the idyllic image of casual porch-front lounging so nostalgically and photogenically rendered in typical New Urbanist propaganda, at River Garden the presence of actual residents gathering conjured only hostility.

Owens discovered some residents eager to build bridges, but for the most part she found River Garden to be a place of separate worlds. Even community events sponsored by HRI tended to "lack cross-tenure appeal." These attracted chiefly former public housing residents and Section 8 voucher holders, aside from the market-rate renters drawn by the prospect of a Dog-Costume Parade. Owens concluded that the management seemed to hold events "just for the sake of being able to say that attempts were made to bring residents together."[43] Meanwhile, other management decisions played up differences through differential rule enforcement. Barbara Jackson observed that HRI prohibited residents from placing items outside their units. In December, they let only "the people in market rate" put out Christmas decorations. "Why would you tell public housing residents they can't put out Christmas decorations?" she asks. "That's so obviously discriminatory." Similarly, while residents paying market-rates "have flags out front," she resented how public housing tenants could not even keep a grill outside.[44] Another longtime former resident, Ronald McCoy—who moved out of River Garden to buy a nearby home in 2012, added:

> It's the way the management treats the different individuals based on income. If they are a low-income family they may not even be able to put patio furniture out, and they have a cement patio. But their next-door neighbor is market rate, and they can have a big barbecue every weekend if they want to.[45]

Jackson saw this as deliberate: "They want to get people so frustrated and so disgusted that they just want to leave. But ultimately, this just hurts many of those who give up: they 'go live somewhere else' where they pay more rent and wind up getting evicted and getting in more trouble."[46]

Owens observed that Walmart picked up the slack in social space that had been quashed by control measures imposed in the adjacent development, in part because the supercenter employed many River Garden residents and also because it informally provided "reunion" space for former residents to reconnect. The store—however controversial its origins—supplied local residents with inexpensive "one stop" shopping, including a pharmacy, cell phone store, hair salon, vision center, and a McDonalds. Many residents regard it as a key part of their daily or weekly social life, not just a place to shop. By contrast, many homeowners headed further inland to Magazine Street shops and restaurants. Like a neighborhood version of Venn diagram, they had some overlap in River Garden, but largely managed to travel in different circles.[47]

The tensions that Owens observed in 2011 continued to mount, causing HRI to install thirty-six cameras around the community that September. The management also hired "a private police detail, six police officers living onsite and a third party security firm that patrols the area." Some of this became controversial, especially when a journalist pointed out that one of the on-site NOPD officers, Jayson Germann, had "had 37 complaints filed against him in a three-year period," including "allegations of excessive use of force, verbal intimidation, theft, wrongful arrests and the filing of false reports," prompting the New Orleans Police Department to assign him to "a program to modify his behavior." Whether harmed or helped by Germann's patrols, River Garden's greater level of attention to security—presumably prompted by three murders that occurred on-site during 2011—seemed to lead to a decline in the number of voluntary move-outs due to fears about personal safety. Meanwhile, evictions slowly crept up: eighteen in 2010, nineteen in 2011, and twenty-two in 2012.[48]

In early 2012, HRI appointed Terrie McCurdy as the new site manager and added Armand Clavo as a "quality of life director" to work with the community. Neither of these hires sat well with the most vocal low-income residents. Clavo had previously served as a NOPD officer for almost a decade, during which, the *Times-Picayune* reported, he had "21 complaints filed against him that resulted in five suspensions," two of which explicitly blamed him for "unprofessionalism." Don Everard at Hope House questioned why HRI would employ such a person. "If you hire an ex-cop to be your quality of life officer instead of someone like a community organizer," he wondered, "what does that say about your value system?"[49]

Longtime leader Barbara Jackson continues to fight for her community in River Garden but has little positive to say about HRI's staff. Interviewed in 2013, she complained that site manager McCurdy was "terrorizing people" to the extent that "they're even scared to walk out their door because [HRI] hired someone off the police force." Jackson found McCurdy totally disrespectful, with "no compassion for people, especially people of public housing."

> They're just totally like you are on a plantation, or you is just the help. You are not judged on doing the right thing, on going to work and working hard, on trying to be a mother, taking care of your kids. You're not even looked at like that.

In contrast to previous River Garden site managers who held to the rules but did not proactively patrol the development, McCurdy "personally goes out. She don't sit behind a desk; she goes out with an officer, Clavo, so that's her protection. Then she can talk to people any kind of way she wants." She uses "vulgar language" and treats residents "like they are children." The clear message is: "I have a hold over your life. Whatever I say I can get you put out any minute." In turn, Jackson blamed Clavo for "going into people's apartments without authorization."[50] Ronald McCoy described Clavo's role as "intimidation—that's exactly what he's there for," observing that he treats women with particular disdain. "He talks with his 'library voice' when he talks to a man, but when he talks to a female he screams at the top of his lungs. And he gets this crazy look on his face. . . . And that's why a lot of people are afraid to speak out."[51]

David Abbenante, as HRI Management's president, vigorously defended Clavo, noting that the firm had carefully reviewed him, including a criminal background check, and had found nothing of concern. "We talked about everything and we feel very comfortable with what Armand has done for the community and he has the support of HRI. You can slam me up and down the street but I don't like it to get personal with my staff. I don't think it's fair. It's like character assassination."[52]

In early January 2013, in one particularly unfortunate incident, River Garden management unfairly maligned the character of residents. HRI's site office sent letters to those living on St. Andrew and Adele Streets that triggered tenants' worst fears about excess surveillance and its consequences. As the *Times-Picayune* reported, the letter "stated that management inspected the residents [*sic*] apartments and found the following violations: missing cabinet knobs, door stoppers, toilet papers, tub stoppers, light bulbs and broken blinds and door frames." Further, this memo came with a stark warning: "If they didn't fix these problems they could lose their housing subsidy and face eviction after which their apartment could be converted to a market rate unit." Residents reacted with understandable puzzlement and distress. Although individuals knew that no such items were "missing" in their particular apartment, they wondered what sort of secret inspection had prompted the charges. Moreover, the threat to evict and replace them with those who could pay market rates simply confirmed long-standing conspiracy theories—even though HRI could not in fact legally alter the subsidy status of their unit. Manager McCurdy quickly realized the "mistake," indicating that the letters had been sent out "by accident" and had not been authorized by her. Instead, new letters went out to clarify that there would be a *future* inspection in advance of an upcoming audit by HUD.[53] By then, however, the damage had been done.

On January 23, sixty or so River Garden residents, former St. Thomas tenants, and their allies marched from Hope House to the River Garden Apartments leasing office to protest against discrimination and mistreatment by HRI management (figure 5.5). Specifically, River Garden's public housing residents complained that they had been "harassed and intimidated by management, subject to unlawful invasion of their apartments, threatened with eviction for minor offenses, and denied due process through a grievance procedure." Brandishing a variety of signs calling for "No More Harassment" and "People Over Profit!" the residents stressed HRI's lack of respect. Ronald McCoy described River Garden as a "dictatorship" and "the new Jim Crow."

They chanted "Terrie Must Go! Terrie Must Go!"—and, someone added at the end, "Take Clavo with you!" HRI leaders continued to defend their

Figure 5.5. Protests against River Garden Management
Caption: River Garden residents staged a protest against HRI Management in January 2013.
Credit: Annemarie Gray.

employees, and Abbenante countered by blaming Don Everard for creating the trouble. "We ask that Mr. Everard promote the mission of Hope House, help foster the spirit of community in River Garden and abandon his current tactics which are creating unfounded fear and unnecessary concern in our community."[54]

A few months after the protest, HRI let Armand Clavo go and subsequently shifted to a private security company with a less overt police pedigree. Terrie McCurdy also later resigned from River Garden. To replace her, David Abbenante brought in manager Carlos Rivera, described by Everard as "a pleasant guy with a quiet demeanor, who seems a good bit more willing to work with residents." "On at least a few occasions," he notes, if there are neighbor-to-neighbor conflicts, "management has arranged to move a tenant to one of HRI's other developments, rather than simply evict."[55] Five years after the protest, River Garden seems calmer, and violent crime is down. Conversely, prices are up—both market-rate rentals at River Garden and throughout the larger gentrifying neighborhood. Pres Kabacoff views the periodic tensions with River Garden residents as necessary part of pursuing HRI's own difficult mission: "We try to be a good-guy developer," he averred. "We're driven by making tough inner-city neighborhoods work."[56]

POST-KATRINA PUBLIC HOUSING TRANSFORMATION

The advent of Katrina and subsequent housing market challenges delayed or canceled some later phases of St. Thomas, but this did not prevent St. Thomas from becoming a precedent for the post-Katrina transformation of many of the remaining large public housing developments in New Orleans (figure 5.6). As Pres Kabacoff saw it: "River Garden became the model for the rest of the projects in the city."[57] Michael Kelly, who helped launch the St. Thomas redevelopment when he was HANO director in the late 1990s, agreed: "Katrina clearly expedited the effort, but the idea was the St. Thomas model was what needed to happen throughout the New Orleans portfolio."[58] As Peter Burns and Matthew Thomas observe in *Reforming New Orleans*, in a city where "business interests and developers supported mixed-income housing on the sites of former public housing complexes," the New Orleans governance constellation marginalized the poor: "Neither HUD, HANO, the city council, the mayor, the Louisiana Recovery Authority, nor Congress rushed to get public housing residents back in their homes."[59]

To many politicians and developers, Katrina brought devastation, but also opportunity for elites to reshape communities that had been dispersed. Pre-Katrina, the deeply troubled HANO public housing portfolio had more than two thousand vacant apartments and accommodated 5,158 families, plus an

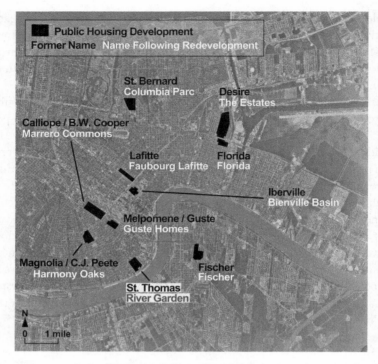

Figure 5.6. Beyond River Garden: Public Housing Redevelopment in New Orleans
After Katrina, much of New Orleans public housing has been rebuilt as mixed-income
communities, often following the model developed for River Garden.
Credit: Author with Jonathan Tarleton; aerial photograph 1VCUI00010057 courtesy of
the US Geological Survey.

additional 8,981 supported in private housing by housing choice vouchers,
much of this in locations that received heavy flooding.[60] Before the storm,
New Orleans had already been shifting toward reliance on vouchers, as city
leaders clearly found it impossible to manage huge housing projects that
averaged a thousand units each.

Eight months after the storm that forced mass evacuation, HUD secretary Alphonso Jackson encouraged HANO not to reopen public housing,
blaming the inadequacy of infrastructure in New Orleans. "Most of the
public housing developments are in areas where electricity has not been
turned on, schools are not open, there are no grocery stores, and we have
a serious mold and lead problem in some of those buildings." He regarded
the ongoing closure as a favor to residents, noting that they had "already
lived in pretty much substandard conditions" and that it would be "inhu-
mane and wrong" to "condone further substandard conditions." Others

frequently voiced an alternative explanation: the city was far more interested in redeveloping public housing than in reopening it. Laura Tuggle, a legal aid attorney, observed that empty public housing would be much easier to demolish. "One of the hardest parts of redevelopment is having to relocate residents of public housing," she commented. "That job was done for them."[61] Congressman Richard Baker from Baton Rouge infamously cast this as divine intervention: "We finally cleaned up public housing in New Orleans. We couldn't do it, but God could."[62]

While some wished to shut down public housing because of poor conditions, others blamed poor tenants. Responding to a rally urging HANO to reopen the St. Bernard development, New Orleans city councilor Oliver Thomas insisted that any returning residents should be those with jobs: "We don't need soap opera watchers all day."[63] Although all HOPE VI efforts, in New Orleans and elsewhere, had previously used redevelopment as an opportunity to reselect residents, post-Katrina New Orleans heightened the drama. Secretary Jackson phrased it bluntly: "Some of the people shouldn't return." Acknowledging the past history of gang violence, he added, "Only the best residents should return. Those who paid rent on time, those who held a job and those who worked." Advocates derided Jackson for stereotyping public housing residents as unemployed, criminal, or both, but plans went forward.[64]

In June 2006, Secretary Jackson announced that HANO's "Big Four" projects—St. Bernard, Lafitte, B.W. Cooper, and C.J. Peete—should be demolished, causing widespread protests from former residents. An architectural analysis conducted by MIT professor John Fernandez concluded that "no structural or nonstructural damage was found that could reasonably warrant any cost-effective demolition." In papers filed in court, Fernandez observed that "replacement of these buildings with contemporary construction would yield buildings of lower quality and shorter lifetime duration," noting that "the lifetimes of the buildings in all four projects promise decades of continued service that may be extended indefinitely." Similarly, Tulane law professor Bill Quigley pointed out, HANO's own documents showed that

> Lafitte could be repaired for $20 million, even completely overhauled for $85 million while the estimate for demolition and rebuilding many fewer units will cost over $100 million. St. Bernard could be repaired for $41 million, substantially modernized for $130 million while demolition and rebuilding less units will cost $197 million. BW Cooper could be substantially renovated for $135 million compared to $221 million to demolish and build less units. Their own insurance company reported that it would take less than $5,000 each to repair each of the CJ Peete apartments.[65]

None of this mattered to HUD or New Orleans city officials. This was never only about costs; it was about who would pay and who would benefit. And, ultimately, the example of turning St. Thomas into the mixed-income River Garden—despite its arduous process—offered the desired model. Accordingly, in December 2007, the New Orleans City Council voted seven to zero to go ahead with the demolitions. Raw feelings persisted. As one commenter described it: "The City Hall gates were locked. Hundreds of protesters, wanting to testify, were kept out with pepper spray and taser guns. The scene was reminiscent of a third-world revolution."[66]

A decade later, the New Orleans public housing landscape is vastly smaller and wholly different. HANO reached its latest nadir in 2009 following a series of financial scandals that ultimately caused HUD to send a whole new team of overseers, led by seasoned public housing "turnaround" specialist David Gilmore, to run HANO between 2009 and 2014. Gilmore did much to stabilize the system, despite the exigencies of the Great Recession, paving the way for a return to local control with the appointment of executive director Gregg Fortner in late 2014. Under Gilmore, HANO altered its board meeting procedures to permit public comments *before* policies had been voted upon, rather than after; HANO increased its distribution of housing vouchers by forty-five hundred; and made fitful if fateful progress on redeveloping much of the city's remaining public housing.[67]

C.J. Peete (originally called Magnolia) is now known as Harmony Oaks, a name chosen by "the investors' marketing people." Developed by the famed St. Louis–based firm McCormack Baron Salazar, 1,403 public housing apartments have been converted into just 460 mixed-income units, with "50 for-sale affordable homeownerships units" to be scattered into the surrounding neighborhood. Since fewer than one hundred families had lived at Peete even *before* Katrina struck, it seemed possible to envision a wholly new start. Even so, mistrust reigned, centered on the usual issues of residents' right of return, project design and services, and management roles for tenants. Eventually, just 15 percent of former residents were able to return to what is described in the Harmony Oaks marketing brochure as a "gated community [that] features a sparkling pool, playground, fitness center with free weights, and a business center." The flyer makes no mention of its mixed-income nature, although an electronic version has a notation that reads, "*Income restrictions apply on some apartments, call for details.*" In fact, this particular development included a plurality of public housing units (44 percent), with the remainder split fairly evenly between "affordable" units and "market-rate." David Gilmore viewed this as a marked improvement, since "Nobody in his right mind would ever build a C.J. Peete again." At base, the source of capital for redevelopment both revealed and determined the priorities: HOPE VI funds contributed $20 million—less than one-tenth the cost of this $250 million transformation.[68]

The B.W. Cooper project (formerly known as Calliope), which once featured 1,550 units, is now Marrero Commons, named for Yvonne Marrero, community leader and former president of the Cooper RMC. Although construction of the development hired an unusual number of public housing residents, the redevelopment faced protracted delays, caused in part by severe soil contamination on the site. The resultant community contains only 143 public housing units, approximately one-third of its 410 apartments. Since it is also managed by McCormack Baron, it uses the same style of marketing brochure as Harmony Oaks and, similarly, remains silent about its mixed-income aspect.[69]

By contrast, the website for the former St. Bernard development, now known as Columbia Parc at the Bayou District and managed by Columbia Residential, explicitly highlights its social experiment: "Columbia Parc is proud to be a mixed-income community." The website has a section for former St. Bernard residents considering a return. The development actively recruits them but reminds them that they will need to pay for utilities, be "legally employed with verifiable income," be drug free, have a clean criminal background, and undergo additional background checks on credit and rental history. That said, the print brochure handed out to prospective residents makes no mention of the development's mixed-income character when extolling "the community inspired by New Orleans and perfected by you." Instead of the 1,464-unit original development, Columbia Parc has 683 units, allocated fairly evenly among market-rate, "affordable," and public housing / project-based voucher units.[70] Of the 900 households living in St. Bernard at the time of Katrina, however, only 120 managed to return.[71]

Lafitte, the last of the demolished "Big Four"—is now fancified as Faubourg Laffite. It has been redeveloped by the not-for-profit firm Providence Community Housing, in partnership with Enterprise Community Partners and L&M Development. They have adopted a gridded New Urbanist plan filled with porch-fronted, single-family cottages and shotgun-style singles and doubles. Although not as dense as the 896-unit original project, the first 517 units completed on-site contained about two-thirds public housing or project-based vouchers, including a separate 100-unit building serving the elderly. Faced with numerous financing delays and recession-induced barriers to meeting goals for additional homeownership components, the team nonetheless plans to infuse hundreds of additional housing units into the surrounding Treme neighborhood.[72] In other words, there can sometimes be nonprofit-dominated constellations even in cities that typically favor big private developers.

Finally, there is the ambitious plan for the 821 units of Iberville, rechristened as Bienville Basin. This brings the story back to HRI. Pres Kabacoff had long coveted the redevelopment possibility of this prime site adjacent to the French Quarter, and successfully sought out the contract. Because it is being redeveloped under the federal Choice Neighborhoods program that succeeded HOPE VI, HRI had to accept one-for-one replacement of lost public housing—a far cry from their approach at St. Thomas. HRI proposed to accomplish this with about half public housing (412 units), and half project-based vouchers (446). To keep the overall complex from being dominated by those with the lowest incomes, however, HRI proposed a much larger overall development, expected to contain 1,841 units once completed.[73] If successful, this would bring Kabacoff close to meeting his stated preference for communities that would have no more than 40 percent extremely low-income households.

Meanwhile, a few other large projects—Guste, Fischer, Florida, and Desire (now "The Estates") became markedly smaller but remained overwhelmingly occupied by public housing residents.[74] Overall, though, the dominant result of public housing transformation in New Orleans has been a shift from projects to vouchers. A decade after Katrina struck, fully 91 percent of HANO-subsidized households received their aid in the form of a housing voucher, while just 1,820 households remained in public housing.

For many households, the voucher program has proved successful: a safer alternative to life in large public housing projects. That said, an overall assessment in the *Times-Picayune* in 2015 concluded that "a large percentage of Section 8 families are clustered in low-income, largely black neighborhoods, many in eastern New Orleans"—a part of the city with spotty public transportation and distant from French Quarter jobs. Faced with entry into a rental housing stock after half of it had been destroyed by Katrina, low-income households still had limited choices a decade later—especially in so-called high-opportunity communities with better schools, jobs, and less crime. And, as with the relocations launched after St. Thomas was first torn down, many households seeking to use vouchers faced resistance from landlords on racial grounds. Still, despite the problems, the supply of vouchers falls well short of demand. As of 2015, 13,000 households remained on the New Orleans wait list that hadn't been opened for new names since 2009. HANO director Fortner estimated that opening it would cause an additional fifty thousand people to sign up. Meanwhile, in the decade after Katrina, median rents rose by 50 percent while wages stagnated. In 2017, HANO gamely continued to weather reduced payouts from HUD, even as one study found that New Orleans had "a dire need of at least 33,000 affordable units just to deal with the current market conditions."[75]

CONCLUSION: SATISFYING THE DEVELOPERS, PURGING THE POOREST

Pres Kabacoff insisted that the development income mix at River Garden ended up "not much different" than what had been proposed in the initial HOPE VI project that HRI inherited.[76] This is not entirely disingenuous. Seen more than two decades later, despite an enormously wide oscillation between proffered alternatives over the course of many years, what has been actually built out does bear some resemblance to the initial HOPE VI vision. In sharp contrast to the pointed drama of Brod Bagert's claims in 2002 about a development that would be 78 percent market rate, HRI built nothing of that sort. HRI very much *wanted* to build a very different community mix, but just couldn't pull it off. On one side, persistent resident activism and lawsuits gradually increased the number of public housing units; on the other side, a combination of Katrina displacement and housing market conditions made the bulk of the planned high-end components financially infeasible. The numbers now suggest a development that is 52 percent market rate. Yet even that figure is misleadingly high, since this does not include those who are using housing choice vouchers to live in some of the market-rate apartments. The surprising reality is that River Garden really *does* house primarily low-income households, many of them extremely-low income. Despite his determination to "hold the line" at 40 percent "affordable" because HOPE VI is "about attracting market rate," Pres Kabacoff could not do that. One might well update Congressman Baker's observation: "We couldn't keep public housing from gentrifying, but the market did."

Still, the irony of a development that bears little resemblance to the caricatures drawn by the conspiratorial fears of its earliest critics has nonetheless done nothing to quiet multisided reproach. The River Garden that resulted—home to so few former St. Thomas households—bears little resemblance to the early dreams for a New St. Thomas that would feature 51 percent resident control, a resident management corporation, and apartments sized and located to maximize the return of residents. The similarities in market-rate housing percentages between HOPE VI and the eventual reality cannot mask the dashed hopes of the earliest promises. The resulting community bears little resemblance to the ideals that first prompted residents to offer their buy-in at the time of the ULI visit back in 1994. Given the injustices of the subsequent process and the frequent changes of plan, Jay Arena is surely correct to view River Garden as causing too many low-income residents to be "driven from New Orleans." At the same time, however, from the self-styled "good guy" developer's standpoint, HRI has had to face the backlash from middle-class residents who feel that the developer/

manager has done too little to shield them from Pres Kabacoff's wish to engage in "tough inner-city neighborhoods."

To Don Everard at Hope House, the necessity to rely on the HOPE VI program for redeveloping St. Thomas derailed the high promise of the initial ideas floated by ULI and dramatically shifted the focus away from the needs of existing public housing residents.

> HOPE VI had the process where you pretty much had to cut off two legs in order to get funding: it had to be a mixed-income community, it had to be less dense poverty rates. . . . And so in trying to write the grant application for funding, residents really offered up a lot. In order to get what they want they agreed to basically amputate part of themselves.

And then, as Everard saw it, the grant itself got amputated, too. "We had asked for forty million dollars, we got twenty-five. And in a sense, it was downhill from there." As a savvy participant-observer for more than three decades, Everard recognized a single searing truth: HOPE VI is "a very strange process" because "resident input was very important up until the time that the grant was gotten." After that, he realized, "Resident input was obstructionist and [something] to be gotten around."

> And so it was a real change in attitude once the grant was there. People began to realize that this seems to be the way it's set up. That you have to agree to this but everything can change afterwards. And really everything changed afterwards.[77]

Erstwhile HANO director Kelly acknowledges this. "Like a lot of HOPE VI applications, [the St Thomas proposal was] submitted with an optimal vision." Resolving the details is "where the tensions start. . . . The actual number of low-income residents who returned was a lot less than what was initially agreed to with the neighborhood and the residents right when I left [in 2000]."[78] In the Big Developer constellation of New Orleans, HOPE VI provided little more than an entry point for a private sector-dominated deal to be determined later.

Looking back at her own experience with HOPE VI, even when seen from the comfort of her home in River Garden, Barbara Jackson felt profoundly misled. "With HOPE VI," she underscored, "we were there up front. It could have been a good program, but it was a trial, it was something new to them. So if they failed, they could say, 'Well, it was new to us.'" Ultimately, Jackson resented the extent to which developers "make deals all the time behind doors." She saw the St. Thomas to River Garden saga as one big manipulation: "They had the original HOPE VI plan, and they had the one that they executed. They didn't want nobody to have any kind of comprehensive

[view] of how everything was working, and how to make sure that the community could really be a working community." At base, Jackson lamented the extent to which HANO, HUD and the developers failed to appreciate the St. Thomas community that existed *before* HOPE VI. "We had everything going. We had strong economic development and . . . all the stuff they say they wanted. They wanted to have a community that was mixed-income, a strong community, people striving. It was there." To her great disappointment, however, "The powers that be wanted more than that."[79] To many onetime St. Thomas denizens, River Garden meant being sold down the river, cast out from the garden.

Bill Quigley, who has worked as an attorney for St. Thomas residents since 1982, also regretted the outcome, calling River Garden "a disgraceful memorial to our loss." Looking back, he observed that "the people of St. Thomas were bribed, scared, intimidated and seduced into leaving their apartments as government and private people kept telling them they would be evicted and the property was going to come down." However, Quigley also emphasized the extent and duration of resistance—"protests, pickets, sit-downs to prevent bulldozers, and nearly constant meetings with every person in local, state and federal government who would listen." In contrast to his more conspiratorial friend Jay Arena, Quigley was far less willing to impugn the motives of those residents and allies who long fought for a more just result. Quigley resisted the idea that "some or all of the resident leaders sold out or were bought out." He acknowledged that he was mistaken not to have himself taken "a more active and confrontational role" and regretted that he was not more suspicious of the ULI involvement right from the start. Still, he saw the larger saga as more than the inevitable operation of what Arena called a "government- and foundation-funded nonprofit complex."

> Personally, I do not think these mistakes were made from greed or self-interest or selling out. I think people fought for their homes for years and summoned allies to help them whenever they could, but were ultimately overwhelmed by the combined forces of local, state, and federal government along with the economic waves that continued to crash against them. . . . Jay and the many [others] who view this tragedy differently may indeed be right, but from my perspective, I dissent.[80]

Even if there remain disagreements among New Orleans progressives about the nature and extent of co-optation and blame, it seems overwhelmingly clear that the long, sad tale of St. Thomas is dominated by systematic injustices. River Garden and Walmart remain, but the neighborhood's poorest residents have largely been purged.

Fortunately, other cities have approached public housing redevelopment differently.

Part III

PLEBS IN BOSTON

Figure III.1. Boston's Plebs Governance Constellation
Boston's HOPE VI governance constellation is found in the community-centered sector
of the firmament.
Credit: Author with Suzanne Harris-Brandts.

Figure III.2. The Plebs Constellation in Boston: A Telescopic View
This telescopic view of the Plebs constellation depicted in figure III.1 has Orchard Park resident leader Edna Bynoe as its orienting pole star. The Boston Housing Authority and a strong not-for-profit developer also matter, but the constellation is skewed toward the needs of the low-income community, with the private for-profit sector playing a secondary role.
Credit: Author with Suzanne Harris-Brandts.

[Resident leader] Edna Bynoe carried a *huge* amount of weight [in the redevelopment decision-making].
                                      —Boston Housing Authority administrator Bill McGonagle

OVERVIEW: HOPE VI WITHOUT HOPING THE POOR WILL LEAVE

When compared to the saga of public housing in New Orleans, the story of Boston's experience with the Orchard Park public housing development demonstrates both a parallel early trajectory and a strikingly different outcome during and after redevelopment. Part III of this book conveys this story across two chapters. Chapter 6 narrates the rise and subsequent struggles of Orchard Park while also explaining the origins of Boston's Plebs governance constellation that brought such deeply felt community and resident engagement to the cause of public housing (fig. III.1), while chapter 7 traces the resident-centered, successful effort to transform Orchard Park into Orchard Gardens using the HOPE VI program (fig. III.2).

As with much early public housing across the United States, Boston's city leaders created Orchard Park in 1942 to clear slums, generate construction jobs, build modern housing, and—because it opened after active US involvement in World War II had commenced—house war workers. This reiterated the Boston Housing Authority's prewar efforts to purge the poorest from the slums and to use the new projects to rehouse others who were more economically and socially stable. In this way, Orchard Park began as a place intended for low-income households, while resisting those with the lowest incomes. The early determination to build a highly selective community composed of the upwardly mobile "worthy poor" did not survive much past the late 1950s—much like other public housing in large American cities. Yet here is the puzzle: When Orchard Park itself became so rundown that it urgently needed to be redeveloped under the HOPE VI program of the 1990s, somehow Bostonians—unlike New Orleanians—resisted the temptation to replace it with a community emphasizing market-rate housing. Instead, the Boston Housing Authority (BHA) chose to retain fully 85 percent of apartments for use by low-income households. These families now reside in the community known as Orchard Gardens. The next two chapters recount the story of that transformation but also step back to ask the more fundamental question: What is it that gave rise to a political culture in Boston that privileges the rights of the poor in ways that can explain this city's approach to HOPE VI?

Despite Boston's well-known associations with many progressive movements across the eighteenth and nineteenth centuries, little about the city's deeply conservative politics during the mid-twentieth century would make one expect the city to emphasize the rights of its poorest minority citizens. Yet Boston's governance constellation became dramatically reconfigured between the 1950s and the 1980s. A city once polarized around the parochial politics of Irish politicians and Yankee businessmen wrenchingly grappled with racial and ethnic diversification. Elected officials in the 1960s increasingly found it politically imperative to pay attention to residential neighborhoods rather than just downtown business interests, and faced increased backlash against their efforts to implement ambitious urban renewal programs across the city. The situation worsened once this effort was coupled with an ill-advised attempt to ram the Southwest Expressway and Inner Belt highway through the heart of the city's black community. Rather than mere protests, however, the reaction to forced displacement generated new institutions and empowered individuals to instigate what I have termed the Plebs governance constellation. Multiple not-for-profit community development organizations sprouted in most neighborhoods, helping low-income residents gain both welcome amenities and sustained voice. Roxbury's Dudley Street Neighborhood Initiative (DSNI), whose community land trust gained its own power of eminent domain,[1] is but the most celebrated of such efforts to permit communities to shape their own development.

Orchard Park—situated within the DSNI sphere of influence, located between three of Boston's urban renewal zones, and positioned immediately adjacent to the swath of land cleared for the Inner Belt—could not help but be shaped by these larger forces. At the same time, the patronage-riddled and nearly bankrupt Boston Housing Authority of the 1960s faced its own tenant-centered revolution. In sharp contrast to practices elsewhere in the country, one mayor permitted the BHA board to gain a "tenant-oriented majority," and two subsequent mayors named former BHA tenants as chief administrators of the agency. The BHA's turnaround also importantly benefited from a period of court-ordered receivership in the 1980s, which led to dramatic transformations of several deeply troubled developments. And because the BHA demonstrated that it could sometimes be possible to turn around its worst projects without also turning those projects over to high-income occupancy, a pattern of public expectations had been set. So by the time HOPE VI funds became available in the 1990s, activist Boston citizens had every reason to assume that public housing transformation would overwhelmingly serve those with the lowest incomes. To do otherwise would be politically dangerous.

Still, that did not mean that any of this would be easy.

6

The Rise of Orchard Park

THE ORIGINS OF ORCHARD PARK

The Boston Housing Authority (BHA), established in 1935, enthusiastically embraced public housing for families. It completed eight prewar projects— one under the terms of the Public Works Administration and seven more with the US Housing Authority (USHA). The Orchard Park public housing development, built in the city's Roxbury neighborhood, served as the city's sixth project, gradually receiving its initial tenants between 1942 and 1944. In its lavishly illustrated annual report for 1945, the BHA paused to congratulate itself for having constructed "eight, clean, shining Developments rising fresh to the sun where once in dreary, dirt-filled dilapidation slum dwellings had shambled in contaminating hopelessness against a gray and somber sky." Having seemingly both cleared slums and fixed Boston's weather while housing nearly twenty-five thousand low-income families in 5,975 new apartments, the BHA also self-assuredly celebrated its institutional capacity to replace "vociferous antagonism" with "open approval."[1] But not everyone remained so openly acquiescent.

Developing the new 774-unit complex entailed demolishing hundreds of homes and businesses and displacing well over a thousand people. The BHA duly photographed the buildings on the site in October 1940, then took the land by eminent domain two months later. Many of the single-family and triple-decker wooden homes, brick apartment structures, and neighborhood corner stores looked relatively sound to others (figure 6.1). Boston's 1935 Real Property Inventory Report found that two-thirds of housing in the tracts cleared for the project could be considered in "good" condition or needing only "minor repairs." Nonetheless, the housing authority's lawyers assured doubters that the site met the legal threshold "wherein dwellings predominate which, by reason of dilapidation, overcrowding, faulty arrangement or design, lack of ventilation, light or sanitation facilities, or any combination of these factors, are detrimental to safety, health or morals." The BHA regarded the site as "fast becoming severely blighted" and viewed public housing as the chance to save it for desirable residential occupancy. Not all tenants and

Figure 6.1. View of Neighborhood Cleared to Build Orchard Park
In late 1940, Boston Housing Authority staff photographed the homes and businesses
that were taken by eminent domain to make way for the Orchard Park public housing
project.
Credit: Courtesy of the Bostonian Society.

owners left willingly and peacefully; several residents refused to depart, and
police needed to forcibly remove them from their homes. Throughout 1941,
police struggled to prevent arson in the transitioning neighborhood. During
one month in late spring, neighbors called firefighters to extinguish twenty
different fires, causing the city to station a nightly patrol of sixty men in the
area. Public officials worried about vandals, but departing residents faced
the largest frustration.[2]

Unease about displacement certainly had a logical basis: the new public
housing would not be targeted to the households being forced out. My own
previous study of the first four USHA projects in Boston showed that 50–
70 percent of displaced households applied for such housing, yet the BHA
accommodated only 2–12 percent of them.[3] For this fifth effort at Orchard
Park, the advent of war yielded an additional exclusionary twist.

Originally planned to house low-income families and to address a
shortage of affordable housing, many public housing developments, including the not-yet-complete Orchard Park, were repurposed by the federal

government into housing for "war production workers" once American war preparations ramped up in 1941. This gave defense workers (such as shipbuilders and munitions factory employees) and families of soldiers and veterans first priority in the initial lease-up. It did not simply grant an occupational preference; it also markedly altered the low-income character of the development. Orchard Park could be advertised in 1940 as accommodation for those with annual family income that could not exceed $1,050 to $1,490, depending on apartment size—figures that were equal to approximately 50 percent of area median income (AMI) at the time. By 1942, however, with the need to accommodate higher-income war workers, the BHA essentially doubled the income ceilings, initially to $2,200, then to $2,800. Although the BHA quickly amended its policy to permit some local families requiring large apartments to occupy apartments in Orchard Park and other affected projects, this had relatively little effect. Prodded by patriotism and exigency, the BHA purged the poorest from the neighborhood razed to build the project. Careful review of Boston's "police lists" (an annual census of every household in the city) reveals that just eleven families from the neighborhood—equal to about 2.5 percent of those displaced—made it back into the completed Orchard Park. With war workers as primary tenants, the BHA happily anticipated that rent receipts would exceed operating expenses by nearly 35 percent each year.[4]

The housing authority platted new streets and culs-de-sac, giving some patriotic names taken from the wartime headlines: Bataan Court and Corregidor Court, which commemorated losses in the Philippines during 1942 (figures 6.2–6.3). The new public neighborhood of Orchard Park took its name from the local open space—once a place for growing apples. With twenty-eight three-story, modernist, garden apartment buildings spread across two adjacent fan-shaped parcels, the plan of Orchard Park resembled a sixteen-acre bowtie. Cheered by the prospect of a proposed Roxbury Crosstown Highway that would "form a splendid boundary for the project," within the project itself the housing authority touted its plan for "desirable super-blocks" that could "eliminate through traffic."[5] Demographically, as architecturally, the new neighborhood bore little relation to the old.

The households occupying the new housing project tended to be both smaller and, on average, ten years younger. Many more women listed "housewife" as their occupation, while men were most likely to work as welders, machinists or electricians or serve in the navy—a far cry from the previous denizens, who most commonly toiled as laborers, drivers, or clerks. A US citizen now headed every household in the new project. Whereas 97 percent of the residents of the razed neighborhood came from Boston, almost one-third of the new Orchard Park households moved there from outside the city—from sixty-seven different Massachusetts communities

Figure 6.2. Rendering of Orchard Park Housing Project, Boston
Architect John McPherson's rendering of the Orchard Park project shows its unusual
bowtie layout. The four buildings at the top, at the corner of Albany and Yeoman
streets surrounding the smokestack, were devoted to black-only occupancy, while the
rest of the development was initially targeted to whites.
Credit: Boston Housing Authority.

and nineteen different states. Both whites and blacks converged on Boston
for wartime jobs, and the BHA accommodated this at Orchard Park by
permitting quasi integration—a biracially segregated project that concentrated black residents into four adjacent buildings. This accorded well
with the immediate neighborhood composition, which stood at a kind of
crossroads. Northwest of the project area, African Americans dominated,
whereas to the south and east, whites of Canadian, Irish, and Italian heritage far outnumbered blacks.

In 1944, two-year-old Edna Bynoe arrived with her parents and siblings
as one of the first few black households to inhabit the new development.
Interviewed more than sixty years after her arrival, she recalled her
childhood neighborhood as full of flowers, trees, grass, and play yards, with
four different schools within walking distance. As a teenager in the 1950s,
she had Dudley Station transit available little more than a block away—yet
much of value was even more readily at hand. The neighborhood itself featured approximately 150 retail establishments within six hundred feet of the
project, including thirty-three places to buy food, fourteen restaurants, fifteen drinking places, five drugstores, twenty-four clothing stores, six barbers
and two beauty parlors, four laundries, eight general merchandise stores,
ten places to purchase furniture or appliances, four shops selling used items,
and eighteen repair shops. Amid such vibrancy, however, by 1957 there were
also forty-nine vacant stores.[6]

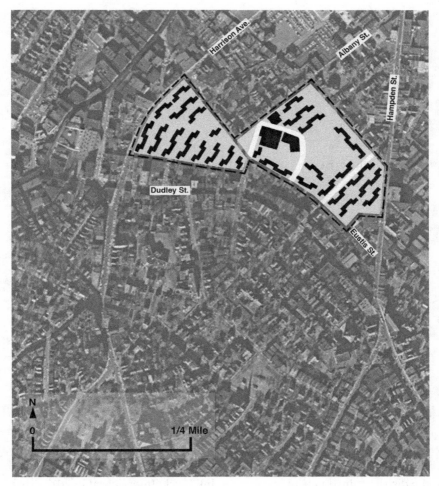

Figure 6.3. Orchard Park as Built
The BHA inserted the Orchard Park housing development into a dense residential and commercial urban fabric, as revealed by this aerial photograph from 1955.
Credit: Author with Jonathan Tarleton; aerial photograph 1VKF000010020 courtesy of the US Geological Survey.

Many members of Edna Bynoe's large extended family achieved prominence in politics, business, and civic affairs, but her own achievements happened closer to home. She remained at Orchard Park for the rest of her life, while working thirty-five years for the state government and raising her own children in the development. For decades, she remained the community's most important leader—the central force behind the Orchard Park Tenants Association and a key impetus behind the project's eventual redevelopment into Orchard Gardens. In so doing, she personally witnessed the rise, fall, and rebirth of Boston's public housing.

Throughout the 1940s and 1950s and into the 1960s, Orchard Park remained quite a desirable place to live. Meanwhile, however, the winds of change swirled all around it. Just as the prewar BHA leapt at opportunities for slum clearance, so too city agencies in the 1950s and 1960s eagerly embraced possibilities for large-scale urban renewal.

RENEWING BOSTON

Urban renewal in Boston is often treated as synonymous with the infamous clearance of the city's West End, but this is certainly incomplete. The West End was not even the first Boston neighborhood to crumble before the era's bulldozers. The Red Sox had failed for decades to vanquish the Yankees, but in 1956 it proved relatively easy to annihilate the neighborhood known— at least to planners—as New York Streets (because its roads were named after seven upstate New York places).[7] This small, multiethnic community, constructed on landfill in the northeast corner of the South End, offered up few audible protests but nonetheless sustained lingering indignation. More than six decades later, longtime Boston black activist Mel King, who grew up on Seneca Street, remembered hearing about the planned clearance from an article in the *Boston Traveler*: "The early 1950s headline said that I lived on 'skid row,' in a 'slum.' I was amazed. After all, we called it 'home.'" King loved the "richness of the community and its relationships" and only later discovered that the city needed to declare it "blighted" in order to access urban renewal funds and convert the area to commercial use. After the neighborhood was rebuilt to house the *Herald Traveler* newspaper plant, the district gained new nickname: the Ink Block. Interviewed in 2013, King was still outraged: "I used to live there, yet they had the audacity to call it the Ink Block, memorializing the paper that benefitted from using negative descriptions as a weapon of mass displacement and demeaning what folks called home."[8] Such are the long memories of urban renewal in Boston.

In this respect, Boston's other early adventure with urban renewal— the storied clearance of the West End—has remained the city's most dramatic touchstone. In part, this is because of the high visibility of the demolition—forty-eight acres near the heart of downtown—but much had to do with its location adjacent to Massachusetts General Hospital (figure 6.4). Working on a grant from the National Institute for Mental Health, teams of researchers—most famously including sociologist Herbert Gans, psychologist Marc Fried, and planner Chester Hartman, soon provided an unprecedented level of documentation. Gans wrote compellingly of the lives of

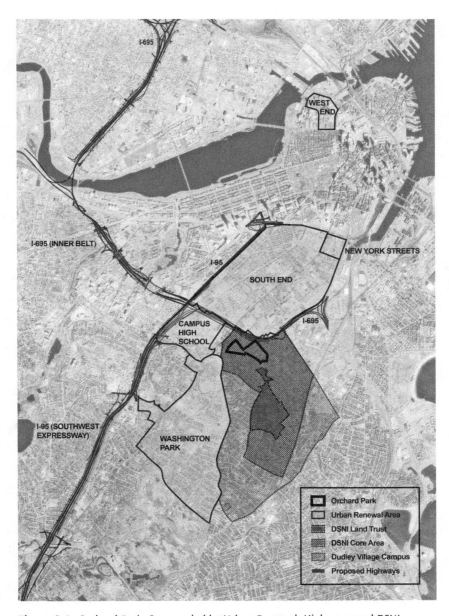

Figure 6.4. Orchard Park: Surrounded by Urban Renewal, Highways, and DSNI
By the 1960s, Orchard Park residents found themselves surrounded on three sides by
urban renewal districts—South End, Campus High School, and Washington Park—
and threatened by the incursion of the Inner Belt highway. More encouragingly,
by the 1980s, Orchard Park also benefited from the activities of the Dudley Street
Neighborhood Initiative (DSNI), operating in the neighborhood just to the south.
Credit: Author with Jonathan Tarleton; aerial photograph 1VECR00010087 courtesy of
the US Geological Survey.

"urban villagers" before their neighborhood was razed; Fried documented their displacement in a classic article, "Grieving for a Lost Home," and Hartman analyzed the contested politics of the whole saga, tracing the outcomes for residents. Taken together, these studies showed how a tax base definition of a "slum" and a growth-oriented political economy could yield the removal of a working-class neighborhood that had remained, at least to its residents, "a good place to live."[9] To this day, in addition to the rich academic literature, there is an active West End Museum and periodic reunions of now-elderly displacees who gather to remember their disrupted childhoods. At the time, though, Boston's general plan of 1950 assuredly proposed replacing this "obsolete neighborhood" with new superblocks punctuated by tower-in-the-park urbanism. These, civic boosters hoped, would repatriate a suburbanizing middle class and bring the city "quality shoppers." It proved to be a remarkably drawn-out, decade-long process just to get to the point of razing the neighborhood, followed by many more years before the site could be fully built out. Equally important, the demise of the West End marked a profound broken promise: when the West End project had been initially announced in April 1953, Mayor John Hynes said it would contain low-rent housing for 1,175 families, 200 middle-income apartments, and just 640 high-rent apartments. Even though 2,248 households would be "displaced," they were told that many could move to the new low-rent housing. Instead, by the time the city sent out eviction notices in 1958, all references to any subsidized housing on the site had disappeared.[10] In part, this alteration happened because oversight for the federally funded redevelopment program shifted in 1957 from the BHA to the newly established Boston Redevelopment Authority (BRA), but mostly it marked passage of the Housing Act of 1954, which provided even less incentive to build public housing. Moreover, as historian Thomas O'Connor remarks, "The apparent ruthlessness with which the demolition program was carried out in the West End produced such a wave of horrified revulsion that the future of any further 'urban renewal' projects was much in doubt."[11]

Edward J. Logue arrived in Boston in 1960 and became development administrator of the BRA under newly elected mayor John Collins. Logue came from New Haven, Connecticut, where he had launched the nation's fifth-largest urban renewal program in terms of capital grants (and largest on a per capita basis), enough to force the displacement of about 20 percent of the city's population. Coming to Boston, he faced the contested legacy of the total-clearance approach.[12] Determined to alter this image, Collins introduced Logue's "90 Million Dollar Development Program for Boston" by promising that "neighborhood committees" would have "a key partnership role in the carrying out of renewal plans." "I would call it planning *with* people," he summarized, "instead of planning for people."[13] *Fortune* magazine marveled that the BRA's bold plan could affect fully 25 percent of Boston's land and half its population. Clearly, there would be a lot of people to plan with. Each of the largest neighborhood plans—in Roxbury (Washington Park), the South End, and Charlestown—covered more than five hundred acres, more than ten times the size of the erstwhile West End. Planner Lawrence Kennedy observes that Logue considered himself "a leader in incorporating community participation and social reform into the process of rebuilding the physical city." Given how little had been done to engage communities in the earlier clearance processes, Logue at first appeared to be progressive. Intent on keeping to the "planning with people" slogan, Logue's team made clear that most of the BRA's work would focus on rehabilitation of existing structures, while acknowledging that "about 20 percent of the residential structures in each project area should be cleared."[14]

This meant there could be losers as well as winners in what planner Langley Keyes called "the Rehabilitation Planning Game." To Keyes, writing in 1968, "The renewed Washington Park was simply not producing rentals that could be afforded by low-income people of any kind." Moreover, this was quite intentional, since "the people who had put [the vote for] urban renewal over the top in Washington Park during the planning game—the Negro Elite and Blue-Collar Workers—had predicated that support on the emergence of a middle-class life-style community in Washington Park."[15] Kennedy credits the BRA team behind Roxbury's Washington Park for engaging with "at least some important elements of the community leadership" and the plan initially did receive considerable community support,[16] but most other assessments of the era view the consultation less generously.[17] To urban activists Peter Medoff and Holly Sklar, the Roxbury and South End urban renewal efforts illustrated a central "problem": "The city wanted to plan *with* like-minded people, mainly middle-class homeowners, while planning displacement *for* low-income residents."[18]

PLANNING WITH (SOME OF THE) PEOPLE

Boston's urban renewal program regularly displaced the poorest residents, but refused to acknowledge this. One South End advocacy group put it bluntly: BRA stands for "Blacks Run Again." As early as 1963, *Boston Globe* real-estate reporter Anthony Yudis pointed out "some glaring inconsistencies" in the claims about family relocation. The BHA insisted that priority for placement in public housing went to those displaced by urban renewal, yet figures consistently showed that few displaced families ended up in these projects. The BHA deemed 70 percent of the first 439 families relocated from the Washington Park area eligible for public housing, yet just

13 percent moved there. Similarly, for the first households relocated from the Castle Square area in the South End, 63 percent had public housing eligibility, but only 13 percent found homes in public housing. Seeking an explanation for the contradiction between policy and practice, Yudis concluded, "The BHA has been unable—or unwilling—to fully honor the priority statements. Relocation workers are somewhat reluctant to say so publicly, but privately they admit it." The agreements with the community centered on elaborate promises to stage relocation and demolition over a period of four years to permit new construction and rehabilitation of existing structures, but yielded far more displacement than rehousing.[19]

In 1964, in his role as chair of the mayor's Advisory Committee on Minority Housing, Reverend Robert Drinan wrote to Mayor Collins to complain that "the Boston Public Housing program is in trouble" and that "families displaced by Urban Renewal refuse to enter Public Housing, thus hampering relocation efforts." In other words, not only had public housing's "debased image" increased resistance to its own expansion, the resistance to existing projects forced "families and individuals with inadequate incomes" to treat "substandard housing as their alternative." The "bitterness engendered by such a choice," in turn, "builds resistance to urban renewal."[20]

Julius Bernstein and Chester Hartman, who cochaired the Massachusetts Committee on Discrimination in Housing, took a particularly dim view of Logue's mantra about "planning with people." Observing the implementation of Roxbury's Washington Park Urban Renewal Plan in 1966, they saw a process wholly "directed toward moderate-income residents":

> The entire "planning with people" process was carried out with the area's more articulate, educated, established residents. Those whose needs are greatest, the community's low-income, deprived segment, were never a part of the planning process, only its victims. The "planning" was only with some of the people.

With two thousand families displaced from this "renewal area," most of them low-income, Bernstein and Hartman complained that only four hundred replacement housing units had been built, and that these were "too expensive" for the displaced households. Meanwhile, the BHA had "not built a single new unit of family-size public housing for 12 years." The urban renewal program lacked its own "sufficient tools to produce low-rent housing," yet the BRA failed to bring "the public housing program into renewal areas as a prerequisite to displacing thousands of families."[21]

Logue himself regarded Boston's public housing program as "a bust," noting that "few Bostonians today look on a nearby public housing project as a community asset." Looking back at the end of the 1960s, Logue called urban renewal "the most flexible and potentially the most effective city rebuilding tool yet devised." He lamented its "increasing disfavor, even among some of the high-ranking feds who were supposed to administer it." Logue refused to place the blame on "Negro removal," since "the amount of Negro removal has been greatly exaggerated." Nor did he impugn the "banal design of too many projects." Instead, for Logue the problem inhered in the inadequacy of federal funds and the "thicket" of federal bureaucracy that proved too difficult for most local governments to navigate. He reiterated the refrain about "planning with people, instead of for them," insisting that this had been "part and parcel of the Boston Redevelopment Program from its inception." At base, he felt the participation challenge could be solved; the real problem was what he called the "delivery capacity—the ability to produce the results the citizens seek."[22]

Meanwhile, residents of Orchard Park found themselves at the center of all this. Since Orchard Park itself already represented "new" housing, it was not part of an urban renewal area. Yet urban renewal effectively surrounded the project on three sides, as figure 6.4 shows. The South End urban renewal area came within two blocks of Orchard Park's northern edge, and the tip of the Washington Park urban renewal zone reached to within two blocks of Orchard Park's southern boundary. Equally important, the 120-acre Lower Roxbury urban renewal area known as Campus High School loomed just two blocks to the west, with its 57-acre Madison Park district designated for clearance to feature a new high school. Many residents liked the idea of the school, but complained that the initial plan entirely lacked low- or moderate-income housing. They enlisted Urban Planning Aid—a nonprofit group of advocacy planners, architects and social scientists with links to MIT and other universities—to analyze a community survey and help them develop a "counter plan" that would contain the community's "own ideas on how the area should look."[23] Neighborhood activists established the Lower Roxbury Committee Against Urban Development. Vincent Haynes—who had once been Mel King's football coach—had witnessed the destruction of the West End while working nearby, and was "adamant" that such a fate would not befall Roxbury once urban renewal and associated highways threatened. If city and state officials "had been able to do what they'd done in the West End," Haynes later insisted, "they would have done it and thought, 'Great!'" Instead, Haynes and his allies won "a binding commitment" from the BRA to "build replacements in the area for housing that was razed." Determined to control the character of that housing, Haynes and colleagues themselves became developers and formed the Lower Roxbury Development Corporation, later renamed Madison Park, to honor a park that had been demolished. This became one of the first and largest community development corporations in Massachusetts, initially responsible for 546 units of low-income housing known as Madison Park Village. They would later play a vital role in the remaking of Orchard Park, too.[24]

To public housing residents flanked on all sides by the backlash against a supposedly inclusive processes, demands for more community input continued to reverberate—both in Orchard Park and across the city. To Mel King, the new activism of the 1960s and 1970s had a clear basis: "The New York Streets and the West End were the catalysts for folks in other parts of the city to demand urban renewal committees and develop CDCs. People understood they could take on City Hall and the BRA and create change."[25] Oddly enough, Albany Street—the last of the New York Streets to survive—actually has its western terminus right at the heart of the Orchard Park project.

FROM "PLANNING WITH PEOPLE" TO THE "ILLUSION OF INCLUSION"

Boston's political culture privileging the rights of the poor developed in large part because, starting in the 1960s, elected officials repeatedly learned that ignoring those rights led to political defeat. John Collins and Ed Logue, tainted by the heavy-handed displacement and destruction of urban renewal, found their political futures stymied by the very constituencies they had marginalized. In 1967, when Collins (who had already lost an election for Senate in 1966) decided not to seek another term as mayor, Logue jumped into the breach. But, despite (or because of) his considerable visibility as director of the BRA and status as promoter of the "New Boston," he failed to gain traction. An ascendant black constituency and white ethnic enclaves that bore the brunt of his policies resented the way Logue "chafed at the demands of community activists who insisted that all displaced persons in urban renewal areas be allowed to move back into rehabilitated units" and distrusted his perspective that "there was something un-American about returning to where you had already been."[26] In the primary, Logue finished a distant fourth.

Other politicians taking a more participatory approach to city-making saw their fortunes rise. In 1967, mayoral aspirant Kevin White stated, "All urban renewal plans must be based on close consultation with the affected neighborhoods."[27] White courted Boston's growing black community. He visited black neighborhoods, cultivated black leaders as supporters, and ultimately received the endorsement of the influential black-oriented newspaper the *Bay State Banner*.[28] When he won election, White ordered the doors of City Hall be open 24/7, and created a series of little city halls in the neighborhoods through which more citizens could ostensibly access government services more easily. Some regarded this move with great suspicion.

Architect-activist John Sharratt asserted that White "didn't want anybody working for the people," so "he put neighborhood planners into the BRA site offices and the Little City Halls to try to co-opt the community development movement." In the aftermath of Martin Luther King Jr.'s assassination and ongoing racial unrest in 1968, White chiefly sought neighborhood stability and safety, rather than community empowerment. As Mel King pithily explained: White wanted to project "the illusion of inclusion."[29]

Privileging the rights of the poor became good politics, even when this favoritism proved superficial and short-lived. As Boston shifted from a sheltered world of Yankee-Irish tensions to a more globally engaged city of increased racial and ethnic diversity, the political calculus of neighborhood redevelopment altered rapidly. Between 1929 and 2017, Bostonians elected as mayor an unbroken succession of ten white Roman Catholic Democrats (all of them Irish, except Tom Menino—in office from 1993 until succeeded by Marty Walsh in 2014). Beneath that seeming continuity, though, has been a massive shift in orientation toward neighborhood politics, much of it driven by the travails of urban renewal. Between 1940 and 1960, Boston's black population nearly tripled, reaching 63,000, and the political competition between ethnic white neighborhoods and black neighborhoods solidified as resources declined in an age of urban crisis.[30]

In 1951, a change in the Boston City Charter shifted city council voting procedures from a ward-based system in which every resident had a district representative, to a nongeographic system, in which all councilors were elected at large. Over the ensuing thirty years, just one black candidate won election to the city council—Tom Atkins, who served for four years. This system kept the city largely under the control of Irish and Italian leaders from white-dominated neighborhoods while starving other districts from the political access that could result from having a councilor wedded to local needs. And, similarly, it made these politically marginalized neighborhoods vulnerable to urban renewal.[31] Accordingly, neighborhoods had to find new ways of pushing back against government. Particularly within black neighborhoods, this spurred the emergence of new leaders and organizations eager for greater self-determination. In 1981, indicative of new political pressures, Boston voters shifted the council to thirteen members, nine of whom would be elected at-large, and the composition of the council quickly diversified.

MANAGING RACE AND POVERTY IN BOSTON PUBLIC HOUSING

As the BHA wrenchingly and reluctantly moved toward an emphasis on the rights and preferences of its tenants, conditions in its developments continued to deteriorate. To a great extent, the decline in maintenance and management coincided with a shift in the racial occupancy patterns at BHA developments. In contrast to many other American cities, Bostonians built public housing almost entirely to serve whites. Between 1938 and 1954, the BHA constructed just three of its twenty-five large family projects in neighborhoods with a nonwhite majority. During that period, local elected officials welcomed public housing into nearly every ward of a city that was, in 1950, still 95 percent white. Then, in 1954, the BHA ceased building any more large projects for families. In the late 1950s, only about 10 percent of residents in the BHA's twenty-five projects were nonwhite. Soon afterward, though, working-class whites—who had lots of other opportunities for housing—simply stopped applying. Similarly, a downward trend in incomes set in. A program that had commenced with families who "used the projects well and happily" because they were "middle class as to living standards but caught in the depression" had been superseded by those of a lower "cultural level" who lacked "the expectations or actualities of rising income," a study by famed houser Elizabeth Wood concluded. By 1961, only half of BHA households reported income from employment. In 1967, whites still occupied about three-quarters of BHA apartments, but constituted only 41 percent of the applicant pool, so changes in class and race continued in tandem.[32]

As nonwhite demand for public housing continued to increase, this meant inevitable change—project by project, neighborhood by neighborhood. Still, as a whole, Boston retained an overall white majority in its public housing all the way until 1990. Five of the twenty-five projects more or less mirrored the gradual racial shift, but the housing authority managed the composition of the others much more directly. The BHA attempted to "protect" certain family projects located in historically Irish Catholic neighborhoods such as South Boston and Charlestown, keeping those places overwhelmingly occupied by whites all the way through the 1980s. Meanwhile, four other projects in Roxbury had been targeted for nonwhite occupancy right from the start. In this context, Orchard Park represented a fourth kind of racial trajectory. Although nominally racially mixed from the start, its racial transformation did not happen gradually. Rather, like five other projects in Roxbury and Dorchester, it transitioned rapidly from white to black. Just 12 percent black in 1957, the black population doubled to 23 percent by 1963, then rapidly accelerated to 59 percent by 1964.

As the racial mix of the development altered, occasional spates of violence broke out. On a late Saturday afternoon near the end of May 1963 at the corner of Adams and Eustis streets, a "broken bottle fight erupted between a Negro youth and a white boy." Within ten minutes, this escalated into a full-fledged "riot" involving one hundred fighters, while "another 600 ringed the fight area and pushed and shoved their way toward the combat area," and "many combatants brandished knives." Once police arrived, according to press reports, "an additional 300 poured from the project's buildings into Adams street" armed with "bats, rocks and bottles." Police managed to de-escalate the situation fairly rapidly, despite several injuries and multiple arrests. A year later, in a development that now suddenly was about evenly split between black and white residents, 335 Orchard Park residents, organized by their "Block Group tenant organization," sent a petition to the BHA:

> We, the tenants of the Orchard Park Housing Development, would like to make it known that we feel Negro and White people can live together harmoniously. We have demonstrated that people of good will, regardless of race or cultural background, can and will work with one another to achieve a decent neighborhood. Therefore, we are asking for co-operation from the Boston Housing Authority to help maintain a racial balance in this development.

The BHA's Advisory Committee on Minority Housing went so far as to propose that the backlog of vacancies be managed according to a simple rule: "Process the entire 'white' backlog through Orchard Park and other predominantly Negro projects. Process the entire 'colored' backlog for predominantly 'white' projects." The housing authority had no interest in trying anything of the sort, especially since even such a "benign quota" would clearly be illegal. By 1969, Orchard Park was fully 89 percent nonwhite—a near-complete reversal in little over a decade.[33]

In the midst of such momentous demographic change, seventy members of Orchard Park's self-described "Men's Alliance" formed the Orchard Park Security Patrol, where, sporting yellow jackets and carrying walkie-talkies, they vowed to work "seven nights a week to prevent violence." More controversially, however, twenty black Men's Alliance members accused the BHA board of turning "a deaf ear to the demands of its tenants." They insisted that all remaining white BHA employees be transferred out of Orchard Park. Should the board fail to listen, they promised "drastic action," and would seek the support of groups such as the Black United Front, a newly established "coalition of activist and social service organizations supporting black constituencies."[34]

Tensions continued to mount. In early 1968, a citywide tenants group put together "a statistical breakdown of muggings, assaults and break-ins" in Boston's projects and urged Mayor White to greatly enhance the police presence in these developments. They documented that Orchard Park residents had faced fifty break-ins during the first month of 1968 alone. As the number of teens proliferated, large family projects such as Orchard Park struggled to provide appropriate recreational outlets. Resident Pearl Wise, mother of two teenage boys, asserted that "Roxbury's number one problem is that teenagers have been ignored." Confined during the summer to "hot and crowded apartments," they had "no recreation center where they can gather to play cards, enjoy themselves." Even worse, the *Globe* editorialized, "The only neighborhood house in the area of the Orchard Park projects is due to be torn down this fall to make way for the Inner Belt Highway."[35]

TIGHTENING THE INNER BELT

As Orchard Park struggled with disinvestment, violence, and racial turn-over, the larger neighborhood faced a different threat in the late 1960s, given the proposed alignment of the Inner Belt expressway. Apart from the West End, the battle over the Inner Belt may be the most significant development fight in the history of Greater Boston. As its name implies, the Inner Belt was to connect a planned Southwest Expressway to the rest of Boston's existing interstate highway system. But this necessitated passage through some of the most densely built areas of three cities. The highway plans seemed logical as a paper diagram but made little sense politically. Closely tied to the boundaries of urban renewal plans, the highway plans sparked community organizing across the city—hardly surprising since the Inner Belt was to loop right past Orchard Park while threading through Roxbury and the South End, then hook through the Fenway neighborhood. It would then continue across the Charles through Cambridge and Somerville, while the Southwest Expressway was to stretch outward from the South End through Roxbury, Jamaica Plain, and Hyde Park (see figure 6.4). Vociferous opponents managed to stop the Inner Belt in Cambridge and Somerville before much of any land taking and demo-lition had transpired, but this was not the case in Roxbury and elsewhere in Boston. The state's Department of Public Works continued to acquire and demolish houses along the right of way for Inner Belt and Southwest Expressway throughout the 1960s, acquiring 80 percent of the land and razing half of the existing buildings.[36]

Once neighborhood organizations combined to form the Greater Boston Committee (GBC) on the Transportation Crisis, real political progress proved possible. Formed in December 1968, the GBC bought together a broad and multiracial collection of allies.[37] GBC held a "People Before Highways" rally on Boston Common in January 1969 that gained significant attention, in part because it had grown to include not just antihighway pro-mass transit activists but also "those concerned about the environment, lack of housing, unemployment, and other social and economic issues related to transporta-tion."[38] As journalist Alan Lupo put it,

The common man in these groups was as interested in preserving trees as he was in preserving inner-city homes. He was as likely to be an Italian from East Boston as a WASP from Milton or a black militant from Roxbury; he was as likely to be a stoic undertaker from Jamaica Plain as a radical from Cambridge. Such heterogeneity impressed vote-conscious politicians. It said to them "All those people are angry about the highways. Put them together and you've got damned near all Greater Boston."[39]

Activists could rail against the development-induced displacement of past and present urban renewal ventures—and past experiences with highway construction also directly mattered. Karilyn Crockett, whose book contains the most detailed discussion of Boston's "people before highways" revolt, situates the Southwest Expressway and Inner Belt opposition in relation to the earlier highway-induced clearances that created the Southeast Expressway ("Central Artery") and the Massachusetts Turnpike Extension—which cut off Hudson Street in Chinatown and ripped up neighborhoods in Brighton and Newton, among many other places. This armed activists with "a cityscape full of cautionary tales," culminating in "a radical grassroots political agenda intolerant of government-led efforts to reorder urban space through exclusionary, abusive, and anti-democratic means." Like "Remember the West End" for urban renewal, there was "Don't be the next Hudson Street" for highways.[40]

Crockett focuses on three organizations: the Greater Boston Committee, Urban Planning Aid, and the Black United Front. Taken in tandem, this fascinating and effective federation "merged black nationalist demands for local decision-making control with a critique of state-sponsored planning methods in hopes of creating a multi-racial, multi-ethnic regional coalition."[41] Combined with objections from whiter, wealthier areas and intense discontent and strong demands for community control within the black community, the diverse group gained influence. In February 1970, acting governor Frank Sargent—a liberal Republican facing an election battle against Mayor Kevin White later in the year—went on television to pose some momentous questions and answers:

Are we really meeting our transportation needs by spending most of our money building roads? The answer is no. Are the roads we are building too costly—not merely in dollars, but in what they cost us in demolished homes, disrupted communities, dislocated lives, pollution in the air, damage to our environment? The answer is yes—they are too costly.[42]

To the delight of the activists, Sargent imposed a partial moratorium on highway construction within Greater Boston's Route 128 circumferential roadway, thereby halting the project. As Alan Lupo put it in 1971, "Poor and working-class people, aided by underpaid, committed professionals, built a strategic alliance responsible for fundamentally reorienting the transportation policy of the Commonwealth of Massachusetts."[43] Whereas New Orleanians resisted the Riverfront Expressway but ignored the elevated I-10 through Treme, Bostonians conjoined their antihighway battles—both racially and politically—and gained a single victory.

Following extensive input from a Transportation Planning Review committee, Boston leaders successfully convinced Congress to allow federal interstate highway funds to be used for transit. Notably, this review committee included involvement from both the Greater Boston Committee and the Black United Front. In November 1972, with the review completed, Sargent turned to television again to announce, "We will not build expressways," concluding that a transit and commuter rail system would avoid "further ravaging an already devastated section of the city."[44] This ultimately led to the participatory planning process for the "Southwest Corridor," seeding "the idea that nearly 200 acres of land in the center of the city could be repurposed to meet the needs of nearby low-income residents."[45] Over the next decade, planners and designers famously turned the Southwest Expressway part of the project into a splendid mass transit corridor and series of linear parks. As for the Inner Belt, though, cleared properties in the "Crosstown" area near Orchard Park languished vacant, sometimes for decades, contributing to the overall decline in economic vibrancy of the Dudley Square area.[46]

More broadly, the pushback against the early excesses of urban renewal gave Boston its core strengths in neighborhood-based development. As Tom Lewis put it in *Divided Highways*, "The only thing that lasts longer than a highway battle is the bitterness of the individuals caught in the struggle." In thinking back about the highways and the Dudley neighborhood, planner Russell Tanner commented, "It's so obvious that this entire area was first traumatized, and then organized, by that process. And you have many individuals active in the community who were *forged* in that process." Paul Grogan and Tony Proscio, authors of *Comeback Cities: A Blueprint for Urban Neighborhood Revival*, stress that the "first critical step" in the late twentieth-century revival of Boston's low-income neighborhoods began in the 1970s with the efforts to "build and support an emerging network of competent grass-roots development organizations," now called community development corporations (CDCs). Overwhelmingly, these CDCs "grew out of opposition to '60s urban renewal efforts," yielding not just the Madison Park Development Corporation in Roxbury, but also Inquilinos Boricuas en Acción (IBA) and the Tent City Corporation in the South End, and, in Jamaica Plain, Urban Edge and the Jamaica Plain CDC.[47] In time, these organizations would also engage with public housing, but this would be predicated on significant changes in the way Boston managed its program. Ultimately, the most illustrative fight for self-determination with the largest possible direct effect on the future of the Orchard Park redevelopment occurred within the Boston Housing Authority board itself.

BUILDING A PRO-TENANT BOSTON HOUSING AUTHORITY

In the early 1960s, with the West End flattened and a newly reinvigorated BRA seeking to extend its urban renewal reach across the city under the leadership of Ed Logue, the Boston Housing Authority remained in the firm grip of City Hall. The BHA, like most other housing authorities elsewhere, was governed by its board. This board constituted the actual "Authority" in the BHA's name, and its members fully embraced that moniker. Perhaps more than anywhere else in the country, Boston's housing authority micromanaged its public housing operations. By the end of the 1960s, Boston would become an exemplar of tenants' rights, but when that tumultuous decade began, the vast patronage operation of the BHA could not have been further from such a pro-tenant model.

Under Massachusetts law, the mayor could choose four housing authority board members while the governor picked the fifth, each for a five-year term that was potentially renewable. In Boston, it had become long-standing practice to let these constituent members of the housing authority dole out political favors in keeping with the wishes of the elected official who had sponsored them. As late as 1968, five such well-connected men—four white and one black—directed the BHA. Four members of the board—Edward Hassan, Victor Bynoe, Jacob Brier, and Charles Savage—had served since near the beginning of the Collins administration in 1960, and the fifth, Cornelius Kiley, had acted as the state's representative ever since 1949. The BHA was largely theirs to run. Francis Lane had formally served as the BHA's administrator since 1938, but the board progressively stripped him of his powers. Indicating his irrelevance to the BHA's governance, when Lane died in 1960, the board left the position vacant until 1963. Instead, its members preferred to act themselves as both day-to-day administrators and policymaking board. Each member received a private office and secretary and a per diem salary permitted to total as much as $10,000, while chairman Hassan—then in his seventies—had two secretaries and a chauffeured limousine, with a salary of up to $12,500. These men were not housing professionals and could retain their other occupations—three were attorneys—while simply putting in appearances at the BHA in order to collect their per diem payment. The federal public housing program prohibited payments to board members but, since Massachusetts had its own housing program, the BHA got around this restriction by paying the board from that.[48]

It took vociferous complaints and a lawsuit from civil rights groups to get Mayor Collins to bypass the board and appoint an "acting administrator." In 1963 he named Ellis Ash, who had been Logue's deputy and had previously held senior housing posts in Baltimore and Seattle. Ash certainly had the right qualifications but could not even get the "acting" part of his title removed until 1965. Meanwhile, the board conducted all substantive business in closed executive sessions and "continued to hire key personnel without Ash's knowledge, much less his recommendation." Board member Victor Bynoe—a lawyer-engineer and the uncle of longtime Orchard Park resident Edna Bynoe—quietly evinced concerns about hiring practices in a confidential letter to Mayor Collins. He pointed to the need to upgrade the aptitude of the BHA staff and hoped there could be "a formula" that would "establish a framework of competent personnel which would be able to carry in a large degree the less competent." Still, he recognized that the "political implications" of this might damage "the only area where political patronage is available in the City." Given the patronage pull, Bynoe's more recalcitrant colleagues continued to resist Ash.[49] Finally, with the election of Kevin White in November 1967, everything seemed to change—even if much of the change swapped out one form of rancor for another.

With White in office, Ash started talking more openly about building what he called a "tenant-oriented" BHA. He emphasized ways to give residents more of a voice in policy and supported the creation of tenant organizations in each development, as well as citywide task forces.[50] At first, White seemed like the ideal partner for this. Soon after taking office, the initially progressive new mayor proposed filling Hassan's board seat with civil rights activist Julius Bernstein. This was a particularly radical move since Bernstein served as chairman of the state's Socialist Party, a staunchly prolabor (but anticommunist) group. White reportedly wanted Bernstein to chair the board, but the conservative holdover members preemptively re-elected Jacob Brier for that role before Bernstein could join. Other wheels of change continued to turn, however. During the previous spring, the Massachusetts General Court (state legislature) removed the prohibition against tenants serving on housing authority boards. A citywide tenant group, the Tenants Policy Council (TPC), soon put forth two candidates for Governor Frank Sargent to consider as Cornelius Kiley's fourth five-year term approached its end. The TPC, established in 1968 to give tenants greater control over a $13 million federal modernization program, itself represented a strong affirmation of the growing voice of Boston's low-income residents. And the TPC had many allies. The Massachusetts Conference on Human Rights, the Citizens' Housing and Planning Association, together with both Mayor

White and Senator Edward Kennedy, all urged the governor to appoint a tenant to the BHA board. Sargent picked John Connolly, a twenty-one-year-old Harvard undergraduate who had lived his whole life in the Mary Ellen McCormack development. Notably, Connolly worked as a "housing specialist" for the city's antipoverty agency, Action for Boston Community Development, and had already been active in drafting legislation to enhance state funding for public housing.[51]

Even with Bernstein and Connolly on board, BHA tenants and the lingering Collins appointees remained "at odds on almost every issue, be it broad policy or daily maintenance practices" through early 1969. The old guard gained a brief victory in June when Ellis Ash—the BHA's more progressive administrator who had battled against them for six years—resigned his post. Ash cited health reasons to explain his departure, though much of it had to do with his frustrations over the board's unwillingness to tackle what he termed the "social issues of housing." As he exited the BHA, Ash concluded that the necessary changes could only come from expanding the power of residents. "The only choice is to go to the constituency, the public and the tenants," he explained to the *Bay State Banner*. A month later, White appointed a second tenant, Doris Bunte, to the board to replace its lone black member, Victor Bynoe. Although Bynoe had frequently voiced sympathy for the plight of low-income residents, the substitution more unambiguously tipped the balance to what the new leadership touted as the "tenant-oriented majority." Bunte, a black, thirty-six-year-old tenant activist, had lived in Orchard Park for more than a decade while raising three children in the development and serving as chair of the development's tenant task force. She also served as recording secretary of the TPC and promised "more and better low-income housing" that would be "oriented towards the tenants." In January 1970, the newly reformulated board elected Bernstein as its chairman, thereby marking what the *Globe* called "a high point in an increasing movement toward power of public housing tenants in the state."[52]

Kevin White and Frank Sargent had apparently reshaped the board, but this did not necessarily mean that the new "tenant-oriented majority" would continue to do the bidding of their backers. White, with concurrence of the board, appointed Dan Finn as BHA administrator. Finn had worked under four mayors and two governors, creating the city's housing inspection department under Collins and setting up eleven "little city halls" in Boston neighborhoods to support the work of White. Despite his administrative experience, Finn quickly ran afoul of what the *Globe* termed the board's "New Triumvirate." The board gained an administrator who would actually run the BHA but then resented his decisions. Finn resisted efforts by the progressive board to rein in patronage and reduce racial segregation. At base, Bunte later recalled, "We didn't own the executive director—Dan

Finn was the Mayor's Man." As tensions mounted, White and Finn held a press conference on January 21, 1971, to denounce Julie Bernstein for "blatant misuse of public funds" while a board member. The very next day, during a televised BHA board meeting, Bernstein calmly read out a six-page statement defending his actions and lambasting the mayor. Bunte spoke next, calling for a motion to fire Dan Finn. Connolly seconded the motion, and the tenant-oriented majority duly voted Finn out.[53]

Finn angrily termed this a "pure act of retribution," even as Mayor White candidly admitted that the preemptive effort to discredit Bernstein and his mounting concern about the board's view of Finn were "not unconnected." White quickly moved on to retribution of his own, launching a new set of trumped-up charges against Bunte in March 1971. Undaunted, the tenant-oriented majority went on with their work, issuing a "Statement of Objectives," which included a pledge to perform maintenance tasks more equitably across developments, and a commitment to a merit-based personnel policy, one that entailed hiring more tenants into positions with managerial responsibilities. The three also favored a new "model lease" with "unprecedented grievance rights" for tenants. Even as the trio made its public calls for the end of patronage, Kevin White himself presided over a thirteen-day "trial" of Bunte. In an unprecedented joint hearing with the city council, White served simultaneously as "prosecutor, petitioner, judge and at least half of the jury." The mayor's charges were technical, but his efforts clearly political.[54]

In an eighteen-page finding announced in June, White quietly dropped his most incendiary accusations but found Bunte guilty of three charges of administrative misconduct. The mayor urged the city council to vote to remove Bunte from office. In an editorial entitled "Mayor White's Hatchet Falls," the *Globe* commented: "The original strong suspicion that Mrs. Bunte was the intended victim of a political purge now stands confirmed." The lone black city councilor, Tom Atkins, characterized the BHA as "a political dumping ground" and regarded Bunte's ouster as "a personal vendetta." Three weeks later, the all-male city council voted five to four to oust Bunte. This result, however, would not stand. Following months of appeals and court procedures, the Massachusetts Supreme Judicial Court ruled unanimously in favor of Bunte and ordered her reinstatement. Afterward, Bunte demurely yet defiantly told an interviewer, "I was just a little black lady from Roxbury fighting a mayor, but I was right, and I won."[55]

In the short period between 1968 and 1972, the BHA underwent nothing short of a revolution in its governance, as it shifted allegiances and adapted a self-styled "pro-tenant majority" stance. Although the specific details of this board arrangement did not outlast the mid-1970s, since White predictably retook control from "tenant-oriented majority" and eliminated all current tenants from the board by 1977, the centrality of tenant voices could no longer be ignored.[56] As a governance constellation, Plebs shone brightly above the projects of Boston.

Bill McGonagle has a particularly long perspective on this, since he grew up in the Mary Ellen McCormack development with John Connolly (who later became his brother-in-law), started working at the housing authority in 1980, and rose to become its administrator in 2009. When asked, in his role as administrator, to explain why the BHA favored a version of HOPE VI that emphasized the public housing side when proposing mixed-income developments, McGonagle put it bluntly: "BHA has been pro-tenant since the so-called pro-tenant majority days of the board in the 1960s."[57]

More immediately, the painful saga of the "tenant-oriented majority" also revealed what Boston neighborhood chronicler J. Anthony Lukas called a "new Kevin White." In this same mode of retrenchment, White "downplayed his Office of Human Rights, Model Cities, and other programs to aid the black community, while talking tough on crime and drugs, beefing up the police, and holding the line on taxes." To many Bostonians, Lukas observed, White's treatment of Bunte and her colleagues sent "a clear signal that henceforth the Mayor would adopt a more skeptical attitude toward the black and the poor."[58]

Boston's local struggles with public housing deepened with the cutbacks of the Nixon administration, which severely squeezed necessary modernization funds. Worse, once Congress agreed in 1969 that public housing tenants should pay no more than 25 percent of their income in rent, Nixon's HUD stalled on asking Congress to authorize increased operating subsidies to make up for the lost revenues that inevitably followed. The decision to reduce rents helped more low-income (and no-income) households to afford public housing, but added to the financial precarity of housing authorities during a time of deferred maintenance and rapid inflation of operating costs.[59]

MASTERING AND RECEIVING THE BHA

Starting in 1970, Boston tenants and their allies launched a succession of lawsuits to protest deteriorated conditions in the developments. Finally, in March 1975, the class action complaint filed by Greater Boston Legal Services on behalf of Armando Perez and eight other BHA tenants convinced Judge Paul Garrity, then chief justice of the Housing Court in Boston, to demand immediate redress. Garrity found "countless violations of the State Sanitary Code" and concluded that "those violations result from vandalism and from BHA's financial inability to conduct routine maintenance at its developments and to replace antiquated heating, plumbing, electrical and other systems." Garrity soon concluded that the BHA itself lacked the expertise to produce a plan to remedy the situation and ordered the appointment of Robert Whittlesey as master.[60] Whittlesey, a professional housing reformer in the Ellis Ash mode, realized "an indifferent mayor and a misguided Board of Commissioners" would make his job exceedingly difficult.[61] With the BHA under a series of short-term administrators, it could not make much progress on Whittlesey's recommendations. Even a 250-page consent decree signed in 1977 did not prevent the BHA from continuing to engage in what an exasperated Garrity called "gross mismanagement, nonfeasance, incompetence and irresponsibility," leading to "incalculable human suffering" in Boston public housing.[62]

In May 1979, Garrity visited six projects. When he got to Orchard Park, he documented leaking apartments, rubbish-filled basements, and stench. Outdoors, conditions were no better. "I observe reinforced concrete picnic tables which have been totally destroyed," he intoned into his tape recorder.

> I am observing a dumpster which is filled to overflowing. . . . There is a very small play area for tots that is absolutely filthy and filled with debris. There are no children playing there. I am observing pools of stagnant water with abandoned automobile tires, trash can lids and other debris.[63]

The judge's observations corresponded quite closely to what the BHA's own staff documented at Orchard Park that October.

Orchard Park, this assessment began, "could almost be classified as an 'island,'" given that "most of the land adjacent to the development is vacant." Yet life on the "island" itself offered little reprieve. The project "serves as an anonymous environment for criminals to escape into after committing a crime in the Dudley Terminal area," adding to an already high rate of crime within the development. Further, the BHA self-report continued, "The horrible condition of the grounds is striking: broken glass and burning over-flowing dumpsters are common." Twenty-one percent of the development's units lay vacant, and the number of vacancies had doubled from 75 to 153 between 1975 and 1979. There were 198 households on the waiting list, but the BHA proved incapable of managing move-outs, as "vandalism of unoccupied units (particularly the theft or damage of pipes and broken unboarded windows) . . . led to water damage in other apartments, thus producing a domino effect." Consequently, "A large number of units could be classified as 'bomb-outs.'" Project maintenance lagged badly in the inhabited units, too—there were almost 500 work orders outstanding (316 of them for plumbers). An annotated map showing "social usage" focused on such things as undesirable "gathering areas," shortcuts, no man's

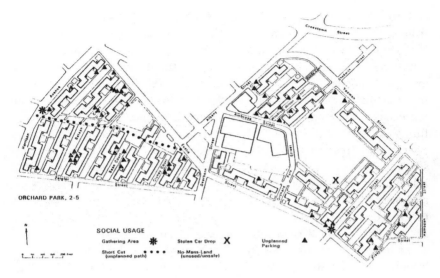

Figure 6.5. "Social Usage" at Orchard Park in 1979
A BHA report from 1979 mapped the "social usage" of Orchard Park, annotated to show spaces that served as a "gathering area, short cut (unplanned path), Stolen Car Drop, No-Mans-Land (unused/unsafe), and Unplanned Parking."
Source: Boston Housing Authority, "Orchard Park 2-5," 1979.

land, unplanned parking, and a "stolen car drop"[64] (figure 6.5). At one point the BRA grew so concerned about Orchard Park's capacity to drag down its efforts to increase investment in the Dudley Street area that the BRA proposed construction of a series of three-story garages to create a wall between the project and the retail area. Neighbors predictably objected, and the BRA dropped the idea, but it underscored the dismal reputation of the city's public housing.[65]

With Orchard Park unfortunately typical of conditions prevailing in Boston's family public housing developments and the current structure of the BHA unable to right the ship, Garrity ordered the nation's fourth-largest public housing program into receivership—the first time a US court had ever taken over a publicly financed independent authority.[66] The BHA board fought the ruling, but the Massachusetts Supreme Judicial Court affirmed it, permitting receiver Lewis H. (Harry) Spence to take over in February 1980. Spence, a charismatic thirty-three-year-old Harvard Law School graduate who had previously made excellent progress with the housing authority in nearby Cambridge, took on a difficult challenge with considerable support, at least from tenants and from the judge. Kevin White seemed glad to be rid of the problem, commenting, "That's all right. He's got it. He can have it."[67]

Garrity's announcement of the receivership received widespread acclaim from public housing residents. At Orchard Park, tenant Thomas Harris saw it as overdue: "We should be under receivership because the management's not doing anything to help us. There are all these empty apartments here and yet people can't get in. In the wintertime it's cold and in the summer the radiators are on full blast."[68] Judge Garrity granted his receiver "full power to direct, control, manage, and administer and operate the property, funds and staff of the BHA." With the board completely abolished, Harry Spence could reshape policy, too. He regarded the BHA as "by far the most severely distressed public housing program in any major city," noting that it had an average vacancy rate more than twice that of any other housing authority."[69] In fact, Orchard Park's vacancy of about 20 percent was only the fourteenth worst—thirteen other family developments had between 26 and 57 percent of their apartments unoccupied.[70] Over the next four and a half years, Spence took full advantage of the opportunity to build a brand-new senior staff, many of whom—such as David Gilmore—would go on to distinguished careers both in Boston and around the country. By late 1984, when Spence left the receivership and Garrity left the Housing Court to become a superior court judge, the judge credited the BHA with "numerous and significant" achievements. Under Spence, the BHA managed to balance its budget, markedly curtail the cycle of vacancy and vandalism in its developments, and regain the confidence of state and national funding agencies. Spence pointedly worked to ramp up tenant involvement in security and modernization efforts and increased the hiring of tenants for BHA jobs.

Most visibly, Spence presided over the investment of tens of millions of dollars needed to launch comprehensive redevelopment of three troubled BHA developments: West Broadway, Franklin Field, and Commonwealth, all of which remained as 100 percent public housing even after their transformation. Meanwhile, he also inherited—and moved forward—the makeover of New England's largest project, 1,502-unit Columbia Point, yielding the mixed-income alternative of Harbor Point. This celebrated rebuilding venture retained 400 units for public housing residents while providing the rest as 883 market-rate rental apartments. Spence says he accepted the Harbor Point approach "very reluctantly," because the old project (with just 350 units still occupied) was "dragging down" the whole program.[71]

Still, at least in Boston, this kind of market-oriented transformation has remained a stark anomaly. Nothing like it would be allowed to happen again for the next thirty years, even with the advent of HOPE VI. Elsewhere, the Harbor Point approach became a much-visited national model, inspiring cities such as Chicago and Atlanta to reimagine public housing as privately managed communities containing no more than one-third public housing residents. In other words, Boston spawned this developer-friendly seaside precedent, but in its own city this practice has remained a fish out of water ever since. City officials acquiesced in the Harbor Point project because it seemed the only way to "save" *any* units in the mostly abandoned project that had deteriorated during the worst of the BHA's mismanagement.

Since Harbor Point, especially under HOPE VI, Boston's approach to public housing redevelopment has been at the opposite end of the spectrum. Although the city has not continued to advocate for 100 percent public housing redevelopments in the manner of Commonwealth, West Broadway, and Franklin Field, the BHA has consistently minimized the role of market-rate units in each of its HOPE VI developments, as well as in most of its HOPE VI–like developments that have been produced by other financial mechanisms. Boston's unusual HOPE VI prehistory seems particularly salient. A full decade before HOPE VI even existed, the Boston Housing Authority—by consolidating unspent funds and obtaining large grants from the Massachusetts legislature—established its own extensive track record of public housing redevelopment. And, because these redevelopment efforts relied heavily on tenant initiatives and significant roles for tenant organizations—detailed in my earlier book *Reclaiming Public Housing*—these precedents set important expectations for the role of low-income residents in any future effort to remake public housing in Boston.

Arguably, Harry Spence's emphasis on resident organizing became one of his longest-lasting accomplishments as receiver. He recognized that, in 1980, "the residents, like the staff, were deeply discouraged and depressed and believed nothing could improve." Once the receivership began, he "quickly realized" it would be a mistake to "just take good care to these tenants" in a carefully tended "hothouse atmosphere," because "one day the judge is going to go away." Spence wanted to be certain that residents had learned "how to fight the good fight":

> If they haven't learned how to beat a bureaucracy or a political institution and make that institution do for them what they need it to do, you haven't done them any favors. As our adversaries, they really, in truth, would be our allies. We both wanted to improve the projects.[72]

In the rapidly evolving governance constellation of Boston, the tenants did not simply orbit some bureaucratic sun; they were encouraged to shine on their own.

RAY FLYNN AND DSNI: ACTIVIST GOVERNANCE AND ITS LIMITS

When Kevin White's fourth term approached its end in 1983 and he declined to run again, this signaled a turning point. White had largely abandoned the neighborhoods despite initially embracing them, and establishment politicians seeking to succeed him failed to garner enough votes to make it into the runoff, despite their institutional advantages. Instead, black community organizer-politician Mel King and populist Ray Flynn went head to head, marking a dramatic political shift. King later noted that the most important thing about the 1983 campaign was its "focus on communities. In prior years the campaigns were focused on downtown. It was easy to show graphically how the neighborhoods had been cleaned out, in terms of urban renewal and lack of attention. . . . And you could make the case for turning it in the other direction."[73]

Flynn defeated King but still, as Jim Vrabel notes in *A People's History of the New Boston*, "brought many activists into City Hall with him." Some had even supported his opponent. "Many of the older activists were veterans of the fights against urban renewal and the highways and for civil rights and rent control," Vrabel comments, "whereas the younger ones were coming out of CDCs, Fair Share, and the Boston Community Schools."[74] Peter Dreier of the Massachusetts Tenants Organization joined the Flynn team, working to allocate public land to the purpose of affordable housing development in conjunction with a rising cadre of community development corporations.[75] Even as some activists moved into government, their counterparts remained in the communities, where they gained increasing power.

Most strikingly, the city granted power of eminent domain to the nascent Dudley Street Neighborhood Initiative (DSNI), established in 1985, using the Dudley Neighbors Incorporated community land trust. This marked the first time in US history that a city agency had granted such control to a community group, and it enabled DSNI to consolidate land for building new housing. Importantly, the Orchard Park public housing development itself fell within DSNI's neighborhood focus, so the Orchard Park Tenants Association (OPTA) joined DSNI as a member.[76] Although the Orchard Park site is a few blocks north of the Dudley Triangle where DSNI's own eminent domain powers held sway, the public housing project still sat squarely in the "core area" of DSNI's purview (see figure 6.4). Accordingly, any would-be public housing developers needed to take heed, not just take land.

The approach to Orchard Park redevelopment carried much the same spirit as the DSNI, an organization that a *Globe* reporter hailed as a bastion of "Urban Self-Renewal." The distinction between the old "urban renewal" and the new effort to "create a vision for change that came not from professionals but from the community" could not have been put more pointedly. A *Globe* editorial reflected back on the legacy of previous approaches in Roxbury, reminding readers that "after 31 years, the city has never fully recovered from the tensions and suspicions of urban renewal." In its first decade of operation, DSNI transformed more than three hundred of the neighborhood's thirteen hundred vacant lots into new buildings or public space. In 1996, filmmakers Leah Mahan and Mark Lipman released their award-winning documentary *Holding Ground: The Rebirth of Dudley Street*, a key step in transforming public perceptions of the area. By this point, the *Globe* noted, the City of Boston had "adopted DSNI's resident-inspired redevelopment plan; City Hall routinely sends any and all developers who want to work in the Dudley Street neighborhood to DSNI's office on Dudley Street." Meanwhile, the city's own efforts to promote investment in the Dudley Square area also helped engage local banks, greatly enhancing the availability of inner-city lending.[77]

Beyond the DSNI, Flynn's administration established a series of neighborhood councils and planning and zoning advisory councils to monitor development throughout the city. Seeking more influence than this, a network of fifty grassroots groups from across the city formed the Coalition for Community Control of Development (CCCD) to propose a new system of neighborhood councils. Initial proposals included veto power, though later ones pushed for the provision of city funding and required review over all development proposals before they could go forward. The ordinance never passed, but the group did once again use an existing, improved mechanism of community engagement as a point of opposition to propose something more radical in terms of community control. Planning scholar Pierre Clavel notes that "CCCD had achieved a great deal. It captured the involvement of neighborhoods of different stripes across the city, and articulated a vision of neighborhood participation that many supported."[78] At the extreme, however, some activists regarded mere participation as insufficient: they preferred neighborhood exodus.

FREEING MANDELA

Under the banner of the Greater Roxbury Incorporation Project (GRIP) a small cadre of black residents—none of whom had grown up in Boston—dreamed up the idea of "municipal incorporation." The activists sought to peel off "Greater Roxbury"—Roxbury, Mattapan, and parts of surrounding neighborhoods—to become a separate city to be known as Mandela, named for then-imprisoned anti-apartheid activist Nelson Mandela. Rather than "incorporation," opponents viewed this as an ill-advised "secession" from Boston. At twelve square miles, Mandela would lay claim to slightly more

than one-quarter of the Boston's land area, neighborhoods housing 22 percent of the city's population. Faced with sobering if self-interested analysis produced by the Flynn administration showing that an independent
Mandela would be "financially bankrupt" in its first year, the ballot item lost
75 percent to 25 percent.[79]

Still, the idea of Mandela proved a successful way to articulate a demand
for greater community voice. As Medoff and Sklar observe, "Many Mandela
referendum supporters did not actually want Roxbury to secede, but thought
passage of the nonbinding referendum would place greater pressure on the
Flynn administration to support more community control over development and a fairer distribution of city resources." The organizing tool showed
how the neighborhood had been shortchanged, but in 1988, voters in the
affected neighborhoods again defeated a referendum calling for the incorporation of an independent Mandela, this time by a two to one margin, with
one-third of ballots left blank.[80]

From John Collins to Ray Flynn, each successive Boston mayor routinely
criticized the prior administration's handling of neighborhoods. Sometimes
with reluctance and sometimes with gusto, they proved increasingly willing
to allow the city's low-income and minority residents to gain greater roles
in their own governance. Constantly prodded by advocates and citywide
alliances, Boston's political culture gradually began to privilege the rights of
the poor. Boston citizens broadly resented the top-down planning of urban
renewal, exemplified by the demolition of New York Streets and the West
End, and many criticized the inadequacies of subsequent "planning with
people." Faced with insistent demands from civil rights groups and a Black
Power movement that advanced self-determination for the black community, Boston's elected officials made modest progress. From the movement
against the Inner Belt highway and Southwest Expressway to the formation
of GRIP and the vote for an independent Roxbury to the city's relationship
with DSNI, Boston's governance constellation began to shift. In this context,
the histrionics of Kevin White's struggles with the BHA board, paired with
the historic receivership that followed, served as proving grounds for the
power of Boston's low-income residents.

AFTER THE RECEIVERSHIP: HOPE AND DECLINE

With Kevin White finally out of office as 1984 began, Judge Garrity optimistically viewed "malign neglect" as likely to be replaced by "competence, concern, and care."[81] He therefore turned the BHA over to mayoral control. Ray
Flynn brought the contested leadership of the BHA full circle by appointing
Doris Bunte as the new administrator, succeeding Spence. Bunte, who had

parlayed her well-publicized battle with White into a twelve-year stint in the Massachusetts legislature, thus became the first African American woman and first former public housing resident to head a major US public housing agency.[82]

Moreover, the legislature amended state law to abolish the BHA's board of commissioners, thereby giving Bunte a level of control previously available only under a receivership. The new governance structure permitted the Boston mayor to appoint the BHA's administrator, who would in turn have the powers of both executive director and board. A nine-member BHA monitoring committee, introduced in 1986, assesses performance and provides initial budgetary review, while also reviewing proposals to modernize development as well as any proposed "property dispositions which would reduce the total number of housing units owned by BHA." Most remarkably, at least five of the nine members of the monitoring committee are required to be BHA residents—with the remaining four selected from the community by the mayor. Two citywide resident groups that had been established during the receivership—Tenants United for Public Housing Progress (TUPHP—pronounced "tough") and the Committee for Boston Public Housing (a better-funded successor to the Tenants Policy Council)— helped select the tenant representatives. Even now—more than three decades later—the description of the monitoring committee appears on the BHA website under the broader category of "Resident Empowerment."[83] As a form of governance, this resident-led oversight would simply be unimaginable in many cities, certainly including New Orleans.

Despite the efforts of the receivership to orchestrate dramatic turnarounds in a few developments and significantly reduce vacancies, conditions at Orchard Park continued to plummet through the late 1980s. More generally, as one senior administrator complained, some of Spence's reforms were "systematically dismantled." Even with erstwhile Orchard Park tenant leader Doris Bunte in charge of the BHA, necessary maintenance and repairs lagged. Fifteen hundred BHA residents from across the city, led by tenant leaders at Bromley-Heath, signed a petition supporting Bunte's overall performance. Soon afterward, however, a much-anticipated federal review faulted the BHA for "poor rent collection, shoddy contract management, high administrative costs, accounting problems and delays in getting vacant apartments rented." The BHA, on HUD's "troubled list" since 1979, remained there.[84]

By 1991, dogged by federal investigations into alleged corruption, Bunte's influence in the Flynn administration flagged. She resigned in November, commenting that she had "never been allowed close enough" to be a major player. She thought this could be because she was black or female, though she also acknowledged that some of the distance could be because BHA headquarters was located several blocks from City Hall. Six weeks later, Flynn named Bunte's successor, thirty-six-year-old attorney David Cortiella. Cortiella, of Puerto Rican descent, had previously worked with Flynn as the city's affirmative action director and as director of the mayor's policy office. He then served as executive director of the Boston Fair Housing Commission, and BHA tenants also knew him from his role as one of the four nontenant members of the BHA monitoring committee. Cortiella immediately pledged to support more "tenant empowerment." He inherited significant financial problems, but less than a year into his tenure HUD formally removed the BHA from its list of "troubled" housing agencies for the first time in fifteen years—based on an audit that actually covered the final year of Bunte's administration. Mayor Flynn termed this "a significant breakthrough for public housing in this city." Nevertheless, at many developments such as Orchard Park conditions remained dire.[85]

7

The Fall of Orchard Park, the Rise of Orchard Gardens

GUNS, GANGS, AND "GOD": ORCHARD PARK REACHES ITS NADIR

In the late 1980s and early 1990s, crime in and around the Orchard Park project peaked. A surge in drug-related violence associated with the rise of crack cocaine sent the development to its nadir, consolidating its well-earned reputation as one of the most dangerous parts of Boston. Taxis refused to take residents home; even the milkman asked for a police escort. The Boston Police Department annually recorded more than one reported crime per unit in Orchard Park—double the rate at other family public housing developments in Boston.[1] Fully 86 percent of households offered a spot at Orchard Park turned down an apartment in the half-vacant project, "even though such a decision meant that they went to the end of the 20,000-person waiting list."[2]

In the first eleven months of 1988 alone, Orchard Park residents called for police help almost three thousand times—the most in the city.[3] If reporting on Orchard Park at all, the Boston papers focused on stabbings and shootings. Many articles featured just a succinct headline and three or four sentences of text that did little more than locate the violence and name the victim: "Youth Shot in Neck in Roxbury Project," "Roxbury Man, 39, Stabbed at Project," "2 Shot at Roxbury's Orchard Park Project."[4] In some cases, moreover, it was enough just to be "near" Orchard Park in order to blame the "project." Situating the violence in its habitual territory thereby set a boundary on mayhem for those who lived safely beyond it.[5] It is also worth remembering that many lived relatively safely *within* Orchard Park, too, placing great value on community ties. Interviews conducted with 10 percent of the households in the early 1990s, at the very beginning of my research, confirm that residents found empathy as well as pathology in this place. The Boston press, however, focused chiefly on the latter.

Globe columnist Mike Barnicle repeatedly contributed lurid comments about the "graffiti-scarred hallways" where "drugs and guns dominate." Fellow *Globe* contributor Alan Lupo mordantly commented, "Any more shootings, drug-related or otherwise, at Bataan Court in Roxbury's Orchard Park housing project, and the place will start to resemble its namesake, the site of the World War II death march." A longer and more reflective piece entitled "A City Life, Short, Sad, Ends by Gun," described the demise of a young man called over to a car parked in Orchard Park, only to be shot and killed by the vehicle's passenger. Here, though, the death is contextualized, seen as the consequence of tangling with "New York-based crack cocaine drug rings."[6]

The New York reference proved apt. This period was marked by the reign of notorious drug kingpin Darryl Whiting, a native of Queens, who used Orchard Park as a base of operations to sell up to six kilograms of cocaine each week and became known by the nickname "God" (or 'G' to area youth)—a testament to his control over the area.[7] Between 1987 and 1990, Boston gang analyst George Hassett estimates, "Nearly 100 drug dealers from Whiting's old neighborhood of Corona, Queens, arrived—usually in groups of two or three—to work the growing industry."

By 1990, "The dirt path around Orchard Park projects known as Bump Road was a 24-hour cocaine depot that grossed as much as $100,000 a day."[8] As Bill McGonagle remembered, Whiting and those known locally as the New York Boys would "infiltrate the development" by "setting up shop" in apartments and intimidating the women to let them use their place. Journalist Ric Kahn adds, "Whiting preyed on young single women with children, offering them drugs and/or money—$150 a day" to operate his business from their apartments. An Orchard Park resident, twenty-two years old at the time, recalled the devastation on her community:

> This guy, they called him God or something, started bringing more and more people from New York to gradually take over the crackhead people's houses. I lost a lot of friends. . . . It was really sad to see because the kids that were going to school and getting ready for college never got to do their goal.[9]

In a subsequent interview with Whiting himself, Hassett learned some details:

> Security measures were elaborate. Crew members had binoculars, walkie-talkies, and headphones; one project apartment was used solely to store an arsenal of weapons, ranging from riot-pump shotguns to Uzis. Pitbulls roamed off-leash in project hallways used for dealing.

Meanwhile, "The Boston police were caught off guard, unable to respond to such a sophisticated operation."[10] McGonagle recalled it as a "horrible period" of "war." "Darryl Whiting, aka 'God,' was running the place," he readily conceded. "It was not run by BHA. It was 'New Jack City'—as close as we, or anyone in the world ever got to that."[11]

Whiting was never an official tenant of Orchard Park—and the BHA formally, if ineffectually, barred him from entering any of its developments. Still, he profoundly influenced the local OP Trailblazers gang, drawn by his flashy dressing and fancy cars, and impressed by what Kahn terms Whiting's "Fortune 500 ego." Boston rapper Mann Terror, who grew up in Orchard Park, was twelve years old when Whiting first arrived, and remembers his mesmerizing effect. "When God walks through the projects, it was like everything just kind of stopped." Such actions had complex consequences. "As the New York boys pumped poison in the projects," Hassett points out, "Whiting was getting recognition for his good deeds."[12]

Whiting opened a series of businesses a few blocks south of Dudley Square—Crown Video, Crown Barber Shop, Crown Sneaker, all part of his Corona Enterprises portfolio. Audaciously, Whiting even offered 25 percent discounts to "public servants" such as the police. Still, police considered these businesses to be all part of a scheme to launder drug money, while shamelessly permitting Whiting to build and burnish his reputation as someone productively investing in the neighborhood. As Mann Terror recalled, "When God came around, the day turned great. He might buy out the ice-cream man and make him serve the whole projects." In late 1989, Whiting threw a Christmas party at his nascent Crown Social & Recreation Hall where he "played Santa and distributed 250 [free] toys," part of a larger pattern of offering field trips to water parks for area youth, sponsoring dances and prizes for honor roll students, and paying for a new basketball hoop at Orchard Park.[13] With a quarter-century to reflect, the BHA's McGonagle still marveled at the extent of Whiting's impact: "The calculation and cynicism with which he approached that [Orchard Park] community were nothing short of breathtaking."[14]

Boston police struggled to bring down Darryl Whiting. Kahn's *Boston Phoenix* article in April 1990, entitled "Gang Godfather or Mean Streets Robin Hood?," garnered widespread attention, especially since it was accompanied by a brazen interview where Whiting claimed to be "a role model for black people" who would "do something positive for the community," and cast himself as "a humanitarian." African American US attorney Wayne Budd bristled at this effrontery: "[Whiting] threw down the gauntlet, in a way . . . when he had the audacity to appear in the newspaper." Budd viewed him as "the perfect negative role model for inner city kids. . . . He was just the kind of guy I thought was deserving of the full weight of the federal government's resources.[15] Budd chose to make prosecution of this case a top priority.

Eventually, in December 1990, the gang was brought down by what McGonagle calls "extraordinary police work."[16] The authorities relied heavily on Jeff Coy, a streetwise undercover Boston Housing Authority cop working for the DEA. Posing as a flashy Rhode Island drug dealer named Jay Reed, Coy became intimately involved with Whiting's networks. Beginning in September 1988, "Coy walked and talked like a gangster, carried Uzis around Orchard Park, and snorted cocaine chased by Valium," while once also shooting "two local stick-up men in an Orchard Park hallway who mistook him for an average drug customer." Meanwhile, Coy also provided information to the DEA about drug and weapon sales. This evidence proved crucial to convicting Whiting, who became the first person in Massachusetts to receive a life sentence for selling drugs. Eventually, the indictment against Whiting and his associates expanded to encompass fifty-one people, with forty-six sentenced to prison terms of various lengths.[17]

Without this first step in breaking up the major drug ring that had overtaken Orchard Park from the outside, Bill McGonagle argued, "The redevelopment couldn't have been done successfully." This is certainly true, but ending the rule of the New York Boys did not stem the gang-related violence at Orchard Park. The mainstream press continued to situate violent acts as happening "near" Orchard Park, even when project residents or their residences were not involved. A review of more than six hundred articles in the *Boston Globe* and *Boston Herald* that mention Orchard Park, written by dozens of different journalists, reveals a central focus on drug-related violence, with most of the attention concentrated on period between the late 1980s and the mid-1990s.[18] Edna Bynoe, who arrived in the project as a toddler in the mid-1940s and—a half-century later—served as the chairwoman of the Orchard Park Tenants Association (OPTA), lamented in 1992 that, even after Whiting's downfall, "there are buildings you can't go in" because youths "take over" ground-floor entries and brazenly sell drugs (figure 7.1). OPTA's vice chairman, David Gonzalez, concurred: "Everybody in the place is scared to go out." Another resident, Lorraine Robinson, concluded that Orchard Park was irredeemable: "Let me tell you something. They can rehab this place all they want. It's gone."[19]

Press reports emphasize the moments of crisis and tend to seek out the same sorts of "tenant spokesperson," so it is particularly useful to be able to talk to a broader cross-section of residents. Fifty-three interviews conducted with residents in 1993 reveal the extent to which concern over violence and discord coexisted with a lingering genuine affection for the place, coupled with hope that conditions could improve. Significantly, more than two years after the fall of Darryl Whiting, nearly every respondent stated that drugs, violence, and gangs remained major concerns, mirroring the rise of gang violence in Boston during this period when police believed that Orchard Park Trailblazers still had fifty to one hundred teenage members.[20] Still, despite serious crime problems, only one-third of those interviewed indicated

Figure 7.1. Bleak Orchard Park, as of 1993
By 1993, vacancies at Orchard Park had mounted, and much of the development appeared to be an asphalt wasteland with high crime. Even at its worst, however, most residents expressed support for their community.
Credit: Author.

that the ongoing presence of drugs and the lack of personal safety were extreme enough to prevent improvement in the living conditions at Orchard Park. In addition, a majority (53 percent) affirmed that Orchard Park was a "good place to raise kids." Given the dire press reports of gang violence and killing, the percentage of respondents expressing concerns about these problems was startlingly low. It could be that media coverage portrayed an exaggerated picture of unsafe conditions at Orchard Park, but it is also possible that residents were inured to the conditions or simply hopeful and optimistic about their home.

Residents also exhibited a strong sense of community at Orchard Park, born of familiarity based on many years of shared experiences. Some residents started living at Orchard Park at an early age, leading to strong bonds. "I grew up with everybody here. [I] know everyone here." "[There is] a lot of togetherness [and] unity after you've been here awhile." For other residents, this even produced a kinship-like network: "It feels like I'm at home with a big family." Despite serious socioeconomic problems in their community, interview respondents emphasized close ties to other residents of Orchard Park.

Even with the socioeconomic challenges, most of those interviewed expressed satisfaction with Orchard Park. When asked, "How satisfied are you with this development?" two-thirds of respondents stated they were very satisfied or somewhat satisfied. In addition, 68 percent of respondents indicated they definitely would or probably would recommend Orchard Park to a friend looking for a place to live. When asked, "How long do you want to live in this development?" over half of respondents stated they wanted to live at Orchard Park as long as possible. Given that these interviews took place two years before the BHA applied for HOPE VI funds to renovate the development, these shared sentiments seemed surprisingly hopeful.

David Gilmore, the BHA's chief of operations at the time, remembered having to balance "two opposite perspectives." On one hand, having spent more than his "fair share of nights at Orchard Park putting out fires and emergencies and dealing with the police," Gilmore regarded it as "an awful place to be," somewhere "nobody should have to live." On the other hand, he marveled that "it also produced some of the most extraordinary human beings, [as many] leaders as any community in the city of Boston." He singled out two: "My love Doris Bunte came out of Orchard Park. Miss Bynoe was a product of Orchard Park." Gilmore greatly respected the "people who just said, 'The way you describe life at Orchard Park may be true, but it doesn't mean that I can't do what I gotta do here.' That same community gave birth to them."[21] At base, Orchard Park's rebirth depended on re-establishing a basis for mutual trust between the BHA and its residents.

MODERNIZATION BEFORE HOPE VI

The BHA, with planner Amy Schectman playing a key role, prioritized its first HOPE VI application for its Mission Main[22] project—arguably the other most "severely distressed" property in the inventory—but it also moved forward with efforts to reinvest in Orchard Park. In 1992, the BHA received $35 million from HUD through the Comprehensive Improvements Assistance Program, the Comprehensive Grant Program, and the Comprehensive Modernization Program, each of which permitted rehabilitation of public housing, but not demolition. Initially, OPTA leaders mistakenly believed that all of this money would be dedicated to renovation at Orchard Park (entirely understandable, since a *Globe* editorial stated that "the BHA is sitting on a $35 million federal grant for a renovation of the Orchard Park project"). Angered that this was not to be the case, relationships soured, though OPTA leaders still felt supported by BHA architect Hank Keating, who "consistently treated them honestly and respectfully."[23]

In 1993, without yet seeking a HOPE VI grant, the BHA estimated
that it would cost HUD $41.6 million to complete a full redevelopment
of Orchard Park in three phases over the course of three to four years.
Working with a team of faculty and students from MIT, Orchard Park
residents developed a separate $11 million plan for an on-site Family
Investment Center (FIC), to be located in the on-site Dearborn School,
which had been closed and boarded up since 1981. The team proposed
this FIC as a resident-managed "one stop" multiservice facility intended
to provide "opportunities for informal interaction, positive activities for
youth, and self-help programs for adults" through education and job
training.[24] As the BHA and OPTA began to think through ways to redevelop the full Orchard Park site, several urban design principles emerged
that would remain salient in the years to come. All agreed that it would
be valuable to create a greater sense of "defensible space" through clearly
delineating all parts of the site for particular uses, including provision
of semipublic front yards and stoops, and semiprivate rear courtyards.
Design ideas included introducing a new street system to break up the
"superblock" layout and "replicate typical Boston street patterns." The
BHA imagined a 36 percent reduction in on-site unit density, leaving just
460 apartments, with replacement housing distributed into "large family,
townhouse units on parcels adjacent to the site." This, the BHA averred,
would "solve two problems with one program"—replacement housing
would be "convenient for people used to living in Orchard Park," while at
the same time "fill the current vacant lots, which create a sense of empti-
ness around the site and an urgent public safety concern." At base, a full
"modernization" of Orchard Park would "reintegrate the development
into the surrounding neighborhood" and also "build up a neighborhood
around the development."[25] Although HUD did not supply the influx of
funds to undertake this plan, this work proactively set the agenda for a
future HOPE VI bid.

Eventually, in April 1995, the BHA released $20 million in "moderniza-
tion" funds to carry out the work on phase 1 of what the *Globe* termed a
"face lift" of nine vacant Orchard Park buildings that had been previously
gutted and boarded up.[26] Given that residents had watched buildings get
closed and partly demolished, causing many to fear that the entire development could be taken from them, this news came as a great relief. BHA acting
administrator Joseph Feaster (who succeeded David Cortiella) described the
310 families remaining on the site as "survivors" who "took a big leap of faith
when they let us do the demolition." "Now," he insisted, "they have a done
deal."[27] In fact, many more deals would remain to be negotiated, but it certainly marked a start.

TOWARD HOPE VI PLUS

In August 1995, aided by consultants from The Community Builders (TCB), the BHA submitted its proposal for the "Orchard Park Neighborhood Revitalization" to HUD, seeking $33 million funding from what was now called "HOPE VI Plus." As previewed by the BHA's earlier planning efforts, the "plus" here meant both greater engagement with the surrounding neighborhood and greater reliance on the private sector, through inclusion of units funded by Low-Income Housing Tax Credits (LIHTC). At the time, the idea of a mixed-finance HOPE VI still remained novel, so BHA leaders, joined by TCB president Patrick Clancy and project manager Russell Tanner, went to Washington to meet with HUD sell the idea, emphasizing that TCB had already obtained the tax credits. As Tanner recalled, "The pitch to HUD was, 'We got our tax credit award, but we have not picked the developer yet.' Clancy, with political support, had convinced the state to allocate the credits to the BHA, so that the BHA could go out with an RFP, handing the credits to the developer."[28]

Submitted during Feaster's sixteen-month administrative interregnum, this successful proposal stands out as his greatest achievement. Rather than focus on Orchard Park itself, the BHA addressed neighborhood conditions on a much larger scale, using not-for-profit developers, akin to the work of the nearby DSNI. The HOPE VI application acknowledged that such high levels of "overall coordination and collaboration"—expected to encompass "over $755 million in city, state, federal and private dollars" in ten years—would once have been termed an "urban renewal master plan." But, acutely aware that reference to such a "bygone initiative" in 1990s Boston would never fly, the BHA took special pains to point out that this sort of "top down planning" was "no longer viable." Instead, the BHA pledged to work with the "sophisticated" agendas of the locally active community development corporations (CDCs). In short, it vowed to build an "overarching vision from the bottom up."[29] At its core, the BHA needed to do this because so much impetus came from the tenants themselves. Tanner remembered Edna Bynoe and OPTA "driving the train to a surprising extent"—and that the BHA saw the advantages of this. "To their credit," he continued, "Feaster and [BHA staff] were not trying to direct us to do just what *they* wanted. They wanted engagement. They knew they had a 'tiger by the tail' with the Residents Association, and that that was powerful."

> The financial part of it was not what was catching everybody's interest; it was not having the Boston Housing Authority as your landlord anymore—having a private owner. I very much remember Edna saying, "We would like to have private management." She named other privately managed properties nearby

and said, "Those are run pretty well. Why can't *we* be run like that?" And she
was very in your face about it. I'm paraphrasing it, but it was basically, "We
gotta get rid of the BHA to do that, and so if HOPE VI will do that, let's do it'"
That was very impressive. I was blown away by that.[30]

Rather than get defensive when faced with a Plebs constellation built around
Edna Bynoe, BHA staff embraced an innovative plan.

Instead of the 711 remaining public housing units at Orchard Park (only
half of which were then occupied), the BHA's HOPE VI Plus application
proposed a total of 635 units, including 60 intended for homeownership
(with 15 of these to be subsidized to reach those with incomes between
45 and 60 percent of AMI). This initial application spread 544 public
housing across the original site, adjacent empty lots, and surrounding
neighborhoods. Only 330 of these units would be on the original fifteen-
acre site, including the 126 units already underway as part of the pre–HOPE
VI phase 1 plan—90 of which were also subsidized by LIHTC. The remaining
335 units of in-fill housing—both newly built and rehabilitated—would be
divided into several smaller projects intended to engage "community development corporations and both small and large developers." Indicative
of a commitment to rehousing larger families, 47 percent of the proposed
apartments contained three, four, or five bedrooms. OPTA leadership
agreed to an income mix that targeted only about half of the total units
to occupancy by those with the lowest incomes, while leaving 25 percent
for "moderate" incomes and 30 percent for "market"-rate occupancy. That
said, the proposal defined moderate incomes as those earning between 45
and 60 percent of AMI and therefore the target demographic for LIHTC,
and defined "market-rate" as targeted to those earning "up to 80 percent"
of the AMI—equal to about $50,000 for a family of four—so technically the
proposal could be construed as reserving *all* units for some form of "low income" occupancy—albeit across the full range of public housing eligibility.
The OPTA leadership recognized that this income mix might mean that
some households then living on-site would not be able to return, but favored this set of definitions because it seemed to offer an "opportunity to rid
themselves of certain 'trouble' tenants."[31] At the same time, Tanner pointed
out, "There was no appetite to do a major displacement. [BHA HOPE VI di-
rector] Deb Goddard had no interest in cutting the population in half and
dispersing them." "Another way to look at it"—the attitude of BHA leaders
and long-serving mayor Tom Menino—was that "the *people* who live there
aren't the problem. It's the *place*, the services, the concentration of poverty. We can diminish that. We can change behavior. The residents were not
vilified or labeled as *the* problem." Tanner also acknowledged that "*some* of
them were a problem—Edna was the first person to say that—but there was a

sense that those aren't the people who are going to stay."[32] This basic belief undergirded Boston's approach to HOPE VI. Unlike in other cities, this was just not going to be about kicking low-income people out of newly desirable neighborhoods.

OPTA also stood to gain further influence. This initial HOPE VI application promised that "long-term management of the site" would involve what was rather vaguely termed a "private partnership between the OPTA and a development partner," aided by Boston's vast network of low-income housing support institutions. Still, this stopped well short of a call for resident management. It offered residents a role in management oversight, but clearly stated that "this new partnership will hire a professional management to oversee day-to-day operations at the site."[33] Significantly, the HOPE VI application contained a letter of support from Madison Park Development Corporation, the same trusted nonprofit that had already developed affordable housing in Orchard Park's immediate neighborhood. This preexisting relationship proved immensely helpful once Madison Park was selected as part of the development team.

HOPE VI COMES TO ORCHARD PARK

Following receipt of a $400,000 planning grant in May 1995, in September the BHA and OPTA triumphantly secured a $30 million HOPE VI grant. The *Herald* explained that this could "turn the slum into a homey, suburban-like neighborhood," even as the *Globe*'s headline ambiguously framed the victory as "Orchard Park to Undergo Rehab"—terminology that sounded a bit too much like treatment for drug addiction. Nonetheless, the mayor, BHA and OPTA leaders were understandably thrilled. Goddard, who took over from Amy Schectman to lead the BHA's HOPE VI efforts, stressed that the money "goes much beyond public housing" and "helps the whole neighborhood." Instead of a hindrance to private investment in the neighborhood, the revitalized development could now be "the leverage." Goddard immediately credited the tenants who had "been fighting for their own housing for more than 10 years." Edna Bynoe, as OPTA chairwoman, praised Senators Edward Kennedy and John Kerry together with Representative Joseph Kennedy II for helping to secure the grant, underscoring the political sensitivities of the process. Also, a couple of years earlier, Bill McGonagle, the BHA's deputy administrator at the time, had cleverly arranged to have HUD secretary Henry Cisneros, in Boston to check in on Mission Main, also pay a brief visit to Orchard Park. As McGonagle recalled, it was after dark, around eight or nine o'clock, and they went "to shoot some hoops."

In retrospect, once the BHA submitted the HOPE VI application, "It put the pitch on a more personal level. That may or may not have made a difference."[34]

Whatever the relationship between hoops and HOPEs, Sandra Henriquez's appointment as the new BHA administrator in 1995 definitely proved to be a difference maker. A trained housing professional, Henriquez gained considerable management experience working for Judge Garrity and then for Spence when the BHA was under court supervision. She then moved to work for the Massachusetts Department of Housing and Community Development, before shifting to the private management sector for nearly a decade with Maloney Properties. Henriquez returned to the BHA only after receiving assurances that she would have political independence. Menino appointed her to serve in his cabinet, making her the first public housing chief to gain entry into a Boston mayor's inner circle. Described in a lengthy *Globe* profile as "upbeat, nonconfrontational, consensus-oriented,"[35] Henriquez kept her BHA post all the way until 2009 when Barack Obama appointed her assistant secretary at HUD, putting her in charge of the entire nation's public housing. In the interim, Boston's public housing residents, and the rest of the city, benefited greatly from having consistent and compassionate leadership at the helm of the BHA.

The BHA quickly moved forward during February and March 1996 to select a development team to implement and manage the project. The BHA, continuing to rely on its consultants from TCB, produced an extremely detailed request for proposals (RFP). The RFP again called for 635 units, with 350–370 of these to be located on or adjacent to the existing site, and with "approximately 85 percent" of these units "available to public housing eligible households." In terms of design, the RFP asked for "a typical urban family housing neighborhood, one which cannot be readily recognized as 'public housing.'" Prior to issuing the RFP, BHA planners reached agreement with OPTA that redevelopment would entail phased demolition of all remaining structures on the site. This commitment to phasing thereby reduced the likelihood of future confrontation over a matter that proved so contentious elsewhere. The RFP urged respondents to plan on making significant use of tax credits, but urged that the winning developer "establish rent levels significantly below the tax credit maximums" so that it would be possible to engage in "broad marketing to households below the ceiling of eligible income." The BHA clearly sought to maximize the chance that existing Orchard Park residents (or others on the BHA public housing waiting list with very low incomes) would be able to find homes in the LIHTC units. Similarly, the RFP stressed that the goal was to house "a broad range of incomes . . . side-by-side" but emphasized this still meant housing for "low- and moderate-income families," defined as those earning less than

50 percent of AMI—in other words, targeted to those that HUD would actually term "very low income" households. The RFP mentioned households
paying market rates, but asked developers to work assiduously to make sure
that many units in this category could still be affordable to those earning
under 80 percent of AMI. The BHA also affirmed that TCB would remain
its partner in overseeing these financial aspects of the program, thereby
reminding potential developers that there would be both a sophisticated
not-for-profit watchdog and an engaged public sector team.[36]

In other words, even as the BHA artfully made use of the slippery term
"public housing eligible" just like other housing authorities such as HANO,
there was a significant difference. The BHA framed its language about income mixing quite narrowly—as a way to *maximize*, rather than minimize,
the number of its own households that could be served. Although the BHA
did not promise to bring back all public housing units, since it now operated
on the assumption that "the 'one-for-one' requirement will be eliminated,"
it nonetheless sought to keep very low-income families as the principal
beneficiaries of HOPE VI redevelopment.[37] In Boston, it proved possible to
use common HOPE VI parlance about "attracting a broad range of incomes"
without this ever becoming code for handing much of the land over to private developers to find market-rate renters or owners. Instead, the BHA and
its partners operated under a mandate—partially self-imposed and partially
imposed by decades of pressures levied by tenant coalitions, community-
based organizations, and pro-poor city councilors—that sought to retain and
maximize opportunities for the city's poorest households. The same terminology about income mix carried different political implications under
Boston's tenant-friendly Plebs governance constellation.

Developer selection relied on a nine-person committee, with three
individuals appointed by the BHA administrator, three appointed by
the director of the Boston Redevelopment Authority, and three representatives from OPTA, all advised by representatives from TCB. Four
teams submitted bids, though two later withdrew. In April 1996, Mayor
Menino announced that a development consortium led by Madison Park
Development Corporation had been selected. The team, known as Madison/
Trinity Ventures to take note of the key role played by Trinity Financial,
soon contracted with Maloney Properties (and later Trinity Management) to
provide overall site management for the development. Madison and Trinity,
as general partners, shared ownership on a 51 percent / 49 percent basis,
but the resident organization (now known as the Orchard Gardens Tenants
Association) also obtained a nominal 1 percent ownership stake as a limited
partner, thereby giving their president rights to attend owners' meetings,
while also providing additional legal protection should anyone ever wish to
try to convert the development to market rate.[38]

Chrystal Kornegay's MIT master's thesis about the redevelopment of Orchard Park, written in 1996-1997 just as the redevelopment was being launched, provides a real-time window into the views of key participants. Kornegay—who would two decades later serve as Massachusetts undersecretary for housing and community development and then as head of MassHousing, the state's affordable housing finance agency—emphasizes the overall sense of "trust and reciprocity" between OPTA and its development partners.[39] She characterizes the developer selection process as "uneventful" since "all parties agreed that the proposal submitted by Madison/Trinity was the perfect match for the Orchard Park redevelopment"—a far cry from the multiphase contested process at places such as St. Thomas in New Orleans. The BHA's HOPE VI program director Deb Goddard concurred, asserting that this "proposal was the best" because it emphasized "the human element, [and] the real emotional integrity and understanding of the program came through. It was really enjoyable to read." Bill McGonagle, another BHA representative on the committee, commented that Trinity was "really surprised" to be selected, since it was a small player and others were much more established. "We really put them on the map," he noted. Madison Park CEO Jeanne Pinado concurred that "Trinity was a very young company," whereas her organization had "a much bigger balance sheet at the time." Importantly, "We knew Edna and had the community relationships." Moreover, Trinity's Patrick Lee had worked as a consultant on Madison Park Village and also knew Pinado's predecessor, Danette Jones, from their days working in the Dukakis administration.[40]

It seems no coincidence that a not-for-profit housing developer played such a central role in the creation of Orchard Gardens. Pinado commented that the "CDCs in Boston have always had an ability to organize the residents and a good *reputation* as developers or community-based organizations—and therefore had the respect of the city government." She remembered Tom Menino telling her that "other mayors around the country think that he's crazy for hanging out with the CDC people." They would joke, "Aren't they a bunch of hippies with long hair and earrings?" Yet Boston's city hall leadership remained steadfast: "We've had the sort of mayors that supported community activism. They weren't afraid of it, and good people went into that field. It wasn't just the community organizers; you had people with technical skills."[41] The relative strength of Boston's CDCs is also underwritten by "this whole cadre of funding mechanisms for CDCs that don't exist in other places," particularly the Hyams Foundation and the Boston Foundation. Additionally, Boston's nonprofit housing agencies gain tremendously from the Community Economic Development Assistance Corporation, a public-private finance institution providing financial resources and technical expertise, and from the Community Development Financial Institutions Fund, as well as other state-supported grant opportunities. Boston is a major national hub for these sorts of resources and supports, and the Massachusetts Association of Community Development Corporations has more than eighty-five members. On top of this, Pinado pointed out, "There's all the advocacy people"—groups such as the Massachusetts Affordable Housing Alliance, Mass Alliance of HUD Tenants and City Life/Vida Urbana. "*Those* folks," she observed, "would also never let Boston get rid of public housing." And, especially in the context of DSNI, "There wasn't going to be a lot of tolerance for replacing low-income people."[42] In Boston's governance constellation, CDCs and housing advocacy groups clearly constitute what astronomers would call a "multiple star system."

Given this, the signal importance of Pinado and her allies certainly makes it tempting to treat the emergence of Orchard Gardens as the work of a Nonprofitus governance constellation. To do so, however, would miss out on the even greater centrality of tenant leader and guiding spirit Edna Bynoe. In the shift from Orchard Park to Orchard Gardens, there was no more powerful force than Bynoe herself. She seems to have been consistently accorded a special level of deference by all other players—whether developers, community groups, fellow residents, the BHA, or the mayor. Many HOPE VI processes have featured charismatic tenant leaders (often black women), but they nonetheless usually remain no more than points of consultation, rather than as sources of core direction. Boston's Orchard Gardens aligns most fully as a Plebs constellation because its governance is so dependent on the voice of Bynoe as a resident leader. While it can certainly be argued that the solo centrality of Bynoe makes her more "Pleb" (a single figure) than "Plebs" (one of many), the overall import of resident preferences in decision-making seems incontrovertible.

Bynoe, as OPTA chairperson and therefore a key member of the selection committee, regarded the Madison/Trinity development partnership, and their management collaborator, Maloney Properties, as "a terrific team." Interviewed in 1996, she underscored that Maloney "only works with non-profits and resident controlled housing" so "they know the issues we'll have to deal with."[43] McGonagle added that "Edna really liked them because she appreciated how they—particularly [Trinity's] Patrick [Lee]—developed a "rapport with the tenants." And "Edna," he affirmed, "carried a *huge* amount of weight" in the decision-making.[44] Another OPTA representative on the developer selection committee, John Bowden, remained a bit more circumspect, commenting that "some of the residents around here are skeptical because we've been waiting so long for this. But the more we see that's getting done, the more optimistic they'll get."[45]

Not all aspects of the HOPE VI rollout proceeded smoothly. In late 1996, a year after the BHA received its HOPE VI grant, the 126 units that had been rehabbed under the pre–HOPE VI modernization grant readied for occupancy. This triggered discussion of whether these units should go solely to existing public housing residents living in decrepit apartments elsewhere on the site. The BHA team worried that this would cause phase 1 to be stigmatized as the place "where the poor people live" and that it would be difficult to move extremely low-income public housing residents out to create a broader mix at some future date. Further, the BHA feared that "families occupying these units would result in wear and tear and reduce the units' [future] marketability." Accordingly, the BHA pushed OPTA to countenance a broader mix. OPTA resisted, arguing that existing residents had suffered through the upheaval of poor conditions and redevelopment already and "should reap the rewards of their patience and commitment." Despite cordial relations, some OPTA leaders also feared an "attempt on the part of BHA to permanently dislocate residents who had been moved off-site for this phase of the development." Kornegay notes that members of the development team viewed the controversy over phase 1 income mixing "as an opportunity to win points with the OPTA, and therefore sided with them." Ultimately, the parties reached a compromise whereby the BHA agreed to house existing tenants in the phase 1 apartments, with the proviso that some would need to move again once the HOPE VI phases were completed.[46]

Before submitting its HOPE VI application, the BHA conducted a market study to assess what rents could be charged to those in the upper tiers of the income mix. They based the finances for the development on setting rents about 20 percent below comparables in the surrounding neighborhood, thereby setting up a "considerable market advantage" for the future development. This pricing did not, however, fully factor in how ongoing perceptions of crime might deter potential residents.[47]

CLEARING OUT DRUGS AND CRIME

As work on the development progressed, the BHA, the development team, and the Boston police department assiduously worked to reduce the scourge of drug-related violence. Without this crucial intermediary step, the new community could not be ready for safe occupation. Yet periodic proclamations of victory over the drug trade consistently proved premature. In 1993, the BHA regarded the worst to be over. BHA administrator Cortiella reassuringly wrote HUD secretary Cisneros that Orchard Park was "once dominated by a development-based criminal enterprise," but "through the work of the residents, in cooperation with BHA police, the Boston police department, and federal authorities, the activities were brought to a halt [so] the community no longer lives in this shadow."[48]

Still, even with Whiting and associates in prison, problems remained. In November 1995, Boston police shut down a major heroin distribution center, located "just across the street from the Orchard Park projects." A year later, the police made another heroin bust when police nabbed the suspect "as he headed back into the project." Separately, they caught and arrested another dealer operating from within Orchard Park. Two months later, following a period of undercover surveillance, they arrested two additional heroin dealers in the project. A police officer, extolling the significance of the arrest, rather ambiguously called it "a blow to the Orchard Park development right now," thereby conflating its impact on the stature of the drug trade with its impact on the larger community. In 1997, the *Herald*'s artful headline announced, "Police Prune Orchard Park; Officials Say They Nabbed 16 'Baddest' Apples." Police insisted that this raid finally decimated the Orchard Park Trailblazers, "long known as one of the most violent and dangerous Boston street gangs in Boston's history." "They were ruthless, the baddest of the bad," one police source told the paper. "But we smoked everybody who's anybody down there. It was a beautiful thing." Police regarded this as cleaning up the residue of Darryl "God" Whiting's network: "Most of those kids were lookouts for Whiting" who had "grown up and stepped up to the plate." The arrests, authorities hoped, would "put a significant dent, not only in the distribution of crack cocaine in Roxbury, but also in the wild gunplay that is a regular occurrence in the Orchard Park development where they were based."[49]

The HOPE VI redevelopment of Orchard Park into Orchard Gardens came with major improvements in neighborhood crime and safety. These changes were part of an overall decline in crime known as the Boston Miracle, but far surpassed the city's overall improvement.[50]

Sometimes, housing authority leaders like to tout a decline in crime without mentioning that it occurred largely because a development was fenced off during construction, but that is not the case here given the extensive use of phasing that kept many residents on-site. A comparison that measured the area both pre–HOPE VI and soon after the opening of the new housing clearly indicates a remarkable transformation, and one that did not depend on a full-scale replacement of the people in the community: "Comparing 1995 to 2000, aggravated assault at Orchard Gardens dropped by half. Burglary was six times less common. Assault was down by two-thirds. There were 73 drug violations in 1995; in 2000, there were four." Meanwhile, comparison with crime levels at a nearby housing project that had not undergone such redevelopment showed no parallel decline. Seen more broadly, the total number of crimes in the

Orchard complex dropped from 752 in 1989 to just 57 in 2002. Instead of 202 violent crimes in 1989, there were just 3 in 2001. Similarly, "nuisance crimes" plummeted from 454 to 39. In 2008, recognizing the impact of community organization and community-oriented policing, the Orchard Gardens/Commons Public Safety Committee won a national award from the MetLife Foundation.[51]

Prominent housing analysts also regarded the redevelopment of Orchard Park as a spectacular success (figure 7.2). The project garnered several awards for the developers and architect Fernando Domenech, including a Best Practices Award from HUD, a Builder's Choice Award from the National Association of Home Builders for excellence in residential design, and a Community Building by Design Award from the American Institute of Architects and HUD, given to projects with an "exemplary role in helping to revitalize the communities in which they are located by enhancing the community's physical fabric." These many awards affirmed not just the value of the HOPE VI transformation but also the ongoing efforts at community building that continued for many years after completion of the physical reconstruction.

Figure 7.2. Orchard Gardens, Phase 1 and Phase 2
Orchard Gardens opened in 1998 and 1999 with neotraditional streetscapes of wood-frame homes. An example of the pre–HOPE VI first phase of redevelopment, which rehabilitated "the bricks," is visible at the rear.
Credit: Author.

MIXING INCOMES OVER TIME

With the shift from Orchard Park to Orchard Gardens, the BHA tried to strike a delicate balance. Politically, it needed to make the new development available to house hundreds of extremely low-income families that wished to return, yet BHA leaders (and the development team) also wished to diversify the incomes of those they housed without resorting to a substantial tier of market-rate apartments, as was done in New Orleans and elsewhere. Orchard Park household incomes averaged just 17 percent of the area median, and the push for work associated with the end of welfare and its replacement with Temporary Assistance for Needy Families (TANF) had not improved the situation. Interviewed in 2000, Sandra Henriquez observed that "people are getting jobs," but these were at "subsistence-level, at break-even with where they were when they were on TANF."[52]

The BHA accordingly set a goal of diversifying the public housing side of its Orchard Gardens occupancy by creating an income mix *within* the low-income group, that is, those earning less than 80 percent of area median. The development allocated 12 percent of units for families earning below 10 percent of AMI, another 12 percent for those between 11 percent and 20 percent of AMI, 23 percent of units for households in the 20–40 percent of AMI range, 41 percent of units for families earning between 40 percent and 60 percent of AMI, and the remaining 12 percent of units for households at the upper end of the low-income spectrum, that is, those with incomes between 60 percent and 80 percent of AMI. Since this wishful mix of incomes bore little relation to the incomes of existing Orchard Park residents, the BHA deliberately chose not to enforce it during the initial occupancy of the redeveloped property; instead, as BHA deputy administrator Kate Bennett put it, it would happen by "attrition." Program director Goddard explained further: "The mix was to be achieved over time through unit turnover. OPTA agreed because it did not affect the right to return." To facilitate this transformation toward its income-mixing goal, the BHA and developer established a targeted waiting list, which quickly grew to eight thousand households. Even with this, however, in 2000 the actual incomes of those on the waiting list skewed heavily toward the lower tiers—the majority had incomes below 20 percent of AMI, and just 10 percent of households had incomes over 40 percent of AMI (instead of the target of 53 percent in the idealized tiering plan).[53] This tilted a little higher than the incomes of former Orchard Park residents who had already moved in, and showed hints of future income diversity, but the shift would clearly take a long time. Spinning these figures optimistically, Henriquez argued that the separate development-based waiting list at Orchard Gardens meant that "you still see a lot of people who are at the lower end of the economic spectrum but you see many more people coming in who are working with higher incomes who can afford whatever the going rate is for those units."[54]

The management duly monitored the income tiering, though this proved difficult. As longtime Madison Park CEO Pinado described it, "They set up these buckets, and I remember Maloney complaining about how expensive it was to set up a computer database to track all these *thousands* of applications that came in into those buckets. It wasn't just a waiting list; it was *five* waiting lists. You had to constantly send notices out and figure out where people fit into those buckets. And then when somebody moved out that was low income, if you needed to fill up a more high-income unit, you were supposed to pick from that waiting list first." Still, the slow transition to having more tenants in the higher tiers helped with revenues. Longtime Orchard Gardens property manager Sharon Russell-Mack added that some of the increase came from Orchard Park residents whose own incomes also went up over time. Russ Tanner, now director of real estate at Madison Park, confirmed that this has enabled some of the "returnees" to reach the incomes needed for the "moderate" or "market" tiers.[55]

Nearly twenty years into full occupancy, Orchard Gardens has made some gradual progress toward the goals of the idealized mix. Still, as the comparison shown in figure 7.3 makes clear, the population remains skewed toward lower incomes. That said, compared with 2000, the majority is now no longer below 20 percent of AMI, and nearly one-third of households reported incomes over 40 percent of AMI—three times the rate in 2000. In other words, even though it isn't the income mix posited as the long-term goal, Orchard Gardens still accommodates a full range of lower-income households.

Boston's policy therefore has kept to its double goal: planning a development that would be able to attract those who might otherwise never deign to put themselves on a public housing waiting list, while still seeking to serve the neediest. In seeking to implement its income mix slowly, as units turned over, the BHA did not let its long-term desire to attract a somewhat broader income mix become an excuse to permanently displace the lowest-income families at the time of redevelopment. As of 2016, the median income for Orchard Gardens households stood at about $20,000—equal to about one-quarter of the median income for the Boston area. The BHA wished to keep Orchard Gardens as a resource for many extremely low-income households and retained that promise.

HUD data show that the BHA helped 330 households relocate when the HOPE VI redevelopment commenced and evicted an additional 20 households. Of those relocated, 244 moved temporarily to other public housing units (mostly to other parts of the Orchard Park site, since the redevelopment occurred in phases), while others accepted an offer of a

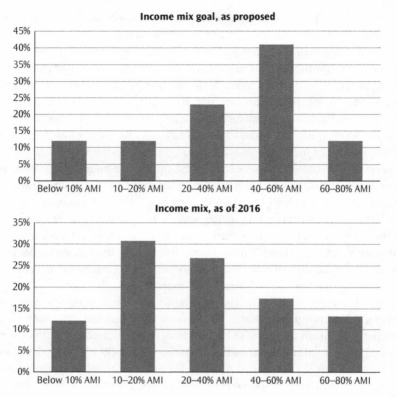

Figure 7.3. Income Mix for Orchard Gardens: Aspirational versus Actual
The BHA and its development partners proposed a target mix of low incomes,
skewed toward the less impoverished, but chose to implement this over time through
attrition, rather than displace extremely low-income households at the time the
development opened. Seen more than fifteen years later, as the bottom part of
the chart shows, there has been modest progress toward this aspirational income
diversity, but Orchard Gardens still mostly houses very low-income and extremely low-
income households.
Source: Derived by Author and Nicholas Kelly from data supplied by Boston Housing
Authority and Orchard Gardens staff.

housing voucher, which enabled them to utilize their subsidy in the private market. Some older residents also chose the option to move to a BHA
project for the elderly. For most, though, the question of whether they
would be able to return to the new Orchard Gardens was a moot point.
As one resident put it, "I never moved out of it. I never moved out. They
transferred me from this side to the other side." Another commented that
she feared she wouldn't get back if she moved to "the place they call 'off-
site,'" so she insisted on remaining until her new apartment was ready;

"I didn't care, even though I was [left] in that building by myself." Edna Bynoe was herself one of the last to move to a new apartment, recalling that her priority was "to make sure my tenants came back." She insists that the relocation "went well, because I had my tenants that lived here doing it. They would go in and help a lot of my seniors pack their stuff up." In the particular social dynamic of Orchard Park, Bynoe's consistent use of possessive pronouns seems quite apt. Ultimately, 226 of the 330 former Orchard Park households remained or returned to the new developments built to replace the project.[56]

NEIGHBORHOOD HOUSING BEYOND ORCHARD GARDENS

Reflecting a "joint decision" between residents and management, the BHA renamed the on-site part of the new development "Orchard Gardens," but the redevelopment work did not stop there (figures 7.4–7.7). The BHA retained 292 of 331 units in Orchard Gardens as public housing, but this constituted less than half the number of apartments previously on the site. This was logistically possible because Congress had lifted the one-for-one replacement rule and politically feasible because of the high pre-redevelopment vacancy rate, but the BHA still insisted on minimizing the net loss of units. To do so, the agency employed a scattered-site approach to replace lost housing elsewhere in the area. Consequently, the redevelopment yielded a total of 635 units of on-site and off-site housing, which is still a net reduction of 76 units. These off-site components included Orchard Commons, rowhouses located on previously vacant land parcels in the neighborhood, completed by Cruz Development in 2001. Madison Park Development Corporation added Shawmut Estates on nearby Ruggles Street—fifteen condominium units offered for sale to first-time homebuyers in 2000. The BHA again partnered with Madison Park to develop another small nearby project, Twenty at Luma, which opened in 2010. This consisted of twenty subsidized homeownership opportunities targeted to lower-income households, which must be below 80 percent of AMI to qualify. Finally, the BHA completed the off-site component of the Orchard Park redevelopment by adding Long Glen Apartments in the Allston neighborhood, some of which were allocated to extremely low-income households, while others used LIHTC subsidies to attract households earning up to 60 percent of AMI. Taken together, the HOPE VI effort at Orchard Gardens and its off-site adjuncts raised $60 million in loans and LIHTC equity, while permitting nearly 70 percent of the remaining 330 Orchard Park households to return, and also doing a great deal to shore up investment in the surrounding area and beyond.[57]

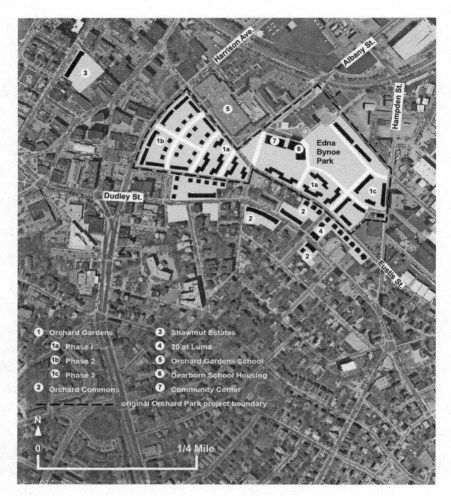

Figure 7.4. Orchard Gardens and Associated Developments
The Orchard Gardens part of the development is complemented by other new housing
spread into surrounding neighborhoods beyond the footprint of the old project.
Credit: Author with Kristin Simonson and Jonathan Tarleton.

LIFE AT ORCHARD GARDENS

As the first part of Orchard Gardens opened in spring 1998, the *Boston
Globe* hailed the magnitude of the change. Instead of control by "a notorious drug dealer, Darryl 'God' Whiting, control rests with a committed
tenant task force, an efficient property manager, and one of the city's
most effective nonprofit housing groups, Madison Park Development
Corporation."[58] This brief editorial endorsement of Boston's distinctive

Figure 7.5. Orchard Gardens Front Porch
The rental component of Orchard Gardens presents a streetscape of front porches and white wooden fences.
Credit: Author.

Figure 7.6. Orchard Commons Homes on Zeigler Street
Across Zeigler Street from Orchard Gardens, the duplex homes of Orchard Commons extend the impact of HOPE VI into the surrounding neighborhood.
Credit: Author.

Figure 7.7. Orchard Gardens and Twenty at Luma
The intersection of Adams Street and Eustis Street shows the confluence of new on-site and off-site housing, with part of the Twenty at Luma housing in the foreground, and phase 3 of Orchard Gardens across the street.
Credit: Author.

governance constellation—emphasizing the role of residents and not-for-profit institutions—succinctly underscored the difference between Boston and many other cities that deployed HOPE VI through other means and with other aims. Grogan and Proscio described the emergence of Orchard Gardens as a key example of Boston's "rejuvenated" neighborhoods, following decades of declining population, racial unrest, and market disinvestment. Orchard Gardens, they exulted, showed "a wholesale transformation of both the physical appearance and social dynamics at work in places once so isolated that they had become economic leper colonies."[59] Instead, the new development faced overwhelming demand for rental applications. "You would have thought they were dropping money from the sky," Madison Park's Pinado recollects. "The place just got bombarded with people the first day from every direction. Diana Kelly from Maloney Properties was there with a bullhorn trying to control the crowd."[60] An article in *Business Week* more prosaically credited the success of Orchard Gardens to the LIHTC program, noting that "the place is almost unrecognizable, thanks to tax-subsidized investments from BankBoston, DaimlerChrysler, and Allmerica Financial, plus federal grants." In this formulation, the $30 million from HUD's HOPE VI seemed almost an afterthought. Still, even *Business Week* admitted that "the tax credit doesn't solve everything," noting that the BHA had to pair tax credits with federal funds to reach the "70 percent of the original tenants [that] had no earned income at all." Otherwise, HUD secretary Andrew Cuomo affirmed, LIHTC couldn't "house the poorest of the poor."[61]

In 2000, President Bill Clinton visited the development so that Mayor Menino could show it off. "Everything the president and vice president have been talking about for the last seven years" in terms of urban redevelopment "is there at Orchard Gardens," Menino declared: "economic development, better education, a safe neighborhood."[62] Taking note, another *Globe* editorial praised the "relative peace that has descended on Boston," commenting that "the Blooming of Orchard Gardens is proof to a nation that no blighted neighborhood is beyond repair."[63] A study of neighborhood economic development subsequently found that surrounding areas "experienced positive, statistically significant differences" in the ten years following the HOPE VI grant, with an "average property appreciation of nearly $198,000 in the Dudley Square area." Similarly, average incomes in the neighborhoods surrounding Orchard Gardens increased by about $40,000, while violent crime declined by 66.2 percent. Analysts interpreted much of the neighborhood's economic gains to the transformation of Orchard Park into Orchard Gardens, while also finding that reinvestment in the Dudley area also benefited considerably from the area's designation as an Enhanced Enterprise Community and, subsequently, an Empowerment Zone.[64] At the same time, many of the gains at Orchard Park stemmed from attentive site management and increased professionalism at the BHA.

BHA administrator Sandra Henriquez had come to her job with managerial experience in both the public and private sector and sought to deliver the best of both. She preferred to think of herself not as the administrator of the city's once-benighted housing authority but as the CEO of Boston's largest realty firm. She emphasized an attitudinal shift in the BHA's approach to management As the *Globe* summarized it: "Tenants who often complained of being treated as mere welfare recipients by housing employees are being called 'assets' and 'valued clients.'" And, correspondingly, the Henriquez-led BHA embraced "tax credits and the whole set of tools that have always been used before by the private-sector and real estate types."[65] In Boston, however, reliance on the private sector toolbox would be tempered by a political culture emphasizing maximum attention to the needs of the poorest.

Although OPTA leader Edna Bynoe had an income from her job as a supervisor in the state welfare office that would enable her to afford housing elsewhere, she had no desire to move on from the place where she had lived for more than five decades. "This is my home, it's convenient to Dudley, it's safe, and it's all I know." Because she had a higher income, her monthly rent of $900 was higher than what more impoverished neighbors would pay for the same size apartment, and she paid it happily. Henriquez recognized that there was a downside here, since so many thousands of households remained on the agency's waiting list. Still, she insisted, "The value of having the Ednas of the world stay is a tradeoff I am willing to make." At a time when some other housing authorities defended the mixed-income housing ideal by emphasizing the transformative presence of wealthier residents paying market rates, Henriquez saw the value and relevance of a more prox-imate sort of mix: "Folks like Edna moved in very poor, struggling, and they progressed along the way. Who else can be a better role model?" Bynoe's own intent remained clear: "I'm not leaving. I tell my children that if I die, just spread my ashes around Orchard Park."[66]

Bynoe, who died from cancer in 2010, is not buried at Orchard Park, but her name is on the library of the Orchard Gardens K-8 Pilot School, opened in 2003, that she championed. And, in 2011, Mayor Menino formally named the development's community park for Bynoe.[67] The new Orchard Gardens school got off to a rocky start, "wracked with leadership turnover and mass confusion" and saddled with poor standardized testing results. Approximately two-thirds of the students—who were uniformly low income and 98 percent black or Hispanic—came from the neighborhood. Half spoke a first language other than English.[68] After 2010, however, under the lead-ership of principal Andrew Bott—who replaced 80 percent of the teachers—the school rapidly transformed. Instead of a place regarded as "one of the worst in the state," its "180 degree turnaround" was celebrated with a trip to the White House. Bott views the school as an extension of Bynoe's goals for the redevelopment: "I think we are returning to Edna Bynoe's vision," he commented. "Every family has a dream. For kids, a bad school can crush that dream."[69]

Residents and housing officials universally remember Bynoe as key to the transformation of the neighborhood where she spent her life. Many residents helped OPTA move forward, but Bynoe set the expectations high. Sandi Henriquez observed that "developments have personalities," and that Orchard was just "a more personable overall development, no matter how bad things got." Much of this has to do with "the leadership of the tenant body." A longtime Orchard resident underscored this point: "Edna Bynoe was a wonderful person. Her name is just about all over the place. . . . She was a very hard lady but she got what she wanted done. She was not playing around and that's why it's like it is now." Manager Russell-Mack concurred: "Working with Edna Bynoe was one of the biggest privileges. I can't even say it in words." Russell-Mack frequently sought out Bynoe for advice. "She and I would have very serious, deep discussions. Her perseverance—regardless of whether the other board members stepped up to the plate—it didn't matter; she kept the ball rolling. She was the *last* to be relocated; she [initially] went into the bricks [the phase I renovation]. She could have had any apartment she wanted. She was not about that. She said, 'Take care of my residents first.' It wasn't a show. She really meant that."[70]

Interviews conducted with seventy-seven residents who moved into the redeveloped neighborhood between 1998 and 2003 convey overwhelming support for the transformation. Orchard Gardens looked and felt like a new environment due to both physical and social transformations. "It is cleaner, more sophisticated, better. Custodians are on the premises now."[71] The redesigned buildings featured porches and backyards to give residents a sense of responsibility over outdoor space. As Edna Bynoe put it, "It's such a joy not to be on top of each other, to have our own parking space, entrance. Now I can have a barbecue in my own fenced-in yard."[72] The defensible space extended into homes, as residents exercised visual control over territory, even if they did not actually own it. The perceived changes in the safety conditions were demonstrated in everyday social interactions; the sense of ownership and investment was evident in the details of how residents cared for their living environment. As Bynoe observed,

> People in the summer time are more friendly. At Christmastime, people decorate their houses like it's a little town. Lots of Santa Clauses and lights outside—and people don't mess with the stuff.

And the youth who strayed from the phase 1 "bricks" to the new houses knew not to mess with Edna Bynoe herself:

> They hang at the bricks. They don't hang in front of people's houses. If they stand in front of houses, people tell them to move. They were standing in front of my house one day and they were smoking, and I told them, "Just get outta here." They all just looked at me and said, "I'm sorry, Miss Bynoe. We forgot you lived here." They moved.

Bynoe's insistent focus on the behavioral and cultural adjustment that is necessary in a move from a streetscape of brick apartments to one of wooden homes underscores a point made in anthropologist Catherine Fennell's study of households "transitioning" during the redevelopment of Chicago's Henry Horner Homes. To Fennell, "The sociability of those who had spent lifetimes 'on front' diverged" almost irreconcilably from that of "those who had passed them in 'nice backyards.'"[73] At Orchard, too, returning residents faced new scrutiny, most of it from fellow residents.

Former residents had a right to return to the redevelopment provided that they were current on their rent payments, had no history of property damage, and did not have anyone on their lease with a drug or felony crime conviction. Residents repeatedly credited the BHA for keeping out those whose family members had been selling drugs: "They got rid of people who couldn't be helped." "Certain undesirable people were weeded out because of redevelopment, which is good." "They made the right decision in releasing some of the families that had altercations." One resident put it more bluntly: "They didn't let bad people come back. That's fine. If anyone sells drugs, [they] better not come back."

Most residents felt far safer in the new development, due to changes in the security presence and tenant composition. Orchard Gardens benefited from "more police activity throughout the area [and] more crackdown" on individuals engaged in criminal activity. In addition, respondents observed a change in the population of residents at Orchard Gardens, particularly among young people who were perceived as troublemakers: "[It's] not the place that's changed, it's the teenagers that's changed. A lot of teens don't even live here. Some kids [have grown] respectful." Management also tried to reinforce this, in ways that skirted the boundary between sensible administration and neoliberal paternalism. As sociologist Laura Tach comments, Orchard Gardens "management also conducts routine 'house-keeping' inspections to make sure that units are in good condition, and families who do not keep their apartments up to standard are required to receive counseling on how to maintain their homes. Ultimately, they are evicted if they cannot satisfy these requirements, though this is a rare event."[74] Evictions happened, both before and after the new development opened, but it always remained well short of a wholesale purge. At first, Edna Bynoe worried that it had not gone far enough: "We haven't rooted out all the bad actors," she noted in late 2000. Still, "The tenants keep pressure on to keep the buildings clean and safe. Everyone has their own front and back yards, so everyone is responsible for their own property."

Residents consistently praise the value of private entrances instead of the violence and frightening uncertainty of the old project's common hallways and stairways: "You have your own front entrance and back entrance." "Nobody don't have to come in your door but you." "No more jumping from roof to roof. No more running from hallway to hallway." "The kids don't mark up with graffiti and stuff all over the place, like they used to." Instead of apartments, residents feel like they have individual homes: "It's like houses to me." "When I lived in Orchard Park, it felt like I was living with somebody. Right here this is mine. This belongs to me."

For others, however, skepticism lingers: "The fact that they took down those buildings and built houses makes it look a little less than what it really is, the projects."

Many residents stress the importance of having a new name for their development, even if others choose not to notice the change. "That was a good thing that they changed the name too because everybody used to the project calling it OP and all of that. It's not OP. This is Orchard Gardens, I live here in Orchard Gardens." A second proud resident insisted: "I don't live in the projects; I live in a development. I correct people [who say,] 'You in the projects.' I say: 'No, I live in a development, thank you.' There's a difference." A third was more skeptical: "Nobody likes Orchard Park. Nobody cares we're Orchard Gardens." A fourth added: "Some people even still call it 'the projects.' I guess it's still Orchard Park to them; it's not Orchard Gardens. And I hear people say 'down the projects,' but it's not the projects anymore to me." Perhaps outsiders perceive the development differently depending on how much history they know: "Only people that are from Massachusetts are able to tell" that Orchard Gardens is public housing. To locals who have internalized the lingering stigma of the geography, though, "We just haven't been able to live down the reputation."

Most of those interviewed see the architectural transformation as signaling a distinct break from the Orchard Park "projects," though others emphasized that too much of the older project mentality has not changed: "The hanging out, the cussing and swearing." "Some of the people are just so lowdown acting." "They make it look so ghetto." As another long-time resident expressed it, "In the old court they didn't do all that swearing at old people, whatever, but now you look at them, they will curse you out." One forty-year resident saw both continuity and change: "It's different people in it, and it's not as ghetto and hood even though it's in the hood. It's more respectful, maintenance is up to standards, and there are more groups to help."

At nearby Orchard Commons, there is a similar effort to undertake careful screening. Orchard Commons developer Daniel Cruz, vice president of Cruz Development Corporation, insisted that all prospective tenants undergo a credit and reference check, along with a criminal offender record check. "If someone bounced a check for $10 in 1990 we won't hold that against them," Cruz remarked. "But if you had anything to do with drugs, you're disqualified." Lolita Kelsey, an African American administrative assistant at Beth Israel Hospital, was thrilled to get a market-rate unit in Orchard Commons. "I was looking for a place where the rents were stable and I was lucky enough to win a lottery for one of the few market-rate units," she commented. "A few years ago, I wouldn't have chosen to live near Dudley Square because it was unsafe and rundown, but now I feel comfortable because they're cleaning up the neighborhood and a different group of people are moving in."[75]

By 2017, as the last remnants of land cleared for thwarted highway projects finally moved toward redevelopment around Dudley Square, Orchard Gardens Tenants Association president Valerie Shelley feared gentrification. Shelley, who succeeded her sister Edna Bynoe as the de facto center of the Plebs constellation, rhetorically asked: "Who doesn't want a better community?" Yet she worried about its consequences. "Let's not move us out. Don't make it better on the backs of other people." Tito Jackson, as Roxbury's city councilor, made affordable housing the central issue of a bid to unseat Marty Walsh as mayor. Although Walsh easily won reelection in November 2017, many in Boston's communities of color seemingly shared Jackson's concern that Boston "will soon be San Francisco if we do nothing." By contrast, John Barros, the Walsh administration's chief of economic development, sought to strike a difficult but pragmatic balance that would "attract market-rate, moderate and low-income opportunities" to Boston's neighborhoods.[76]

Many residents of the new Orchard Gardens consistently stress the value of proximity to Dudley Station for transportation and the availability of nearby supermarkets and shopping. Conversely, others express concerns about intrusions coming from this neighborhood: the homeless people, alcoholics, and drug addicts who come by the development from nearby shelters and a methadone clinic. Others worry about speeding cars. Many other factors compensate. Those who remembered the frequent blackouts and insecurity of the old Orchard Park value consistent electricity, better outside lighting, the absence of rats and roaches, the safe delivery of mail, the newfound willingness of taxi drivers to come to the neighborhood, the presence of well-maintained parks, gardens, the new school, and the increase in programs for youth, seniors, and job seekers. Importantly, recent interviewees consistently praise the quality of the management and maintenance, and the "respect" they get from staff, including manager Sharon Russell-Mack. Many residents also value the way community services are delivered.[77] One stated, "We feel less like a number, just a tenant. They seem to cater to us, seem to care more. And they listen to what we really have to say. That in itself is a big plus."

As a particular plus, Orchard Gardens residents have had the same manager since July 1999. And maintenance director Mike Palmer has been in place even longer, since 1997. The managing agent shifted from Maloney Properties to Trinity Management in 2012, but retained Russell-Mack, Palmer, and other employees. Russell-Mack, who is as ebullient as she is respectful, is careful to credit her full staff, emphasizing that the multiethnic and multiracial team includes many residents. "Because we've incorporated a diverse mix and also staff members that live here, it's made a difference." At base, though, is a culture of mutual regard. "Everybody's treated the same here. Even with the residents association. There's no special passes or privileges [for leaders]. If somebody comes in here, whether they pay rent or don't pay rent, whether they live in the brick buildings or the townhouses, it doesn't matter. Everybody's treated respectfully."[78]

Even so, residents still must face up to sporadic violence, much of it drug related. As one resident puts it, people "like to look at the buildings, so it changed that way. The only thing what didn't change is the violence." Much of this, though, seems to stem from the ongoing visitations of former residents and others who do not respect the changes that have occurred. "Outsiders want to come back and destroy the community that has been rebuilt. That's my biggest fear." "I know people come from other places to buy drugs down here." "It's outsiders making it bad for the people that's here. Some of these dudes that I see hanging around here, they live nowhere around here. They just come around here and do bad stuff." "Rival gangs know where to come—they come right here 'cause this is where they used to hang at. . . . They get locked up, they come back. . . . They got released and want to come back and claim their corner." Another resident added, "People from the outside come here with the trouble. All because you used to live here back in the days. Back in the days you used to could do anything." But the excuse that you "'used to live here' don't count" because now they "could hit you with the [charge of] trespassing." Another resident, however, pointed out that many Orchard Gardens families are in denial about the complicity of their own children. "I shouldn't say this, but a lot of parents would say, 'My son ain't into this, my child ain't into that.' No, that's not true; you're lying to yourself. Your child *is* doing what they doing out there."

Some households clearly did come back with "children or grandchildren who were ruthless gang bangers." Many residents believe that management adjusted quickly, but others would have preferred even more expansive criteria for blocking the return of their neighbors, including "ones causing damages to property." They wished that more had been evicted or denied the opportunity to return simply "because they were troublemakers." Since not all problem-creating households got put out, "There's some slipping-ins. There's some loose ends on a tied knot." Another framed it more optimistically: "I do know of some that they let them come back, they did change, they got better." Yet Edna Bynoe—to the end of her life a tough critic of fellow residents—blamed some of her neighbors for failing to change: "They still think they're in the projects. They sit outside like they got no class. They gave 'em front and back yards and they don't sit in the back, they sit out in the front." Such lingering concerns seem justified.

In 1997, seven years after arresting drug kingpin Darryl "God" Whiting, officials raiding Orchard Park claimed they had again "broken the back" of the drug gangs. Yet, seven years further on, in June 2004, police once more raided the new Orchard Gardens, arresting fifteen men—several from the still-functioning Orchard Trailblazers gang—for selling drugs. The raid police nicknamed "Operation Bad Apple II" did not target Orchard Gardens residents only, but "most" had ties to the development. Still, police were quick to point out that they did not believe this revealed "a gang problem as menacing as that of fifteen years [earlier]."[79] But then, the same week at two in the morning, a fatal murder "shook many residents from sleep." The *Herald* now referred to the development as "tidy," but its reporters continued to visit only when it was not. To *Herald* reporters, whatever its HOPE VI new look, serial unsolved "assassinations" continued in the place the paper persisted in calling "the Orchard Park Projects."[80] Subsequent periodic shootings prompted a *Globe* editorial in 2007 entitled "Fear Grows in This Orchard," which pointedly asked: "What value is derived from urban place making if no one wants to live there?"[81] Fortunately, however, the demand for housing at Orchard Gardens has remained strong.

Interviews conducted with twenty-five residents in 2013–2014—fifteen years after most of the redevelopment had been completed—continued to reveal fairly high levels of satisfaction with Orchard Gardens and Orchard Commons. Indicative of this, approximately three-quarters of the former Orchard Park households that moved to the new development still remain there nearly two decades later.[82] "Satisfaction," in this sense, presumably entails a combination of improved conditions and coveted housing subsidies that makes departure unappealing. Most respondents emphasized improvements to safety but stated that there are still some "bad areas," at least some of the time. "The drugs are still here, but it is more safe; you don't mind inviting nobody over." "People can't just hang on the side of the street and hide behind the buildings and doing things out in the open like they did before, because they do have cops here to try to straighten some of that out." "The area gangs have calmed down a bit." "It's not as wild as it was before." Another resident, who had not previously lived at the old Orchard Park, noted, "It's gotten somewhat better over the years, but every now and again you have an outbreak." Another concurred: "Every now and then they have somebody selling drugs and stuff, but they try to catch them, and they keep the trespassers out." Some saw this as seasonal: "In the winter time it's more quiet. Summertime is more ghetto, and it's just a lot of hanging out." Reflecting on her first seventeen years as manager, Sharon Russell-Mack acknowledged issues with ongoing violence but said,

> I don't accept it when they say, "It happens in *those* communities," because we shouldn't look at it that way. It's not something we should get accustomed to. Each time it happens, it should fire us up more so to say, "OK, this is *totally* unacceptable anywhere." And it *has* decreased, even if it has a little roller coaster with it. I am very optimistic. . . . We're getting there.

She observed that only older residents talk about the Trailblazers. Others prefer to "identify the ones that are involved by name" because "they don't even give them the identity of any connection" to a larger entity: "They're 'trouble,' not 'the Trailblazers.'" As for those that bring trouble from outside, she hopes that judges will enforce antitrespass regulations and will "understand that it's the *community* that's affected and not be so lenient."[83]

Although some still find other residents "unfriendly," most emphasize that Orchard Gardens has developed into a more of a community. It is "mostly a quiet neighborhood" where you can "sit outside and [don't] have to worry about gunshots." "I got to know my neighbors." "It's more open. You feel a little bit more closeness. Most will go outside and sit on their porch." One grandmother added; "Everybody speaks, even the police. My son-in-law was on the porch and they didn't see me. They backed up and wanted to know where the blessed lady was."

Residents from Orchard Park and Orchard Gardens have few issues with the BHA's decision to seek out residents who have a range of low and moderate incomes. All seem to be aware that their neighbors may have higher or lower incomes and pay different levels of rent. Most view this positively, since it permitted a range of people including many with steady outside employment. One noted that "it lifts the stigma of public housing," and other lower-income residents appreciate that some people with higher-paying jobs and more choice about neighborhoods have nonetheless chosen to live in Orchard Park and Orchard Commons. As one resident put it, "The mixed income over here is good, because some people make more, pay more. Some can't afford it and they pay less. So it is a good fit." Despite some interpersonal tensions, residents of Orchard Gardens and Orchard Commons evince very little of the "us" and "them" dichotomy that seems to prevail in so many other mixed-income communities with a stark divide between "market rate" residents and those who are "subsidized." Manager Russell-Mack sees little conflict over incomes, remarking that most people "wouldn't [even] know who is in what income" tier. The only time she sees resentment is from some people who fail to pay rent and use the excuse, "'I'm paying more than half of the other people.' That's their defense." "Otherwise," she contended, "I don't hear that they really care."[84] Either because there are so few residents living at Orchard Gardens without some form of subsidy, or because the range of incomes is not so great, this particular tension seems far less prominent there than it does in HOPE VI communities in cities such as New Orleans, Chicago, or Atlanta. At Orchard Gardens, there seems little mention of role models or instrumental modes of social capital transfer, but vigilant management contributes to informal social control, and investment in building this mixed-income community seems to have improved the economic prospects of the neighborhood.

Still, tensions occasionally carry a racial or ethnic tinge. The development retains a black majority, but about 40 percent of the residents are Latinx, plus three Asian households; the last white resident moved out in December 2016.[85] Most of the mixing of African Americans with immigrant households from the Caribbean and Latin America is supportive, though not always. A black male Haitian resident complained that he had been assaulted by a Latino while picking up his mail: "The guy just walked in the middle of the road and tried to kill me." On other nights, he hears "all that Spanish music," grousing, "My neighbors over there are making parties at 1:00 a.m., 2:00 a.m." so "we cannot even sleep." Other black residents spoke more positively: "We have a lot of foreigners. But they're very nice people. They say 'Hi' to you, they speak to me. Last summer the lady had a baby shower next door. She invited me to the baby shower. I had to call AAA for my car two weeks ago and she came out asked me if I need a ride somewhere." Still, this resident indicated she continues to hear "negative talk" about how "all the black people are going to be moved out because the foreigners are taking control of everything." Another African American resident mixed praise with surprise, noting that her neighbors were "Dominican, but they're nice." Put a different way, "We are starting to get people from different cultures and stuff, and they seem to be nice. So far." Still, some African American tenants resent it when such "foreigners" gain apartments: "I know a lot of people of color have put in for here, and most of the time it would be a Spanish person" that gets the apartment. "I don't think that's right."

Other than the episodic violence and lingering presence of drugs, many residents expressed concern about a seemingly prosaic issue: parking. To some it is the lack of visitor parking that creates tension when neighbors host nighttime visitors: "They park in someone else's parking space and sometimes there do be a little chaos." To others, the problem is daytime parkers from outside the neighborhood: "People that work in the hospitals park over here for free because they don't have to pay" their garage rates. The problem lessened after Orchard Gardens added signs for "resident only" parking. But manager Sharon Russell-Mack viewed cars parked by nonresidents as a marker of progress. "Years ago, you wouldn't get people parking here with their hoopty, let alone their nice Mercedes. I see it as a compliment for Orchard Gardens."[86] To some more conspiratorially minded residents, however, it signaled an early sign of gentrification, especially as white households moved into the area more frequently. Having resident parking signs "shows you white people coming back—they want the city back and they want Dudley back, and we're going to be thrown out." Another added, "They want to put you out of here because the white people want to come back; they want to get all this back because it's closer." Others, however, saw this as an opportunity—with more white people around, maybe the neighborhood would become "more upscale," and there would be fewer liquor stores surrounded by people begging for "spare change." At base, low-income residents of color in Orchard Gardens did not wish to lose their homes. Many remembered the worst of the drugs and violence and still feared a return to those times, but they also did not want to lose out because conditions had improved.

In 2014, with long sentences for drug offenses now being reconsidered, Darryl Whiting applied to have his sentence reduced. In 2016, however, Judge Patty B. Saris rejected the appeal, noting that she had read Whiting's 2013 book, *Takin' It to Another Level*. Self-published under the name Darryl "God" Whiting through Corona Crown Books with the editorial assistance of Darryl Whiting Jr., it is a revenge fantasy novel in which the incarcerated author imagines a released prisoner named Darryl Whiting torturing and killing those who once testified against him. The novel, which lawyers and both Whitings insisted was "pure fiction," nonetheless discusses the Boston-based targets by name. Judge Saris easily matched some of the names in the novel with the presentencing report, commenting that "the use of real names, places, and events in the book convinces me that the defendant poses an ongoing threat to the community." Whiting remained in prison. BHA administrator McGonagle commented: "The residents of Orchard Gardens can breathe a collective sigh of relief."[87]

BOSTON'S OTHER HOPES

In Boston, the HOPE VI program has brought relief to low-income residents in developments across the city. In contrast to cities that have emphasized the need to focus extensively on bringing in a substantial market-rate component to redeveloped public housing, Boston has consistently resisted this. Orchard Gardens allocated just 14 percent of units to those with incomes sufficient to pay market rates. At Boston's other two early HOPE VI sites, the figures were only slightly higher: 18 percent at Mission Main and 23 percent at Maverick Landing in East Boston. Since then, BHA deputy administrator Bennett noted, "If anything we have moved in the direction of mixing *less* than Orchard." Moreover, she pointed out, some of those in the market-rate units at Orchard, Mission, and Maverick are there with mobile housing choice vouchers—so many of those units, too, are occupied by extremely low-income tenants. At the BHA's final two HOPE VI developments—Old Colony (now the Anne M. Lynch Homes at Old Colony) in South Boston and Washington Beech in Roslindale—there are both public housing units and LIHTC units, but no market-rate housing at all. Throughout the entire eighteen-year period of HOPE VI funding, Boston had just one mayor. And Tom Menino, Bennett points out, consistently "championed" both public housing and investments through HOPE VI. The key thing, though, is that the mayor embraced HOPE VI, "not as a gentrification program but as a neighborhood revitalization program."[88]

At base, this decision to emphasize lower incomes in any income mix is a moral stance, though it is also conditioned by the particularities of Boston's expensive housing and construction market that made it hard for market-rate units to "stand on their own" financially when built in the context of public housing. Fundamentally, though, according to former BHA administrator Henriquez, who served from 1995 to 2009, the BHA's focus on those with "public housing eligible incomes" is "by policy and design." "Philosophically," she believes, "if residents lived through the 'difficult' times, then they should be able to share in the better ones." Henriquez's successor, Bill McGonagle, shares the same fundamental approach. He has accepted the "mixed-income concept," but only "reluctantly and pragmatically." "At the end of the day," he reflected, "I'm in the affordable housing business, not the mixed-income business. My business is to take care of poor people."[89]

CONCLUSION: HOPE FOR THE POOR

Boston's approach to HOPE VI has been consistently pro-tenant—even if not all expectations have been fulfilled. Given the growth of neighborhood political power since the 1960s, it would have been treacherous for leaders to do otherwise. Forged in the backlash against urban renewal in low-income neighborhoods—and particularly in low-income neighborhoods of color—Boston has greatly benefited from a broad collection of community-based nonprofit housing corporations. Groups such as TCB and Madison Park have been eager and available partners in pursuit of the kind of HOPE VI redevelopment that has minimized displacement. That said, in its eagerness to reduce the density of apartments on its public housing sites and deliver larger units with higher percentages of private entries, the BHA has typically fallen at least 20 percent short of providing 100 percent replacement of its stock. Acknowledging this, deputy administrator Bennett insisted that any loss of units "has not been about wanting less poor people than there were." To underscore this point, the BHA sought to "rationalize" its modest shortfall by getting "replacement Section 8 added to our allotment for any public housing unit that we lost." Administrator McGonagle concurred: "My job is to preserve every single hard unit" of public housing." It really involves "walking a tightrope" to do this while also remaining "competitive" to get the grants. This meant not just replacing units for those who are merely "public housing eligible," but providing no loss of one-for-one availability for those with extremely low incomes who most need public housing. McGonagle marveled that other cities have assiduously worked to rid themselves of such housing: "If I'd tried to do anything like they've done, I would have been run out of town on a rail. It's just not politically possible to do in Boston, and I wouldn't want to do it anyway."[90]

At its core, the relative success of Boston's experience with HOPE VI does indeed rest on this question of what is "politically possible." As the eight-decade evolution of the BHA has shown, such possibilities are hardly static. Instead, they are crafted from hard, neighborhood-based work, not simply handed down from on high. Boston's governance constellation shifted its configuration not just because Harry Spence or Judge Garrity once shone brightly, but because low-income tenants—and particularly poor people of color—insisted on greater visibility. This gave the transformation of Orchard Park into Orchard Gardens its particular form, what I have dubbed "Plebs." Triggered by the sustained backlash against the dubious premises and promises of urban renewal and high-handed expressways, buoyed by the initiatives of Dudley Street neighbors, prodded by the ascent of a "tenant oriented" housing authority board, provided with successful exemplars of redevelopment by the BHA receivership, championed by passionate resident leaders, and supported by increasingly tenant-centered city officials, this transformation could not help but be centered on the needs of extremely low-income residents.

Part IV

PUBLICA MAJOR IN TUCSON

Figure IV.1. Tucson's Publica Major Constellation for Posadas Sentinel
Viewed from Tucson, the Publica Major constellation shines prominently in the public
sector of the sky.
Credit: Author with Suzanne Harris-Brandts.

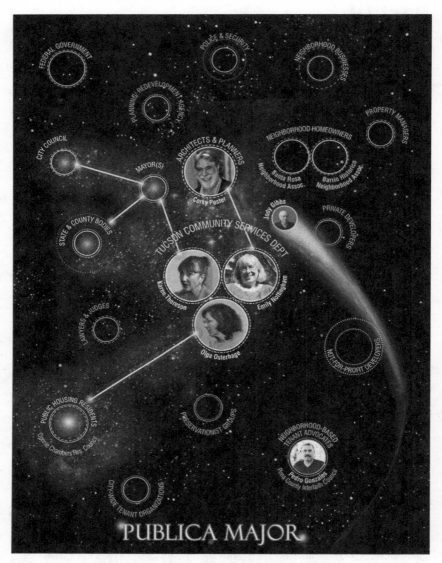

Figure IV.2. The Publica Major Constellation in Tucson: A Telescopic View
This telescopic view of the Publica Major constellation depicted in figure IV.1 has
Tucson's Community Services Department as its orienting pole star. Architect Corky
Poster and public housing residents also mattered, but Tucson's public sector played
the dominant role.
Credit: Author with Suzanne Harris-Brandts.

We always expected to have a relatively low rate of return. They were getting good relocation choices. We bought brand-new houses in new subdivisions, three-bedroom homes that were more spacious than they'd been living in. Our public housing stock is quite good. They were given a lot of choice about where they could move, and we worked closely with them.

—Emily Nottingham, deputy director, Tucson Community
Services Department

OVERVIEW: SCATTERING THE BARRIO WITHOUT PURGING THE POOREST

Public housing in Tucson is far less discussed than public housing in New Orleans or Boston or other major American cities, in part because there is so much less of it. Yet Tucson's approach to public housing reveals a third possible attitude to public housing governance and redevelopment, typifying what I have termed the Publica Major constellation (figures IV.1 and IV.2). Part IV is split between two chapters that show what happens when responsibility for public housing remains more wholly vested in the public sector—subject neither to the whims of private developers, as in New Orleans, nor to the sway of empowered low-income tenants, as in Boston. Chapter 8 narrates the complex and reluctant emergence of Tucson's Connie Chambers public housing development, intertwined with a deeply contested process of urban renewal. Chapter 9 follows with an account of the demise of Connie Chambers and its replacement by Posadas Sentinel, a transformation made possible by a broader public sector strategy to decentralize public housing.

Given that the burgeoning urban growth of Tucson occurred much later than in the other cities discussed in this book, many might guess that the phenomena of slum clearance and urban renewal would bear little or no relevance in such a place. Sadly, this is far from the case. In May 1958, Tucson city officials gained federal approval for one of the largest urban renewal schemes in the country—clearance of 392 acres of the city's residential and commercial heart. The ambitious scale of this venture marked it as more than eight times larger than the contemporaneous—and still-infamous—clearance of forty-eight acres in Boston's West End. Tucson's downtown barrio had nothing like the population density of a compact eastern city, but objections remained intense. Although the urban renewal effort would take more than a decade to realize and would eventually take a much smaller form, its contested legacy has deeply affected the course of community relations and public housing in the city.

Tucson's housing authority built its first project, known as La Reforma, in the 1940s. Located in the Santa Rosa barrio, south of downtown, this project was extended through construction of the two-hundred-unit Connie Chambers public housing development in 1966–67 during the urban renewal era. Thirty years later, after a period of decline, the City's Community Services Department (which took over as Tucson's housing authority in 1971) received a HOPE VI grant to redevelop the property as Posadas Sentinel, part of a wider revitalization effort in the surrounding barrio. The name "Posadas Sentinel," chosen by residents, refers to "Posadas," a Mexican tradition that recounts the Nativity story of Joseph and Mary looking for a place to stay in Bethlehem, and "Sentinel," the name of the peak directly west of the neighborhood.[1] Although the Posadas story is ultimately meant to celebrate the birth of Jesus in a manger, it is also an account of repeated failures to find housing, so its resonance is as powerful as it is ambiguous. Acutely conscious of neighborhood critics who viewed HOPE VI as no more than another round of insensitive urban renewal, the city assiduously worked to maximize housing opportunities for residents of Connie Chambers. The result is a heartening effort to improve a centrally located neighborhood, tempered by the fact that most of the original residents did not return to live there after redevelopment.

As with Orchard Gardens but unlike River Garden, Tucson's city leaders premised the redevelopment on occupancy by very low-income households, while seeking other ways to diversify range of incomes. Moreover, Tucson's Community Services Department (CSD) accomplished this while replacing *all* two hundred public housing units. Rather than put these all back into the original barrio site, however, it took advantage of the city's peculiar housing market and scattered much of the housing across the city by purchasing homes in a variety of new or vacant subdivisions—chosen for their proximity to transit and quality public schools. Because many of the former Connie Chambers households who gained the most were not rehoused on-site (but often gained new, single-family homes), the story of Posadas Sentinel questions the conventional kneejerk critique that any HOPE VI success must entail rehousing most former residents in that new community.

Instead of following its Star of Bethlehem into the realm of private developers, the proponents of Posadas formed a more tightly drawn governance constellation from within Tucson's own public sector. Relying on close partnership with a local architect-planner combined with sincere outreach to residents, the CSD nonetheless kept much of its process in-house, thereby epitomizing a third approach to HOPE VI governance, one that has retained a significant role for the public sector.

Despite CSD's ample goodwill, significant dissenters still see Posadas as another unfortunate round of discriminatory urban renewal. Taken overall, Tucson's story still suggests that it is possible to have both an equitable process and a widely apportioned set of equitable outcomes for public housing residents.

8

The Rise of Urban Renewal and the Connie Chambers Project

DOWNTOWN AND LA CALLE

Very little in Tucson's early development history would give reason to associate this place with the idea of equitable housing. It is a place that has endured profound spatial and social conflicts among *Los Tucsonenses* (those of Mexican origin with deep roots in the region), the Hohokam (who hold an even longer claim), and the various other groups that have come to join them or push them aside. This is obviously quite different from the dominant black-white dynamic that is more commonly discussed in other American cities, such as New Orleans or Boston. Tucson's initial growth reflected its Spanish and Mexican origins; Mexican troops vacated the city only in 1856, three years after the territory was annexed under the terms of the Gadsden Purchase. By the 1880s, however, the growing Anglo presence gradually forced the Mexican American population southward from the presidio toward what effectively became a parallel central business district (CBD) located just south of the Anglo one, a new barrio centered around the Plaza de la Mesilla. As Lydia Otero puts it in her book on Tucson's urban renewal impacts, this area, soon known more simply as La Placita, "became the focal point of the displaced Mexican American community." Centered on the commercial area referred to as *la calle*, the new barrio recreated "a landscape that looked and felt like their homes in Sonora or in Tucson before the arrival of Anglos." By the 1940s, the vast majority of Tucson's Mexican Americans occupied the barrios south and west of the Southern Pacific Railroad tracks, with Anglo occupancy dominating the city to the east.[1]

Downtown, located just south of the original townsite boundary and on the *Tucsonenses* side of the tracks, soon became contested territory. Although Tucson's Mexican Americans constituted no more than about 15 percent of the metropolitan area's residents during the mid-1950s, they often formed a near majority of downtown pedestrians, due to the proximity of their residences to the city's center. To Tucson's city officials and most of their consultants, *la calle* and its adjacent residential barrios seemed "outdated" and "marginal," and this area's vibrancy and centrality to the *Tucsonenses* community (and to the city's Chinese and African American residents) merited little scrutiny. Instead, especially following the spate of small, outlying shopping centers built during the late 1950s and the establishment of the El Con Mall three miles east of downtown in 1961, many city leaders came to feel that drastic transformative action would be needed to sustain Tucson's traditional CBD as a viable economic center. This conviction intensified once a 1960 plan presciently predicted "spectacular" regional growth that could yield "1,400,000 persons in metropolitan Tucson by the year 2000." A research team based at the University of Arizona provided a multifaceted analysis of Tucson's evolving downtown in 1960, concluding that "the survival of retailing in the CBD will depend on the ability of the CBD to develop as a center of other activities." They suggested greater reliance on making downtown Tucson a center of office jobs, but also sought "some other source of strength" and hoped that "planned nuclei of recreational and cultural establishments might achieve this." Notably, they even recommended that the city "set aside an area devoted to the preservation of Tucson's Spanish and Mexican heritage," pointing out that this held "rich potential for the tourist industry." Moreover, almost in passing, they added that razing these areas "and relocating residents to other parts of the community may substantially interfere with the well-established shopping pattern in the downtown area."[2]

Despite such suggestions and warnings, most of those involved with charting a course for Tucson's center cared little about either the heritage or the purchasing power of its Latinx community. Ultimately, as Otero observes, urban renewal proponents "did not seek to revitalize the area or to improve its retail potential. Instead, they wanted a 'cleansed' downtown with a new purpose. City leaders wanted tourists and a 'new' breed of people to take pleasure in the new downtown they promised and eventually developed."[3] In Tucson, however, the fitful movement toward slum clearance and urban renewal did not proceed in tandem with the reluctant embrace of public housing. Rather, they occurred almost as alternating impulses, each championed and opposed by different constituencies. As one long-serving Tucson city official astutely noted, "They were separate, with each going its own way."[4] Tucson city officials, much like the business community, preferred that the private sector take responsibility for any low-rent housing and did not view urban renewal and new public housing as part of a planned relationship. As a result, public housing came to the fore only in the interregnum between efforts to implement an urban renewal plan.

LA REFORMA AND ITS REFORMS

In Tucson, as in other American cities, passage of the 1937 Housing Act prompted more excitement about slum clearance than about new public housing. Roy Drachman, soon to become one of the city's most prominent postwar real-estate developers and civic leaders, championed the slum clearance effort in 1939, as head of Tucson's chamber of commerce. He remained deeply disappointed that the efforts yielded more units of public housing than cleared slums. According to Tucson Housing Authority executive director William Walsh, the city destroyed fifty slum dwellings as part of the exchange for what became 160 new public housing apartments. For Tucson's persistent critics of public housing, such limited clearance stopped well short of what the city needed. And, like Drachman, these detractors also insisted that the private sector ought to be in charge of any replacement housing that might result.[5]

The Tucson Housing Authority (THA) targeted its first foray into public housing to what were then called "Spanish American families." Prompted by a Chicano member of the THA board, the city named it La Reforma, seeking to recall the period of mid-nineteenth-century liberal reforms in Mexico. The first Tucson-based reforms, however, occurred even before the project was ready for occupancy. As at Boston's Orchard Park, the entry of the United States into World War II dramatically affected the entry of residents into public housing. Instead of a new enclave of modern dwellings for Mexican Americans, La Reforma housed primarily Anglo war workers. After 1946, as the war workers moved on from its eight large perimeter blocks of brick, single-story housing, La Reforma gradually regained much of it intended constituency. By 1954, Pat McLaughlin could regard her family as "the last of the Anglo families in there." In 1947, however, La Reforma still housed only a dozen low-income families, prompting the federal government to urge the THA to do more to "oust the higher income tenants." In 1949, an *Arizona Daily Star* editorial summed up much of the local opposition to using public housing for the poor, questioning why a Tucson taxpayer should have to "support his less frugal or less capable fellows." Others raised a different issue, noting that the managers of La Reforma refused to admit black households of any income.[6]

The whole concept of public housing remained highly controversial in Tucson. As former housing authority official Cressworth C. (Cress) Lander commented, when it came to public housing, "Tucson was one of those reluctant communities. We had 150 units when most cities had 5,000. The citizens who were running the board at that time kept it segregated." More pointedly, this board "didn't want to have housing for poor folks" of any kind. Roy Drachman (by then a real-estate developer) lambasted public housing as a dangerous form of "socialism." He pointed out that every Russian city had public housing and pointedly questioned "whether we want that here." In a debate with Drachman, William Shaw, executive secretary of the Tucson Citizens' Committee for Better Housing, pointed out that if public housing was socialism, it was no more so than the Federal Housing Administration: "The two programs are the same, the one providing loans for those with middle incomes and above, the other for low income groups." Drachman retained deeply engrained suspicions about Tucson's poor, fearing that there would soon be calls to buy them food and clothing, and arguing that if they were ever to attain "equality of opportunity," they would need to "go out and work for it." Ultimately, he pointed out, "There's always going to be a certain amount of slums. It's unfortunate, but that's the way it is. Everyone can't be rich."[7] For the time being, Drachman's sentiments won out.

In February 1950 the city council voted down a proposal to build more public housing. Following this rebuff, the council faced complaints from the Tucson Urban League, whose members remained upset that no blacks could live in the segregated La Reforma, and that a planned project for blacks to be known as Crispus Attucks had not been built. This citizens' group felt that the city owed them "Negro housing," even though Tucson was no more than about 3 percent black. That fall, after public housing supporters forced the issue onto the ballot, Tucson's voters rejected the idea of expanding La Reforma by a margin of more than five to one.[8]

Eventually, during the 1950s, La Reforma itself began admitting black families, becoming 15 percent black by 1962. The THA continued to resist using La Reforma to house Tucson's poorest households. Out of 160 households, only 33 received welfare. The THA conducted regular inspections to insure cleanliness and evicted nearly 10 percent of households annually. Reasons for ouster varied from "non-payment of rent, immorality [or] continued disturbances" to the more vaguely termed charge of "nonconformity," revealing a complex mix of cautious economics and paternalist moralism.[9]

PURGING THE *TUCSONENSES*

With La Reforma a controversial presence, but still safely located a fifteen-minute walk south of *la calle* and the rest of downtown, Tucson city officials continued to debate the matter of slum clearance in the older adobe districts that lay in between. From the late 1930s through the late 1950s, officials pondered whether the area could be rehabilitated or must face wholesale clearance.[10] Thereafter, as Otero demonstrates in her quietly devastating account of Tucson's urban renewal saga, "Officials would fail to provide city services to *la calle* and would allow building and sanitary regulations to go unenforced. For their part, bankers would deny *la calle*'s home owners and landlords access to loans to maintain, let alone improve, their properties." As urban renewal official Don Laidlaw later recalled, starting in the 1950s "There was some zeal on the part of building inspectors to rein in improvements, because the conclusion had already been reached that everything was gonna get torn down—why spend public money on buying back improvements." Local attorney Carlos Robles, engaged in assisting residents fight condemnation orders, concurred: by the late 1950s residents "were told not to improve their property because it had no future."[11]

The efforts of Tucson's civic leadership to recast the city's Mexican American center took at least three decades to realize. In 1958, twenty years after the first stirrings of slum clearance, city officials proposed clearing 392 acres of the city's core, stretching all the way south to Twenty-Second Street. This first plan proposed to acquire all property in the area at once in order to discourage inflated prices if the project were to proceed in phases. Planners then wished to begin development at the south end of the district, designating the area near La Reforma for "low-cost private housing" intended to rehouse those soon to be displaced from other parts of the urban renewal area (figure 8.1).

Tucson gained approval of its Workable Program and, in March 1961, Mayor Don Hummel appointed attorney S. L. (Si) Schorr as director of urban renewal and gave him substantial authority for preparing the plan. Schorr explicitly counseled property owners to refrain from further investment that "would be a step against the tide in the area." "Naturally," he added, lending institutions understood this, so "satisfactory financing is unavailable." City officials envisioned the urban renewal scheme as a "single long-range project," but in the near term they needed to come up with a plan for relocating the residents. In his memoir, Hummel recalled "innumerable neighborhood sessions" and "good support from residents who lived in the affected areas, on assurances that they would have an opportunity to get improved housing after the land was cleared and redeveloped." Planners knew that they had to comply with federal requirements for rehousing displaced residents, but many in Hummel's own central constituency continued to balk at the very concept of public housing.[12]

In 1961, Schorr authored a report, tellingly entitled *Urban Renewal: A Teamwork of Private Enterprise and Government for Slum Clearance and Redevelopment of the Old Pueblo*—a clear indication of the tightly delimited form of governance constellation still in place for managing Tucson's economic health. The report made the same arguments used throughout the

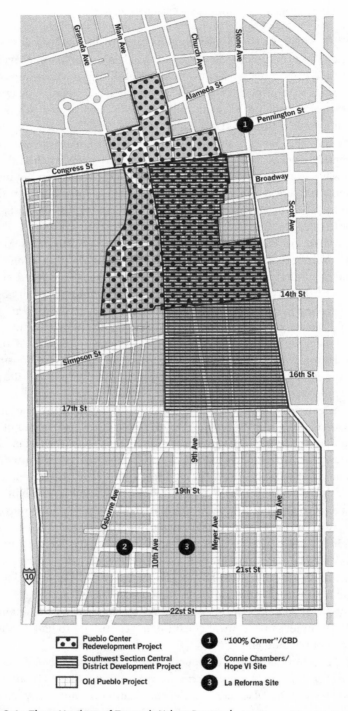

Figure 8.1. Three Versions of Tucson's Urban Renewal
Although Tucson's urban renewal plans shifted from 392 acres to 76 acres to 80 acres, each plan targeted the barrios closest to the CBD. The initial proposal extended all the

country about the "cost of slums," pointing out that the area's high rates of crime, fires, and juvenile delinquency caused the district to draw disproportionately on city services, thereby placing an unfair burden on Tucson's taxpayers. Officials claimed that the Pueblo Center district housed 2 percent of the city's population but accounted for 37 percent of crimes against persons. Instead of "pointless" financial support of "blight" subsidized by those already paying higher property taxes, Schorr's team promised to make central Tucson "the Southwest's outstanding cultural magnet and tourist attraction." The entire report mentioned public housing only twice. The city assumed that nearly all relocatees would find "adequate housing in the normal private market," but estimated that 12 percent might be able to make use of available units in La Reforma over the next two years.[13]

William Matthews, editor and publisher of the *Star*, responded to Schorr's report with a rare editorial warning about the cultural costs of the Old Pueblo District Project. He noted that urban renewal advocates object to "wasteful street design" and "plead that structures are too near property lines and that family dwellings are intermingled with business and industrial areas" but forget that this was "the way the Mexicans built their villages." He wondered: "Must the people of Tucson destroy this remaining area of Mexican life just because the streets are too narrow and buildings old? . . . Maybe someday Tusconans would look back at urban renewal and wonder why they authorized such a project which wiped out at one stroke what remained of Mexico in Tucson." As Hummel, a Democrat, reached the end of his third and final two-year term as mayor in December 1961, progress on the Old Pueblo District plan remained stalled. City elections then yielded a Republican mayor, Lew Davis, as well as an all-Republican city council. Davis held mixed opinions about urban renewal, and five-sixths of the new council were openly opposed.[14]

On January 12, 1962, the five anti-urban renewal council members "met secretly" and drew up a memorandum asking for the resignations of both Schorr and the city manager. Schorr refused to resign and instead went

---

Figure 8.1. Continued
way south to Twenty-Second Street, where it reached the La Reforma public housing site, adjacent to the future Connie Chambers project.
Source: Adapted by author and Yonah Freemark from Rachel Stein Gragg, "Tucson: The Formulation and Legitimation of an Urban Renewal Program," MA thesis, University of Arizona, 1969, fig. 2, p. 37, and from map shown in Roy P. Drachman and Vincent L. Lung, *The Pueblo Center Redevelopment Project*, report presented to the Central City Council of the Urban Land Institute, April 23, 1965 (Tucson: City of Tucson, 1965), between pp. 4 and 5; and S. Lenwood Schorr, *Urban Renewal for Slum Clearance and Urban Development of the Old Pueblo District: Teamwork of Private Enterprise and Government* (Tucson: City of Tucson, 1961), 16.

directly to the press with a markedly reduced plan—only one-fifth of the original size—that he hoped could appease opponents and jump-start a public
reconsideration. The smaller project—now less mellifluously called the
"Southwest Section Central District Development Plan"—would end at sev-
enteenth Street, thereby stopping short of much of the area of older barrio
homes once targeted for replacement by new "low-cost private housing."
Schorr focused this plan on a "convention facility" component and told the
city council that the "economic success of a redevelopment plan" depended
on this. Even this somewhat more modest plan encompassing "only"
seventy-six acres proved too controversial. Schorr's tactics forced a reluctant
mayor and a hostile council into a position of holding public hearings but
did little to alter their views. Despite leadership from a new advocacy group,
the Citizens Urban Renewal Enterprise (CURE), the plan came under attack
in the press. Both the *Arizona Star* and the *Tucson Citizen*, along with many
Tucson residents, raised a litany of highly varied objections: urban renewal
would raise property taxes, or it would distribute property development
rights unfairly or fail to clear enough slums. As Robert Fairbanks points out,
such skepticism typified "the war against slums" throughout the region. "The
use of eminent domain especially struck a nerve in the urban Southwest,"
he stresses, given its "long tradition of suspicion of centralized government
and a commitment to rugged individualism." In Boston, residents objected
to particular projects; in Tucson, like New Orleans, philosophical-financial
opposition came from those who resisted the entire concept. In May, the
council voted to put the urban renewal plan on indefinite hold and allowed
the initial federal approval of its "Workable Program" for housing to lapse.[15]

A PUBLIC HOUSING INTERREGNUM

With the urban renewal plan in protracted limbo, in December 1962 the THA
cautiously requested an additional two hundred units of public housing to
supplement La Reforma. Support from a variety of church and civic leaders
buoyed the housing authority, but, as the *Star*'s headline aptly warned, a
"Housing Battle" loomed. THA chairman Edmund Arriaga pointed out
that Tucson lagged well behind Phoenix in public housing supply. He tried
to put the best possible spin on the city's previous experience with La
Reforma. In the first sixteen years that it had operated under the auspices
of THA, Arriaga pointed out, 424 out of the 904 who had called it home had
"rehabilitated themselves" to the point where they could move on to other
housing. In this way, the THA sought to reassure Tusconans that public
housing residents should be regarded as responsible and upwardly mobile,
thereby making additional housing less of a moral risk.[16] A *Star* editorial

urged the council to "go slow on expanding public housing." Instead, the paper called for opponents to "come forward with a clean capitalist plan," adding, "Think what a feather it would be in Tucson's cap if housing, along with other problems, could be faced and met by private enterprise!"[17]

Many city officials viewed any talk of public housing as a barrier to gaining approval for urban renewal programs, even though the Public Housing Administration in Washington required a Workable Program for relocation. By July 1963, while still stressing a central role for private enterprise, the council agreed to move forward with two hundred more public housing units. THA executive director Cornelius (Connie) Chambers promised that Tucson's new Workable Program would entail corresponding condemnation or demolition of two hundred substandard housing units, adding that those in the cleared areas would have "first choice in the new buildings."[18]

In the winter of 1964-1965, the THA began its arduous effort to acquire 13.5 acres of land immediately across from the La Reforma project. The city had owned the previously undeveloped southern part for decades, but the mostly residential northern part was far from vacant. By August 1965, the THA succeeded in negotiating the purchase of thirty-two out of the forty-five properties it needed but had to litigate the remaining thirteen cases. In addition to homes, the future Connie Chambers site also housed the Lee family's Westside Market. As Ronald Lee, a Chinese American, recalled, "The city took the Westside property; they just took everything." Although his family was able to open a new store on Twenty-Second Street, more than thirty years later he described displaced neighbors as still "bitter about the way the way they were treated." As Lee saw it, "There was a lot of dissension when the city came in to take over and build Connie Chambers on our land but no resistance because we weren't educated on how to fight it. In those days, the government talked and you listened, and you couldn't do anything about it. You just got run over."[19]

PUEBLO CENTER REDEVELOPMENT, REVIVED

Meanwhile, with the plan to double the size of La Reforma public housing in progress under the auspices of the THA, in late 1964 Mayor Davis and the city council separately revived the urban renewal plan, now called the Pueblo Center Redevelopment Project. Tucson's third version of an urban renewal plan now targeted eighty acres to the west and southwest of the CBD. The new incarnation curtailed the southern spread of the first two plans still further, stopping at Fourteenth Street, while adding some land on the north. It still focused on plans for a new community center, government facilities, a transportation center, and shopping areas, but now contained no residences, apartments, or public housing of any kind. Although residential structures comprised 70 percent of the buildings on the existing site, the city sought to supersede such land uses and, by extension, such land users. Just south of Fourteenth Street, the city proposed a sunken new east-west highway, the Butterfield Stage Route, which, if built, would have further separated the urban renewal area from the remaining barrios.

Although many elected officials still preferred a form of "private" urban renewal that did not entail federal funding, the business commu- nity showed renewed interest in a bolder plan. The Build America Better Committee of the National Association of Real Estate Boards produced "An Action Program for Tucson," which drew sharp contrasts between modern Tucson and the "mud huts a stone's throw from the central business dis- trict," and stressed that the commercial center of *la calle* had "no future." If it were to be "cleared of present structures and completely redeveloped," the realtors opined, this could "open the heart of the city to view by creating a magnificent new entrance from the freeway to downtown." Tucson Broadcasters, an organization representing twelve radio and three televi- sion stations, spoke out strongly in favor of a community center that could host conventions. Roy Drachman, as chairman of the Citizens Committee on Municipal Blight, and Vincent Lung, Tucson's assistant city manager and coordinator of community development, obtained "an expert stamp of approval" from key officials of the Urban Land Institute in April 1965— the same organization that would jump-start plans for redevelopment of St. Thomas in New Orleans three decades later. Tucson's ULI consultants agreed that the proposed community center and cultural facilities would give the downtown area a necessary "shot in the arm." Moreover, at a time when Tucson faced signs of economic decline, reactivating the demolition and construction industry enabled backers to see urban renewal as "in- stant industry."[20] Buoyed by new supporters, the council voted to reinstate the urban renewal program and create a new Department of Community Development.

On March 1, 1966, Tucson's voters approved the city's plan to borrow up $14 million to support the Pueblo Center Redevelopment Project. Still con- troversial, the project passed by a margin of 10,193 to 7,129. The surprisingly low number of total votes reflected both a 32 percent turnout and the more salient fact that the city permitted only those 55,000 citizens who owned Tucson real estate and paid property taxes to cast ballots. In short, only about 3 percent of the Tucson's population of 300,000 actually voted to approve the plan. Moreover, the various citizens' committees associated with urban renewal planning since the 1950s had all failed to include membership from citizens who actually lived in the communities targeted for clearance. Taken together, especially given that more than 80 percent of those to be displaced

Figure 8.2. Tucson's Urban Renewal Clears Eighty Acres of the Downtown Barrio
An aerial photograph taken in 1969 shows the extent of Tucson's urban renewal
clearance south of the downtown.
Credit: Photo © Fred Wehrman photography, 1969, files of Lydia Otero.

were renters, very few of those most directly affected by the proposed purge
had much of any opportunity to weigh in on it. Ultimately, Tucson's civic
leadership cared most about altering negative aspects of the city's image, so
it made no sense to consult those judged responsible for that negativity. As
Drachman put it,

> We must have a convention facility so that we can develop a more complete
> image as a place to visit. We must expand our cultural facilities. We must do
> something to clean up and clear out the unsightly near-downtown slum areas.

Cleaning up and clearing out meant removal of a population that was 91 percent Mexican American, African American, or Chinese. Although drastically scaled down from the gargantuan 392-acre original vision, the Pueblo
Center project nonetheless cleared 80 acres of the downtown barrio, said to
be the most densely populated place in Arizona (figure 8.2).[21]

Not coincidentally, the deeply racialized project targeted the commercial center of the *Tucsonenses* community and also displaced a substantial
percentage of the city's other nonwhite residents. The city's *Final Relocation
Report* gave the transition the best possible spin, insisting that "human

renewal was linked with the goal of physical renewal." The report immediately made clear, though, that this essentially meant replacing one set of
humans with another, leading to the "upgrading of the families, individuals,
and businesses in the target area." "By the mid-1960s," Otero observes, "'la
calle' had become synonymous with 'old,' 'dilapidated,' and 'dangerous.'"
In other words, its denizens faced a catch 22—they were forbidden to improve their homes and businesses and then victimized for the failure to do
so. In this way, over the course of two decades of manipulated disinvestment, the area's designation as a "slum" became a self-fulfilling prophecy. If
Tucson's leaders had termed the area merely "blighted," Arizona law would
have required redevelopment to be primarily residential, but, because of
the "slum" designation, the district could be redeveloped for any purpose
(figure 8.3). Because the changeover of the community could be couched in
the language of "highest and best" land uses, and because "social evils" could
be replaced by "carefully designed facilities," city officials had no need to
deploy the language of race.[22] Confronted with the center of a community,
city officials preferred to substitute a community center.

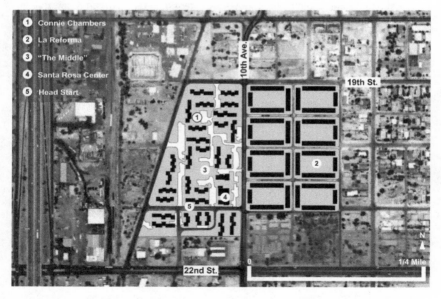

Figure 8.3. Connie Chambers and La Reforma Public Housing Developments
Residents often referred to the Connie Chambers development, completed in 1967,
as New Reforma, since the courtyard dwellings of La Reforma were located just across
the street.
Credit: Map produced by author with Kristin Simonson and Jonathan Tarleton.

Seeking to reclaim the affection of suburbanites and attract new visitors, the Tucson Community Center (TCC) opened in 1971. Later renamed the Tucson Convention Center, its arrival epitomized the fiscal imperatives of urban renewal, since it focused on the city-region as a whole.[23] To the promoters of Greater Tucson, the city-region's economic future seemed to reside in enhanced tourism and convention business and cultural programming, not to mention the perpetually elusive efforts to regain downtown retail vibrancy. As Schorr had put it in 1961, "Because we do not live in a neighborhood only but in a *total* city, it is in the interest of every Tucsonian to have a sound downtown area." Still, as Fairbanks has shown for other cities in Arizona, Texas, and New Mexico, even when cities are dominated by a business elite, urban renewal proponents experienced increasing difficulty making arguments that projects would be good for "the city as a whole."[24]

In Tucson, many of those forced from the hundreds of homes and businesses demolished by the urban renewal process resisted their eviction, forcing the city to file condemnation suits on 117 different parcels. About half of those who owned properties accepted the buyout money offered as the result of appraisals, even though these marked the low point of valuation following two decades of disinvestment and did not take into account the enhancements likely to result from the forthcoming new construction. A court ruling in 1969 eventually determined that some of the increased property values due to accrue from neighboring new civic facilities ought to be factored in when making appraisals, but this interpretation came far too late for most owners to obtain fair value for their homes and businesses. And, as Otero points out, because renters made up the overwhelming majority of affected residents but had no legal standing to sue, "No court records document their dissatisfaction." Moreover, as attorney Carlos Robles observed at the time, even those owners who could have fought the city did not do so, partly due to cultural and language barriers: "When the city threatened suits against them if they didn't move, they left without going to court. They thought there was something criminal about courts. They didn't understand that these were civil cases." As Hector Morales, the Ward 5 city councilor at the time, later recalled, "I tried to stop urban renewal. I had families come to me, and I tried to help them. But the council refused to give them a break."[25]

The city's *Final Relocation Report* candidly recounts that "many site residents" distrusted the relocation staff. First, they resented the long period of uncertainty that had preceded demolition and blamed the staff that "symbolized this project." Second, many of those who owned property in the urban renewal project area complained about the "prices and methods" used to acquire their homes, especially since the appraisers came from out of state. Some in the barrio, residents protested, were rewarded because they proved adept at negotiating good prices, while others failed to obtain enough compensation to be able to purchase a comparable home elsewhere. Ultimately, out of nearly three hundred households that still needed to be relocated once the clearance finally moved forward, forty-four were able to purchase their own homes. Much of this limitation, presumably, had to do with low incomes, but urban renewal officials matter-of-factly stated the larger problem: "Tucson loan officers were often reluctant to extend loans to project residents." Cress Lander, who served on the housing authority board during this period and soon became the long-serving head of the city's Community Services Department, pointed out that the relocation of homeowners from the barrio proved to be one of the project's greatest shortcomings. "When they had urban renewal they basically bought out all of the Hispanic and black and low-income people around Meyer Street. They were supposed to get a new form of FHA deal that [meant] they could have a new house for only seventy to eighty dollars a month in payments." Unfortunately, "The administration at that time allowed the developers to sell these houses to just anybody in Tucson," so the "good deals" did not go to the intended beneficiaries. Instead, as Lander recalled with frustration, the FHA program "ended up serving higher-income people," and these loans enabled just twelve families from the razed part of the barrio to purchase a home.[26]

As for renters, the city's first priority was to protect their landlords. Fearful that well-founded rumors about property sales to the City of Tucson would cause "tenants to vacate units early in the project," landlords got the city to delay notifying tenants about the need for them to vacate until after the property had been duly acquired. The city still gave tenants ninety days to relocate and proudly noted that "there were no evictions." That said, finding new homes for those departing households that asked for assistance proved to be "one of the biggest problems faced by the relocation staff." Despite optimistic predictions about the availability of inexpensive housing made at the time the city applied for urban renewal funding, once relocation began, "this anticipated housing supply shrank drastically," due to competing demand from new employees in the aircraft and mining industries, as well as from university students and winter visitors. The urban renewal staff also soon discovered that "Tucson realty companies usually did not handle rentals for low-income families or individuals" and that market sales prices "were often out-of-reach for low-income project residents." Moreover, despite Tucson's antidiscrimination ordinance passed in 1965, many black relocates faced considerable resistance from potential landlords.[27]

The relocation staff interviewed some of the families who chose substandard housing in an effort to understand why. One Mexican American woman with seven children moved into a windowless home with a sagging kitchen floor and unventilated bathroom so that she could remain nearby in the barrio:

> Although public housing was strongly suggested, she adamantly refused to move. Uneducated herself, she felt a strong allegiance to the local school and did not wish to move to another school district. Also, as in many poverty families, possessions such as chickens and a garden are highly valued. One cannot raise chickens in public housing. Therefore, this mother chose to remain in the substandard home that she could afford on her low income.

An elderly, single, black veteran also chose to remain in the area, even though it meant living in a substandard dwelling with inadequate heating or plumbing. When queried, he explained that the new home was "private, quiet, and close to the central business district," and rented for only twenty dollars a month. "I'm satisfied," he noted, "and it is just about what I can afford to pay." As the relocation report put it, "His comment could be the words of any of the residents who moved to substandard housing." In the end, Tucson city officials seemed to understand why some displaced residents preferred to move into other substandard housing rather than try life in public housing. Private housing, however low in quality, "represents a social environment comparable to that of the old home. The substandard homes are primarily located close to the central business district with cheap restaurants, stores and taverns nearby." Such private homes also provided greater perceived freedoms, since they had "none of the aura of regulations linked with public housing." Taken together, the paucity of written accounts about the purging of the *Tucsonenses* community does not tell the whole story. As Lydia Otero observes, "Although those displaced by urban renewal did not come together in large numbers to protest, many opposed their removal in ways that remain undocumented."[28] And collective memory has remained a form of resistance.

THE RISE OF CONNIE CHAMBERS

The Connie Chambers Homes project, designed by the firm of Edson and Goldblatt, opened in the fall of 1967, just as the nearby downtown demolition ramped up. Named in memory of the former THA executive director who had died in 1965, the THA promised to give priority to those displaced from the urban renewal area. With two hundred new units becoming available, plus additional vacancies at the adjacent La Reforma, the resource at first seemed to be an appealing way for the 161 families and 120 individuals forced out of the Pueblo Center Redevelopment area to find new homes that were little more than a ten-minute walk from the razed parts of the barrio.

By August 1967, sixty-six families from the urban renewal zone had applied for residence in what they usually called "New Reforma," but soon became known as "the projects," or "The PJays." THA executive director Paul McCoy conceded that "not all families from the urban renewal area will qualify for residence in the housing project" but insisted that "we will have room for all those who do qualify." Once again, the availability of public housing depended on what it meant to "qualify." On the surface, the THA framed qualification around issues of residency and income. Households needed to have lived in Arizona for a year and within Pima County for at least six months, and they needed to have incomes lower than $3,000 unless they were supporting an unusually large number of children. Rents, which included utilities, varied from $28 to $78 per month, depending on family size. Tucson's urban renewal staff expected "public housing to be "a major relocation resource," and estimated that fully 40 percent of the "site occupants" would go there. To the surprise of many, however, only thirty-six families from the barrios razed to build the community center or the new public housing itself actually moved into either Connie Chambers or La Reforma by 1970.[29]

The housing authority did not retain records of these early tenants, but the *Final Relocation Report* issued by Tucson's redevelopment agency coupled with various newspaper accounts and oral histories provide some sense of the variety of reasons why public housing officials resisted some tenants and some tenants resisted public housing. First off, for 120 lodgers and other single individuals purged from the barrio, "family" public housing simply was, by definition, not a viable alternative. Many larger households presumably failed to meet income or residency requirements. Although public housing rents sometimes compared favorably to what was available elsewhere in the barrio, a survey of displaced households conducted by the Tucson Redevelopment Agency in 1965 had found that "the average monthly income of the non-white residents was less than $100 per month," suggesting that public housing rents could be out of reach, especially for larger families.[30]

The public housing option simply held no appeal for many people, either because its social environment seemed both isolating and socially disruptive, or because its design bore little relation to preferred modes of living. As resident Sarah Valencia complained to a reporter in 1970, "There is no quiet here, always disorder, confusion, mischief. And vandalism, always they are breaking things, windows, cars. There are too many children running around." She much preferred her old home in the barrio, even though "the roof leaked and the wallpaper was falling off." At least there she had her old friends, whereas "none of them moved [to Connie Chambers], and I only see them once in a while." Another woman said she was dissuaded from public housing by a friend who pointed out that her children would have no yard to play in and that "everyone lived too close together, and there was a lot of stealing going on." The relocation staff interviewed twelve of the thirty-six households that moved into public housing. Respondents discounted the problem of excessive regulations or inspections, and most found modern plumbing and spaciousness of their public housing apartments "definitely a physical improvement over their old homes." That said, ten of twelve complained about what the staff termed "the children problem"—groups of kids "uncontrolled by parents, [who] roam noisily about late at night annoying neighbors and each other." Many objected to "feuds between neighbors that sometimes led to actual fights." A social worker noted that the combined population of La Reforma and Connie Chambers included 1,615 legal residents but estimated the real total closer to 2,000 due to the presence of extra "relatives and illegitimate children." At base, urban renewal officials blamed the parents and the conceptual design of the project: "Because families are concentrated in a small area, parents themselves have problems with neighbors and there is little energy left to control the children. . . . While public housing has represented physical upgrading for many project families," its "close, community living" has also "presented new interpersonal living problems." Such commentary provided little insight given that most households had presumably come from markedly denser living environments elsewhere.[31]

Connie Chambers nonetheless did mark a significant environmental shift (figures 8.3–8.4). In contrast to the barrio composed primarily of one-story structures, much of the Connie Chambers architecture contained two-story parts. This increased the perception of density, even though the project offered large expanses of open space between buildings. At least La Reforma had been organized around internal courtyards, a more culturally familiar form for the project's Mexican American majority.

At the time Connie Chambers opened, the THA board remained aloof and suspicious of its low-income tenants. This quickly changed once the mayor appointed Cress Lander to the board. But Lander, an African American who had good relations with both the business community and the civil rights community, soon found himself "out of sync" with the rest of the board. Lander recalls that the board supported midnight inspections of public housing apartments so that "they could see if a man was living in the house" but was not on the lease. Lander objected to a level of paternalist intrusiveness that "made it difficult for people to live a normal life," a surveillance that he notes was made possible by a project design that "wanted everything open." Lander refused to allow inspections to happen and took steps to acquaint the board with the actual clientele. When he first joined, the board used to meet over a "nice dinner" on the tenth floor of the Pioneer

Figure 8.4. Connie Chambers Project: Palms and Problems
Despite its appearance as a motel-like complex fringed by palms, many in Tucson
considered Connie Chambers to be a dangerous place to live in or visit.
Credit: Courtesy of Poster Frost Mirto, Inc.

Hotel. This was an elite institution well distant from both the agency headquarters and the public housing, and "there was no way for a public housing
resident to appear before the board. They didn't allow people to come with
any kind of grievance or statement or recommendation. They were shut
out. I told them that they couldn't meet in the Pioneer Hotel and be the
board for the Housing Authority." Lander insisted that they meet instead at
the Connie Chambers site so that residents could take part. Early in 1968 at
Lander's urging, newly elected mayor Jim Corbett, a Democrat, forced just
such a meeting and attended it himself. Paul McCoy, the THA executive
director in charge of La Reforma and Connie Chambers, then "got up and
said that 'there's a nigger in the woodpile' because we were being forced to
move the meetings down to the project," Lander recalled. "The mayor was
there and asked for his resignation. Not only did the mayor ask for his resignation but the *rest* of the board all resigned, all except me." Mayor Corbett
then named Lander board chairman and filled the remainder with new
people. According to the *Citizen*, this was all no more than a "temporary
uproar," caused by Democrats seeking to replace McCoy with a "closer political friend." McCoy actually remained in his post, while the THA board

quietly embarked on various reform efforts. At Lander's urging, by summer 1968 the THA finally appointed a bilingual employee at a project whose occupants were two-thirds Mexican American, created a tenants' council "to allow tenants some voice in the affairs of their projects," invited a tenant representative to attend THA meetings, and added a nighttime foot patrolman.[32] Hardly the same story as the contemporaneous "tenant-oriented majority" in Boston, but still hinting at progressive politics, even in Tucson.

Despite Lander's leadership, project-based public housing remained a contentious issue. Completion of the additional public housing in the Santa Rosa barrio south of downtown reignited concerns about whether this represented the right development direction for such a centrally located neighborhood. As early as 1972, the city began asking HUD for permission to "close out" La Reforma, and, in 1974, a *Star* editorial stated that building the two projects had delivered "an instant ghetto." The *Star* favored dispersing the residents and replacing both projects with middle-class homeownership opportunities targeted to "non minority" families so as to "bring a new balance to the neighborhood and its schools and bring an economic lift to the neighborhood and to downtown, just a few blocks away." With Tucson's leaders having already purged the poorest from the urban renewal area, the paper wished to see the remainder of low-income households moved out as well.[33]

Meanwhile, the city continued to consider new ways to upgrade residential areas located beyond the bounds of the Pueblo Center clearance. Even after the Pueblo Center renewal plan cleared eighty acres, the city and its consultants never abandoned the larger aim of eliminating all substandard housing. Throughout the 1960s and into the 1970s, the city set out plans for a broader program of "community renewal." As a report by the planning firm of Candeub, Fleissig titled "Preliminary Proposals for Area Treatment" put it in 1968, "The Community Renewal Program represents an ongoing continuous effort to replace, maintain, conserve and develop portions of the Tucson community to provide a good living environment for its residents." This meant that residents of the barrios spared by the first phase continually felt under siege and distrustful of the city's motives, unsure what "treatment" their "area" would receive. In 1968, the Community Services Department's consultants conducted nearly a thousand household interviews to determine the "prevalence of social problems." They defined such problems with an aggregate rank based on poverty, low education, broken homes, welfare cases, overcrowding, presence of the elderly, renter status, and unemployment. Not surprisingly, they found that a key concentration of "#1 rank problems" remained in the barrios just south of the urban renewal clearance, in the vicinity of La Reforma and Connie Chambers. In addition to economic, educational, and environmental factors, the city's list of "blight indices" also included factors such as "population with Spanish surname as a percent of total population" and "Negroes as a percent of total population." Even if race and ethnicity did covary with many indicators of socioeconomic distress, labeling minority status as itself a marker of blight is as revealing as it is impolitic. With "social problems" duly racialized, Tucson officials embarked on an effort to use public housing as a means to scatter the barrio.[34]

SCATTERING PUBLIC HOUSING

With about four hundred Tucson households on the waiting list for public housing (a modest number but still larger than the entire stock), the city sought to acquire additional units without building new projects. This philosophical preference for deconcentration both anticipated and mirrored the larger federal effort to shift more of the nation's subsidized housing onto a certificate and voucher basis through the Section 8 program introduced in 1974. Section 8, however, relies on the private market, whereas Tucson's leaders wished to scatter the city's publicly owned stock as well.

Cress Lander began working directly for the city in 1969 as head of the Model Cities division of the Community Planning and Development Department and gradually took on increased leadership roles. He was chiefly responsible the decision to incorporate Tucson's housing authority into the city's Community Services Department in 1971 and headed the combined department all the way until 1992. His move to make the THA part of city government had several repercussions. First, since those who had crafted Arizona's enabling legislation for housing authorities distrusted the very concept, Arizona law denied them the power to own land; moving the THA into a larger community services city agency that had no such restrictions made new property acquisition much simpler. Second, moving the THA into this particular city agency set public housing on a much more spatially integrated course, embedding it in larger questions of neighborhood well-being in ways that differ from most other cities. In this way, Tucson's approach to poverty governance retained—and enhanced—the role of the public sector. Instead of a THA concerned with projects, Tucson's public housing would be based in an agency concerned with economic development at larger community scales. For Lander, however, taking control of the city's public housing portfolio offered the opportunity to shift away from the old "project" mentality completely.[35]

For both social and political reasons, Lander wanted Tucson's public stock to grow in a scattered manner. As he phrased it, "I had a plan to decentralize housing, and that's what we were able to do. We were able to get units into all of the councilmanic wards in Tucson." With sites scattered across the city, "We used to brag that we had 1,500 units and the mayor didn't know where they were." Eventually, Tucson managed to distribute its housing into four hundred different sites, many of them no more than a single house. As Lander observed, "When we had fifteen hundred units and the mayor didn't know where they were, then we didn't *have* public housing—unless the people living in it told the people next door that they were living in public housing." Tucson's urban renewal proponents had scattered the residents of the barrio unwillingly; Lander's second-generation scatterplot purported to do so more proactively, focused on diversifying the city's neighborhoods. Because Tucson's public housing chiefly housed Mexican Americans, blacks, and Native Americans, scattering it "had a big effect on the desegregation of the schools." Although Tucson nominally had integrated schools, having neighborhood-based schools in substantially segregated neighborhoods meant that, basically, "the schools were still segregated." Moving low-income non-Anglos all over town helped alter schools as well as housing.[36]

THE END OF LA REFORMA

With public housing projects politically unpopular and Tucson headed down a new policy path of scattered-site development, the ultimate fate of La Reforma—whether the new part or the original—soon looked bleak. It had taken thirty years to build 360 units of project-based family public housing and, within five years, the city had already commenced serious discussions about how to get rid of it. This, too, would take nearly thirty years to accomplish. As the city explored HUD's willingness to let it tear down the older portion of its "instant ghetto," residents also joined the fray. In 1972, a group calling itself "La Reforma Angry Tenants," claiming to represent both parts of the development, publicly threatened a rent strike to protest inadequate maintenance. They complained about "leaky stoves, furnaces, and water heaters [that] present a health as well as a fire hazard." They added that "cracks in walls, holes in floors, [and] inadequate plumbing make living itself a hazard." The disgruntled tenants objected to unchecked vandalism, drinking, and drug use within the two projects and resented being charged extra for broken windows since these were "items over which they have no control." They also objected to policies that raised their rent immediately after they left welfare or got a better job, commenting that "we want to live better, but how can we when we keep getting hit down each time we raise our heads?" They "insisted" on a six-month delay in such rent increases. As tenants fumed about conditions, many others in the city schemed to get rid of the problems by getting rid of the projects. By 1975, the Tucson Trade

Bureau proposed the "removal" of both La Reforma and Connie Chambers, even though it recognized that a mass relocation project could result in "resentment, increased social problems and community disruption." A *Citizen* editorial praised the trade bureau for exercising "the kind of initiative required from the community to keep the ball rolling toward a vigorous, healthy inner city."[37]

As the wrecking ball swung closer to La Reforma, housing officials blamed lack of funding for its maintenance woes. To Cress Lander, upkeep "was always the battle." It was "one thing to get your subsidy in terms of the rent," he noted, but the "other big battle was to get some money for the ongoing maintenance and upkeep of the housing." Eventually, in 1979, Tucson again applied to HUD for permission to shut down the old part of La Reforma, promising to clear the site and replace the lost units with scattered-site public housing. In addition to skeptics at HUD, Lander faced many local critics who resisted the idea of tearing down such a major source of well-located public housing. "A lot of people thought it was a real nice place, but it wasn't," Lander insists. "La Reforma looked like a million dollars" because it was brick construction, but he contended that it was structurally unsound due to a lack of steel reinforcement caused by materials constraints during the war. Part of the problem, he asserted, is that the concrete floors had been built too thin, only one to three inches, and once they cracked, all sorts of problems ensued. The city provided HUD with city and federal engineering reports to demonstrate that such shortcomings made it "unsuitable" for housing and "not feasible" for renovation. Tucson's housing and community development officials also considered the current *policy* to be structurally unsound, since it "contributes to undue concentration of low income families in the area which is inconsistent with city and HUD objectives." Lander justified the closure mostly in physical design terms but also recognized the social struggle that this entailed. "We just had to get rid of people a little bit at a time," he recalled, but Lander and other Tucson officials felt certain that scattered-site public housing offered better options than projects. Ultimately, HUD acquiesced, and demolition commenced in November 1983. It proved easier to disperse buildings than people. AAA Demolition happily sold off the La Reforma salvage, characterized as being in excellent condition—"mission tiles, 2 million kiln-fired Red Jumbo bricks, clear lumber with a decorative V-groove that was used for the ceilings, wood doors, evaporative coolers, and gas heaters."[38]

With La Reforma's tenants relocated, the city struggled to redevelop the empty site. Emily Nottingham, who began working for the city in 1978 and would eventually be in charge of its housing and community development programs, took part in the disposition of La Reforma. "We didn't want the property to be an abandoned nuisance," she recalled. The city wished to "redevelop it for the private market and bring some more private sector investment in and get rid of the 'donut hole' in the neighborhood." Unfortunately, the city initially sold the site to a poorly capitalized developer who went under, and subsequent development efforts also faltered.[39]

Just as Tucson's downtown barrio had given way to overstated hopes of a private sector revival under the banner of urban renewal, public housing renewal seemed the next logical step. La Reforma fell first, but the demise of Connie Chambers would not be far behind.

9

The Fall of Connie Chambers and the Rise of Posadas Sentinel

THE FALL OF CONNIE CHAMBERS

With La Reforma demolished by 1984, the city gradually turned its attention to Connie Chambers, its largest remaining family public housing development. As with most other urban public housing developments, residents recall its history with a mixture of nostalgia and clear-eyed skepticism. It is therefore easy to understand both the CSD's interest in redeveloping the project and the reluctance of others to see this happen. In 2000, during the HOPE VI transformation process, a local nonprofit worked with ten Connie Chambers youth to produce a bilingual collective memoir, entitling it *Don't Look at Me Different / No Me Veas Diferente*, intending it to counter stereotypes by presenting "Voices from the Projects." Based mostly on interviews with residents, the memoir provides a balanced historical account, emphasizing the lingering pride of residents about the strengths of their community without glossing over serious shortcomings and dangerous conditions. Taken together, residents recall an early period of stability, with little evidence of turf battles between the La Reforma and Connie Chambers sides of the development. Into the 1970s, they describe a world of "two-parent families [with] everybody looking out for each other" and an active Connie Chambers Neighborhood Association.[1]

A key turning point came in February 1975 with the murder of twenty-one-year-old Connie Chambers resident Bobby Ray Harris, gunned down in the project's Santa Rosa Center gym in front of one hundred witnesses. Carrie Bryant Joe, who lived in Connie Chambers as a youth from 1979 to 1982, remembered the lingering effect of the Harris killing, especially since the killer had come from the La Reforma side. "A lot of people back then were real close and when that happened it made things a little bit more complicated and worse." The murder put a "burden on the families" and left people "scared to socialize with people outside the area." By the early 1980s, Arnold Moreno recalled, "Everything was changing. The people in the neighborhood weren't the same anymore. There was more alcoholism than anything else. More drug addicts." Ismael Galindo, whose family moved into Connie Chambers in 1980, remembered the nighttime comradeship in the "Middle," the area at the center of the project where Coleta Avenue intersected Twentieth Street and "where everybody hung out when the sun went down, tagging on walls, getting drunk, getting high." He also recalled the danger—"all the gunshots, police sirens, and the helicopter lights flashing through the windows nightly." "Everybody from the pjays got along well," he continued, "but anybody from another neighborhood wasn't allowed to walk through the projects. If anybody was caught walking through at night, that person would get beat down by whoever was hanging out in the Middle." At the same time, however, Galindo praised the availability of the Santa Rosa Center, with its indoor gym and many programmed activities. Adolfo (Chico) Figueroa recalled block parties and Thanksgiving football, but also rampant drug use and car break-ins. He resisted the notion that Connie Chambers residents constituted a "gang" but acknowledged that outsiders "weren't welcomed." "They'd come here to start trouble, they wouldn't come here to get along." Repeatedly, residents blamed most of the "trouble" on "outsiders" intent on vandalism. To curtail graffiti, in 1986 the CSD hired Chicano artist Alfred Quiroz to supervise project youth in painting seven murals he designed with them on "key walls" of the development. The murals depicted everything from mountains, jungles, and beaches to Aztec wind gods and internationally collaborating astronauts. One depicted five faces, representing the unity of the project's Anglo, Chinese, Native American, Chicano, and African American residents, and another proudly called out the name of the "10th Avenue Projects" (figure 9.1).[2]

Seeking funds from the federal Public Housing Drug Elimination Program in 1991, the city presented a dire picture of Connie Chambers, noting that fully 42 percent of households had vacated the development in the preceding year. The CSD evicted a few of those households, but a larger number had simply "abandoned their homes." Most tenants who left did not explicitly document their reasons, but the CSD blamed drug-related crime: "Because the neighborhood has become a dangerous area to live in, tenants will not stay, even if their need for housing is critical." With the arrival of crack cocaine in the late 1980s, the Tucson police department documented an upsurge in arrests on Connie Chambers property, rising from an already-high 300 in 1987 to 566 by 1991. Police reported a "call load" of more than one hundred per month throughout this period. By 1991, larceny, assault, narcotics arrests, vandalism, disorderly conduct, and liquor violations each occurred on a weekly or near-weekly basis in the development. Seeking to discourage drive-by drug trafficking, the CSD posted signs against trespassing and loitering and installed gates across several throughways to create a series of dead-ends. More generally, city

Figure 9.1. 10th Avenue Projects Mural, Connie Chambers
The Community Services Department asked Chicano artist Alfred Quiroz to work with
youth from Connie Chambers to create a series of murals as a means to discourage
graffiti, including this one calling out the name of the "10th Avenue Projects."
Source: Charlene Vega (2000), youth photographer, Voices, Inc. From *Don't Look at Me
Different / No Me Veas Diferente*, 133.

leaders came to regard Connie Chambers itself as a dead-end and sought
out alternatives.[3]

When Cress Lander retired as director of the CSD in 1992, his colleague
Emily Nottingham succeeded him on an interim basis. As she put it, the CSD
started to focus on Connie Chambers in the early 1990s, because it "was our
one development that felt like 'the projects'":

> Although occupied and relatively well maintained, it had its own little gang,
> the PJays. It was referred to as "the projects," and the neighborhood didn't like
> it. There were a lot of tenant complaints and tenant-to-tenant disagreements.
> We didn't think it was functioning well.

Karen Thoreson, who came to Tucson as CSD director in 1993 after having
headed the housing authority in tony Boulder, Colorado, reacted even more
harshly. "Connie Chambers frankly just offended me," Thoreson recalled.
"It was old public housing and in poor repair. It was crime ridden, but you
couldn't do anything about it." Just as bad, directly east of the site she found
the aftermath of La Reforma, "a big vacant lot full of broken glass where
folks would shoot up and drink beer. It was just a disaster, just disgusting."
She blamed the public housing, past and present, for causing disinvestment
in "everything around it." Thoreson, with Nottingham now as her deputy,
immediately thought to try for a HOPE VI grant but didn't think the city
would qualify.[4]

Initially, the department tried to get funding from HUD's MROP (Major Reconstruction of Obsolete Projects) program but failed twice. In 1994, the department launched a community development effort to assess the larger Santa Rosa neighborhood because, even without money, "at least we could plan." Thoreson and Tucson planner William Vasko worked closely with a team led by architect-planner Corky Poster from the University of Arizona's Roy P. Drachman Institute for Land and Regional Development Studies (a community outreach unit named after the legendary developer and university benefactor). Among many questions, Poster's team asked, "What is the future of Connie Chambers?" and "Can we end its isolation?" Without specifying just who this "we" should be, the planners recognized that they operated on contested terrain. They asked: "Can we construct a future for Greater Santa Rosa that satisfies the legitimate concerns and interests of its diverse populations? Is there room in the area for everyone to win?" The plan stopped short of answering such questions. As Emily Nottingham put it, Poster was involved in "a lot of shuttle diplomacy" due to the "lack of a shared vision" and high level of "discord in the neighborhood unrelated to Connie Chambers." The plan—much of which would eventually be implemented—proposed multiple alternatives for placing housing and community facilities on the former La Reforma site, including a new Drachman School and community center. It also envisioned an enhanced commitment to in-fill housing in the broader neighborhood, led by nonprofit organizations, as well as investment of "substantial and sustained capital and maintenance resources" to sustain Connie Chambers. The plan also proposed a variety of economic development and social services initiatives, but stopped short of proposing resources or asserting consensus.[5]

The Community Services Department, because it was more than a housing authority, remained committed to broader community development efforts. The CSD, in collaboration with Poster, successfully applied for a HOPE VI planning grant in 1995, targeted to both Connie Chambers and its surrounding environs. To prepare the application, Poster and CSD teamed up with TAG Associates, the Boston-based housing consulting firm led by Jeff Lines. Indicative of the ways that many HOPE VI constellations share stars and histories, decades earlier Poster's roommate at Harvard had been Harry Spence, and Lines had served as chief financial and administrative officer for the Boston Housing Authority during Spence's receivership. Spence led Poster to Lines, but "Once they got the grant," Lines recalled, "the mayor and the housing authority wanted it to be local. Corky was local."[6] Poster and the CSD public sector leadership remained in the driver's seat and continued to pursue a broad neighborhood vision.

As Emily Nottingham framed it, "We really did want to do neighborhood work as well as public housing work." Like her deputy, CSD director

Thoreson wanted large-scale transformation, even if some of it proved un-realistic. "We had really big goals for that neighborhood," she recalls. "I thought I could stop teen pregnancy and change graduation rates over a short period of time." Short of that, she wanted to use HOPE VI to "help change the residents' lives, and then to bring investment to that neighbor-hood, while we invested in affordable housing development throughout the neighborhood."[7] Thoreson's idealism notwithstanding, CSD's top-down approach ensured that middle-class values would continue to come into conflict with the preferences of low-income residents.

As part of the $379,000 planning grant, Poster and the CSD deployed a bilingual team of neighborhood residents and students to conduct two surveys, one involving Connie Chambers residents and the other soliciting the opinions of those in the surrounding barrios. Based on responses from one hundred Connie Chambers residents (a 50 percent return), the planning team drew several important conclusions. Most important, perhaps, they estimated that 45 percent of the households wished to remain in the neigh-borhood following redevelopment. The actual question as posed read, "If you had the opportunity to move into a new or rehabilitated public housing unit, where would you rather live?" It then gave two choices: the "same neighborhood" or some "other neighborhood." Ambiguity is encoded into both the question and the answers, since respondents might welcome "new" but not "rehabilitated" public housing or might be unclear about whether this referred a new multifamily project or one of Tucson's scattered-site homes. Similarly, they might view staying in the "same neighborhood" as meaning a return to the current site of the project itself or might interpret "neighborhood" as referring to the broader environs. Given the considerable interest voiced in leaving the neighborhood, Poster and the CSD judged that retaining eighty public housing units on-site (a number reduced to sixty as of June 1996) would be sufficient to house all those who wished to remain. As Thoreson put it, the mix of units proposed for the site "represented what the residents said." She insisted, "We were really committed to involving the residents in this plan, and not simply shooing them away."[8]

The second survey, conducted in the surrounding barrios, revealed less reticence about such shooing. Most respondents, especially those answering in English, offered disparaging comments about the physical presence of Connie Chambers, though many remained uncertain about how many public housing residents ought to remain on-site or in the neighborhood following redevelopment. Clearly, however, many neighbors wanted change: "Tear it down." "Low-income housing should be dispersed throughout Tucson." "Get rid of Connie Chambers." "It should be leveled." "Get rid of the Riffraff." "Transform the area so that it resembles the rest of the neighborhood." "Split it up, take it to a different neighborhood in the city." "Rip it down, [it's a] bad idea [to have] all poor people together." "Get rid of it and place them in low cost housing in different parts of the city." "Everyone should move." Or, most succinctly, "Bulldozer!"[9]

TENANT ORGANIZING

In dealing with its constituency both within and beyond Connie Chambers, Tucson's Community Services Department needed both to organize residents and to appease neighbors. HOPE VI sagas range from developments with strong and active residents' councils to situations where a housing authority essentially has had to invent a resident group to talk to for the purposes of demonstrating necessary community involvement. The Connie Chambers to Posadas Sentinel story is closer to the latter mode. Olga Osterhage, who oversaw the redevelopment for CSD, acknowledged that "we were more on the weak end. We worked to form a residents' council during the time of the planning grant. There was a lot of apathy there. They definitely didn't feel united for a cause." Determined to use HOPE VI as a vehicle for transformation, the CSD itself had to court resident "involvement"—a far cry from the proactive insistence of Edna Bynoe at Orchard Park or the withering demands of Barbara Jackson at St. Thomas. Osterhage and her colleagues sought to identify "born leaders." Emily Nottingham, then the CSD deputy director, concurred with Osterhage: "We tried to form a tenant council early on because we wanted them to have a voice. We spent a lot of time putting on barbecues, things to invite tenants to, to become organized themselves." All in the department also praise Grace Johnson, a single parent in her twenties who, CSD director Thoreson said, "was really a champion." Johnson, as president of the residents' council beginning in January 1996, "became the spokesman." She told the *Star,* "I want to be optimistic. I want to believe that the federal government and the city have our best interests at heart." Johnson and her two-year-old daughter did not intend to make Connie Chambers a permanent home, but Johnson wanted to use her remaining time at the development to help the CSD "make it better for people." She sometimes struggled to gain participation but doggedly "knocked on door after door asking people about their concerns and recruiting them to come to public meetings."[10]

As the CSD quickly found out, however, the city did not hold a monopoly on the wish to organize tenants. Neighborhood activist Pedro Gonzales, who spent his youth as a Connie Chambers resident after his family was twice displaced from homes in the urban renewal area, emerged as a persistent critic of the city's intentions and tactics. As the HOPE VI process took hold, Gonzales did his own organizing, and remained deeply suspicious of the organizing done by the city. Gonzales and his family had doggedly lingered in the neighborhood and retained strong connections to Connie Chambers. "Because we'd lived there, they knew the family," Gonzales pointed out. "They trusted me, and a lot of the elderly there knew my mom and my dad. They called us and we went over there and talked to them. They were telling us that the city wanted to get the money and move them out." Gonzales took it upon himself to "make sure that the city didn't do what they did in the sixties to us." As Gonzales saw it, the city formed a "hand-picked committee" of residents, the "ones they could manipulate." "They made this young mother, Grace Johnson, the president, and they used her. To this day, I don't know what she got out of it, but she really went to bat for them." Gonzales said the city promised tenants money to start small businesses and played up the possibility of homeownership. "That was the thing they were selling us," he commented. "Our whole argument was that these were just false promises." It is certainly true that the city's HOPE VI team raised expectations about both resident businesses (related to property maintenance and entrepreneurship training) and homeownership early on. In the resident survey, for instance, the CSD noted, "Under HOPE VI, home ownership might be a possibility for some residents." Not surprisingly, fully 90 percent of respondents expressed interest in this. Subsidized homeownership in the adjacent neighborhoods did indeed become a notable part of the HOPE VI strategy, but nearly all of it was financially beyond the reach of Connie Chambers residents. The mythic pull of homeownership also held sway because the Tucson CSD and press continued to translate the HOPE acronym as "Homeownership Opportunities for People Everywhere" even though HUD's original version actually read "Homeownership and Opportunity," and had already been more realistically transmuted into "Housing Opportunities."[11]

Whatever their prospects for future homeownership, Connie Chambers residents continued to debate the extent of existing problems in the development. Although many chose to exit, those who remained tended to be less critical of its conditions than were city officials who needed to play up its deficiencies in order to obtain federal funding. When surveyed in 1996, three-quarters of respondents from Connie Chambers expressed support for the on-site management, and most also approved of building maintenance. At the same time, however, the vast majority complained about plumbing deficiencies and pest infestations, including health problems resulting from application of pesticides. Beyond such matters, residents most resented the stigma of being saddled with "the reputation of the Projects." Citywide, the turnover in Tucson's public housing approached 25 percent annually, far higher than in most cities.[12] Clearly, this bore little resemblance to cities where public housing residents held multigenerational attachments to particular projects.

ORGANIZING AGAINST THE TENANTS AND AGAINST THE CITY

Just as some in the community sought to help the tenants organize, others took the opportunity to organize against them—either explicitly through hostility to public housing or implicitly (and often ambivalently) through support for alternative neighborhood visions and investments. The initial challenges to the Posadas Sentinel HOPE VI planning process came from community groups: the Santa Rosa Neighborhood Association (with jurisdiction for the area between Eighteenth and Twenty-Second Streets that included Connie Chambers) and the Barrio Historico Neighborhood Association (covering the swath of gentrifying barrio between the Fourteenth Street edge of the urban renewal site and Eighteenth Street). Because HOPE VI had been rooted in a "Comprehensive Community Development Plan for the Greater Santa Rosa Area," these groups understandably claimed jurisdictional relevance. Both organizations gained seats on the Project Advisory Committee set up by the city, which had representation from nearly a dozen neighborhood organizations and service providers. The overall mix of opinions yielded a tense atmosphere. As the *Tucson Weekly* put it, "The neighbors are ticked, City of Tucson officials are defensive, and everybody seems to be dancing ever so gingerly around questions of race, culture and integration. . . . Improving Connie Chambers and installing services for the poor, neighborhood residents argue, will only bring down their housing values by increasing poverty levels."[13]

During March 1996, David "Chance" Reyes, as president of the Santa Rosa Neighborhood Association, and Mary Lou Heuett, as president of the Barrio Historico Neighborhood Association, escalated their concerted campaign to steer the HOPE VI project toward their own interests. As work on the planning grant progressed, they sent five letters in a single two-week period to the CSD complaining about various aspects of the process. They insisted on conducting their own survey of neighborhood residents because the one being implemented by Corky Poster and the CSD had ignored fifty-one of the fifty-two questions the associations wished to have asked. Poster responded that, even though the draft questionnaire had been shared with the Project Advisory Committee well in advance, the associations had submitted their "dramatically different" questions only after the questionnaires had already been delivered to the printer and had provided no Spanish translation. As a result, the contested neighborhood received dueling surveys, leaving the CSD frustrated by what it considered to be a misrepresentation of its intentions for the project. In May and June, the associations campaigned directly to the mayor and council, providing them with the results of their survey. The survey deployed a series of leading questions, such as, "Do you support the continued presence of Connie Chambers as a concentrated public housing project in its current location?" and "Do you think Connie Chambers residents in poverty should be given the choice of participating in the Section 8 Program (where residents are allowed to live in the location of their choice)?" Not surprisingly, the 122 respondents overwhelmingly indicated disapproval of Connie Chambers, affirmed that "concentrated public housing increases crime in the neighborhood," and expressed the wish to have public housing residents leave the area. Reyes and Heuett, joined by architect Jody Gibbs of the Centro de Arquitectura y Urbanismo para la Communidad, reported some of the survey's findings back to neighborhood residents. Their letter blasted the city for ignoring the results of the survey while "instead planning what appears to be a massive Urban Renewal Project encompassing 18 square blocks." They claimed that the enormous amount of money the city intended to spend on the project would be enough to give more than $50,000 to every resident of the area—an alternative use of funds that "would immediately solve the problem of poverty and home ownership."[14]

In July, still seeking to stop Tucson from receiving a HOPE VI implementation grant for the CSD's current plan, the neighborhood associations, joined by Gibbs, took it upon themselves to write a four-page letter directly to HUD secretary Henry Cisneros and three key HUD officials responsible for administering HOPE VI. They wished to "inform" HUD that the city's plan (which contained sixty on-site replacement public housing units) "is not supported by the residents of the neighborhood." Stressing that the neighborhood was predominantly minority and that it had five times the number of poor people as Connie Chambers itself, the neighborhood associations argued that the HOPE VI project merely "reconstructs on the same site yet another concentrated public housing project" where public housing residents "would stand out like a sore thumb." They claimed that Tucson's Community Services Department "has refused to listen to input from the neighborhood associations, has failed systematically and consistently to notify neighborhood residents of public meetings, and has controlled information and agendas to block the concerns and proposals from the neighborhood." If public housing residents were to remain in the neighborhood, they preferred that they be scattered across it, not housed on the old Connie Chambers site. The proposed plan, they claimed, would threaten the viability of the new school and adjacent community center. They attached their survey of neighborhood residents showing that "a majority will not use nor send their children to such a center if a concentrated public housing project is located across the street." Moreover, the neighborhood associations claimed, the plan failed to do enough to increase neighborhood homeownership or improve economic conditions. Equally bad, the proposed community center failed to provide the swimming pool that the neighborhood wanted, and included a drug treatment center that it had resisted.[15]

Although three organizations had cosigned the letter to Cisneros, Corky Poster contended that they really only represented the combative spirit of a single person, architect Jody Gibbs. Gibbs and Poster had run the Tucson Design Center together from 1974 to 1984 and had once been "like brothers, very close." Poster explained that Centro de Arquitectura y Urbanismo para la Communidad, the third institutional cosigner of the letter to HUD, was simply the remnant Spanish version of this defunct community design center's corporate name; it was an organization that had not actually employed anyone since the 1980s. "Jody uses it when he wants to sign things with other than his name" or "needs to have it in Spanish." Meanwhile, Poster continued, the second signatory was Gibbs's then-girlfriend, archaeologist Mary Lou Heuett, who served as president of the Barrio Historico Neighborhood Association. The third signatory, David "Chance" Reyes, president of the Barrio Santa Rosa neighborhood organization, was a friend of Gibbs's who soon moved back to his native Texas. As Poster saw it, Gibbs simply enjoyed being an obstructionist and wanted to support his "girlfriend that lived in the neighborhood in one of the gentrifying homes."[16]

Whatever the in-grown ties behind the complaint letter to HUD, however, it seems clear from the surveys that many more than three people in the neighborhood distrusted the city's affordable housing goals and motives. The CSD was worried enough to hire a Washington lobbyist firm, Bracy Williams & Company, to help with HUD relations and, in Tucson, made the case that the authors of the damaging letter to HUD largely represented only themselves.[17] As August began, the city's HOPE VI proponents aired their side at a two-hour public meeting. CSD representatives stressed "dramatic differences between the urban renewal 30 years ago and the HOPE VI Plan." They insisted that "the plan respects people's desire to stay in the community and improve their quality of life," adding that "this plan is not about displacing anyone, [and] in fact it protects against displacement." The CSD contrasted urban renewal that "demolished homes for a convention center, music hall and La Placita" with the current plan "to demolish obsolete public housing and construct good, affordable housing for low income people with needed support services." Despite such arguments, Tucson's city council initially refused to approve the CSD's $15 million HOPE VI application, citing fears about excessive costs to the city, concerns from neighbors about gentrification pressures, and the inadequacy of plans for economic development and job creation. Following further negotiations, however, two weeks later the council relented, and the CSD submitted the plan to HUD.[18]

Tucson duly received its HOPE VI implementation grant in October 1996, and an exultant CSD director Karen Thoreson declared, "It's going to eliminate our only family public housing project. There will never be a project in Tucson again. That's good. Projects have stigmatized the residents and the whole neighborhood." Others, in the neighborhood, however, were not ready to give up their fight. The Pima County Interfaith Council (PCIC), a community advocacy group founded according to the confrontational organizing principles of Saul Alinsky (and therefore not unlike STICC in New Orleans), also took a strong interest in Connie Chambers and its environs. The mayor, city manager, and council agreed to let Angie Quiroz of PCIC be cochair of the advisory board for the project, along with Eb Eberlein, a teacher and musician who lived three blocks away from the development. The CSD met regularly with the advisory board, but—as is already clear from the actions of the neighborhood associations—some of the advisers quickly moved toward radically different ideas.[19]

PCIC's intervention, led by Pedro Gonzales, carried multiple objectives, some of them explicitly aimed at protecting Connie Chambers from perceived city malfeasance, and some centered on strengthening the political position of the larger barrio. Gonzales distanced his stance from the gadfly role of Jody Gibbs and his colleagues:

> It was really hard to tell where he was coming from. He was working with the Santa Rosa Neighborhood Association even though he didn't live here. I'm not sure what his agenda was. At times, I found him very [much] for the families; at other times, he sounded against. We were never sure where he was coming from, so we ignored him and tried to get him out of our way.

Gonzales argued that what the city called the Greater Santa Rosa Plan had little respect for the long-term low-income residents of the barrio, because the planners dealt chiefly with the neighborhood associations that were composed largely of gentrifying Anglo newcomers. "They were having meetings with the *associations*, and they were excluding us from the conversations. I started attending the meetings and becoming very vocal." Karen Thoreson and Corky Poster had "no interest" in hearing my perspective, Gonzales asserted. "They actually treated me more like an outsider." That was one of his "big fights" with them. "You're not going to treat me like that in *my* neighborhood," Gonzales retorted. "This is mine, not yours." As Gonzales saw it, "They were able to pimp the newcomers, get them to buy into that [project], but they didn't get buy-in from the longtime residents here." Gonzales also bristled at the notion that Connie Chambers "declined." That sort of interpretation, he argued, takes responsibility away from the city. "It never really went downhill," Gonzales claimed. "The city *ran* it down. The city was the landlord, and just like with La Reforma, they neglected it, wouldn't fix the coolers, the heaters. They really wanted to frustrate people, and that's how people wound up leaving."[20]

Gonzales questioned nearly everything the CSD proposed during 1997 and argued that Connie Chambers did not need to be razed. "They were saying the foundations were bad," he comments, but "We actually had pro bono structural engineers come in who said the structures were sound." Gonzales championed the development's existing social structure as well: "We talked to a lot of the families. The families didn't want to leave." From the start, PCIC expected that it would be able to name the project manager for the implementation grant, and when Karen Thoreson told them it would be Olga Osterhage (then second in command at the public housing program), they reacted with "hostility." They insisted on interviewing her to make sure her Spanish was fluent. "It was a strange start for me," Osterhage drily comments. PCIC asked the city to scrap the idea of using the HOPE VI grant to build public housing and instead argued that the funds could be better spent on job training. Osterhage gently explained that 100 percent of the grant could not be diverted to this purpose, and this led to "some friction." As Poster narrated it, "Pedro Gonzales was trained by the Alinsky Industrial Areas Foundation people. They targeted this [HOPE VI project] and said it was culture-cide." Poster countered critics such as Gonzales by citing the findings from the earlier interviews with residents. "Look, the people we're talking to say they want to move out of this neighborhood. You're speaking for them, but when you actually talk *to* them, they say they don't want to stay." Dueling interpretations of residents' preferences remained unresolved.[21]

As usual with HOPE VI, winning the grant did not necessarily grant the win to the original proposal. The CSD still needed to obtain consensus on what the city would actually build. When the CSD readied its implementation plan for approval by Tucson's mayor and council on October 13, representatives from the PCIC came to the meeting and demanded that the residents first be able to put the plan to a vote. They questioned, "Why are they just being told that this is the plan?" They marched in with signs saying, "Let Them Vote, Let Them Vote." This action seems to have caught the CSD staff completely off guard. "We didn't even think to have them vote," Osterhage recalled. The city had held many gatherings with residents on topics including design of the new homes, community facilities, infrastructure, and economic development, and "We told residents that they could be part of all of those groups." In all, Osterhage estimated, the community services staff had convened "over a hundred meetings" during the summer of 1997 and felt entirely ready to have the plan move forward.[22]

After the PCIC's intervention at the council meeting, the CSD readily agreed to put the plan to a vote of residents, using an independent community development organization, Chicanos Por La Causa, to conduct the poll in mid-October. As the voting date approached, another group calling itself the Inner City Forum (El Foro de los Barrios Centrales) handed out flyers urging Connie Chambers residents to vote down the plan and "demand that the City draw up an alternative," citing a version of options proposed by Jody Gibbs and the neighborhood associations (figure 9.2). "The current plan," the handouts charged, "just like the Urban Renewal of the 1960s, will drive most Connie Chambers residents out of the area, destroy houses that could serve other needy low income families, and raise property values and rents in the area which will drive additional low income minority families out of the neighborhood." The flyers contained provocative block-print drawings urging the need to struggle against class-based eviction and depicting the

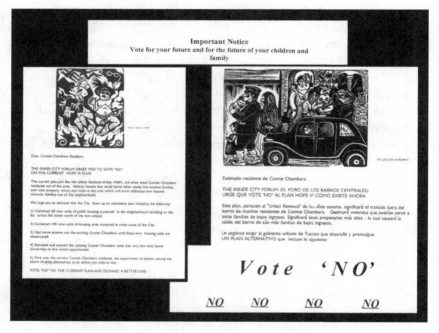

Figure 9.2. Anti–HOPE VI Flyer from Tucson's "Inner City Forum"
Tucson's "Inner City Forum" urged Connie Chambers residents to vote down the HOPE VI plan with this flyer distributed in October 1997. Promising that rich people would end up in hell for having evicted poor Mexicans, neighborhood activists urged residents to fight for alternatives.
Credit: Inner City Forum, files of Olga Osterhage, Tucson Community Services Department

suffering of "Rich People in Hell" that would result from such policies. On the day of the vote, Osterhage remembered, "We just stayed in our offices, but we had calls from residents saying PCIC was at their door telling them to vote no, and they were feeling a little intimidated." To Osterhage, they were telling residents "if they voted to approve the plan, they were going to end up on the street, and that it was a plan to get rid of poor Mexicans on that side of town." As someone determined to do the right thing for residents, she was nonplussed: "Why would I do that?" she wondered aloud. PCIC told Connie Chambers residents "not to trust us, that we had ulterior motives. They said it was 'son of urban renewal,' and that we were going to just start knocking on doors and telling people they had to leave. Some people were told that we were not going to build anything back." To those residents who asked her, Osterhage said, "Just vote what you think. You saw the plan." Out of 181 eligible households, 107 cast a vote, and nearly 80 percent of them (84-23) voted to support the city's plan.[23]

The vote of confidence did not surprise Osterhage: "It was the trust issue—that what we were saying in the plan was what we were going to do." Pedro Gonzales, by contrast, saw not trust but intimidation. Because "HUD insisted on 'participation' from the people," Gonzales claimed, the city embarked on schemes for "buying the people" by "feeding them at the meetings" and "offering vouchers to go to Target." Moreover, he charged, the CSD tried to make the prospect of remaining at Connie Chambers as unappealing as possible: "They started harassing them about their yards; they didn't help when their coolers or heaters weren't functioning right. They really frustrated the people. They were doing everything they could, but people didn't want to go." To architect Corky Poster, with the numbers on his side, the result of the vote proved the fundamental irrelevancy of the neighborhood opposition, revealing it to be "more grandstanding than anything else."

> There wasn't any sophistication in that opposition that carried to the next level. There wasn't a public housing constituency, a political auxiliary. Those folks were scattershot. That vote was a critical thing. Once that happened, all the air went out of that balloon entirely, and people just got real quiet. They kept speaking *for* the residents and saying, "They don't want this project." And then they voted and said, "Yeah, we do, actually."

PCIC and Pedro Gonzales moved on to "other wars," but Gonzales stead-fastly maintained that "Corky Poster and the city are a bunch of liars" who "manipulated the people."[24]

Meanwhile, some of "the people" strongly resented negative portrayals of project life in the Tucson media during the waning days of Connie Chambers. Although acknowledging a difference in scale, the *Star* compared "problem-riddled" Connie Chambers to the "worst of the worst public housing," such as "Cabrini-Green in Chicago." Its reporter called the project "outdated and troubled by gangs" and derided its appearance as a "no-frills military barracks," an "isolationist . . . clump of buildings that sticks out from the rest of the downtown-area neighborhood." A *Star* editorial called Connie Chambers "a crime-plagued symbol of 'project' housing" that "effectively warehoused the poor in . . . ghettos." The *Tucson Weekly*'s writer disparagingly maligned a landscape of "weed-fringed dirt" where "laundry hangs like wilted wildflowers over faltering balconies, and clusters of trash skitter up windswept drives." Residents did their best to counter such portrayals, including "An Open Letter to People Who Are Against Public Housing," from young Connie Chambers resident Aracely Carranza. If Connie Chambers was not a "pretty place," she argued, it was not the fault of residents: "Yeah, they might look ugly from the outside. But why? Because you guys make them look like that. We weren't the architects. On the inside, the projects look pretty because we decorated them our way, our taste."[25]

FROM CONNIE CHAMBERS TO POSADAS SENTINEL

Armed with its $15 million HOPE VI implementation grant, the city embarked on plans to make the project look very different. Architecturally, Corky Poster delivered an attractive low-rise landscape of 120 highly varied pastel homes that exuded the feel and low density of the surrounding barrios, while providing a more modernist twist (figures 9.3–9.5). No two homes look alike, even though many share common floor plans. The development draws on a variety of cottage styles and flat-roof Sonoran influences. With six different roof forms and nearly a dozen color schemes intermixed, the new development resists any attempt to identify it as a single project. This design, carried out at twelve units per acre to mimic what Poster terms "the healthiest acre of the adjacent neighborhood," promised a dramatic reversal in appearance. Instead of Connie Chambers—"built as if it were a fortress" as "an island of isolated poverty in a neighborhood of historic Hispanic architecture," the new development stressed integration in all dimensions. Because the old Connie Chambers "looks like 'the projects,'" Tucson's HOPE VI application had pointed out, "Everyone knows it and acts accordingly." Project design, in short, encoded a behavioral politics. The old design encouraged disrespect for property because it lacked "defensible space," thereby relegating its open areas to "the gangs and criminals, little used in the day and feared at night."[26] By contrast, the new design promised not simply new construction but a reunified street grid and a clear

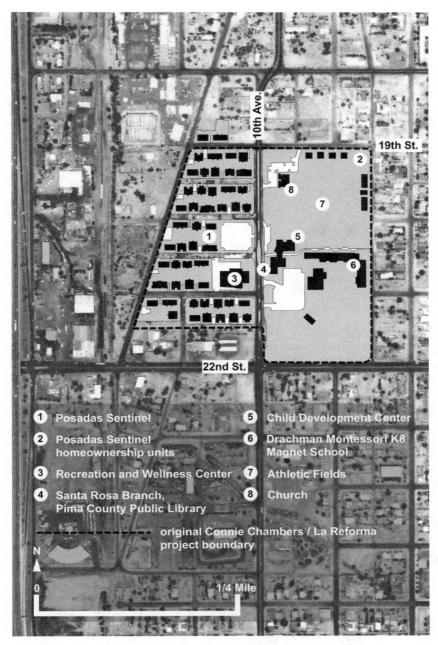

Figure 9.3. Posadas Sentinel and the Drachman School Complex
With the old La Reforma project razed, the HOPE VI grant replaced the Connie
Chambers side of the site with Posadas Sentinel and devoted the former La Reforma
site to a new school and other community facilities.
Credit: Author with Kristin Simonson and Jonathan Tarleton.

Figure 9.4. Posadas Sentinel Homes
The low-rise homes of Posadas Sentinel evoke the older barrio. Sentinel Peak is visible in the distance.
Credit: Author.

Figure 9.5. Shaded Street in Posadas Sentinel
Posadas Sentinel features a variety of architectural styles and colors.
Credit: Author.

articulation of front and back yards to be maintained by their residents, all part of a welcoming and reassuring familiarity.

Beyond the bounds of the new housing, the CSD worked with several community development organizations that developed more than sixty additional units intended to provide opportunities for affordable homeownership in the immediate neighborhoods. Some of these ownership units occupied land on the original La Reforma site. The rest of that empty tract was dramatically transformed into the new Drachman School, with associated athletic fields and parkland, along with new buildings for a Learning Center / Library and a Child Development (Head Start) Center (figure 9.6), supported by HOPE VI funds. On the west side of Tenth Avenue, the HOPE VI program provided funds for the design of an expanded Recreation and Wellness Center built with city bond money, and located directly adjacent to the homes of Posadas Sentinel.

The CSD wished to honor its commitment to permit all interested Connie Chambers households to remain for the new Posadas, but also wanted to build a very different community from what had gone before. In the old Connie Chambers, single women headed 91 percent of households, and only

Figure 9.6. Santa Rosa Public Library Branch
In addition to the new housing, the dual transformation of the sites that once held the Connie Chambers and La Reforma housing projects featured a new public library, the Drachman K-8 Magnet School, a Recreation and Wellness Center, and a Child Development Center.
Credit: Author.

one in five families reported that their primary source of income came from employment. The CSD met its twin objectives—responsiveness to the wishes of existing residents and responsiveness to a community and policy environment demanding deconcentration of poverty—in several innovative ways.[27]

By staging the demolition and development of the project in two phases, the CSD offered every Connie Chambers household the opportunity to remain. The CSD's plan replaced sixty public housing units on-site and mixed in sixty tax-credit units targeted to those with somewhat higher incomes who could afford to pay rents at near market rate. Since only fifty-eight Connie Chambers households initially indicated a wish to remain on-site and wait for new apartments during eighteen months of construction, these sixty units more than covered the expressed demand from current residents. This decision to phase the construction enabled those who wished to stay on-site to then move directly into a new unit at Posadas without having to make an interim move away from the development. Corky Poster observed, "People appreciated the theoretical option [to stay on-site] even though they may or may not have chosen to do that, ultimately. They liked the idea that they were being treated with enough respect, that they just weren't people to be moved around at will, that the school their kid goes to and the relationship they have in the neighborhood were important enough that it actually became a basis for planning, the basis for the staging of the development. It was as much principle as anything else."[28] This strategy enabled the CSD to avoid some of the pitfalls typical in other places, where long construction delays and moves to distantly located temporary housing often severely compromised the return rate. Even so, few Connie Chambers households ultimately ended up in Posadas.

By 2003, as Posadas moved toward full occupancy, only forty-five of the fifty-eight Connie Chambers households that had initially elected to stay on-site and wait still remained in place or had returned. Osterhage attributed this notable attrition to several factors. Some people belatedly realized just what it would mean to "live in the middle of a construction site," while for others this was outweighed by proximity to downtown and their church. Most residents did not have the option to move away from Connie Chambers during the construction phase and then return only when a new unit at Posadas was ready, so their only chance for these homes was to remain there continuously. As Osterhage put it, "They really had to want to stay." Others who decided to leave may well have had some concerns about policies and expectations at the new development: they would need to be financially responsible for paying all utilities (water, gas, and electric bills), could no longer keep a large dog, could no longer hang laundry to dry outdoors (and would therefore have to purchase their own dryer), and could not store any belongings outdoors. Most people who left after construction started, however, changed their minds because they had little attachment to the neighborhood and saw better alternatives. A more conspiratorial Pedro Gonzales saw it very differently: "They were thinking of the people they wanted there. They didn't want the people that lived there before, even though they're saying that they gave them that option. They're a bunch of liars. They were handpicking the people they wanted there."[29]

Osterhage acknowledged that critics from outside Connie Chambers sometimes accused the city of "moving [out] all these people with ties to the neighborhood," but she countered this by noting that most residents actually had much weaker ties to the development and the area, as indicated by the high turnover rate and relatively low average length of occupancy—just five years. Some had deep roots in the neighborhood, but many of those living at Connie Chambers resided there only with great reluctance. Most had arrived at the project from a centralized waiting list, and only those in the most "desperate situation" had chosen to move in. Most others preferred to turn it down and just wait until some other opportunity arose. "It was not their choice." Some in the development, however, actively resisted change. Margie Noriega said she "just loved the projects the way they were" and "fought and fought for them not to knock them down." The city, Noriega argued, "had enough money just to get them repaired" but "didn't listen to us at all." Still, she acknowledged that hers was not the majority opinion: "We couldn't win. There was too many people in the projects that just wanted to get out of here."[30]

FROM CONNIE CHAMBERS TO SINGLE-FAMILY HOMES

Most Connie Chambers households expressed the desire to leave. For some, it may well have been due to the sorts of pressures and frustrations with the city that Pedro Gonzales described, but many others left because they perceived genuine advantages to the other options the CSD made available to them. In stark contrast to housing authorities such as HANO that used HOPE VI as a way to reduce their stock of public housing, Tucson's CSD insisted on one-for-one replacement of the units lost on the Connie Chambers site, even as Tucson's housing planners preferred to continue their long-standing practice of scattered-site public housing. The CSD acquired an additional 130 public housing units, many of them in newer subdivisions being built across the city, never purchasing more than a couple of units on any given street (figures 9.7–9.8). They also arranged for 10 units within Tucson House, a development for seniors. In this manner, the CSD replaced all 200 of the units that had once existed at Connie Chambers, but did so in a decidedly nonconcentrated manner.[31]

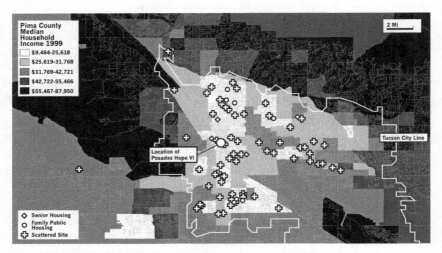

Figure 9.7. Scattering the Barrio: Tucson's Scattered-Site Replacement Public Housing
Given options to move to public housing, much of it in single-family homes located across the city, most Connie Chambers residents took up this option and did not remain to live at the new Posadas. Because most of greater Tucson's wealthier neighborhoods lay outside the city line in unincorporated Pima County, many neighborhoods across the city proved to be politically plausible sites for low-income housing.
Source: Compiled by author with Carrie Vanderford and Yonah Freemark from address data supplied by the Tucson Community Services Department.

Figure 9.8. Single-Family Replacement Public Housing for Connie Chambers
One of the single-family public housing units purchased by the City of Tucson.
Credit: Author.

Because Tucson had managed a scattered-site public housing portfolio since the early 1970s, the Community Services Department knew how to do this effectively. As Osterhage saw it, "You buy units all throughout the town in different neighborhoods, so that a person is not associated with a certain public housing development. They're associated with the neighborhood in which they live." She acknowledged that a scattered-site system is "more work for management" and more expensive, but Tucson had been successful with this approach and "wanted to continue that trend." When purchasing new houses and apartments, the CSD paid careful attention to qualities such as proximity to shopping and schools and availability of public transportation, and included information about these sorts of attributes when sending letters out to prospective residents. Osterhage could point to only three or four homes that suffered from excess isolation, due in each case to the failure to build previously promised public transportation. Taken overall, given that the city now owned several hundred scattered-site units and gave relocating Connie Chambers households a priority for all vacancies, it appears that more than eighty of them chose this option. Osterhage commented that these residents "got the best of the best units, by far."[32]

Emily Nottingham stated that she "personally went out and looked at every proposed house we acquired," with assistance of Sandy Horvitz of Housing Development Partners. "I was pretty tough on him because I really wanted it to be scattered. I didn't want more than three or four in a subdivision. I didn't want them right next to one another." With the housing market "booming" and no shortage of willing buyers, not all builders cared to have the Community Services Department buy up units for public housing residents or, if they did, wanted them to purchase more than just three or four, or did not wish to have the CSD purchase scattered units across the site. Moreover, because HUD had to approve the feasibility of each house proposed for purchase, the process took a lot of time, and many builders simply lacked the patience to deal with the red tape, given that they had other, simpler alternatives. When this worked out, however, as it often did, the city gained new housing units (what Nottingham called "acquisition without rehab") in desirable neighborhoods for "less than what it would have cost to build them in consolidated projects." They were "standard units built for the market, and we didn't have to oversee a contractor." She regarded the system as both cost effective and also "community-process effective." With land prices relatively affordable, and with white racial prejudice against accepting Latinx neighbors arguably less virulent than in cities faced with rehousing large numbers of displaced African Americans, Tucson's persistent but modestly scaled effort to scatter public housing proved workable.

Still, management of such a scattered-site portfolio has had both upsides and many challenges. Nottingham argued that it has worked out well for residents. They take good care of the units, but it entails a lot of driving around on the part of the manager to look for problems. Sometimes, though, the subsidized tenants face unusual scrutiny, since "each house has four neighbors who know it is public housing, and sometimes can be quick to call in complaints." With "eyes on the prize" watching from either side, from behind, and from across the street, surrounding public housing with private sector homeowners has added its own unofficial form of on-site management. "But this is also how we sell it—we tell neighborhoods, 'You couldn't really have a better neighbor'—if the resident is doing something wrong, you get to call the mayor and the city council person who's very responsive to constituents in a way that a private sector landlord is not going to be. We sell it that way, so we have to mean it when we do."[33]

Many residents were pleasantly surprised that they actually had options across the city. "When we started working with the clients, a lot of them thought all we had was Connie Chambers" or that "if we had anything else, it was very similar." To Osterhage, this lack of information about options explains why, at the time of the city's survey in 1996, fully 45 percent of Connie Chambers residents initially told Corky Poster's researchers that they would prefer to remain in the neighborhood.[34] With the HOPE VI grant in place, to make sure that residents really did understand their choices, Osterhage embarked on a series of tours. She drove a van around the city seven hours a day every Tuesday to show them the range of available housing. "People were amazed. They would say, 'I didn't know you had single-family homes. I didn't know I could live in this neighborhood.'" Single-family homes constitute fully 40 percent of Tucson's scattered-site public housing options, and the CSD made sure that prospective residents could go see their potential options as often as they needed to, so that they could feel fully comfortable with their choice. Often, family members from different generations did not agree about a particular moving option, and the CSD would endeavor to help them reach consensus. In some cases, "It took a long, long time." Osterhage remembered "weeks where I saw the same families on the tours. That was OK; I understood why it was so difficult for some families to make a decision. Some felt that "this is too good to be true. What are they not telling me?" The second time some residents went out on one of Osterhage's tours, they would bring along relatives who didn't even live with them, who could serve as a sounding board and a reality check about the move they were contemplating.[35]

The terms of Tucson's HOPE VI agreement stipulated that the CSD would endeavor to place relocated residents in neighborhoods with minority concentration no more than twenty percentage points higher than the city's 38 percent average, but permitted exceptions if the neighborhoods had fewer than 30 percent of residents living in poverty. In practice, most relocation occurred to neighborhoods that met the rather liberally defined lower-poverty threshold, even if these neighborhood choices did little to reduce ethnic or racial concentration. If they were headed into higher-income neighborhoods, the CSD attempted to educate residents about the sorts of standards they could expect. Osterhage freely admitted that the city's own previous lax standards had contributed to the problem. At Connie Chambers, "Part of it was management's fault. We allowed them to have inoperative vehicles. We allowed them to have that broken window a little longer. We allowed them to hang their laundry on the fence. We weren't there on top of it. So we had to educate them, and say, 'If you're choosing to live in this neighborhood, fine, but know that you won't be able to do this, this, or this.'" At base, the city's housing officials did not want to set up residents for failure. As Osterhage put it, "We didn't want to move them and have them fail, because then we would have failed." The CSD put together a set of neighborhood standards for Posadas Sentinel, but essentially conveyed the same expectations for those moving into scattered-site properties. "There was a lot of handholding, and sometimes other staff not associated with HOPE VI would say, 'You're spoiling these people.'" The move to scattered sites left some former Connie Chambers residents distant from friends and family, but one survey found that the "improved housing conditions and safer neighborhood outweighed the isolation they felt."[36]

Some residents emphatically agree that they had genuine choices. Roberta Harris, who continued to live at Connie Chambers for more than two decades after her son Bobby's murder, described her experience:

> I think HOPE VI was the best thing that came to the projects. I went to every meeting they had. . . . They didn't tell you, "You have to go here, and if you don't go here, you're out." They didn't tell you that. They take you to the apartments, and you look at them, and they tell you about the neighborhood. It was *my* choice. I said, "I think I want to move out. I need to try another area, another place, for a while."

Aracely Carranza's family was one of the few offered a temporary off-site move with an option to return after redevelopment. Writing in 2000, she criticized this process: "They picked a place for us. . . . They just moved us wherever they wanted. . . . But we are coming back." Most of those who initially remained on-site during construction but then decided to leave Connie Chambers permanently did so because they found better options. As Osterhage commented, "Some of it was talking to an old neighbor and seeing, 'Oh, they chose a house, and they're doing well. Maybe I can still find something.'" Once they saw the other choices available, the prospect of waiting around a construction site in a nonrenovated Connie Chambers apartment may well have seemed less appealing. For those who initially trusted the city less, it took the successful relocation of others to convince them to explore other options.

Ultimately, Osterhage was "not at all" surprised that so few Connie Chambers residents chose to stay on for the new Posadas. Similarly, Emily Nottingham explained,

> We always expected to have a relatively low rate of return. They were getting good relocation choices. We bought brand-new houses in new subdivisions, three-bedroom homes that were more spacious than they'd been living in. Our public housing stock is quite good. They were given a lot of choice about where they could move, and we worked closely with them.

At base, whatever the more conspiratorial accusations of neighborhood critics, Tucson officials seemed genuinely committed to giving Connie Chambers residents a real choice, one comprising several desirable alternatives.[37] Still, public housing communities are always worlds of deeply felt ambivalence. Even when city officials believed themselves to be well meaning, this did not always mean that residents believed all promises had been fulfilled.

POSADAS SENTINEL: MANAGING THE NEW COMMUNITY

Posadas Sentinel, completed in 2002, has already faced many challenges, affecting both its tenant composition and its management. Initially, Tucson housing officials decided to place the new Posadas Sentinel under private management, part of the larger effort "to disassociate the development" from the old Connie Chambers, as Olga Osterhage phrased it. They chose the Metropolitan Housing Corporation, already linked to the project as the city's general partner in the tax-credit financing deal. At first, everything went well with the move-in of residents, and the CSD believed that the management had "capable staff doing a good job." After a few years, however, the staff changed, and, Osterhage observed, "There was nobody checking on them, making sure there was consistency." Osterhage received complaints about gang activity and noticed many problems with record-keeping, as well as a broader "unprofessionalism" and "inconsistency in enforcing the rules."

> I was the one who would get calls from residents about illegal activities. They'd say, "I called this in to the office and they're not doing anything about it." They would ask why the police had come to make an arrest for drugs, and yet the person was still living at Posadas. They were very slow about getting and acting on police reports.

Osterhage kept telling Emily Nottingham, "We need to take the property back." Eventually, in September 2008, the city did so. As one resident put it during a focus group interview, it was like "an apple with a rotting piece; they came in and cut out that piece."[38]

To fix the management, the CSD brought in Bobbi Stone, who had proved herself to be an effective public manager of Tucson House, a 408-unit development serving elderly and disabled residents. To Stone, this transition was not easy. The former management company treated her arrival "like a hostile takeover" and was "not very forthcoming with a lot of information that we needed. The on-site manager would spend a little time with us and then just disappear." Stone found not just disorganized files but social disorganization, as well: "There were people on one street that were afraid to go to their mailboxes because there were gangs right there at that corner of the property every day." Stone needed to reintroduce a culture of community responsibility. "I would come into work on a Monday," she recalls, "and there would be beer bottles all over the place on a corner, cases of beer, broken bottles." Stone would then go from neighbor to neighbor and "would call them to task for lease violations" because they had allowed drinking. "That was very controversial." Stone credits the turnaround of safety at the development to the willingness of residents to be more proactive in surveilling the territory immediately outside their homes. As Stone put it, "You have a responsibility to your neighborhood, instead of just closing your blinds and ignoring it." By dissuading large gatherings of gang members from assembling at night, this prevented the situation from escalating to the point where "rival gangs driving by in carloads start shooting at each other. If they're not gathering there, then that's not a problem." The turning point for Stone occurred December 2008, soon after she had arrived, when a sixteen-year-old youth was shot and almost died. "Something had to be done. That's when I started coming down hard. I evicted one of the main characters in that whole drama. That family was evicted," along with another one later. In all, the eviction of "three key families" quickly made "a huge difference." The community policy at Posadas, as revised under Stone's direction in January 2009, stressed the value of neighborhood solidarity: "Your home does not begin and end at your own front door. When you turn down the street, you are home. When you walk down a sidewalk, you are home. This entire neighborhood is your home."[39]

The neighborhood is still primarily home to Hispanic residents, who made up about three-quarters of the population as of 2017. Five percent are African American, nearly 5 percent are non-Hispanic whites, and most of the remaining 15 percent are African refugees, principally from Somalia or Sudan.[40] Unlike in other cities, at Posadas there is almost no difference in the racial and ethnic breakdown between those living in the public housing

units and those residing in the tax-credit / market dwellings, though cultural and linguistic barriers remain, especially with regard to the Africans.
Since the 1990s, Arizona has been a national leader in refugee resettlement,
including nearly eight thousand from war-torn Somalia and Sudan. To the
surprise of Posadas management, there are sometimes more serious ethnic
and tribal rivalries between the Somalis and the Sudanese, some of whom
are also unhappy about having to replay intra-African struggles in Tucson.[41]

Olga Osterhage recalled little gang activity during the 1996–2000 period of the HOPE VI grant, but acknowledged that some of this resumed
after Posadas opened. To some extent, the new and expanded community
facilities have helped, but problems remain. At the time when families
needed to decide whether to stay on for a place in the new Posadas or disperse into other housing options, the CSD did not attempt to dissuade any
particular families from remaining. In contrast to other cities where housing
authorities used the occasion of redevelopment to clear out their most problematic households, in Tucson—for better or worse—city housing officials
say, they offered everyone who wished it the full opportunity to remain at
the development. Looking back, Osterhage observed that they simply did
not know which families had gang ties. "We didn't have the information
that, oh, this family has three PJay family members, and this family has two
PJays." Although the sprawling motel-style Connie Chambers was hardly the
Cabrini-Green environment portrayed in the press, in the context of Tucson
it had still seemed a daunting managerial challenge. Osterhage blamed part
of the information absence on its "being such a *huge*, two-hundred-unit complex, designed with dead-end streets." As a result, "Management didn't even
know about half of what was happening. If we had known about a family
that was causing problems and had proof, we would have taken action then"
and not "waited for the new Posadas." Instead, she noted, "There was not
one family where we said, 'You're not welcome back.'"[42]

Unlike many other housing authorities and private management
companies implementing HOPE VI grants, the Tucson Community Services
Department insists that it made no attempt to keep the former public
housing residents from gaining homes in the new replacement development.
To the contrary, the CSD and management team did no additional screening
to keep particular families out. They simply told them they would need
to meet higher standards of behavior spelled out in the Posadas Sentinel
Community Policy. The policy set rules against gang activity, stipulated zero
tolerance for drug-related criminal activity either on or off the premises,
prohibited alcohol abuse, stipulated the terms for "quiet hours," regulated
behavior of guests, outlined which items could be kept or used in outdoor
yards, prohibited vehicle repairs on-site, and set expectations for apartment
maintenance. As Osterhage commented, "We worked with the families that

were gonna stay. We said, 'Remember, these are the new rules. We used to let you have two pets and they were bigger than the policy. Not anymore. Before, we said this was a high-crime area, so we said it was OK for you to have a pit bull. Now our policy says no aggressive breeds. It's different now. If you're willing to abide by these new rules, you'll be fine here.'" In addition to the promise of stricter lease enforcement, however, the CSD relaxed certain other expectations. Although, for many years, all other families entering into the public housing component of the development needed to take part in a Family Self Sufficiency (FSS) program intended to get them financially stable enough to leave subsidized housing, the CSD exempted the former Connie Chambers residents from participation.[43]

At the same time, as the introduction of an FSS requirement made clear, the CSD also sought to substantially reconfigure its definition of public housing residents when tenanting the rest of Posadas Sentinel. Corky Poster put it bluntly: "They were clearly cherry-picking residents. They were trying to make HOPE VI successful by picking successful residents, as opposed to making the housing turn residents into successes." The CSD sought to move public housing away from "housing of last resort" and to view it instead as "temporary housing during a move up to a different market." In Emily Nottingham's phrase, "We wanted it to be a 'new day dawning' sort of development." We had been "lazy in our management as far as expectations of tenants, [and] we didn't want that to be the case in the new Posadas. We wanted to set a new level of expectation, and also a new level of support, so that people could meet those expectations."[44]

As in Boston at Orchard Gardens, Tucson's leaders sought to attract a less impoverished constituency to Posadas while still supporting the needs of former Connie Chambers households. Their strategy included several approaches intended to diversify incomes over time. First, the city established a site-based waiting list, meaning that prospective residents could line up for possible entry into Posadas without having to put themselves on a citywide waiting list for something called "public housing." At the same time, those who were already in the Tucson public housing system did not have the option of requesting a transfer to Posadas. Taken together, this had the effect of attracting many households with higher incomes—incomes that fit well with the tiers established as part of the tax-credit deal. Because the tax-credit housing had been spread across both the Posadas site and eighty of the scattered-site units, and because the city had gained extra points by agreeing to target some of those tax-credit-financed units to those with incomes of below 20, 30, 40, or 50 percent of area median income (instead of the usual higher cap of 60 percent of area median), the CSD could choose how to allocate each type of subsidy. Instead of putting those with the lowest income thresholds on the Posadas site, they elected to put those

with the *highest* income eligibility threshold there, and to place those with
lower incomes into the scattered sites. In this way, the city used the variation
within its financing structure to help further reduce project-based poverty.[45]

Closely linked to this wish to accommodate more households nearer to
the higher end of eligibility for access to public housing, the city also made
use of a "work preference" for new entry into Posadas (a preference subsequently adopted throughout Tucson's public housing system). At Posadas,
for those who were not in school, the CSD mandated participation in the
FSS program, intended to provide them with a five-year "passage out of
poverty" toward employment and sufficient income to exit completely
from public housing. Posadas seemed a particularly encouraging site for
an FSS program since the development already had an award-winning K-2
elementary school across the street and a Head Start program, as well as
a library branch with active programming. In terms of incomes and work
status, then, the new arrivals in Posadas were initially not so socioeconom-
ically distinct from the sixty households living on-site in units subsidized
solely by tax credits. As recently as 2006, for instance, the FSS and work
requirements skewed the incomes of public housing residents at Posadas
to fully 49 percent of the area median income, about triple the average
incomes of Tucson's public housing residents systemwide at the time. With
the economic downturn and joblessness that followed the Great Recession,
however, the incomes of public housing residents at Posadas declined and
averaged only about 30 percent of median as of 2017. The incomes of those
in the tax-credit portion of the apartments have remained at about 50 percent of the area median.[46]

Indicative of the ongoing economic struggles on the public housing
side, the FSS program proved to be a mixed success at best and is no longer
a requirement for entry into Posadas public housing. Of the thirty-one
graduates of the FSS program during its first ten years, nine (including
Grace Johnson) were able to move out of public housing, and six of these
were able to purchase their own homes. Five individuals also managed to
obtain a certificate or degree while participating in the program. Many
others, however, either failed to complete the program or did not gain sufficient economic independence to be able to leave public housing. With
the economic downturn after 2008, many households lost their service
industry jobs, leading to a large number of evictions from the subsidized
units due to nonpayment of rent. Indicative of Tucson's affordable
housing shortage, there is a remarkably high number of other households
in line to take their place. The Community Services Department (recently
renamed the Department of Housing and Community Development) had
expected the demand for the tax-credit-subsidized units to outstrip the
demand for the public housing units, but this has consistently not been

the case. As of May 2017, 119 households with moderately low incomes remained on the waiting list for one of the sixty tax credit subsidized apartments (which range from two to four bedrooms). Meanwhile, indicative of the exponentially higher demand for more deeply subsidized housing targeted to those with the lowest incomes, nearly seven thousand households awaited an empty unit in the sixty units of public housing at Posadas.[47] Clearly, most will be waiting for a very long time.

CONCLUSION: SCATTERING THE BARRIO

In Tucson, never a city to champion public housing in a large way, the transformation of Connie Chambers to Posadas Sentinel has nonetheless been successful in many dimensions.[48] As elsewhere, however, it has been a significant double struggle both to build public housing and to replace it. In Tucson, these two struggles have been intimately connected, since many in the Chicano community believe that the old urban renewal policy never really stopped. Even as a consensus has emerged that urban renewal brought neither commercial nor residential success to central Tucson, the program still has its defenders. In 2010, a half-century after he directed Tucson's early renewal efforts, Si Schorr continued to praise Tucson's "prudent civil decision" to remove "the heart of the blighted and deteriorated slum area." Schorr sees this as the "stimulus" that prevented further deterioration of downtown, though he laments the private sector's failure to build more housing. By contrast, the equally long memory of Pedro Gonzales framed urban renewal in religious terms, viewing the legacy of the Tucson Convention Center as a profound moral affront:

> I'm a person of God. I believe that when you do bad things to people, bad things happen to you. It's like Cesar Chavez said, "They will be judged." What they did here with urban removal with the TCC—that's why nothing has happened there and nothing *will* ever happen. The way we say it, they left the rattlesnake rattles there. Whatever they try there is never gonna work, because they moved people against their will. And those are God's people.

Those who work for the city of Tucson must grapple with the perspectives of both Schorr and Gonzales.[49]

Former CSD director Karen Thoreson grasped the anger of neighborhood activists such as Gonzales and PCIC and regarded them as a "legitimate voice." She credited PCIC for having done many good things in Tucson, but imagined that the "longer history of mistrust" made it impossible for the city to engage productively with them in the Santa Rosa barrio.

The city had plans to just raze that neighborhood. People hadn't forgotten that. The city had so little respect for the people in that neighborhood and the conditions in that neighborhood that they were willing to just get rid of it. That was what fueled all of it. Posadas was characterized as another urban renewal project. I think Pedro knew better, but it served his purpose to keep the anger alive.

For her part, Emily Nottingham fully understands that PCIC and others in the surrounding barrios did not want to see the tenants get used, and that they feared a repeat of the worst aspects of urban renewal. She emphasized that the CSD had a broad mandate: the HOPE VI initiative was "primarily about the residents and the future residents, but we *are* a community development department." This meant that she also needed to worry about "what the neighborhood wanted" and about "how the development should fit in." The objections from neighbors proved personally and professionally frustrating, since "a lot of the residents took the position that 'we don't trust the city so we'll not participate in the discussion, but just fight whatever the city proposes.'" Nottingham insisted that "we honestly wanted to work with them and knew that they had been fighting for thirty or forty years" and did not trust the city.[50]

Albert Elias, who succeeded Nottingham as CSD director in 2008 and at this writing serves as Tucson's assistant city manager, comes from a deeply rooted *Tucsonenses* family and feels the impact of long community memory even more acutely. Elias, who began working for the city's Planning Department in 1984, saw the legacy of urban renewal as "an incredible obstacle that has been a yoke placed on all city actions."

No matter how great of a person you are, no matter how hard you try, it's shaped virtually my entire career with the city. It's always been a factor in anything the city's trying to do in this general vicinity. . . . That's the yoke of working for government. You have to effectively own all these decisions that happened before you.

Elias understands the resistive power of collective memory. Even though it has been well over a half-century since the first stirrings of urban renewal, and one might think "the people have died or gone away," this is actually not the case. As Elias commented, deeply rooted memories of maltreatment and expulsion remain part of the oral tradition of Tucson's Mexican American community: "Their *nana* told the story to their *tia*, and my *tia* told me that twenty years ago, so here we are forty years later and this person who may be thirty years old and never really experienced this has a whole backstory that they're completely aware of because their family and friends have relayed it to them." The new development may have been named Posadas Sentinel, but some sentinels of the community still saw it as Pueblo Center revisited.[51]

The saga of public housing in Tucson's Santa Rosa barrio reveals the complexity of neighborhood reaction. To some, HOPE VI represented merely the latest edition of "Mexican removal," a process with a near-continuous history. Other residents seemed perfectly happy to see a dramatic reduction in the number of public housing residents in their neighborhood but feared gentrification would soon follow, causing their own property taxes to rise to unaffordable levels. They ignored the city's tax abatement plan, intended to prevent just such an occurrence.[52] Meanwhile, some feared a continued downward trend: building back public housing on the site would recreate the problem of concentrated poverty that had doomed Connie Chambers. At the opposite extreme, others saw no reason to tear down Connie Chambers at all; the buildings simply needed to be repaired and were already "good enough for public housing residents."

Urban renewal purged the poorest; HOPE VI Tucson-style operated more subtly and benignly than its precursor, even though it ultimately led to the same result—at least for those residing in the city's central barrios. Good-hearted people in the CSD such as Olga Osterhage and Emily Nottingham certainly had no wish to "purge the poorest" and did nothing of the sort. Instead, they presided over an innovative system designed to offer genuine choices to extremely low-income households. Because Tucson phased the development of Connie Chambers and offered *all* households the choice to stay on to live in the new Posadas, and because the CSD offered some first-rate relocation options, including many opportunities for new single-family homes in diverse neighborhoods, Tucson's version of HOPE VI achieved its goal of deconcentrating poverty in a much more positive way than most other cities. As Osterhage put it, "The key point is that our other housing is also really good. If our other housing were bad, it would be really hard" to justify this use of the Posadas site for so few Connie Chambers residents. She visited Atlanta and toured their "beautiful" Centennial Place development but quickly realized that this was not the Tucson model. "When I heard they didn't do one-for-one replacement, it felt to me like they used the best property for non-public housing and they did the minimum for the public housing."[53] As in Atlanta, Tucson's leaders wished to eliminate "projects," but Osterhage and her colleagues believed this could be accomplished by doing as much as possible for public housing residents.

Tucson's own policies did not succeed in appeasing critics in the neighborhood, but it is significant that far fewer complaints seem to have come from the public housing residents themselves. This remains a major achievement. That said, as in other cities, Tucson's leadership used policy mechanisms and federal funding to replace a well-located but extremely low-income project community with a much more upwardly mobile alternative.

Despite some legitimate criticism from local activists, Tucson's processes have still yielded a more equitably implemented displacement than the heavy-handed removals that have prevailed elsewhere in cities such as New Orleans. Although still a displacement, it is one that has been accompanied by some careful and humane administration, genuine attention to tenant needs, and respect for tenant choices. At the same time, by replacing half of the on-site units with less deeply subsidized tax-credit units that can command near-market rents, and—at least initially—by shifting the public housing side of the Posadas population toward those who could meet "working preference" and "family self-sufficiency" standards for admission, the CSD deliberately skewed occupancy of this choice location toward a far less impoverished population and thereby facilitated the further gentrification of the surrounding barrios. If the "creaming" of the poor at Posadas had been part of a general policy, Tucson's system would not stand out as a progressive example as much as it does. It is therefore important to note that, despite a system-wide "working preference" in place for several years, Tucson still uses its (admittedly undersized) public housing portfolio to serve those who, on average, earn only 21 percent of the area's median income. Even so, however, Tucson's fifteen hundred public housing units and more than five thousand vouchers, taken together, serve but a small fraction of the more than fifty thousand Tucsonans whose low incomes make them eligible for housing subsidies.[54]

Paradoxically, while Tucson's approach to the Connie Chambers redevelopment exemplifies the Publica Major poverty governance constellation, the overall contribution of Tucson's public sector to affordable housing provision remains disproportionately tiny. Other cities of roughly similar population—such as San Francisco, New Orleans, Atlanta, Baltimore, Cleveland, and Boston—each devote two to seven times as large a percentage of total housing units to public housing. Correspondingly, Tucson has just twenty-three affordable and available housing units for every one hundred households earning less than 30 percent of the median income—much lower than any of these other cities.[55] Tucson has succeeded in assembling an excellent inventory of scattered-site public housing over nearly a half-century, but, after the projects have been removed, city leaders still choose to house a very small percentage of the city's poorest residents.

Part V

NONPROFITUS IN SAN FRANCISCO

Figure V.1. San Francisco's Nonprofitus Constellation for North Beach Place
Viewed from San Francisco, the Nonprofitus constellation shines prominently in the
sector of the sky dominated by not-for-profit organizations.
Credit: Author with Suzanne Harris-Brandts.

Figure V.2. San Francisco's Nonprofitus Constellation: Telescopic View
This telescopic view of the Nonprofitus constellation depicted in figure V.1 shows
San Francisco's BRIDGE not-for profit housing developer and key community-based
tenant advocacy groups—Tel-Hi and the CCDC—as its dominant features. Public
housing residents, Mayor Willie Brown, private developers, and the San Francisco
Housing Authority also mattered, but San Francisco's not-for-profit sector played the
dominant role.
Credit: Author with Suzanne Harris-Brandts.

> For Chinatown, we fought for one-for-one replacement . . . so I just used
> the same values we have here for our community for the HOPE VI.
>   —Reverend Norman Fong, Chinatown Community Development
>   Center and former San Francisco Housing Authority commissioner

OVERVIEW: RESISTING GENTRIFICATION BY REPLACING ALL PUBLIC HOUSING

Part V, divided into three chapters, narrates how a fourth form of poverty governance—one centered on the role of not-for-profit community organizations and housing developers—has shaped the HOPE VI experience in San Francisco. Unlike Tucson, where the public sector held sway, San Francisco had a weak housing authority; unlike Boston, no single tenant emerged as a Plebs pole star; and unlike New Orleans, San Franciscans refused to leave the fate of public housing to the unchecked preferences of for-profit developers. Chapter 10 charts the rise and fall of the North Beach Place public housing development, demonstrating how the city's Nonprofitus constellation (figure V.1) burst forth from the cataclysm of urban renewal. Chapter 11 maps out the application of this approach to the redevelopment of North Beach Place (figure V.2) by charting the decade-long struggle from initial HOPE VI proposal (1995) to completed development (2005). Part V concludes with chapter 12, which investigates life in the post–HOPE VI version of North Beach Place, while discussing how San Francisco's leaders sought to make this a model for public housing transformation citywide.

In San Francisco, housing activists and a strong not-for-profit housing sector have played important roles in preserving public housing occupancy for low-income residents despite the city's rampant gentrification pressures. The North Beach Place housing development—built in 1952 and redeveloped a half-century later—stands as an unusual model for what HOPE VI can be. Located in a rapidly gentrifying part of San Francisco full of expensive dwellings and a thriving tourist economy centered around nearby Fisherman's Wharf, the fate of North Beach's public housing could easily have been yet another tale of market-driven development chasing the "highest and best" use for land. Instead, local officials, not-for-profit developers, community groups, and the residents they served responded by treating the retention of public housing units as their highest priority.

In contrast to the overwhelming majority of HOPE VI developments nationwide that have assumed that the reduction of on-site public housing units is both a necessary and desirable aspect of what it means to replace the projects, the proponents of North Beach Place insisted on retaining every single one of the 229 deeply subsidized apartments that had been located on those blocks. Moreover, in addition to one-for-one replacement of public housing, the North Beach team actively committed another HOPE VI heresy: they increased, rather than decreased, the density of housing on the site. And, as another stark repudiation of typical mixed-income housing doctrines and majority practice, the additional housing included not a single market-rate apartment. Instead, the housing heretics of North Beach deployed an unprecedentedly large allocation of Low-Income Housing Tax Credits to produce an additional 112 units of housing intermixed with the public housing, with this portion targeted to those who could be considered the higher end of San Francisco's poor—families whose jobs earned them no more than 60 percent of the area's median income.

Despite San Francisco's current reputation as a mecca for progressive politics and tenant empowerment, this outcome at North Beach was far from preordained. Rather, it results from a long and partially successful struggle, one piece of a larger and less successful effort to enable one of the nation's most expensive cities to retain its lower-income residents. The redevelopment of North Beach Place resisted the frenzy of high-end market-rate development sweeping San Francisco (and sweeping out its lowest-income citizens). In the context of a weak and unstable housing authority, the city's strong nonprofit housing community, joined by empowered tenant groups and supported by Mayor Willie Brown (in office, 1996–2004), embarked on a public housing redevelopment effort that preserved and enhanced the last remnants of affordable housing in an otherwise gentrifying neighborhood.

At North Beach, highly engaged neighborhood organizations together with an empowered not-for-profit housing developer supported the needs of low-income residents while also enhancing the neighborhood. Not only did the process unleashed by a HOPE VI grant actually increase the number of on-site affordable housing units, it also added a new supermarket, additional below-grade parking, and new street-level retail. At the same time, however, the struggle to rehouse former residents proved contentious and protracted and, ultimately, only 36 percent of the original households chose (or were able) to return to the new development. Most of the initial tenant leaders did not come back, and many current residents—while grateful for their housing—lament the strictures of life under the close surveillance of private management.

This saga again underscores just how complicated it is to pull off the redevelopment of an American public housing project. Although the overall outcome is better than most, the process endured multiple setbacks and required dogged efforts by a wide variety of parties. By examining the interplay of many powerful and less powerful voices, the politics of urban redevelopment stands out in sharp relief.

10

The Rise and Fall of North Beach Place

NORTH BEACH: CANNED FRUIT, LITTLE ITALY

The future site of North Beach Place began as a nineteenth-century tenement district housing a variety of European and Latin American immigrants drawn there by the promise of waterfront employment. Italian fisherman from the town of Sestri settled in large numbers along Bay Street and Francisco Street near the waterfront.[1] After the 1906 earthquake and fires, however, the rebuilding of Bay Street increasingly brought industrial and commercial facilities. The site still housed many apartments, but the cutting, packing, warehousing, and receiving facilities of the California Fruit Canners Association took up more than half of the block between Mason and Taylor Streets. Established in 1899 by Marco Fontana, this cannery was for many years the state's largest fruit- and vegetable-processing company.[2]

By 1920, the larger North Beach neighborhood had coalesced into San Francisco's Little Italy. Although the Italian population hit its peak during the 1930s, when fully fifty-seven thousand residents identified as either Italian born or of Italian descent, the district retained its Italianized reputation for several more decades. By the 1930s, however, the adult children of the immigrants who had settled in the area "began leaving in large numbers"; by the 1960s, the remaining Italians were "mostly old people."[3]

For Italians and others in Depression-era San Francisco, quality housing affordable to those with low incomes remained in very short supply. A 1939 Works Progress Administration survey showed that San Francisco had more than thirty-two thousand substandard dwellings that could be rented for less than thirty dollars a month; meanwhile, however, the city had only twenty-two hundred vacant *standard* dwellings available at such low rents. The WPA survey, completed just a year after establishment of the San Francisco Housing Authority (SFHA) in 1938, helped make the case for creation of substantial public housing. As elsewhere, public housing gained supporters because it could be appealingly paired with the legally mandated "equivalent elimination" of slums. The SFHA managed to launch five projects—Holly Courts, Potrero Terrace, Sunnydale, Valencia Gardens, and Westside

Courts—before American involvement in World War II halted construction of six additional ventures. North Beach Place, for which the housing authority had completed at least half of the necessary land acquisition, was among the many real-estate casualties of war.[4]

First proposed in early 1941 with designs completed in 1942, the project was "temporarily shelved" due to the nonavailability of steel and cost of materials and the need to shift to the "new, urgent objectives" of housing families of defense workers as well as army and navy enlisted personnel. In 1944, to illustrate its "Plans for Peace," the SFHA offered a full-page rendering of the future North Beach Place, noting that it would rise "hard by Fisherman's Wharf."[5] A year later, near the end of the wartime hiatus, the journal *Architect and Engineer* published many more of the drawings, noting that "no finer example of public housing could be selected." It urged immediate construction of the project, but little happened on the site for several more years.[6]

Like other agencies of the era, the SFHA touted public housing as a testament to the city's fortitude in the "war against slums." The same San Franciscan spirit that had built "a magic city" out of the ashes of the 1906 fires and had conceptualized the Golden Gate and Bay Bridges also infused public housing. "Just as the building of the two great bridges marked the passing of the ferry boats and the closing of one chapter," the 1946 *Annual Report* intoned, "so the creation of the Housing Authority meant the ultimate elimination of all blighted areas and the complete restoration of the city to a vital, virile community." In San Francisco, as elsewhere, public housing inhabited a world of binary aesthetics in which "families moved out of the squalor and into the bright sunshine and fresh air of a modernly planned apartment type neighborhood." Fog-free and flawless, the new housing could be marketed as a new moral beginning. "No more alleyway play yards for children, no more wretched poverty but in place of these all of the safety factors for moulding good, clean youth into future useful citizenship," emboldened by a "new concept of community responsibility." With the end of the war on the other side of the Pacific, it was time "to resume the offensive against the slum way of life" and to move forward with the "imposing development in North Beach" (figures 10.1–10.2)[7]

With passage of the Housing Act of 1949, the SFHA moved quickly to restart its war-waylaid projects. By the end of that year, it completed relocation of "all families living in the substandard housing" on the North Beach site and immediately drew up plans for the demolition of this "slum site." Arguing that the city's persistent postwar housing shortage was "felt most seriously by veteran and other low-income families with children," the SFHA assiduously worked to develop new housing to serve this constituency. By 1949, more than half of the SFHA's public housing accommodated

Looking North to Alcatraz Island

Figure 10.1. North Beach Place and Alcatraz
The San Francisco Housing Authority touted the future North Beach Place development in its 1946 annual report. This rendering of the project designed by Born and Gutterson depicts a gleaming future emerging from the soot of an industrial waterfront, with the Alcatraz Island prison visible in the Bay.
Source: 1946 SFHA annual report, San Francisco Housing Authority.

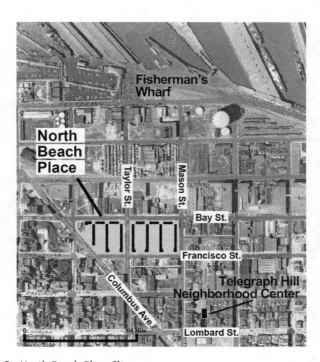

Figure 10.2. North Beach Place Site
The SFHA sited North Beach Place in a mixed industrial and residential district near Fisherman's Wharf in an era before the advent of new hotels and mass tourism.
Credit: Author with Kristin Simonson and Jonathan Tarleton.

families of veterans, and these households accounted for fifteen hundred out of the eighteen hundred families on the waiting list. Each year, about ten thousand households made inquiries, but most didn't even bother to sign up, dissuaded by the list's length.[8]

North Beach residents initially viewed the housing project site as a potential neighborhood amenity, eager to see it developed with a playground and nursery school that could also benefit residents from the surrounding area.[9] The SFHA intended its North Beach Place project, located in "San Francisco's widely-known Latin quarter," to be occupied entirely by whites. Accordingly, an SFHA annual report observed, "Both in architecture and in landscaping, it reflects the color and feeling of the Mediterranean."[10] Arrayed in three-story walk-ups with balconies, plus one building with four floors, the project combined stark modernism with clear references to local character. The initial drawings for the project, produced by well-regarded architects Ernest Born and Henry Gutterson, with landscape design by Thomas Church, showed clear outreach to Italians in the neighborhood, replete with Italianate plantings and even a bocce court (figures 10.3–10.4).

The social center and building No. 11

Figure 10.3. Italianate Rendering of North Beach Place
Architectural renderings show courtyards planned with tall Italian poplars and a grape arbor, although SFHA administrator John Beard refused to allow the proposed "social center" to be built.
Source: San Francisco Housing Authority, 1946 Annual Report.

1952 | **NORTH BEACH PLACE**

North Beach Place in San Francisco's widely-known Latin quarter, and next in point of congestion to Chinatown, followed closely the opening of Ping Yuen. Completed in early 1952, it made available 229 greatly-needed apartments. It was quickly filled. Both in architecture and landscaping, it reflects the color and feeling of the Mediterranean.

Figure 10.4. San Francisco's "Mediterranean" Project for the "Latin Quarter"
Although it is more obvious in the renderings of Mediterranean plantings than in the concrete reality of the built housing project, the SFHA viewed North Beach Place as catering to the Italians of the city's "Latin quarter." Despite the willful images and rhetoric, North Beach Place soon faced intense pressures to admit black residents and later became predominantly Chinese.
Source: San Francisco Housing Authority, *Road to the Golden Age: A Report on the First 20 Years of Operations, 1940–1960.*

More pointedly, by clarifying its cultural context during an era of lingering racial and ethnic segregation, the drawings signaled who would be welcomed. Since comparatively few dwellings were to be demolished to make way for the project, neighborhood residents with low incomes had some hope of entry. For nonwhite residents, however, the situation remained far more complex.

HOUSING RACE

As in nearly every American city, issues of race and racial change lie close to the heart of the public housing story in San Francisco. In San Francisco, however, the story has long been more than a black-white matter, and the saga of North Beach Place is no exception. Starting in the 1940s, as local planners contemplated an expansion of the city's public housing commitment, housing officials struggled over questions of desegregation. In 1942, on a three to two vote, the SFHA commissioners passed a resolution

vowing to provide racial representation in public housing that was propor-
tional to the need of low-income households in each group, but added that
"this Authority shall act with reference to the established usages, customs
and traditions of the community and with a view to the preservation of
public peace and good order and shall insofar as possible maintain and preserve the same racial composition which exists in the neighborhood where
a project is located."[11]

In October 1949, as postwar construction plans ramped up, the SFHA
commissioners voted to uphold the prewar policy that targeted public
housing admission on the basis of "neighborhood pattern," thereby
reinforcing segregation. Given that the city's black population had swelled
eightfold from only five thousand in 1940 to more than forty-three thousand in 1950—making this population more than twice as large as those self-
identifying as Chinese—the issue of where African Americans could live had
rapidly become highly visible.[12] The Council of Civic Unity (CCU), an interracial civil rights organization led by white housing activist Edward Howden,
worked hard to increase public pressure on the SFHA, convening forums
throughout the city. Most significantly, the CCU convinced supervisor (and
future mayor) George Christopher to take on the issue directly.[13] Typifying
the frequent standoffs that would come to characterize SFHA relations with
the city's Board of Supervisors and mayor, in November the more liberal
supervisors tried to undermine the SFHA Board of Commissioners' policy
by voting eight to three in favor of a nondiscrimination clause for entry into
all new public housing supported by federal funds from the Housing Act of
1949. This action forced the SFHA to accept these terms if it wished to apply
for $30 million to support three thousand new public housing units, since
this application needed approval from the supervisors.[14]

Socially conservative SFHA executive director John Beard pushed back.
As a former tenant manager, historian John Baranski notes, Beard "had
considerable experience filtering out nonwhite applicants from white-
only projects and this segregationist expertise was what [won] him the
position" back in 1943. "Public housing," Beard maintained, "is intended
to serve not only the tenants but the community as a whole. We don't
want any cultural islands scattered about the city. An effort to change the
character would be accompanied by social disturbances of considerable
degree." He insisted that the policy was "not discrimination" and that it
had been "borrowed from Philadelphia." Supervisor Chester MacPhee
offered a sharp counterargument: "Segregation in public housing is no
more to be tolerated than segregation in any other Government activity.
If we followed the Commission's plans, we'd be having separate libraries
and separate hospitals. Imagine the fire department turning out only for
fires in the houses of white people." The *San Francisco Chronicle* viewed

the underlying impasse as a power struggle over the very nature of the city's governance: "Who is boss, the Housing Authority or the Board of Supervisors?"[15]

On February 20, 1950, the supervisors and the SFHA reached a so-called compromise, promising to open new public housing on a racially integrated basis, but grandfathering in North Beach Place (and several other delayed developments) on the grounds that these had been planned prior to the war. As the *Chronicle* noted, the agreement "represented little compromise at all. It was nearer a retreat by the Housing Commissioners."[16] Although the Board of Supervisors could not make desegregation retroactive, the decision firmly altered future policy.

North Beach Place opened in early September 1952 as San Francisco's final development to be tenanted on an officially segregated basis. The SFHA gave preference to veterans and to those who had been displaced by the project's construction. It set a maximum monthly income for admission between $180 and $249, depending on family size. Rents ranged from $13.50 to $51 per month, initially set as a percentage of tenant income. Two-person households paid 22 percent of their income in rent, whereas the rent for the largest households (containing six or more people) consumed only 17 percent of household income. Three-quarters of the apartments contained two or more bedrooms, including fifty-nine with three bedrooms and nine with four. The housing authority filled these with young families, headed by American citizens with stable incomes, even though those incomes needed to be fairly low.[17] These income and family composition preferences, however, remained silent on the matter of race.

This did not go unnoticed, especially since court hearings on its racial composition commenced that same week the project opened. With black families in search of public housing limited to a single development (Westside Courts, located in the Fillmore), the NAACP helped African American tenants challenge the SFHA system. Attorneys worked with three black households denied entry into North Beach Place despite being income eligible and holding veteran status. Even though black veterans officially qualified for priority housing, the NAACP documented that the SFHA preferred to house fifty-two white nonveterans in North Beach. Beard testified that the SFHA conducted "complete credit investigations" of all sixteen black applicants—all of whom failed to qualify—while acknowledging that no similar checks had been conducted on the eighty-six white households that had thus far been admitted. Moreover, the SFHA bent over backward to seek out white veterans, even if it meant importing them from outside of San Francisco. Having an extra cache of white veterans available to house instead of black nonveterans girded the housing authority against the possibility that the NAACP might win its case.[18]

When the SFHA did lose, its appeals kept the case moving through the state courts during 1952 and 1953. Ultimately, in 1954, the *Banks v. Housing Authority of San Francisco* case reached the US Supreme Court. Only after the Court refused to hear the case—a decision announced just one week after the celebrated *Brown v. Board of Education* decision—did the SFHA relent and begin to integrate all of its projects.[19] The concept of "neighborhood pattern," every court agreed, was no more than a euphemism for an unconstitutional form of segregation.[20]

Meanwhile, presaging future apprehensions about who would be housed in North Beach Place, legal advocates from San Francisco's Chinese community actually downplayed concerns about segregated public housing—fearing that full racial integration could cause them to lose their hold over the first "Chinese project," Ping Yuen.[21] For North Beach Place, nominally integrated a couple of years after it had first opened, race relations remained fraught for decades, greatly influencing its redevelopment, as well.

NORTH BEACH PLACE IN THE 1950S

North Beach Place opened with several distinctive amenities, including an "experimental kitchen," rooftop laundry, and drying yards—but plans for a large "social room" proved too controversial to implement.[22] John Beard regarded past provision of social space in the prewar Holly Courts project as a clear mistake, according to Baranski, since it "facilitated tenant (and subversive) organizing." At North Beach Place, Beard argued against including any community meeting space. Civic groups provided careful documentation of heavy past and present use of community space in San Francisco public housing, but the commissioners agreed with Beard that public housing funds should be spent on housing rather than "recreation facilities."[23] In this domain, too, early battles would continue to be refought for decades to come.

As befitting a former site manager, John Beard kept a close watch over tenants. Like many other housing authority leaders of his era, he took full advantage of the high demand for public housing to be very selective about who would be allowed to occupy it. Baranski argues that Beard "turned his managerial paternalism into policy" by hiring a separate police force that provided him "with his own surveillance crew." Even more proactively, "Beard and his staff weeded out tenants for character flaws by constantly tinkering with tenant eligibility standards. Low-income nuclear families headed by veterans had the highest priority."[24] Moreover, even after the federal Public Housing Administration ceased requiring household heads in public housing to be US citizens, the SFHA preferred to retain this prerequisite, "thus setting in policy . . . a right to discriminate against immigrants." Residents who made it through the screening, however, greatly appreciated the low rents, careful maintenance, and numerous services provided at all of the early SFHA projects.[25]

URBAN RENEWAL, FREEWAYS, AND THE RISE OF TENANT-ORIENTED INSTITUTIONS

As in New Orleans, Boston, and Tucson, the governance of early public housing in San Francisco took place in accordance with the wishes of a small circle of public sector players, eager to work closely with the business sector to improve the economic prospects of the postwar American city. Low-income residents and not-for-profit community groups held no visible place in this constellation. The subsequent power of San Francisco's tenant-oriented institutions did not appear by magic; rather, it arose in tandem with an initial round of neighborhood fights. As in Tucson, where the upending of the downtown barrio to build the convention center caused lingering resentments, or in Boston, where the battles over development-induced displacement from urban renewal and highway construction led to protracted struggles, San Francisco's activism was forged in reaction to the city's own racially charged upheavals during the 1950s, 1960s, and 1970s. San Francisco's version of the antihighway revolt commenced in 1959 and stopped completion of the waterfront Embarcadero Freeway; the "elevated stub of Interstate 280 . . . became a legend for highway protesters across the nation."[26] The city's political culture may now be firmly associated with empowered left-wing politics, but this had to be created as a countermovement to policies judged to be unfair and discriminatory.

Writing in *Local Protest, Global Movements*, Karl Beitel sees San Francisco as emblematic of a "distinctively American brand of Populist social protest," one that has "consistently celebrated locally embedded forms of community-based self-governance." The future struggles by North Beach Place tenants and their allies for what Chester Hartman famously termed "the right to stay put"[27] depended on earlier efforts to gain control over the management of their lives through partnerships with local organizations and persistent calls for enhanced autonomy. Beitel highlights the "persistence of local protest" in San Francisco across diverse federal policy regimes and shifting mayoral priorities, which have long oscillated between prodevelopment and community-focused polarities. He laments that these protest movements have remained fragmented and unable to transform market-dominated practices but points out that "San Francisco has perhaps the most developed system of participatory governance of any major city in the United States."[28] Things did not start out that way.

During the peak of the postwar era of urban renewal in the 1950s and 1960s, San Francisco's progrowth regime delivered an alliance of business, labor, and government through the auspices of the city's redevelopment agency (SFRA), under the heavy-handed direction of Justin Herman from 1959 until his death in 1971. The Blyth-Zellerbach Committee, a group of the city's influential businessmen established in 1955, worked to jump-start what they judged an initially laggard urban renewal program. They commissioned a report in 1959 from Philadelphia-based consultant Aaron Levine that urged more aggressive business leadership, coupled with enhanced investment in expanding the City Planning Department and SFRA. The report also called for an "independent citizens organization to assist the planning program" so as to overcome public "apathy and usually opposition and resentment to most planning proposals."[29] The committee duly established and initially funded the San Francisco Planning and Urban Renewal Association (SPUR) to take up this task. Meanwhile, following a national search, Mayor George Christopher responded by hiring Herman. "Within months," historian Alison Isenberg observes, "the SFRA was buying properties, clearing parcels, and selling land."[30] By the end of the 1950s, San Franciscans had assembled "a powerful growth coalition capable of rebuilding downtown."[31]

Political scientist John Mollenkopf observes that Justin Herman "knew the federal program and the urban development business backwards and forward, had close personal ties to the Washington bureaucrats whose co-operation would speed his activities, and had strong views about the importance of public control over urban design." Herman's vision for San Francisco's development included a vastly expanded central business district that entailed substantial clearance of minority-dominated neighborhoods near downtown and rehabilitation of other areas "where 'blighting' so-cial groups occupied Victorian housing stock likely to be desirable to the growing middle class that the new downtown office buildings would gen-erate."[32] Chester Hartman, who moved to the Bay Area in 1970 to work for the National Housing Law Project, acknowledged Herman's "incredible energy, tenacity and political talent," but pointedly resisted his projects. He viewed Herman's redevelopment agency as "a powerful and aggressive army out to capture as much downtown land as it could. . . . Under the ru-bric of 'slum clearance' and 'blight removal,' the Agency was systematically sweeping out the poor, with the full support of the city's power structure."[33]

The two major redevelopment projects in the Western Addition, known as A-1 and A-2, displaced as many as 20,000 people, many of them concen-trated in the predominantly black Fillmore area at the center of the demoli-tion (figure 10.5). The A-1 project of the late 1950s and early 1960s uprooted

Figure 10.5. Urban Renewal and Freeways Come to San Francisco
Urban renewal projects A-1 and A-2 decimated the core of San Francisco's growing
black community in the Fillmore, while citizen activism curtailed the incursions of
freeways, including an extension of the Embarcadero Freeway that would have been
routed directly past North Beach Place.
Credit: Author with Jonathan Tarleton; aerial photograph 1VLX000010087 courtesy of
the US Geological Survey.

four thousand households, and fully one-quarter of them ended up in nearby
substandard housing, just in time for them to be displaced again during the
clearance associated with larger A-2 initiative, responsible for removing
13,500 more people from the district, while providing remarkably little new
affordable housing.[34] Clearly, while this Western Subtraction left the Fillmore
far less filled with black people, it also left a fractured city filled with anger.

Thomas Fleming, editor of the *Sun-Reporter*, a weekly newspaper
oriented to African Americans, viewed the SFRA's efforts at land control
as a shameless campaign of racially motivated displacement. Writing about

Herman in 1965, he observed that "Negroes and the other victims of a low income generally regard him as the arch villain in the black depopulation of the city."[35] Although the A-1 project had proceeded relatively unimpeded, "Project A-2 faced opposition from the beginning." The NAACP's housing director strongly objected to the lack of alternative housing and relocation resources; one organization, Freedom House, even came up with an alternative plan for the area; and the Western Addition Community Organization (WACO) mobilized to lead the resistance. In 1968, with the help of a legal aid organization, WACO even won a federal injunction that forced the SFRA to review renewal plans with a community panel.[36]

Justin Herman bitterly resented the litigation launched to slow or stop these and other renewal projects and lashed out those who instigated these delays. When attorney Sidney Wolinsky from the San Francisco Legal Assistance Foundation hired his own attorneys to demand an apology from Herman for calling him an "S.O.B.," "ambulance chaser," and "shyster" who was "intellectually dishonest," Herman doubled down on his criticism of his critics. "Regarding your formal request for a retraction for anything I might have said about you: Nuts." Then, "with official business out of the way," he truculently offered up "some advice acquired from 35 years of public service":

> When you get into government work as you recently have, and then go about trying to halt the only two multi-million government projects in the City which will provide housing for low income people (the Western Addition) and which will provide the badly needed revenues to support the jobs and aids to enable those people to move into those homes (Yerba Buena Center), then you have to expect a little criticism now and then.

He went on to accuse Wolinsky and his colleagues of "practicing a new kind of guerilla law—you know, the exploiting and manufacturing of phony incidents to win public support and discredit a fellow public agency." He warned them that "the criticism can sometimes get even hotter." Ever confident in his institutional aims, he dismissed his critics as playing a "game of using vast sums of Federal money to thwart Federal programs to the bewilderment of some Federal taxpayers and the wails of the genuinely disadvantaged." Herman half-jokingly concluded that, in these "Days of the Absurd," he just might himself seek assistance from Wolinsky's Neighborhood Legal Assistance Foundation to file a counterclaim. Seeming to acknowledge his own reputation for effective autocracy, Herman entitled his talk at the 1968 national conference of the American Society of Planning Officials "Planners and Politicians: A Machiavellian Team."[37]

However bombastic his rhetoric, Herman viewed himself as an urban renewal progressive who remained sensitive to "land grab" critiques and engaged in ways to retain public ownership over land. Once backlash accelerated in 1968, he even gained some credit for constructive response to protests.[38] In 1974, three years after his death, the city ceremoniously named the major plaza at the foot of Market Street in his memory.[39]

Despite such a forceful redevelopment regime, from the mid-1950s to the mid-1970s San Francisco's neighborhood-based activists fought substantially successful battles, especially against freeway extensions. This proved that victory for citizen-centered neighborhood movements could be possible. Stopping the Embarcadero Freeway did more than leave an emblematic aerial stub; it also meant that the larger project of extending I-480 along the waterfront all the way to the Golden Gate Bridge did not proceed. Specifically, since the anticipated alignment went down Bay Street before bending slightly at Columbus Avenue, the antihighway movement stopped North Beach Place from being severed from Fisherman's Wharf (see figure 10.5). Just as with the thwarted Riverfront Expressway extension in New Orleans and the aborted Inner Belt in Boston, the San Franciscan revolt against I-480 kept planners from their wish to pair public housing and public highways. These episodes reveal a consistent spatial politics—an index of relative power and vulnerability—even if the contestation played out differently in each city.

In San Francisco, despite community-based success in freeing themselves from freeways, the mostly unsuccessful efforts to halt other urban renewal projects undercut confidence—most notably the failure to prevent the razing of the Fillmore. Still, the protracted skirmishes meant that the language and tools of zoning and land use had been appropriated by local leaders, rather than left to "the experts." "Most notably," Beitel points out, "defeats being handed to activists in the Fillmore District and the spread of the gentrification frontier throughout San Francisco's working class neighborhoods would spur the formation of a citywide umbrella organization of nonprofit, community-based housing developers—the Council of Community Housing Organizations." CCHO offered an alternative development model centered on the concerns and needs of low-income working-class neighborhoods. In short, San Francisco's housing and land-use activists learned their lessons from urban renewal. This relatively small cadre, many of them inspired by the San Francisco State student strike of 1968–1969, mastered the lingo and practices of legal-regulatory administration so that they could "use various measures—ballot initiatives, testimony before local planning and housing commissions, direct action and mobilization around district elections—to impose some limits on developer prerogative."[40]

Starting in the 1970s, with cities accorded greater leeway to prioritize their spending of federal Community Development Block Grant (CDBG) funds, having a neighborhood-based counterweight to the mayor's office proved highly significant. An administrative complaint issued by CCHO and its legal allies caused HUD to withhold San Francisco's CDBG allocation until, in the mid-1980s, the city committed itself to allotting the majority of its housing funds to nonprofit organizations. With not-for-profit housing corporations afforded increased centrality, San Francisco's approach to future federal programs such as HOPE VI could not help but be affected by increasingly entrenched expectations for participation and inclusion in decision-making. Epitomized by the subsequent struggle to redevelop North Beach Place, the result has been "a culture of local dissent and the ability to extract meaningful concessions from private developers"—even though none of this has been sufficient to preserve the overall affordability of the city's housing stock.[41]

As neighborhood-based organizations flexed their development muscles, other events focused attention on the plight of existing low-income tenants. CCHO not only created a "credible counterpole" to conventional market-centered development practices; it also contributed to a broader tenant movement that led to rent control provisions and eviction protections and, more generally, increased the regulation of rental housing in San Francisco.[42]

Much of this came to a head in the decade-long fight over preservation of the International Hotel, a 155-room residential building occupied primarily by older male Filipino and Chinese laborers, located downtown in the seam where an expanding financial district uneasily intersected Chinatown (figure 10.5). When a developer, seeking to demolish and redevelop the "Manilatown" property, proposed to evict existing residents, this sparked a pivotal round of neighborhood backlash, dramatically altering the local political landscape of landlord rights. From 1968 to 1977, community activists organized mass rallies attracting as many as five thousand participants.[43]

Despite protracted legal maneuvers and efforts to find solutions, however, at 3:00 a.m. on August 4, 1977, four hundred San Francisco police broke through a human barricade of two thousand supporters and forcibly evicted the tenants. Chester Hartman (a participant) comments: "It was brief, brutal, and effective." As Beitel describes it, "Officers broke into tenants' rooms, smashed personal possessions, and destroyed toilet facilities to ensure that tenants would have no way to return."[44] Those particular tenants did not return, but the I-Hotel ignominy remained a touchstone for subsequent generations of activists.

In 1980, San Francisco's Residential Hotel Demolition and Conversion Ordinance banned the demolition and conversion of such places, unless sufficient fees were provided to the city's affordable housing replacement fund. Such preservation efforts soon gained counterparts in new forms of affordable community housing to supplement the public housing stock, as well as the city's Rent Stabilization and Arbitration Ordinance, passed in 1979, which now covers 170,000 rental units. An inclusionary zoning ordinance has contributed to the development of more than a thousand additional affordable housing units, and the SFRA embarked on a long-term

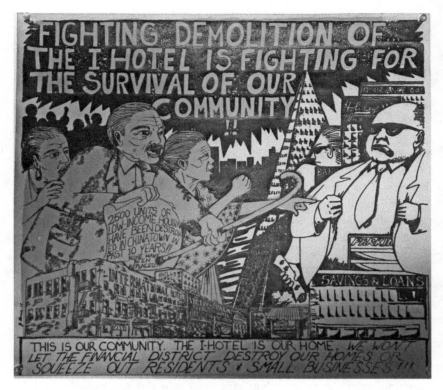

Figure 10.6 The Battle over the I-Hotel
Starting in the late 1960s, San Francisco's tenant activists rallied to save the
International Hotel (I-Hotel), located on the edge of Chinatown and the Financial
District. Although they lost the I-Hotel battle in 1977, the backlash led to landmark
ordinances aimed at preserving affordable housing. Several decades later, this
poster still adorned the office wall of Calvin Welch, who cofounded the Coalition of
Community Housing Organizations in the late 1970s.
Credit: Collection of Calvin Welch, photo by author.

plan to replace the net loss of 6,709 units that had resulted from its urban
renewal activities. All told, despite the extent of gentrification and some of
the highest housing prices in the country, it is also the case that more than
half of San Francisco's entire housing stock now carries some form of "price
control." A quarter-century after the I-Hotel's demise, a report by housing
activists could plausibly claim that a city "once notorious for urban renewal
that diminished housing affordability and displaced tenants" could now be
"renowned nationally for its best practices in housing and community development."[45] As Beitel puts it, "The value of maintaining neighborhood diversity, the right of low-income tenants to remain in the city, and an ethos

of environmental and neighborhood preservation are now embedded in the taken-for-granted rhetorical framework for conducting deliberations over the goals and priorities to be served by local development." In a city where 65 percent of residents are renters rather than homeowners, it is hardly surprising that San Francisco's governance constellation developed a notable protenant, Nonprofitus skew.[46]

SAN FRANCISCO HOUSING AUTHORITY STRUGGLES

The rise of community-based housing organizations paralleled the decline of the SFHA, as the agency faced its own internal governance transformation. In the 1950s, public housing could still be framed as a bulwark against subversion of all sorts. After two decades of operations, the SFHA praised the contributions of public housing to the "moral, spiritual, intellectual and physical stature" of the citizenry.[47] Yet the new North Beach Place housing project joined a changing neighborhood, soon to be both ridiculed and acclaimed for the short-lived literary counterculture of the Beats. Three years after the project opened, Allen Ginsberg wrote most of *Howl* in an apartment on Montgomery Street, less than a mile away.[48] Ginsberg, needless to say, would have hardly been a welcome tenant at North Beach Place.

A gradual loss of institutional self-confidence and financial viability soon overcame even the most ardent efforts to spin the San Francisco public housing story in rosy terms. The ample doses of heady self-praise that permeated the annual reports of the SFHA during the 1940s were followed by a succession of terse but upbeat typescripts throughout the 1950s and early 1960s, but the picture darkened soon afterward. Tenants, both in public housing and elsewhere in the city, gradually began to raise their voices. Residents at many SFHA developments formed tenant associations, and, in December 1964, North Beach tenant Marjorie Bezzone, acting on behalf of the North Beach Tenants Association (NBTA), became the first tenant representative ever to speak at a SFHA commissioners' meeting; soon afterward, this sort of thing became commonplace. Within a decade, public housing residents even gained two seats on an expanded seven-member board of commissioners—not quite the equivalent of Boston's "tenant-oriented majority" board, but similar in spirit.[49]

In August 1965, North Beach residents finally convinced the SFHA to create permanent space for resident social gatherings and meetings. John Beard's longstanding objection to any possible spatial facilitation of resident organizing had been overcome. Coincidentally or not, Beard's twenty-two-year reign as executive director ended just two months later, following many years of increased rancor over his treatment of tenants. Mayor Jack

Shelley—whose election in 1963 ended a fifty-year string of Republicans in that office and launched what has thus far been more than fifty consecutive years of mayoral Democrats—replaced Beard with his aide, friend, and former law school classmate, Eneas Kane.[50]

With Beard's exit, the housing authority began to acknowledge the scope of its challenges. As Kane put it, "Annual reports usually glow with pride and optimism. This, the 29th Annual Report of the San Francisco Housing Authority, . . . recounts the problems as well as the achievements." As larger numbers of residents entered the system with greater impoverishment, rent delinquencies mounted, as did mistrust between tenants and the housing authority charged with managing them. "Rising costs and diminishing income" rapidly destabilized the SFHA's finances. It sought out greater opportunities for social services and, by necessity, embraced the idea of tenant councils. The Hunters Point project, located in the city's far southeast, faced the worst conditions. By 1966, the SFHA acknowledged, "The wanton destruction of buildings . . . is rampant and adds to widespread despair in the area." Apartments faced vandalism as soon as they were vacated, and maintenance costs were "skyrocketing." More generally, SFHA leaders worried about "the sense of isolation many [tenants] feel. They feel cut off from the city's quest for jobs and opportunities, and sense little community with San Francisco."[51]

Many San Franciscans soon credited Kane for improving morale, pursuing closer ties with residents, and offering greater respect for tenant councils. Still, even as the housing authority embarked on new programs to lease housing, develop public housing on scattered sites, and engage in turnkey arrangements with private developers to produce new housing for seniors, Kane acknowledged that more of the existing tenants could not meet their rent obligations.[52] By 1969, fiscal problems mounted. As Kane described the situation in a letter to new progrowth mayor Joseph Alioto (in office from 1968 to 1976), "The Authority continues to be caught between the horns of the wage-price spiral and statutory limitations on the cost of new construction," even as many existing developments faced "a vandalism problem that continues unabated."[53] In 1970, Kane expressed further worries to Alioto. "The demand for public housing exceeds the supply and shows no signs of leveling off," he noted, but the SFHA could provide housing for only about one-quarter of its annual applicants and "faced a critical financial situation."[54]

Kane lasted almost a dozen years as SFHA executive director but, like his long-serving predecessor, left office under a cloud. He resigned in January 1977 following an indictment for embezzling housing authority funds, pleaded guilty to grand larceny, and received a sentence of three years' probation. Soon afterward, the SFHA entered into a protracted period of decline, and a long succession of executive directors struggled. In 1980, during the mayoralty of Dianne Feinstein (in office from 1978 to 1988), HUD branded the SFHA as a "Troubled Housing Authority." San Francisco thereby joined New Orleans and Boston among the twenty-two cities in the country (out of more than three thousand housing agencies) to warrant this dubious distinction. In 1985, HUD placed the SFHA on probation and, in 1988, a HUD regional official complained to the commission chairman that "the authority has virtually lost control of entire developments." Half the city's projects, HUD charged, were managed more by drug dealers than by the SFHA, leading to extensive vandalism and an incapacity to maintain apartments.[55]

CHANGING NEIGHBORHOODS AND NEIGHBORS

As the SFHA staggered through its decades-long cycle of instability, the neighborhoods surrounding its developments continued to change as well. When North Beach Place opened, the imposing diagonal of Columbus Avenue still marked a clear boundary between the world of the "Latin quarter" and the life of San Francisco's legendary Chinatown, generally seen as extending north only as far as Broadway (see figure 10.5).[56] Despite periodic efforts to continue to market North Beach as culturally Italian, Chinese residents gradually moved northward, especially once their numbers increased following the easing of immigration restrictions in 1965. With Chinatown seen as encroaching from the south, the North Beach neighborhood faced newfound interest from many quarters. Historian Amy Howard notes, "The national and international fascination with the Beats in the late 1950s and the rise of the topless clubs in the 1960s drew a wide range of new visitors to the district, including 'Summer of Love' participants in 1967." On the waterfront side, in 1961, North Beach Place architect Ernest Born (together with Esther Born and John Bolles) prepared a Plan for Fisherman's Wharf, envisioning enhanced open space, restaurants, and cafés.[57]

Throughout the 1960s and 1970s, the tenant population of North Beach Place itself continued to diversify. With linguistic divides hampering communication, Chinese residents felt left out of the development's initial tenant association, launched in 1964. Consequently, the NBTA gained a Cantonese-speaking counterpart in 1966, the North Beach Place Chinese Improvement Association. By 1969, Chinese tenants constituted approximately 30 percent of the households in the development. Meanwhile, to the development's north, additional challenges mounted with the growth of mass tourism along San Francisco's waterfront. Instead of fishermen and wharves, there was now Fisherman's Wharf.

Increasingly the Italian names of North Beach Place's neighbors were replaced by the monikers of Hilton, Marriott, Sheraton, and Travelodge, yielding more nearby hotel rooms than apartments or houses. The Powell and Mason cable car line, which terminated at Bay Street and Taylor Street in the midst of the development, now formed a key link in the tourist route from Chinatown to Fisherman's Wharf. Of the more than thirteen million tourists who flocked annually to the shops and ambiance of this district, local officials estimated that more than one million arrived by cable car, itself a tourist destination. This odd juxtaposition of low-income housing and high-impact tourism, many commentators wryly noted, made North Beach the most heavily visited public housing project in the United States. For most, however, such visits were inadvertent at best.

By the 1980s, arriving at the North Beach project triggered feelings of danger and disruption: public housing residents resented the noise of the tourists just outside their windows, and tourists (and many businesses dependent on their patronage) regarded the denizens of the projects as a source of crime and depredation. At one point, Mayor Feinstein seriously entertained a $35 million proposal from a developer to turn the North Beach Place site into yet another hotel. Denise McCarthy, long-serving executive director of the Telegraph Hill Neighborhood Center (Tel-Hi), recalls, "There was a huge discussion about how much better it would be to take the money and build all this new housing somewhere else more 'appropriate.'" Tel-Hi responded with extended organizing and outreach to the press, and "it died. She couldn't pull it off." Tel-Hi, founded in 1890 as a settlement house in the manner of Chicago's Hull House, would remain a key ally for North Beach Place for many decades.[58]

To some extent, McCarthy observes, the effort to preserve low-income housing succeeded because "there were a lot of liberals in that neighborhood," and a lingering "sense of bohemianism" in a place that is "not that many blocks from City Lights bookstore." Perhaps more surprisingly, Tel-Hi relied substantially on support from "almost the entire power structure of the main merchants' group, the Fisherman's Wharf Merchants Association." They supported keeping it because it was the last "sizable development" left; "everything else had been gentrified." The group's secretary, Al Baccari, McCarthy found, "just had a very strong social conscience." Baccari was joined in this by Chris Martin (whose father Leonard had preserved and redeveloped the nearby Cannery in the mid-1960s).[59] "They both really cared. They had spent years there. Chris grew up around that place." Even though the Wharf had "lost its connection to the Italian community in terms of tenancy," the old families realized "you couldn't have a community with just businesses, and they certainly didn't want to have a hotel." Longtime housing activist Calvin Welch, who cofounded the Council of Community

Housing Organizations in the late 1970s, concurs: "Chris understood what it meant to be in a neighborhood, and saw the projects as part of the neighborhood." "It really was just people who had values," McCarthy adds. "It's kind of nice, isn't it?"[60]

NORTH BEACH NADIR

Although North Beach Place avoided redevelopment into a hotel, conditions continued to deteriorate between the mid-1970s and the early 1990s. Neighborhood residents frequently blamed North Beach Place tenants for disturbing the tourists, while residents blamed outsiders for invading the all-too-permeable precincts of the development. A *Chronicle* reporter seemed to blame both residents and their friends, noting that "rampaging teenage thugs keep most of the poor and elderly tenants in terror." Police officer Edward Rodriguez blamed the design of the project for some of the trouble, noting that suspects "watch us from one end [of the project] and see us two blocks away."

Given the complaints about excessive permeability and rampant crime, it is surely ironic that architect Oscar Newman singled out North Beach Place for special praise in his landmark book, *Defensible Space: Crime Prevention through Urban Design*, first published in 1972. In a five-page spread of photos and text, Newman emphasized the way that ground-floor units along Bay Street could be entered directly from the street via a small "semi-private" landing and featured well-placed windows that permitted the kind of surveillance that "clearly will not tolerate ambiguous use or loitering." He found these "symbolic, territory-defining devices" to be "a particularly fascinating feature of the project's design," since the entrances were treated "as if they were single-family houses within a row-house configuration." Still, Newman noted, the other sides of the project had no such territorial definition, and the place as a whole suffered from "a factory or bunker aesthetic." Even worse, he wrote, the project's Garden Courts isolated the children's play areas from any direct access to the interior of buildings and "seem to have worked out poorly." Although Newman did not mention it, the ease of pedestrian access through these low-surveillance Garden Courts surely contributed to their value as escape routes for criminals. These nondefensible features of the space, it seems, more than overcame the innovations of the Bay Street frontage, yielding many of the same problems that Newman had identified as endemic to fully open superblock configurations.[61]

Crime continued to mount. Residents complained that unlocked garbage wells acted to harbor muggers, and investigators noted that about half of the lights in stairwells and along balconies had missing bulbs. As robberies tripled from eleven in 1977 to thirty-six in 1978 and automobile theft remained a weekly occurrence, tenants declined to identify suspects by name, fearing retaliation.[62] By 1979, North Beach Place tenants met with Mayor Feinstein and called upon the SFHA to step up security and improve lighting. They threatened a rent strike (a tactic that had proven successful elsewhere in San Francisco and in other cities).[63] Hope Halikias, representing the North Beach Tenants Association, complained to the Board of Supervisors in 1985 that no one from SFHA was willing to listen, charging the agency with having a "plantation mentality."[64] Following the rise of teenage gangs in 1970s, drug sales and drug-related violence escalated in the 1980s with advent of crack cocaine. This is confirmed by residents who experienced that era directly. One tenant, who first moved to North Beach Place in 1981, dated the decline to 1986, "when the big big crack cocaine came out" and "every nationality from other places used to come here and try to do their drugs." Another resident, tenant leader Cynthia Wiltz, experienced the effects of the drug scene quite personally. She lived next door to a new community resource center that was torched by drug dealers just before it was due to open. "My life's in jeopardy," Wiltz told the *Chronicle*. "They say they're going to burn me out next."[65] Although, statistically, crime in and around the North Beach complex never reached the levels seen at some other San Francisco public housing sites, in this location it was just much more visible.

When interviewed many years later, long-term residents who had lived through the old project's worst days uniformly deplored those conditions. Alma Lark arrived at North Beach in June 1958 as one of the first African American residents and spent much of the next five decades advocating for the rights of North Beach tenants. Lark, described admiringly by other North Beach residents as "feisty," "powerful," "strong," "Malcolm X–like," "out-spoken," "nationalistic," and "about 5'3"," became particularly vociferous in the run-up to redevelopment. By 1992, when she testified in a congressional hearing devoted to problems with public housing in San Francisco, she described "stopped up" gutters, an "intolerable problem" with "enormous cockroaches" and mice, "urine and human feces" on the stairway, heaters that did not work, and a delay to get a nonfunctioning stove replaced. Lark sued the SFHA and put her rent in an escrow account, pending settlement of her case. She blamed SFHA recalcitrance on her being "a tenant activist."[66] In that, she was not alone.

Greg Richardson arrived at North Beach in late 1993 as a homeless single parent and lived there for the remainder of the decade, all the way until the redevelopment. Moving in, he considered it a "hellhole," with "so much isolation from the rest of the city."

[There was] garbage all over the place, broken windows, crying and screaming all the time. Tourists getting harassed and robbed by the cable car, [with the perpetrators] running into buildings after they robbed them. People were always breaking car windows out every ten minutes. Old ladies being beat up, mugged. Domestic violence was just rampant.[67]

Richardson viewed North Beach as "controlled by drug dealers" but quickly tried to get involved with improving the governance of his new neighborhood. He sought to work with "at-risk youth, drug dealers, any form of negativity that existed in the complex." To him, this was the only way to improve a community that "was so afraid." As an African American male, he viewed much of the multiethnic community with puzzlement:

The Chinese and Pacific Islanders kept their doors locked. They didn't come outside. They were just like a closed community. Hispanics kind of stayed to themselves. Samoans and African Americans kind of mingled together. But a lot of the single women there just stayed in their houses and dealt with the elements of the drug world.

Interviews with many other long-term residents, conducted with the promise of anonymity, round out the picture. Whether male or female, Chinese, white, black, or Hispanic, they shared widespread distress.

Residents consistently emphasized problems with various building systems— clogs and floods, poor drainage on balconies, wintertime lack of warmth, or unwelcome steam heat in the summer. Pest infestations also prevailed. In the kitchen, one resident recalled, "The whole wall was collapsing, and rats were coming in"; another drew a finer distinction: "The big rats were outside, those that comes in the house are small." Others emphasized the misbehavior of fellow residents, manifested by "tenant fist fights," "problem dogs in the stairwells," "loud music," trees that died because "kids threw ice on them," and once-peaceful courtyards that became the site of staged pit bull fights." Some also opted to highlight "outsiders committing crimes," but mostly they lamented the state of North Beach Place itself: "messed up," "really bad," "an embarrassment," "raggedy"—one person compared it to Folsom Prison, even though "you are not confined."[68]

Periodic surveys of residents conducted by the SFHA and community organizations during the run-up to redevelopment provide more quantifiable confirmations of these anecdotes. One survey of more than a hundred households, undertaken shortly before the redevelopment commenced, found that most residents listed bathroom and kitchen plumbing, cockroaches, and broken windows as among their "most serious" interior maintenance problems. A majority also stressed problems with unsafe stairwells, exterior painting, site drainage, and broken walkways. Although three-quarters of respondents said that they "felt safe" at North Beach, they blamed "troublemakers," mostly those living outside the development. By contrast, they consistently valued the same things: location, transportation, and convenience to shopping; they would either walk to the nearby Safeway or take a bus to Chinatown.[69]

Demographically, North Beach Place had changed dramatically. Few Italians remained in either the project or the neighborhood. Instead, in a city where the Chinese population had doubled between 1960 and 1980,[70] North Beach Place was half Chinese and one-third African American, with much of the remainder of its polyglot and polyethnic populations hailing from Latin America, Africa, and Asia. As the diversifying residents tried to cope with poor conditions, this effort was matched by constant turmoil in the housing authority.

SEARCHING FOR SFHA LEADERSHIP

In May 1989, Art Agnos, who had succeeded Feinstein as mayor in 1988 and served until 1992, appointed David Gilmore as SFHA executive director to try to right the ship. Gilmore had prepared himself for the task in San Francisco by playing important roles in the celebrated turnaround of the equally dysfunctional Boston Housing Authority during the remarkably effective receivership led by Harry Spence in the early 1980s.[71] Agnos, who held an MSW degree, had served as a social worker at the SFHA during the late 1960s, so he was well versed in the workings of the agency. He proved to be a strong advocate for low-income housing while mayor. With Gilmore in charge, the SFHA made rapid progress. Believing that "the days of large infusions of federal dollars for the construction or rehabilitation of new public housing are long over," Gilmore regarded the preservation of rental public housing of the "highest possible quality" to be a "moral imperative."[72] Within his first two years of leading the SFHA and establishing a series of performance standards, Gilmore reduced the unacceptable 10 percent vacancy rate to less than 1 percent, repaid more than $12 million of SFHA debts, built up operating reserves, and instituted an extensive series of resident initiatives.[73] By June 1991, HUD assistant secretary Joseph Schiff could praise the SFHA for reversing its downward spiral, and, in April 1992, it achieved a passing score under HUD's new Public Housing Management Assessment Program (PHMAP), enabling the agency to be removed from what Gilmore called the "infamous list of troubled Public Housing Authorities." He boldly asserted: "We have ended the most dismal era in the history of public housing in San Francisco."[74]

Despite this seeming progress, in September 1992 a congressional sub-committee held a hearing in San Francisco to investigate the HUD inspector general's charge that the SFHA should not have been removed from the "troubled" list. The audit found that "the agency provided HUD with un-supported and unreliable information" and itemized numerous specific concerns regarding accounting practices, rationales for treating seventeen thousand work orders as completed, and processes for counting units as "occupied," among many other matters. Moreover, the IG's site inspections found that 87 percent of randomly sampled apartments failed to meet HUD's "Housing Quality Standards" due to maintenance operations that "were not efficient or economical."[75] Not surprisingly, the SFHA took "strong exception" to the findings. Gilmore defended his record of accomplishment during the first two years of a five-year plan, and insisted:

> We have never attempted to fool anyone into believing that we are better than we are. . . . We were a deeply troubled housing authority and we are now a good housing authority working hard to become better. We claim no more lofty status than that, but will accede to nothing else.

Gilmore reiterated the immense gains the SFHA had made under his watch and lambasted the "slipshod, politically charged manner in which this re-view has been conducted."[76] This dispute revealed both the questionable advisability of self-scoring management performance and the high drama of election-season politics, since the hearing occurred shortly before the George H. W. Bush administration would be voted out of office.

Meanwhile, however, Art Agnos had already completed his single four-year term as San Francisco's mayor, succeeded in 1992 by the city's progrowth, tough-on-crime former police chief Frank Jordan for the next four years. With that shift, David Gilmore's days were numbered. As Gilmore himself puts it, "I am either loved or hated by mayors."[77] He later told a reporter: "My arrogance, for which I am well known, got in the way."[78] Agnos remained in San Francisco as the HUD regional administrator from 1993 to 2001, while Gilmore went on to develop a national reputation as a public housing turnaround specialist, asked to run the housing authorities in Seattle, Washington, DC, and New Orleans.

With Gilmore's departure, SFHA promoted architect Michael Kelly (who had worked at the authority since 1983) as acting executive director. Kelly remained only until 1994, when he left to join HUD as a troubled-agency re-covery specialist—skills he would soon put to good use when directing both the New Orleans Housing Authority from 1995 to 2000 and the Washington, DC, Housing Authority from 2000 to 2010, before subsequently taking senior housing authority leadership roles in both Philadelphia and New York City.

While Gilmore and Kelly managed to build similar, if differently ordered, nationally visible resumes, the SFHA remained in flux.

After Kelly's departure, the SFHA struggled. Its PHMAP score again plummeted, and an in-depth *Chronicle* investigation found "a pattern of bureaucratic inertia, questionable use of money and entangled political interests that raise serious management, safety and legal issues."[79] The "persistent bungling" of housing administration took its toll on the underfunded housing developments. Barbara Smith, then head of SFHA's housing development division, matter-of-factly enumerated some of the problems that would take at least $350 million to repair: "We have leaking roofs, we have bad electricity, we have heaters that need to be replaced, we have plumbing problems."[80]

The remarkable career trajectory of Smith as a San Francisco housing official clarifies the city's fundamental instability in its low-income housing bureaucracy. She had been well groomed to withstand the leadership challenges of the SFHA, which she joined in 1991. Before that, she spent more than fifteen years in the Mayor's Office of Housing, working under four different mayors, eventually becoming that agency's director in 1989. Then, in the quarter-century since her move to the SFHA, she served, she estimated, under twelve to fifteen different SFHA leaders. Eventually, in 2013, she took on the title of acting executive director herself.[81] Smith's stamina and longevity in the face of an ever-changing cast of characters, both inside the housing authority and beyond, certainly stands out. In many ways, she is the one constant in the saga of North Beach Place: she oversaw its redevelopment while also helping to coordinate the rest of San Francisco's engagement with HOPE VI and beyond. Her strategy was as simple as it was daunting: "We just did our thing. I had a great staff. Our philosophy was, keep your heads down and do your work. Barrel ahead with these projects and we'll make them happen."[82] With Smith as the lone source of stability, a growing array of old and new players emerged to shape the governance constellation necessary to reimagine North Beach Place.

11

Renewing North Beach Place

SEEKING REDEVELOPMENT OPTIONS

At the heart of the North Beach redevelopment impulse, city leaders and neighborhood proponents sought to transform the negative image of the troubled project, seen as a detriment to tourism at nearby Fisherman's Wharf.[1] For several years in the mid-1990s, city officials considered extending the cable car route toward the water. In 1996, Frank Jordan's mayoral successor, Willie Brown, remarked—with some ambiguity—that extending the line "would enable tourists to see Fisherman's Wharf without running the gauntlet of dangers associated with street walking." Some North Beach Place residents agreed that moving the terminus could improve safety, while others claimed that "the development is wrongly blamed for the crime that occurs" and complained that "the city is more concerned with its image than the welfare of its poorest citizens."[2] Ultimately, the cable car extension proved too logistically and financially difficult to implement, so discussion remained centered on how to eliminate the negative impact of the North Beach Place project itself. It comes as no surprise that, when San Francisco eventually submitted a HOPE VI application to redevelop the property, its cover illustration of featured a full-color drawing of a revitalized tourist-filled cable car terminus, in which the flanking buildings of the housing development are almost unrecognizable as such. It is a vibrant world of happy visitors in I-heart-SF T-shirts and lively ground-floor retail, as if Fisherman's Wharf had moved inland to claim new territory (figure 11.1).

In San Francisco, as in gentrifying neighborhoods elsewhere, private developers proactively stepped up to propose alternative uses for public housing sites. In San Francisco, however, any move to alter public housing has been met by countermoves by increasingly empowered tenants and their ever-vigilant allies. Any workable governance constellation for North Beach Place would need to be an inclusive one. Precisely because city officials knew there would be pushback, and because many of their consultants and partners respected the views of tenants, even the *starting point* for discussion needed to assume a level of resident empowerment that would be

Figure 11.1 North Beach Place HOPE VI Application
The cover of the North Beach Place HOPE VI plan provided as full a contrast as
possible to the bleak reality of the troubled housing project, emphasizing a newly
vibrant tourist zone at the heart of the development.
Credit: Seifel Consulting, Inc., and Peter M. Hasselman, graphic illustrator.

unthinkable in many other US cities. This did not mean that it would be easy
for tenants and their allies to dictate parameters, but it did mean that they
were not alone in their wish to retain as much affordable housing as possible
in North Beach.

In 1993, the SFHA commissioned architectural consultants Kaplan
McLaughlin Diaz to explore a potential "planning process and design
alternatives" for North Beach Place. Funded by a family foundation and a
private developer, the report set out a variety of design principles for any
future redevelopment on this site.[3] The report previewed strong tenant
feelings that would re-emerge once HOPE VI became a reality: residents
made clear that any redevelopment proposals must offer all possible
safeguards against displacement. If new investment were to come to North
Beach Place, residents wanted to be certain that they would still be there to
enjoy it.

Michael Kelly's brief time at the helm of SFHA included stepped-up
discussions about the future of North Beach Place, even though he left San
Francisco before an actual HOPE VI application could be submitted. As Kelly
recalls, North Beach was "one of the sites that had been teed up." North
Beach seemed a place where "the economics are just so obvious that you

knew it was going to happen. It was just a question of how and when." And, like Kelly, wary residents knew that "the real estate was just too valuable to leave it in its existing use."[4] The fact that North Beach Place ultimately did retain its existing use is a testament to the power of San Francisco tenants and their advocates.

Meanwhile, as redevelopment options started to be discussed more seriously, tenant leadership schisms emerged, both within the African American part of the community and between the black leaders and other ethnic communities at the development. Soon after his arrival at North Beach, Greg Richardson started attending tenant meetings, as one of the few males to take part. He viewed the organization as basically "defunct." As he later recalled, "They'd have meetings and I'd say, 'What type of training or programs has the housing authority given you because you don't know the rule of order, you take things personally, and you're yelling and screaming at each other. You're not accomplishing anything.' They were dysfunctional." Eventually, as elections approached, he says that other tenants tauntingly approached him. "They said, 'Oh, Mr. Richardson, you think you know everything. Why don't you run for the president?' So I said maybe I just might." He did and won. His leadership caused some tensions with long-standing African American residents such as Alma Lark. Richardson saw Lark as "an old fox" who "would battle the SF Housing Authority on every front—on every application, on every front to stop them in their tracks." As Richardson put it,

> Alma was there long before I lived there, and she was the one always schooling the ladies, schooling the tenant's board on what they need to do. So she was more like the queen behind the scene. So all the ladies listened to Alma. What Miss Lark said, they kinda trusted that opinion. Miss Lark looked at me as a threat.

Redevelopment efforts at North Beach faced many other kinds of threats, both internal and external.

HOPING FOR HOPE

With the SFHA in disarray and under HUD oversight, local officials needed to sort out how a dysfunctional agency could best apply for a HOPE VI grant. Not surprisingly, having received a HOPE VI planning grant from HUD in December 1995, they chose to outsource preparation of the full revitalization grant application. SFHA consultant David Cortiella, who had preceded Sandra Henriquez as Boston Housing Authority administrator, suggested that they bring in Boston-based planner Amy Schectman to prepare the bid. She had successfully masterminded Boston's first HOPE VI proposal for Mission Main—scored nationally as the top application during the very first cycle of grants. But Schectman, unavailable to move to San Francisco on short notice, turned down the opportunity. Instead, MIT housing scholar Langley Keyes, Schectman's former adviser when she was a master's student, proposed another MIT graduate, San Francisco–based Elizabeth (Libby) Seifel.

Seifel, who had recently started her own consulting firm, took on the job with gusto. Aided by Schectman and Keyes, she brought the necessary energy and organization to pull together the full application in only six weeks. Attuned to the emergent "Boston Model" by her colleagues, Seifel found that a version of this made abundant sense in San Francisco—another city where tenants and their advocates expected to have a major say in any plans for public housing redevelopment. She immediately discovered two key factors: "the dysfunction of the housing authority" and the parallel strength of "the neighborhood activists," based out of the Chinatown Resource Center (CRC) and Tel-Hi. By connecting first to these groups, she quickly ascertained that these organizations "did not want *any* reduction of public housing on that site." As Seifel recalled, "They were just *adamant* about one-for-one replacement. At that time, there was no way HUD was going to do it. They didn't want to hear about it. But it was really clear it had to happen." With the application due in a month, Seifel and the SFHA HOPE VI team launched "this incredibly intensive tenant outreach," one that utilized the previous work from the Kaplan McLaughlin Diaz report. They held seven meetings with residents during August and early September and took full advantage of the relationships that had already been built with tenants by their vibrant community-based organizations. Staff from those groups knocked on residents' doors to alert them to upcoming meetings, and several of those meetings attracted more than forty tenant participants from a range of races and ethnicities.[5] Meanwhile, Seifel's team persuasively pulled together a strong case to attract a variety of supportive letters from neighborhood organizations and future partners in the grant.

The process of creating the HOPE VI case for North Beach Place underscored the importance of many players who were neither mayors nor housing authority personnel nor even residents. Rather, this particular governance constellation had neighborhood-based nonprofits as its pole star. Libby Seifel immediately recognized that any viable action had to heed the voices and interests of progressive housing organizations. Importantly, Seifel also understood the fundamental importance of this connection to past battles: "Urban renewal, which was handled so poorly in some of the poorest and most diverse neighborhoods in the city . . . caused such a scar that it created this activism." The redevelopment of the Western Addition and battles over the I-Hotel and other demolished single-room occupancy dwellings, she commented, "really got people motivated to say, 'Wait, this is just not acceptable.'"[6]

In San Francisco, local housing activism and land-use politics jointly shape the terrain of action for the Housing Authority. CCHO cofounder Calvin Welch saw this as rooted in geography. "Land-use politics is at the heart of politics of San Francisco," he observed, because it's a peninsula where "everything is developed"—so "any new development means displacing an existing use."

> It gives land-use politics a certain hard edge that is not often found in cities. In many cities, land-use politics is the stuff of the urban financial elite. In San Francisco, it's the stuff of neighborhood and community organization. It's talked about on the street. People's livelihoods and lives are affected, and it's of interest. The politics of zoning and development in San Francisco is neighborhood politics, is community politics. You don't play those politics well, you're gone.

To Welch, this is the racially charged lesson of past urban renewal. "Ask the African American community. You get co-opted, you're gone. That's what happened to African Americans." They came to San Francisco at mid-century in search of work but were unable to defend their neighborhoods. "In an essential way," Welch contended, "they took the jobs, and they lost the land, to put it most brutally."[7] All future development related to affordable housing would need to contend with this legacy.

For the entire period of HOPE VI redevelopment, the SFHA remained an unstable player; although the agency was necessary to make the redevelopment happen, in many ways redevelopment occurred in spite of the SFHA rather than because of it. In large part, this was because of the important roles played by successive mayors and by the powerful agenda-setting capacity of the city's community-based housing groups. At base, San Francisco has developed a civic culture supportive of low-income housing. As housing scholar Jane Rongerude observes,

> Much of the political process in San Francisco involves extensive public meetings and opportunities for public comment. These might be in the form of public commission meetings with formal comment periods, collaborative neighborhood planning meetings, mayoral taskforces or advisory boards, or rallies outside city hall. Though these processes, stakeholders such as public housing residents, who might be excluded elsewhere, often manage to find a voice through the support of well-established community organizers and advocacy organizations such as ACORN, the San Francisco Organizing Project, the Council of Community Housing Organizations and the Housing Rights Coalition.[8]

With numerous well-established not-for-profit housing firms and a variety of legal assistance agencies, low-income residents had no shortage of potential allies. Moreover, as Libby Seifel pointed out, "Renters are the biggest voting bloc in this city. So they have very significant rights in the view of the supervisors and the mayor."[9] Whereas in many cities, local housing authorities tried to house the political minimum of extremely low-income public housing residents when redeveloping sites under the HOPE VI program, this could not be the case in San Francisco. As Welch put it, "In San Francisco, the political minimum was [rehousing] *all* of them."[10] This was not lost on city housing officials. SFHA's Barbara Smith acknowledged their power: "We have a very strong group of housing advocates in San Francisco. That was a lot of the push."[11]

Some of this housing activism inhered in established private housing developers, both nonprofit and for-profit, but much of it carries deep neighborhood-based heritage. The residents of North Beach Place have benefited tremendously from two community organizations in particular: Tel-Hi and the Chinatown Community Development Center. This was already clear during the abortive effort in the 1980s to replace public housing with a hotel, but the roots go much deeper. Soon after North Beach Place opened, Tel-Hi consciously moved to larger quarters at 660 Lombard Street, just two blocks away from the development and has continued to assist its residents with on-site and off-site services for two-thirds of a century (see figure 10.2).[12] The current Chinatown CDC, established in 1998, represents the coming together of many housing and tenant advocacy organizations established during the late 1960s and 1970s, including the CRC. Although the Chinatown CDC now operates citywide, its roots are in Chinatown, with a long history of outreach into North Beach.[13] At the same time as Tel-Hi and the Chinatown CDC have been a boon to North Beach Place tenants, however, these organizations have—perhaps inadvertently—also contributed to internal schisms. As Amy Howard puts it in *More Than Shelter*, "The longstanding support of Tel-Hi and the Chinatown CDC strengthened North Beach Place—but it also demonstrated the racial and ethnic divide that separated tenants, with many African American tenants drawing on the resources of Tel-Hi while Chinese Americans went to the CDC for assistance."[14] This partial division of allies, too, has been part of the complexity of the North Beach Place governance constellation.

Ever since the foundational litigation of the 1950s, North Beach Place residents have understood the larger civic implications of their struggles. Older resident leaders remembered earlier neighborhood contests; for the Chinese, it was the fight for the I-Hotel; for North Beach's blacks, it was urban renewal. As James Tracy, leader of the Eviction Defense Network (EDN) that worked with North Beach residents, commented: "Historically a lot of them came out of the Western Addition and Fillmore [urban renewal battles]. They know the history, that no matter what progressive public policy wonk is out there to talk about how beautiful this new HOPE VI New Urbanist thing is, that they're promises that are being made by a white establishment with Willie Brown funding it." They remembered that "we had black leaders sell us out at Western Addition and Fillmore." For some, it is a quite visceral sense of oppression that comes from being "driven out of my community." Tracy added: "I actually remember seeing Greg Richardson break down and cry when he talked about what happened at Western Addition."[15] Moreover, Tracy observed, several North Beach tenants had previous organizing experience. In addition to Richardson's activism in the Western Addition, Tracy noted, "Alma Lark, a dynamic and cantankerous elder, did trench work in the Southern Christian Leadership Conference; Bethola Harper was a former member of the Black Panther Party, [and] other key leaders, such as David Hesbitt and Thomas Toy, had taken part in strikes as union members."[16] The North Beach approach to HOPE VI combined ample tenant activism and pro-tenant support networks with vibrant not-for-profit housing firms and their public-spirited for-profit private developer partners.

HOPE VI APPLICATION, SAN FRANCISCO STYLE

The SFHA sought $30 million from HUD—but recognized that this was a lot of money for a relatively small 229-unit project—so the HOPE VI planning team needed to find ways to "tell a compelling story." Residents and their advocates complicated the situation because, Seifel noted, they wanted "one-for-one replacement on-site, and *nothing* more." They did not want any additional housing to be added to the site, believing that it "was already dense enough." "In fact," Seifel added, they didn't even want to have to *move*—they would have been happy to rehab the bloody place, and not blow it up." Some residents argued that those extra units would directly result in smaller apartments for everyone. Meanwhile, the Fisherman's Wharf Merchants Association wanted the redeveloped project to maximize the number of working folks who could be their employees. As a result, the HOPE VI team proposed what, at least in the political context of San Francisco, seemed to be "the ultimate compromise."[17] To have a shot at getting $30 million, they felt the need to propose a plan with more units.

Recognizing the dramatic need for affordable housing that affected far more than the city's poorest, they offered up a San Francisco version of income mixing. Using Low-Income Housing Tax Credits, it would be possible for households earning up to 60 percent of AMI—currently about $60,000 for a family of four—to move into North Beach Place. In Seifel's view, this permitted explicit cultivation of "the working poor, or even what we used to call 'working middle income.'" To make this narrow income mix (containing only extremely low-income, very low-income, and low-income households) seem more palatable to HUD, the team emphasized the demographics of the surrounding neighborhood to show that it was indeed mixed income in a much broader sense; "it was not an isolated public housing development." Given the overall gentrification of the district, the HOPE VI team opined, only this kind of all-low-income "income-mixing" could "preserve the neighborhood character and the opportunities for people to live in this area."[18] Meanwhile, the deeply dysfunctional SFHA had been placed under the control of a "HUD recovery team"—an arrangement orchestrated in January 1996 by the newly sworn-in mayor Willie Brown working with his "old friend [HUD secretary] Henry Cisneros" and Art Agnos.[19]

Libby Seifel credited a substantial range of key players for pulling off a successful HOPE VI application: the "political strength" of Mayor Brown, the quality of the HUD recovery team, and the availability of Keyes and Schectman as advisers "helped run interference with HUD and others in Washington, DC." This enabled SFHA to make an argument for one-for-one on-site replacement— at precisely the same time as Congress and HUD were moving to legislate that option out of existence, or at least make it easier for developers to ignore it. Even more remarkable, Seifel pointed out, North Beach emphasized one-for-one replacement while also being "the first case in the country" to propose to build back all public housing without including a market-rate component. Ultimately, though, success in obtaining HOPE VI support depended on the capacity of the application to distance itself from the actual track record of the SFHA. The presence of the HUD recovery team made it possible to propose the redevelopment as a public-private partnership that could be developed and managed by the private sector, with no expectation for site-based direction from the housing authority. Accordingly, the application was chock full of support letters from many of San Francisco's not-for-profit (and for-profit) development and management organizations, each expressing interest in bidding on the project if it were to be funded. The presence of the HUD recovery team also worked internally to make it possible for the SFHA commissioners to give this strategy their own necessary approval.

Underscoring that even a "dysfunctional" housing authority had "some bright stars," Seifel also gave a lot of credit to the housing authority's "incredible HOPE VI team"—including Barbara Smith, project manager Sean Spear, and Juan Monsanto. Ultimately, though, Seifel credited "the support of the North Beach collective of social service associations and the Chinatown service organizations" for enabling the team to meet its tight deadline. "It was pretty miraculous in any case. I pulled so many all-nighters."[20]

The "miracle" of the application, though, was hardly without its ongoing challenges. Financially, despite repeated requests, the mayor's office never formally committed to the $10 million of local matching funds that everyone had told the HOPE VI team would be necessary to make the application nationally competitive, even though the application implied that it had been promised.[21] In the long saga of struggles between the SFHA and the Mayor's Office of Housing, this silence (and its misleading representation) signaled another chapter of mutual unease.

LURCHING TOWARD REDEVELOPMENT: CONFLICTS WITH RESIDENTS

The HOPE VI proposal as submitted outlined a three-part process of phased demolition and construction and explicitly stated that "assuming normal turnover rates at this development, it will not be necessary to involuntarily relocate any residents off-site." "Our relocation plan," the application continued, is "greatly influenced by the views of residents voiced during the HOPE VI planning process," openly noting that "most importantly, a great many residents have indicated that their support for the proposed development is contingent upon their being allowed to remain on-site during construction." In the weeks preceding submission of the application, residents and their advocates believed that they had a commitment from the SFHA to stop renting vacated units at the development. Although there were only two empty apartments at the time of the HOPE VI application, redevelopment proponents assured residents that a moratorium on filling vacancies would enable enough apartments to accumulate by the time of demolition so that residents would not have to be temporarily displaced off-site. Members of the architectural team apparently estimated that there was a "95 percent chance that residents would not need to relocate."[22] The HOPE VI team reassured residents that "no residents in good standing will be displaced," and that each household would have the choice of remaining on-site or taking a Section 8 voucher. The residents therefore thought they had gained assurances about a multiphase redevelopment to "maintain the stability of the community," but once the HOPE VI project lurched toward implementation, these assumptions would quickly face the tough financial and political scrutiny of the team chosen to lead the redevelopment.[23]

On October 6, 1996, advocates for low-income housing in San Francisco got mostly good news. HUD agreed to fund the SFHA's HOPE VI proposal for North Beach—but offered only $20 million, just two-thirds of what had been requested. The SFHA's Barbara Smith recalled, "HUD said, 'Well, you don't really need $30 million; we'll give you $20 million, take it or leave it.'

So, we took the twenty but that $10 million gap stayed with us."[24] Actually, this left the project with a double $10 million shortfall—since it now lacked firmed-up funding on both the federal and local fronts. On the federal side, a HUD inspector general analysis later explained the shortfall by noting that the selection panel "felt strongly that the site had extraordinary potential for commercial and upper/middle income residential" that was "not effectively exploited by the SFHA's plan." Doing this would "better reach the full creative potential of the site." Perhaps true, but doing that would do little to fulfill the promised intent of the application.[25] As usual with HOPE VI, simply winning the grant did little to guarantee the reality of the implementation. More pointedly, especially given the large gaps in financing, changes to the plan became almost inevitable. Moreover, as is also always the case, the postgrant dealmaking and recalculating would be very difficult to explain to residents who had gamely entered into the process with a set of expectations that might no longer be realistically sustained.

In addition to the reduced dollar amount, another aspect of the grant announcement caught residents by surprise. At a news conference held in Mayor Brown's office, HUD regional director Agnos said that the work to redevelop this "obsolete, blighted housing" would be done in a single phase, necessitating relocation for everyone. Existing residents would get a written guarantee about their ability to move back. Phasing the project, he noted, would just be too expensive: "We can't afford that. It adds to the cost." Needless to say, this twist did not sit well with North Beach tenants. NBTA president Greg Richardson, who knew that his fellow residents had backed the application because it stipulated phased redevelopment, told the *Chronicle* that they were "going to be upset."[26] For the most vocal tenants, that was an understatement.

Once she heard about the new terms of relocation, strident tenant leader Alma Lark told a reporter at the *San Francisco Independent* that residents had never even agreed to back the application to demolish North Beach. Instead, she claimed, those at the meeting had been tricked into signing the support statement that accompanied the HOPE VI bid. Two other African American tenant leaders, Bethola Harper and Cynthia Wiltz, concurred that they thought they were merely signing an attendance sheet.[27] Lark, a vociferous advocate for resident management, insisted that most tenants wanted the complex modernized rather than demolished and rebuilt. Wiltz added, "I didn't want it to go through. We have been used and we don't know what's going on." For his part, NBTA president Richardson regarded these comments as wholly disingenuous: "All of us knew," he insisted. "Everybody that came to that meeting was in support." Richardson, recognizing that his fellow residents were "going nuts," vowed to "make sure [housing officials] abide by the [original] plan."[28] His colleagues remained skeptical. As Harper later lamented to housing activist James Tracy, "We learned that we couldn't sign anything without it being used against us."[29]

The HOPE VI application itself, however, shows that the signed pages clearly state that these were intended as HOPE VI grant application "Support Letter Signatories," thereby buttressing Richardson's version of the events. Lark, Harper, and Wiltz are all among the sixteen signatories of a clearly labeled printed page. Examination of six of the seven sign-in sheets for the resident meetings held in the run-up to the HOPE VI application shows that those, by contrast, were informally handwritten and not done on printed forms. Moreover, the sign-in sheets asked for name, address, and phone number, whereas the support letter form provided spaces for signature, name, and address. Still, some ambiguity remains. Lark, Harper, and Wiltz were among many who entered their names into the support letter form with answers corresponding to the format used in the sign-in sheet categories, perhaps indicative of some confusion. Moreover, in the HOPE VI application, this page appears separately and ahead of Richardson's own endorsement letter, which was signed only by him. Still, there is little evidence to support the more conspiratorial conclusion advanced by Tracy that "a sign-in sheet for a community meeting had been cut-and-pasted into a petition asking HUD to demolish the property."[30] In any case, what seems to matter most here is the widespread sense of mistrust between many resident leaders and the housing authority (and among the residents themselves), tensions that would only increase once it became clear that many provisions of the original HOPE VI proposal most favored by tenants would prove unworkable. And this was even before the SFHA sought a developer to implement the project.

Indicative of the vast capacities for small misunderstandings to spread across a tangled bureaucracy, it was not yet even clear that Agnos's comment about the need for one-phase development represented settled policy. Seeking to diffuse controversy, Washington-based HUD staffer Adam Chavez stated that he "probably shouldn't have mentioned" the one-phase plan to Agnos and the local HUD press secretary since "it's still under discussion" and HUD hoped it would be possible to do "minimum relocation." Meanwhile, just to confuse things further, SFHA spokesman Patrick Lynch opined that it remained the housing authority's "intention to do a phased development."[31] Nervous, factionalized, and befuddled North Beach residents did not know who could be trusted. Divided governance of North Beach Place had met the divided governance of HUD.

In the meantime, the initial HOPE VI application raised expectations about a second contentious issue of import to some residents: the possibility that North Beach might be redeveloped and managed by its own tenants. This discussion had roots that predated HOPE VI. In the early 1990s, some

North Beach tenants, aided by the San Francisco–based Center for Self-Governance, began debating this matter. Inspired by HUD secretary Jack Kemp's advocacy of resident management and eventual tenant ownership of their developments, North Beach residents led by Alma Lark wholeheartedly embraced the possibility. The SFHA resisted this but knew that, as the possibility of HOPE VI redevelopment emerged, the National Affordable Housing Act of 1990 required the agency to offer a resident group the "opportunity to purchase" the property for less than its market value (preliminarily assessed at $19 million)—as long as the group notified SFHA by October 7, 1996.[32] In the run-up to the application, Seifel's team devoted two meetings to this topic, though these discussions did not lead to a proposal from Lark's nascent North Beach Resident Management Council (NBRMC) before the HOPE VI application could be submitted.[33]

Even so, another part of the application stated outright that a future management company "will be required by its agreement with the SFHA to enter into negotiations with the RMC concerning resident management." Underscoring both the attention to this matter and the ambiguity of its resolution, the proposal further specified that "the management company and the RMC will be required to agree on performance standards for the RMC which will determine whether and when the RMC will assume dual and sole responsibility for specified property management functions."[34] In other words, the proposal made it a requirement to discuss possible involvement, but deftly made no real promises. Not surprisingly, this allowed plenty of leeway for misinterpretation.

Shortly after Agnos triumphantly announced the compromised grant, residents and the community organizations that supported them bonded together as the "North Beach Coalition" to try to get a better deal. The executive directors of the CRC (Gordon Chin) and Tel-Hi (Denise McCarthy) joined with four North Beach tenants and representatives from Kai Ming Head Start, Asian Neighborhood Design, Asian Law Caucus, and several other groups to send a pointed letter to Emma McFarlin, HUD's executive monitor at the SFHA. They also made sure to copy their concerns to everyone from Mayor Brown to HUD secretary Henry Cisneros. The coalition reiterated highly conditional support for the HOPE VI grant, asserting in boldface type that would be forthcoming **"only if the SFHA, the HUD Recovery Team and HUD follow through"** on the previous agreement to provide **"one-to-one on-site replacement** of the existing very low income public housing units"** and "proceed with **phased demolition, with on-site relocation**, as was consistently promised to North Beach Place tenants by SFHA throughout the HOPE VI application process." Further, the coalition insisted that no request for proposals should go forward to developers without "an **alternative revitalization plan, satisfactory to tenants** and community members" that would explain how the $20 million short-fall could be addressed. The group called for full tenant and community access and input into the process, funding for translators, and a written guarantee that tenants in good standing "can either continue to live at North Beach Place during the revitalization process, or if they choose to temporarily be relocated outside the site, that they can return to North Beach Place once the revitalization is completed."[35] The battle lines were drawn, and North Beach residents remained savvy, engaged, and empowered by their many allies.

HOPE VI planning meetings continued through 1997, with several dozen residents (including Harper as NBTA treasurer and Wiltz as NBTA president) present at many gatherings. The tenants kept raising the issue of relocation, and SFHA project manager Dale Royal still talked about on-site options, thereby keeping that version of HOPE alive.[36] The meetings and the tenant leadership remained ethnically and racially diverse and, in April, the NBTA board agreed to add one Chinese-speaking vice president and one Spanish-speaking vice president. Some residents also expressed confusion about why North Beach should have two different tenant groups, the NBTA and the NBRMC. Tenant Thomas Toy, newly appointed as acting vice president of the NBTA to provide "better communication with the large group of non-English speaking Asian residents," joined the fray. He pointedly questioned "why the SFHA is recognizing the NBRMC and giving it all the authority when it has not had elections."[37]

The growing schism among tenant leaders surfaced more openly that June when Cynthia Wiltz, who at this point was both the NBRMC's vice president and the NBTA president, wrote a terse letter to NBRMC president Alma Lark announcing her resignation from Alma's organization. In this missive, which she copied to SFHA officials and Mayor Brown, she accused Lark of failing to hold either a meeting or an election of officers for three years. Meanwhile, Wiltz pointed out, "You attend meetings as a representative of North Beach? How can that be? . . . How can you know what the residents want?" Two weeks later, Toy wrote Lark again. In a letter endorsed by Wiltz and Hesbitt and signed by many "concerned residents," he stated that North Beach residents "do not recognize the NBRMC (in which you claim to be the president) as an official organization." If Lark failed to hold a meeting, with translation available, within two weeks to start the election process, Toy threatened to make "formal announcements" about this nonrecognition to all residents, the mayor's office, the Board of Supervisors, the chief of police, and the HUD regional office.[38]

The struggle over resident organizations also pointed to tensions between African American leaders and their Chinese counterparts. Ethnographers Patricia Gutherie and Janice Hutchinson, who interviewed black and

Chinese North Beach Place residents in 1988–1989, emphasized their lack of interaction. At base, in those pre–HOPE VI days, African Americans said they felt isolated in the project, whereas the North Beach Place Chinese had the welcoming environs of Chinatown as an extension of their own world. Conversely, historian Amy Howard argues that the common challenges and opportunities of redevelopment helped unite residents, including Chinese and African Americans.[39] HOPE VI extended both tendencies; some resident leaders found means for cross-group collaboration, while more skeptical participants felt victimized by divide-and-conquer politics.

In July, with the NBRMC still intact, Alma Lark and six members of the NBTA board submitted what they called "The Petition of North Beach Public Housing Residents" to SFHA's acting director Ronnie Davis. Significantly, the petition carried endorsement from the CRC and Tel-Hi, signed by their executive directors, Chin and McCarthy. In the petition, the residents and their allies repeated the familiar demands: "one-to-one on-site replacement of public housing," a "phased demolition and on-site relocation guarantee," and "no RFP/RFQs until the San Francisco Housing Authority discloses [an] alternative revitalization plan satisfactory to all North Beach Public Housing residents."[40]

In response, just three days later Ronnie Davis held an evening meeting with North Beach residents. To their delight, he agreed to "immediately commit" to everything in the petition. The next morning, July 16, he put it all in writing in a detailed four-page letter addressed to "All Identified North Beach Resident and Surrounding Community Leaders." "In no uncertain terms," Davis underscored, "the San Francisco Housing Authority is committed to seeking to implement the revitalization plan spelled out in the grant application (phased demolition and new construction of all 229 public housing units with an on-site relocation option)." To help move things forward, Davis created a formal working group combining board members from the NBTA and NBRMC, plus representatives from the CRC, Tel-Hi, the Mayor's Office of Housing, and the Parking Authority (which was expected to commit $10 million to the project for an underground garage). He also proposed to hire a "professional group facilitator specific to North Beach" to "insure that the planning process proceeds in a timely and orderly fashion."[41]

Meanwhile, the unsettled issues of development phasing and even the question of one-for-one on-site replacement of public housing still remained on the table, at least in the view of the SFHA commissioners. In summer 1997, as part of an overhaul of the housing authority's board, supervisor Mabel Teng helped convince Reverend Norman Fong of the CRC to join. Fong, who had previously been involved in many meetings about North Beach public housing, recalled that "the one thing that I did on the commission was to say I would not support the North Beach HOPE VI unless they required one-for-one replacement." His reason for this actually had little to do with North Beach. "For Chinatown, we fought for one-for-one replacement and got that in the 1986 zoning, so I just used the same values we have here for our community for the HOPE VI. . . . I did not know that that was a significant event, but I laid down my body." At first, he wasn't sure that other commissioners would support this demand, due to what he termed "pressures from outside."

> But I didn't care. I worked with the commissioners, and it was *our* decision. And slowly, one by one, [they] supported me. To President Sulu[lagi Palega] I went, "Come on, Bro, that's why we're here. You're a community guy like me." Actually, it was *easy* with the commissioners. [Commissioner] Shirley Byrd was a resident of Sunnydale, a tenant, too—so I had her on our side. So by the end the commission totally agreed that this was the right thing to do.

Reverend Fong, in his uniquely irrepressible way, also "pushed for phased development." He played up his role as a minister: "I wore my collar to every meeting—I tried to tell people we gotta do the right thing. I was still worried about what would happen with displacement. . . . We wanted it phased because we wanted to keep [just] as many tenants there." He later heard that there were meetings held about him in city hall, asking, "Who's this crazy reverend here?" but his well-placed allies "always told them, 'No one can control the reverend.' "[42]

As it turned out, no one could control HUD, either. In 1997, the SFHA failed to secure an additional $6.5 million HOPE VI grant to cover some of the shortfall. Still, the reapplication process provided an opportunity to remind HUD that the Bay Area is "home to the strongest non-profit affordable housing sector in the country," while also reassuring the feds that "for-profit developers . . . also expressed an interest in North Beach." The application duly invoked HUD's then-preferred language about creating a "Campus of Learners" that would enable residents to "graduate from public housing" and proposed to help residents start and maintain new businesses. In a development where only 6 percent of adult residents were employed and where household incomes averaged only 16.7 percent of San Francisco's median, the HOPE VI team anticipated that fifteen "highly motivated resident-entrepreneurs" would begin the training, ten would complete it, and five would "develop profitable ventures."[43] But resident development would be a moot point unless the team could sort out other financial mechanisms to make the property development part of HOPE VI financially feasible.

To do this, the team needed to attract a much larger allocation of tax-credit financing—the funds that could be raised from investors by selling the development's tax benefits. The HOPE VI application had projected

$19.5 million of equity funding derived from easily available federal 4 percent Low-Income Housing Tax Credits, but much more would be needed.[44] Meanwhile, the SFHA and its working group received a sign-off from what the CRC dexterously termed "the tenant 'leaders' (including Alma)"[45] and proceeded with the developer RFP.[46]

The RFP stipulated that developers must plan for one-for-one on-site replacement of all 229 public housing units, phased demolition ("with the option of on-site relocation), and 126 "affordable" rental housing units. The RFP further specified that the development should be built upon a "platform" above a garage and new retail space and explicitly stated that "development is to occur in three phases in order to minimize potential displacement of current residents." The RFP left the question of future management deliberately unresolved and asked potential developers to "present the pros and cons of management by the SFHA, resident management, private management, or some combination thereof," noting that "it is the desire of the resident organizations to be in partnership with whatever management structure is eventually chosen."[47] In short, the RFP reiterated everything that North Beach residents, the CRC, and Tel-Hi had been insisting upon.

In mid-October 1997, with no resolution on how to select a developer, CRC and Tel-Hi leaders met to strategize.[48] The CRC/Tel-Hi summit agreed to push for inclusion of all working group members on the selection committee.[49] The CRC/Tel-Hi idea was that the working group should manage developer selection and "make recommendations to Ronnie Davis and the SFHA Commission, which has the final say."[50] In other words, the initial evaluation of proposals would be conducted by residents and their allies (with some participation by other city agencies), rather than by the SFHA itself. This usurpation proved too extreme to pass muster, but it is indicative of the kind of governance structure that the Nonprofitus world of San Francisco actually thought plausible.

SFHA project manager Dale Royal worried that the working group lacked sufficient financial expertise to review the proposals and instead proposed an "independent group" ("cleaner, and less self-interested") to handle this, with the working group and SFHA staff as "advisors." Some CRC staff saw this as an advantage, quietly voicing "concern about having Alma on the Developer Selection committee and having her influence the other tenants on the committee."[51] Ultimately, the nine-member evaluation team included two North Beach public housing residents (Thomas Toy and Lorraine Bender), two SFHA project managers (Dale Royal and Ernie Monaco), a local architect (George McLaughlin), and representatives from the Mayor's Office of Housing (deputy director Daryl Higashi), Tel-Hi (community organizer Gentle Blythe), the Fisherman's Wharf Merchants Association (executive secretary Al Baccari), and the City Planning Department (zoning administrator Bob Passmore). In addition, a "Technical Team," which included two people with financial expertise, provided initial scrutiny.[52]

PICKING A WINNER, MANAGING A LOSER

The evaluation team assessed four bids, significantly preferring the one from a consortium calling itself North Beach Development Partners, although there was one other strong contender, North Beach Opportunity Partnership (a consortium of San Francisco–based Citizens Housing, Telesis, and Michael Willis). The other two bids lagged far beyond, and one—from a Florida-based consortium calling itself Human Technology Partners—earned less than half the point total of the winner. Underscoring the contentiousness of the process, this latter bid had been developed in partnership with Alma Lark and her NBRMC. Tenant association leaders had been "warned against signing onto a particular developer as a financial partner," but this did not dissuade Lark.[53]

In contrast to the other bids, Human Technology Partners proposed to purchase the site for $20 million and inaccurately assumed that the SFHA could simply transfer its HOPE VI grant to other projects. The proposal combined 229 public housing units with 126 for-sale apartments, half subsidized and half market rate. This bid also called for a 3,200-square-foot gym, a 3,000-square-foot crafts shop, and a 5,000-square-foot artists' studio. When the selection team asked where the money to purchase the site would come from (let alone the source of $92 million that the team proposed to spend on redevelopment), they received only "very evasive" responses, stating that there would be "Triple A Corporate Bonds" but refusing to divulge the name of an actual corporate lender. Moreover, they proposed an exorbitant developer fee of $11.9 million. Worse still, SFHA's Barbara Smith recalled, "If you called their phone number, you got a used car sales office."[54] Lark "brought these guys out from Florida," and "we interviewed them," she continued, "but it wasn't really realistic." At base, the evaluation team doubted that the RMC had the capacity to oversee the property, even if they were to hire private management.

SFHA commissioner Fong recalls that Lark and her supporters sought him out. "I remember being approached by about nine North Beach African American residents who were pushing for this Florida company. I said innocently, 'Aren't there some Asian residents there?'" They agreed that any successful solution would need to "get the Chinese residents involved." Reverend Fong recognized the uneasy dynamic: Lark was "very tough and controlling. It was hard with the Chinese."[55] A review of the scoring sheet shows that her Human Technology bid fared best in the hybrid category

called "Plans to work cooperatively with residents; options for limited equity ownership for tenants; maximizing role of NB Resident Management
Corp." In sixteen of seventeen other categories, it ranked dead last. To Lark,
the fix was in: "The Housing Authority has never wanted empowerment of
residents," she told a reporter. "We developed a proposal to tear down and
rebuild this one ourselves. The voted in and out what *they* wanted."[56]

The winning proposal accepted by SFHA commissioners in July 1998
brought together a team led by the nationally prominent but locally based
BRIDGE Housing Corporation, a not-for-profit housing developer that had
already built almost seven hundred units in San Francisco and nearly seven
thousand in California. BRIDGE was joined in the bid by two other San
Francisco firms, Em Johnson Interest (led by African American developer
Michael Johnson) and the John Stewart Company (JSCo, a for-profit twenty-
year-old housing development and management firm that already managed
more than twenty-eight hundred units in the city and eleven thousand
statewide).[57] Picking the team with BRIDGE, Ronnie Davis added, had an
important symbolic component for building the city's governance constellation: "The Housing Authority can benefit politically by demonstrating its
willingness to work with local non-profit developers."[58]

According to the John Stewart Company's eponymous chairman, the idea
for a partnership with BRIDGE to redevelop North Beach Place actually
predated the award of HOPE VI funds—and even predated the grant proposal itself. Stewart "vividly" remembered a call from BRIDGE founder Don
Terner, who noted that his firm had not yet done much work with "very-low
income populations where there was a high crime rate," whereas, as Stewart
put it, "Our company had specialized on 'brain-damaged' challenging
projects." JSCo also happened to have its offices across the street from the development. Some of its windows had been shot out, and Stewart considered
the location "a turnstile when it came to crime." Eager to upgrade his own
neighborhood, he was "absolutely" interested.

> We were very familiar with the project, and we had pretty much given up
> on the housing authority as being able to do much of anything in the way of
> correcting it. So we had a big motivation to share the risk on the development
> side. So I immediately said yes, and we started working on it.

Tragically, Terner died in a plane crash in early April 1996, but Stewart
continued to collaborate with his successor at the helm of BRIDGE, Carol
Galante.

Their initial plan stipulated 229 public housing units, but instead of
the remainder being below-market subsidized apartments, they proposed
91 "income-restricted units" and 40 market-rate units, for a total of 360
apartments. Moreover, North Beach Development Partners recommended

segregating the market-rate units from the rest of the development, ostensibly because this would minimize the need for intradevelopment relocation of existing residents and because they could obtain higher market rents by clustering these units on the west side of the development where there were better views. When the proposal evaluation team pushed back on this, the BRIDGE team "offered to integrate the market units, recognizing that rents may need to be lowered." The selection team asked that the final developer agreement stipulate this "to guarantee that no segregation would occur."[59]

As it turned out, after "running endless pro forma projections," the team itself decided that market-rate rentals were "much higher risk" and dropped the idea completely.[60] John Stewart also felt that it would be difficult to get financing for subsidized homeownership. And market-rate condos were a political nonstarter. He recognized that "condos in that area would have sold well" but understood that "it was clear all along that we weren't going to displace the people." Secondarily, placing condos on top of the existing mix would have "necessitated a height variance." Stewart decided that the team "should focus on the 'art of the possible': mixing-in tax-credit units that—given San Francisco's extremely high AMI—could house those with "incomes ranging from $45,000 to $70,000 a year." To Stewart, this was not just an economic calculation but a social one: "We knew that population would be very stable, and we knew that they would have at least one if not two breadwinners that were actually *working*." By contrast, the developers looked at a public housing population with an average income of $15,000 and saw "multiple generations of nonworkers." The solution: "Combine the two populations, and do so where we had them integrated structurally into the design."[61]

Internal documents reveal that the SFHA also explicitly realized that it could increase revenues by upping "the amount of market rate units and commercial space at the site" or could "sell a portion of the land at market rates to commercial developers or educational institutions." These approaches were politically nonviable, however, since they would "prevent the one-to-one replacement of public housing units needed and promised to residents."[62] San Francisco's initial forays into HOPE VI—at Bernal Dwellings, Plaza East, and Hayes Valley—had each failed to replace all public housing units, and the SFHA—prodded by its critics—was determined not to let this happen again.[63] Whatever else may be said about the travails of North Beach Place, this fundamental commitment to the principle of public housing—and to at least some of the many promises made to residents—remains striking. And, clearly, to date this is not a commitment that leaders in most other cities have chosen to sustain.

PROMISES AND PROTESTS

The SFHA needed to work with its new development partners but also had to improve relations with its old tenants. In mid-May 1998, fifty Chinese residents, upset at rumors (which proved accurate) that Cantonese-speaking North Beach Place manager Henry Kwan would be transferred by the SFHA, petitioned executive director Davis. Calling for Kwan's retention, they emphasized that "current tenant representatives" failed to be "accountable to the tenants at large."[64] Five days later, Davis came out to the development for an "emergency residents' meeting" and promised to find a new bilingual manager, though this remained an ongoing issue. Chinese residents again asked why North Beach had two tenant organizations and were told that the NBRMC's corporation status was "suspended" and "inactive." Davis promised them that North Beach residents could vote on whether to be represented by the NBTA, the NBRMC, both, or a joint organization, with new elections to follow once that issue was resolved.[65] Residents also continued to complain about poor maintenance, and the NBTA and NBRMC jointly sent a petition to Davis to again ask the SFHA to cease renting vacant apartments so as to maximize the chances for on-site relocation.[66]

On August 10, Ronnie Davis sent a formal letter (printed in English, Spanish and Chinese) to all North Beach residents to let them know in bold-faced, italicized terms that *"The San Francisco Housing Authority has made and continues to make the following commitments to the residents of North Beach*:

- *All 229 public housing units will be rebuilt on site.*
- *Construction . . . will be phased to minimize the need for relocation off-site.*
- *Residents will not be permanently displaced as a result of HOPE VI."*[67]

Although the reassurances from Davis remained consistent, only the first of these three pledges would prove enforceable.

Three days after Davis's letter had been sent (and perhaps even before it had been seen), James Tracy's Eviction Defense Network helped to organize a rally at the development. Approximately thirty people gathered near the cable car turnaround, brandishing signs that read, "Don't take our homes." Flyers claimed endorsement by the NBTA and the NBRMC plus other support from various named housing and human rights organizations from elsewhere in San Francisco. Tracy explained to a *Chronicle* reporter that many residents "have absolute distrust of the Housing Authority due to their past record." Intentionally or not, he helped to foment discord by emphasizing the SFHA's failure to pick the redevelopment proposal submitted by Alma Lark's group; the *Chronicle* framed this as a rejection of a "$100 million proposal by a group of tenants." "We believe the tenants have the right to run their own place, and the chance to own it as well," Tracy asserted. For their part, many residents remained more cautious than their advocates. Some, such as NBTA board member Bethola Harper, participated, but she kept her focus on worries about relocation, and the potential for displacement if the redevelopment venture failed to find its full funding.[68] Others, such as NBTA president Cynthia Wiltz, chose not to join in, and she took a job with the housing authority. The alignment between residents and their externally affiliated advocates remained imperfect at best, not unlike the tensions between residents and Alinsky-inspired community organizers in Tucson.

Thinking back on the event, Tracy explained the political dynamics of the Eviction Defense Network's work with the residents. "We were very influenced by the politics of the Zapatistas," he stressed. "We were very aware of coming into their community . . . [with] political ideas." The EDN endeavored to get a dialogue going, rather than simply do "whatever the people want." Tracy and his team would ask, "Hey what about this?" They recognized that "we were always to the left, and they'd have a counter proposal, and we'd meet somewhere in the middle. . . . It wasn't always peaceful, but it was a dialogue, and we built up a lot of trust." The cable turnaround rally, however, demonstrated the limits of this trust and revealed the high stakes for residents. As Tracy recalled, "We were out there trying to convince everyone to do a civil disobedience where we would all sit down at the cable car and stop all the tourism, and the tenants association came back and said, 'We can't do that. We got Child Protective Services to worry about.'" So the EDN instead proposed, "Why don't you be the spokespeople and we do the sitdown?" But residents responded: "We don't want to have you guys doing anything we wouldn't do."[69] Additionally, Tracy worried that "arrests of allies would signal that resistance to HOPE VI was only the work of outside agitators."[70] In the governance constellation of North Beach Place, Comet Tracy functioned much like Comet Bagert in New Orleans and Comet Gibbs in Tucson: a brief, high-visibility feature that demanded notice but rapidly moved on.

As residents and their allies continued to meet and trade their concerns, the HOPE VI development team worked with its own partners to pull together the necessary financing. Plans for the redevelopment slowly moved forward during the fall of 1998, and the SFHA continued to tell residents that the new development would be constructed in two phases, starting with the larger eastern block.[71]

Moreover, seeming to keep another promise to support "residents who want to start their own businesses," the developer committed to 10 percent of the leased commercial space.[72]

Meanwhile, SFHA staff continued to worry about ongoing mistrust. A thoughtful memo from Dale Royal, written soon after he left his job at the housing authority, addressed to SFHA planning and programming manager Juan Monsanto, outlined the problems and proposed possible solutions. "In my opinion," Royal told his former supervisor in January 1999, "there is a sense of panic and suspicion among North Beach residents and the surrounding community about the HOPE VI revitalization."

> Bay Area housing activists have capitalized on this sense of uncertainty to frighten residents and neighbors with exaggerated worst case scenarios. Housing Authority staff organizes lots of meetings with resident leaders but the general level of distrust continues. Meanwhile the surrounding community, influenced by the local newspapers who portray the Housing Authority as a clumsy corrupt government agency, is getting nervous about what the agency will do to their neighborhood.

While seeking solutions, Royal suggested that SFHA staff should "just accept the fact that not everybody is going to like HOPE VI regardless of how many meetings are scheduled to discuss it. And clearly the North Beach resident leaders don't like HOPE VI." He suggested that the housing authority should rely more on the HOPE VI working group and should try to do more direct outreach to a broader cross-section of residents and community members. He followed with a set of specific suggestions for improving the quality of communications.[73]

At base, residents still wanted their communications to take the form of written guarantees about key matters of concern.[74] With most promises still intact, Wiltz and Davis signed an MOU in January 1999, and the SFHA soon moved forward with demolition plans for the east block of the development. With assistance from the EDN's James Tracy and Connie Jacobs, on March 11, several nervous North Beach residents—including Harper, Richardson, Toy, and Hesbitt—obtained a hearing at the San Francisco Human Rights Commission. They repeatedly itemized their reasons for past distrust of the SFHA and questioned the reliability of MOUs. Juan Monsanto responded on behalf of the SFHA, reiterating that there would be a "two-phase demolition and new construction." The idea, he indicated, was to relocate all the residents from one side, either by consolidating them on the other side "by attrition" or "relocating them throughout the city or elsewhere." He tried to reassure those present that "up to 80 percent of the total population" could then move into the site that was being built first "because we're building more units than we are demolishing." He repeated the party line that "as many residents as possible have the option to remain on site during demolition or new construction."[75]

As tenant activists complained, many other North Beach households relocated following the east block closure. Tel-Hi and the newly consolidated Chinatown Community Development Center (CCDC) attempted to keep track of the dispersed households. The vast majority moved on to other public housing sites across the city, and twenty-eight scattered with Section 8 vouchers (with half of those certificates deployed outside of San Francisco). Only a couple of dozen households from the east side relocated to vacancies on the western part of the site, where they joined the remaining westside residents.[76]

Davis, always popular with the tenants he sought to appease, continued to work with North Beach residents to meet their many demands. In September 1999 Davis signed an exit contract with residents, following almost a year of periodic debate about its language. According to James Tracy, Davis needed to do this because more than 60 percent of the tenants signed "pledges not to move until the exit contract was delivered with real guarantees." Intended for use with each relocating leaseholder, the contract reiterated the MOU and gave the NBTA more say in defining the "fair screening criteria" when residents returned, so that there would be less disagreement about which of them remained "in good standing."[77] Marking this occasion, James Tracy wrote an article for the progressive housing journal *Shelterforce* entitled "Tenant Organizing Wins One-for-One Replacement." Tracy termed this exit contract a "modest victory" due to its legally binding guarantees about "one-for-one replacement" at a time when HUD and much of the rest of the public housing system was pushing against this.[78] Tenant organizing had certainly helped, though it is worth remembering that the entire HOPE VI process at North Beach had *commenced* with the premise that none of the 229 public housing units would be lost. Certainly, though, the work of the tenants, the EDN, and their work with the Fire By Night Organizing Committee, contributed a lot to maintaining that initial commitment. As Tracy puts it in his book *Dispatches against Displacement*, "The EDN brought with it a willingness to organize alongside tenant leaders, instead of usurping their power."[79] That said, a lot of power lay elsewhere.

THE WILL OF WILLIE BROWN

Ronnie Davis had managed to work out an agreement with residents but struggled to work with the North Beach Development Partners team—many of whom probably wished they could exit from their contract, too. John Stewart regarded Davis as "impossible" to reach by phone, because he "was hell bent to keep the management [within SFHA]."[80] With HUD complaining that the housing authority was lagging behind on all of its HOPE VI grants, the long stalemate over North Beach threatened to put $20 million at risk.[81] Moreover, the development team needed to raise large amounts of private equity and needed to do everything possible to heighten the confidence of investors. As Stewart recalled, "We finally broke the logjam because we had a meeting with Willie Brown." At the meeting, Ronnie Davis and his attorney began by insisting that they wouldn't do the deal unless SFHA could keep the management; Stewart wanted no part of that:

> I remember saying, "Here's our problem—you're on the 'watch list' at HUD and your management has been scored way below norms. We have to raise about $48.5 million worth of equity (which we did); we have to make certain loan guarantees (which we did); we have to bring third-party lenders in there with hard debt as well as soft debt, and we have to be comfortable that this project is going to make it, and so do they. I don't think there's *any* chance with roughly $48 million of hard, at-risk, equity—let alone the debt structure—that anybody is going to accept the housing authority [as manager]."

As Stewart remembered it, when Davis tried to rebut, Brown interjected:

> "Mr. Davis"—he called him Mr. Davis because he wanted to be called Mr. Davis—"Mr. Stewart has made this point and he's right. I don't think you can get this financed. This issue is over. Let's move to the next point." Willie Brown laid down the hammer.[82]

Brown's hammer also deeply affected the "next point" as well.

Discussions with the mayor centered on more than questions of management; they also focused on what would be needed to make a tax credit deal work for North Beach Place—and for San Francisco. BRIDGE consultant Ben Golvin explained the local and state politics affecting tax credits:

> San Francisco had its own geographic allocation, and so a project from SF is effectively competing for SF's by-population percentage of the total pool of federal tax credits. Getting one project from San Francisco is usually what happens—it just happened to be one project that sucked up not only San Francisco's but all of twelve other counties' as well.[83]

Even though Willie Brown later complained in his memoir about the "sacred cartel" of San Francisco's top not-for-profit housing organizations, the mayor helped the North Beach team orchestrate a massive infusion of Low-Income Housing Tax Credits—"$38 million out of the overall federal allocation and a one-year shot of $17 million in state credits, totaling $55 million"—enough to generate the $48 million in equity finance that the project needed to move forward. With this sale of equity, the developers could buy down a

$72 million construction mortgage to about $25 million. As a result, their debt service per unit could be locked in at a very low rate, thereby making it possible to keep the development affordable.[84] Denise McCarthy gave Brown a lot of credit: "It wouldn't have happened without the mayor. We had been working and working on it and kept getting closer with the money," she observed, "but there wasn't enough." The whole deal could have failed "if he hadn't pulled off what he did with the tax credits for the state. . . . He pulled it off because of his years in the Assembly, and everybody agreed, including LA, to give up a whole bunch for one year so he could do it. It was amazing."[85]

Willie Brown had many reasons to care about North Beach Place. First, he knew and trusted the people from BRIDGE, JSCo, and their team. Also, he had met with many neighborhood groups and, as Denise McCarthy from Tel-Hi pointed out, he "knew how much the [Fisherman's Wharf] merchants were pushing it." He also knew this business support insisted that "it would *not* be managed by the housing authority." In Stewart's diagnosis, the merchants "were *hugely* supportive because we had added 120-plus units on top of the public housing, so we added a *working* population. . . . They knew that construction was going to be good, that we had reserves and we were well financed, and that the operating budget included a lot of money for security."[86] Even if tolerated locally, the North Beach Place promoters had further hurdles to leap.

Before tax credits could be deployed, the development team had to obtain a variety of approvals and permits, from matters of zoning to issues of historic preservation and environmental impact. It took a lot of time, but the project eventually received permission to build a mixed-use complex in a residentially zoned neighborhood. Similarly, a historic preservation assessment—while laudatory of the work of Gutterson, Born, and Church—judged it sufficient simply to document their work extensively prior to demolishing it, rather than to call for the original project to be preserved.[87] The project also passed scrutiny in terms of its environmental impacts, despite minor concerns about traffic increases.

While the city debated environmental impacts, the SFHA faced impacts of its own. In February 2001, Matt Gonzalez and Tom Ammiano, two city supervisors who formed part of a new eight-to-three progressive majority on that board, pushed back against the progrowth politics of Willie Brown and the agencies he controlled. Ammiano had run against the incumbent Brown in the 1999 mayoral election after Brown had famously said, "Democracy is best served by my running unopposed."[88] Although Brown prevailed in a runoff, he was forced to shift further to the right to court Republican voters. Then, with San Francisco supervisor elections held on a district basis for the first time since 1979, voters handed Brown a broad rebuke. As Richard DeLeon observes, they "rejected his plans for land use and development, defeated virtually all of his anointed and lavishly funded candidates, and elected a new, progressive supermajority to the board,"[89] which then opposed him for the remainder of his final term. Ammiano and Gonzalez called for legislation to dissolve the housing commission and let the Board of Supervisors run the SFHA themselves. Intended as a challenge to Brown's authority from the left, they cited a HUD audit from 2000 that blasted SFHA practices, as well as ongoing corruption probes. Brown's spokesman responded with much the same aplomb as his boss: "I would liken having the Board of Supervisors sitting on the Housing Authority to replacing the National Security Council with the cast of 'Hair,'" P. J. Johnston jousted. "It's a power grab that doesn't make sense for the people living in public housing."[90] Then, barely a month later, Ronnie Davis—the mayor's man who had been brought in to fix public housing in San Francisco—was put on unpaid leave, indicted by a federal grand jury in Ohio and accused of stealing public funds during his stint as chief operating officer at Cleveland's public housing agency.[91]

CLOSING THE FINANCIAL GAP, OPENING A GAP WITH RESIDENTS

Gregg Fortner, deputy to Davis, took over as acting SFHA director in time to participate in two key meetings with Mayor Brown and the North Beach development team. To John Stewart, this was a key turning point. "Gregg was a wonderful, delightful, proactive anomaly in a chain of dysfunctional managers. He was a 'How can we get this done?' guy. Ronnie had this huge cloud over his head, and he could not run that authority. Gregg could."[92] At a first meeting in April, they agreed on the urgency to raze the long-vacated east block by fall 2001, due to "health, safety, [and] security concerns"—facilitated by an extra $3.2 million HOPE VI demolition grant to cover the costs. A month later, the mayor met again with the North Beach development team and key SFHA leaders, where they discussed the "schedule required to obtain [the] tax credit allocation for the development," concluding that it would be a "single allocation in 2002."[93] This meant that—while North Beach would utilize a hugely disproportionate amount of tax credits—it would do so entirely within one round of allocations, thereby freeing up San Francisco to put in for a different project in the next round. The implications of that would soon erupt into the next major controversy.

These seemingly arcane and cryptic details about tax credits had profoundly matter-of-fact consequences for North Beach tenants: because the timing of tax credits directly affected construction phasing, it therefore also directly impacted promises about tenant relocation. The flip side of the immense success with cornering tax credits was that these tax credits would need to be deployed in a single year—and would therefore require the demolition and construction to proceed in a single phase. As JSCo executive Jack Gardner explained: "If it was broken up into two rounds, San Francisco would have used *two* of its period rounds of 9 percent tax credits. . . . Willie Brown basically said, 'No, screw that—do it all in one.'"[94]

Brown had to explain the North Beach Place deal to other tax-credit-seeking players in the city, some of whom regarded BRIDGE and its partners with jealousy if not outright resentment. Calvin Welch, who uneasily served as chief housing adviser to Brown, described BRIDGE as "a great shark," adding, "This was just the latest incarnation of BRIDGE soaking up tax credits." He marvels at BRIDGE's political connections, at both at city and state levels, noting its capacity to work with Mayor Brown and steer him toward a mutually desirable outcome. "If Willie was told, 'Pick up the phone and call,' he'd pick up the phone and call. [But] Willie had to be *told* to pick up the phone and call," Welch observed.[95] In turn, as John Stewart described it, Brown handled the rest of the internal politics himself: "He said to other nonprofits and developers, 'Guess what, this year almost everything is going to go into this one project, so they can do it in one fell swoop—we got the pain over with.'"[96]

Obtaining the tax credits all at once also meant all construction would need to start in 2002, so that it could be completed by December 2004, when the tax credits would expire.[97] As John Stewart put it, his team realized that "we really need to do this in one fell swoop." Tax-credit timing mattered most, but avoiding the need to "string out the project" into phases also offered better "economy of scale." "Most importantly," Stewart averred, JSCo worried that trying to "go in for credits in two different bites" would be too risky. As a frequent and well-placed player in these sorts of deals, Stewart "knew State Treasurer Phil Angelides personally, and he kind of said, 'You'll be taking your chances; what's gonna happen if you don't get an award of credits in the second year?'"[98] North Beach Development Partners did not want to take any such chances.

Despite the political sensitivity of this change of plan—or, more precisely, *because* of this sensitivity—there seemed to be no comparable rush to inform the tenants during spring 2001. In fact, this deal had already been struck during the preceding year. Asked about this long afterward, Barbara Smith recalled, "The developers did say very clearly, 'We can't deliver it,'" adding, "I don't think they ever committed to two phases."[99] Tenant activists eventually discovered a memo from BRIDGE to SFHA officials, dated all the way back in January 2000, suggesting that the exit contract not use the language about two phases, and that it was time for "the merits of one phase to be introduced to tenants."[100] In any case, eighteen months after this internal admission, the team finally divulged the revised strategy to residents. "We wanted to reveal that to the residents [earlier]," JSCo's Jack Gardner insisted, "but then-executive director Ronnie Davis prevented us from doing so." When the truth was later revealed, "We got pilloried for our 'bait and switch,' and everybody had to be displaced off-site, temporarily." Meanwhile, "Ronnie Davis was already gone."[101]

Throughout the summer of 2001, the SFHA and its partners tried to find ways to rebuild trust with residents. In June, BRIDGE hired back Ben Golvin (who had worked with them as a project manager from 1983 to 1995) as a consultant to help manage the project and work with North Beach tenants. As Golvin recalled, he was immediately sent over to meet with residents. "The task for North Beach Associates and for the Housing Authority was to go explain to the residents why it was that it was going to be done in one phase instead of two." Together with Gregg Fortner, Golvin—as a young, white planning and development professional—had to bear the brunt of the resident turmoil. There were many meetings that also included Gardner and Stewart, as well as Carol Galante from BRIDGE and Michael Johnson, but it fell to Golvin to lead "the day-to-day work of rebuilding trust with the tenants."[102]

As Tel-Hi's Denise McCarthy noted, this was more than a problem for the developers; it also affected resident relationships with staunch neighborhood supporters.

> All we had was the mayor saying, "Has to be one phase, guys, or it ain't happening." We said, "Oh my God, oh my God, we promised them." . . . Some of the tenants, like Alma, went wacko and hired lawyers. It was crazy.

Reneging on the promise from Davis, McCarthy continued, triggered memories of all the "promises that had been made and broken in the Western Addition. Part of the reason it wasn't an easy sell was that people were worried: 'Oh, this is just a scam to get rid of us.'" Reflecting back on the long process, erstwhile NBTA treasurer Bethola Harper felt manipulated and misled. "We learned that agreements we made with the housing Authority were meant to be broken as soon as they could demonstrate enough tenant support to satisfy HUD. Most importantly, we learned never to air out any differences in front of the city. If we had to argue, we needed to meet amongst ourselves to work out our own problems. They were always looking for ways to spread rumors and pit the races against each other. The end goal was to get as many of us out, and pay for as little relocation as possible."[103]

Fortunately, due to the long-standing support from Tel-Hi, residents still had someone to trust. Despite some outliers such as Harper and Lark, McCarthy observed, "We *had* most of the residents. . . . And Ronnie Davis had been discredited by that time, pretty much. I think they trusted *us*." Still, the process remained a leap of faith for Tel-Hi: "All of us were also out on a limb, because we weren't really sure that it was all gonna really work." Not surprisingly, "It took lots and lots and lots of meetings."[104]

Residents met with Fortner on July 21 to air their distress. Some focused on relocation, while Alma Lark enlisted the support of an outside activist group, Housing as a Human Right, to push for the resident management agenda, expressing "fundamental concern that residents were denied ownership of the development." Fortner explained that, while all residents would indeed have to relocate, they were not being evicted. At the top of the participant sign-in list, underscoring previous discord, one attendee scrawled, "This doen't [*sic*] mean we agree to anything."[105]

The following week, NBTA board members flatly refused to meet with anyone from the SFHA and the development team to discuss design and security issues affecting the new development. This placed Cynthia Wiltz—by then an SFHA employee as well as the NBTA president—in an extremely awkward position.[106] Tenants instead met among themselves. Seventeen tenants from the NBTA and NBRMC banded together on July 28 to write up a position paper announcing that they would "accept no relocation" that violated the exit contract that had been signed by Ronnie Davis and by the SFHA's general counsel. They vowed to "stay on site" and refused to accept any change that "might violate their promised, continuous residence at the North Beach Development." Moreover, they revived the idea that the NBRMC should be accorded a "51 percent majority-interest" in the development, asked that 10 percent of the interest from the $20 million HOPE VI grant be allocated to the RMC to "address tenants' desires for maintenance and self-improvement on-site," and demanded that all rents be counted as "equity toward purchase" of their apartments.[107]

On July 31, a small group of the usual North Beach resident leaders, joined by Don Paul from Housing as a Human Right, met with SFHA senior officials, together with Ben Golvin and Michael Johnson. Each side restated its position: the development team explained how and why the tax-credit deal drove the schedule, while Paul and the residents expressed concerns about relocation, security, timetables, and construction materials. The impasse continued.[108]

Johnson, Golvin, and their developer colleagues repeatedly tried to make the logical argument that one-phase connection meant that "in the end, all the tenants will be able to get back into the property soon."[109] But residents, prodded by Paul and other activists, remained unconvinced that "all" would ever benefit. In September, the residents held a press conference to voice their grievances about the relocation process and refused to let representatives from the developer team participate in the discussion. If the last residents continued to stay put, Paul believed, the North Beach Place project would become the next I-Hotel fiasco: "a political disaster for the Housing Authority and everyone else."[110]

Gradually, however, the remaining residents of the west block moved out during the fall of 2001 and the early part of 2002.[111] During these tense times, Barbara Smith regarded Tel-Hi as an important "moderating influence" because Denise McCarthy and her staff "were fine with all the public housing residents returning" but "were not as radical as the one-sided housing advocates." Other residents credit Supervisor Aaron Peskin for championing their cause and helping with relocation. In turn, tenant leaders received a "Certificate of Honor" from Peskin to acknowledge the importance of their own contributions.[112] For most, however, relocation remained both frightening and contentious.

Many of the lingering North Beach residents worked individually with lawyers, while some activists considered filing a larger suit charging breach of contract. To John Stewart, having legal assistance available helped everyone since, for residents, "the biggest impediment to making this deal happen was the fear of being relocated out and [then] losing their Section 8." JSCo worked proactively with legal aid attorneys to reassure their North Beach clients that the developer would stick to its promises regarding the right to return. Without such external validation, Stewart asked rhetorically, "Why should they believe *us*?"[113] Barbara Smith concurred that the tenants used the legal system effectively: "They were a pretty smart group of residents. They knew the Asian Law Caucus and Bay Area Legal Aid. They knew their rights."[114] Meanwhile, Golvin and the rest of the development team tried mightily to articulate relocation terms that could be fair to all.

Construction of the new North Beach Place did not begin auspiciously, to say the least. On January 15, 2002—the very first day of demolition— a bulldozer tipped over, crushing its driver atop a mound of rubble.[115] Environmental problems on-site caused other construction delays. Half of the project's units contained lead paint and asbestos, and—hardly surprising given the site's complex early history—the soil had some arsenic, mercury, zinc, and lead contamination. Meanwhile, the SFHA continued to worry about the project's once and future residents.

In March 2002, the SFHA issued a lengthy, thorough, and sensitive "North Beach Relocation Plan," which offered "additional assurances to Residents," promising a "first right to return" to all households "who remain in good standing," while stipulating that they "will not be subject to the screening criteria developed for new applicants" to North Beach Place. Having "Good standing," the agreement defined, meant that a resident "has consistently paid their rent on time, has complied with all the provisions of the lease agreement, and that no member of the Resident household has been convicted of a felony charge." The agreement also stated that residents could remain in their west-block units "until the availability of tax credit financing for the project is confirmed." Finally, the housing authority pledged to "maximize the right of residents to return . . . by identifying any potential obstacles to a Resident's 'good standing' and develop[ing] a program of information, counseling and services aimed at overcoming any obstacles to assure that the current Residents are able to return," including establishing a "repayment agreement" for those owing back rent.[116] By October, the last of the remaining west-side residents relinquished their apartments, just ahead of the demolition crews. About 80 percent found alternative accommodation in San Francisco; the rest moved farther afield.[117]

Another key factor that eased the crisis over relocation, Stewart points out, turned out to be the sheer generosity of the housing voucher offered to residents. "We got through [US Representative] Nancy Pelosi's office a *very* strong allocation of vouchers, at very high rates." The North Beach team offered reluctant relocatees the options of portable housing subsidies that were "way above market, allowing $1,600–$1650 a month for a one-bedroom apartment, $2000 a month for two bedrooms, $2,750 a month for three bedrooms, and $2,975 month for four bedrooms." As Stewart framed it, "We presented to this assembled body [of tenants] an opportunity to 'take the money and run.' And a lot of 'em [did that]."[118]

For those who did come to live at North Beach Place, however, life at the new development offered both excellent opportunities and unexpected challenges.

12

Life at North Beach Place

A Model for Other Places?

The opening of North Beach Place—the east block in 2004 and the west block in 2005—occasioned much praise in the local press, much of it framed in dramatic "before and after" contrasts. Instead of a "dismal yellowish," "cramped," "hulking," "once-notorious," "crime-ridden" array of "crumbling 1950s-era boxes," "hunched over the cable car stop like a monster in the night," "complete with cockroaches, raw sewage leaks and thugs"—a place that had become a "populous public hazard" and "exuded a bleak sadness that seemed to seep into neighboring properties," making it "a bane of the North Beach and Fisherman's Wharf neighborhoods"—the SFHA and its partners had coproduced a "cheery," "shiny," "handsome," "clean," "superlative," and "heralded" development that was "by all accounts . . . a gem"(figures 12.1-12.3).[1] A new world presumably awaited: drug traders replaced by Trader Joe's; muggers supplanted by a coffee shop named JR Muggs.[2]

North Beach Place garnered numerous awards: from the *San Francisco Business Times* real-estate competition and from *Builder* magazine; a "Readers' Choice" award for Family Projects from *Affordable Housing Finance* and designation as a "Green Roof of Excellence" in the category of "intensive residential."[3] Barnhart Associates did most of the architecture for North Beach Place, though the building for seniors had a separate designer, Full Circle Design Group. Architect Paul Barnhart commented, "The neighborhood groups felt it was important to have the project not make too much of a statement, to keep the height limits and architectural limits similar" to the nearby three- or four-story residential structures.[4] Demand for apartments, not surprisingly, was robust.

When North Beach Place opened the east block in September 2004, more than twenty-one hundred people applied for a tax-credit-subsidized apartment during a single three-week period. Still, leasing up occurred slowly. Only a few dozen apartments filled by the end of the year, even though the

Figure 12.1 The Cable Car Terminus at the Redeveloped North Beach Place
The Powell and Mason cable car line still ends at a turnaround between the blocks of
North Beach Place, but the new location has retail and much to offer tourists. A sign
welcoming visitors to Fisherman's Wharf stands prominently at the intersection.
Credit: Author.

SFHA had twenty-seven thousand names on its waiting list.[5] Some of this
bureaucratic complexity occurred because fully 119 of the new units were
funded through project-based Section 8 vouchers, 138 remained part of the
conventional public housing system, and the rest were subsidized by tax
credits that required yet a different entry process. Meanwhile, 48 of the
apartments were constructed for seniors (with one for the resident manager) in a separate building.

Despite these complexities and the attenuated off-site relocation, many
people involved with North Beach Place initially expected about half of the
former residents to come back. An official HUD database about the project even indicates, quite erroneously, that fully 90 percent of the original
229 households were relocated back to the new development.[6] Others
provided different estimates, also all wrong. The construction contractor,
Nibbi Brothers, explicitly asserted that "more than 50 percent of the original Housing Authority residents have returned";[7] newspaper reports in fall
2004 stated that "a little more than half have decided to come back,"[8] and,
accordingly, some of the key players on the development team continued for
years to believe this to have been the case. These estimates, however, seem
to have represented the stated intents of former residents, rather than the

1. Hyatt Hotel
2. Pier 2620 Hotel
3. Holiday Inn Express
4. Marriott Hotel
5. Sheraton Hotel
6. Holiday Inn
7. Courtyard Marriott
8. The Cannery
9. Pier 45
10. Telegraph Hill Neighborhood Center (Tel-Hi)

North Beach Place
Taylor St.
Mason St.
Bay St.
Francisco St.
Columbus Ave.
Lombard St.

0 ————————————————— 1/4 Mile

Figure 12.2 Site Plan and New Neighborhood Context for North Beach Place
The revitalization of North Beach Place occurred in tandem with a broader
transformation of the neighborhood. On the bayside of Bay Street, hotels proliferated,
while inland North Beach continued to gentrify. Instead of the open courtyards of the
old project, the interior outdoor space of the new development is raised one story on
a plinth, with retail and parking entered from the street level.
Credit: Author with Kristin Simonson and Jonathan Tarleton.

reality of their return. In fact, as John Stewart himself admitted, "We only
retained eighty-two units out of 229. Thirty-six percent is the number." "The
rest," he observed, "did a diaspora. And we don't know *where* they went; I expect a lot of them left the city."[9]

Douglas Shoemaker, who served as director of housing for Willie Brown's
mayoral successor Gavin Newsom (in office from 2004 to 2011), put it
bluntly: "[Housing Choice] Vouchers in San Francisco have been synonymous with *flight*, not with choice."[10] Denise McCarthy observed that "several
people who moved got Section 8 *houses* out of the city, and they weren't
about to move back." Others, she recounted, resisted the idea of downsizing
back to the new North Beach Place: "The units are small, the rooms are
small—smaller than they were. The *location* was great, but some people,

Figure 12.3 Trader Joe's Comes to North Beach Place
A Trader Joe's supermarket anchors the corner of Bay Street and Mason Street, with
North Beach Place apartments above and adjacent to it.
Credit: Author.

once they got more room, weren't willing to make that move."[11] JSCo president Jack Gardner agreed that, for some, the appeal of Section 8 trumped anything that North Beach Place might provide. "If you can move into a house, somewhere in the East Bay, in a good school district, and you don't want to live the urban life of North Beach–Fisherman's Wharf anymore, you stay." At the same time, he acknowledged, those contemplating a return had to consider the changes from the old SFHA laxity: "Certainly, you'd be coming back to a different management."[12]

BRIDGE consultant Ben Golvin agreed that most nonreturning residents simply had a better option elsewhere:

> There were people I worked with day in, day out who had been the acknowledged leaders—at some point they'd been the elected leaders of the tenants—who were really interesting, marvelous people, and four out of five of them decided that once they'd gotten Section 8 and were living in a place that was in the private sector and they weren't reporting to the housing authority and they had a landlord and just paid their rent, they just felt like everybody else in the world. I talked to those people; they said, "This is much better for me and my family."

For others, though, particularly if they had been former North Beach Place households with members who were not on the lease, prospects for return seemed highly problematic. While "right to return" proved relatively straightforward for some, for others there were unspoken issues. Golvin illustrated the dilemma: "Nobody wants to say, 'Hey, what about my "baby daddy" who maybe lives here, but doesn't really, 'cause if he did, his income would be counted and—by the way—he wouldn't qualify because of his criminal record.'" Others lived in complex, multigenerational households. "There's a bunch of situations where people have households that don't fit the exact criteria of the housing authority rules or the tax credit rules," Golvin continued. "People know that, and my guess is that there were people who moved out and understood what the place was going to be like, and were clear that they were never coming back."[13]

IS THERE A NORTH BEACH PLACE FOR BLACKS?

For many African Americans in North Beach Place, redevelopment proved to be a battleground, and most black leaders felt that they, in effect, lost a war of attrition. Few returned following redevelopment. Former NBTA president Greg Richardson is among those who resent the rehousing process most bitterly. When he relocated temporarily during the construction processes, Richardson fully expected to return. "I was all excited to go back," he recalled, but felt thwarted at every turn by both the North Beach board and the management. "They all turned on me. . . . They picked everyone off one by one." Richardson thought he was dissuaded from returning because "they knew if I was there I was gonna push certain elements of this HOPE VI program: resident-owned businesses, youth training programs, and the resident management corporation." Richardson also blamed the tenant association for having failed to remain an effective voice in its dealings with JSCo. Instead, "John Stewart chose who they wanted back," and "SFHA lost track of a lot of people." Richardson accused the relocation officers of being "sellouts," adding that "the actual tenants' association sold the tenants down the drain." Richardson described the new North Beach regime as "like a dictatorship." Management did not prevent his return outright, but rebuffed him by creating terms that he would judge unacceptable by refusing to give him a two-bedroom apartment.

> I gave up my house and so what? . . . My family sacrificed, we moved out of here, and you give me this kind of treatment? You want me to come back to this little bitty unit?

Richardson views the one-for-one replacement of public housing as no more than a hollow victory, since cost cutting led to smaller-than-promised apartments, too small to fit a family's furniture.[14]

Most of the other black tenant leaders did not return to live in the new North Beach Place. Their reasons seem to be quite diverse, and their erstwhile fellow residents were only too happy to offer a wide variety of additional explanations. Alma Lark owed the SFHA $3,000 in back rent due to her previous efforts to withhold funds to protest conditions, and several tenants cited this as the reason for her nonreturn. In an August 2005 interview, Lark stated that she had "expected to go back" but the SFHA had "inflated" the rent she owed: "I didn't know they were going to charge me no $3000. Where am I gonna get $3000?" Still, she expressed hope that she might one day "get back up there." SFHA official Barbara Smith acknowledged Lark "owed a lot of back rent" but noted that this "doesn't prevent us from moving people into the new housing. All you have to do is not have been evicted." Instead, Smith insists, Lark didn't return because she was happy with living at the Rosa Parks housing development for seniors.[15] A few months after the new North Beach opened, however, Lark died following a stroke.

The reasons why other leaders did not return vary. Cynthia Wiltz complained that her bed could not fit in the North Beach Place apartment she had been offered. Others, such as Bethola Harper and Beverly Williams, preferred to keep their Section 8 ("housing choice") vouchers and live elsewhere. Many told their former North Beach neighbors that they did not want to return to a place that had so many new rules. Meanwhile, some tenants and their advocates complained that they were falsely accused of being behind on rent, due to the housing authority's poor recordkeeping.[16] In theory, based on their carefully negotiated exit contract, former North Beach residents were to be permitted to return "with just a minimal credit check." Others coming from public housing elsewhere faced a much higher barrier to entry based on credit and other factors. Even so, despite this exit contract guarantee, another black former NBTA leader, Lorraine Bender, recalled that at first the management sought to bar re-entry of former North Beach residents based on credit reasons. Tenant leaders had to argue that "you're not supposed to do that" until the SFHA finally said, "Oh, you're right." As Bender observed, it is not enough to "have an agreement"; you also need to "fight to have it enforced."[17]

Bender returned to the new North Beach Place only to be evicted in 2009 under the "one strike and you're out" policy after her adult son was charged with drug possession. Even though the charges were subsequently dropped and even though she "was not responsible for the conduct," Bender, her nineteen-year-old daughter, and her two-year-old grandson were all forced to leave North Beach Place. Upset about her eviction, Bender complained that she was "put out for so little" and that the "zero [tolerance] policy [is] really heavy." She was offended by what she calls JSCo's "strict military style" and lack of sensitivity, part of a world of excessive rules and pervasive surveillance cameras. In her view, "It may be a race thing" since "Afro-American and Hispanic tenants are not treated equally, especially the ones that spoke out." In Bender's assessment, many of the other African American households from the old North Beach never tried to return: "A lot of families couldn't come back because they heard about the strict rules." Others who did return didn't last long. Bender estimates that fifteen or twenty families had been evicted ahead of her, most of them African American. "The ones with big voices and teenage children are out," she commented ruefully. "I was the last one."[18]

Citywide, at the time of the initial HOPE VI application for North Beach, African Americans occupied about 51 percent of SFHA apartments and more than one-third of those at North Beach, while constituting about 11 percent of the city's population. At North Beach, however, Asian households (many of them not Chinese) occupied a slim majority of apartments, markedly higher than their overall 24 percent citywide presence in SFHA properties. In a housing development founded in an era of extreme tension over African American occupancy of San Francisco public housing, the HOPE VI process and outcome only served to revive this strain. At base, interviews with three dozen current residents and neighborhood leaders suggest, the Chinese occupants of North Beach Place exist in a very different world from their African American co-residents. A quarter-century after HOPE VI planning began, San Francisco as a whole has an African American population of less than 5 percent, and this is still dwindling. Moreover, since most of the black population resides in the southeast of the city, North Beach Place's neighbors typically equate the sighting of a black person with presumed public housing residence.

MIXING IT UP: THE CHALLENGES OF INTERPERSONAL AND INTERGROUP RELATIONS

Lengthy interviews conducted with a broad cross-section of twenty North Beach Place residents several years after the development opened reveal deep-seated ambivalence.[19] These residents—black, white, Chinese, North African, and Latin American with roots in Mexico, El Salvador, and elsewhere—collectively report reasonably high levels of satisfaction with life in the development, but this seems to be in spite of its racial and income diversity, not because of it. Those residing in the shallow-subsidy tax-credit units frequently resent the deeper subsidies allocated to residents in apartments funded by public housing and Section 8: "Psychologically," a Chinese man maintained, "it seems unfair that we get less [space] in proportion to what we pay for versus those who pay less. It's out of balance. For example, some residents [who] don't work and have many children only need to pay $300, but get the same unit as ours." Another Chinese man added:

> Mixed income is not a good thing. We pay over $1,200, while others pay little or nothing, like the woman who lives next to me with three kids. When there's this big gap in rent, there's no sense of responsibility. . . . When you have to pay more out of your pocket, you take care of things better, and not trashing the place.

He resented being treated as part of "government low-income housing" where "people perceive and lump us a bad people and bad image." A female Chinese respondent underscored this connection between financial and behavioral resentment: "I don't want my children get exposed to bad behavior and role models. . . . I don't think it's fair, even though everyone gets subsidies from government, but we pay more."

From the public housing side of the income divide, the picture can look quite different. "I feel like if you have a good job, and you are working, and you are paying good rent, they are going to treat you better and pay more attention to you," a Latina married mother of three lamented. "I feel like property management treats people based on income—they treat those who pay more rent better than those who live in public housing." A Latina senior complained that income mixing is "a bad thing because those who paid more think they have more rights." "Management treat higher-income residents better than people on Section 8 and other low-income people," she added. "They can make noise, hang laundry, keep plants and bicycles [and have] more rights, but low-income people need to put things down there in the parking lot." Specifically, she recalled one resident who was actually told not to talk in the hallway because doing so was "disgusting."

Other public housing residents just do not see why they should share a scarce resource with less-needy tenants. An older, single Latina resident stated this categorically: mixing incomes is "a bad thing, everybody should be in Section 8 or housing authority." Another Latina, who returned after living previously in the old North Beach development, maintained the same thing: "This is government property; all of a sudden they are bringing other people in, and it's not fair for those people who have been on the waiting list for five years to get into housing." A third Latina respondent, who transferred from public housing in Potrero Hill, stated that North Beach should not be for those paying "regular rent." While she acknowledged that the people "paying full rent . . . are the kind of people you want to live with" because "you don't have to worry about them," this has a downside. "Because they just opened it up to everybody," it "takes away from us," since units are "very small" and "so many" are not available to SFHA residents. Similarly, a male Chinese college student observed, "Some people have a lot

of money, but they still apply for the housing. They don't seem like low income, they just somehow got into North Beach. Isn't NBP supposed to be for
low-income people? They just take from others."

Some, though, see value in the mix: "Low income gets the stereotype
tag that you are not good; mixed income changed the image of the place,"
one Latina receiving TANF support commented. A white, employed public
housing resident who considered herself "a hard worker" appreciated
having a larger number of households with jobs on-site: it helps public
housing residents to "keep working for a living when they are around other
people that work for a living. If I was the only person in my neighborhood
that works for a living, I'd feel kind of weird." An employed, Latina public
housing resident suggested that she was a role model for her higher-income
neighbor, since she defied their stereotypes: "It's kind of good to educate
other people that not all public housing people are bad. . . .Not all public
housing residents and families are on welfare, on drugs, or unemployed." In
this way, she flips the assumed directionality of the much-discredited role-
modeling rationale for income mixing.

The working-class households occupying the tax-credit units are disproportionately Chinese in comparison to those in the public housing units
(other than the senior building)—so the income differential is overlaid with
racial tensions. Almost without exception, the Chinese respondents (many
of whom speak little English) expressed particular fear-driven animosity toward the development's black youth. "Black youth, groups of them, their
pants hang down to the knees. I fear their behavior and attitude. They are
weird. They stare at me." Or "Black teenagers are hanging out on the streets,
sitting on parked cars, fooling around, swearing, . . . fighting, urinating,
might be taking drugs." Another worried over "African American teenagers
hanging out at nighttime. Not sure if they are gang. Once the security
kicked them out of the gate area, they moved to the cable car area." An
elder Chinese who used a Section 8 voucher to move with his wife to North
Beach Place from a Chinatown residential hotel observes matter-of-factly
that "those hanging out on the streets are blacks and no Chinese. I fear them
because I don't speak English, and I am a senior. I fear them for the way they
dress and behave. I am afraid they will beat me." Another Chinese resident,
who lived with his wife and children in a tax-credit subsidized unit, said that
he fears black youth just outside the development:

> I don't know if they are high on drugs, [but] they are not rational [and] al-
> ways scream. If I get beaten, when the cops come and [find] that I don't speak
> English, a group of them can gang up and say things differently and reverse
> [the story], saying that I beat them. We talk about America as a democracy—is
> it really fair legally?

In this context, he asks, "Am I a racist?"

Latina residents from public housing units said much the same sorts of things: "Just like before, there were a lot of black people sitting and hanging outside at the entrance. And it's kind of scary for the kids. And former, original tenants who used to be kids here [are] now selling drugs." Someone else added, "It looks like public housing because of the people who hang around—African American young kids, older guys, a white guy, and a Samoan guy hanging around drinking, selling drugs, breaking in cars, robbing, harassing tenants, tourists, and anyone. Those guys make you feel like we are back in the projects." Another declared: "The older and younger kids are destroying the front of the property and making us look bad. The kids are hanging out in the public, in front of the building and at the corner. They [are] smoking, drinking, urinating, insulting people." "I am not a racist," she is quick to add,

> but unfortunately, it's the African American young kids and older guys, and the black African American girls. It's unsafe. These people are more into the gangs. Because all they talk about is violence, all they want to do is hit someone. You cannot talk to them. They are verbally violent. They are not the type of people who you try to go to talk to and resolve problems; they are the people who want to hit you, fight you, attack you.

Several respondents indicated that the development had calmed down after its first few years once a few problem households were evicted. A white, female tenant maintained that "a lot of us are not racist. A lot of us have good relationships with people of all colors. [But] then you have one or two families from Sunnydale that are always upset all the time. It can throw all the chemistry off." Still, she praised "the better screening of tenants," adding, "It's not a dumping ground anymore."

The few remaining African American households notice the challenges posed by youth, but seem much more likely to blame this on the development's lack of dedicated recreational space and opportunities, or to assume that problems are generated by outsiders. One black resident explained: "[Neighbors] still complain about little stuff like teens hanging out at the corner, the little things. It's the drug traffic, but they are not residents; most of them just come here. But they still complain about the little hangout. I guess it will never go away." What to some seems no more than a "little hangout" to others feels like a direct threat.

Sometimes the concerns are focused within the development, not just its outside edges. "When my son played the piano from 7:00 p.m. to 7:30 p.m.," one Chinese resident related, "the upstairs unit tenant complained to management for noise nuisance, and another time, she borrowed money from me, but she never return the money. I believe they picked on me because of my race." In the end, he commented, "They got evicted for not paying rent," adding that "they were Section 8 tenants." Another Chinese tenant reported:

> My next door black neighbor once said to me: "Get the fuck back to China." Isn't it racism? The blacks couldn't tolerate the Chinese. For example, [when] my wife once took the garbage out, the next door kid, not even ten years old, threw a bottle at her. . . . Not all blacks are like that, but those low-income and not educated blacks are not friendly to Asian tenants, and there are still a lot of them here.

Government policymakers, he continued, want "different racial and ethnic groups harmoniously living together, but practically it is unachievable—not just a gap, but absolutely unachievable. . . . The planners, architects and management don't know about it. It actually will lead to an outcome of no one speaking to each other; those who know English pick on those who don't." "I don't understand minority and diversity policy in America," he went on:

> I heard that when we moved in, there was such policy that each Chinese unit has to be next to a black unit. Why do they need to allocate like that? There is an underlying problem that many of you don't know. My white neighbor told me that the rule is that there is no smoking here, [but] the black tenant kept smoking in the open. . . . The smoking tenant is very mean, and if you complain, she will say you are racist. The blacks kept saying that we discriminate against them racially, but isn't this racism against Chinese?

North Beach Place has rules, he concluded, but they are "not enforced consistently and fairly."

Yet some non-Chinese residents saw things as skewed to favor the Chinese. They pointed to rules that seem to be enforced to permit some cultural preferences but not others: "Asian people hang a lot of laundry on the railing on the balcony, [but] for three years, nobody say anything," one Latina declared. "We see more help for the Asian people than for other cultures. Management treats Chinese a hundred percent better." Another Latina insisted that she has been discriminated against because she is "not Chinese."

Some of the intergroup tensions have been enhanced by the nature of the development's architectural and urban design. One of the most innovative aspects of North Beach Place's physical transformation has been its inclusion of ground-floor retail all along the development's commercial edge on Bay Street. This is in keeping with the nature of the surrounding neighborhood and also carries the added advantage of working well with the slope of the site, which made inclusion of the extra level of retail on the downhill side especially inviting. The incorporation of a Trader Joe's supermarket, although too up-market to be of much daily relevance to many public housing residents who have a cheaper alternative nearby, has created a broad draw from across a quadrant of the city.[20] Similarly, the inclusion of several hundred units of parking helped with project financing and endeared the project to many in the larger community.

This inclusion of ground-floor accessed retail and parking, in turn, pushed much of the residential portion of the development one story above street level. The development is, essentially, built on a plinth above the parking and supermarket, a key design decision that has triggered both gains and losses. On the plus side, the interior courtyards of North Beach Place are a separate internal world, raised above the street, and accessed only by a card-controlled gated entry (figures 12.4–12.5). Long gone is the freely accessed project, in which visitors (including escaping criminals) could easily take refuge or make strategic shortcuts. Now, except for those who manage to sneak through the automated garage door of the parking lot and thereby gain access to the development from below, North Beach Place functions as a far more private and privatized gated community than its open-access

Figure 12.4 Courtyard-Facing Apartments on the Plinth of North Beach Place
Many of North Beach Place's apartments can be accessed from the raised plinth inside each of the blocks. While the courtyards, plantings, and playgrounds are certainly photogenic, many residents complained about a lack of privacy, excessive rules, and intrusive surveillance by management.
Credit: Author.

Figure 12.5 Gated Entrance to North Beach Place
From the Bay Street side, access to North Beach Place is through an intercom-based
gated entry. Once inside, stairs or an elevator lead up to the plinth from which
courtyard-facing apartments may be accessed.
Credit: Author.

precursor. For many residents, this gain of security and privacy is of paramount importance and thoroughly welcomed. One returning resident praised the new development as "very quiet, a gated community." Another resident, a black male in his fifties, also defended the gates. The new North Beach Place is "off the street and safer." "People used to just walk in," he observed. "People can't walk in now."

For others, however, this outward sense of security is merely illusory and instead supports the architectural equivalent of a police state. One African American tenant went so far as to liken North Beach Place to "concentration camp life"—by which she seemed to mean something akin to the World War II Japanese internment camps—somewhere you go "to be safe from war." Others remarked that the courtyards on the plinth lent themselves to near-complete surveillance by cameras. "They have too many," a black resident opined, noting that a guard admitted to her that there were 144 of them. Moreover, the cameras are not entirely fixed. "A camera is not directly on the house unless your house is a problem house," this resident observed. "Then they can move the cameras." A white resident had a somewhat different take: "I don't like the cameras, but they are a deterrence." John Stewart insists that there are only thirty-nine cameras, though he concedes that nearly all of them are trained on the inside of the development, a system that costs JSCo "$25,000 a month" to implement. In an effort to curtail North Beach drug dealing, there is also surveillance of "one street corner on the outside, on Mason and Francisco, which is where they did all their business." When dealers tried to re-establish their operations after the new development opened, Stewart says, "We let them know; we focused our security service and had a camera, and basically said, 'There's a new sheriff in town. You're not going to be coming down trying sell drugs to our people.' That became a *huge* issue."[21]

Other residents of North Beach Place feel betrayed by the failure of the promised business incubators to yield viable opportunities for resident-owned businesses in the new ground-floor retail spaces along Bay Street and, of equal importance, lament the lack of funding stream for resident services that was expected to result from the income generated by this retail component. As former board member Lorraine Bender put it, although the board negotiated an agreement on business incubator space for residents, the "criteria [were] too high" and we were "not educated on how to do it." Once the NBTA realized that public housing tenants would not be taking advantage of the incubator space, Bender said, the tenants put forth the idea of renting out the incubator space to private sector organizations, such as a coffee shop or cell phone provider. As she sees it, the SFHA liked the idea and was willing to work on it, but John Stewart remained nonresponsive. Instead, they appropriated the idea of giving the space over to the private sector (which came to include a Starbucks, a Budget Rental Car outlet, and a ballet school) but kept the money and chose not to inform the NBTA. "Tenants were supposed to get one-third of the incubator space and all the proceeds from that," Bender complained, but ultimately "It was not a participation partnership. This is a moneymaking thing here. They want to pay their debt. The residents want a simple business and can't do it. This is not the independent way that HOPE VI was supposed to go."[22]

Interviews with some other returning public housing residents also evince thwarted hopes. A single parent on TANF commented, "I wanted to start a business at the incubator space. I was thinking to start a translation services or an arts and crafts business, but it just died, and I heard nothing since." Another woman, currently employed, views the incubator promise to have been a cynical ploy: "They promised many things, like finding jobs for people; they even asked tenants what kinds of businesses they want, just to make people believe. I was dreaming at that time of opening a business, my own cafeteria." Others involved with trying to help residents negotiate this process consistently pointed to ways that residents, and those who sought to empower them, underestimated what would be needed. Tel-Hi's Denise McCarthy observed, "The incubator space sounded like a great thing at the time. The residents said, 'Oh, I'm gonna do catering' or this or that." Ultimately, "They had ideas but didn't understand all of the costs." The SFHA's Barbara Smith concurred, noting that "the residents wanted space for resident-owned businesses" until they realized what was really involved. Then they said, 'Go ahead and lease it and we'll just share in the rental income.'"[23]

John Stewart offered a similar view: "None of the residents really said, 'We want those leases.' There was not a lot of initiative there." The "surprise retail" success, according to the JSCo chairman, is the ballet studio, Tutus.

> They've done extremely well. Who would have ever thought? Tutus has a scholarship program for some of the kids that live up above. They have all learned their tour jetés. You can hear the strains of *Swan Lake* if you go there on a Saturday morning.[24]

While to some the new ballet skills marked a literal turnaround to go with the real-estate one, to others Tutus depended on attracting an upscale clientele and signaled a swan song for the pregentrification neighborhood.

MANAGING LIFE ON THE PLINTH

Interviews with a broad cross-section of North Beach Place residents reveal a mixed picture about life in the gated community on the plinth that replaced the permeable old project. One of the signal changes brought on by

HOPE VI redevelopment—in San Francisco as elsewhere—has been careful attention to rule setting and rule enforcement by the private management companies charged with delivering and maintaining attractive, secure, and orderly communities. The obvious upside to this has been a marked increase in the safety of these communities, especially in comparison to the "anything goes" mentality of the pre-redevelopment project. The downside, however, is that many residents feel that the management has gone too far in policing behavior.

Manager Felicia Chen took over as JSCo's site administrator in late summer 2005 and served for many years. Systematic analysis of the first few years of her monthly newsletters and intermittent memos from JSCo provide a clear sense of the ongoing struggle to maintain control over the appearance of the development and the behavior of its tenants. Chen issued repeated warnings about littering, dumping, ball playing, scooter riding, gate tampering, noise, vandalism, and "unruly children from our property" playing football on a neighborhood street. She anticipated the backlash: "Believe me, I have heard all the complaints you can possibly imagine about how we have no space for kids to play and that they should have designed the property differently." This kind of argument was a nonstarter for Chen: "The fact remains that we need to work with what we have." One memo in 2007 even banned play with nerf balls: "In the past," Chen intoned, "we thought nerf/foam ball was OK, but we have gotten so many complaints about kids getting into residents' patios to retrieve balls (trespassing), damage to the screens (when balls hit windows/screens) and destruction of landscaping. This has led us to ban all ball playing at North Beach Place."[25] With nerfs duly neutralized, in midsummer the management unleashed its legal armor on squirt guns and water balloons, sending some residents a "30 Day Notice of Change to Terms of Tenancy" to let them know about these additional banned substances and practices. "**Failure to comply**," the notice stated in bold print, "**shall constitute good cause for eviction**."[26]

Chen reminded residents that they "chose to move to North Beach Place" and that, if they now think this was a bad idea, "it is not all that difficult to rectify the mistake." Public housing tenants could request a transfer, since "there are always vacancies in Sunnydale, Potrero Hill, Pitts Plaza, Alemany, etc." For those in the apartments subsidized solely by tax credits—revealingly if undiplomatically described by Chen as "those who pay their own rent"—"you can move out any time you wish."[27] Vigilant management, coupled with barely disguised contempt for those whose contribution of 30 percent of their income apparently did not count as "paying their own rent," focused on rule enforcement.

The concerns over youth got paired with other reminders of behavioral expectations, including prohibitions against smoking, eating, or drinking in common areas. The more specific hints—reminiscent of the most paternalistic excesses of early public housing practices from the 1940s[28]—urged residents to "clean up daily and avoid messy build up," "do laundry weekly," "wipe up spills immediately," "pick up misc. items off the floor," and "sweep and mop often." In July 2008, JSCo management required all adult residents to sign off on a set of seventy-four "New House Rules," which basically codified the earlier behavioral concerns, while adding an explicit prohibition against wearing pajamas, nightgowns, or bathrobes—or going shoeless—in any common areas.[29]

To some extent, after these first few years of perpetual admonitions, rules gained traction and rule breakers departed, so life at North Beach Place settled down. Still, many residents felt that rule enforcement had become racialized. They viewed rules as associated with particular cultural practices, which then got interpreted, rightly or wrongly, as favoring one community over another.

Some African American households at North Beach Place had high hopes for the courtyards, viewing these as the primary source of public space available to them. By contrast, one black resident observed, the Chinese "don't come out. It's only the Afro-Americans and the Latinos. They got Chinatown. They got the Chinese Resource Center. They got the Chinese playground. We don't have resources in this area, except Tel-Hi." Erstwhile tenant leader Lorraine Bender remembered long discussions about the rules between the board and the new management company. Some of the rules "got amended" after the discussions ended and, as a result, "We can't do a lot of things that we thought" would be possible. "We didn't understand that it would be like this." Initially, she insisted, there was a clear agreement to have a BBQ area (as had existed in the older development) as well as a minigym for teens. In Bender's view, these were amenities that had particular resonance and importance for the African American portion of the community, so she was particularly resentful that they were omitted or prohibited.[30]

Reflecting back on the social world of the old North Beach Place, Tel-Hi's Denise McCarthy remembered when the NBTA purchased "a big barbeque." In the old development, "the housing authority didn't care" if people had large gatherings. In the new North Beach Place courtyards, "It's hard for everybody to have to give up doing things when you have people living together so close."[31] Yet, just as many residents pointed out, the counterargument also holds weight. The old development had too much permeability, with everybody coming through and nobody taking responsibility, leaving lots of hiding places for illicit things to happen. The new design deploys positive sounding things like "courtyards" and "patios" but couples this with discordant surveillance.

The result, it seems, is that North Beach Place delivered the *image* of the patio and the BBQ space, but has had trouble in delivering anything more than that image. With so many people all looking across and down at you in such close proximity, augmented by all the cameras, there is a basic contradiction. The photogenic backyard Americana culture is surely there, but the plethora of rules discourages residents from having the independence and the freedom to actually take advantage of control over their space. Many residents feel they are on a stage set, being watched by an audience, either directly or indirectly—not unlike the Hitchcock cinematic classic *Rear Window*. In effect, the design says yes, while the politics says no.

Repeatedly, and disturbingly, many of the concerns about life in North Beach Place rapidly turn into discussions about the challenges of diversity—centered on issues of race, ethnicity, and generational divides, but also closely interwoven with the effort to integrate the working-class residents of the tax-credit units with the extremely low-income, and more frequently jobless, residents of the public housing.

Despite significant ongoing tensions, North Beach Place's many triumphs—rooted in long memories and a decade-long struggle by residents to improve their housing environment, and supported by the tireless work of multifarious advocates and professionals—reveal a mostly successful struggle to develop a partially successful place. As such, the HOPE VI experiment at North Beach Place has been a learning experience for all concerned but continues to have its critics.

Perennial public housing skeptic Howard Husock scoffs at the purported success of North Beach Place. As the new development prepared to open, he ridiculed city and HUD officials for being proud of failing to "support higher end uses" in San Francisco. "If something else had been built there," he quoted HOPE VI director Milan Ozdinec in 2003, "it would have been a tremendous economic boon for the city of San Francisco." Husock could not understand why such a boon should be resisted: "Under a Republican administration," he lamented, "such cavalier dismissal of urban prosperity, even by a career HUD official, is dispiriting."[32] Not surprisingly, affordable housing developer Ben Golvin saw it differently. He understood that some would rather have seen the North Beach property sold off, with funds used to "build far more affordable housing in other parts of the city." Golvin resisted that temptation with a twofold logic: "First, there are people who had been living there [in North Beach public housing] for fifty years. It is their community and their neighborhood and we are displacing them temporarily in order to rebuild their homes." And, more broadly, Golvin understood the issue in more than cold economic terms, asking rhetorically, "What is the justification, aside from pure economics, to say we will rebuild your home but it is going to be in Hunters Point?"[33]

Meanwhile, Hunters Point itself would indeed become the next point of contention and opportunity. With North Beach Place allowed to remain in North Beach, San Francisco's housing leaders soon turned their attention to the city's few remaining areas of disinvestment. For those most concerned with preserving the remaining affordability of San Francisco's housing stock, North Beach Place seemed a viable model for the future.

FROM HOPE VI TO HOPE SF

During July 2003, as then-supervisor Gavin Newsom moved forward in his successful campaign to be elected mayor that fall, his staff suggested that he undertake a series of tours of San Francisco's public housing developments. This began with the most troubled places, located in Bayview–Hunters Point. Deputy Field Director Ahsha Safaí (who would himself one day be elected to the Board of Supervisors) focused Newsom's tour on San Francisco's "Big Four"—Sunnydale, Alice Griffith, Hunters Point / Hunters View, and Potrero Terrace / Potrero Annex (figure 12.6). Together, these places included well over half of the city's public housing apartments for families—places that had been entirely untouched by the HOPE VI program. And since African American households occupied approximately two-thirds of these twenty-three hundred units, these large developments housed a substantial proportion of San Francisco's rapidly disappearing black population. Safaí warned Newsom that "the majority of the constituent services, neighborhood complaints, and department work will be focused on the residents of the Big Four." "To know the Big Four intimately," he continued, "will allow you to anticipate many of the policy changes you will have to implement to further reform public housing in San Francisco."[34]

Such reforms took renewed urgency for Mayor Newsom in 2004.

By August, just before North Beach Place was due to open, HUD once again placed the SFHA on its "troubled" agency list due to concerns about financial management.[35] As mayor, Newsom's predecessor, Willie Brown, had taken an interest in public housing, but many other San Francisco leaders had preferred to regard it as federal property that had been ignominiously tied to inadequate federal funding—rather than something that belonged at the top of the city's own policy and budget agenda. Newsom's director of housing, Douglas Shoemaker, understood the city's frustration with the elusive and inadequate HOPE VI program and strongly supported the new mayor's willingness to "try something else." As Shoemaker commented, "This issue that the housing authority's problems are not the city's problems is bogus. At first it was, 'Why do we want to bail out the Bush administration just because they wanted to divest?' It felt awful. But the properties were

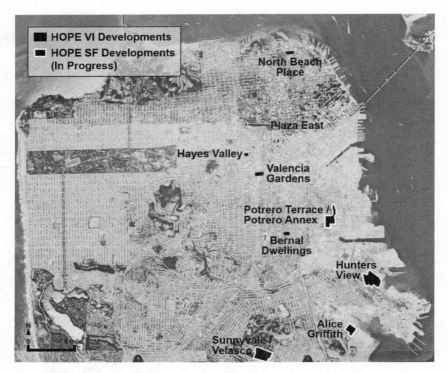

Figure 12.6 Locations of HOPE VI and HOPE SF Developments in San Francisco
Following on HOPE VI, the Mayor's Office of Housing and the SFHA embarked on an
effort to extend mixed-income redevelopment efforts to the southeast part of the city
using the city's own HOPE SF program. As at North Beach Place, HOPE SF endeavored
to replace all public housing while building additional housing to serve those with
higher incomes.
Credit: Author and Jonathan Tarleton; aerial photographs N10NAPPW10532097,
N10NAPPW10532099, N10NAPPW10535012, and N10NAPPW10535014 courtesy of the
US Geological Survey.

crumbling and the housing authority was on the troubled list. We just had
a lot of problems."[36]

In March 2005, Mayor Newsom told reporters that, because "HOPE VI has
been essentially gutted by the Bush Administration," San Francisco would
move forward with its own efforts to replace and revitalize public housing.
"Rather than waiting for Air Force One to come to SFO [San Francisco's air-
port], we are acknowledging there is a problem (in public housing) and we
are taking responsibility."[37] In September 2006 he pledged to devote "all of
his political capital" to ensuring that city voters passed a $95 million bond to
support this initiative, and Gregg Fortner promised that no public housing
residents would be permanently displaced.[38]

That fall, Newsom and Supervisor Sophie Maxwell (whose district encompassed the Bayview–Hunters Point neighborhoods) appointed a "broad-based task force," charged with providing "recommendations for addressing the conditions in San Francisco's most distressed public housing while also enhancing the lives of its current residents." The twenty-seven-member task force entitled its report, released in March 2007, *HOPE SF: Rebuilding Public Housing and Restoring Opportunity for Its Residents*. Not surprisingly, it featured a large color photo of the revitalized North Beach Place on its cover. The report began by noting SFHA's dire financial state: the federal government provided the agency about $16 million a year to address the physical needs of its properties, yet the backlog of unaddressed immediate needs had already reached nearly $200 million by 2002 and was continuing to escalate by more than $26 million every year. To address the shortfall, the task force proposed that the city take advantage of the relatively low densities of the SFHA's major projects by replacing them with higher-density, mixed-income neighborhoods that would be similar in unit-per-acre density to other thriving San Francisco districts. Instead of eight "highly distressed" sites constructed at an average of only seventeen units per acre where "the buildings are now falling apart," the task force argued for new communities to be constructed at forty units per acre. This seemed eminently plausible in a city where zoning permitted densities 25 percent higher than that. It is one of the glaring oddities of land-poor San Francisco that public housing sits on huge swaths of underdeveloped territory. Increasing density would let the new housing developments "match their surrounding communities," all while retaining the same number of apartments dedicated to occupancy by low-income, public housing households. The overall difference, however, would be stark: the twenty-five hundred units of rebuilt public housing on these sites would be collectively joined by as many as thirty-five hundred new housing units serving those with higher incomes (while also providing approximately 20 percent of these units with subsidies for both affordable rentals and ownership).[39]

Later in 2007, Newsom and the Board of Supervisors authorized the $95 million in local bond funding needed to launch HOPE SF and embarked on the initiative's pilot project at Hunters View. As head of the Mayor's Office of Housing under Newsom, Shoemaker remained a key staff participant in the task force process. He recognized that the decision to increase housing density bore little resemblance to past HOPE VI efforts in most American cities, noting that San Francisco's practice "makes us a sort of strange beast." Still, he noted, this was the only way forward. "If we're going to make this work, it's with the premise that we're going to rebuild all of the public housing in some way, shape, or form." For Shoemaker and other San Francisco housing advocates, the central question became "What can we add to it to make these communities function better and to add to our overall affordable housing stock?"[40]

Like others who take a long view, Shoemaker observed that current policy arose from the "strong residential hotel conversion ordinance . . . which basically requires full replacement or payment of full replacement value." He saw this as the impetus for San Francisco's not-for-profit "housing movement," confirming the prevailing view that the current generation of leaders in community development organizations still trace their roots to the "fight against redevelopment and its combination with Model Cities." "When you get weaned on all this," Shoemaker noted, "you learn that you are the successor to the International Hotel and to the north of Market work that stopped the expansion of the hotels into the Tenderloin."[41]

Ever sensitive to the city's larger development history, the HOPE SF website contrasts the new process with the old:

> In San Francisco, many remember callous and misguided efforts to redevelop the Western Addition / Fillmore neighborhood. Under Urban Renewal, the City abused its power of eminent domain, displacing thousands of residents and relocating much of the neighborhood's African-American population. This story resembles hundreds like it across America. HOPE SF will not repeat those mistakes.[42]

Similarly, a *Chronicle* reporter reassured readers that the HOPE SF approach is "a departure from earlier urban renewal schemes because at the core of its plan is the idea that existing residents will not be made to move. In contrast to the Fillmore redevelopment of the 1960s . . . H[OPE] SF builds first—existing residents are moved into new buildings before the old, dilapidated ones are torn down."[43] Despite the deep commitment to progressive ideals, however, HOPE SF got launched just in time to meet the Great Recession, making market-rate investment in marginal neighborhoods a much dicier proposition.

HOPE SF proposed to "create an economically integrated community" while ensuring "no loss of public housing"—just as had been accomplished at North Beach Place.[44] Yet the neighborhoods around most of San Francisco's remaining non-redeveloped public housing bore little relation to the rising fortunes of North Beach. As Shoemaker observed in 2009, in places like Hunters Point, "There aren't grocery stores; there's low-performing transit; public services are not high performing; schools are among the worst performing in town. You've got all the issues that surround monoculture housing." In short, "These are not the highly marketable sites compared to North Beach. You could have built anything in North Beach and sold it for $800,000. They didn't do that, but that would have been easy enough to do." Meanwhile, the financial model proposed under HOPE SF assumed that both land sales and the sales of bonds that were predicated on future expected higher tax revenues would be sufficient to cross-subsidize the rest of the development in terms of infrastructure and hard costs of replacing units. This initially proved to be a risky formula, since the recession meant that the city could not get anyone to build market-rate housing. Shoemaker candidly admitted, "We're struggling with the fact that we don't know who our future market-rate buyers are going to be. We're rolling the dice that we're going to find people that want to buy these homes."[45]

Housing activist Rene Casenave, who cofounded the Council of Community Housing Organizations with Calvin Welch, rhetorically wondered: "Who's gonna want to pay $600,000 for a condo in the projects?" He worried that "they're going to cut the number of public housing units if they don't move people in." Despite the promises about one-for-one replacement and phased on-site relocation, Casenave and others feared that "anyone who has a problem with the Housing Authority is getting evicted to make room for relocation on-site." Sara Shortt, executive director of the Housing Rights Committee and a member of the HOPE SF task force, expressed concern that attending to the preferences of newcomers might marginalize public housing residents in their own neighborhoods. "There are certain amenities homeowners that buy condos there are going to want to have. They're going to want to see a Starbucks and a Jamba Juice," she observed. "This could really change the neighborhood's demographics."[46] To the proponents of HOPE SF, however, the prospects of changed demographics and new investment were precisely the reasons to undertake the initiative—as long as it could be accomplished without losing public housing units.

Construction commenced on the first phase of new homes in Hunters View in late 2010 but proceeded without the inclusion of the market-rate component. The *Examiner*'s reporter phrased it succinctly: "The most radical element . . . will be dumped due to the real estate slump." Eventually, however, the intended mix will include one-for-one replacement of all 267 public housing units, together with at least 83 "affordable" rental units, and at least 300 market-rate homeownership units, with a small percentage of these subsidized to attract lower-income buyers. With the homeownership component "on hold" until future phases, the development team opened the first phase during 2013 and 2014. This included eighty new homes for public housing residents, while also incorporating twenty-seven additional "affordable" apartments, thereby creating a narrow mix of incomes not unlike what had been tried at North Beach Place.[47]

As the initial HOPE SF efforts got underway at Hunters View, replacing a scattered compound of more than fifty buildings constructed across twenty-two acres in 1956, the many accomplishments of North Beach Place continued to inspire. As Shoemaker put it, "North Beach Place has been phenomenally successful. Everybody points to it. In trying to think through HOPE SF, we went down there to think about it from a design perspective, what worked."[48] North Beach also clearly stands as a landmark for residents and their activist advocates, since it has raised expectations for equitable treatment of tenants. "Today," economic justice organizer James Tracy observed in 2014, "the exit contract won by the North Beach Tenant Association is the base level of protections for planned public housing renovations" elsewhere.[49] JSCo president Jack Gardner explicitly cited the hard lessons from North Beach Place when explaining why his firm was determined to avoid the "You're not going to let us come back" problem from HOPE VI: "We're doing the HOPE SF project in phases now to allow for no involuntary off-site relocation, even temporary."[50]

In other dimensions, however, the precedent established with North Beach Place and other HOPE VI sites in San Francisco has proved more contentious. Even Ed Lee, Newsom's successor as mayor who came into office in 2011 with strong bona fides in progressive housing circles due to his past activism with the Asian Law Caucus and his leadership of the city's Human Rights Commission, quickly faced pressures from unions that felt the city's growing reliance on private developers spelled trouble. Developer John Stewart, whose firm has taken the lead on the first HOPE SF development at Hunters View, views the SFHA's practice of having "ten separate unions" as entirely unworkable. He characterized the "housing authority model on labor costs as a perfect storm leading to bankruptcy."[51]

Stewart views the challenges at Hunters View as more daunting than what JSCo faced at North Beach Place. "Hunters View is much tougher because it's a very rough neighborhood and you're following a pattern of terrible management from the housing authority." At base, he worries that residents who had previously experienced extremely lax rule enforcement will have a difficult time with new team.

> So you have a lot of people out there that think if they don't pay on time that we can just "add it to the tab." We've said it's not going to work that way. We've had to be unpopular. You have to absolutely make sure that people know that housing is not a right; it is a privilege. . . . We're working with them to make sure they understand what the house rules are.

At its core, the returning public housing residents are faced not just with a new type of manager; they are faced with a new type of neighbor—and a new kind of investor oversight. "They're living with a different population; when you bring in tax-credit people you've got a different population."[52]

In August 2011, San Francisco won a $30.5 million grant from HUD's Choice Neighborhoods program—the more inclusive neighborhood redevelopment program intended to improve upon, and succeed, HOPE VI. This eventually enabled progress on redeveloping the Alice Griffith development (often referred to as "Double Rock"), located near the old Hunters Point Naval Shipyard. Constructed in 1962 and named after the cofounder of Tel-Hi, Alice Griffith contained 256 two-story townhouse apartments for public housing residents. The new plan, led by developer McCormack Baron Salazar, promised that all of these units would be replaced in advance of moving anyone off-site, and that these would be part of a new community of 1,126 residences, built out to include—and be dominated by—the usual HOPE SF mix of "affordable" and market-rate units. In turn, this could be touted as part of the larger Hunters Point Community, to be led by Miami-based developer Lennar—a $275 million project proposed to include more than ten thousand housing units in the redeveloped shipyard, together with commercial activities, parks, and space for research-and-development activities.[53] Here, as elsewhere, islands of public housing affordability would remain, even as one of San Francisco's last remaining districts of high poverty gained a wave of new investors and wealthy denizens.

Meanwhile, in addition to JSCo, the other key partners on the North Beach Place development team each gained a foothold in HOPE SF: Em Johnson Interest was selected to rebuild 136 existing units and 220 new units at Westside Courts in the Western Addition, and BRIDGE Housing Corporation received the contract to build 619 replacement public housing units for Potrero Terrace and Potrero Annex while also interspersing 187 below-market-rate housing units, and another 817 market-rate rentals and condos into the larger Potrero Hill neighborhood. Similarly, the city also tapped Mercy Housing, working with Related California, to transform Sunnydale into 775 replacement public housing units plus another 219 units of tax-credit "affordable" housing and about 600 market-rate apartments, while also adding a small retail district, parks, and a new recreational and educational center. In 2015, San Francisco voters approved a $310 million bond to support affordable housing in the city, and in late 2016 the Board of Supervisors approved $20 million support for each of the Potrero and Sunnydale initiatives.[54]

As HOPE SF slowly moved forward under mayors Gavin Newsom and Ed Lee (who served from 2011 until late 2017), the SFHA continued to struggle. In July 2008, the board of commissioners brought in Henry Alvarez as director to succeed Gregg Fortner, who had been forced to resign in 2007 under pressure from Newsom, who wanted to take on greater city control over public housing.[55] At the time of the search, Lee was city administrator and led the transition team at the Housing Authority. Alvarez developed close ties with both mayors and worked with a more mayor-driven commission than previous directors. Still, the overall dynamic remained consistent: the Mayor's Office of Housing continued to drive HOPE SF, while the SFHA endeavored to become a more reliable partner. The long legacy of SFHA's disconnection from the larger housing goals of the city, combined with its long history of management shortcomings, proved difficult to overcome. The agency reduced its annual shortfall of uncollected rents from a peak of $3 million in 2007, but faced a backlash from tenants who claimed to have been erroneously charged. Meanwhile, complaints about conditions in the non-redeveloped projects continued to mount. In 2012, the SFHA's management score from HUD plummeted from 75 to 54, placing the agency on the "troubled" list yet again and generating the need for a corrective action plan.[56]

Then, in late 2012, Alvarez himself came under attack, facing three lawsuits from subordinates who accused him of racism, vindictiveness, bullying, and other discrimination, coupled with a possible criminal probe into accusations that SFHA had steered contracts to vendors linked to City Hall.[57] Alvarez asked for a medical leave, and Lee quickly floated ideas about overhauling the SFHA and turning it into a new model built around public-private partnerships—explicitly based on the experiences at North Beach Place and Valencia Gardens. In February 2013, echoing the bold action of Willie Brown in 1996, Lee purged the housing commission, replacing all but one member—a public housing tenant, appointed by Lee two months earlier. The other appointees were all senior city employees who worked for the mayor or one of his appointees, plus one who served as a deputy district attorney. The new SFHA commissioners formally ousted Alvarez that April. Lee made his purpose clear: "My intent is to end the Housing Authority as it functions today, because it doesn't do well."[58] To do so, it seems, would entail reconfiguring the city's governance constellation to shine more brightly on the office of the mayor, while also continuing to capitalize on the strengths of the city's nonprofit housing organizations.

Resolution of the legal disputes against Alvarez cleared him of many allegations, but the SFHA paid $1.3 million to settle other claims. In the meantime, he decamped for Berkeley to open a restaurant, appropriately named Next Door. The eatery received generally favorable reviews for its "comfort food," but was listed as "permanently closed" as of 2014.[59] The SFHA's own doors remained open, though just barely.

Barbara Smith, who had been appointed interim director when Alvarez went on leave and who subsequently took on the position on a regular basis, brought a trusted voice and deep knowledge of housing development. She inherited a housing authority that was "hurtling toward collapse, projected to run out of cash in two months and have a deficit of $6.4 million by the end of its fiscal year in September 2013"—a shortfall significantly exacerbated by federal budget sequestration that slashed HUD's contributions. Without finding ways "to become more efficient and lower our costs," Smith observed, "we're going to be out of business."[60] That June, the city released the results of a "scathing audit of the troubled agency." This blamed SFHA mismanagement for losing out on significant federal operating subsidies, overpaying for city services such as police protection and trash collection, poor contracting and procurement services, and using long-outdated waiting lists for prospective residents. The audit found that almost half of tenants were delinquent on their rent, and that the authority had failed to collect $9.1 million since 2007.[61] The following month, a team led by city administrator Naomi Kelly and Mayor's Office of Housing and Community Development director Olson Lee presented Mayor Lee's alternative approach.

Titled *SFHA Re-envisioning*, the team's plan sought nothing less than a new mechanism for transforming the business of the SFHA. The report drew on four months of meetings involving six working groups, which engaged more than a hundred residents and seventy-two different agencies, and also reflected input from separate review and analysis from the CCHO and the San Francisco Planning and Urban Research Association (SPUR)—an organization whose acronym had been prudently altered to promote "urban research" instead of "urban renewal." The report blamed "a severe decline in federal funding" for the incapacity to deliver adequate public housing and services to residents but also sharply criticized the SFHA "mismanagement" for making a bad situation worse. At base, Lee's team concluded, the only way forward for SFHA would be for the agency to become more closely aligned with the city, and for it to take full advantage of public-private partnerships involving developers, community-based organizations, and residents. Part of this, the report suggested, would encourage use of all possible sources of funding, including participation in HUD's Rental Assistance Demonstration (RAD) program, which would enable the city to convert its public housing into Project Based Rental Assistance developments—a long-term contract that could permit the city to leverage debt and raise the funds necessary to rehabilitate the properties. This public-private partnership emphasis would also entail an enhanced commitment to raise funds to complete four HOPE SF sites (Hunters View, Alice Griffith, Potrero, and Sunnydale). The plan also proposed efforts to upgrade the remainder of the "non-HOPE SF" SFHA portfolio within eight years, while also seeking greater production of housing units that would be affordable to public housing residents as part of the city's other affordable housing construction. The report urged creation of "maintenance mechanic" positions (a clear rebuke to the existing ten-union system) and called for a better system of rent collection to be coupled with an "eviction prevention strategy" that would help residents "get current on their rent if they fall behind." The report also called for improvements to resident services and tenant leadership, based on practices that had emerged in HOPE SF sites. At its core, the plan called for the SFHA to become more reliant on "the city's strengths": San Francisco's "ability to produce and maintain affordable housing through a strong network of community based affordable housing developers."[62] Once again, the model for much of this is North Beach Place.

Extending the trend previewed by the North Beach version of HOPE VI, and building upon the ideas of the HOPE SF initiative, Mayor Lee's vision for "re-envisioning" public housing in San Francisco placed its ultimate trust in the financial acumen of the private sector while endeavoring to justify this trust through the kind of enhanced public oversight and accountability that is possible because of the city's long legacy of activism over issues of housing affordability. As the 2013 report observed, public housing has struggled in many places, but "What is unique about the history of public housing here in San Francisco is that it has failed while the development and preservation of affordable housing has been such a success."[63]

Ultimately, as SPUR's input to the report suggested most explicitly, the SFHA could either be completely dissolved or could "transfer the development and management of all public housing developments to third parties." In this model, the "re-envisioned" authority becomes almost invisible, largely superseded by a new world of asset management, private developers, and public land trusts.[64]

Starting in late 2013, the cash-strapped housing authority opened thousands of public housing units to private investors partnering with not-for-profit housing organizations. Many in the city viewed this as the last, best chance to pay for repairs and redevelopment. As Ed Lee put it, "Ultimately, we want every site we invest in to become investments for the private sector as well."[65] In January 2014, HUD approved San Francisco's participation in the RAD initiative, promising the city twenty years of guaranteed voucher funding that would enable a variety of community-based nonprofit owners to access resources such as debt financing and Low-Income Housing Tax Credits, expected to "leverage approximately $180 million in investor equity and other new resources to rehabilitate up to 4,584 public housing units." Even the CCHO seemed cautiously optimistic. Codirector Peter Cohen trusted that the city's robust array of community-based affordable housing developers would be up to the task. "I think there's a sensitivity and a commitment to housing the poorest of the poor in San Francisco that is much stronger than you'll probably find elsewhere," he noted. "This is essentially extra money from the federal government to make the whole thing work."[66]

In March 2015, Mayor Lee and the Board of Supervisors launched phase 1 of the RAD implementation, intended to assist 1,425 units of public housing located across nine of the supervisory districts. By the end of 2016, the *Chronicle* headlined the result: "SF's Public Housing Is Now All

Privately Run." The reporter actually felt the need to remind readers that "the San Francisco Housing Authority still exists." The SFHA continued to own land and retained responsibility for ensuring continued affordability, administering vouchers, and managing waiting lists.[67] Even so, with public sector buy-in and lots of private sector equity, the changes meant the Nonprofitus constellation shone more brightly than ever.

As San Francisco continues to seek innovative ways to repair and retain public housing, while also pursuing other paths to affordable housing,[68] the bold HOPE SF initiative causes public housing residents, activists, and policymakers to ask multiple questions: What happens to residents who are not able to remain on-site during construction or rehabilitation? Will HOPE SF or RAD participants lose housing assistance faster, and, if so, will this because they have suffered or because they have prospered? Will HOPE SF succeed in enabling the return of middle-income blacks to San Francisco? What will its impact be, regionally, on ethnic and racial distribution and housing costs? How will the enhanced reliance on the private sector—both through HOPE SF partnerships and through RAD—change the self-identity of the slowly dismantled SFHA? These questions are currently unanswerable.

One certainty, though, is that San Francisco's Nonprofitus governance constellation exists in a very different part of the political universe from that of the progrowth regime that oversaw the city a half-century earlier.

Still, the haunt of urban renewal endures. In the political posturing of progressive San Francisco, even the name "Justin Herman Plaza" has become anathema. In September 2017, the Board of Supervisors voted eleven to zero to ask the Recreation and Parks Commission to rename the plaza for a person who could be considered an "honored resident"—someone who "should embody San Francisco values of equity, inclusion and forward-thinking." That October, the commission duly voted to implement the proposal. The supervisors' accurate if tendentious resolution recounted the displacement saga of the Western Addition and quoted Herman as saying, in 1970, that "this land is too valuable to permit poor people to park on it." Continuing to honor Herman, they argued, would "give credibility to this 'urban renewal' project that sought to buy up buildings and evict people who were poor, old, black and brown."[69] The president of the Board of Supervisors, London Breed, could take this quite personally. Hardly someone bred in London, she is an African American raised by her grandmother in public housing in the Western Addition. In the context of a city that has long strained to retain its black population, Breed's political ascent was already a remarkable story.

Then, on December 12, 2017, Ed Lee suddenly died, making Breed acting mayor of San Francisco. Subsequently elected, she thereby inherited central responsibility for making San Francisco affordable to more of its residents—a macrocosm of the epic struggle that has shaped and reshaped North Beach Place.

CONCLUSION: GENTRIFICATION AND ITS DISCONTENTS

In the end, it is not easy to assess the saga of North Beach Place. Clearly, it is a struggle that has profoundly influenced the future directions of public housing in San Francisco. As a hard-fought process to keep deeply subsidized apartments in a gentrifying and well-located neighborhood, it is surely a triumph, especially given that the development team managed to add substantial numbers of affordable units to the same site and did not need to resort to market-rate dwellings to make their numbers work. At the same time, however, it is a familiar tale of broken promises and conflicting priorities. It yielded lingering bitterness among some residents, much of that thoroughly racialized and deeply rooted in the urban renewal losses of an earlier era.

At base, when they look at the processes that recreated North Beach Place, developers and residents do not see the same project. To the developers, there is a single holistic "deal" dependent on intricate funding mechanisms. It is obvious to them that it was better for the project finances and for the city's future tax credit flow to have proceeded with a one-phase development. Surely, they think, if that fact were explained logically, residents would understand the difficult predicament the developers faced in bringing the redevelopment plan to a financially feasible fruition. And surely, if assessed rationally, stricter management and rule enforcement should be in everyone's best interests.

In the minds of public housing residents, however, the deal is quite differently framed. First, it is not a singular deal; it bears the weight of history. To low-income residents, hardened into suspicion by decades of false starts and fractured pledges, every deal is presumed to be a "raw" one until proven otherwise. They have no great interest in seeing the developers use their tax-credit allocation all in one year. If they think about this subject at all, they see those tax credits as subsidizing the wealthier people that they never thought were needed on "their" property in the first place. Creating all those extra units probably meant smaller apartments for them and less privacy in the courtyards and could explain the extra surveillance and all those cameras. To residents, the question of two phases morphing into one had nothing to do with the logic of efficiency. Rather, it represented two much more visceral and fundamental matters: a betrayal of trust, and a loss of home. The single-phase deal conjured the very real and frightening possibility that they would struggle to find a new place to live in the city or would have to move to an unfamiliar and likely dangerous housing project elsewhere, far from the supports of Chinatown or Tel-Hi. This was not simply inconvenience; it entailed life-altering disruption and ongoing uncertainty.

In San Francisco as elsewhere, the HOPE VI program provided an important impetus for redevelopment action, but ultimately the specific fate of North Beach Place and its residents depended on particular economic conditions and political machinations. Well over three-quarters of the $113 million total cost to remake North Beach Place came from sources beyond the HOPE VI grant itself. In fact, the HOPE VI funds were just the third largest source of capital, trailing both tax-credit equity and mortgage debt financing.[70] San Francisco's Nonprofitus governance constellation ensured that the stars aligned differently than they did in many other American cities, yet even this could not keep the hopes of some low-income residents from being eclipsed.

Part VI

CITIES OF STARS

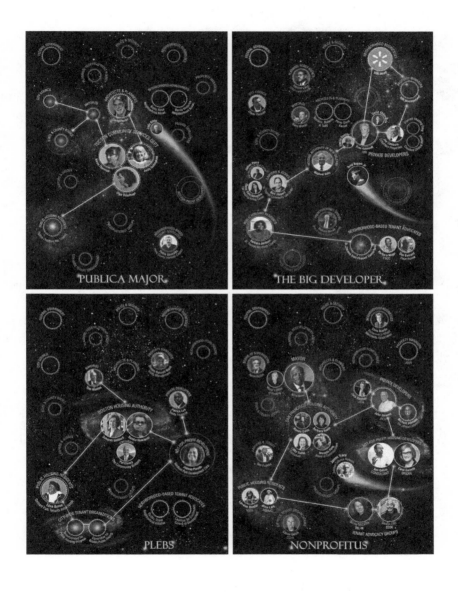

13

Housing the Poorest: Hoping for More

The four tortuous sagas of public housing development and redevelopment in New Orleans, Boston, Tucson, and San Francisco have much to teach us about housing policy, urban governance, and the place of the poorest in American cities. Specifically, I have deployed the HOPE VI program as a diagnostic tool to see how city leaders identify and treat larger urban maladies (whether real or imagined) triggered by the struggle with public housing. To observe HOPE VI implementation is to watch governance in action. This provides a deeply revealing look at the priorities of city leaders and citizens as they jointly confront the dire challenge of inadequate affordable housing.

Public housing redevelopment in all cities faces some common challenges, but these have been met by quite different approaches, led by distinctly different constellations of players, and structured by particular political histories. All HOPE VI is not alike because all cities are not alike. Instead, cities, and the public housing neighborhoods within them are led by different constellations of stars. These celestial networks each stretch across broad swaths of the institutional universe but allow us to find an orienting polestar in different specific corners.

The constellations I have named Publica Major, the Big Developer, Nonprofitus, and Plebs are abstract diagrams that encode particular patterns of poverty governance. In what follows, I revisit these cities of stars and then discuss how particular configurations of HOPE VI affect governance in two settings: the phased implementation of projects and the management of completed neighborhoods. The relative power of public, private, not-for-profit, and community voices shapes the choices about how quickly to implement a project, and whether or not to prioritize on-site rehousing of the existing extremely low-income community. And, following on this, the second key arena of poverty governance entails decisions about selecting and managing residents in the completed development.

Reflecting on the lived reality of the four communities discussed in this book thereby provides an opportunity to revisit the stated rationales for income mixing. Finally, I will assess the difficulties of redeveloping public housing in the context of ongoing (self-inflicted) economic austerity and lingering resentments, and conclude by examining emergent directions for housing and planning policy.

WHAT'S THE DEAL WITH HOPE VI?

HOPE VI is not a grant to pay for housing redevelopment; it is an invitation to leverage a deal. What happens next depends on housing markets, development history, and the planning culture of the locale. Deals are differentially situated; it's not just "capitalism" or "growth machines," "urban regimes," or "public-private partnerships," it is also specific ideas put out for bid. Yet the same particularities of markets and history also shape what sort of bid seems politically possible in the first place.

Importantly, HOPE VI deals vary greatly even when one focuses only on those neighborhoods facing gentrification pressures. Certainly, many of the 260 HOPE VI initiatives targeted places that were not "islands of poverty in seas of renewal" but, rather, neighborhoods where the seas were just as impoverished as the islands. This book has not been about those sorts of places. Instead, I have focused on neighborhoods where the suffering of residents is matched by the salivation of developers. Yet salivation may not always yield salvation, at least not of an equitable sort. Still, for the leadership in many cities, HOPE VI sites were selected not just because they could be justified as "severely distressed," but because they could also be pegged as "most likely to succeed." Mike Kelly, who has led housing the authorities in San Francisco, New Orleans, Washington, DC, and Philadelphia at various points in his career, noted the appeal of "the low-hanging fruit in terms of a very strong market and the ability to leverage private dollars." In New Orleans, he observed, "St. Thomas was key because of its location, like the North Beaches and the Techwoods [in Atlanta]." Places that had this sort of upside formed "the cornerstone to the kind of stuff I was doing, as well as other directors in the midnineties. The enlightened ones were drinking the Kool-Aid, and we knew that this was the future of development."[1] But HOPE VI also had much to do with the past of development, too. HOPE VI may have been a program of the 1990s and 2000s, but its roots hold firm to earlier eras in each city.

At its core, a HOPE VI development trajectory emerges from the frequently conflictual relationships among key players: a housing agency, a development team, and a resident organization, coupled with variable input from mayors, city councils, citywide tenant organizations, neighborhood-based advocacy groups, lawyers, architects, planners, and denizens of adjacent neighborhoods. It seems no coincidence that the examples that proved most protective of low-income tenants' rights were either those with prominent not-for-profit development firms (Boston and San Francisco) or high-level direction from a public agency working directly with a design team (Tucson). In sharp contrast, the interests of for-profit developers remained much more central in New Orleans.

Not-for-profit developers—especially if they are community based—are concerned with neighborhood stabilization and, as Chrystal Kornegay puts it, "are in the business of housing production to first meet the requirements of the existing neighborhood." In this context, "the profitable sale or rental of housing is their secondary objective, and serves to support the first."[2] Conversely, the world of for-profit developers, such as HRI in New Orleans, is by definition a profit-driven business, one that may be steered by greater or lesser degrees of social conscience or neighborhood engagement. To them, community involvement is merely contingent—rather than intrinsic— to their mission. The larger question for this book, though, has been *why* some cities, or at least some neighborhoods within them, rely upon for-profit developers, while others do not. Or, more broadly, regardless of the profit motive of the developer: Why have some HOPE VI development teams sought to retain a maximum number of the very low-income poor, while others have endeavored to house only the politically acceptable minimum? Teasing this out, I argue, is a complex matter deeply rooted in decades of past experience with development and redevelopment. This larger urban and neighborhood history has emerged in tandem with each city's political culture and, with that, its constellation of governance.

CITIES OF STARS

Four types of governance constellation have been illustrated here: the Big Developer (New Orleans), Plebs (Boston), Publica Major (Tucson), and Nonprofitus (San Francisco). Taken together, these four examples help explain how the complexities of urban governance and housing market conditions led to such diverse outcomes. In dissecting the governance constellations that undergird HOPE VI in each city, two things become clear. First, the constellations differ, in large part because they emerge out of distinct political histories. Second, the list of players may be the same in every city neighborhood, but the relative level of power and visibility among them certainly is not. To aid in our celestial navigation, each constellation has its polestar. Like Polaris in Ursa Minor, in New Orleans, HRI dominates the Big Developer; in Boston, Edna Bynoe orients us to Plebs; in Tucson, the CSD centers Publica Major; and, in San Francisco, the tri-star brilliance of BRIDGE, Tel-Hi, and the Chinatown CDC draws the eye to Nonprofitus. In turn, depending on which stars shine brightest, different definitions of HOPE VI success will prevail. In other words, which of the six hopes for HOPE VI have predominated? Who gains, and who loses, in redevelopment efforts centered on reimaging stigmatized places, reinvesting in neglected neighborhoods, reforming low-income residents by giving them more upscale neighbors, releasing other residents from the constraints of projects to pursue other opportunities with vouchers, reinventing housing authorities as better market actors, and reprioritizing beneficiaries to make sure HOPE VI serves chiefly the deserving poor?

Some of these impulses—especially the ones centered on reimaging and reinvestment—are benefits centered on a particular place, while others—especially the yearnings for reform and release—are ostensibly centered on the well-being of low-income residents. The other two hopes for HOPE VI—reinvention and reprioritzation—recall other challenges for the definition and governance of poverty, as these center on issues of political economy, power, and markets. HOPE VI, as a funding mechanism that mandated complex public-private partnerships, transformed the role of housing authorities and dramatically altered the political economy of low-income housing development by positioning these public agencies as market actors. Similarly, by using the logic of poverty deconcentration as the reason to favor broader mixes of incomes, HOPE VI processes reprioritized beneficiaries in ways that could either negate or affirm the power of resident voices. By viewing each of these four HOPE VI sagas from the perspectives of housing authorities, mayors, developers, advocacy groups, and residents, it becomes clear whose definition of success predominates, and whose gets marginalized. In so doing, moreover, dissecting the HOPE VI program reveals much about the changing nature of urban governance in the American city.

In the mid-twentieth century, all four cities embraced a progrowth agenda, and business leaders enjoyed close relationships with elected government officials. Yet only Boston, Tucson, and San Francisco translated this into a robust urban renewal agenda, whereas New Orleans leaders faced a backlash from conservative Louisiana state legislators who repealed the necessary enabling legislation in 1954. As a result, Ed Logue in Boston, Si Schorr in Tucson, and Justin Herman in San Francisco had no counterpart in New Orleans. For better or worse, this also meant that New Orleans did not experience a full-bodied revolt against the perceived excesses of development-induced displacement.

In fighting for their neighborhood, St. Thomas tenants and their supporters had to produce their own social movement. They did not inherit, borrow from, or build upon the power of an earlier generation's struggles. By contrast, in other cities with long and painful memories of urban renewal, advocates for low-income tenants of color frequently occupy city council seats. Or there are, at least intermittently, sympathetic mayors. In cities such as Boston and San Francisco, the backlash against urban renewal and the struggles to stop highways from flattening neighborhoods bequeathed a legacy of activism and, beyond that, a number of not-for-profit housing developers committed to retaining and enhancing the affordability of dwellings. Alternatively, even if these other civic and electoral forces fall short, in cities such as Tucson it is possible to count on principled public sector officials who are acutely aware of past injustices, and who have been able to retain both respect and resources. Not-for-profit organizations in New Orleans, even after I-10 left Treme in its shadows, failed to develop effective countermeasures to the power of private developers. Urban renewal backlash, or lack thereof, is certainly not the only force shaping late twentieth-century political pressures, but it did help sculpt the approaches each city took to HOPE VI. That said, the mere existence of a traumatic urban renewal experience is not enough to predict a propoor approach to future low-income housing redevelopment. Having an urban renewal experience may be a necessary but not sufficient condition, since some places had ample exposure to urban renewal without generating a sustained backlash.

The complex governance constellations that succeeded the simpler cosmology of the old urban renewal order present the astropolitical viewer with quite different images. In the transition from St. Thomas to River Garden in New Orleans, private developer Pres Kabacoff shone brightest, in clear alignment with Walmart, despite strong efforts from residents and community-based resident advocacy organizations to remain visible. By contrast, in Boston, residents and a partnership led by the not-for-profit Madison Park Development Corporation worked in tandem with a proactively engaged Boston Housing Authority and a highly supportive mayor to make sure that the transformation of Orchard Park to Orchard Gardens favored the needs of very low-income households. In Tucson's shift from Connie Chambers to Posadas Sentinel, the governance constellation remained quite small. As in Boston, the local housing authority—known then as the Community Services Department—took the lead. Here, however, the CSD partnered directly with architect Corky Poster to realize the project. The team respectfully built up a small set of residents to work with but faced nothing like the oppositional feistiness of St. Thomas's Barbara Jackson and North Beach Place's Alma Lark—or the insistent spirit of Orchard Park's Edna Bynoe. Instead, the Tucson constellation included more backlash from neighborhood associations eager to see fewer poor people remain in the gentrifying barrio, as well as lingering distrust from those who remembered the lore of urban renewal and feared another purge of Mexican Americans. The governance constellation behind San Francisco's North Beach Place reveals yet another distinct configuration of operations. Here, the long-standing weakness of the San Francisco Housing Authority gave way to a strong developer partnership led by the not-for-profit BRIDGE housing, working with public-spirited private developer partners, including the John Stewart Company and Em Johnson Interest, as well as a strong-willed mayor, Willie Brown. The North Beach Tenants Association, together with the ill-fated North Beach Resident Management Council, asserted a moderate level of influence on the process, powerfully aided by two community-based organizations, the Chinatown Community Development Center and the Telegraph Hill Neighborhood Center (Tel-Hi). In each case, the nodes of governance charted a constellation, yet each looked distinctive.

Governance constellations are more than just diagrams of battling or cooperating stakeholders. They provide clues to the process of new community formation. One pole star stands out as brightest and orients the whole—whether it be a for-profit developer, a not-for-profit developer, a housing authority, or a group of residents and their advocates. Each of these types of constellations had quite different approaches to getting a HOPE VI project built.

HOPE VI projects are not just real-estate ventures; they are also adventures in governing the poor. At the same time as complex physical construction efforts need to manage money and timetables to produce affordable buildings, equally complex social construction processes are needed to sort out which people will get to live in the new community—and which will not. After analyzing these four HOPE VI sagas, it seems worth reiterating Katz's penetrating observation that "the quintessential act of policy" entails "identifying and administering the grounds for exclusion."[3] For HOPE VI implementation, this happens at two key stages: first, the complex sociofinancial drama of decisions about the phasing of a project and, second, the management challenges centered around which households are selected to return and permitted to remain. Decisions about construction phasing can be de facto decisions to exclude. And, similarly, targets for income, requirements for work, and expectations for behavior can send clear messages about who is wanted in the new community and who is not. These dynamics varied considerably from neighborhood to neighborhood.

GOVERNING HOPE VI IMPLEMENTATION: THE POLITICS OF PHASING

All public housing redevelopment efforts face a common challenge: determining who deserves to benefit from the new investment. To be sure, in any community there will be some members whose past track record of illegal behavior or disruptive tenancy should legitimately make them ineligible to return. The reasons for such exclusion should genuinely be rooted in instances of problematic actions, not primarily dictated by reasons of persistent poverty (as self-evidently demonstrated by such criteria as a poor credit score). Tenant leaders are frequently the harshest critics of fellow tenants, recognizing that part of the problem in socially dysfunctional projects had been that lax rule enforcement permitted some of their neighbors to behave in dangerously disruptive ways. In this sense, both tenant leaders and private developers shared the objective of ridding a community of its troublemakers. Meeting that objective could happen slowly, through the process of evictions, or in a more abrupt and wholesale manner by using the complete razing of the property as an occasion to move everyone off-site, while permitting only a select subset to return. In this context, the seemingly technical issue of project phasing holds clear political implications: a multiphase project could allow some residents to move temporarily within the site facilitating the ease of return, whereas a single-phase effort would force all to be dispersed much further. For those residents and their allies intent on maximizing the rate of return, single-phase options carried an overwhelming downside. Alternatively, for developers already drawn to the economic efficiency of a single-phase construction process—and for those residents eager to have some fellow tenants denied the opportunity to return—a full-scale relocation offered appealing opportunities for selectivity.

In New Orleans, while development of River Garden proceeded in phases, this did little to protect the capacity of former St. Thomas residents to remain. Instead, the phasing truly commenced only after the entire site had been cleared and its residents shunted elsewhere. The site thus cleared, it even became possible for the colossal Walmart and its associated parking lot to take up some of the land once occupied by public housing. With the old boundaries obliterated, the developer could make uncontested claims about the retail being "adjacent" to the new housing without having to account for why it parts of it had been allowed to take up the space once allocated to the old housing. Some of the phasing at River Garden understandably followed from the exigency of Katrina in 2005 and the market challenges that followed for many years, including the additional impact of the Great Recession. Yet the term "phasing" does little justice to the steady stream of broken promises and fundamental alterations of plans that went on for more than a decade. This decimated any possibility for trust between residents and either the developer or the housing authority. With Pres Kabacoff's HRI as the third developer tasked with implementing the project, bewildered residents still remembered the promises of the first two—let alone the more resident-friendly proposals that had preceded HOPE VI entirely. By the time HRI finished building River Garden, onetime notions of resident ownership and managerial control, resident-owned microenterprises, and STICC control of the self-sufficiency component of the HOPE VI grant all simply vanished from the picture. Moreover, unrealizable phasing affected all corners of the constellation: extremely low-income households never received the perpetually promised allocation of one hundred units of off-site rental housing for large families, but HRI also failed to build most of the market-rate housing intended to go on the River Garden site itself.

In Boston, by contrast, the propoor governance constellation proposed a process intended to maximize the capacity of Orchard Park residents to gain access to the redeveloped Orchard Gardens. Here, phased construction facilitated tenant retention. In many cases, residents never even needed to leave the site—the moved directly from their old home to the new apartment. This helps explain why nearly three-quarters of those living at Orchard Park at the time of its phased demolition proved willing and able to return to Orchard Gardens. The key point is not the return rate itself; it is the underlying willingness to want to maximize this. Despite the harrowing history of drugs and violence at Orchard Park, the BHA and its partners stuck to its fundamental premise: HOPE VI was not there to replace public housing; its purpose was to help previously ill-served residents gain more respectful treatment. In Boston, given the pressures that had built up over a period of three decades at the housing authority, among neighborhood-rooted developers, and within the elected municipal bureaucracy—not to forget the crucial role of empowered tenant leaders—public housing redevelopment needed to proceed in ways that advanced the needs of the lowest-income residents. Indicative of the stark contrast in approaches to poverty governance, at Orchard Gardens, the park is named in memory of Edna Bynoe; at River Garden, the park's name commemorates the cofounder of HRI.

In Tucson, like Boston, the Community Services Department structured the phasing of Posadas Sentinel to accommodate all who wished to stay on the site. Although it is true that architect Corky Poster's own pre-redevelopment survey showed that the numbers of planned on-site units would never have permitted all to remain, the CSD found ways to ensure that demand would not exceed supply. They did so not by turning away those who wished to return or by insisting on the use of unpredictable vouchers, but by working closely, one on one, with each family to identify alternative housing. By purchasing new housing scattered across the city, strategically selected to afford proximity to better schools and public transit, the CSD helped ensure good options for most residents. Even though the majority chose not to take advantage of phased implementation and endure a multiyear existence on a construction site, this seems to have been a genuine choice. The Tucson story depends on the unusual market circumstance of a dramatically overbuilt subdivision supply that made purchasing new units financially attractive to the city, but it also depended on a quarter-century of preferences for shifting the CSD's housing portfolio away from multifamily projects. And, certainly, the long-standing and highly questionable undercommitment of Tucson to the whole idea of public housing provision made the task of scattering Connie Chambers households all that much easier. Still, the offer of phasing coupled with the care with which the CSD worked to help residents find desirable new homes within the CSD system, bespeaks a fundamental respect for the needs of low-income residents. Tucson's leaders clearly could have handed over the prime site of Connie Chambers to a private development team intent on maximizing its financial return. Instead, they invested in a broad array of new community facilities, while choosing not to devote any of the HOPE VI mix to market-rate apartments. Some of this seems explainable by the predilection for scattered-site public housing, but much of it also reveals a sensitivity to those once victimized by the bulldozers that flattened much of the city's Mexican American barrio, actions that seemed both indiscriminate and discriminatory. Here, too, the governance constellation of the late 1990s had formative roots in memories that lingered from the 1960s.

Persistent fear of development-induced displacement during HOPE VI could never be just a rational—or irrational—response to a singular development proposal. It could look that way to a developer, to be sure, but not to residents in cities and neighborhoods that had built up layers of mistrust. In Tucson, the mistrust at Connie Chambers grew in the same neighborhood as the housing; in Boston, mistrust at Orchard Park emerged in the context of massive clearances associated with highway-induced and renewal-induced residential and commercial displacement that virtually encircled the site.

In San Francisco, the urban renewal memories were somewhat less spatially proximate, but nonetheless just as powerful. This helps explain why North Beach Place resident leaders and their influential advocates remained so adamant that any redevelopment on the site needed to proceed in phases. ·Even though San Francisco's post-urban renewal embrace of countervailing social movements had brought forth citywide pro-tenant groups and many sympathetic elected officials, North Beach Place tenants entered the HOPE VI process with a wary vigilance. SFHA leaders, and their HOPE VI consultant Libby Seifel, knew right from the start that it would be politically necessary to replace all public housing on the site, especially since earlier HOPE VI efforts in San Francisco faced backlash for failing to do that. They consistently kept to this part of their deal with residents. Still, this was not enough. Caught up in the spirit of a tenant-centered process, SFHA director Ronnie Davis had also promised residents that the redevelopment would occur in phases. Instead, it turned out that Davis himself was just a passing phase. The city and its development team reversed course and tardily revealed that the entire site would be cleared for a one-phase construction, which meant all households would need to vacate. As perceived by residents and their allies, this caused the North Beach Place governance constellation to suffer the political equivalent of a belated Big Bang. In fact, though, little realignment of the development cosmos actually occurred. It just reminded the community corner of the constellation that they were but fragile pieces of a universe they could not control. Even under the progressive governance of San Francisco, the timing of tax-credit allocations to powerful developers outweighed adherence to promises about timing made to residents. Most residents nevertheless gained good opportunities, due to the provision of high-value vouchers. Still, reneging on the promise of multiphase development surely reduced the number of households that returned to the new North Beach Place.

Many scholars and practitioners have focused their attention on the governance of mixed-income sites once they are built and occupied, yet doing only this misses much of the battle over governance that had already occurred. The acrimony over HOPE VI stems largely from a loss of trust during project implementation. Mistrust happens because various members of the governance constellation, beholden to different constituencies, have different baselines for measuring promises. The hopes of residents are rooted in the original deal they struck when asked to sign off on a HOPE VI grant application. Every change to the project is calibrated against that initial set of expectations. And, in most cases, they entered into HOPE VI agreements already with a great deal of mistrust for the agencies that had let their homes and communities turn into such "severely distressed" conditions. What may look to other members of the constellation to be fairly minor details—units left unbuilt, a tax-credit deal that occurs in one year instead of two, a project implementation that occurs in one phase instead of spread across several—to low-income residents can trigger more than disappointment. It registers as deeply felt acts of betrayal, disempowerment, and marginalization. In some cases, the anger may be felt by a small corps of agitated residents—or even by their self-styled advocates—and may not represent the community as a whole. Still, this does not mean that the anger is any less real, less disruptive, or less deserving of a response.

GOVERNING HOPE VI SITES: SELECTING AND MANAGING RESIDENTS

Development phasing is just the first part of governing the poor under HOPE VI. It also matters how many lowest-income residents reside in the completed community, what proportion of the total population they constitute, where they live within the development, and how they are treated by management and by fellow residents. In New Orleans, developer Pres Kabacoff explicitly viewed success in HOPE VI as "finding a way to attract market rate" households. Although the market did not cooperate, HRI fought hard to cap "affordable" housing at no more than 40 percent of the total at River Garden. As HRI's David Abbenante put it, "100 percent affordable" developments are a form of entrapment—they deprive low-income households from "the ability for growth" because they lack proper role models. Once market conditions and resident pushback forced HRI to accommodate more than 40 percent low-income households, the developer countered by proposing that nearly all of the largest families should be housed separately and away from the site. And then—with that additional public housing kept separate from the HOPE VI funding—HRI never made it a priority to have that housing actually get built. At the River Garden site itself, the developer kept the homeownership units spatially separate from the renters and also kept many of LIHTC-subsidized rental apartments in different buildings, segregated from both owned homes and the public housing units. Not surprisingly, ethnographer Kelly Owens found that this polarized allocation of units yielded a great deal of mutual self-segregation, even in the more public areas of the development. Her findings echo the research findings from Chicago, site of the most extensive studies of mixed-income dynamics. There, Robert Chaskin and Mark Joseph found that "to some extent spatial proximity did make interaction easier, but cross-class exchanges for the most part have been both limited and either extremely casual, failing to yield instrumental benefits for the poor, or contentious, contributing to conflict between low and higher-income residents."[4] Such nonproductive mixing continues to be the common refrain at many mixed-income sites, especially where large numbers of market-rate households are mixed with those receiving public housing subsidies. At River Garden, this tension is compounded by resident resentment of HRI Management's intrusive surveillance, seen as an excessive constraint on outdoor socializing.

In Boston, the attitude of the BHA and its development team could hardly have been more different. Boston's leadership deliberately chose to remake Orchard Park in a way that still permitted Orchard Gardens to be overwhelmingly occupied by extremely low-income households. They refused to buy in to the idea that the community would rapidly revert to the chaos it experienced in the late 1980s and early 1990s unless the occupancy was forcibly skewed toward households able to afford market rates. Instead, the BHA and its partners worked to diversify incomes in a slower manner and across a broader spatial domain. Rather than set tight income thresholds, or construct only small apartments in ways intended to preclude substantial numbers of Orchard Park families from returning, they pursued a more aspirational set of income tiers. Most of the existing households with their extremely low incomes could return, but, over time, the BHA and private management company hoped that many of those public housing families could increase their incomes into higher brackets. Or, if and when an extremely low-income household left Orchard Gardens, they aimed to select a somewhat higher-income household from the site-based waiting list. Although, after more than fifteen years of occupancy, the reality of the income mix has not caught up with the aspiration of the tiers, there has certainly been some notable progress. Moreover, by integrating LIHTC-funded apartments into the mix in a seamless way, the BHA strategy pursued a narrower range of incomes and largely managed to avoid the socioeconomic schism that prevails in many mixed-income communities with a more economically polarized constituency. At the same time, the Boston version of HOPE VI extended development into the surrounding community and built a variety of new housing on previously vacant parcels. The multideveloper team also introduced a modest amount of market-rate rental housing and opportunities for homeownership, without yielding the more rampant sort of gentrification that has overtaken many other parts of Boston. Residents of Orchard Gardens and its sister developments must still face up to periodic outbursts of violence, but life is generally peaceful. Importantly, the Orchard Gardens community has had just one manager in the twenty-first century, Sharon Russell-Mack, who continues to enjoy widespread acclaim.

In Tucson, the Community Services Department pursued an innovative approach to poverty deconcentration when planning Posadas Sentinel, determinedly seeking to eliminate all vestiges of "project" life. The CSD accomplished this while still remaining respectful of existing residents. They devoted all HOPE VI resources to building various forms of subsidized housing but deployed a site-based waiting list and attempted to steer many of the best-off among public housing residents to the site itself, while encouraging those with the lowest incomes to consider the scattered-site opportunities, which also often provided larger apartments or even single-family homes. Although the CSD invited back nearly all former Connie Chambers households, for any new households entering public housing apartments, they imposed strict new requirements. Combining a "work preference" with initial insistence that they participate in a Family Self Sufficiency (FSS) program, the CSD made clear that it regarded impoverishment as no more than a temporary life stage that could be overcome relatively quickly through education, training, and hard work. At the same time, the HOPE VI program infused new affordable homeownership options into the Santa Rosa neighborhood, along with investment in new buildings for a Learning Center / Library, a Child Development (Head Start) Center, and a Recreation and Wellness Center. Having fewer extremely low-income people in the neighborhood appeased some neighbors, and both the homes and the residents of Posadas have blended in with no obvious major tensions. Although the initial private management plan did not work out, yielding a return to public sector control, this too seems to have been handled well by what is now known as Tucson's Housing and Community Development Department.

At North Beach Place, as at Posadas, the SFHA and its development partners also entirely eschewed provision of market-rate housing. Instead, the entire governance constellation agreed that HOPE VI should enable at least one last piece of the neighborhood to hold out against rampant gentrification. North Beach Place seamlessly integrated public housing funds, project-based vouchers, and LIHTC support to return 229 deeply subsidized apartments to the site, all intermixed with 112 units of LIHTC-only housing that helped diversify the range of incomes. On this site, surrounded by wealth, it made little sense to talk about deconcentrating poverty. Instead, the San Francisco team sought ways to ensure that a higher percentage of residents had jobs, believing that this narrower mix of incomes would be sufficient. In terms of site management, there have been some tensions among residents, often tied to linguistic and cultural differences between Chinese Americans and African Americans—the development's two largest constituencies. Many residents also complain about what they perceive to be the John Stewart Company's excessive surveillance and paternalist attitudes, while others appreciate the plethora of rules and the stricter enforcement.

In all cases, new management regimes sought to impose and enforce new behavioral norms on low-income residents. Typically, this has entailed reliance on private management, though Tucson remains an exception. At Posadas, the shift of management back to the city after seven and a half years of failed private management represents a mirror reversal of the trend in other places. In cities such as New Orleans, Boston, and San Francisco, the pre–HOPE VI management problems sounded distressingly familiar to the post–HOPE VI problems that plagued Posadas until 2008, but in Tucson the subsequent management shift went in the other direction. In Tucson, everything that city officials said *private* management failed to do paralleled the complaints made about the inadequacy of public management elsewhere. The tale is similar, but the players are reversed. That said, the city's own management had certainly failed once previously at Connie Chambers.

All such discussion of the management of poverty should acknowledge that sweeping charges of "neoliberal paternalism" need to be examined in a nuanced, case-by-case manner. All managers of HOPE VI developments understandably seek ways to enforce shared norms, but it is those places (such as River Garden) that need to cater to (or appease) sizable constituencies paying market rates that seem most likely to overreach and thereby court backlash. In those settings, which have been found to be particularly prevalent in Chicago, it seems wholly justified to highlight what Chaskin and Joseph have termed "incorporated exclusion"—the tense relations that result when public housing residents get treated as less than full participants in their own mixed-income community. "Regulatory regimes established to maintain order," they argue, "largely aim to enforce middle-class norms, in part to keep the developments viable to the market, and in practice they target low-income residents."[5]

By contrast, in communities where the mix of incomes is narrower or where extremely low-income households predominate—such as Orchard Gardens, Posadas Sentinel, and North Beach Place—the pressures for exclusion may be far less extreme.[6] Some residents, as at Orchard Gardens, may complain about the "ghetto" behavior of fellow residents, and North Beach Place continues to experience interracial tension, but there seem to be fewer instances where cultural preferences, such as socializing on front stoops, become treated as rule violations. Even so, in narrow-mix communities, there can be other sources of externally imposed judgmental authority. Tax-credit investors may well serve as a kind of absentee proxy for the sorts of paternalist rule enforcement otherwise associated with proximate homeowners or market-rate renters. Managers, whether private as in San Francisco and Boston or public as in Tucson, are now inescapably market actors. Their records are closely monitored and they are broadly accountable—to investors, if not always to residents. The broad governance constellations of HOPE VI have necessarily brought with them a far greater level of external behavioral scrutiny than the narrower regimes of earlier eras.

Brother Don Everard, from his base at Hope House in New Orleans and his past roles leading the St. Thomas Irish Channel Consortium (STICC), became a thoughtful observer of housing managers. As he saw it, there are "two different ways of managing":

> You can have the hard-nosed, my-way-or-the-highway type management. Or you can incorporate people into the process and make them feel like they have some power to help make this community work, a real community-based kind of model where you ask, "What rules do you think are important? How do we write that rule? How do we enforce it?" and have a real dialogue about that where people feel that they own it in some sense.

Brother Don saw public housing residents as "very communitarian." They insist on being "taken seriously" and "having some control." Yet some managers fail to appreciate this. Their attitude is: "This is the rule, and if you don't like it go somewhere else. And if you don't like it and you break it, well then we'll send you somewhere else." Wistfully, he conceded that this may be "a good business model." "But," he felt certain, "it's not a good human model."[7]

Tenant-management relations are one key measure of HOPE VI success, but it is also worth reconsidering the larger set of assumptions about what mixed-income housing is supposed to deliver.

REVISITING THE RATIONALES FOR INCOME MIXING

Scholars examining mixed-income housing have consistently found that some of the most frequently voiced rationales bear little relevance in practice. Many previous studies have debunked rationales for income mixing that stressed the importance of role modeling or posited ameliorative contagions of social capital. In the communities discussed in this book, these seem again to be little more than evanescent aspirations. They are sometimes voiced but rarely acted upon. Meanwhile, other assumptions about the value of income mixing warrant additional scrutiny. The idea that informal social control will yield safer communities for everyone remains pertinent, especially since the communities discussed here have each been explicitly designed to replace sites of protracted violence and extreme insecurity. Yet it is less clear whether management practices intended to ameliorate this owe much to income mixing, let alone to income mixing that emphasizes the presence of higher-income households. Instead, as at Orchard Gardens and Posadas Sentinel, good management relations seem rooted in a much more basic matter: respect for residents. By contrast, the social control associated with a shared upholding of rule enforcement may be much more difficult to achieve if residents perceive that rules are enforced differentially depending on income level or subsidy type. This, again, is the "incorporated exclusion" problem, though it doesn't seem to be found everywhere equally.

The fourth commonly voiced rationale for mixed-income housing is that the inclusion of higher-income residents will leverage additional political interest and generate greater market investment, thereby improving wider community fortunes. All four stories in this book seem to support this. Whatever one's view of Walmart, it has been a much-praised addition to the neighborhood, as a source of employment, low-cost shopping, and venue for sociability. It is less clear how to judge the small-scale retail that appeared elsewhere within River Garden or what to make of the Kupperman warehouse's reinvention as a SWAT headquarters. Some residents may still recall broken promises about resident-owned businesses, yet those ventures may never have been little more than wishful thinking. Similarly, at North Beach Place, some returning tenants resent the failure to implement the once-promised row of resident-run incubator businesses proposed for Bay Street. Instead, there is Starbucks—redundantly matching the one that already existed across the street. To Elvin Wyly and Daniel Hammel, these sorts of neighborhood investments seem to epitomize "neo-liberal American urbanism." "Are Starbucks and Wal-Mart the new urban pioneers," they ask, "working with city and federal officials to spur a 'renaissance' by erasing the old welfare-state landscapes of the 1960s?"[8]

Without waxing nostalgic for such "welfare-state landscapes" of large-scale public housing that could be isolating, single function, and uniformly bleak, it is certainly worth questioning the new political economy of the investment that HOPE VI has helped generate. Whatever the value of Walmart for the Lower Garden District, it should not be forgotten that Pres Kabacoff enticed this behemoth as a way to make the *market-rate* housing at River Garden more profitable to HRI. It may have saved the financials for a deal that also brought a modicum of public housing back to the site, but this merely underscores the extent to which HOPE VI sometimes permits the private sector to leverage a large amount of public money to pursue investments that actually yield a sharp reduction in the amount of public housing.

This New Orleans version of HOPE VI plays right into the expectations of those looking for evidence of neoliberal paternalism at work. Here, the neoliberal impulse of HOPE VI enabled the state to apply market principles to public housing. Applying the framework from *Disciplining the Poor*, this means that "neoliberalism and paternalism . . . converge on the idea that governance itself must be transformed in order to more effectively manage the poor." In New Orleans, the public institutions of the state deputized the private sector to take the lead, with a mandate to oversee community-based not-for-profit groups and their low-income constituencies. In this developer-skewed constellation, neoliberalism and paternalism "promote efforts to extend the state's governing capacity by using privatization and collaboration to enlist civil society institutions. Paternalism emphasizes that such cross-sector collaborations be state led, while neoliberalism emphasizes that they must be organized on market terms." Increasingly, as Soss, Fording, and Schram argue, "State and market operations have become integrated and . . . state authority is used affirmatively to meet market needs." Applied to HOPE VI, this explains why the New Orleans city council allowed city tax revenues to be used to make building market-rate housing more attractive to HRI, why the SFHA sequenced North Beach Place construction to accommodate tax-credit investors, and why the Tucson Community Services Department could bail out the market by purchasing new public housing in overbuilt subdivisions.[9]

Yet it seems overly simplistic to treat every place as the same story of neoliberalism run amok. Instead, the processes of developing and managing HOPE VI initiatives reveal quite different strategies of governance that vary from city to city, and even from neighborhood to neighborhood.

Excavating the deeper planning histories of each particular place uncovers layers of contested development that, at least in some cities, force contemporary privatization efforts to rise from destabilized ground. As Brenner and Theodore observe, to understand neoliberalism as it actually exists means situating today's practices within "inherited institutional landscapes and power configurations."[10] Moreover, such inheritances foster more than just neoliberalism; there are also deeply rooted patterns of spatial and racial segregation expressed through housing discrimination. In this way, neoliberal practices share space with other governance strategies that operate simultaneously.

Even if there is some shared state-led predilection for market rule over social relations, past political struggles establish path dependencies that sustain quite different tactics for governing the urban poor. This has enabled seemingly similar development practices to carry quite different local meanings. Just as Walmart rises partially from the rubble of St. Thomas, it is also true that North Beach Place is built partly on top of a sizable Trader Joe's supermarket. But such superficial similarities do not make the overall dynamic identical. Trader Joe's did not function the way Walmart did for Trader Pres. In San Francisco, the inclusion of a supermarket and parking did nothing to prevent the SFHA and its development team from building back all of the public housing on-site and adding in even more affordable housing. Instead, it brought some additional funding that helped ensure that the affordable housing got built. Including the supermarket presumably made the overall development more appealing to upscale neighbors, but it was all in service of a larger aim: increasing the supply of badly needed subsidized housing. In a world where the choices are Tall, Grande, Venti, and Trenta, perhaps neoliberalism also now comes in many sizes.

North Beach Place supported economic growth of the broader neighborhood but did so without displacing the poorest from a gentrifying area. As JSCo president Jack Gardner put it, in a conversation joined by development consultant Ben Golvin, the redevelopment of North Beach Place was meant to signal a counterpoint to the previous rounds of probusiness and wanton real-estate urban renewal that transformed the Fillmore and Yerba Buena: "By the time it gets to North Beach," Gardner remarked, "there is a sense that 'that's not how SF does things, we don't displace our poorer citizens'"—"At least not *intentionally*!" his colleague Golvin interjected. Skipping past that important qualification, Gardner continued, "We replace one-for-one public housing when it's demolished; we embrace an urban, dense lifestyle." Gardner's point is that public housing in San Francisco actually *lacked* adequate density, so that developers could introduce both additional housing and other land uses that would not take the property "beyond the density of the surrounding neighborhood." To this public-spirited, for-profit partner in the North Beach Place venture, everything added up: "There's social policy, there's compassion, and there's good, hard real-estate sense. And so, there wasn't ever any serious consideration that there wouldn't be replacement of those public housing units on site." Yet Golvin's jovial caveat also applies—in pricey San Francisco, sometimes displacement happens despite the best of intentions.[11] Even so, intentions do matter. Tellingly, both New Orleans and San Francisco got less funding than asked for from HOPE VI, but in San Francisco this did not become an excuse to build back fewer units than had been promised in the HOPE VI application. This, too, highlights the importance of the governance constellation in place at the time the grant is requested.

When told about alternative approaches to HOPE VI in San Francisco, Pres Kabacoff fired back:

> San Francisco ain't New Orleans. You get it, right? It's who you're dealing with. In cities that are desperately poor and people don't have educations and are not functioning, then filling up your project with them and expecting market-rate to come is a tough task. In San Francisco, where your tax-credit people may be making seventy thousand bucks, that's a different crowd. You get that, right?

Similarly, Kabacoff dismissed the relevance of the Boston approach with its insistence on redeveloping HOPE VI sites that reserve the overwhelming majority of units for public housing residents. "Boston's a healthier town," he snapped.[12] It is indeed true that Boston and San Francisco have far healthier economies and median incomes than New Orleans. Yet in both of these other cities, public housing residents also suffer from poor education and extreme poverty. In Boston and San Francisco, however, the collective expectations of their governance constellations do not make it easy for private developers to regard the functionality of the poorest residents with such scorn. And once private developers are no longer at the center of the development universe, the problem is no longer framed as the challenge of how to get "market rate to come." Instead, the problem is how to reduce the prevalence of poor *housing*, not the prevalence of poor *people*.

It is not as if New Orleans lacks the affordable housing problems of Boston or San Francisco and can therefore blithely give free rein to the market. Quite the opposite. As previously noted, New Orleans has only 30 percent of the affordable and available housing it needs to serve extremely low-income households. This is virtually identical to the figure for San Francisco (29 percent) and much worse than Boston (46 percent). Decisions to reduce the amount of housing that affordably serves the poorest cannot be explained solely by housing markets.

There are important historical and economic reasons why the HOPE VI approaches pursued in some cities differed from those undertaken in other places. The "New Orleans Model," for instance, would never fly in San Francisco or Boston, where tenants' rights are firmly ensconced and carry broad institutional support. Nor, conversely, does it seem likely that the powerful real-estate interests in New Orleans would ever countenance redeveloping public housing without a market-rate component, even though this could surely be accomplished in some high-demand areas. Tucson's unusual approach to scattered sites works best in communities that have small public housing programs, high residential vacancies, and high-quality construction. In Boston, by contrast, a tight housing market meant that scattering new subsidized housing into other neighborhoods required entirely new buildings.

One remaining question is whether cities can shift their constellation type, especially if that city lacks a citywide galvanizing moment, rooted in massive urban renewal that yielded consequential backlash. Can such a city shift away from a Big Developer orientation toward constellations that rely upon powerful neighborhood organizations? In considering this, it is first worth recalling that all cities with Nonprofitus, Publica Major, or Plebs constellations have already moved far beyond the narrow public-private constellation of the urban renewal era, so clearly change is possible. Moreover, the examples of governance constellations described here have focused on particular neighborhoods within cities and need not describe every neighborhood in that city. While it does seem the case that there are indeed citywide tendencies for HOPE VI (as suggested by figure 1.6), it is also true that city leaders are pragmatically responsive whenever substantial sources of federal funding become available. In New Orleans, for instance, Big Developer Pres Kabacoff and HRI won the right to develop Bienville Basin (née Iberville), even though the terms of the federal Choice Neighborhoods program required his firm to accept one-for-one replacement of any demolished public housing units. In this instance, it would seem, a well-designed policy initiative forced an alteration of preferred practices. Then, with the November 2017 election of African American LaToya Cantrell, New Orleans gained a neighborhood activist as its first female mayor. New Orleans is still not San Francisco, but the arc of its governance universe may be bending more toward social justice. Still, change does not come easily.

In any case, it seems worthwhile for anyone seeking ways to redevelop public housing to be more fully aware of the practices that others have tried. Moreover, whether a city's governance constellation leads to policy and design approaches that favor mixing out the poorest or retaining them, it can be demonstrated that there are more equitable and less equitable forms of practice. In the end, depending on the particular strengths and weaknesses of a city's governance constellation, it is much harder in some places to align the stars in service of greater equity for the poorest.

THE LIMITS OF ONE-FOR-ONE REPLACEMENT

When the mandate for one-for-one replacement proved difficult for developers to achieve, HUD and the elected officials that approve its budget basically had two choices: either dramatically increase the size of HOPE VI grants to permit them to cover more of the costs of replacing housing, or drop the mandate. In the context of the mid-1990s revolt against "big government," it was no surprise that Congress and HUD chose to do the latter. This left housing authorities with three possibilities: (1) build back smaller, (2) engage in a spatially broader initiative to return public housing units on a more decentralized basis, or (3) ignore the repeal of one-for-one replacement and build back all units anyway. New Orleans, with the transformation of St. Thomas into River Garden, chose the first option by drastically reducing the count of public housing units, while also reneging on a promise to do even a little bit of the second. Tucson, by contrast, went from Connie Chambers to Posadas Sentinel by retaining the original number of deeply subsidized units and did so by scattering many of them across the city—the second tactic. Boston, with the shift from Orchard Park to Orchard Gardens, tried a much less drastic version of unit reduction and made some inroads into decentralization. Finally, San Francisco's North Beach Place managed to avoid both forms of compromise and instead embraced the third option; the city's leadership refused to build back smaller but retained all public housing units on the same site by building a more dense mixed-income development.

The examples from San Francisco and Tucson show that it is sometimes possible for HOPE VI to replace all hard units of public housing on a one-for-one basis, at least in the case of reasonably small projects. Yet such strategies are much harder to pull off for larger projects, even if this should be desired. In Boston, the planners of Orchard Gardens and the other offshoots came fairly close to matching the units once present in Orchard Park, which once had more than seven hundred apartments. They fell short because this is financially, logistically, and politically difficult to accomplish, especially since twenty-first-century occupancy standards call for much larger apartment sizes than those found in the old projects. To attempt anything like one-for-one replacement for a large project virtually necessitates taking a broader neighborhood strategy. The Boston team did that with Orchard Gardens, with substantial success. On a much larger scale, a developer-centered governance constellation in Chicago has grappled with the replacement of Cabrini-Green, which once held thirty-six hundred apartments. In that case, however, nearly a quarter-century after an initial HOPE VI grant, just a few hundred low-income apartments have been mixed into what is a now fully gentrified larger neighborhood.[13] In Chicago, community-based actors proved much less influential than elsewhere. "The approach to community-based public housing reform in Chicago," Chaskin and Joseph point out, "has been to engage 'community' principally as a target of intervention rather than as a unit of action, emphasizing planning, design principles, and the primacy of development professionals rather than the mobilization of community-level actors, processes, and resources."[14] This reveals the operation of a governance constellation quite different from those in San Francisco or Boston. In those places, community voices had important structural roles, and any loss of public housing units could be considered a failure of both process and outcome.

During the Barack Obama administration (2009–2017), national housing officials quickly concluded that the loss of units under HOPE VI constituted a serious flaw. Their successor program to HOPE VI, Choice Neighborhoods, restored the mandate for one-for-one replacement. Like the HOPE SF initiative in San Francisco (which received one of these grants) Choice Neighborhoods embraced a larger community frame, distributing a large amount of new housing into a wider area in a way that deconcentrates poverty without losing public housing units. Still, Choice Neighborhoods never came close to the levels of funding enjoyed by the earliest rounds of HOPE VI and remained a small program of just twenty-two implementation grants through 2016.

In 2017 and 2018, Congress generally resisted the Trump administration's more extreme efforts to erode the HUD budget, but halting the growing backlog of deferred maintenance in public housing has remained a seemingly unattainable quest. Even so, in May 2018 some congressional Democrats pushed back and proposed to invest $70 billion over five years in public housing operations and capital needs. Such ideas gained little initial traction. Meanwhile, inadequate HUD budgets struggled to fund the current outlay of housing vouchers, let alone expand it. Instead of increasing funding, the Trump admistration proposed that tenants should pay more than 30 percent of their income for rent (thereby conflicting with the most commonly used definition of "affordable" housing). New emphasis on introducing time limits for residents in public housing may well follow, much like the earlier shift from AFDC to TANF.[15]

Efforts to impose work requirements for public housing entry and ongoing occupancy continue to mount. Selecting higher-earning residents can help with rent rolls and fiscal stability for housing authorities, just as it did back in the 1940s and 1950s. And, at base, reframing public housing as "workforce" housing will increase the ideological resonance with long-standing efforts to connect housing assistance to work responsibility and moral worth. While perhaps financially necessary at a time of squeezed spending on domestic programs, this does nothing to close the widening deficit of affordable housing supply. New policies, rooted in paternalist management and aspirations for self-sufficiency, revive old notions of public housing as a reward for good citizenship, yet reiteration of this civilizing mission only worsens the problems for the city's poorest residents.

As of 2018, other options for expanding investment in deeply subsidized housing remain fraught with obstacles. In 2016, the national Housing Trust Fund (HTF) distributed its first $174 million to states, followed by a distri-bution of $219 million in 2017 and $267 million in 2018—the beginning of what could be one promising piece of the solution. The HTF targets 75 per-cent of its funds to support extremely low-income (ELI) households (those earning no more than 30 percent of the area median income or the fed-eral poverty limit)—and the rest goes to those with very low incomes (below 50 percent of AMI). Unfortunately, Congress has to date shown no inclina-tion to scale this up in a way that could significantly address the scope of the shortfall, despite a letter signed by nearly 1,300 organizations urging that the HFT be funded with at least $3.5 billion per year. By contrast, the ini-tial Trump administration budget proposed defunding the HTF completely. Although the Federal Housing Finance Agency encouragingly announced in February 2018 that it would protect funding for the HTF, its future remains uncertain.[16]

Meanwhile, the much-heralded LIHTC program also faces stiff challenges due to the effects of the major tax reform legislation passed at the end of 2017. The value of tax credits depends on corporate investors viewing their current tax burden as onerous enough to warrant seeking this form of relief. With corporate tax rates plunging from 35 percent to 21 percent as of 2018, interest in using LIHTC is expected to decline as well.[17]

Seen more broadly, the steady erosion in the percentage of American households receiving deeply subsidized rental housing seems likely to continue—even as extreme housing need continues to grow. It is worth reiterating that only one-quarter of very low-income American households receive a housing subsidy. Nationally, the situation for those with extremely low incomes (below 30 percent of AMI) is particularly dire. Nearly three-quarters of such households face severe cost burdens, meaning that they pay more than half of their income on rent and utilities. Such excessive spending on housing can mean too little income remains to cover other expenses such as healthy food, necessary medicine, or higher education. The situation for extremely low-income renters in the New Orleans and Tucson metropolitan areas is even worse than the national average, and—despite the sustained investment in public housing—it is only slightly better for those living in and around Boston (60 percent with severe housing cost burdens) and San Francisco (70 percent). The Boston area has forty-six affordable and available units for every one hundred ELI households, whereas there are just thirty-three for New Orleans, thirty for San Francisco, and twenty-three for Tucson.[18] Given the large net loss of units under HOPE VI, that program only exacerbated the shortfall.

Not-for-profit developers have played important ameliorative roles in HOPE VI and elsewhere but cannot be counted upon to solve the problem, especially not for households with the lowest incomes. As Calvin Welch of the Council of Community Housing Organizations commented, CDCs "have a difficult enough time housing poor people" and "simply didn't have the capacity [to serve] the *extremely* poor." To Welch, this explains why community-based housing groups argued so strongly for retaining public housing units in San Francisco. "We *needed* public housing to function," he declared. "Supporting one-for-one public housing replacement" was "self-protective for the CDC community." Community-based organizations have long tried to figure out which of the poor they can really afford to help, and have concluded that they need to have a public agency willing to grapple with the very poorest of the poor. Welch stated it bluntly: "We were terrified with the prospect of having to take on the responsibility of housing public housing tenants."[19] In a world of diminished public agencies (and, more broadly, public agency), sheer desperation drives community-based participation in progressive governance constellations. And, with HOPE SF and RAD in San Francisco, not-for-profit agencies will now be asked to shoulder more of the burden for housing those with the lowest incomes.

All four of the HOPE VI epics chronicled here have paired residents with advocacy organizations based outside their development, most prominently in New Orleans and San Francisco. To the harshest critics, however, such partnerships are far from benign. Jay Arena, writing about St. Thomas, views the "government- and foundation-funded nonprofit complex" as the "Trojan horse of neoliberalism." To him, organizations such as Hope House and STICC may seem an "inoffensive humanitarian and even progressive force," yet they actually hurt residents by facilitating dependence on services previously delivered by the state. Worse, Arena charges, "The nonprofits channeled residents and activists away from protests and into a negotiating process that conferred legitimacy on the black urban regime's privatization, demolition, and displacement agenda." As Arena narrates the story, low-income residents lost out by being duped into collaboration with private developers, a process that gradually stripped them of their once-radical sense of personal and collective agency.[20]

It is hard not to share many of Arena's doubts about St. Thomas—and doubting Thomases have a storied history. Still, the serial sellouts conveyed in Arena's sobering interpretation do little justice to the powerfully supportive work of Hope House and other agencies. Moreover, however great the temptation to find co-optation, this is not the only model for HOPE VI. At North Beach Place, both Tel-Hi and the Chinatown Community Development Center seem to be local nonprofits that remain genuine heroes to residents. And, at both Orchard Park and Posadas, it would seem that more conciliatory and collaborative approaches managed to maximize benefits for low-income residents, even if the results are less than perfect. Given the cost and complexity of what it takes to redevelop public housing, what is gained by eschewing every tactic that is not obstructionist?

Tel-Hi and the CCDC were not able to help North Beach Place residents win every fight, but it seems unduly cynical to dismiss their motives as no more than a pacifying form of controlled dissent—just enough to register displeasure without forestalling the march of development. Seen more positively, as in San Francisco, committed nonprofit actors helped low-income residents get their voices heard loudly enough to maximize the chance that the large capital-bearing and capital-seeking forces that could be arrayed against them would instead accommodate their needs as much as possible. This did not stop a tax-credit deal from nixing the promise about multiphase development, but it does seem to have helped preserve the commitment to one-for-one replacement. At a time when the public sector fails to make adequate investments in public housing and the social programs that support it, it makes little sense to castigate those who come closest to devoting their lives to the service of others. Even worse, perhaps, is the accusation that participants in some sort of nonprofit-industrial complex are mere dupes, unaware of the extent that they have been co-opted by larger forces of neoliberal capitalism. This merely adds insult to injury, and does nothing to improve the circumstances of the least advantaged.

It seems one dimensional to suggest that urging low-income tenants into even more protracted struggles based on extended obstructionism will yield better outcomes. There have been some notably confrontational efforts in public housing redevelopment—such as the lawsuits undertaken on behalf of tenants at Chicago's Cabrini-Green and Henry Horner Homes—that have gained somewhat better deals for low-income people, but these, too, are ultimately consent decrees based on negotiated compromise. For residents whose activism could cause them to lose the deep housing subsidy that they were fortunate enough to receive and which enables them to afford to live where they do, it is too easy for well-meaning activists who do not themselves face those same consequences to urge tenants to sustain or enhance levels of militancy that could lead to their eviction.

In all too many instances, low-income residents have been treated with deep disdain and lack of fairness, and these occasions should be called out, condemned, and—if possible—prevented. In other instances, however, those who profess to support low-income residents actually do so. Tucson officials spent their days showing Connie Chambers residents opportunities to move to single-family homes in neighborhoods with better public transit and public schools. San Francisco community leaders and staff members spent their nights giving wise counsel to public housing residents about their rights and helped them maximize their chance to return. There are developers who take the time to find ways to rehouse a tenant with a problematic rent-paying history, rather than seek the first possible excuse to deny her re-entry. There are mayors, city council members, and housing authority leaders who remain dedicated to serving those with the lowest incomes and providing them with the highest possible standards of housing, even at a time when budgets are decimated and morale has sunk.

San Francisco activist James Tracy astutely points to the important ways that "success" is differentially defined by the various players that make up a governance constellation. "The success of HOPE VI depends on your standard," he notes. "For the housing authority and the developer, once a new building is up, that defines success. But from a standpoint of community preservation, losing units in the San Francisco housing market is not a successful project."[21] In contrast to the relentless negativity of Arena's assemblage of uniformly misbehaving participants in New Orleans, Tracy takes a more pragmatic view of the role of community groups. "While it is foolish to believe that a nonprofit housing developer will build a movement," he writes, "it also isn't strategic to automatically dismiss the lot as automatically part of a nonprofit industrial complex."[22]

FROM RADICAL TO RAD

Just as housing authorities once often called HOPE VI "the last, best hope for public housing,"[23] city housing officials have now anxiously turned to the Rental Assistance Demonstration (RAD) program for deliverance. Introduced by HUD in 2011, RAD quickly generated interest across the nation, not just in San Francisco. Though initially conceived as a demonstration limited to 65,000 units, by late 2015 it reached its new cap of 185,000 units with a wait list. In 2017, Congress raised the cap to 225,000 units, with proposals to remove it completely. In the context of decades of declining federal support for capital improvements and steadily aging buildings, RAD enables local housing authorities to open up new sources of funding by permitting them to convert their conventional public housing apartments to long-term project-based rental assistance or project-based vouchers. This switches that housing into a form of HUD "assisted" housing, rather than conventional "public housing." After conversion, these properties would continue to receive an annual allocation of federal funds, but the new ownership entity would gain greater flexibility to leverage other capital to make up for the insufficiency of that federal contribution. The underlying idea is that RAD could stem the ongoing losses of deeply subsidized housing without requiring Congress to make a significant increase to the HUD budget. By August 2017, RAD had raised $4 billion of additional capital to pay for public housing improvements.[24]

Importantly, RAD responds to some of the key shortcomings of the HOPE VI program that proved so contentious in many of the places discussed in this book. Although some advocacy groups and tenants understandably remain skeptical based on decades of broken promises, HUD has stipulated that participation in the RAD program entails a one-for-one unit replacement commitment, includes enhanced assurances about residents' right of return, and requires long-term renewal of subsidies. Following conversion, residents even have the right to opt for a tenant-based housing voucher, if available.[25]

The success of RAD, though, depends on at least three things: the willingness of Congress to keep up the federal side of funding for project-based and tenant-based subsidies; the interest and capability of private sector and not-for-profit partners to take on the complex sociopolitical task of repairing or redeveloping public housing following decades of disinvestment; and the capacity of the public sector to provide appropriate ongoing oversight. In its initial years, RAD has proved to be particularly popular in small cities that have few public housing units and modest capital needs. For large projects in large cities, the challenges are greater, especially in expensive housing markets. Still, assuming there are willing and competent partners, transferring ownership through RAD may be the best remaining way to obtain necessary capital. After decades of squeezed budgets and deferred maintenance, this consequential shift away from the public sector is yet another step in a fifty-year march. Even though RAD does not require private ownership unless there are LIHTC units involved, RAD is in many ways the logical culmination of the "privatization of public housing" that has been underway since the 1960s.[26]

As privatization and fiscal desperation converge, it is hard to be fully hopeful. Still, RAD may carry an upside for public housing communities repeatedly threatened by displacement. To many in the governance constellations that hover above public housing, part of RAD's appeal is that it seems more socially navigable simply because it does not presume the wholesale substitution of one community with another. Even so, if caps on conversion get lifted, RAD could portend a future in which conventional public housing in the United States disappears almost entirely.

AFTER THE PROJECTS: THE ONGOING NEED FOR PUBLIC HOUSING

Ultimately, if the first eighty years of public housing history have shown anything, it is that Americans remain uneasy about offering deeply subsidized housing to some people seen as doing little to deserve this largesse—especially given that millions of other hard-working households are granted no such financial reprieve. There is a limit to empathy, and it has deep cultural roots in a polity that views poverty as evidence of personal moral failing rather than structural economic inequity. This remains the core problem facing many of those in public housing—and many of those desperately seeking to get into it: full-time, low-wage employment does not provide adequate income for a household to affordably rent market-rate apartments in most American cities.

Future redevelopment of public housing needs to find some form of middle ground. Public subsidies should not be used to turn mixed-income housing into maxed-income housing—biased toward those able to pay market rates. Skewed too far to meet the market, such communities unfairly deploy public money to reduce housing supply for the neediest households. But neither should future public funds go to versions of mixed-income housing that are effectively nixed-income housing, serving chiefly the un-employed. This would replicate the concentrated poverty of the old projects at their economic nadir. Housing serving only the very neediest will continue to promote socioeconomic marginalization of all kinds—and will never hold political appeal for funders. Narrow-mix versions of mixed-income housing—places that combine working-class, low-income households with those having incomes that are extremely low—seem to hold the most promise for building communities that are both desirable and socially equitable. This is also consistent with George Galster's summation of the economics and planning literature showing that "disadvantaged residents" can sometimes benefit from "social mix," but "this appears most likely when the social gulf between groups in the neighborhood is not excessive."[27]

Whatever the particularities of the social mix, the protracted struggles necessary to transform housing projects into HOPE VI projects make clear that these ventures have been financially and politically treacherous. At the same time, these tales of four cities suggest that there can be outcomes for extremely low-income residents that are least partially successful—and that those successes can take more than one form. One core principle shines through: given the past history of poorly maintained and ill-managed properties, equitable treatment for residents should be measured by their option to return to the redeveloped site of their former homes. It is possible that they will choose not to exercise that option, but this should be because they believe they have a genuinely preferable alternative available elsewhere. Positive outcomes could therefore include not just the opportunity to return to a new apartment in a well-governed HOPE VI project on a desirable site but also the possibility of a well-utilized housing choice voucher (where the actuality of "choice" is as important as the housing or the voucher). Finally, an equitable outcome could even entail successful relocation to another property managed by the housing authority or its deputies if those properties are desirable. In the end, equitable outcomes are those that residents themselves deem to be equitable.

As the number of conventional public housing projects continues to shrink, the very concept of "the projects" will inexorably disappear from the lexicon. HOPE VI has itself been another form of "project" that has already reached the end of its statutory life, even as its 260 iterations continue to try to build their communities. Still, both public housing and HOPE VI remain part of a much larger American cultural project: the effort to set the boundary for public sector intervention in the lives of the least economically advantaged. That project of poverty governance will continue long after the other projects are gone.

Notes

CHAPTER 1

1. For a three-hundred-year prehistory of public housing, see Lawrence J. Vale, *From the Puritans to the Projects* (Cambridge, MA: Harvard University Press, 2000).

2. Rhonda Williams, *The Politics of Public Housing* (New York: Oxford University Press, 2004), 45, 46; see also Vale, *Puritans to the Projects*, chapter 3; Robert Fairbanks, *Making Better Citizens* (Urbana: University of Illinois Press, 1988), 2; J. S. Fuerst, *When Public Housing Was Paradise* (Urbana: University of Illinois Press, 2005).

3. James Fraser, Deirdre Oakley, and Joshua Barzuin, "Public Ownership and Private Profit in Housing," *Cambridge Journal of Regions, Economy & Society* 5 (2012): 397–412; Robert Lang and Rebecca Sohmer, "Legacy of the Housing Act of 1949," *Housing Policy Debate* 11 (2000): 291–98; Alexander von Hoffman, "A Study in Contradictions: The Origin and Legacy of the Housing Act of 1949," *Housing Policy Debate* 11 (2000): 299–326; Douglas Massey and Nancy Denton, *American Apartheid: Segregation and the Making of the Underclass* (Cambridge, MA: Harvard University Press, 1993); Richard Rothstein, *The Color of Law* (New York: Liveright, 2017).

4. Michael B. Katz, "What Kind of Problem Is Poverty?," in Ananya Roy and Emma Shaw Crane, eds., *Territories of Poverty* (Athens: University of Georgia Press, 2015), 43.

5. Katz, "What Kind of Problem," 70–71.

6. Katz, "What Kind of Problem," 45.

7. Mulvaney quoted in Caitlin Dewey and Tracy Jan, "Trump to Poor Americans: Get to Work or Lose Your Benefits," *Washington Post*, May 22, 2017; Carson quoted in Jose DelReal, "Ben Carson Calls Poverty 'a State of Mind' during Interview," *Washington Post*, May 24, 2017; Carson quoted in Tessa Berenson, "Working in Trump's Washington Is Testing Ben Carson's Beliefs," *Time*, November 6, 2017.

8. Julie Zauzmer, "Christians Are More Than Twice as Likely to Blame a Person's Poverty on Lack of Effort," *Washington Post*, August 3, 2017. In contrast to Republicans, just one-quarter of Democrats blamed poverty on a lack of effort.

9. Center on Budget and Policy Priorities, "Policy Basics: Public Housing," as updated May 3, 2017, https://www.cbpp.org/research/policy-basics-public-housing.

10. Quoted in Annie Lowrey, "With Rental Demand Soaring, Poor Are Feeling Squeezed," *New York Times*, December 9, 2013.

11. National Low Income Housing Coalition, *The Gap: A Shortage of Affordable Homes*, March 2018, http://nlihc.org/sites/default/files/gap/Gap-Report_2018.pdf, 2.

12. NLIHC, *The Gap* (2018), 2–5; National Low Income Housing Coalition, *The Gap: The Affordable Housing Gap Analysis 2016*, http://nlihc.org/sites/default/files/Gap-Report_print.pdf, 2–6. These figures actually understate the gap, since the data—based on the 2014 American Community Survey—do not include the homeless. For those earning less than $15,000 annually—approximately equal to full-time work at minimum wage—nearly three-quarters faced such severe cost burdens; Harvard Joint Center for Housing Studies, *America's Rental Housing: Evolving Markets and Needs* (2013), http://www.jchs.harvard.edu/sites/jchs.harvard.edu/files/jchs_americas_rental_housing_2013_1_0.pdf, 30. See also HUD, "Trends in Housing Costs: 1985–2005 and the 30-Percent-of-Income Standard," June 2008; Christopher Herbert, Alexander Hermann, and Daniel McCue, "In Defense of the 30 Percent of Income to Housing Affordability Rule—in Some Cases," *Shelterforce*, April 25, 2017; Jeff Larrimore and Jenny Schuetz, "Assessing the Severity of Rent Burden on Low-Income Families," *FEDS Notes*, December 22, 2017, https://www.federalreserve.gov/econres/notes/feds-notes/assessing-the-severity-of-rent-burden-on-low-income-families-20171222.htm; Joint Center for Housing Studies of Harvard University, *America's Rental Housing 2017*, 26–31, http://www.jchs.harvard.edu/sites/jchs.harvard.edu/files/harvard_jchs_americas_rental_housing_2017.pdf. The 30 percent of income standard is also facing challenges. With the Make Affordable Housing Work Act of 2018, the Trump administration proposed to increase rents from 30 percent of household income to 35 percent and to eliminate all deductions that could lower that number, while also tripling the minimum monthly rents; https://www.hud.gov/sites/dfiles/Main/documents/RentReformLegislativeText.pdf.

13. G. Thomas Kingsley, "Trends in Housing Problems and Federal Housing Assistance," Urban Institute, October 2017, https://www.urban.org/sites/default/files/publication/94146/trends-in-housing-problems-and-federal-housing-assistance.pdf, 13.

14. US Department of Housing and Urban Development, *Worst Case Housing Needs: 2017 Report to Congress*, August 2017, https://www.huduser.gov/portal/sites/default/files/pdf/Worst-Case-Housing-Needs.pdf, ix.

15. Harvard Joint Center for Housing Studies, *The State of the Nation's Housing 2015*, http://www.jchs.harvard.edu/sites/jchs.harvard.edu/files/jchs-sonhr-2015-full.pdf, 33; Matthew Desmond, *Evicted: Poverty and Profit in the American City* (New York: Crown, 2016).

16. HUD, "Report of Total Proposed and Total Actual Unit Activity for Each Project," http://portal.hud.gov/hudportal/HUD?src=/program_offices/public_indian_housing/systems/pic/sac, data as of December 19, 2012. See also Edward Goetz, *New Deal Ruins: Race, Economic Justice, & Public Housing Policy* (Ithaca, NY: Cornell University Press, 2012), 4, 48–74.

17. Cuomo quoted in William C. Symonds, "Public Housing Finally Gets It Right—but It's Not Enough," *Business Week*, April 19, 1999.

18. Lawrence J. Vale and Yonah Freemark, "The Privatization of American Public Housing: Leaving the Poorest of the Poor Behind," in Katrin Anacker, Mai Thi Nguyen, and David Varady, eds., *The Housing Policy Handbook* (New York: Routledge, forthcoming). See also Lawrence J. Vale and Yonah Freemark, "From Public Housing

to Public-Private Housing: 75 Years of American Social Experimentation," *Journal of the American Planning Association* 78, no. 4 (2012): 379-402.

19. Henry G. Cisneros and Lora Engdahl, eds., *From Despair to Hope* (Washington, DC: Brookings Institution Press, 2009); John Arena, *Driven from New Orleans* (Minneapolis: University of Minnesota Press, 2012); Goetz, *New Deal Ruins*.

20. William Julius Wilson, *The Truly Disadvantaged* (Chicago: University of Chicago Press, 1987); William Julius Wilson, "Another Look at *The Truly Disadvantaged*," *Political Science Quarterly* 106, no. 4 (1992): 639-56; Lawrence J. Vale, "Beyond the Problem Projects Paradigm: Defining and Revitalizing 'Severely Distressed' Public Housing," *Housing Policy Debate* 4, no. 2 (1993): 147-74; Gayle Epp, "Emerging Strategies for Revitalizing Public Housing Communities," *Housing Policy Debate* 7, no. 3 (1996): 563-88; Susan J. Popkin, Bruce Katz, Mary K. Cunningham, Karen D. Brown, Jeremy Gustafson, and Margery A. Turner, *A Decade of HOPE VI* (Washington, DC: Urban Institute and Brookings Institution, 2004); Robert J. Sampson, *Great American City* (Chicago: University of Chicago Press, 2012).

21. Edward G. Goetz, *Clearing the Way* (Washington, DC: Urban Institute Press, 2003). See also Douglas S. Massey and Shawn Kanaiaupuni, "Public Housing and the Concentration of Poverty," *Social Science Quarterly* 74, no. 1 (1993): 109-22; Robert J. Sampson, "Moving to Inequality: Neighborhood Effects and Experiments Meet Social Structure," *American Journal of Sociology* 114, no. 1 (2008): 189-231; Stephen Steinberg, "The Myth of Concentrated Poverty," in Chester Hartman and Gregory D. Squires, eds., *The Integration Debate* (New York: Routledge, 2010); David Imbroscio, "'United and Actuated by Some Common Impulse of Passion': Challenging the Dispersal Consensus in American Policy Research," *Journal of Urban Affairs* 30, no. 2 (2008): 111-30; Xavier de Souza Briggs, "Maximum Feasible Misunderstanding: A Reply to Imbroscio," *Journal of Urban Affairs* 30, no. 2 (2008): 131-37.

22. Laura Tach and Allison Dwyer Emory, "Public Housing, Neighborhood Change, and the Restructuring of Urban Inequality," *American Journal of Sociology* 123, no. 3 (2017): 723.

23. Lawrence J. Vale, Shomon Shamsuddin, and Nicholas Kelly, "Broken Promises or Selective Memory Planning: A National Picture of HOPE VI Plans and Realities," *Housing Policy Debate*, 2018; https://doi.org/10.1080/10511482.2018.1458245.

24. Jason Hackworth, *The Neoliberal City* (Ithaca, NY: Cornell University Press, 2007), 8-9, 11, 16.

25. Matthew F. Gebhardt, "Politics, Planning and Power: Reorganizing and Redevelopment Public Housing in Chicago," PhD diss., Columbia University, 2009, 41.

26. Loretta Lees, Tom Slater, and Elvin Wyly, *Gentrification* (New York: Routledge, 2008), 61, 138-41, 220; Jason Hackworth and Neil Smith, "The Changing State of Gentrification," in Lees, Slater, and Wyly, eds., *The Gentrification Reader* (New York: Routledge, 2010), 65-76; Robert J. Chaskin and Mark L. Joseph, *Integrating the Inner City* (Chicago: University of Chicago Press, 2015), 160.

27. Robert Beauregard, "The Chaos and Complexity of Gentrification," in Neil Smith and Peter Williams, eds., *Gentrification of the City* (Boston: Allen and Unwin, 1986), 36.

28. Cassim Shepard, "Interview with Gerald Frug," *Urban Omnibus*, August 27, 2013.

29. Rowland Atkinson and Gary Bridge, eds., *Gentrification in a Global Context: The New Urban Colonialism* (New York: Routledge, 2005), 5; Edward G. Goetz, "Gentrification in Black and White: The Racial Impact of Public Housing Demolition in American Cities," *Urban Studies* 48, no. 8 (2010): 1581–604. Others have pointed out that sometimes "black gentrification" has yielded more diverse beneficiaries. See Derk S. Hyra, *The New Urban Renewal* (Chicago: University of Chicago Press, 2008).

30. Elvin K. Wyly and Daniel J. Hammel, "Islands of Decay in Seas of Renewal: Housing Policy and the Resurgence of Gentrification," *Housing Policy Debate* 10, no. 4 (1999): 711–71; Goetz, *New Deal Ruins*, 162–63; Peter Marcuse, "Comment's on Elvin K. Wyly and Daniel J. Hammel's 'Islands of Decay in Seas of Renewal: Housing Policy and the Resurgence of Gentrification,'" *Housing Policy Debate* 10, no. 4 (1999): 784, 796.

31. Deirdre A. Oakley and James C. Fraser, "U.S. Public-Housing Transformations and the Housing Publics Lost in Transition," *City & Community* 15, no. 4 (2016): 350, 353.

32. Neil Brenner and Nik Theodore, "Cities and the Geographies of 'Actually-Existing Neoliberalism,'" in Brenner and Theodore, eds., *Spaces of Neoliberalism* (Oxford: Blackwell, 2002) 14.

33. Robert Fairbanks, *The War on Slums in the Southwest* (Philadelphia: Temple University Press, 2014), 91, 121.

34. Christopher Klemek, *The Transatlantic Collapse of Urban Renewal* (Chicago: University of Chicago Press, 2011), 244.

35. For detailed analysis of the range of income-mixing practices deployed in the HOPE VI program, see Lawrence J. Vale and Shomon Shamsuddin, "All Mixed Up: Making Sense of Mixed-Income Housing Developments," *Journal of the American Planning Association* 83, no. 1 (2017): 56–67; Hackworth, *The Neoliberal City*; Lawrence J. Vale, *Purging the Poorest* (Chicago: University of Chicago Press, 2013).

36. Vale and Shamsuddin, "All Mixed Up"; Chaskin and Joseph, *Integrating the Inner City*,11.

37. Vale and Shamsuddin, "All Mixed Up."

38. Felice L. Michetti, "New 'Hope' for Public Housing: Asset Management Shows the Way," *HOPE VI Developments* 26 (March–April 1998), 1–2.

39. Yan Zhang and Gretchen Weismann, "Public Housing's Cinderella: Policy Dynamics of HOPE VI in the Mid-1990s," in Larry Bennett, Janet L. Smith, and Patricia A. Wright, eds., *Where Are Poor People to Live?* (Armonk, NY: M.E. Sharpe, 2006), 42.

40. Henry Cisneros, "A New Moment for People and Cities," in Cisneros and Engdahl, *From Despair to Hope*, 8–9; Bruce Katz, "The Origins of HOPE VI," in Cisneros and Engdahl, 15, 18, 26; Richard D. Baron, "The Evolution of HOPE VI as a Development Program," in Cisneros and Engdahl, 31, 34, 37; General Accounting Office, *HUD's Oversight of HOPE VI Sites Needs to Be More Consistent*, GAO-03-555, May 2003, 10–11. The one-for-one replacement rule was suspended in 1995 and repealed in 1998; even before the rule ended, housing authorities were permitted to replace up to one-third of their public housing units with vouchers; Cisneros and Engdahl, *From Despair to Hope*, 46 n. 20.

41. Goetz, *New Deal Ruins*, 4, 50, 64.

42. "Major Themes of the HOPE VI Program," as the title of the article has it, are sequentially outlined in Housing Research Foundation, *HOPE VI Developments* 30 (September 1998): 1, 2; Merrill H. Diamond, "In My Opinion: One Consultant's View of HOPE VI," *HOPE VI Developments* 35 (April 1999): 2; Congress for the New Urbanism and HUD, *Principles for Inner City Neighborhood Design: HOPE VI and the New Urbanism*, January 2000.

43. Interviews with Thomas Kingsley, Milan Ozdinec, and William Murphy conducted by Nicholas Kelly, August 2016.

44. *FY 2010 HOPE VI Revitalization Grant Agreement*, 26, https://www.hud.gov/sites/documents/10REVIT_GRANT_AGREEMENT.PDF; National Housing Law Project, the Poverty & Race Research Action Council, Sherwood Research Associates, and ENPHRONT, *False HOPE: A Critical Assessment of the HOPE VI Public Housing Redevelopment Program* (2002), https://www.nhlp.org/files/FalseHOPE.pdf; Abt Associates, "Interim Assessment of the HOPE VI Program: Case Study of Ellen Wilson Dwellings in Washington, DC. Final Report, Vol. 1," 2003, http://www.abtassociates.com/Reports/2001409176851.pdf; Bennett, Smith, and Wright, *Where Are Poor People to Live?*; General Accounting Office, *HOPE VI Resident Issues and Changes in Neighborhoods Surrounding Grant Sites*, GAO-04-109, November 2003; Vale, *Purging the Poorest*; Vale, Shamsuddin, and Kelly, "Broken Promises."

45. General Accounting Office, *HOPE VI Resident Issues*, 4, 8, 10; return rates calculated from dashboard data about the entire HOPE VI program supplied by HUD to the author in January 2015.

46. Interview with Jeffrey Lines, April 2014. Unless otherwise indicated, all interviews were conducted by the author. For details on unbuilt homeownership units, see Vale, Shamsuddin, and Kelly, "Broken Promises."

47. General Accounting Office, *HUD's Oversight*, 10–11.

48. Robert J. Chaskin, "Between the Idea and the Reality: Public Housing Reform and the Further Marginalization of the Poor," *City and Community* 15, no. 4 (2016): 373. For a sample of the large literature on housing vouchers and the Moving to Opportunity experiment, see David Varady and Carol Walker, "Vouchering Out Distressed Subsidized Developments: Does Moving Lead to Improvements in Housing and Neighborhood Conditions?" *Housing Policy Debate* 11 (2000): 115-19; Rachel Kleit and Lynne Manzo, "To Move or Not to Move: Relationships to Place and Relocation Choices in HOPE VI," *Housing Policy Debate* 17 (2006): 271-308; Deirdre Oakley and Keri Burchfield, "Out of the Projects, Still in the Hood: The Spatial Constraints on Public Housing Residents' Relocation in Chicago," *Journal of Urban Affairs* 31 (2009): 589-614; Edward Goetz, "Better Neighborhoods, Better Outcomes? Explaining Relocation Outcomes in HOPE VI," *Cityscape* 12 (2010): 5-32; JoDee Keller, "Experiences of Public Housing Residents Following Relocation: Explorations of Ambiguous Loss, Resiliency, and Cross-Generational Perspectives," *Journal of Poverty* 15 (2011): 141-63; Deirdre Oakley, Erin Ruel, and Lesley Reid, "Atlanta's Last Demolitions and Relocations: The Relationship between Neighborhood Characteristics and Resident Satisfaction," *Housing Studies* 28 (2013): 205-34; Xavier de Souza Briggs, Susan J. Popkin, and John Goering, *Moving to Opportunity: The Story of an American Experiment to Fight Ghetto Poverty* (New York: Oxford University Press, 2010); Sampson, "Moving to Inequality"; Edward G. Goetz, "Your 'Opportunity' Map Is Broken: Here Are Some Fixes." *Shelterforce*,

November 16, 2017, https://shelterforce.org/2017/11/16/your-opportunity-map-is-broken-here-are-some-fixes/; Lawrence J. Vale and Nicholas F. Kelly, "From Public Housing to Vouchers: No Easy Path Out of Poverty," *The Dream Revisited*, Furman Center, New York University, May 2016, http://furmancenter.org/research/iri/essay/from-public-housing-to-vouchers-no-easy-pathway-out-of-poverty.

49. Janet L. Smith, "Public Housing Transgression," *City & Community* 15, no. 4 (2016): 377.

50. Mark Joseph, "Is Mixed-Income Development an Antidote to Urban Poverty?," *Housing Policy Debate* 17, no. 2 (2006): 209–34; Mark L. Joseph, Robert J. Chaskin, and Henry S. Webber, "The Theoretical Basis for Addressing Poverty through Mixed-Income Development," *Urban Affairs Review* 42, no. 3 (2007): 369–409; Chaskin and Joseph, *Integrating the Inner City*; see also http://nimc.case.edu/library/.

51. Joseph, "Is Mixed Income Housing an Antidote," 219–22; Chaskin and Joseph, *Integrating the Inner City*, 130; Many subsequent studies have also found little evidence of significant cross-class interaction, especially in mixed-income communities with a market-rate component; Mark Joseph, "Early Resident Experiences at a New Mixed-Income Development in Chicago," *Journal of Urban Affairs* 30, no. 3 (2008): 229–57; Laura Tach, "More Than Bricks and Mortar: Neighborhood Frames, Social Processes and Mixed Income Development of a Public Housing Project," *City & Community* 8 (2009): 273–303; Robert Chaskin and Mark Joseph, "Building 'Community' in Mixed-Income Developments: Assumptions, Approaches, and Early Experiences," *Urban Affairs Review* 45 (2010): 299–335; James DeFilippis and Jim Fraser, "Why Do We Want Mixed-Income Housing and Neighborhoods?," in Jonathan S. Davies and David L. Imbroscio, eds., *Critical Urban Studies: New Directions* (Albany: State University of New York Press, 2010); Diane Levy, Zach McDade, and Kassie Dumlao Bertumen, *Effects of Living in Mixed-Income Communities for Low-Income Families: A Review of the Literature* (Washington, DC: Urban Institute, 2010); Mark Joseph and Robert Chaskin, "Living in a Mixed-Income Development: Resident Perceptions of the Benefits and Disadvantages of Two Developments in Chicago," *Urban Studies* 47, no. 11 (2010): 2347–66; Erin Graves, "The Structuring of Social Life: A Case-Based Analysis of a Mixed Income Community," *City & Community* 9 (2010): 109–31; Erin Graves, "Mixed Outcome Developments: Comparing Policy Goals to Resident Outcomes in Mixed-Income Housing," *Journal of the American Planning Association* 77, no. 2 (2011): 143–53; Robert J. Chaskin and Mark Joseph, "Relational Expectations and Emerging Reality: The Nature of Social Interaction in Mixed-Income Developments," *Journal of Urban Affairs* 32 (2011): 209–37; Rachel Garshick Kleit and Nicole Bohme Carnegie, "Integrated or Isolated? The Impact of Public Housing Redevelopment on Social Network Homophily," *Social Networks* 33, no. 2 (2011): 152–65; Robert Chaskin, Amy Khare, and Mark Joseph, "Participation, Deliberation, and Decision-Making: The Dynamics of Inclusion and Exclusion in Mixed-Income Developments," *Urban Affairs Review* 48, no. 6 (2012): 863–906; Mark Joseph and Robert Chaskin, "Mixed-Income Developments and Low Rates of Return: Insights from Relocated Public Housing Residents in Chicago," *Housing Policy Debate* 22 (2012): 377–406; Vale, *Purging the Poorest*; James Curtis Fraser, Ashley Brown Burns, Joshua Barzuin, and Deidre Oakley, "HOPE VI, Colonization, and the Production of Difference," *Urban Affairs Review* 49 (2013): 525–56; James Fraser, Robert Chaskin, and Joshua Barzuin, "Making Mixed-Income Neighborhoods

Work for Low-Income Households," *Cityscape* 15 (2013): 83–100; Chaskin and Joseph, *Integrating the Inner City*.

52. DeFilippis and Fraser, "Mixed-Income Housing," 136, 138.

53. Oakley and Fraser, "U.S. Public-Housing Transformations," 357.

54. Hackworth, *The Neoliberal City*, 52; Jason Hackworth, "Public Housing and the Rescaling of Regulation in the USA," *Environment and Planning A* 35 (2003): 531–49.

55. Shomon Shamsuddin, "Preserved for Posterity: Public Housing Redevelopment and Replacement in HOPE VI," paper presented at the Association of Collegiate Schools of Planning conference, October 2017.

CHAPTER 2

1. Erik Swyngedouw, "Governance Innovation and the Citizen: The Janus Face of Governance-beyond-the-State," *Urban Studies* 42, no. 11 (2005): 1999. See also Michel Foucault, "Governmentality," in Paul Rabinow and Nikolas Rose, eds., *The Essential Foucault* (New York: New Press, 2003), 229–45.

2. Clarence N. Stone and Robert P. Stoker, eds., *Urban Neighborhoods in a New Era* (Chicago: University of Chicago Press, 2015), xiv.

3. Martin Horak, Juliet Musso, Ellen Shiau, Robert P. Stoker, and Clarence N. Stone, "Change Afoot," in Stone and Stoker, *Urban Neighborhoods*, 1.

4. Audrey G. McFarlane, "When Inclusion Leads to Exclusion: The Uncharted Terrain of Community Participation in Economic Development," *Brooklyn Law Review* 66, no. 3 (2000): 870–71.

5. James Q. Wilson, "Planning and Politics: Citizen Participation in Urban Renewal," in Wilson, ed., *Urban Renewal: The Record and the Controversy* (Cambridge, MA: MIT Press, 1966), 409.

6. Economic Opportunity Act of 1964, Public Law 88-252; Lillian B. Rubin, "Maximum Feasible Participation," *Annals of the American Academy of Political and Social Science* 385 (1969): 14–29.

7. McFarlane, "When Inclusion Leads," 876, 880–81, 885–86.

8. Georgette C. Poindexter, "Who Gets the Final No? Tenant Participation in Public Housing Redevelopment," *Cornell Journal of Law and Public Policy* 9, no. 3 (2000): 663–64.

9. Poindexter, "Who Gets Final No," 666.

10. Poindexter, "Who Gets Final No," 672.

11. Poindexter, "Who Gets Final No," 673–75, 679.

12. Lisa Alexander, "Stakeholder Participation in New Governance," *Georgetown Journal on Poverty Law and Policy* 16, no. 1 (2009): 117–85.

13. Sherry Arnstein, "A Ladder of Citizen Participation," *Journal of the American Institute of Planners* 35, no. 4 (1969): 216–24.

14. Rachel G. Bratt and Kenneth M. Reardon, "Beyond the Ladder: New Ideas about Resident Roles in Contemporary Community Development in the United States," in Naomi Carmon and Susan S. Fainstein, eds., *Policy, Planning, and People: Promoting Justice in Urban Development* (Philadelphia: University of Pennsylvania Press, 2013), 356–81; Manuel Castells, *The City and the Grassroots: A Cross-Cultural Theory of Urban Social Movements* (Berkeley: University of California Press, 1983).

15. Vale and Freemark, "From Public Housing."

16. Robert P. Stoker, Clarence N. Stone, and Martin Horak, "Contending with Structural Inequality in a New Era," in Stone and Stoker, *Urban Neighborhoods*, 210.

17. Archon Fung and Eric Olin Wright, "Thinking about Empowered Participatory Governance," in Fung and Wright, *Deepening Democracy* (New York: Verso, 2003), 3–42; Xavier de Souza Briggs, *Democracy as Problem Solving* (Cambridge, MA: MIT Press, 2008). For discussion of networked governance, see Ismael Blanco, "Analysing Urban Governance Networks: Bringing Regime Theory Back In," *Environment and Planning C* 31 (2013): 276–91.

18. See http://govinfo.library.unt.edu/npr/library/announc/hudwinnr.html.

19. Clarence N. Stone, preface to Stone and Stoker, *Urban Neighborhoods*, xvi–xvii.

20. Clarence N. Stone, *Regime Politics: Governing Atlanta, 1946-1988* (Lawrence: University of Kansas Press, 1989), 3.

21. John R. Logan and Harvey L. Molotch, *Urban Fortunes: The Political Economy of Place*, 20th anniversary ed. (Berkeley: University of California Press, 2007);

22. Logan and Molotch, *Urban Fortunes*; Horak et al., "Change Afoot," 12–13. Stone's regime types are described in Clarence N. Stone, "Urban Regimes and the Capacity to Govern," *Journal of Urban Affairs* 15, no. 1 (1993): 1–28. See also Clarence N. Stone, "Looking Back to Look Forward: Reflections on Urban Regime Analysis," *Urban Affairs Review* 40, no. 3 (2005): 309–41, and Karen Mossberger and Gerry Stoker, "The Evolution of Regime Theory," *Urban Affairs Review* 36, no. 6 (2001): 810–35.

23. Peter F. Burns and Matthew O. Thomas, *Reforming New Orleans* (Ithaca, NY: Cornell University Press, 2015), 4–5.

24. Mary Pattillo, *Black on the Block* (Chicago: University of Chicago Press, 2007), 8.

25. McFarlane, "When Inclusion Leads," 928–29.

26. Horak et al., "Change Afoot," 5.

27. James C. Fraser and Edward L. Kick, "The Role of Public, Private, Non-profit and Community Sectors in Shaping Mixed-Income Housing Outcomes in the US," *Urban Studies* 44, no. 12 (2007): 2357–77; Katz, "What Kind of Problem," 44.

28. Fraser and Kick, "Role," 2361–62.

29. Joe Soss, Richard C. Fording, and Sanford F. Schram, *Disciplining the Poor* (Chicago: University of Chicago Press, 2011), 1.

30. Soss, Fording, and Schram, *Disciplining the Poor*, 2, 3, 5, 15–16, 46.

31. Frances Fox Piven and Richard A. Cloward, *Regulating the Poor*, 2nd ed. (New York: Vintage, 1993); Michael B. Katz, *The Undeserving Poor* (New York: Pantheon, 1989); Herbert J. Gans, *The War against the Poor* (New York: Basic Books, 1995).

32. Vale, *Puritans to the Projects*.

33. Soss, Fording, and Schram, *Disciplining the Poor*, 4; Chaskin and Joseph, *Integrating the Inner City*, 229.

34. Soss, Fording, and Schram, *Disciplining the Poor*, 37, 38, 50, 264, 291; Robert Greenstein, "Welfare Reform and the Safety Net," Center for Budget and Policy Priorities, June 6, 2016.

35. Soss, Fording, and Schram, *Disciplining the Poor*, 5.

PART II

1. In 1971, a multivolume assessment of the New Orleans built environment referred to the area as "Lower Garden District" just as gentrification took hold; Samuel

Wilson Jr. and Bernard Lemann, *New Orleans Architecture*, vol. 1: *The Lower Garden District* (New Orleans: Friends of the Cabildo, 1971). The "Lower Garden District" was added to the National Register of Historic Places in 1972 and expanded in 1990, http://www.nationalregisterofhistoricplaces.com/la/orleans/districts.html.

2. Alexander J. Reichl, "Learning from St. Thomas: Community, Capital, and the Redevelopment of Public Housing in New Orleans," *Journal of Urban Affairs* 21, no. 2 (1999): 173, 174.

CHAPTER 3

1. Cited in Burns and Thomas, *Reforming New Orleans*, 11, 12.

2. HANO, 1942 Annual Report (HANO, 1943), 59.

3. Martha Mahoney, "Law and Racial Geography: Public Housing and the Economy of New Orleans," *Stanford Law Review* 42, no. 5 (1990): 1270; Elizabeth Fussell, "Constructing New Orleans, Constructing Race," *Journal of American History* 94, no. 3 (2007): 851.

4. 1930 US Manuscript Census.

5. HANO, Report of the Housing Authority of New Orleans for the Year Ending December 31, 1939 (HANO, 1940), 17-18, 28; HANO, 1940 Annual Report (HANO, 1941), 18.

6. HANO, 1939 Annual Report, 17-18.

7. HANO, 1939 Annual Report, 17, 18, 27.

8. HANO, 1938 Annual Report (HANO, 1938), 7, 12.

9. HANO, 1941 Annual Report, 13; HANO, "Public Housing in New Orleans," (HANO, 1947), 4, 8; Alvin M. Fromherz, "Development and Operation . . . The Early Days," in HANO, *Twenty-Five Years of Community Service in the Field of Low Rent Housing* (HANO, 1962), 31.

10. Mahoney, "Law and Racial Geography," 1269. HANO reported that white families on relief averaged $462.34 in annual income during 1939, and only the lowest tier of rent at St. Thomas—accommodating just 12 percent of accepted households—accepted those with less than $450 of annual income (HANO, 1939 Annual Report, 34); HANO, 1940 Annual Report, 23.

11. HANO, 1941 Annual Report, 57.

12. HANO, "New Orleans Public Housing Market Review," August 1947, 21-22, New Orleans City Archives.

13. HANO, "Public Housing in New Orleans," 14.

14. Mahoney, "Law and Racial Geography," 1271, 1274-75.

15. Arnold R. Hirsch, "Race and Renewal in the Cold War South: New Orleans, 1947-1968," in Robert Fishman, ed., *The American Planning Tradition* (Washington, DC: Woodrow Wilson Center Press, 2000), 219-20, 229.

16. Harland Bartholomew & Associates, *A 25 Year Urban Development Program: New Orleans, Louisiana*, prepared for the New Orleans City Planning and Zoning Commission, February 1952, iv, 32, table G; Fussell, "Constructing New Orleans," 847, figure 1.

17. Housing Authority and Planning Commission, City of New Orleans, "Progress in Slum Clearance and Urban Redevelopment," November 1952, 1; City Planning and Zoning Commission, "Report and Recommendation for Selection of Low-Rent Housing Project Sites for Negro Occupancy," September 1952, 1.

18. Hirsch, "Race and Renewal," 228–29, Schiro quoted, 230.

19. Hébert quoted in Kent Germany, *New Orleans after the Promises* (Athens: University of Georgia Press, 2007), 185.

20. "Urban Renewal Plan Is Opposed," *Times-Picayune*, April 30, 1954, 26; "Urban Renewal Plan Criticized," *Times-Picayune*, September 14, 1961, 12; Frank Schneider, "Halt Slums, Barnett Urges," *Times-Picayune*, March 25, 1966; "9th Ward Plans Appeal Slated," *Times-Picayune*, January 18, 1967; Paul Atkinson, "City Receives Renewal Grant," *Times-Picayune*, March 5, 1970, 1.

21. Germany, *New Orleans*, 199.

22. Frances Frank Marcus, "New Orleans Disputes Future of Park on Site of Treme, Where Jazz Dug In," *New York Times*, March 23, 1983.

23. Ethel Goodstein, "A Tale of Two Civic Centers," Proceedings of the 84th ACSA Annual Meeting, 1996, 228–33.

24. Hirsch, "Race and Renewal," 235.

25. Tom Lewis, *Divided Highways* (Ithaca, NY: Cornell University Press, 2013), 181, 185–87, 192, 196, 199–210.

26. Lewis, *Divided Highways*, 187–89; Mark H. Rose and Raymond A. Mohl, *Interstate: Highway Politics and Policy since 1939*, 3rd edition (Knoxville: University of Tennesee Press), 106, 113.

27. Huey Perry, "The Evolution and Impact of Biracial Coalitions and Black Mayors in Birmingham and New Orleans," in Rufus P. Browning, Dale Rogers Marshall, and David H. Tabb, eds., *Racial Politics in American Cities*, 3rd ed. (New York: Longman, 2003), 231.

28. Mahoney, "Law and Racial Geography," 1276–77.

29. Mahoney, "Law and Racial Geography," 1280.

30. "Calling Car 65," editorial, *St. Thomas News* 2, no. 3 (March 1967).

31. Arena, *Driven from New Orleans*, 5; Germany, *New Orleans*, 201; City of New Orleans, "St. Thomas NSA, Strategy Statement and Survey," n.d. (ca. 1979), New Orleans City Archives.

32. Mahoney, "Law and Racial Geography," 1280.

33. Arena, *Driven from New Orleans*, 7, 13.

34. Interview with Barbara Jackson conducted by Annemarie Gray, January 2013.

35. Interview with Jackson.

36. Interview with Jackson.

37. Arena, *Driven from New Orleans*, xvii, 23–26; interview with Jackson.

38. Arena, *Driven from New Orleans*, 26.

39. Christine C. Cook and Mickey Lauria, "Urban Regeneration and Public Housing in New Orleans," *Urban Affairs Review* 30, no. 4 (1995): 539.

40. Sheila Stroup, "Hope House Shines On," *Times-Picayune*, November 1, 1994.

41. Lynne Jensen, "Book Circuit Tour Awaits Death-Row Activist Prejean," *Times-Picayune*, June 14, 1993.

42. Andrea R. Vaucher, "'Dead Man' Moves On," *Times-Picayune*, June 3, 1995.

43. Sister Helen Prejean, *Dead Man Walking* (New York: Vintage, 1994), 3–4.

44. Coleman Warner, "Police, HANO Seek Ways to Curb Violence," *Times-Picayune*, March 16, 1993.

45. Interview with Brother Don Everard conducted by Annemarie Gray, January 2013.

46. Bill Walsh, "Psychological Scars Deeper," *Times-Picayune*, July 27, 1993; Walsh, "After the Gunshots—No More Child's Play," *Times-Picayune*, July 27, 1993; Michael Pearlstein, "Arrests May Break Gang," *Times-Picayune*, November 3, 1993; Ronette King, "Groups Joining Hands to Help Lower Garden District Bloom," *Times-Picayune*, December 11, 1993; John Deshazier, "Solid Sterling: On Court, in Class, Xavier Prep Standout a Busy Bee," *Times-Picayune*, February 16, 1993.

47. Iris Kelso, "Housing Idea," *Times-Picayune*, December 5, 1993.

48. Michael Pearlstein and Christopher Cooper, "Suspects' Gang Ties Infamous," *Times-Picayune*, June 7, 1995.

49. Walt Philbin, "17 Suspects in 'Heroin Network' Indicted," *Times-Picayune*, June 17, 2000.

50. Bob Ussery, "3 Are Shot to Death within 16 Hours," *Times-Picayune*, January 13, 1994. This kind of stigma is not atypical. See Lawrence J. Vale, "Destigmatizing Public Housing," in Dennis Crow, ed., *Geography and Identity: Exploring and Living the Geopolitics of Identity* (Washington, DC: Institute for Advanced Cultural Studies / Maisonneuve Press, 1996).

51. Coleman Warner, "Restaurant, Residents Both Seeing Green," *Times-Picayune*, October 22, 1994; Siona LaFrance, "Where Hope Sprouts and Pride Blooms," *Times-Picayune*, November 23, 2000; Sarah O'Kelley, "Going Places with Pasta," *Times-Picayune*, January 4, 2001; Nikki Usher, "A Garden of Hope," *Times-Picayune*, July 21, 2003; Deshazier, "Solid Sterling"; Coleman Warner, "2nd Front Opened in Crime," *Times-Picayune*, October 12, 1995; Leslie Williams, "St. Thomas Group Creating Opportunities," *Times-Picayune*, October 19, 1997.

CHAPTER 4

1. Arena, *Driven from New Orleans*, 45–50.

2. Arena, *Driven from New Orleans*, 72–75.

3. Interview with Pres Kabacoff, April 2010.

4. St. Thomas / Irish Channel Consortium, "Accountability Statement" (Draft), November 19, 1992; Arena, *Driven from New Orleans*, 62–64.

5. Urban Land Institute Advisory Services, *Lower Garden District, New Orleans, Louisiana* (Washington, D.C.: ULI, 1993), 9.

6. Urban Land Institute, *Lower Garden District*, 13, 14, 16, 17, 24, 25, 74.

7. Urban Land Institute, *Lower Garden District*, 75, 76, 87–88.

8. Urban Land Institute, *Lower Garden District*, 25; Arena, *Driven from New Orleans*, 77–79; Bolan quoted in King, "Groups Joining Hands."

9. Lane, quoted in Iris Kelso, "Lane's Concept," *Times-Picayune*, December 12, 1993.

10. Urban Land Institute, *Lower Garden District*, 25, 55, 76–82.

11. Interview with Brother Don Everard conducted by Annemarie Gray, January 2013.

12. Arena, *Driven from New Orleans*, 84.

13. Minutes of September 1994 STICC meeting, Hope House files.

14. "A Neighborhood Success Story," editorial, *Times-Picayune*, April 11, 1994; Perez Ernst Farnet, *A Master Plan for St. Thomas Housing Development LA 1-1 & LA 1-9*, 1994; Wallace, Roberts & Todd (with Perez Ernst Farnet), *Plan for the Lower Garden District*, 1995.

15. Tucker and Associates, Inc., Strategic Plan, Prepared for the Housing Authority of New Orleans, May 26, 1995, 6–8, 14–15.

16. Greg Thomas, "Rebirth of the St. Thomas Housing Development Is at the Heart of Hopes for the Lower Garden District," *Times-Picayune*, October 22, 1995; Leslie Williams, "N.O. Zeroes In on Blight," *Times-Picayune*, March 21, 1996.

17. Kelly quoted in Greg Thomas, "The Plan," *Times-Picayune*, October 22, 1995.

18. Leslie Williams, "St. Thomas 'Guide' to Oversee Facelift," *Times-Picayune*, January 4, 1996.

19. Landry quoted in Williams, "St. Thomas 'Guide.'"

20. Arena, *Driven from New Orleans*, 99.

21. HANO, "A Cooperative Endeavor to Rebuild Public Housing," (HANO, 1996), 2; "Forward on Public Housing," editorial, *Times-Picayune*, September 8, 1997.

22. Demetria Farve and Fannie McKnight, "Give Credit to Residents," letter to the editor, *Times-Picayune*, April 15, 1996.

23. Williams, "N.Y. Firm May Lead HANO Project"; interview with Kabacoff.

24. HUD, *FY 1998 HOPE VI Guidebook*, "Resident and Community Involvement."

25. Interview with Michael Kelly, March 2009.

26. Memo from Michael Janis to Chet J. Drozdowski, Director of the Louisiana State Office of Public Housing, "Approval of the Housing Authority of New Orleans' (HANO) Request to Demolish . . . ," March 20, 1997, 4; interview with Kelly; Arena, *Driven from New Orleans*, 107–8.

27. Tucker and Associates, Strategic Plan, 1; Arena, *Driven from New Orleans*, 109–10.

28. Reichl, "Learning from St. Thomas," 181.

29. HANO Continuous Improvement Plan, Section V (HANO, April 1998), 5; Letter from Barbara Jackson (STRC) to Pres Kabacoff (HRI) and Benjamin Bell (HANO), May 26, 2000, Hope House files; HRI and HANO, "Revitalization Plan Cover Sheet," July 2000; Don Everard, "St. Thomas HOPE VI," memo for Hope House files, May 12, 2000; Reichl, "Learning from St. Thomas," 181.

30. Brod Bagert Jr., "HOPE VI and St. Thomas: Smoke, Mirrors and Urban Mercantilism," master's thesis, London School of Economics, September 2002, appendix D.

31. HANO, HOPE VI Grant Application, cited in Bagert, "HOPE VI," 8, 20.

32. Interview with Kelly.

33. HUD Office of the Inspector General, "Audit of the Fiscal Year 1996 HOPE VI Grant Award Process," 98-FO-101-0001, October 20, 1997, appendix M, 12.

34. "Groundbreaking at St. Thomas," editorial, *Times-Picayune*, October 11, 1996; Housing Authority of New Orleans, Urban Revitalization Demonstration Grant Application for St. Thomas Housing Development, August 1996; Arena, *Driven from New Orleans*, 121.

35. Greg Thomas, "Neighborhoods Rejoice," *Times-Picayune*, April 26, 1996.

36. Arena, *Driven from New Orleans*, 121–22; Letter from HUD Deputy Assistant Secretary Michael B. Janis to HANO Executive Director Michael Kelly, "Approval of the Housing Authority of New Orleans' (HANO) Request to Demolish . . . ," March 20, 1997; Memo from Janis to Drozdowski, 3–6.

37. Letter from Janis to Kelly; Memo from Janis to Drozdowski, 3–6.

38. Leslie Williams, "HANO Signs Pair of Firms," *Times-Picayune*, July 15, 1997.

39. Arena, *Driven from New Orleans*, 122–23.

40. Leslie Williams, "Residents Issue Ultimatum on St. Tammany [*sic*] Deal," *Times-Picayune*, July 15, 1997.

41. Memo from D. Michael Beard, HUD Director Inspector General for Audit, 6AGA, to HUD Deputy Assistant Secretary Elinor Bacon, July 24, 1998, 1–14; Mary Swerszek, "Report Slams HANO Deal," *Times-Picayune*, August 9, 1998.

42. Memo from Beard to Bacon, 1–14; Mary Swerszek, "HANO to Rebid Flawed Rehab Deal for St. Thomas," *Times-Picayune*, July 14, 1998; Swerszek, "Complex Residents Want Say in Rehab," *Times-Picayune*, July 25, 1998; Swerszek, "Report Slams HANO Deal," *Times-Picayune*, August 9, 1998.

43. Creative Choice Homes, "Final Response to HUD I.G. Report on the St. Thomas Developer Procurement," Draft for Discussion and Comment, August 13, 1998; files of HOPE House, St. Thomas Box.

44. James Varney, "HANO Chooses Local Developer: HRI Chosen over National Rivals," *Times-Picayune*, October 29, 1998; Arena, *Driven from New Orleans*, 125.

45. Jackson quoted in Varney, "HANO Chooses Local Developer."

46. Varney, "HANO Chooses Local Developer."

47. Varney, "HANO Chooses Local Developer."

48. James Varney, "Kabacoff Wins Rehab Contract: Residents Favored Another Company," *Times-Picayune*, October 31, 1998.

49. Kabacoff quoted in Varney, "HANO Chooses Local Developer."

50. Interview with Kabacoff.

51. Alma H. Young and Jyaphia Christos-Rodgers, "Resisting Racially Gendered Space: The Women of the St. Thomas Resident Council, New Orleans," in Michael Peter Smith, ed., *Marginal Spaces* (New Brunswick, NJ: Transaction Publishers, 1995), 102.

52. The St. Thomas Community Law Center commenced operations in September 1996, as "an unofficial offshoot of the Loyola Law Clinic." Based on the principles of "self-determination for residents of public housing," the law center's nine-member board of directors included seven who were residents of St. Thomas or members of community organizations; Bart Stapert, "Summary of Qualifications," accompanying letter from Stapert to Alvi Anderson-Mogilles, "Response to RFP Legal Assistance for the St. Thomas Resident Council," May 11, 1999, Hope House files.

53. Arena, *Driven from New Orleans*, 128–30.

54. Arena, *Driven from New Orleans*, 130–31.

55. Interview with Kabacoff.

56. Susan Finch, "Grant Sought to Start Razing Project," *Times-Picayune*, April 28, 1999.

57. Interview with Everard.

58. Robert George, "Man Is Killed outside His Sister's Window," *Times-Picayune*, August 22, 2002; Michelle Krupa, "Violence Sprouts after St. Thomas Uprooted," *Times-Picayune*, August 25, 2002; Tara Young, "Second Relative Killed in Three Weeks," *Times-Picayune*, September 9, 2002; Tara Young, "Turf War Rises Out of Ashes of St. Thomas, Trapping Family," *Times-Picayune*, February 9, 2004; Brittany Libson, "River Garden: New Orleans' Model for Mixed-Income Housing?," *Social Policy* 37, nos. 3–4 (2007): 101.

59. Data compiled from HANO, "St. Thomas Relocation Report as of 1/29/01 for Phases 1, 2, and 3," Hope House files.

60. HANO, "St. Thomas Relocation Report."

61. Susan Finch, "Suit Targets HANO Utility Subsidy," *Times-Picayune*, May 15, 2001.

62. Stevens quoted in Rhonda Bell, "Apartments Scarce for Section 8 Renters: Displaced Residents Need Homes," *Times-Picayune*, June 6, 2000; Bell, "Housing Vouchers Are No Guarantee," *Times-Picayune*, October 26, 2000.

63. Sheila Stroup, "Images Show Life before Demolition," *Times-Picayune*, July 11, 2002; Stroup, "'I Love the People of St. Thomas,'" *Times-Picayune*, April 15, 2004.

64. Don Everard, "A Team Effort at St. Thomas," *Times-Picayune*, July 17, 2001.

65. Email correspondence from Don Everard to Lolis Elie, *Times-Picayune*, January 2, 2001, Hope House files.

66. Kabacoff quoted in Lisa Selin Davis, "New Orleans Faces Off with Wal-Mart," *Preservation*, March 19, 2004, http://www.preservationnation.org/magazine/story-of-the-week/2004/new-orleans-faces-off-with.html.

67. HRI and HANO, "St. Thomas Revitalization Plan," January 2000, executive summary, 7.

68. Don Everard, "Some Notes Concerning the Planned Revitalization of St. Thomas," n.d. (but likely 2001), Hope House files.

69. HRI and HANO, "St Thomas Revitalization Plan," January 2000, 6.

70. HRI and HANO, "Revitalization Plan Cover Sheet," July 2000.

71. Bagert, "HOPE VI," 24.

72. Shelia Danzey quoted in Stephen Stuart, "Residents Anxious over Revamp of St. Thomas," *New Orleans City Business* 21, no. 26 (December 25, 2000): 4.

73. HANO, "St. Thomas Relocation Report."

74. HRI and HANO, "St. Thomas Revitalization Plan, Unit Mix Summary Assumptions—Preliminary: For Discussion Only," July 2000.

75. Memo from Tom Crumley, HRI to HANO, STRC, and HUD, "St. Thomas Redevelopment HOPE VI Status Report and Commitment List," June 13, 2000, Hope House files.

76. Don Everard, memo for Hope House files, June 23, 2000.

77. Letter from Barbara Jackson (STRC) to Pres Kabacoff (HRI) and Benjamin Bell (HANO), December 13, 2000, Hope House files.

78. Jackson and Nicotera quoted in Rhonda Bell, "A Complex Undertaking," *Times-Picayune*, October 26, 2000.

79. HRI, "Request for Qualifications for the Housing Authority of New Orleans Development Partner for the St. Thomas HOPE VI Off-Site Housing Program," March 9, 2003, 3.

80. Interview with Kabacoff.

81. Don Everard, "St Thomas HOPE VI Revitalization, Proposal Concerning Income-Tiering for Placement in On-Site Public Housing Units," October 19, 2001, Hope House files.

82. Memo from Don Everard to Individuals and Groups Involved in the St. Thomas HOPE VI Revitalization, "Why Income-Tiering Is Inappropriate and Unjust," September 19, 2001.

83. Letter from Barbara Jackson (STRC) to Pres Kabacoff (HRI) and Benjamin Bell (HANO), May 26, 2000, Hope House files.

84. Burns and Thomas, *Reforming New Orleans*, 111-12.

85. Bruce Eggler, "Residents Break Off Talks with Developer," *Times-Picayune*, September 5, 2001.

86. Lili LeGardeur, "Law Clinic Director Says Bye to N.O," September 24, 2001.

87. "Based on New Study of St. Thomas HOPE VI Plans, Former Residents Considering Lawsuit," press release, September 30, 2002.

88. Bruce Eggler, "St. Thomas Revamp Shorts Poor, Foes Say," *Times-Picayune*, October 1, 2002; Eggler, "Developer Defends Wal-Mart Plan," *Times-Picayune*, October 16, 2002.

89. Bagert, "HOPE VI," 1-2, 27, 29, 31. Bagert reports (p. 26n) that, when he asked HANO officials to see a copy of the original HOPE VI application in 2002, he was assured that the current plans were "identical"; after searching for three hours, however, HANO was unable to find a copy of the original, indicating "just how closely they had been following its stipulations."

90. Eggler, "Developer Defends Wal-Mart Plan."

91. Kabacoff quoted in Eileen Loh Harrist, "The Challenger," *The Gambit*, December 3, 2002, http://www.bestofneworleans.com/gambit/the-challenger/Content?oid=1240950.

92. Interview with Kabacoff.

93. Kabacoff quoted in Harrist, "The Challenger."

94. Interview with Kabacoff.

95. Interview with Kabacoff.

96. Kabacoff quoted in Greg Thomas and Robert Scott, "Wal-Mart May Build Supercenter Uptown," *Times-Picayune*, July 21, 2001.

97. Kabacoff quoted in Bruce Eggler, "Panel Postpones Taking Vote on Parking Lot Plan; Proposal Would Save 4 Buildings," *Times-Picayune*, August 15, 2001.

98. The Coliseum Square group had been established in 1972 to fight against a proposed new Mississippi River bridge that would have impacted the neighborhood; Joan Treadway, "Lower Garden Variety Tackles Issues Together," *Times-Picayune*, November 15, 1993.

99. Arena, *Driven from New Orleans*, 140.

100. Interview with Kabacoff.

101. James R. Elliott, Kevin Fox Gotham, and Melinda J. Milligan, "Framing the Urban: Struggles over HOPE VI and New Urbanism in a Historic City," *City & Community* 3, no. 4 (2004): 383.

102. Bruce Eggler, "Breaking New Ground," *Times-Picayune*, October 14, 2001.

103. Interview with Kabacoff.

104. Bruce Eggler, "Project's Developer Is Having a Rough Month," September 10, 2001.

105. Kabacoff quoted in Elizabeth Mullener, "Thinking Outside the Big Box," *Times-Picayune*, June 9, 2002. Chicago developers also faced this challenge of needing subsidies to build market-rate units in high-poverty neighborhoods; Chaskin and Joseph, *Integrating the Inner City*, 91, 105.

106. Bruce Eggler, "Wal-Mart War Winding into Home Stretch." *Times-Picayune*, December 17, 2001.

107. Tony Gelderman, "This Giant Will Suck Small Businesses Dry," op-ed, *Times-Picayune*, November 10, 2001.

108. Kabacoff, "Weighing the Impact of a Wal-Mart," op-ed, *Times-Picayune*, November 10, 2001.

109. Galatas quoted in Bruce Eggler, "Cries of Racism Enter Debate over Wal-Mart," *Times-Picayune*, November 13, 2001.

110. Galatas and Kabacoff quoted in Eggler, "Wal-Mart Developer Denies Impropriety," *Times-Picayune*, May 1, 2002.

111. Email correspondence from Don Everard to Lolis Elie, *Times-Picayune*, January 2, 2001, Hope House files.

112. Elliott, Gotham, and Milligan, "Framing the Urban," 391.

113. Kabacoff quoted in Mullener, "Thinking outside the Big Box."

114. Patricia Gay, "There Are Alternatives to a Super Wal-Mart," *Preservation in Print*, October 2001, 22.

115. Eggler, "Panel Postpones Taking Vote."

116. Kabacoff and Balart quoted in Greg Thomas, "Parking Lot Reduced to Save Historic Site," *Times-Picayune*, September 11, 2001. Once it became clear that the Walmart and new housing would go forward, HRI dropped the plan for an adaptive reuse of the Amelia/Kupperman property. Kabacoff sold the buildings to businessman-developer Kevin Kelly in 2002, who said he planned to store metals in them; Bruce Eggler, "Building on St. Thomas Site Set to Begin," December 21, 2002.

117. Bruce Eggler, "Vote Expected Today on Wal-Mart Plan," *Times-Picayune*, October 17, 2002; Kabacoff and his letter quoted in Eggler, "St. Thomas Plans Again on Agenda," *Times-Picayune*, November 22, 2002; Bruce Eggler, "Panel Faults Pace of St. Thomas Project," February 12, 2003.

118. Bagert quoted in Bruce Eggler, "N.O. Council OKs Financing for St. Thomas Complex," *Times-Picayune*, November 23, 2002.

119. Kabacoff quoted in Eggler, "N.O. Council Oks Financing."

120. Kabacoff quoted in Harrist, "The Challenger."

121. Kabacoff and Bagert quoted in Harrist, "The Challenger."

122. Greg Thomas, "Comply and Conquer: Retail Giant Wal-Mart Shows Willingness to Adjust to Strictures of Urban Setting," *Times-Picayune*, March 5, 2004.

123. Bruce Eggler, "Wal-Mart at St. Thomas Opens with Second-Line," *Times-Picayune*, August 26, 2004.

124. Bruce Eggler, "Wal-Mart Foes Try Again to Stop Construction," *Times-Picayune*, December 27, 2003; Eggler, "City Council Defers Action on Wal-Mart for 2 Weeks," *Times-Picayune*, October 18, 2002; Eggler, "Legality of Wal-Mart Tax Deal Debated," *Times-Picayune*, January 3, 2003; Lynne Jensen, "Expert Delved into N.O. History," *Times-Picayune*, October 4, 2004.

125. Rhonda Bell, "St. Thomas Families Get Latest on Revamp," *Times-Picayune*, March 14, 2001; Letter from HRI to HANO Executive Director Benjamin Bell, January 18, 2001, Hope House files.

126. Letter from Shelia Danzey, HRI to STRC President Barbara Jackson, April 3, 2000, Hope House St. Thomas files.

127. HRI and STICC, "Community and Supportive Services Program Agreement," September 28, 2000, Hope House files.

128. Shelia Danzey, HRI Development Project Manager, Letter to Tammi Fleming and Bro. Don Everard, Co-chairmen, STICC, November 21, 2001; Letter from Danzey

to Fleming and Everard, April 19, 2001; HRI, "St. Thomas Community and Supportive Services Program Evaluation," May 9, 2001.

129. Barbara Jackson and Donald Everard, Letter to Pres Kabacoff, July 26, 2001, Hope House files; Matt O'Connor, "Ex-CHA Gets Prison: Lane Sentenced to 2½ Years in Loan Fraud Case," *Chicago Tribune*, August 29, 2001.

130. HRI, "Steering Committee Minutes," October 11, 2001, and November 8, 2001, Hope House files.

131. Danzey quoted in Lolis Eric Elie, "The Lost Residents of St. Thomas," op-ed, *Times-Picayune*, January 2, 2002.

132. Email correspondence from Don Everard to Lolis Elie, *Times-Picayune*, January 2, 2001, Hope House files.

133. Memo from Don Everard to Shelia Danzey, January 30, 2002; Letter from Shelia Danzey to Don Everard, February 1, 2002; Letter from Don Everard to Shelia Danzey, February 5, 2002, Hope House files; Shelia Danzey, "Consortium's Efforts Fell Short, HRI Says," Letter, *Times-Picayune*, January 15, 2002.

134. Arena, *Driven from New Orleans*, 130.

135. Fair Housing Complaint, Greater New Orleans Fair Housing Action Center, December 16, 2002, Hope House files.

136. Stacy Seicshnaydre, "St. Thomas Will Be Fair," *Times-Picayune*, January 22, 2004; National Fair Housing Advocate Online, "N.O. Housing Authority, Fair Housing Group, Settle Fair Housing Complaint," press release, October 10, 2003.

137. Gordon Russell, "Wal-Mart Opponents Gain Some Grist By DEQ Finding," *Times-Picayune*, September 3, 2003.

138. White quoted in Walter Gabriel Jr., "Developer Blamed for Homes Flooding," *Times-Picayune*, June 4, 2004; White and Kabacoff quoted in Gordon Russell, "St. Thomas Neighbors Appeal to HANO," *Times-Picayune*, June 25, 2004.

139. April Yee, "Scars of Renewal," *Times-Picayune*, June 27, 2005; Letter from Concerned Citizens for St. Thomas to Oliver Thomas (president, New Orleans City Council) and Renee Gill-Pratt (local council member), June 6, 2005; Letter from Nadine M. Jarmon, HANO Administrative Receiver to Pres Kabacoff, HRI, "Re: Concerned Neighbors of St. Thomas," April 28, 2005, Hope House files.

140. Boettner quoted in Bruce Eggler, "Ex-St. Thomas Site to Be River Garden," *Times-Picayune*, November 19, 2003.

CHAPTER 5

1. Elizabeth Mullener, "Transformation," *Times-Picayune*, March 13, 2005.

2. HRI Properties, River Garden Apartments brochure, as of 2010.

3. "River Garden Development Celebrates Grand Opening," *Hope House Journal*, Winter 2004, 1, Hope House files.

4. Abbenante quoted in Mullener, "Transformation."

5. Interview with David Abbenante, April 2010.

6. Jarmon quoted in Gwen Filosa, "Housing Blunders Admitted: Tenants, Families Were Hurt by Ousters," *Times-Picayune*, June 30, 2005.

7. Mullener, "Transformation."

8. Gwen Filosa, "HANO Says It Has No Plans to Demolish Iberville Complex," *Times-Picayune*, July 1, 2005.

9. Interview with Abbenante.

10. Liu quoted in Leslie Williams, "Home, Sweet Home," *Times-Picayune*, November 17, 2004.

11. Bruce Eggler, "St. Thomas Housing Design Deal in Works," *Times-Picayune*, February 11, 2004.

12. Everard quoted in Brian Thevenot, "Land Use Debate Recalls St. Thomas Controversy," *Times-Picayune*, March 19, 2006.

13. Bill Quigley, "Comments," C3 NOLA website, September 11, 2005, http://www.c3nola.org/node/61.

14. Bill Walsh, "Official Blunt on Public Housing," *Times-Picayune*, April 25, 2006; Libson, "River Garden," 102.

15. Interview with Pres Kabacoff, April 2010.

16. Gwen Filosa, "Tenant Admitted to River Garden after Suing," *Times-Picayune*, December 7, 2006.

17. Susan Finch, "Plan for Resettling Public Housing Residents OK'd," *Times-Picayune*, July 10, 2007.

18. Finch, "Plan for Resettling"; Gwen Filosa, "HANO Residents Ask U.S. Judge to Block Demolition," *Times-Picayune*, November 3, 2007; Gwen Filosa, "Housing Authority Told to Return St. Thomas Families," *Times-Picayune*, November 14, 2007; Filosa, "HANO Delivers List of Residents," November 15, 2007.

19. Libson, "River Garden," 101-2.

20. Abbenante quoted in Filosa, "HANO Delivers List of Residents."

21. HRI, "Request for Qualifications for the Housing Authority of New Orleans Development Partner for the St. Thomas HOPE VI Off-Site Housing Program," March 9, 2003, 3-8; HRI, "Report on the Progress of the St. Thomas Development," updates for March 7, 2000, May 2, June 6, August 1, October 5, December 5, 2003; HRI, "Report on the Progress of River Garden Development," April 2, 2004, Hope House files. In addition to the ninety off-site rental units proposed to be developed by OMP, ten units were previously allocated for development by Shedo, LLC, a firm co-owned by HRI consultant Shelia Danzey.

22. HRI, "Report on the Progress of River Garden Development," March 20, 2007.

23. HUD, "HOPE VI Revitalization Grant Program: Phase Narrative Report," quarterly reports as of the fourth quarter 2014.

24. Interview with Kabacoff.

25. Ragas quoted in Mullener, "Transformation"; Greg Thomas, "Condominiums Planned for Abandoned Hospital: Home Values Are Increasing in Irish Channel," *Times-Picayune*, September 19, 2006.

26. Greg Thomas, "New Phase to Start in June at Former St. Thomas Site," *Times-Picayune*, March 30, 2005; Thomas, "Homes Planned Near CBD," March 23, 2006.

27. HRI and HANO, "St Thomas Revitalization Plan," January 2000, 22.

28. Interview with Michael Kelly, March 2009.

29. Gallas quoted in Molly Reid, "St. Thomas Reborn in River Garden," November 2, 2007.

30. Letter from Laura Tuggle, New Orleans Legal Assistance to Barbara Jackson, STRC and Don Everard, Hope House, "Re: Follow Up from Meeting with HANO about Concerns at River Garden and Request for Information on CSSP," March 7, 2008, plus notes from River Garden tenants, Hope House files; HRI Properties, "Residential

Lease Agreement and House Rules," River Garden Community Service Requirement Procedures, 40–42, 2004.

31. Interview with Abbenante.

32. Interview with Don Gault, April 2010.

33. Interview with Gault. The "Bout It" name is a reference to a 1997 film, *I'm Bout It*, made by New Orleans rapper Master P, and is variously defined to mean "down for whatever," "all about the 'hood," or "generally better or more 'all about' whatever is being compared," http://www.urbandictionary.com/define.php?term=bout%20it.

34. Interview with Abbenante.

35. Kelly D. Owens, "The Social Construction of a Public/Private Neighborhood: Examining Neighbor Interaction and Neighborhood Meaning in a New Orleans Mixed-Income Development," PhD diss., University of New Orleans, 2012.

36. Owens, "Social Construction," xiii, 2.

37. Owens, "Social Construction," 162–63. This practice is confirmed in Mullener, "Transformation." Some managers of mixed-income developments in Chicago also did not choose to reveal the fact of this mix; Chaskin and Joseph, *Integrating the Inner City*, 99.

38. Owens, "Social Construction," 139–40.

39. Owens, "Social Construction," 138, 156.

40. Owens, "Social Construction," 87, 90.

41. Owens, "Social Construction," 44, 77 n. 18.

42. Chaskin and Joseph, *Integrating the Inner City*, 171.

43. Owens, "Social Construction," 93, 103.

44. Interview with Barbara Jackson conducted by Annemarie Gray, January 2013.

45. Interview with Ronald McCoy conducted by Annemarie Gray, January 2013.

46. Interview with Jackson.

47. Owens, "Social Construction," 95–98, 146.

48. Richard A. Webster, "River Garden Residents March in Protest, Management Pushes Back," *Times-Picayune*, January 24, 2013; Jarvis DeBerry, "River Garden Manager Appears to Be Too Trusting of the New Orleans Police," *Times-Picayune*, February 15, 2013.

49. Everard quoted in Webster, "River Garden Residents March."

50. Interview with Jackson.

51. Interview with McCoy.

52. Abbenante quoted in Webster, "River Garden Residents March."

53. McCurdy quoted in Webster, "River Garden Residents March."

54. Abbenante quoted in Webster, "River Garden Residents March." Additional information about the protest comes from my research assistant Annemarie Gray, who observed and photographed the event.

55. Personal communication with Don Everard, March 2017.

56. Kabacoff quoted in DeBerry, "River Garden Manager." In 2016, Kabacoff stepped back from his role as HRI's CEO, but remains chairman of the board.

57. Interview with Kabacoff.

58. Interview with Kelly.

59. Burns and Thomas, *Reforming New Orleans*, 123.

60. Jennifer Duell Popovec, "Five Years after the Storm, Affordable Housing Scarce in Post-Katrina New Orleans," September 1, 2010, *GlobeSt.com*; Richard A. Webster, "New Orleans Public Housing Remade after Katrina: Is It Working?" *Times-Picayune*, August 20, 2015.

61. Jackson and Tuggle quoted in Walsh, "Official Blunt on Public Housing."

62. Baker quoted in John Harwood, "Louisiana Lawmakers Aim to Cope with Political Fallout," *Wall Street Journal*, September 9, 2005. The comment, said to be something overheard in Baker's conversation with lobbyists, became widely disseminated in other media. Baker regretted the flippancy and insisted he had long supported efforts to improve low-income housing in New Orleans.

63. Martin Savidge, "What's Next for Public Housing in New Orleans," *NBC Nightly News with Brian Williams*, February 21, 2006, http://www.nbcnews.com/id/11485681#.V31pJ1ceioJ.

64. Jackson quoted in Walsh, "Official Blunt on Public Housing."

65. Bill Quigley, "Bulldozing New Orleans," *blackagendareport.com*, January 3, 2007; Fernandez quoted in Quigley.

66. Roberta Brandes Gratz, *We're Still Here Ya Bastards* (New York: Nation Books, 2015), 282.

67. Katy Reckdahl, "Housing Authority's Turnaround Team Gets Three-Year Contract," *Times-Picayune*, July 16, 2010; Richard A. Webster, "HANO's David Gilmore to Step Down Tuesday," *Times-Picayune*, April 7, 2014.

68. Katy Reckdahl, "The Long Road from C.J. Peete to Harmony Oaks," *Shelterforce*, Spring 2013, http://www.harmonyoaksapts.com/brochure.aspx; Gilmore quoted in Pam Fessler, "New Orleans' Public Housing Slowly Evolving," *NPR Weekend Sunday Edition*, August 29, 2010; Reckdahl, "New C.J. Peete Complex is Solid, Shiny—but Not as Social, Some Residents Say," *Times-Picayune*, August 21, 2011.

69. Katy Reckdahl, "HANO to Remove Tons of Contaminated Dirt from Former B.W. Cooper Cite," *Times-Picayune*, November 25, 2011; Katy Reckdahl, "B.W. Cooper Housing Site's Slow March to Rebirth Reaches Finish Fine," *Times-Picayune*, May 5, 2012.

70. http://columbiaparc.com//st-bernard/faq.php; Colombia Parc print brochure, as of April 2010; "Columbia Parc Apartments in Gentilly to Open Waiting List for Renters," *Times-Picayune*, September 6, 2011.

71. Richard Webster, "Columbia Parc in New Orleans is Showcased as National Mixed-Income Housing Model," *Times-Picayune*, October 3, 2013.

72. Martha Carr, "HUD Secretary in Town to Christen First Phase of Lafitte Redevelopment," *Times-Picayune*, February 4, 2011; Katy Reckdahl, "HANO Set to Approve Faubourg Lafitte Market Rate Rentals," *Times-Picayune*, September 18, 2012, http://faubourglafitte.com/about/about-faubourg-lafitte/; Greg LaRose, "Faubourg Lafitte Adding Affordable Housing Units with Grant Awards," NOLA.com, April 6 2018; http://realestate.nola.com/realestate-news/2018/04/faubourg_lafitte_adding_afford.html.

73. Nicolai Ouroussoff, "To Renovate, and Surpass, a City's Legacy," *New York Times*, April 6, 2011.

74. For an interactive graphic showing New Orleans public housing changes as of 2015, see http://www.nola.com/katrina/index.ssf/2015/08/housing_developments_then_now.html#incart_article_small.

75. Webster, "New Orleans Public Housing Remade"; Chevel Johnson, "Low-Income Residents Losing Homes as New Orleans Rents Soar," Associated Press, June 29, 2017; Jessica Williams, "HANO Balances $194 Million Budget with Surplus Money, Position Cuts," *New Orleans Advocate*, September 14, 2017.

76. Interview with Kabacoff.

77. Interview with Brother Don Everard conducted by Annemarie Gray, January 2013.

78. Interview with Kelly.

79. Interview with Jackson.

80. Quigley, "Comments."

PART III

1. Alexander von Hoffman, *House by House, Block by Block* (New York: Oxford University Press, 2003), 93–94.

CHAPTER 6

1. Boston Housing Authority, *Annual Report of the Boston Housing Authority, 1944-1945*, 4–5.

2. City of Boston, *Report on Real Property Inventory* (1935), Census Tracts Q-2 and Q-3; "Police, Firemen Patrol Roxbury Housing Project," *Boston Globe*, June 17, 1941, 26.

3. Vale, *Puritans to the Projects*, chapter 3. Displacement estimated from household data reported in City of Boston, *List of Residents 20 Years of Age and Over* (aka "Boston Police Lists") (City of Boston Printing Department, 1941, and 1945), Ward 8, precincts 6, 7, and 14.

4. "Announce Low Cost Housing Rentals Here," *Jamaica Plain Citizen*, August 8, 1940; "New Housing Project Asks Applications," *Jamaica Plain Citizen*, October 8, 1942; "Low Income Families Will Be Allowed in War Housing Units," *Boston Globe*, October 16, 1942; Boston Housing Authority, legal document specifying eminent domain takings for "Project Mass. 2-5-R," December 18, 1940; "New Housing Will Be Available to War Workers," *Globe*, January 23, 1942; "Public Housing Units Now Open to Servicemen," *Globe*, February 18, 1944; Boston Housing Authority, "Resolution Establishing Policies Relating to the Granting of Preference to Families of Defense Workers," April, 1, 1942; BHA, "Average Annual Estimate of Income and Expense, Mass. 2-5," Boston Housing Authority archives; City of Boston, *List of Residents 20 Years of Age and Over* for 1940, 1941, 1942, 1943, 1944, and 1945, Ward 8, precincts 6, 7, 8, 14, and 15.

5. Boston Housing Authority, *Review of the Activities of the Boston Housing Authority, 1936-1940*, 1941.

6. Interview with Edna Bynoe conducted by Kim Alleyne, October 2005; John Carter, "Distributional Patterns in Boston Public Housing," unpublished master's thesis, Boston University, 1958, 69–79.

7. Christopher Marshall, "Boston's Vanished New York Streets," *Globe*, August 19, 2012.

8. Mel King, "Community Activist Mel King Questions New Luxury Development at Former Boston Herald Site," *Bay State Banner*, June 19, 2013. See also Mel King, *Chain of Change* (Boston: South End Press, 1981), 20–23.

9. Herbert Gans, *The Urban Villagers* (New York: Free Press, 1962), 16; Marc Fried, "Grieving for a Lost Home," in Leonard Duhl, ed., *The Urban Condition* (New York: Basic Books, 1962); Robert Hanron, "West End Project Could Be Spark to Revitalize Boston," *Globe*, December 20, 1959.

10. Thomas H. O'Connor, *Building a New Boston* (Boston: Northeastern University Press, 1993), 126, 137.

11. O'Connor, *Building a New Boston*, 288; Lawrence W. Kennedy, *Planning the City upon a Hill* (Amherst: University of Massachusetts Press, 1994), 162-66.

12. Douglas Rae, *City: Urbanism and Its End* (New Haven: Yale University Press, 2003), 324, 330-39.

13. John F. Collins, "The 90 Million Dollar Development Program for Boston," *Boston City Record*, September 24, 1960.

14. Walter McQuade, "Boston: What Can a Sick City Do?," *Fortune* 69, no. 6 (June 1964): 132-34; Langley Keyes, *The Rehabilitation Planning Game* (Cambridge, MA: MIT Press, 1969), 22, 31; Anthony Yudis, "Housing Rehabilitation Called 'New Frontier' of Renewal," *Globe*, June 28, 1970.

15. Keyes, *The Rehabilitation Planning Game*, 226-27.

16. Kennedy, *Planning the City*, 187; Anthony Yudis, "Renewal Project Goes over Big with Roxbury; Logue Cheered," *Globe*, January 15, 1963.

17. Anthony Yudis, "Housing Program Assailed," *Globe*, November 29, 1963; Keyes, *The Rehabilitation Planning Game*, 199-201.

18. Peter Medoff and Holly Sklar, *Streets of Hope* (Boston: South End Press, 1994), 18.

19. "Blacks Run Again" quoted in King, *Chain of Change*, 68; Anthony J. Yudis, "Do Displaced Get Housing?" *Globe*, November 18, 1963.

20. "[Confidential] Memo to Mayor, with Copies to Ellis Ash and BHA Board from Robert Drinan and the Advisory Committee on Minority Housing," March 5, 1964, John Collins Papers, Box 244; Boston Public Library.

21. Julius Bernstein and Chester Hartman, "Must There Be Two Cities?," letter to the editor, *Globe*, June 1, 1966.

22. Edward Logue, "The Urban Crisis II," *Globe*, February 3, 1969.

23. Anthony Yudis, "Madison Park People Ready for Hearings," *Globe*, November 13, 1966; Elliot Friedman, "Madison Park Renewal Plan Approved," *Globe*, December 29, 1966; Anthony Yudis, "U.S. Aids Hub Campus High," *Globe*, January 9, 1969; "Campus High School Renewal Plan Advances," *Boston Globe*, May 26, 1971.

24. Haynes quoted in Charles Radin, "Roxbury's Quiet Hero," *Globe*, January 14, 1999; http://www.madison-park.org/who-we-are/history/; King, *Chain of Change*, 204-5.

25. King quoted in Jim Vrabel, *A People's History of the New Boston* (Amherst: University of Massachusetts Press, 2014), 111.

26. Vrabel, *People's History*, 19.

27. White quoted in Vrabel, *People's History*, 89.

28. O'Connor, *Building a New Boston*, 268.

29. Sharratt and King quoted in Vrabel, *People's History*, 122, 92.

30. O'Connor, *Building a New Boston*, 295-96.

31. J. Anthony Lukas, *Common Ground* (New York: Vintage, 1986), 60-61; O'Connor, *Building a New Boston*, 215.

32. Anthony Yudis, "Wood Study Finds Downward Trend in Tenant Incomes," *Boston Globe*, January 30, 1963; Wood quoted in Vale, *Puritans to the Projects*, 246, 282–85, 324.

33. Vale, *Puritans to the Projects*, 321–22; Orchard Park Tenants, "Petition to the Boston Housing Authority," June 12, 1964, BHA Central Administrative Files; BHA, "Responses to Recommendations Made By the Advisory Committee," February 3, 1965; BHA Advisory Committee, "Report of Subcommittee to Analyze Responses to Recommendations of the Advisory Committee," July 22, 1965, 3.

34. Judson B. Brown, "Project Blacks Demand Jobs," *Globe*, July 11, 1968; Karilyn Crockett, "'People before Highways': Reconsidering Routes to and from the Boston Anti-highway Movement," PhD diss., Yale University, 2013, 41.

35. Wise quoted in "Teenage Recreation," editorial, *Globe*, August 8, 1967.

36. Kennedy, *Planning the City*, 198.

37. Vrabel, *People's History*, 145.

38. Kennedy, *Planning the City*, 199.

39. Alan Lupo, Frank Colcord, and Edmund Fowler, *Rites of Way* (Boston: Little, Brown, 1971), 163.

40. Crockett, "People before Highways," 9, 10, 31. The dissertation has subsequently been adapted into a book: *People before Highways: Boston Activists, Urban Planners, and a New Movement for City Making* (Amherst: University of Massachusetts Press, 2018).

41. Crockett, "People before Highways," 44.

42. Francis Sargent, Transcript of WHDH Television Broadcast, February 11, 1970, quoted in Crockett, "People before Highways," 138.

43. Lupo, Colcord, and Fowler, *Rites of Way*, 106–7, 111.

44. Francis Sargent, WCVB-TV Broadcast, November 30, 1972, quoted in Crockett, "People before Highways," 177.

45. Crockett, "People before Highways," 208.

46. Sean Zielenbach, "Catalyzing Community Development: HOPE VI and Neighborhood Revitalization," *Journal of Affordable Housing & Community Development Law* 13, no. 2 (2003): 56.

47. Lewis, *Divided Highways*, 192; interview with Russell Tanner, February 2017; Paul Grogan and Tony Proscio, "Our Other Renaissance," op-ed, *Globe*, January 7, 2001.

48. May Boulter Hipshman, "Public Housing in Boston: Changing Needs and Role," master's thesis, MIT, 1967, 35–40; Vale, *Puritans to the Projects*, 307–15.

49. Vale, *Puritans to the Projects*, 308–10; interview with Ellis Ash, May 1997; Victor Bynoe, "[Confidential] Letter to John Collins," March 13, 1964, John Collins Papers, Box 244.

50. Ash quoted in Laura Griffin, "Tenants Get Voice," *Globe*, February 18, 1968.

51. "Jacob Brier Chairman, BHA Votes," *Globe*, February 29, 1968; Janet Riddell, "1st Tenants Up for BHA, Both Doers," *Globe*, February 3, 1969.

52. Ash quoted in "Ash Resigns from BHA," *Bay State Banner*, June 26, 1969; Ash quoted in Judson Brows, "Ash Leaving 40,000 Friends Behind," *Globe*, June 22, 1969; Bunte quoted in Alan Lupo, "BHA Majority 3-2 in Hands of Tenants," *Globe*, July 31, 1969; Danice Bordett, "Mrs. Bunte Speaks on BHA Role," *Bay State Banner*, August 14, 1969; John Plunkett, "Tenants Gain Power with BHA," *Globe*, January 11, 1970.

53. "New BHA Board Meets," *Bay State Banner*, September 25, 1969; Janet Riddell, "Boston Housing Authority: Running Hard to Stay Even," *Globe*, May 31, 1970; Fred Pillsbury, "Firing of Finn from BHA Political Setback for White," *Globe*, January 24, 1971.

54. Robert Jordan, "Finn, Fired by BHA, Charges 'Pure Act of Retribution,'" *Globe*, January 23, 1971; Fred Pillsbury, "Mayor Levels Charges against Another BHA Member," *Globe*, March 30, 1971; Ann Mary Currier, "Mrs. Bunte Refuses Mayor 'as Judge,'" *Globe*, April 13, 1971; Julius Bernstein, Doris Bunte, and John Connolly, "A Statement of Objectives," included in CHAPA et al., *A Struggle for Survival: The Boston Housing Authority, 1969-1973* (Boston: Citizens Housing and Planning Association, 1973), appendix B, p. 3; David Wilson, "If He Ousts Mrs. Bunte, White Could Still Lose," op-ed, *Globe*, May 1, 1971; "BHA Votes Anew on Model Lease," *Bay State Banner*, November 4, 1971.

55. Christopher Wallace, "White Finds Mrs. Bunte Guilty, Demands Ouster," *Globe*, June 19, 1971; "Mayor White's Hatchet Falls," editorial, *Globe*, June 23, 1971; Atkins quoted in S. T. Curwood, "Council Vote on Bunte Set July 12," *Bay State Banner*, June 24, 1971; Robert Jordan, "Council Votes, 5-4, to Oust Mrs. Bunte from BHA," *Globe*, July 13, 1971; Robert Jordan, "BHA Chief Charges 'Political Pressure' by White," *Globe*, July 30, 1971; Joseph Harvey, "Mrs. Bunte's Reinstatement to BHA Upheld," *Globe*, February 8, 1972; Bunte quoted in Maria Karagiansi, "Doris Bunte— the Pain and Triumph," *Globe*, February 16, 1974.

56. Robert Jordan, "White Expected to Act on Appointments Giving Him BHA Control," *Globe*, April 2, 1973; "Public Housing Tenants Ask for BHA Seat," *Globe*, February 12, 1977.

57. Interview with Bill McGonagle, August 2014.

58. Lukas, *Common Ground*, 210.

59. Richard H. Stewart, "Brooke's Amendment Opens Public Housing to the Very Poor," *Globe*, September 28, 1969; "Public Housing in Trouble," *Globe*, October 19, 1969; Eugene Meyer, "Poor Left Out of Many Housing Programs," *Globe*, December 17, 1972.

60. "Tenants Council Sues HUD, BHA," *Bay State Banner*, November 26, 1970; Vale, *Puritans to the Projects*, 338–65.

61. Robert B. Whittlesey, *Social Housing Found* (Bloomington, IN: AuthorHouse, 2016), 173.

62. Paul Garrity, "Opinion," in *Armando Perez et al., vs. Boston Housing Authority*, "Findings, Rulings, Opinion, and Orders," Commonwealth of Massachusetts Superior Court, Civil Action No. 17222 (1979), 102–3.

63. Paul Garrity, "Memorandum of Recorded Observations at the Orchard Park and Mission Hill Extension Developments during the View on May 8, 1979," *Perez* case, Appendix 3, 147–51.

64. BHA, "Orchard Park 2-5," 23 October 1979, 3, 7, 8, 11; BHA Project Files.

65. Zielenbach, "Catalyzing Community Development," 60.

66. Jerry Taylor, "BHA Threatened with Receivership," *Globe*, June 15, 1979; "An Admission of Failure," editorial, *Globe*, June 27, 1979; "Rebuilding Public Housing," editorial, *Globe*, July 27, 1979.

67. White quoted in Whittlesey, *Social Housing Found*, 190; Mac Margolis, "High Court Holds Fast," *Bay State Banner*, February 7, 1980; Bernard Cohen, "Is Harry Spence God? Or Is He Just Damn Good?," *Boston Magazine*, December 1981.

68. Harris quoted in James Stack and Jerry Taylor, "Project Tenants Praise BHA Receivership Order," *Globe*, July 27, 1979.

69. Lewis Spence, "The Plight of Public Housing," speech to the United Community Planning Corporation, April 23, 1980.

70. BHA, "Occupancy Analysis by Development Classification," 1979.

71. Vale, *Puritans to the Projects*, 357–61.

72. Spence quoted in Norman Boucher, "People Live Here, Too," *Globe Magazine*, March 12, 1989.

73. King quoted in Vrabel, *People's History*, 210.

74. Vrabel, *People's History*, 213.

75. Pierre Clavel, *Activists in City Hall* (Ithaca, NY: Cornell University Press, 2013), 68.

76. Medoff & Sklar, *Streets of Hope*, 38, 51, 104.

77. Sara Terry, "Urban Self-Renewal," *Globe*, May 12, 1996; "New Homes for Old," editorial, *Globe*, April 5, 1996; Zielenbach, "Catalyzing Community Development," 65–66.

78. Clavel, *Activists in City Hall*, 82–83.

79. Clavel, *Activists in City Hall*, 81–82; Ed Quill, "HUD Study Puts Mandela in Red," *Globe*, October 4, 1986; Charles Kenney, "The Aftershock of a Radical Notion," *Globe Magazine*, April 12, 1987.

80. Medoff and Sklar, *Streets of Hope*, 132; Joanne Ball, "For Many, Mandela Bid Lacks Fire of '86," *Globe*, October 5, 1988; Kevin Cullen, "Hub Voters Again Defeat Mandela Question," *Globe*, November 9, 1988.

81. "Findings, Rulings, and Orders," *Perez et al. v. Boston Housing Authority*, October 18, 1984, 1.

82. Kirk Scharfenberg, "Bold Choice for BHA," op-ed, *Globe*, October 20, 1984; Joanne Ball, "Bunte: From Public Housing Tenant to Public Housing Administrator," *Globe*, October 27, 1984.

83. Bonnie V. Winston, "Nine-Member Board Created to Monitor BHA," *Globe*, April 13, 1986; https://malegislature.gov/Laws/SessionLaws/Acts/2013/Chapter139; https://www.bostonhousing.org/en/Center-for-Community-Engagement/Resident-Empowerment/Monitoring-Committee.aspx.

84. Peter Canellos, "City Warns the BHA Over Orchard Park," *Globe*, September 13, 1990; Peter Canellos, "BHA Head Gets Support," *Globe*, October 16, 1990; Peter Canellos, "HUD to Keep BHA on 'Troubled' List," *Globe*, November 8, 1990.

85. Peter S. Canellos, "For BHA's Bunte, New Troubles Echo the Past," *Globe*, February 7, 1991; Matthew Brelis, "Bunte Gets Backing from Roxbury Leaders," *Globe*, April 17, 1991; Peter Canellos, "HUD Aide, in Visit, Hits BHA Finances," *Globe*, August 1, 1991; Michael Rezendes and Peter Canellos, "Bunte, Embattled Chief of BHA, Quitting Post," *Globe*, November 7, 1991; Peter Canellos, "At Housing Authority, Legacy of Improvements and Problems," *Globe*, November 7, 1991; Peter Canellos, "Bunte Reviews Her Successes, Pressures," *Globe* November 8, 1991; Michael Rezendes and Gary Chafetz, "Flynn Aide Cortiella to Get BHA Post," *Boston Globe*, December 24, 1991; Don Aucoin, "Flynn Appoints New Chief of BHA," *Boston Globe*, December 25, 1991; Peter Canellos, "BHA Chief Revels at Chance for Sweeping Changes," *Boston Globe*, July 6, 1992; Peter Canellos, "US Drops BHA from List of 'Troubled' Agencies," *Boston Globe*, January 28, 1993.

CHAPTER 7

1. Interviews with residents; Boston Police Department data for 1994 cited in Lawrence Vale, "Empathological Places: Residents' Ambivalence toward Remaining in Public Housing," *Journal of Planning Education and Research* 16, no. 3 (1997): 169.

2. Zielenbach, "Catalyzing Community Development," 57.

3. Police call statistic reported in Boucher, "People Live Here, Too," 16.

4. "Youth Shot in Neck in Roxbury Project," *Globe*, March 18, 1989; "Roxbury Man, 39, Stabbed at Project," *Globe*, April 17, 1989; "Reputed Gang Figure Sentenced to Prison," *Globe*, August 3, 1989; "2 Shot at Roxbury's Orchard Park Project," *Globe*, September 20, 1989; "Roxbury Man Charged with Firing Gun," *Globe*, October 29, 1989; Robert Ward, "2 Shootings Leave Man Dead, Youth Wounded," *Globe*, December 7, 1989; "Man, 24, Is Shot in Roxbury," *Globe*, December 13, 1989; "Roxbury Girl Stabbed in Neck," *Globe*, April, 26, 1990.

5. "Man, 29, Is Latest Orchard Park Victim," *Boston Globe*, January 25, 1989.

6. Mike Barnicle, "A Little Anger Would Help," *Globe*, April 30, 1989; Mike Barnicle, "Tuned in to Violence," *Globe*, May 14, 1989; Mike Barnicle, "Beyond the Evening News," *Globe*, May 28, 1989; Mike Barnicle, "Driven to Extremes," *Globe*, June 1, 1989; Mike Barnicle, "A Fault Line That Never Ends," *Globe*, October 19, 1989; Alan Lupo, "Protesting the Easy Way," *Globe*, October 18, 1989; John Ellement, "A City Life, Short, Sad, Ends by Gun," *Globe,* December 8, 1989.

7. Elizabeth Neuffer, "31 Indicted in Roxbury Drug Probe," *Globe*, December 13, 1990. Although many in Boston interpreted the "God" moniker as an indicator of Whiting's power, the name carried more complex origins. Whiting was a member of the "5-Percent Nation" cultural movement—an offshoot of the Nation of Islam that believes only 5 percent of the world's people know "the truth" and are committed to enlightening the rest. These 5-percenters typically have a Muslim name that incorporates Allah, so it was not a big leap to anglicize this as "God." More commonly, Whiting was known as Ra-Ra or Rah, short for Rasheem Allah; Ric Kahn, "Gang Godfather or Mean Streets Robin Hood," *Boston Phoenix*, April 27, 1990; George Hassett, "When God Walked through the Projects," *Boston Phoenix*, April 5, 2012; D. L. Chandler, "The Meaning of the 5%: A Look at the Nation of Gods and Earths," *HipHopWired*, June 28, 2012.

8. Hassett, "When God Walked Through"; resident interview conducted in 2014.

9. Interview with Bill McGonagle, August 2014; Kahn, "Gang Godfather"; interview with Orchard Park resident.

10. Hassett, "When God Walked Through."

11. Interview with McGonagle.

12. Hassett, "When God Walked Through."

13. Kahn, "Gang Godfather"; Mann Terror quoted in Hassett, "When God Walked Through."

14. McGonagle quoted in Adrian Walker, "In Orchard Gardens, Awaiting Return of 'God,'" *Globe*, May 15, 2015.

15. Budd quoted in Hassett, "When God Walked Through."

16. Interview with McGonagle.

17. Hassett, "When God Walked Through"; Sean P. Murphy, "Cocaine-Ring Trial a Priority for Budd," *Globe*, June 18, 1991; Sean P. Murphy, "Witness Says Whiting

Led Gang by Force and Largesse," *Globe*, June 26, 1991; Sean P. Murphy, "Testimony Links Whiting to Drug Ring," *Globe*, July 18, 1991; Richard Jones, "Whiting, 5 Others Convicted in Drug Ring Case," *Globe*, July 25, 1991; Shelley Murphy, "Convicted Drug Lord's Slay Rap Dismissed," *Herald*, August 15, 1991; Sean P. Murphy, "Whiting Receives Mandatory Life Term," *Globe*, October 22, 1991; Ric Kahn, "Undercover, on the Edge," *Globe*, October 25, 1992. The sensationalist drama lent itself well to Hollywood, yielding the 1999 film *In Too Deep*, featuring rapper LL Cool J as "Dwayne Gittens" (the violent but community-oriented crack dealer known as "God") and Omar Epps as Jeff Cole (the Jeff Coy character). The film ends with Gittens/Whiting convicted and Cole/Coy advising would-be undercover agents not to get "in too deep." Fortunately for a still-reeling Orchard Park, the film was set in Cincinnati. Less fortunately, the real Jeff Coy never fully recovered from his experiences. Suffering from post-traumatic stress disorder and depression—and unable to close a deal for a film about his experiences—he hanged himself in his apartment, less than three years after the Whiting trial; John Ellement, "Remembering Officer Who Took His Own Life," *Globe*, February 1, 1994; Ralph Ranalli, "Tragic Life and Death of an Undercover Cop," *Herald*, February 1, 1994; Ric Kahn, "Secret Soldier in Drug War Lost Last Battle," *Globe*, February 27, 1994.

18. Interview with McGonagle; references to violent episodes in around Orchard Park described in the *Globe* and *Herald*, author's files. The Orchard Park violence also ensnared famed rhythm-and-blues singer Bobby Brown, who grew up in the development that spawned his well-known group New Edition. In 1995, during one of his visits back to Roxbury, Brown's friend, bodyguard, and future brother-in-law—a suspected "enforcer" for Orchard Park drug dealers—was shot and killed as the two got into a "cream-colored Bentley" on Dudley Street; the suspected shooter "then fled toward the nearby Orchard Park housing development." Beverly Ford and Jules Crittenden; "Brown May Be Hiding from Friend's Killer," *Boston Herald*, October 1, 1995; Beverly Ford, "Brown Pal's Slaying May Have Been Payback," *Boston Herald*, October 24, 1995.

19. Bynoe quoted in Beth Teitell, "Roxbury Project Residents Held Hostage by Crime, Poverty," *Herald*, January 16, 1992.

20. Interviews facilitated by Carla Morelli, 1993; gang statistics reported in Joseph Mallia, "Slain Youth's Mom Testifies," *Herald*, December 29, 1993.

21. Interview with David Gilmore, October 2009.

22. The development was known as Mission Main to signal it as the original 1940s portion of the Mission Hill development that was later augmented in the 1950s with a portion initially known as Mission Hill Extension (now Alice Taylor).

23. "Shortchanging Orchard Park," editorial, *Globe*, March 2, 1992; Chrystal Kornegay, "The Hope of Public Housing: How Income Mixing Is Expected to Transform Public Housing," MCP thesis, Massachusetts Institute of Technology, 1997, 61.

24. Cortiella letter to Cisneros, 2.

25. Boston Housing Authority, "Highlights of the Orchard Park Modernization," and "Highlights of the Family Investment Center Proposal," addenda to letter from Cortiella to Cisneros, 1993.

26. Grunwald, "Orchard Park Face Lift."

27. Feaster quoted in Grunwald, "Orchard Park Face Lift."

28. Interview with Russell Tanner, February 2017.

29. Boston Housing Authority, *Orchard Park Neighborhood Revitalization*, HOPE VI Plus Implementation Grant Application, Final Submission, September 1, 1995, ES-6.

30. Interview with Tanner.

31. Kornegay, "Hope of Public Housing," 62–65; Boston Housing Authority, *Orchard Park Neighborhood Revitalization*.

32. Interview with Tanner.

33. Orchard Park HOPE VI Plus Implementation Grant Application, ES.3.

34. Goddard quoted in Andrea Estes, "Orchard Park Gets $30M Federal Grant," *Herald*, September 26, 1995; Bob Hohler, "Roxbury to Receive $30m in HUD Aid," *Globe*, September 26, 1995; interview with McGonagle.

35. Geeta Anand, "The City's Landlord," *Globe*, April 6, 1997.

36. Boston Housing Authority, "HOPE VI Program Orchard Park Revitalization Initiative Request for Proposals [from] Development Teams," February 2, 1996, 5, 8, 15, 20, 22.

37. HOPE VI Orchard Park RFP, 9.

38. Interview with Tanner.

39. Kornegay, "Hope of Public Housing," 73.

40. Goddard quoted in Kornegay, 66; interview with McGonagle; interview with Jeanne Pinado, February 2017. Lee also knew BHA HOPE VI planner Amy Schectman, since they had been graduate school classmates at MIT; interview with Amy Schectman, November 2017.

41. Interview with Pinado.

42. Interview with Pinado.

43. Beth Rogers, "Orchard Park Is En Route to Rebirth," *Herald*, April 7, 1996; Goddard and Bynoe quoted in Kornegay, "Hope of Public Housing," 66.

44. Interview with McGonagle.

45. Bowden quoted in Richard Chacón, "Orchard Park Set for $50m Makeover," *Globe*, April 7, 1996.

46. Kornegay, "Hope of Public Housing," 67–68.

47. Kornegay, "Hope of Public Housing," 69–70.

48. Cortiella quoted in Peter Canellos, "Shots at Orchard Park Fired Aimlessly, Police Say," *Globe*, May 20, 1992; David J. Cortiella, Letter to HUD Secretary Henry Cisneros, July 1, 1993; BHA files.

49. Sean Flynn, "Trio Arrested in Drug Raid," *Herald*, November 27, 1995; Mark Mueller, "Cops Grab $20G of Heroin in 1 of 3 Busts," *Herald*, October 13, 1996; David Talbot, "Two Arrested in Orchard Park Drug Sting," *Herald*, December 15, 1996; Beverly Ford, "Police Prune Orchard Park; Officials Say They Nabbed 16 'Baddest Apples,'" *Herald*, April 12, 1997; Beverly Ford, "Massive Raid Nabs 16 Accused of Controlling Crack Cocaine Ring," *Herald*, April 12, 1997; Patricia Nealon, "Arrests Break Back of Orchard Park Drug Gang, Officials Say," *Globe*, April 12, 1997.

50. Shomon Shamsuddin and Lawrence Vale, "Hoping for More: Redeveloping U.S. Public Housing without Marginalizing Low-Income Residents," *Housing Studies* (2016), http://www.tandfonline.com/doi/full/10.1080/02673037.2016.1194375.

51. Zielenbach, "Catalyzing Community Development," 62; Local Initiatives Support Corporation (LISC), "MetLife Foundation Community-Police Partnership

Award Winner," 2008, 47, http://www.lisc.org/docs/publications/Orchard%20
Gardens.pdf.

52. Interview with Sandra Henriquez, January 2000.

53. Boston Housing Authority, "Orchard Gardens," data obtained as of February
2000; interview with Kate Bennett, August 2014; personal communication with
Goddard, October 2013 .

54. Bennett quoted in Abt Associates, "Exploring the Impacts of the HOPE VI
Program on Surrounding Neighborhoods" (Abt Associates, Inc., 2003); Goddard,
personal communication with author, October 2013; interview with Henriquez;
Goddard, personal communication.

55. Interviews with Pinado; Sharon Russell-Mack, February 2017; and Tanner.

56. HUD, *HOPE VI Revitalization Grant Program: Quarterly Reports*, as of third
quarter 2014; obtained from HUD in 2015; interviews with residents conducted
in 2013.

57. Interview with Joe Bamberg, BHA Real Estate Department, August 2014;
Zielenbach, "Catalyzing Community Development," 61.

58. "Rehab Success Story," editorial, *Globe*, April 7, 1998.

59. Grogan and Proscio, "Our Other Renaissance."

60. Interview with Pinado.

61. Symonds, "Public Housing Gets It."

62. Menino quoted in Charles A. Radin, "Boston Is Model City for Clinton's
Plans," *Globe*, January 18, 2000.

63. "Clinton vs. Guns in Roxbury," *Globe*, editorial, January 19, 2000.

64. Sean Zielenbach and Richard Voith, "HOPE VI and Neighborhood Economic
Development: The Importance of Local Market Dynamics," *Cityscape* 12, no. 1
(2010): 110, 111, 114, 119, and 121.

65. Tatsha Robertson, "Change of Address," *Globe*, February 11, 2000.

66. Bynoe and Henriquez quoted in Tatsha Robertson, "Playing the Waiting
Game," *Globe*, June 7, 1998. Waiting list figure cited in Robertson, "Change of
Address."

67. Brian R. Ballou, "Honors for Woman Who Wouldn't Move," *Globe*, June
22, 2011.

68. Megan Tench, "New School Symbol of Renewal," *Globe*, August 25, 2003;
Kevin Rothstein, "Toiling in Orchard: New Start for Roxbury's Notorious $30M
School," *Herald*, October 12, 2004.

69. Bott quoted in Meghan Irons, "Orchard Gardens Reclaims Streets," *Globe*,
August 12, 2013.

70. Interviews with Henriquez; anonynmous resident; and Russell-Mack.

71. Resident interviews were conducted in two waves, one in 2005–2006 and
another in 2013–2014, in order to give a clearer sense of how conditions have
evolved.

72. Bynoe quoted in Thomas Grillo, "City Seeks Grant for Franklin Hill
Renovation," *Globe*, January 21, 2004.

73. Interview with Edna Bynoe conducted by Kim Alleyne, October 2005;
Catherine Fennell, *Last Project Standing* (Minneapolis: University of Minnesota
Press, 2015), 166,

74. Tach, "More Than Bricks," 283.

75. Cruz and Kelsey quoted in Thomas Grillo, "Praise Greets Orchard Commons," *Globe*, December 2, 2000.

76. Shelley, Jackson, and Barros quoted in Erick Trickey, "Fixing a Highway-Shaped Hole in the Heart of Black Boston," *Next City*, August 14, 2017.

77. Boston Housing Authority, "Closeout Report, Orchard Gardens HOPE VI Community and Supportive Services," June 13, 2011.

78. Interview with Russell-Mack.

79. Suzanne Smalley, "Raid Hits '24-hour' Drug Ring," *Globe*, June 24, 2004; Brian Ballou, "Hub Cops Take Bite Out of Crime, Round Up Bushel of 'Bad Apples,'" *Herald*, June 24, 2004.

80. Brian Ballow, "Suspects Sought in Orchard Park Shooting That Kills 1, Wounds 1," *Herald*, June 21, 2004; Mike Barnicle, "Bonds, Farrell Miss Reality of Hub Plight," *Herald*, June 22, 2004; Michele McPhee, "Orchard Park Violence Leaves Cops Frustrated," *Herald*, June 19, 2006.

81. "Fear Grows in This Orchard," editorial, *Globe*, September 12, 2007; Jessica Fargen, O'Ryan Johnson, and Richard Weir, "'Sweet Kid' Gunned Down," *Herald*, May 8, 2009.

82. Estimate reported by Russell-Mack, February 2017.

83. Interview with Russell-Mack.

84. Interview with Russell-Mack.

85. Racial and ethnic breakdown reported by Russell-Mack, as of February 2017.

86. Russell-Mack quoted in Irons, "Orchard Gardens Reclaims Streets."

87. Travis Andersen, "Sentenced to Life in '91, Ex-Drug Kingpin Eyes Possible Release," *Globe*, May 9, 2015; Walker, "In Orchard Gardens"; Adrian Walker, "Throw the Book at Darryl 'God' Whiting," *Globe*, February 12, 2016; Saris and McGonagle quoted in Milton J. Valencia, "Darryl 'God' Whiting Loses Bid for Early Release," *Globe*, February 17, 2016; US Department of Justice, "Violent Drug Trafficker's 1990 Life Sentence Upheld," press release, February 17, 2016.

88. Interview with Bennett; "Dems Thump Trump over Public Housing Spending, Tout South Boston Project as Way to Go," *New Boston Post*, May 7, 2018; http://newbostonpost.com/2018/05/07/dems-thump-trump-over-public-housing-spending-tout-south-boston-project-as-way-to-go/#.

89. Sandra Henriquez, personal communication with author, March 2, 2009; McGonagle quoted in "Renewing the Commitment to Lifting People Out of Poverty through Public Housing," *Urban Land Magazine*, June 6, 2016.

90. Interview with Bennett; interview with McGonagle.

PART IV

1. Regina Kelly, ed., *Don't Look at Me Different / No Me Veas Diferente* (Tucson, AZ: Tucson Voices Press, 2000), 145.

CHAPTER 8

1. Lydia Otero, *La Calle* (Tucson: University of Arizona Press, 2010), 16, 20.

2. Otero, *La Calle*, 29, 39, 40; C. L. Sonnichsen, *Tucson: The Life and Times of an American City* (Norman: University of Oklahoma Press, 1982), 283; City-County Planning Department, *General Land Use Plan* (Tucson: City-County Planning

Department, 1960), 39; John H. Denton and William S. King, "The Tucson Central Business District as a Changing Entity," *Arizona Review* 9, no. 5 (12960): 3, 6, 12. Interestingly, the *General Land Use Plan* makes no mention of either urban renewal or public housing.

3. Otero, *La Calle*, 39–40.

4. Interview with Cressworth Lander, November 2010.

5. Otero, *La Calle*, 88; Walsh quoted in "Low-Rent Housing Debate Held Here," *Tucson Daily Citizen*, September 22, 1950, 9.

6. Kelly, *Don't Look*, 16–19, McLaughlin quoted, 39; "Decent Homes or New Federal Controls," editorial, *Arizona Daily Star*, July 19, 1949.

7. Interview with Lander; Sonnichsen, *Tucson*, 285–86; Drachman and Shaw quoted in "Low-Rent Housing Debate Held Here."

8. Interview with Emily Nottingham, November 2010, based on her unpublished notes on the early history of the Tucson Housing Authority; La Reforma vote cited in "Go Slow on Expanding Public Housing," editorial, *Star*, January 4, 1963, D10.

9. Tucson Housing Authority, *La Reforma Project*, 1962. Report quoted in Kelly, *Don't Look*, 19–20.

10. Sonnichsen, *Tucson*, 281–82; Otero, *La Calle*, 88–90.

11. Otero, *La Calle*, 88–91, 100, 108–9; Laidlaw quoted in Margaret Regan, "There Goes the Neighborhood: The Downfall of Downtown," *Tucson Weekly*, March 6, 1997; Robles quoted in "People Removed from 'The Hole' Bear Most Bitterness," *Citizen*, December 12, 1970, 4; Juan Gomez-Novy and Stefanos Polyzoides, "A Tale of Two Cities: The Failed Urban Renewal of Downtown Tucson in the Twentieth Century," *Journal of the Southwest* 45 (Summer 2003).

12. Rachel Stein Gragg, "Tucson: The Formulation and Legitimation of an Urban Renewal Program," MA thesis, University of Arizona, 1969, 76; S. L. Schorr and the Citizens' Advisory Redevelopment Committee, *Urban Renewal: A Teamwork of Private Enterprise and Government for Slum Clearance and Redevelopment of the Old Pueblo* (City of Tucson, 1961), 6; 14, Don and Eugenia Hummel, *One Man's Life* (Bellevue, WA: Free Enterprise Press, 1988), 160. Otero, *La Calle*, 56–57, 103–4.

13. Otero, *La Calle*, 56–57, 103–4; Hummel and Hummel, *One Man's Life*, 160; Schorr et al., *Urban Renewal*, 2, 19, 24–25, 27–29, 34.

14. "La Reforma Additions Advocated," *Star*, April 5, 1963, B1; Otero, *La Calle*, 104–7; William Matthews, "Some Facts about Urban Renewal," *Star*, October 22, 1961, D16; Hummel and Hummel, 161.

15. S. Lenwood Schorr, "Memorandum to the Mayor and City Council," January 24, 1962, cited in Gragg, "Tucson," 41, 70–71, 77, 88–90; "Urban Renewal Plan Should Be Dropped—Now," editorial, *Citizen*, May 4, 1962; Otero, *La Calle*, 105–7; Fairbanks, *War on Slums*, 155–56.

16. "Housing Hearing Slated," *Star*, December 13, 1962; "Tucson Housing Authority Asks City to Add 200 La Reforma Project Units," *Star*, December 15, 1962; Arriaga quoted in Dean Fairchild, "La Reforma Program Placed under Study," *Star*, January 22, 1963, B1.

17. "Go Slow on Expanding Public Housing."

18. Steve Emerine, "Public Housing Bid under Advisement." *Citizen*, January 22, 1963, 1; Chambers quoted in "Housing Program Gets Green Light," *Star*, July 25, 1963.

19. "Tucson Starts Buying Land for Project," *Star*, January 29, 1965; "Council Condemns 13 Parcels of Land: City Needs Area for Housing," *Star*, August 10, 1965; interview with Nottingham; Ronald Lee quoted in Kelly, *Don't Look*, 88–91.

20. "'Private' Urban Renewal Backed," *Citizen*, April 21, 1964; Gragg, "Tucson," 46–51, 78, 95; Otero, *La Calle*, 88–91, 100, 108–9, 112; Build a Better America Committee, *An Action Plan for Tucson* (NAREB, 1963), quoted in Otero, 109; Roy P. Drachman and Vincent L. Lung, *The Pueblo Center Redevelopment Project*, April 23, 1965 (City of Tucson, 1965), ii, iii; Roy Drachman, *From Cowtown to Desert Metropolis* (San Francisco: Whitewing Press, 1999), 184.

21. Otero, *La Calle*, 93, 117–18, Drachman quoted, 93–94; occupancy statistics cited in *Final Relocation Report: Pueblo Center Redevelopment Project R-8* (Tucson: Redevelopment Agency, 1969), 4.

22. Otero, *La Calle*, 2, 90–91; *Final Relocation Report*, 1; Department of Community Development, City of Tucson / Candeub Fleissig, Adley and Associates, *Concept Plan: Pueblo Center Project*, May 1965, 2; Bonnie Newlon, *Pueblo Center Redevelopment Project, 1967-1969* (Department of Community Development, Urban Renewal Division, 1969), 14; *Arizona Revised Statutes*, Section 36, Article 3, "Slum Clearance and Redevelopment," 1471.

23. Although the facility was termed a "Community Center" in public discussions, in 1965 the city commissioned a marketing study for the proposed "Tucson Convention Center"; Development Research Associates, "Preliminary Marketing Conclusions and Recommendations, Pueblo Center Project," May 12, 1965, included in *Concept Plan: Pueblo Center Project*. See also Development Research Associates, *Land Utilization-Marketability Study, Pueblo Center Redevelopment Project* (DRA, October 1965).

24. Schorr et al., *Urban Renewal*, 21; Fairbanks, *War on Slums*, 157–58.

25. Otero, *La Calle*, 118–21; Robles quoted in "People Removed from 'The Hole,'" 4; *Pueblo Center Redevelopment Project, 1967-1969*, 6–7; Morales quoted in Tim Vanderpool, "Poor House Shuffle," *Tucson Weekly*, September 18, 1997.

26. *Final Relocation Report*, 3–4, 29; interview with Lander. In 1978, Tucson set out a much more comprehensive set of protections for displaced residents and businesses; City of Tucson, Community Conservation and Development Division, *City of Tucson General Relocation Plan & Policies* (Tucson: Relocation Office, June 1978), 5, 22, 25, 31.

27. *Final Relocation Report*, 6–9.

28. *Final Relocation Report*, 26; Otero, *La Calle*, 6.

29. *Final Relocation Report*, 9; "Connie Chambers Units Receive Their First Tenants," *Star*, August 24, 1967; Margaret Kuehlthau, "Housing Project Has Happy Ending," *Citizen*, September 4, 1967, 23; "Dispossessed," *Citizen*, special supplement, December 12, 1970, 4. Emily Nottingham, who reviewed all of the land acquisition documents, believes that most parcels on the Connie Chambers site itself had been owned homes, so that it would be unlikely that residents would have wished to move into public housing; interview with Nottingham.

30. *Final Relocation Report*, 9; "Dispossessed," 4.

31. Valencia and others quoted in "Dispossessed," 4.

32. Interview with Lander; Jay Hall, "City's Low-Cost Housing Setup Being Improved," *Citizen*, August 7, 1968, 25.

33. Joel Valdez, "Mayor and Council Communication: Department of Housing approving an application to the Department of Housing and Urban Development supporting disposition and close-out request for La Reforma (AZ 4-1), September 24, 1979, cited in Kelly, *Don't Look*, 23; "Romero's Brave Idea: Reforming La Reforma," editorial, *Star*, June 24, 1974.

34. Candeub Fleissig and Associates, *Report on Preliminary Proposals for Area Treatment, A Part of the Community Renewal Program of the City of Tucson, Arizona, Memo 3*, prepared for the Tucson Department of Community Development, October 1968), 13; Department of Community Development, Tucson, *Community Development Program, Tucson, Arizona* (Community Development Department and Candeub Fleissig and Associates, Consultants, March 1970), 19, 29–30; Candeub, Fleissig and Associates, *Need for Renewal*; prepared for the City of Tucson Community Renewal Program, Memo 2, November 1968, "Blight Indices Utilized in Delineating Study Areas," appendix, 4.

35. Interviews with Lander and Nottingham.

36. Interview with Lander.

37. "Tenants City Unfair Rent, Bad Upkeep," *Citizen*, June 28, 1972; "Trade Bureau Spurs Inner City Effort," editorial, *Citizen*, December 18, 1975, 32.

38. Interview with Lander; Kelly, *Don't Look*, 24–25; Valdez; "La Reforma Demolition Is Under Way," *Citizen*, November 16, 1983.

39. Interview with Nottingham; interview with Karen Thoreson, November 2010; Ann-Eve Pederson, "La Reforma Appraiser Gets License Revoked," *Star*, July 17, 1994.

CHAPTER 9

1. Kelly, *Don't Look*, 47, 75, 83.

2. Kelly, *Don't Look*, 84, 97–98, 100 (Moreno), 101, 112 (Joe), 120–21 (Galindo), 121, 124 (Figueroa), 130–33.

3. Community Services Department, "Plan to Eliminate Illegal Drug Related Activities from Public Housing Project," September 1991, 2–14.

4. Interviews with Emily Nottingham, November 2010, and Karen Thoreson, November 2010. HOPE VI initially targeted only the largest housing authorities.

5. Corky Poster, *Comprehensive Community Development Plan for the Greater Santa Rosa Area* (Drachman Institute, University of Arizona, July 1994), "Plan Issues," n.p.; interview with Nottingham.

6. Interview with Jeffrey Lines, April 2014.

7. Interviews with Nottingham and Thoreson.

8. City of Tucson / Poster Frost Associates / Foreground Architecture, "HOPE VI—Connie Chambers Redevelopment Project Questionnaire," version for Connie Chambers residents; interview with Thoreson.

9. City of Tucson / Poster Frost Associates / Foreground Architecture, "HOPE VI—Connie Chambers Redevelopment Project Questionnaire," version for neighborhood residents.

10. Interviews with Olga Osterhage, October 2010; Nottingham; and Thoreson; Sandra Valdez Gerdes, "Housing," *Citizen*, February 7, 2000.

11. Interview with Pedro Gonzales, November 2010; Memo from Karen Thoreson and Emily Nottingham to Jay Itote, May 31, 1996; City of Tucson et al., HOPE VI

resident questionnaire; Johnson quoted in Kristen Cook, "Leaving the Projects," *Star*, May 21, 1996. An evaluation of Posadas HOPE VI experience found that five residents reported starting their own businesses between 1996 and 2002, that twelve reported receiving homeownership counseling during this period, and that five purchased a home; Adriana Cimetta and Ralph Renger, *Final Evaluation Report for the Greater Santa Rosa HOPE VI Project, Year Ending 2002* (University of Arizona, College of Public Health, 2002), 30, 37–40. The first translation of HOPE as "Housing Opportunities" in the Tucson press occurred in April 1999, but "homeownership" sometimes reappeared in the acronym thereafter.

12. Linda Bohlke, *Unfulfilled Promises: Racial Discrimination and Neglect in Tucson's Public and Federally-Subsidized Housing* (Southern Arizona People's Law Center, 1993), 5, 21, 44, 46–47, 84–85; turnover figure cited in Dan Huff, "Poor Relations," *Tucson Weekly*, April 11, 1996.

13. Huff, "Poor Relations."

14. Karen Thoreson, Letter to David Reyes and Mary Lou Heuett, March 22, 1996; Reyes and Heuett, Letter to Poster et al., March 25, 1996; Heuett and Reyes, Cover Letter to Neighborhood Survey, April 2, 1996; Poster, Letter to Reyes and Heuett, March 30, 1996; Thoreson, Letter to Heuett and Reyes, April 11, 1996; Letter from Heuett and Reyes to Councilmember Molly McKasson (with attached survey results), June 3, 1996; Letter from Reyes, Heuett, and Gibbs to Neighborhood Residents, July 31, 1996.

15. Letter from David "Chance" Reyes, Mary Lou Heuett, and Jody Gibbs to Henry Cisneros et al., July 17, 1996, 1–3.

16. Interview with Corky Poster, October 2010. Jody Gibbs did not respond to my attempt to interview him.

17. Interview with Poster.

18. Memo from Karen Thoreson to Michael F. Brown (city manager), "HOPE VI Barrio Santa Rosa / Connie Chambers Revitalization Plan," summary of comments on HOPE VI public meeting of August 1, 1996, August 2, 1996; Joe Burchell, "Minorities, Women to Receive More City Contract," *Star*, August 6, 1996; Joe Burchell, "City Seeks Grant to Tear Down Projects," *Star*, August 20, 1996; Kristen Cook, "City Submits Grant Applications for New Public Housing," *Star*, September 8, 1996.

19. Thoreson quoted in Kristen Cook, "Public Housing's Rebirth," *Star*, October 26, 1996; Carmen Duarte, "City Is Awarded $14.6 Million for Public Housing," *Star*, October 8, 1996;

20. Interview with Gonzales.

21. Interviews with Osterhage, Gonzales, and Poster.

22. Interview with Osterhage.

23. Joe Burchell, "Connie Chambers Residents Get Project Vote," *Star*, October 14, 1997; Kristen Cook, "Council OKs Rebuilding Connie Chambers," *Star*, October 21, 1997; "Beyond a Bad Idea," editorial, *Star*, October 24, 1997; GAO 2003 Report; interview with Osterhage.

24. Interviews with Osterhage, Gonzales, and Poster.

25. Kelly, *Don't Look*, 138–43; John F. Rawlinson and Alexa Haussler, "Boy Shot to Death in Downtown Fray," *Star*, February 11, 1996; Kristen Cook, "More Than a Paint Job," *Star*, May 20, 1996; Cook, "New Connie Chambers Would Blend into

Surroundings," *Star*, May 21, 1996; "Public Housing: A New Start," *Star*, editorial, October 9, 1996; Vanderpool, "Poor House Shuffle."

26. Enric Volante, "The Modern Barrio," *Star*, March 22, 2001; interview with Poster; City of Tucson, "HOPE VI Barrio Santa Rosa / Connie Chambers Revitalization Plan," Existing Conditions, 1996.

27. Demographic table included with Carmen Duarte, "Struggle for Security," *Star*, May 19, 1996, A6.

28. Keith Bagwell, "Razing Begins Tomorrow on Chambers Complex," *Star*, April 5, 1999; interview with Poster.

29. Interviews with Osterhage, Poster, and Gonzales; focus group with Posadas residents, October 2010; CSD, "Posadas Sentinel Site and Unit Standards," n.d. (c. 2001); final return occupancy data in Cimetta and Renger, *Final Evaluation Report*, 4; and, with somewhat different numbers, in HUD, "HOPE VI Revitalization Grant Program: Phase Narrative Report," quarterly as of third quarter 2014. Initially, only seventeen households remained on-site, but four more later returned; Abt Associates and Urban Institute, *The HOPE VI Resident Tracking Study: A Snapshot of the Current Living Situation of Original Residents from Eight Sites*, prepared for HUD, November 2002, 46.

30. Interview with Osterhage; Noriega quoted in Kelly, *Don't Look*, 113, 115.

31. In terms of financing, the 120 on-site units plus 80 units purchased on scattered sites were all part of the same tax-credit deal associated with the HOPE VI grant. In addition, the City purchased 60 additional scattered-site public housing replacement units that were outside of this deal. The project received 10 percent of Arizona's annual tax credit allotment; General Accounting Office, *HUD's Management of the HOPE VI Program* (GAO, 2003), 67; "Tucson Optimizes its Deal to the Benefit of Residents," *Housing Research Foundation News* 45 (January–February 2001).

32. Interview with Osterhage.

33. Interview with Nottingham.

34. Poster Frost survey, 1996.

35. Interview with Osterhage.

36. Interview with Osterhage; Urban Institute and Abt Associates, *HOPE VI Resident Tracking Study*, 91–92.

37. Harris and Carranza quoted in Kelly, *Don't Look*, 85, 137; interviews with Osterhage and Nottingham. The evaluation of Posadas, conducted by the Urban Institute and Abt Associates as part of an eight-city study, regards the Tucson experience as a conspicuous success, with high resident satisfaction; Urban Institute and Abt Associates, *HOPE VI Resident Tracking Study*.

38. Interview with Osterhage; resident focus group, October 2010.

39. Interview with Bobbi Stone, October 2010; City of Tucson, "Posadas Sentinel Community Policy," 2001, revised January 2009, 7.

40. Posadas demographic breakdown as of March 23, 2010, supplied by Bobbi Stone.

41. Interviews with Osterhage and Stone; focus group; Jason DeParle, "Arizona Is a Haven for Refugees," *New York Times*, October 8, 2010.

42. Interview with Osterhage.

43. Interview with Osterhage; City of Tucson, "Community Policy."

44. Interviews with Poster and Nottingham.

45. Interviews with Poster and Stone.

46. Interviews with Poster and Stone; personal communication with Housing and Community Development Department administrator Erin Arana, May 2017.

47. Interview with Osterhage; FSS data supplied by Osterhage, December 2010; waiting list data supplied by Arana, May 2017.

48. Those contracted to do the evaluation of this HOPE VI project complained that the city and CSD set too few quantifiable goals, and therefore the evaluation is no more than "an assessment of oversight and compliance"; Cimetta and Renger, *Final Evaluation Report*, 2. See also Ralph Renger, Omar Passons, and Adriana Cimetta, "Evaluating Housing Revitalization Projects: Critical Lessons for All Evaluators," *American Journal of Evaluation* 24, no. 1 (2003): 51-64.

49. S. L. (Si) Schorr, "'60s Urban Renewal Removed Blight, Set Stage for Future," op-ed, *Star*, February 5, 2010; interview with Gonzales.

50. Interviews with Thoreson and Nottingham.

51. Interview with Albert Elias, October 2010.

52. Cimetta and Renger, *Final Evaluation Report*, 99-100.

53. Interview with Osterhage.

54. Interview with Nottingham; personal correspondence with Osterhage, December 2010, and with Arana, May 2017. Several thousand people have applied for public housing each time Tucson has opened up its waiting list; Bud Foster, "Thousands Apply for Public Housing," KOLD-12 News, March 29, 2010; housing eligibility statistic cited in M. Scott Skinner, "You Gotta Be Good to Get Public Housing," *Star*, October 12, 1998.

55. Calculated from 2010 US Census and HUD USER, *A Picture of Subsidized Households*; National Low Income Housing Coalition, *The Gap: A Shortage of Affordable Homes*, March 2018, appendix B.

CHAPTER 10

1. Dino Cinel, *From Italy to San Francisco* (Stanford, CA: Stanford University Press, 1982), 118, 123.

2. Richard Dillon, *North Beach: The Italian Heart of San Francisco* (San Francisco: Presidio Press, 1985), 73-74; Sanborn Insurance maps, San Francisco Public Library.

3. Cinel, *From Italy*, 125; Dillon, *North Beach*, 4.

4. Housing Authority of the City and County of San Francisco, *Third Annual Report*, April 1941, 8-12; *Fourth Annual Report*, April 1942; Works Progress Administration, *1939 Real Property Survey, San Francisco, California*, 665-08-3-173, 1940.

5. SFHA, *Fourth Annual Report*, n.p.; *Fifth Annual Report*, 1943, n.p.; *Sixth Annual Report*, 1944, n.p.

6. John Bolles, "North Beach Place Housing Project, San Francisco," *Architect and Engineer*, July 1945, 13-16.

7. Housing Authority of the City and County of San Francisco, *Down through the Years*, Eighth Annual Report, 1946, 5-15, 26.

8. Housing Authority of the City and County of San Francisco, *Eleventh Annual Report*, 1949 (SFHA, 1950), 1-2.

9. Amy L. Howard, *More Than Shelter* (Minneapolis: University of Minnesota Press, 2014), 141.

10. Housing Authority of the City and County of San Francisco, *Road to the Golden Age: A Report on the First Twenty Years of Operations, 1940 to 1960* (SFHA, n.d. [1962?]).

11. SFHA Minutes, May 21, 1942; John Baranski, "Making Public Housing in San Francisco: Liberalism, Social Prejudice, and Social Activism, 1906-1976," PhD diss., University of California, Santa Barbara, 2004, 168-69.

12. Albert S. Broussard, *Black San Francisco* (Lawrence: University Press of Kansas, 1993), 133.

13. Baranski, "Making Public Housing," 231.

14. San Francisco Board of Supervisors, "Resolution Recommending Certain Standards and Policies Relating to the Exercise of Rights as to Land in Redevelopment Projects without Discrimination or Segregation Based upon Race, Color, Creed, National Origin or Ancestry, Applicable to Consideration of Redevelopment Plans Submitted for Approval," November 1949.

15. Baranski, "Making Public Housing," 175-78; "S.F. Housing Board Keeps Racial Policy," *San Francisco Chronicle*, October 28, 1949; "Segregation Ban in New S.F. Housing," *Chronicle*, November 9, 1949; Beard and MacPhee quoted in "Segregation and S.F. Housing," *Chronicle*, January 15, 1950; "Housing Policy Attack: Authority Assailed for Segregation Stand in Defiance of Supervisors," *Chronicle*, January 11, 1950.

16. "Housing Officials Agree to Nonsegregation," *Chronicle*, February 21, 1950.

17. State of California, Department of Parks and Recreation, "Building, Structure, and Object Record," North Beach Housing Project, July 21, 2000, 5; "North Beach Place to Be Built by 1952," *Chronicle*, October 16, 1949, 10.

18. "Segregation Issue: 15 Units Held in North Beach for Possible Negro Tenants," *Chronicle*, September 12, 1952; "New Housing Project Opens," *Chronicle*, September 14, 1949; "Hearings Open in Negroes in North Beach Housing," *Chronicle*, September 23, 1952; "Hearing on Jim Crow Segregation: White Non-vets Favored over Negro Vets," *Chronicle*, October 9, 1952; Paul T. Miller, "The Interplay of Housing, Employment and Civil Rights in the Experience of San Francisco's African American Community, 1945-1975," PhD diss., Temple University, 2008, 149-50. See also Howard, *More Than Shelter*, 147-48, 159-63, and Baranski, "Making Public Housing," chapter 4.

19. Bernard Taper, "Housing Authority Urged to Give Up Segregation," *Chronicle*, June 7, 1953; "Court Voids S.F. Policy on Housing," *Chronicle*, August 27, 1953; Miller, "Interplay of Housing," 151-52; Richard Reinhardt, "S.F. Housing Segregation to End: Supreme Court Ruling," and "Housing Board Bows to Ruling," *Chronicle*, May 25, 1954; *Banks v. Housing Authority* 120 Cal. App. 2d 1.

20. Baranski, "Making Public Housing," 236; Miller, "Interplay of Housing," 147-48; Broussard, *Black San Francisco*, 223-25.

21. Reuel Schiller, "Conflict in the 'Tranquil Gardens': *Banks v. Housing Authority of San Francisco* and the Definition of Equality in Multi-racial San Francisco," colloquium paper, March 2013, http://repository.uchastings.edu/cgi/viewcontent.cgi?article=1984&context=faculty_scholarship.

22. Bolles, "North Beach Place," 15-16.

23. Baranski, "Making Public Housing," 220–22.

24. Baranski, "Making Public Housing," 223, 224 n. 34.

25. Baranski, "Making Public Housing," 223, 225–26.

26. Lewis, *Divided Highways*, 198.

27. Chester Hartman, "The Right to Stay Put," in *Between Eminence and Notoriety: Four Decades of Radical Urban Planning* (New Brunswick, NJ: Center for Urban Policy Research Press), 120–33.

28. Karl Beitel, *Local Protest, Global Movements* (Philadelphia: Temple University Press, 2013), 4, 7, 9. For discussion of shifting regime politics during the 1970s and 1980s, see Richard E. DeLeon, *Left Coast City* (Lawrence: University Press of Kansas, 1992); Richard E. DeLeon, "The Urban Antiregime: Progressive Politics in San Francisco," *Urban Affairs Quarterly* 27, no. 4 (June 1992): 555–79; and for a comparison that includes the 1990s, Richard Hu, "To Grow or Control, That Is the Question: San Francisco's Planning Transformation in the 1980s and 1990s," *Journal of Planning History* 11, no. 2 (2012): 141–59, and Brian J. Godfrey, "Urban Development and Redevelopment in San Francisco," *Geographical Review* 87, no. 3 (1997): 309–33.

29. Aaron, Levine, Report to the San Francisco Planning and Blyth-Zellerbach Committee, 1959; Stephen J. McGovern, *The Politics of Downtown Development: Dynamic Political Cultures in San Francisco and Washington, D.C.* (Lexington: University Press of Kentucky, 1998), 63–64.

30. Alison Isenberg, *Designing San Francisco* (Princeton, NJ: Princeton University Press, 2017), 291.

31. McGovern, *Politics of Downtown Development*, 64.

32. John Mollenkopf, *The Contested City* (Princeton, NJ: Princeton University Press, 1983), 168–69, 179.

33. Chester Hartman with 16 others, *Yerba Buena: Land Grab and Community Resistance in San Francisco* (San Francisco: Glide, 1974).

34. Chester Hartman, "Neighborhood Fightback," in Hartman, *Between Eminence and Notoriety*, 175–76.

35. Thomas C. Fleming, "San Francisco's Land Development Program," November 27, 1965, 3.

36. Miller, "Interplay of Housing," 260–71.

37. Letter from attorney Theodore W. Phillips to M. Justin Herman, January 27, 1970; Memorandum from M. Justin Herman to Mrs. Fisher, Mr. Sims, Mr. Wolinsky et al. (c/o Mr. Phillips), January 30, 1970; Justin Herman, "Planners and Politicians: A Machiavellian Team," remarks at the ASPO Thirty-Fourth National Planning Conference, May 8, 1968; Vertical Files, San Francisco Western Addition Redevelopment, San Francisco Redevelopment Agency Archives.

38. Isenberg, *Designing San Francisco*, 18–19, 292–93, 356.

39. Isenberg, *Designing San Francisco*, 343.

40. Beitel, *Local Protest, Global Movements*, 14, 20–22, 32, 152; Miller, "Interplay of Housing," 231–35.

41. Beitel, *Local Protest, Global Movements*, 16, 34.

42. Beitel, *Local Protest, Global Movements*, 14, 32. On rent control, introduced in 1979, see Edward Goetz, "A Little Pregnant: The Impact of Rent Control in San Francisco," *Urban Affairs Review* 30, no. 4 (1995): 604–12.

43. The protesters included many members of the radical People's Temple—led by Jim Jones, who was appointed to the San Francisco Housing Commission in late 1976 by Mayor George Moscone. Just as the I-Hotel reached its epic denouement, Jones abandoned his new post as chairman of the housing commission and fled to Guyana to escape media scrutiny about his church's practices, establishing an outpost known as Jonestown. On November 18, 1978, Jones ordered more than nine hundred of his followers to commit mass suicide. And, just nine days later, Moscone and Supervisor Harvey Milk were assassinated at San Francisco City Hall by former supervisor Dan White; Michael Taylor, "Jones Captivated S.F.'s Liberal Elite," *Chronicle*, November 12, 1998.

44. Beitel, *Local Protest, Global Movements*, 38. Hartman's detailed account of the I-Hotel saga, originally published in 1978, is reprinted in Chester Hartman, "San Francisco's International Hotel: Case Study of a Turf Struggle," in Hartman, *Between Eminence and Notoriety*, 134–43. See also chapters 4 and 5 in Chester Hartman, *City for Sale* (Berkeley: University of California Press, 2002), a book that is a revised and updated version of Hartman's earlier books, *Yerba Buena* (1974) and *The Transformation of San Francisco* (1984).

45. Marcia Rosen and Wendy Sullivan, *From Urban Renewal and Displacement to Economic Inclusion: San Francisco Affordable Housing Policy, 1978-2012* (Washington, DC: Poverty and Race Research Action Council; San Francisco: National Housing Law Project, 2012), 1, 5, 16-17, 44.

46. Beitel, *Local Protest, Global Movements*, 46, 151.

47. SFHA, *Road to the Golden Age,* 6.

48. Bill Morgan, *The Beat Generation in San Francisco* (San Francisco: City Lights Books, 2003), 25.

49. Baranski, "Making Public Housing," 310 n. 88, 364-65.

50. Baranski, "Making Public Housing," 314.

51. SFHA, *Twenty-Ninth Annual Report*, 1966, 2-9.

52. Eneas Kane, letter to John Shelley, September 13, 1967; San Francisco Public Library, http://www.archive.org/details/annualreport196687hous.

53. Eneas Kane, letter to Joseph Alioto, September 29, 1969, 2; San Francisco Public Library, http://www.archive.org/details/annualreport196687hous.

54. Eneas Kane, letter to Joseph Alioto, September 15, 1970, in *Annual Report to Mayor Joseph L. Alioto*, September 15, 1970; San Francisco Public Library, http://www.archive.org/details/annualreport196687hous.

55. Rick DelVecchio, "Housing Projects in S.F. Reported 'Out of Control,'" *Chronicle*, September 10, 1988; Hartman, *City for Sale*, 371; HUD letter quoted, 372.

56. The famous City Lights Bookstore is located at this edge, near the intersection of Columbus and Broadway.

57. Howard, *More Than Shelter*, 165; Isenberg, *Designing San Francisco*, 36, 74, 106-8.

58. Interview with Denise McCarthy, October 2009. Tel-Hi was initially the Telegraph Hill Settlement House, and later the Telegraph Hill Neighborhood Association. The organization currently abbreviates its name as TEL HI.

59. Isenberg, *Designing San Francisco*, 42-44.

60. Interview with Calvin Welch, October 2009; interview with McCarthy. McCarthy retired from Tel-Hi in 2005, after twenty-three years.

61. Oscar Newman, *Defensible Space: Crime Prevention through Urban Design* (New York: Macmillan, 1972), 131–35.

62. Rodriguez quoted in Frances D'Emilio, "Fed-Up Tenants Fight City Hall," *Chronicle*, February 22, 1979.

63. D'Emilio, "Fed-Up Tenants."

64. Halikias quoted in Reginald Smith, "New Moves to Control Housing Authority," *Chronicle*, February 22, 1985, 8.

65. Wiltz quoted in Catherine Bowman, "S.F. Security Beefed Up after Center Fire," *Chronicle*, November 28, 1995.

66. U.S. House of Representatives Employment and Housing Subcommittee, "San Francisco Housing Authority," statement of Alma Lark, 31.

67. Interview with Greg Richardson conducted by Stephanie Groll, August 2005.

68. Interviews with North Beach Place residents, completed with the assistance of Tan Chow in 2009.

69. "North Beach Development Public Housing, San Francisco: Summary of Survey, June 1997," filed at the Chinatown Community Development Center.

70. Brian Godfrey, *Neighborhoods in Transition* (Berkeley: University of California Press, 1988), 102, 114. For discussion of Chinese integration up through the 1950s, see Charlotte Brooks, *Alien Neighbors, Foreign Friends* (Chicago: University of Chicago Press, 2009).

71. Vale, *Puritans to the Projects*, chapter 5; Lawrence Vale, *Reclaiming Public Housing* (Cambridge, MA: Harvard University Press, 2002).

72. San Francisco Housing Authority, *The State of the Authority and Five Year Work Plan: Executive Director's Second Six Month Report*, September 5, 1990, 2.

73. San Francisco Housing Authority, *Restoring Control: The First Two Years*, Executive Director's Semi-annual Report, October 1, 1990–March 31, 1991, 1–6.

74. Susan Herbert, "Local Housing Authority Is Off HUD's 'Bad' List," *San Francisco Examiner*, April 24, 1992; Suzanne Espinoza, "HUD Praises S.F. Housing Authority," *Chronicle*, August 23, 1992; Gilmore quoted in SFHA, *Executive Director's Report and Revised Five Year Work Plan*, May 1993, i.

75. US House of Representatives, Employment and Housing Subcommittee, Committee on Government Operations, "Issues Involving the Operation of the San Francisco Housing Authority," statement and printed testimony of John Connors, Acting HUD Inspector General, September 14, 1992, 4–22.

76. US House of Representatives Employment and Housing Subcommittee, "San Francisco Housing Authority," statement and printed testimony of David Gilmore, 39–54.

77. Interview with David Gilmore, October 2009.

78. Gilmore quoted in Vernon Loeb, "Resident Expert: DC's Housing Authority Was in the Dumps when David Gilmore Moved In," *Washington Post*, May 7, 1998.

79. PHMAP score of 50.7 percent cited in SFHA, *1997 North Beach HOPE VI Application*, July 18, 1997, 93; Catherine Bowman and Aurelio Rojas, "Chronicle Investigation: When Home's Not Sweet," *Chronicle*, April 3, 1995.

80. Smith quoted in Bowman and Rojas, "Chronicle Investigation."

81. Oddly, five years later, her title was still "acting" executive director.

82. Interview with Barbara Smith, June 2012.

CHAPTER 11

1. Catherine Bowman, "City May Extend Cable Car Line," *Chronicle*, September 1, 1994.

2. Brown quoted in Malcolm Glover, "Off-Duty Cop Hurt in Beating," *Examiner*, November 21, 1996; Bowman, "City May Extend Cable Car Line."

3. Kaplan/McLaughlin/Diaz, "San Francisco Housing Authority, North Beach Tenants Association: Planning Process and Design Alternatives for North Beach Place" (KMD, 1993); Howard, *More Than Shelter*, 176–77.

4. Interview with Michael Kelly, March 2009.

5. Memo from Angela Chu, Chinatown Resource Center, to Cheryl Tsui, Channel 26, August 21, 1996.

6. Interview with Libby Seifel, June 2012.

7. Interview with Welch.

8. Jane Rongerude, "From Public Housing to Regulated Public Environments," Institute for the Study of Social Change Working Paper (Berkeley: ISSC, August 1, 2007), 9.

9. Interview with Seifel.

10. Interview with Welch.

11. Interview with Barbara Smith, June 2012.

12. See http://www.tel-hi.org/pages/tel-hi-s-roots.

13. See http://www.chinatowncdc.org/index.php?option=com_content&view=article&id=47&Itemid=56; interview with Chinatown CDC executive director Rev. Norman Fong, June 2012.

14. Howard, *More Than Shelter*, 171.

15. Interview with James Tracy conducted by Stephanie Groll, August 2005.

16. James Tracy, *Dispatches against Displacement* (Edinburgh: AK Press, 2014), 26.

17. Interview with Seifel.

18. Interview with Seifel; SFHA, *HOPE VI San Francisco Housing Authority North Beach Revitalization Plan*, September 9, 1996.

19. Willie Brown, *Basic Brown* (New York: Simon and Schuster, 2008), 257.

20. Interview with Seifel.

21. Willie Brown Jr., Letter to Henry Cisneros, September 9, 1998, included as part of Exhibit M ("Required Certifications") in the SFHA HOPE VI application.

22. The 95 percent figure quoted in memo from Chu to Tsui, 3.

23. SFHA, *North Beach Revitalization Plan*, Exhibit N, Demolition/Disposition Application, 2–4.

24. Interview with Smith.

25. HUD Office of the Inspector General, "Audit of the Fiscal Year 1996 HOPE VI Grant Award Process," 98-FO-101-0001, October 20, 1997, Appendix M, 12.

26. Agnos quoted in Barbara Nanney, "Mixed Messages at North Beach," *Independent*, October 15, 1996; Richardson quoted in Catherine Bowman, "S.F. Gets Big Grant to Replace Projects," *Chronicle*, October 8, 1996.

27. Howard, *More Than Shelter*, 178.

28. Lark, Richardson, Wiltz, and Harper quoted in Barbara Nanney, "Tenants Furious over Agency's Letter," *Independent*, October 15, 1996.

29. Harper quoted in Tracy, *Dispatches against Displacement*, 24.

30. Tracy, *Dispatches against Displacement*, 24. The originals of the August 1996 sign-in sheets are held in the files of the Chinatown CDC.

31. Chavez and Lynch quoted in Nanney, "Mixed Messages at North Beach."

32. A. Lawrence Chickering, "A Bootstraps Approach to Housing," *Chronicle*, April 15, 1992. Memo from Frederick C. Lamont, SFHA Acting Director of Finance, to North Beach Residents, the North Beach Tenants Association and the North Beach Resident Management Council, "North Beach CAL 1-11, 970.13 Resident Organization Opportunity to Purchase, Section 412 of the National Affordable Housing Act," August 22, 1996.

33. *HOPE VI* Application, September 9, 1996, 7–8.

34. *HOPE VI* Application, "Community and Partnerships," September 9, 1996, 98.

35. Letter from North Beach Coalition to Emma McFarlin, "HOPE VI Project at North Beach Place in San Francisco," November 4, 1996.

36. Chinese Language Group, NBTA, "Meeting Notes," June 26, 1997.

37. Chinese Language Group, NBTA, "Meeting Notes," June 26, 1997.

38. Memo from Thomas Toy to Alma Lark, "Request for Official Elections for the NBRMC within days," 60, June 23, 1997.

39. Patricia Gutherie and Janis Hutchinson, "The Impact of Perceptions on Interpersonal Interactions in an African American / Asian American Housing Project," *Journal of Black Studies* 25, no. 3 (1995), 377–95; Howard, *More Than Shelter*, 171–74.

40. NBRMC, NBTA, Chinatown Resource Center, and Tel-Hi, "The Petition of North Beach Public Housing Residents," July 12, 1997.

41. Ronnie Davis, "North Beach Commitments Letter," July 18, 1997; SFHA, *1997 North Beach HOPE VI Application*, July 18, 1997, signed off by Ronnie Davis on July 15.

42. Interview with Fong.

43. SFHA, 1997 HOPE VI application, 10, 27, 32–38.

44. SFHA, 1997 HOPE VI application, 65.

45. Chinatown Resource Center internal memo, "North Beach Place Update," October 26, 1997.

46. SFHA, "North Beach HOPE VI Update: Presentation for Chinese Language Group," September 23, 1997.

47. SFHA, "Request for Proposals from Potential Development Partners for the Revitalization of Assisted Housing at Cal 1-11 North Beach," September 29, 1997.

48. CRC Internal Memo, "North Beach Place Update," n.d. (ca. October 15, 1997).

49. CRC Internal Memo, "North Beach Place Update," October 26, 1997.

50. CRC, "North Beach Update."

51. CRC Internal Memo, "North Beach Developer Selection Process," October 2, 1997.

52. Memo from The Proposal Evaluation Team to Ronnie Davis, "Evaluation Report for North Beach Developer," June 1, 1998.

53. Ronnie Davis, "North Beach Developer Resolution," June 22, 1998.

54. "Evaluation Report for North Beach Developer"; interview with Smith.

55. Interview with Fong.

56. Letter from Ernie Monaco, SFHA to Alma Lark, June 25, 1998; Letter from Ronnie Davis to Alma Lark, October 30, 1998; Lark quoted in Cassi Feldman, "The Turf War Over Public Housing," *sfbg*, January 21, 2001.

57. BRIDGE Housing Corporation, Em Johnson Interest, Inc., and The John Stewart Company, *North Beach Public Housing Redevelopment*, April 1998.

58. "Evaluation Report for North Beach Developer"; Davis, "North Beach Developer Resolution."

59. "Evaluation Report for North Beach Developer"; Davis, "North Beach Developer Resolution."

60. Interview with Jack Gardner, CEO of John Stewart Company, October 2013.

61. Interview with John Stewart, chairman, John Stewart Company, November 2013.

62. Davis, "North Beach Developer Resolution."

63. Angela Rowen, "Locked Out: Public Housing Tenants Want City to Guarantee They Won't Lose Their Homes," *sfbg*, November 3, 1999.

64. Petition from "Residents of North Beach Public Housing Development" to Ronnie Davis, "RE: Replacement of Property Manager at the North Beach Public Housing Development," May 15, 1998.

65. Letter from Thomas Toy to Ronnie Davis, "RE: Follow-Up on May 20, 1998 Meeting with North Beach Public Housing Residents," June 9, 1998; Letter from Thomas Toy to Ana Bertha Campa, SFHA, "RE: North Beach Public Housing: Process to Survey Residents on Tenant Association Options: NBTA/NBRMC," June 24, 1998.

66. NBTA and NBRMC, "Resolution No. 11," n.d. (ca. August 10, 1998). SFHA documents suggest that the "suspension" of the NBRMC was instituted on April 8, 1998, with an effective date of August 1, 1995; SFHA, "Summary of Documentation," March 1999.

67. Letter from Ronnie Davis to North Beach Residents, August 10, 1998.

68. Tracy quoted in Jason B. Johnson, "Residents of Projects List Demands: Tenants Want S.F. to Let Them Run the Development," *Chronicle*, August 14, 1998.

69. Interview with Tracy.

70. Tracy, *Dispatches against Displacement*, 27.

71. SFHA, "Relocation Services," vol. 1, issue 1, October 1998; NBTA and SFHA, "Memorandum of Understanding between the North Beach Tenants Association (NBTA) and the San Francisco Housing Authority," signed by Cynthia Wiltz and Ronnie Davis, n.d., but January 1999.

72. "North Beach Draft Revitalization Plan," November 1998.

73. Dale Royal, Memo to Juan Monsanto, "North Beach Resident and Community Outreach," January 25, 1999.

74. North Beach HOPE VI Working Group Meeting, "Minutes," January 12, 1999.

75. Human Rights Commission, City and County of San Francisco, "Minutes of the Commission Meeting of March 11, 1999."

76. SFHA, "Moved Residents," as of February 7, 2000; SFHA, "HOPE VI Relocation Report," as of June 28, 2001; files of Chinatown Community Development Center.

77. SFHA, "Memorandum of Understanding between the North Beach Tenants Association and the San Francisco Housing Authority," January 15, 1999; SFHA, "Exit Contract for North Beach Resident," n.d.

78. James Tracy, "Tenant Organizing Wins One-for-One Replacement," *Shelterforce Online*, issue 109, January–February 2000.

79. Tracy, *Dispatches against Displacement*, 29.

80. Interview with Stewart.

81. Jeremy Mullman, "A Moving Experience," *SF Weekly*, December 12, 2001.

82. Interview with Stewart.

83. Interview with Ben Golvin, October 2013.

84. Brown, *Basic Brown*, 313; interview with Gardner, October 2013; interview with Stewart. The tax credits were purchased by Related Capital. BRIDGE's project manager Peter Nichol stated that "they competed very aggressively on price," outbidding competitors by paying a combined 86.3 cents on the dollar for both the state and federal tax credits. Bank of America became the main investor; Beth Mattson-Teig, "Aggressive Growth," *National Real Estate Investor*, July 1, 2003.

85. Interview with Denise McCarthy, October 2009.

86. Interview with Stewart.

87. State of California, Department of Parks and Recreation, "Building, Structure, and Object Record," North Beach Housing Project, May 2000 (Criterion A and B), July 21, 2000 (Criterion C), 1; "Memorandum of Agreement between the City and County of San Francisco, Mayor's Office of Housing, and the California State Historic Preservation Officer Regarding the Demolition and Reconstruction of North Beach Place Public Housing Project," August 3, 2001.

88. Brown quoted in Rebecca Solnit, *Hollow City* (New York: Verso, 2002), 130.

89. Richard E. DeLeon, "San Francisco: The Politics of Race, Land Use, and Ideology," in Browning, Marshall, and Tabb, *Racial Politics*, 168–69.

90. Johnston quoted in Rachel Gordon, "Supervisors Seek Housing Authority Control," *Chronicle*, February 21, 2001.

91. David R. Baker, "Joyful Return for First Bernal Dwellers," *Chronicle*, March 24, 2001.

92. Interview with Stewart.

93. Meeting agendas contained in SFHA internal email correspondence with North Beach resident leaders, July 20, 2001.

94. Interview with Gardner.

95. Interview with Welch.

96. Interview with Stewart.

97. "A Revitalized North Beach," *Nibbi News*, Winter 2004, 9.

98. Interview with Stewart.

99. Interview with Smith.

100. "Minutes of Meeting," North Beach," July 21, 2001; BRIDGE memo from 2000 also referenced in Ilene Lelchuk, "North Beach Project Residents Ready to Fight Eviction," *Chronicle*, August 9, 2001.

101. Interview with Gardner.

102. Interview with Golvin.

103. Interview with McCarthy; Harper quoted in Tracy, *Dispatches against Displacement*, 24.

104. Interview with McCarthy.

105. Letter from Don Paul and Housing Is a Human Right to Gregg Fortner, July 23, 2001; "NBTA in Affiliation with RMC," sign-in sheet for July 11, 2001 meeting.

106. SFHA, internal email correspondence, July 24, 2011.

107. NBTA and RMC, "Positions Adopted at July 28, 2001 Meeting by Unanimous Agreement of 17 Tenants."

108. Barbara Smith, "N.B. Resident Meeting," notes, July 31, 2001; Lelchuk, "North Beach Project Residents."

109. Johnson quoted in Ethen Lieser, "Animosity in North Beach Housing," *Asian Week*, August 17, 2001.

110. Paul quoted in Ethen Lieser, "North Beach Housing Residents Refuse to Give Ground," *Asian Week*, September 20, 2001.

111. Ilene Lelchuk, "Strapped Tenants Hesitant to Move," *Chronicle*, November 23, 2001.

112. Interview with Lorraine Bender, October 2009.

113. Mullman, "A Moving Experience"; Ben Golvin to Gregg Fortner and Barbara Smith, "Information to Make Part of the Meeting with Residents Next Tuesday, 7/31," email correspondence, July 30, 2001; interview with Stewart.

114. Interview with Smith.

115. "Bulldozer Tips, Killing Worker in North Beach," *Chronicle*, January 16, 2002.

116. SFHA, "North Beach Relocation Plan," March 14, 2002, amended February 3, 2004, 4–6, 17–19, 21.

117. Ilene Lelchuk, "A First: S.F. Public Housing at Wharf Gets a Trader Joe's," *Chronicle*, October 9, 2002.

118. Interview with Stewart.

CHAPTER 12

1. Ken Garcia, "S.F. Housing Motto: Hurry Up and Wait," *Chronicle*, November 29, 2004; Keat Foong, "Golden Gate Bridging," *Multi-Housing News*, December 1, 2004; Ilene Lelchuk, "Back Home in North Beach," *Chronicle*, October 2, 2004; Robert Shurell, "North Beach Place: A Colorful Community Replaces a Dismal Development," San Francisco Apartment Association, February 2007.

2. JP Muggs soon gave ground to Starbucks, even though there was already another one across the street.

3. "One of California's Largest Affordable Housing Communities, North Beach Place, Opens to Residents Today in San Francisco," *Business Wire*, October 22, 2004; http://www.greenroofs.org/index.php/events/awards-of-excellence/2005-award-winners; Donna Kimura, "Grand Ideas Realized at North Beach Place," *Affordable Housing Finance*, August 2005, 14–15, http://www.housingfinance.com/affordable-housing/grand-ideas-realized-at-north-beach-place.aspx.

4. Barnhart quoted in "A Revitalized North Beach," 8.

5. Kimura, "Grand Ideas"; Garcia, "S.F. Housing Motto."

6. HOPE VI Quarterly Grant Reports, supplied by HUD to the author, January 2015.

7. "A Revitalized North Beach," 7.

8. Jo Stanley, "North Beach Apts. Reopen," *Examiner*, September 20, 2004.

9. Interview with John Stewart, November 2013.

10. Interview with Douglas Shoemaker, December 2009.

11. Interview with Denise McCarthy, October 2009.

12. Interview with Jack Gardner, October 2013.

13. Interview with Ben Golvin, October 2013.

14. Interview with Greg Richardson conducted by Stephanie Groll, August 2005.

15. Interview with Alma Lark, conducted by Stephanie Groll, August 2005; interview with Barbara Smith, June 2012.

16. Zusha Elinson, "Public Housing Residents Await Urgent Transfers," *Bay Citizen*, July 2, 2010. An SFHA report citing February 2009 data admitted that nearly thirteen hundred households failed to pay their rent on time, including twenty-one tenants who owed more than $10,000 each. The rent backlog had peaked in 2007, with more than $3 million not collected; John Coté, "With Public Housing Rent Owed, Evictions Feared," *Chronicle*, July 16, 2010.

17. Interview with Lorraine Bender, October 2009.

18. Interview with Bender.

19. In these interviews, as elsewhere, I have endeavored to render the language exactly as spoken, even if this retains grammatical oddities. Interviews were completed with the assistance of Tan Chow in 2009.

20. David Bodamer, "Trading Spaces," *Retail Traffic* 34, no. 1 (2005): 14.

21. Interview with Stewart. The camera count is also cited in Art Peterson, "North Beach Place: A Pretty Face and Much More," *The Semaphore* (a publication of the Telegraph Hill Dwellers), issue 176 (Summer 2006): 32. At least North Beach Place stops well short of the way CCTV cameras get deployed in Chicago's Oakwood Shores mixed-income housing development. There, "Cameras are designed to respond to certain behaviors—such as groups of people standing around for a certain time—with recorded messages warning them away"; Chaskin and Joseph, *Integrating the Inner City*, 175.

22. Interview with Bender.

23. Interviews with North Beach Place residents; interview with McCarthy; interview with Smith.

24. Interview with Stewart.

25. Various North Beach Place monthly newsletters, 2005–2009; Memo from Felicia Chen to North Beach Place residents, "RE: Three-Day to Perform Covenant or Quit Notice," May 15, 2007.

26. Memo from Felicia Chen to a North Beach Place resident, July 25, 2007.

27. Memo from Felicia Chen to North Beach Place residents, "Building a Better, Stronger Community Starts at Home with You," January 27, 2006.

28. See Vale, *Puritans to the Projects*, chapter 3.

29. John Stewart Company, "North Beach Place Apartments House Rules," May 27, 2008.

30. Interview with Bender.

31. Interview with McCarthy.

32. Howard Husock, "Public Housing's Hidden Costs to Cities," *New York Sun*, January 7, 2003.

33. Steve Lerner, "Conversations with Advocates of Fair Growth," Commonweal.org, n.d. (2004?)

34. Memo from Ahsha Ali Safaí to Gavin Newsom, "Big Four Public Housing Tour—Phase 1 (July 18th 2pm–5pm)," July 15, 2003. Safaí would later be appointed as a housing commissioner, where served from 2010 to 2013.

35. Rachel Gordon, "Housing Agency 'Troubled' Again," *Chronicle*, August 25, 2004.

36. Interview with Shoemaker.

37. Newsom quoted in Ilene Lelchuk, "New Hope for S.F. Public Housing as Federal Funding Evaporates," *Chronicle*, March 28, 2005.

38. Heather Knight, "Infamous Projects Are Rebuilt and Reborn," *Chronicle*, November 20, 2006.

39. San Francisco Mayor's Office of Housing, *HOPE SF: Rebuilding Public Housing and Restoring Opportunity for Its Residents*, Summary of Task Force Recommendations to the Mayor and Board of Supervisors, March 23, 2007, 1–8.

40. Interview with Shoemaker.

41. Interview with Shoemaker.

42. HOPE SF website, http://hope-sf.org/community.php.

43. J. K. Dineen, "Potrero Hill's Biggest Housing Project Starts with Plenty of Hope," *Chronicle*, January 28, 2017.

44. *HOPE SF: Rebuilding Public Housing and Restoring Opportunity for Its Residents*, 8.

45. Interview with Shoemaker.

46. Casenave and Shortt quoted in "Potrero Terrace and Annex to Be Redeveloped," http://www.porteroview.net/news10076.html, October 2008.

47. Erin Sherbert, "City Nears Launch of Hunters View Work," *San Francisco Examiner*, September 22, 2010; John Upton, "Market Rate Homes Nixed from Hunters View Project," *San Francisco Examiner*, October 8, 2009; John King, "Rehab Planned for San Francisco Housing Project," *Architectural Record*, November 6, 2013; "Improving the Quality of Life in Hunters View," *PD&R Edge*, January 27, 2014; Sophie Novack, "An Experiment in Low-Income Housing in Rapidly Gentrifying San Francisco," *National Journal*, February 4, 2014.

48. Interview with McCarthy.

49. Tracy, *Dispatches against Displacement*, 36.

50. Interview with Gardner.

51. Interview with Stewart.

52. Interview with Stewart.

53. John Wildermuth, "Alice Griffith Renovation Gains Federal Jump-Start," *Chronicle*, August 31, 2011; Donna Kimura, "Hope Grows in S.F.," *Affordable Housing Finance*, November–December 2011.

54. HOPE SF website, http://hope-sf.org/basic.php; Joshua Sabatini, "San Francisco Plans for First Uses of 2015 Housing Bond, *Examiner*, September 15, 2016; Dineen, "Potrero Hill's Biggest Housing Project."

55. Gregg Fortner, "SFHA—Setting the Record Straight," letter, *San Francisco Examiner*, February 11, 2013. Fortner states: "The City wanted me out because they felt that I was not the right person to lead the agency during a transition when the City would take a greater role in SFHA oversight."

56. John Coté, "With Public Housing Rent Owed, Evictions Feared," *Chronicle*, July 16, 2010; Erin Sherbert, "City Freezes Low-Income Evictions," *Examiner*, September 10, 2010; Aaron Peskin, "In Housing Agency Flap, Ask Ed Lee," Commentary, *Chronicle*, December 9, 2012; Larry Bush, "Feds Downgrade Troubled Housing Authority," *San Francisco Bay Guardian*, January 8, 2013.

57. Dan Schreiber, "Housing Authority Chief Henry Alvarez Faces Racial Lawsuit Storm," *Examiner*, December 5, 2012; C. W. Nevius, "Ed Lee Should Remove

Henry Alvarez Now," column, *Chronicle*, January 11, 2013; John Coté, "Mayor Ed Lee Fast-Tracks Decision on Housing Authority Director," *Chronicle*, January 16, 2013; Heather Knight and John Coté, "HUD Probes SF Public Housing Contracts," *Chronicle*, February 21, 2013; John Coté and Heather Knight, "Housing Agency Deep in Red," *Chronicle*, March 28, 2013.

58. Dan McMenamin, "Mayor Floats Idea of Public-Private Housing Authority during State of the City Address," *San Francisco Appeal*, January 28, 2013; Chris Roberts, "San Francisco Seeks Model Approach to Improve Public Housing," *Examiner*, January 29, 2013; Heather Knight, John Coté, and John Wildermoth, "S.F.'s Lee Purges Housing Commission," *Chronicle*, February 9, 2013; Heather Knight, "Commission Terminates Housing Authority Director's Contract," *Chronicle*, April 9, 2013; Lee quoted in John Coté, "Henry Alvarez OKd for Medical Leave," *Chronicle*, February 1, 2013.

59. John Coté, "Ex-Chief a Harsh Boss, Say Staffers," *Chronicle*, May 8, 2013; Chris Roberts, "Ousted SF Housing Authority Director Cleared of Many Allegations, Report Finds," *Examiner*, May 8, 2013; John Coté, "Housing Authority Lawsuit Award a Victory of Sorts," *Chronicle*, August 28, 2013; Heather Knight, "S.F. Housing Authority to Pay Off Former Attorneys," *Chronicle*, June 24, 2014; https://www.facebook.com/nextdoorrestaurant.

60. Smith quoted in Coté and Knight, "Housing Agency Deep in Red."

61. Chris Roberts, "Blistering City Report Rips Housing Authority," *Examiner*, June 3, 2013; Chris Roberts, "Cash-Poor San Francisco Housing Authority Gets Break from City Bills," *Examiner*, June 17, 2013.

62. Office of the City Administrator, City and County of San Francisco, *SFHA Re-envisioning*, Recommendations to Mayor Ed Lee on how to transform the San Francisco Housing Authority, n.d. (June 2013), 1–19; SPUR, "Re-envisioning the San Francisco Housing Authority," SPUR Memorandum, June 24, 2013; Memo from Council of Community Housing Organizations to Mayor Edwin Lee, City Administrator Naomi Kelly, and Housing Director Olson Lee, "Public Housing Re-envisioning," June 21, 2013.

63. *SFHA Re-Envisioning*, 19.

64. SPUR, "Re-envisioning the San Francisco Housing Authority," 4.

65. Lee and Donovan quoted in Chris Roberts, "During San Francisco Visit, HUD Secretary Says Private Sector Will Save Public Housing," *Examiner*, September 25, 2013.

66. Jonah Owen Lamb, "Feds Give SF Big Bucks for Innovative Public Housing Plan," *Examiner*, January 23, 2014; Cohen quoted in Heather Knight and John Coté, "S.F. Wins Spot in New Federal Public Housing Program," *Chronicle*, March 2, 2014.

67. Edwin M. Lee, "Press Release: Mayor Lee & Supervisors Introduce Financing Milestone to Revitalize & Rebuild City's Public Housing," March 25, 2015; Lisa Brown, "Historic Project to Preserve Public Housing," GlobeSt.Com, August 24, 2015, http://www.globest.com/news/12_1181/sanfrancisco/multifamily/Historic-Project-to-Preserve-Public-Housing-360988-1.html; Emily Green, "SF's Public Housing Is Now All Privately Run," November 3, 2016.

68. "Mayor Lee's Unfinished Business: Housing," editorial, *Chronicle*, December 12, 2017.

69. San Francisco Board of Supervisors, "Resolution Urging the Recreation and Parks Commission to Remove the Name of Justin Herman from the Plaza on the Embarcadero," September 11, 2017, https://sfgov.legistar.com/View.ashx?M=F&ID=5335455&GUID=4E4DE877-32D4-402A-B3E4-7956311781F6; Carlos Olin Montalvo, "Here's Why SF Wants to Rename Justin Herman Plaza," *SF Station*, September 28, 2017, https://www.sfstation.com/2017/09/28/heres-why-sf-wants-to-rename-justin-herman-plaza/

70. Foong, "Golden Gate Bridging"; HUD HOPE VI Quarterly Reports, North Beach Place, as of 2014.

CHAPTER 13

1. Interview with Michael Kelly, March 2009.
2. Kornegay, "Hope of Public Housing," 80.
3. Katz, "What Kind of Problem," 45.
4. Chaskin and Joseph, *Integrating the Inner City*, 225.
5. Chaskin and Joseph, *Integrating the Inner City*, 159, 166.
6. Greater amounts of mixing have been found in other communities where the income gap was narrower, such as Chicago's Mixed-Income New Communities Strategy (MINCS), piloted at Lake Parc Place; Chaskin and Joseph, *Integrating the Inner City*, 129; James E. Rosenbaum, Linda K. Stroh, and Cathy A. Flynn, "Lake Parc Place: A Study of Mixed-Income Housing," *Housing Policy Debate* 9 (1998): 703–40.
7. Interview with Don Everard, January 2013.
8. Elvin K. Wyly and Daniel J. Hammel, "Mapping Neo-liberal American Urbanism," in Atkinson and Bridge, *Gentrification*, 18.
9. Soss, Fording, and Schram, *Disciplining the Poor*, 21, 25, 27, 29.
10. Brenner and Theodore, *Spaces of Neoliberalism*, 2, 14.
11. Interview with Jack Gardner and Ben Golvin, October 2013.
12. Interview with Pres Kabacoff, April 2010.
13. Vale, *Purging the Poorest*.
14. Chaskin and Joseph, *Integrating the Inner City*, 218.
15. National Low Income Housing Coalition, "House Subcommittee's FY2019 THUD Bill Maintains Increased Funding for Most Housing Programs," May 16, 2018; http://nlihc.org/article/house-subcommittees-fy19-thud-bill-maintains-increased-funding-most-housing-programs; "A Better Deal for Public Housing & Ladders of Opportunity for American Families;" https://abetterdeal.democraticleader.gov/wp-content/uploads/2018/05/ABD-Public-Housing_Fact-Sheet.pdf; Kriston Capps, "To Fix Housing Aid, HUD Wants Work Requirements and Rent Hikes," *CityLab*, April 26, 2018; Diane K. Levy, Leiha Edmonds, and Jasmine Simington, "Work Requirements in Public Housing Authorities" (Washington, DC: Urban Institute, January 2018); https://www.urban.org/sites/default/files/publication/95821/work-requirements-in-public-housing-authorities.pdf.
16. National Low Income Housing Coalition, "HFT: The Housing Trust Fund," Fact Sheet, March 2017, http://nlihc.org/sites/default/files/HTF_Factsheet.pdf; http://www.politico.com/story/2017/05/19/hud-budget-cuts-housing-programs-238610; National Low Income Housing Coalition, "Housing Trust Fund at Risk Due to Tax Reform," January 16, 2018, http://nlihc.org/article/housing-trust-fund-risk-due-tax-reform; National Low Income Housing Coalition, "Nearly 1300 Organizations

Call for Expanding the National Housing Trust Fund," NLIHC Memo to Members 23, no. 6 (February 13, 2018); National Low Income Housing Coalition, "FHFA Protects Funding to the National Housing Trust Fund," February 14, 2018; http://nlihc.org/article/fhfa-protects-funding-national-housing-trust-fund; National Low Income Housing Coalition, "HUD Issues State Allocations of $266.8 Million for the National Housing Trust in 2018," NLIHC Memo to Members 23, no. 17 (May 7, 2018).

17. Conor Dougherty, "Tax Overhaul Is a Blow to Affordable Housing Efforts," *New York Times*, January 18, 2018; Conor Dougherty, "Budget Deal in Congress Includes Help for Affordable Housing," *New York Times*, March 23, 2018.

18. National Low Income Housing Coalition, *The Gap: A Shortage of Affordable Homes*, March 2018, appendix B.

19. Interview with Calvin Welch, October 2009.

20. Arena, *Driven from New Orleans*, xviii, 157, 225.

21. Tracy quoted in Rachel Peterson, "Hope VI in San Francisco," SPUR, March 2005, http://www.spur.org/publications/urbanist-article/2005-03-01/hope-vi-san-francisco.

22. Tracy, *Dispatches against Displacement*, 99–100.

23. Kevin Marchman, presentation at Fannie Mae Annual Housing Conference, 1993; Henry Cisneros, quoted in Jane Roessner, *A Decent Place to Live* (Boston: Northeastern University Press, 2000), 293–94.

24. James Hanlon, "The Origins of the Rental Assistance Demonstration Program and the End of Public Housing," *Housing Policy Debate* 27, no. 4 (2017): 611–39; Alex Schwartz, "Future Prospects for Public Housing in the United States: Lessons from the Rental Assistance Demonstration Program," *Housing Policy Debate*, 2017, http://dx.doi.org/10.1080/10511482.2017.1287113; National Low Income Housing Coalition, "RAD Update," *Memo to Members*, January 11, 2016; Orlando Cabrera, "Trump's Plan to Cut Public Housing Is a Mistake for America," *The Hill*, June 20, 2017; Carolina K. Reid, "Lessons for the Future of Public Housing: Assessing the Early Implementation of the Rental Assistance Demonstration Program," UC Berkeley Terner Center for Housing Innovation, October 2017, 9.

25. Hanlon, "Origins," 627–29.

26. Hanlon, "Origins," 624–25, 627; US Government Accountability Office, *Rental Assistance Demonstration: HUD Needs to Take Action to Improve Metrics and Ongoing Oversight* (GAO, February 2018), 32-40; Vale and Freemark, "Privatization."

27. George C. Galster, "Neighborhood Social Mix: Theory, Evidence, and Implications for Policy and Planning," in Carmon and Fainstein, *Policy, Planning, and People*, 315.

Index